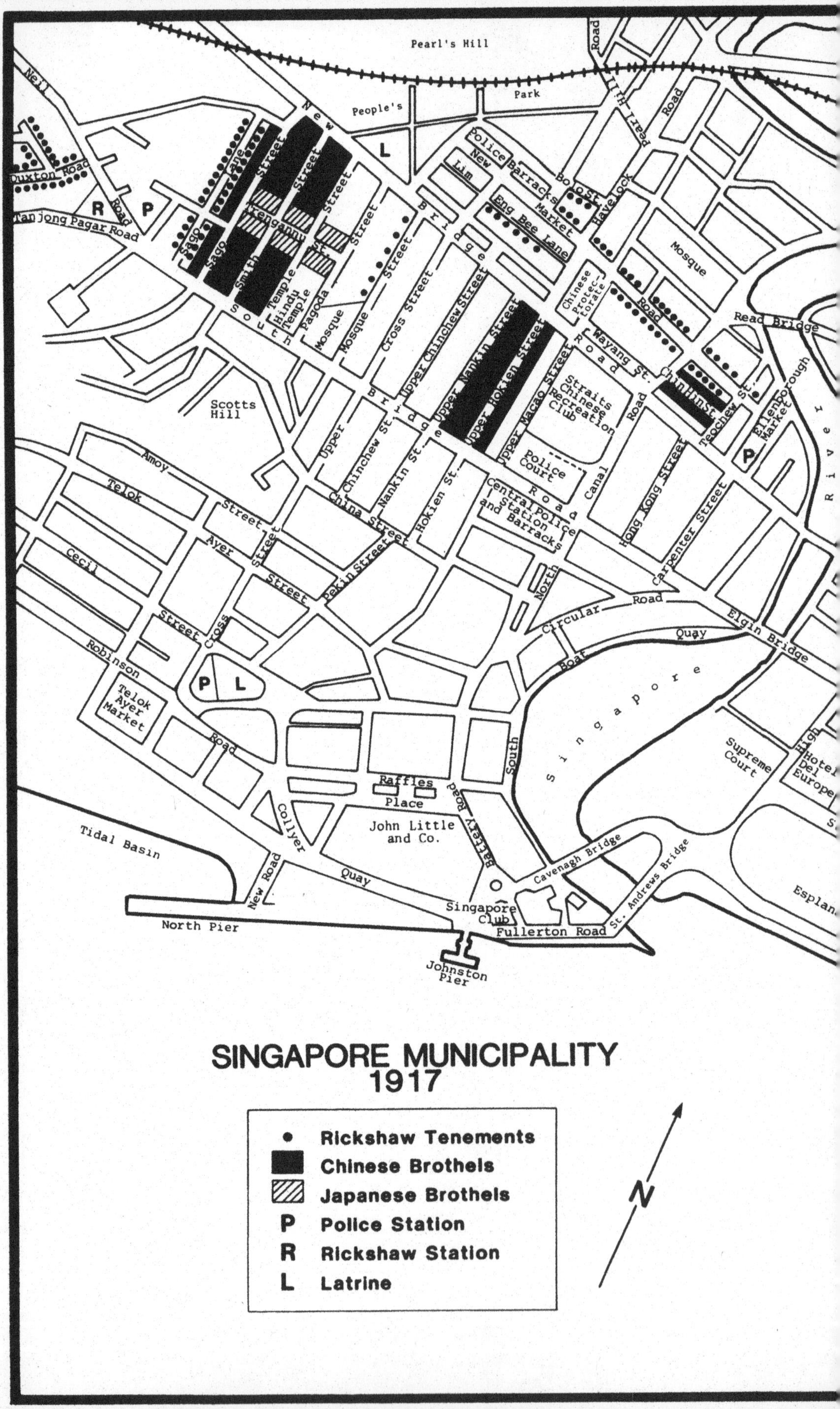

SINGAPORE MUNICIPALITY
1917
Rickshaw Tenements
Chinese Brothels
Japanese Brothels
P Police Station
R Rickshaw Station
L Latrine
N
Pearl's Hill
People's Park
Neil Road
Duxton Road
Tanjong Pagar Road
Sago Lane
Sago Street
Smith Street
Temple Street
Trengannu Street
Pagoda Street
Mosque Street
Cross Street
New Bridge Road
South Bridge Road
Hindu Temple
Scotts Hill
Upper Chinchew Street
Upper Nankin Street
Upper Hokien Street
Upper Macao Street
Upper Cross Street
Chinchew St.
Nankin St.
Hokien St.
China Street
Pekin Street
Police Barracks
New Market
Lim
Eng Bee Lane
Bold St.
Havelock Road
Pearl's Hill Road
Mosque
Chinese Protectorate
Wayang St.
Chin Hin St.
Teochew St.
Straits Chinese Recreation Club
Police Court
Central Police Station and Barracks
Canal Road
Hong Kong Street
Carpenter Street
Read Bridge
Ellenborough Market
River
Amoy Street
Telok Ayer Street
Cecil Street
Cross Street
Robinson Road
Telok Ayer Market
North
Circular Road
Boat Quay
Elgin Bridge
Singapore
South
Raffles Place
John Little and Co.
Battery Road
Collyer Quay
New Road
Tidal Basin
North Pier
Singapore Club
Fullerton Road
Cavenagh Bridge
St. Andrews Bridge
Johnston Pier
Supreme Court
High
Hotel Del Europe
Esplan

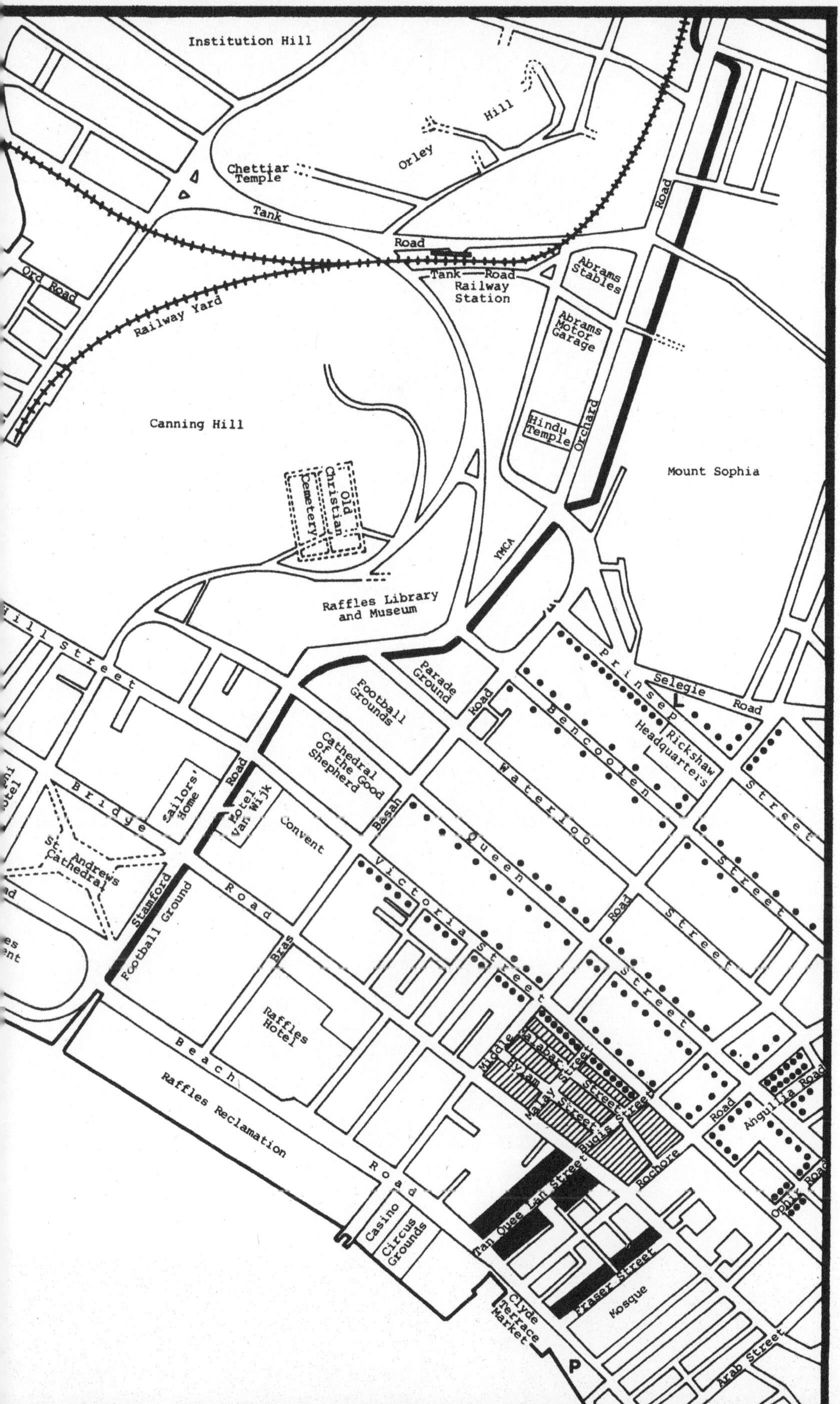

Institution Hill
Orley Hill
Chettiar Temple
Tank Road
Tank Road Railway Station
Abrams Stables
Abrams Motor Garage
Hindu Temple
Orchard Road
Ord Road
Railway Yard
Canning Hill
Old Christian Cemetery
Mount Sophia
YMCA
Raffles Library and Museum
Hill Street
Parade Ground
Football Grounds
Prinsep
Selegie Road
Rickshaw Headquarters
Bencoolen
Waterloo
Cathedral of the Good Shepherd
Sailors' Home
Hotel Van Wijk
Bridge
St. Andrews Cathedral
Convent
Basah
Queen
Victoria Street
Stamford
Football Ground
Road
Bras
Raffles Hotel
Beach Road
Raffles Reclamation
Middle Road
Malabar Street
Hylam Street
Malay Street
Bugis Street
Rochore
Anguillia Road
Ophir Road
Tan Quee Lan Street
Casino
Circus Grounds
Clyde Terrace Market
Fraser Street
Mosque
Arab Street
P

Rickshaw Coolie

RICKSHAW COOLIE

A People's History of Singapore
1880–1940

JAMES FRANCIS WARREN

NUS PRESS
SINGAPORE

Published by:

NUS Press
National University of Singapore
AS3-01-02, 3 Arts Link
Singapore 117569

Fax: (65) 6774-0652
E-mail: nusbooks@nus.edu.sg
Website: http://nuspress.nus.edu.sg

Reprint 2018
Reprint 2019

ISBN 978-981-4722-86-5 (Paper)

The first edition was published by Oxford University Press in 1993 and Singapore University Press in 2003.

Printed by: Markono Print Media Pte Ltd

For

KUO PAO KUN

Pioneer

Exemplary Teacher, Artist and Playwright

Who

Fearlessly Moved the Boundaries of Artistic and Social Inquiry

Preface

The social history of Singapore Chinese society and the city's development, as a commercial centre and entrepot port from 1870 to 1940, has been the setting of virtually all my work for the past two decades. *Rickshaw Coolie* deals with turn-of-century Singapore, wedged between British Malaya and the Netherlands Indies, with its own startling tough "history from below" and idiosyncracies as a Chinese city outside China. This book examines the social conditions that spawned the rickshaw industry and the way rickshaw pullers lived their lives in conjunction with the big changes taking place in the development of colonial Singapore and Asia. Mass migration, rural unrest and change, industrialization in Japan, high finance and the Depression (the dark side of urbanization in Singapore) — these topics all receive their due in this work.

Manuel Castells has argued "cities are made by people". This volume attempts to describe and analyze the urban social history of Singapore through the experience of some of those people; of all the Chinese workers who symbolized colonial Singapore the rickshawmen were, perhaps, in the best position to know the real nature of the city. Using almost two hundred featured individuals and a literary, anthropological-historical technique in the tradition of Emmanual Le Roy Laudurie and Jonathan Spence, *Rickshaw Coolie* is an in-depth historical ethnography. The book describes and analyzes the vital role of rickshaw pullers in sustaining Singapore's pre-war society and economy, as well as the despair, disease and death that had wormed its way, eaten its way to the very core of Singapore under British rule. Here, again, as for historiography: there has not been sufficient imaginative reflection on the significance of particular sources pertaining to death for reconstructing such worlds in Southeast Asian modern history. Indeed, we lag behind our colleagues in countries like France and the United States very considerably and very clearly in recognizing the historiographical importance of a source like the Coroners Records of Singapore. This failure hides from us the stories of the vast number of people for whom death had become an ever-present reality, for themselves, their kindred and their community in the life of the city.

I wanted to write a history of the Chinese in Singapore full of imaginative drama and narrative sweep, one that would be primarily about ordinary individuals and the incalculability of their lives. The stories emerge from the texts of the Inquests and Inquiries complete with deeply impressive dialogue. The Coroner's work is stunning, and thoroughly purposeful. It seemed to me writing about these cases of death from the point of view of anthropological history was a way of framing what had actually happened in life to rickshaw coolies and for giving voice — preferably their own voice or voices of family and friends, and enemies or strangers in association with them — passengers, lovers, Samaritans or assailants. I started with a basic idea in this history of trying to communicate to as wide an audience as possible about what it was like to be a rickshaw puller, what happened to them, how their lives developed within the city and beyond, and that was a very complex process. I have spoken as naturally and compassionately as possible of the individual and collective characters and how they developed within this history — as if Kow Wuh, Ng Kar Eng and Ling Ah Thui and many, many others were old friends. In some ways, many of the individuals in this book were deeply flawed, a tightly tangled knot of desire and despair, of hopes and dreams gone to ruin. I have also written with complete respect and acceptance about their lives. I realized too only some of the extraordinary, enormously moving material in the Coroner's records could enable me to do it.

All the fundamentally great themes of power and innocence, friendship and loyalty, goodness and evil, love and betrayal in all its forms and fathomless complexities were found in the Coroner's cases about the lives of these very ordinary, sometimes dangerous inarticulate men and their women. Until that moment of "discovery" there was no knowledge of such vanished feelings and "events". And I think that was very important because, when I was working on this volume, I tried to recreate such emotions and moments through the complex voices which the Coroner and others spoke of the dead and by travelling back in time in my imagination, not just along the busy thoroughfares lined with rickshaws, but into the kongsi foyers and onto the brothel verandah and beyond. The search for this past reality was my real purpose for having come to Singapore — to resurrect images that would fill out and revise the story in the history books, to mark and memorialize this city as the rickshawmen knew it, and waken the ghosts of Victoria Street and Duxton Road in order to make the memory of dead people live again.

These men and their profession can no longer be considered peripheral to the central concerns of historical study in Singapore. The memory of ordinary Singaporeans has been dominated by those who have held political, economic and ideological sway. Most of the historical records available tend to reflect the overbearing presence of the male: educated, privileged and powerful. As such, their observations were, naturally enough, laden with their own preconceptions, social bias and self-interest. The accounts by the empowered (such as colonial authorities) have often been employed to provide a "contrast" and sometimes a justification for a particular policy or attitude. Meanwhile the history of the "other" — the marginalized or "little people" — is too often lost, overlooked or never recorded. Finding a balance in the historical record requires the historian to seek a wide range of sources in order to tease out the stories of the "little people". The consequence of this volume is the emergence of an alternative memory: a framework of balanced arguments, based on the felt realities of these men, which was fashioned to analyze the history of their past. Stress has been placed on the similarities and differences in the lives and circumstance of the rickshaw pullers, in the variety and complexity of their basic social relations, human condition, and on changes over time, as mirrored in the actual limits of their social mobility. Such an interdisciplinary approach advocates a fairer, more balanced, and realistic account of the past. The historical memory of Singaporean society is constituted not of a single strand, but rather of a tangled skein.

Asia Research Institute
November 2002

JAMES FRANCIS WARREN

Preface to the First Edition

THIS book is about the life and labour of the rickshawmen of Singapore. *Rickshaw Coolie* examines the origin and development of the rickshaw trade in Singapore, its control and regulation from the standpoint of the Chinese and the British, the method of earning a livelihood in rickshaw pulling, and the character of a rickshaw coolie's life. There has been increasing recognition of the need to focus research on the urban work-place, labour and the everyday problems of the coolie class under colonial rule in South-East Asia. Such efforts, if they are to be meaningful, must be posed, theoretically and empirically, against a background of real life. This approach raises grave historiographical problems, for historians, like anthropologists, have tended 'to graze in the fields',[1] focusing their primary attention on the rural societies of South-East Asia. Considerable work has been done on peasant-based movements and opposition to colonial rule, but hardly any historical research has been conducted on the urban labouring class, of which the rickshaw coolies of Singapore formed a part.

The tide-water colonial capitals of the nineteenth and twentieth centuries created new modes of human experience for immigrant Asians, but especially for *singkeh*, the Chinese newcomers to Singapore. At the end of the nineteenth century Singapore rapidly developed as a commercial centre and an entrepôt port dominated by import and export firms and banks, and serviced Britain's imperial expansion and trade-oriented economy in South-East Asia. This development had a profound impact upon every aspect of economic and social relationships, but it was most marked in the labour nexus, in the segregation and extreme overcrowding of the lower-class Chinese who, as rickshaw pullers, coal coolies, and stevedores, provided the sinews of empire and helped to shape the expansion of Singapore.

To reconstruct this 'experience' the notion of work-place and work must be carefully developed and refined within a 'total context and cultural setting'.[2] Thus Singapore, as a Chinese city outside China, is a resource, a field of action, a cockpit or social arena for understanding the economic and cultural aspects of labouring-class Chinese society, as specifically expressed and epitomized in the work entailed in pulling a rickshaw. An account of the material setting of Singapore is vital;

inadequate housing in the form of decrepit, Dickensian buildings, the interdependence of water supply and sewerage disposal problems, too few hospitals and cemeteries affected all areas of life of lower-class Chinese. The material setting includes the place in which rickshawmen laboured. We can gain insight into how Singapore expressed itself in one way to the able bodied but quite differently to the elderly, the sick, and dependants of rickshawmen at stages in the family cycle.

It is this approach which points to the work-place as a 'total context and cultural setting'[3] that enables one to understand how the structure and ideology of a dual framework—traditional China and a colonial society—combined to confine rickshaw coolies to a trade with low wages, hazardous work conditions, poor unionization and uncommon death. By developing our thinking then within the framework of a 'coolie town', some of the unanswered questions about a rickshaw coolie's insight into his work and community will surface from the 'underside'—questions about conditions of hiring, wages and work, conditions of daily life including leisure and violence, the forms of organization which came into being among the Singapore rickshaw pullers, their kind of consciousness and sense of identity. The aim of this book is to reconstitute the world of the rickshawmen and to examine the nature of their interaction with Singapore, and the causes and effects of immigration and colonialism on their lives.

Linked to the structural changes in Singapore's economy was the social impact of mass migration on colonial Singapore, especially with regard to work, behaviour, values and feelings of the Chinese labourers. There was an increasing disparity between the ever-burgeoning Chinese population and the city's ability to deal with growth and change. Singapore's administrators consistently chose alternatives that minimized planning costs but created social conditions which inevitably forced rickshawmen over the poverty line. Despite these problems Singapore, especially at the peak of its growth around 1900, often seemed a place of hope compared to the countryside of China and the treaty ports. In the 1890s, peasants facing poverty and deprivation in China could not keep their growing families fed. Among the rickshawmen in Singapore many had decided to migrate from counties near Foochow.[4] Singapore offered the same hardships, but with a difference, at least for some *singkeh*—the promise of a future. Without such hope life is not worth living at all. By the mid-1920s they had begun to put down their roots for future generations.

By focusing on the rickshawmen of Singapore, with the lens provided by the Coroner's Records, one can also glimpse the society from which the migrants came. The lives of the rickshawmen as revealed primarily in this source open a 'window on China'[5] through which we can view the circumstances of those who stayed behind. We can 'see' the relationship between clan organizations in Singapore and their links with villages and regions in China. The clans emphasized the maintenance of cultural and philosophical traditions with the homeland and the pursuit of special interests within the political and economic order. It is within this context in Singapore that the links between locality, kinship, migration, and the immutability of occupation begin to fall into place. Family circumstances and relationships between family members who emigrated and those who stayed behind can also be identified—the birth of children, illness, destitution and death with their concomitant social and economic repercussions, the unrelenting pressure to remit money and to return, as well as the spiral of failure. In a sense this study of the rickshawmen of Singapore is a way of seeing China from without and, at the same time, looking from China downward at the world of the *Nanyang*.

In order to understand the impact of colonial policy and practice on the lives of the rickshaw coolies, it is important to describe and analyse the key social relationships within the Chinese community between puller and owner, and between the rickshawmen and the Europeans who were administrators, magistrates, and coroners on the one hand, and regular fares, tourists, and motorists on the other. The study of British policies and attitudes with respect to rickshaw coolies will enable us not only to penetrate the myth of the foulness of the rickshaw quarters, of the pullers' supposed propensity to vice and criminality, but also to understand how and why this myth was perpetuated.

In the colonial history of the peninsula it is a fact that changes in Singapore's material circumstance and prosperity have been connected with the period of increased Chinese immigration, and economic and political dominance of the British in Malaya. The role and economic contribution of the Chinese migrant was critical to British development activities in urban settings. The importance of the subject is undeniable. Acknowledged in passing in the historical and developmental literature, it has not yet received the attention it warrants. At the turn of the century, the rickshaw, as a cheap ordinary means of transport, revolutionized the life of Singapore, and although initially encouraged, by the 1920s the British felt that the rickshaw was a challenge to their development policy and the showcase image of Singapore as a 'modern city'. The demand for rickshaw transport throughout the inter-war years, however, continued nevertheless, as did the harsh social conditions for the pullers. The British refused to encourage the trade, at times ignoring it, and then opposing it with a vengeance at the height of the Depression.

Economic and social inequality was linked with high morbidity and mortality in Singapore, because it was a 'coolie town'.[6] Underlying the depressing economics and health hazards of rickshaw pulling there was a demographic pressure crushing the Singapore Chinese that was a direct consequence of the symbiosis between colonial capitalism and migration from south-eastern China. For those living as 'dust to be blown around', the alternative to excessive opium smoking, whoring and gambling, to excessive pain and illness, to excessive loss of strength and ageing, or to excessive loneliness without kin, was suicide. Manuel Castells argues that 'cities are made *by people*'.[7] This book attempts to describe and analyse the urban social history of Singapore through the experience of some of those people; of all the Chinese labourers who symbolized colonial

Singapore the rickshawmen were, perhaps, in the best position to know the city.

I now want to consider briefly the nature, quality, and coverage of the sources for this history. In order to understand what it meant to pull a rickshaw the historian must saturate himself in the whole range of sources available on Singapore in the late nineteenth and twentieth centuries. There is a wealth of information about Chinese labouring classes in the colonial records waiting to be interpreted. The pattern of urban life for the Chinese coolie can be reconstructed in detail with precision and painstaking care from these sources.

Among the most important and interesting of these source materials are the Coroner's Records for Colonial Singapore, 1883–1940. Neglected in a storeroom of the Subordinate Court, these certificates, inquests and inquiries are a historical source of particular interest to historians of the urban poor. When the door was unlocked for me, after several months of searching, to a room in the modern Subordinate Courts Building,[8] I gained access to a collection of several hundred unclassified volumes stacked against a wall to a height of four feet. The records had been moved several times from one repository to another under British rule and again as late as 1975, and this had resulted in a certain amount of damage and loss on each occasion. Most of the volumes of inquests and inquiries and bundles of Coroner's Views lying at the bottom of a stack had suffered due to dampness. In addition to this, there had been, of course, the ravages of white ants. Not sure where to start without a check-list or guide, I began to rummage among the stacks closest to me and soon sensed the historiographical possibilities these documents offered for the study of ordinary Chinese men and women. As I randomly located and read the first inquest statements of rickshaw pullers and their kin, finding expressions of their personal grief, of pain and frustration, of the misery that colonial rule and the Depression had inflicted on them, of an extreme structural poverty reflected in the incidence, the causes and meaning of suicide, and of life's small pleasures like a special meal of chicken, rice wine and noodles shared with friends, I realized that the contents of this repository would yield up, with skill and patience, the living testimony of Chinese people who did not know how to express themselves in print and who did not have access to people with power. These records bring the rickshaw coolies, their clansmen, kinsmen and women of a forgotten past into the historical forefront. They provide empirical evidence on age, sex, marital status, address, place of birth, occupation, length of time in Singapore, diet, dress, sickness, and death. The causes of death often depict the deprivation experienced in pulling a rickshaw. Much also can be learned about housing, health, and poverty, and the almost hopeless struggle to survive in times of recession and depression from literary sources, the detailed accounts of European and Asian observers of Singapore, and photographs that show the Singapore the rickshaw pullers knew. Finally, there is still something to be learned of the experience of the Chinese labouring class by observing the as yet unredeveloped parts of Singapore's Chinatown.

Rickshaw Coolie is not meant to be a curative history. It is written through a concern to understand the structure of experience of Chinese labourers under colonial rule in Singapore. Nevertheless, I hope that this study of the rickshawmen, based on the historiographical principles of a People's History, will contribute to a revision of South-East Asian Modern History, and equally important, in the context of present-day Singapore, to the notion of what is 'historical'.

This book has been an individual project eight years in the making. *Rickshaw Coolie* is based on my experience and vocation as a teacher of the history of non-European culture in a post-colonial world. A passion for a forgotten past of people who have stood outside history and recovery of a whole set of social relations have been a central preoccupation running through my work—teaching and research. This is especially so in the case of *Rickshaw Coolie*. It is also a work that insists on seeing things relationally, using concepts and techniques from anthropology. The lessons in anthropology for the study of history suggest how to create a total set of social relations—a cultural system—in a historical past. This approach involving anthropology and history is something I have stressed in my teaching, and I have tried to make work in my writing.

The research on which *Rickshaw Coolie* is based grew out of a series of special Research Grants from Murdoch University in 1976, 1978 and 1982. I wish to express my gratitude to the University for its generosity and support. I also want to thank the Joint Committee on Southeast Asia of the American Council of Learned Societies and the Social Science Research Council for an award to assist in the writing of the manuscript in residence at Murdoch University between June and December 1982.

The main research was carried out in England in 1979 and in Singapore between 1980 and 1982. In England, I want to thank for their kind assistance all the staff of the Public Records Office, Foreign and Commonwealth Office Library, and Rhodes House Library at Oxford University. Many people have contributed to this study in Singapore. Major sources of encouragement have been Mr Khoo Oon Soo, the former Registrar of the Subordinate Courts, and Ms Seah Poh Geok, Principal Librarian of the Subordinate Courts, and the staff of the library, especially Ms Mahni bte Messod and Ms Loo Swee Yong. I am particularly indebted to Ms Tan Beng Luan and the staff of the Archives and Oral History Department[9] for transcribing and making available portions of the transcripts of interviews with Mr Ho Bee Swee and Mr Ng Kar Eng. I am grateful to Mr Quek Shi Lei and Ms Cathy Lau for assisting me with translation of Chinese materials relevant to my research on the history of the rickshaw coolies. I wish to thank my former student in Singapore, Dr Daniel Chew, who located an important series of photographs for me to examine in the course of his daily work in the Archives and Oral History

Department. Thanks are also due to Mr Murray Austen-Smith and Ms Sonia Illig, Media Services, Murdoch University, for their assistance and advice in rendering the maps of Singapore.

I am indebted to the following colleagues for their incisive comments, criticisms, and encouragement in helping me revise the manuscript for publication: John Butcher, Joe Moore, Carl A. Trocki, Sow Theng Leong, Jonathan Spence, Tim Wright, Wang Gungwu, and Yen Ching-Hwang. The four months spent teaching and writing at Yale University from September to December 1983, and especially my acquaintance with Jonathan Spence, were of importance for bringing my labours to fruition. In this context I wish to thank my friends and colleagues working on South-East Asia at Yale who made me feel my literary home was New Haven—Charles Bryant, Harold Conklin, James Rush, and Jim Scott.

I also appreciate the intelligent and efficient assistance of Melanie Harris, Gail Reekie, Geraldine Antoinette Goodwin, and Irene Finlay in preparing the final draft of the manuscript.

I gratefully acknowledge the permission granted by The University Press of Hawaii to quote from Jean James's translation of *Lo-T'o Hsiang Tzu*. Some parts of the present book have been printed in articles which appeared in *Itinerario* 8 (1984), *The Bulletin of Concerned Asian Scholars* 16 (1984), *Journal of Southeast Asian Studies* 15 (1985), *Journal of the Malaysian Branch of the Royal Asiatic Society* 58 (1985) and *Southeast Asian Journal of Social Science* 13 (1985). I am indebted to the editors of these Journals for permission to reproduce material.

Finally, I wish to thank Carol and Kristin for life rather than art.

Murdoch University JAMES FRANCIS WARREN
July 1985

1. The language of the late Maurice Freedman. Maurice Freedman, *The Study of Chinese Society. Essays by Maurice Freedman* (Stanford: Stanford University Press, 1979), p. 401.

2. Raphael Samuel, 'Local History and Oral History', *History Workshop*, I (Spring 1976), p. 202; the Singapore experience and situation was not unique as all of Monsoon Asia was the home of many other coolie towns. Historians and social scientists who have attempted to break ground investigating the problems of city and country in pre-Second World War South-East Asia include Michael Stenson's attempt to understand the development of the labour movement in Malaya, Ngo Vinh Long's literary documentation of multiple forms of oppression of Vietnamese peasant women forced into towns and cities, Martin Murray's study of how capitalist development in the form of rubber cultivation, metallurgical mining, and manufacturing in urban industrial estates transformed the social structure of colonial Indo-China, and Daniel Doepper's pioneering urban study of the processes and careers responsible for social change in Manila society from 1900 to 1941. See Michael R. Stenson, *Industrial Conflict in Malaya: Prelude to the Communist Revolt of 1948* (London: Oxford University Press, 1970); Ngo Vinh Long, *Vietnamese Women in Society and Revolution: 1 The French Colonial Period* (Cambridge, Massachusetts: 1974); Martin J. Murray, *The Development of Capitalism in Colonial Indochina (1870–1940)* (Berkeley: University of California Press, 1980); and Daniel F. Doeppers, *Manila 1900–1941 Social Change in a Late Colonial Metropolis* (Quezon City: Ateneo de Manila University Press, 1984).

3. Ibid.

4. See, for example, Singapore Municipal Annual Report 1898, p. 102; for 1900, p. 30; Low Ngiong Ing, *Chinese Jetsam on a Tropical Shore* (Singapore: Eastern Universities Press, 1974), p. 73.

5. Freedman, *The Study of Chinese Society*, p. XIII.

6. For a fine discussion of this approach see Louis Chevalier, *Labouring Classes and Dangerous Classes in Paris during the First Half of the Nineteenth Century* (London: Routledge and Kegan Paul, 1973), pp. 320–50.

7. Manuel Castells, *The Urban Question. A Marxist Approach* (London: Edward Arnold, 1979), p. x.

8. I want to thank the former Registrar, Mr Khoo Oon Soo, and the staff of the Subordinate Courts Library, especially Ms Seah Poh Geok, Ms Mahni bte Messod and Ms Loo Swee Yong, for their kind cooperation and assistance in facilitating my researches with the Coroner's Records.

9. The Archives and the Oral History Department were split into two separate units in 1986.

Note on Spelling

Throughout this book, non-English words are spelt the way they appear in the documents which were used as primary sources for the book.

Contents

Appendices

Tables

Maps

Plates

Between pp. 202 and 203

9 Rickshaw stands were an obvious place where pullers came and went, bringing news to relate to fellow pullers. (*Courtesy of the Archives and Oral History Department, Paul Yap's Collection*)

10 The daily activity of the rickshaw pullers around the Raffles Hotel in 1921. (*Courtesy of the Battye Archives, State Government Library of Western Australia*)

11 A row of rickshaws stretching towards infinity along Collyer Quay in the early 1930s.

12 During the rickshaw strike in 1938 thousands of vehicles were impounded for safe keeping at the premises of the Registrar of Vehicles in Middle Road because of fear that striking coolies intended to destroy them.

13 Before the turn of the century over 18,000 rickshaws were in use in Singapore.

14 To reduce the risk of hit-and-run accidents at night, a rear reflector sign which could be attached to the axle was first recommended in 1917, but it was not made a compulsory fitting until 1939.

15 South Bridge Road jammed with rickshaws on both sides of the tram tracks in the vicinity of Temple Street. (*Courtesy of the Archives and Oral History Department, Paul Yap's Collection*)

16 South Bridge Road in 1911.

17 A typical traffic scene in New Market Road in the mid-1930s.

18 One of the most popular motor cars of the inter-war years was the Austin-tourer.

19 Two rickshawmen caught in full stride in front of the Thian Hock Keng Temple, Telok Ayer Street.

20 The local police station near the junction of Pasir Panjang and Clementi Roads. (*Courtesy of the Archives and Oral History Department, Paul Yap's Collection*)

21 A posed photograph/postcard. (*Courtesy of the Archives and Oral History Department, Paul Yap's Collection*)

22–24 Photographs of the type which turned rickshawmen into caricatured specimens for the fashionable genre of magazine pictures and picture postcards associated with imperial tourism. (*Courtesy of the Archives and Oral History Department, Paul Yap's Collection*)

25 A posed photograph of a Malay passenger with umbrella seated in a first-class rickshaw, *circa* 1914. (*Courtesy of National University of Singapore Library, Rare Photographs Collection*)

26 French marines bound for Indo-China going sightseeing in rickshaws in 1938.

Abbreviations

AOHD	Archives and Oral History Department, Singapore
BMOC	British Malayan Opium Commission
CCVS	Certificate Coroners View Singapore
CO	Colonial Office, London
HCR	Housing Commission Report, Singapore
RCAIH	Report of the Committee Appointed to Investigate the Hawker Question, Singapore
SCII	Singapore Coroners Inquest and Inquiries
SMAR	Singapore Municipal Annual Report
SMAR HR	Singapore Municipal Annual Report, Annual Health Report
SMAR JD	Singapore Municipal Annual Report, Jinrikisha Department
SSAR	Straits Settlements Annual Report
SSAR CP	Straits Settlements Annual Report, Chinese Protectorate
SSGG	Straits Settlements Government Gazette
SSOC	Straits Settlements Opium Commission

The Rickshaw Puller

Sob and wheeze, sob and wheeze,
Aching feet, aching knees,
Twist and turn, on I rush,
Through the oily muddy slush
"*Lekas, lekas!* I am late!"
"*Baik, Tuan!*" precipitate:
Red light up: sudden stop,
Threatened by traffic cop,
Toot and whine, toot and whine,
Through traffic, twist and twine.
Arms tired, face is streaming
Cramp in hands, body steaming,
Throbbing heart, throbbing brain,
Struggling on, might and main,
Slop-a-slop, slop-a-slop,
Feel like death, soon shall drop.
Wind and rain, wind and rain,
Slip and slide, on again.
Rain and wind, rain and wind,
Hardly see, almost blind.
Jig-a-jig, Jig-a-jig:
"*Nanti sikit*, you wild pig,"
Want water and some ice.
Execrated—lorry sais,
On and on, start again
Faster, faster, tug and strain:
"*B'renti! B'renti! itu shop!*"
Sit on shaft, slop and mop.
"*Hai yah! mana chukup?*"
"*Sa'puloh, ta'chukup!*"
"*Diam, Diam!* musn't whine!
"Go to hell! lazy swine!"
Jig-a-jog, jig-a-jog,
'Silly fool,' 'lazy dog.'
Life like this, not for men,
Eating, sleeping in a den.
Tug and pull, tug and pull,
Life is short, life is cruel.
Sob and wheeze, sob and wheeze,
Finish up, lung disease.
Nights spent in filthy rooms
Dreaming dreams in opium fumes.

by G. G. D.
The Straits Times Annual 1938

Part I

Rickshaws in Singapore

1 On Sources and an Approach

INTEREST in almost any aspect of economic and social relationships of Chinese labourers—the lower-class culture of a colonial plural society—in the history writing of Singapore is a new phenomenon. There is a historiographical need to focus attention on the history of Singapore as a coolie town to demonstrate the impact of migration and the development of colonial capitalism on the experience of the rickshawmen of Singapore, including labour, exploitation, and conditions of life. What can be revealed by an inquiry into such relationships are the attitudes and behaviour that bound people to one another in the milieu of a coolie town. This approach to the history writing of the 'subject people'[1] of Singapore enables the historian to confront fundamental questions about the nature of migration, colonial urbanism and labour, and to trace how and why a city like Singapore has developed.

What, in fact, the historian must do to accomplish this task is to invert the emphasis which has been placed on Chinese society in Singapore. A dominant theme in conventional historical writing has been to stress the economic success of a handful of Chinese Kapitans and Mandarin capitalists from the beginning of the nineteenth century to the present day.[2] This approach omits the indispensable impact of the coolie on the growth of a city like Singapore. The immigrant Chinese labourer remains hidden from history. There is a mass of documentation available to study his history, politics, and society. But to do so, historians have to commit themselves to a sustained inquiry of those Chinese who came to Singapore to labour, who were hundreds of thousands, poor, who never 'made their fortunes'. It is only by stressing the historic role of labourers like the rickshawmen as a significant subject of study in Singapore historiography that Singapore's overside becomes less prominent. Space is created for the social world of the underside to be seen.

It seems to me incredible to present a history of Singapore without the coolie. Yet historians, who have dealt with the economic, social and political history of Singapore, have, by tracing its progress in terms of development and modernization from colonial past to city-state present, accomplished just this. They have gone astray by not attempting in their analyses to demonstrate the effects of Singapore's economic growth and political influence on the 'other Chinese'. More importantly, this form of historical explanation of Singapore's past has led to little attempt having been made to understand the contribution of the coolie to Singapore society. What I am suggesting is that in a new history of Singapore the Chinese labourers should be visibly present, part of the changing environment of a coolie town under colonial rule. The fundamental problems encountered in the daily lives of ordinary urban dwellers—making their livings and losing them—is the real stuff of urban social history.

Let me now turn to the sources for such a history. The evidence is drawn mainly from official reports and documents, contemporary social description, contemporary statistical analyses, photographs, and oral history, 'tales heard by the eyes'.[3] In these sources exist an astonishing range of facts on all the factors at work in Chinese coolie society, encompassing not only the relative size of the population and the birth, marriage and death rates but also statistics on accidental and violent deaths and suicide, figures for morbidity and mortality from circulatory, respiratory and sexually transmitted diseases, surveys by colonial investigators on the nature of urban housing, on migration and the colonial economy, and several studies of changes in the economy, amount and consumption of opium. A different picture of Singapore emerges with its general trends as a coolie town. It is still a partial picture though, of the city, and of the rickshawmen, their work and needs. There are several reasons for this. First, the evidence does not neatly interlock to spotlight the puller at work because most of the information collected by the British was tangential to the lives of the rickshawmen. Extensive surveys of changes in the economic circumstance of rickshawmen, like those conducted in Peking early in this century, do not exist for Singapore.[4] The sources are partial and fragmentary, making continuity and coherence problematic in an investigation of the Singapore rickshaw puller's life in different periods. Secondly, besides chronological gaps and unacknowledged sources of bias in the documents, some of the decisive records are missing. The Japanese destroyed most of the archives of the Chinese Secretariat in Singapore including detailed statistical series and routine reports on the daily milieu and activities of the Chinese labourers. Crucial evidence in the form of applications for rickshaw licences also could not be found in the offices of the Registry of Vehicles and is presumed to have been destroyed. The lack then of detailed information on aspects of the structure of Chinese society, on rickshaws in Singapore, and on work and experience of the rickshawmen renders a more complete study of their life impossible. Despite these shortcomings there is, nevertheless, buried in the colonial sources a wealth of information on the rickshawmen. The historian of society can, through a controlled and imaginative use of these sources, bring the rickshawmen into the historical forefront of Singapore history and history writing, by focusing on them in the circumstance of their daily lives, its routine, dangers, satisfactions, and accomplishments.

The rapid increase in the 1880s and 1890s in the number of immigrating Chinese workers was the most important single demographic and social development in Singapore's history. During this period the growth of the coolie traffic, and its disquieting biological and social impact on the urban life of Singapore, aroused significant interest and concern among some colonial officials and investigators. Quantitative research was done on this subject in the late nineteenth and early twentieth centuries, and the results of official reports, documents, and statistical surveys were published, in contrast to later years when civil servants frequently asserted that it was financially impossible to carry out similar investigations and difficult to compare current problems and solutions directly with earlier findings.

In 1871, the first modern census was conducted by trained enumerators and thereafter decennial censuses were taken and published up to 1931.[5] As the censuses improved in scope and accuracy, British officials were able to see ordinary aspects of Chinese life in Singapore and not to take them for granted. The census data revealed a vast movement of coolies back and forth between China and Singapore, and a dreadful poverty in the city. The annual police reports and the hospital records, particularly for the Tan Tock Seng Paupers' Hospital, containing mortality statistics with particulars of age and occupation among indigent coolies, provided basic empirical information on destitution and mortality. Here is where the description of the way the rickshawmen experienced life and death in Singapore was to be found. Like the trained colonial servant, the historian, too, can choose to take these quantitative data from the censuses, medical records, police reports, registry of vehicles, and the files of the coroner, and build from them a pattern of urban life and circumstance.

At this juncture I want to turn to the Coroner's Records, hitherto lost documents whose importance for writing about Singapore's past cannot be underrated. The Coroner's Records are available from 1883 to 1940. The emphasis in terms of sheer volume is on the 1920s and 1930s in which there was a steep increase in the number of persons who died under circumstances warranting an investigation; this intensification of the Coroner's work was reflected by the addition of two to three thick quarto-size volumes to record the rise which swelled to over 700 cases per year during the 1930s. There are lacunae in the series for both the 'Certificate of Coroner's Views' and 'Inquests and Inquiries' in the 1890s and partial or discontinuous returns for several years in this century. Chronologically the earliest case pertaining to a rickshaw puller, which involved an altercation with a drunken European passenger, is contained in a slim volume in poor condition for 1895. Thereafter cases of rickshaw pullers, of their wives and kindred, of owners and clansmen, and of passengers and strangers who met natural, accidental, or violent deaths began to build up. Those who were summoned to identify the deceased, who were either involved in brawls, strikes, and dumping bodies, or witnessed the suicide of fellow tenants, traffic deaths, and street crimes, provide the primary source for this exploration of the other side of the Chinese community.

It is in the 1920s and 1930s that the patterns of death among rickshaw pullers become less fragmentary and elusive. In this period particular causes and types of death are plainly encountered. The motor car was a new and dangerous element in the lives of rickshaw pullers while on the streets; traffic accidents between 1920 and 1939 accounted for nearly one-third of all inquests on rickshawmen between 1883 and 1940. Of the 31 cases of suicide among rickshaw coolies known to us from the Coroner's inquests, 26 occurred between 1921 and 1939. All six recorded cases of suicide by wives of rickshaw pullers took place in the desperate years between 1929 and 1935. There is nothing surprising about the chronological scope of these cases except that, when these facts are organized into a temporal series, they reveal the broken and heretofore forgotten lives of pullers and their families in close fearful touch with a world Depression.

The historian must be cautious in evaluating the coroners' returns of the verdict of their juries. The lack of professional training and competence of some early coroners, popular attitudes that might have resulted in concealment of suspicious death among coolies, and difficulties in identifying and recording death among the Chinese populace made the official administrative process uneven, particularly in terms of appraising the reliability of its returns. In 1884 'The Coroner's Ordinance' was enacted by the Governor of the Straits Settlements. It required the Coroner, after holding an inquest of death, to transmit the particulars to the Registrar or, whenever an inquest was held without a jury, to return the depositions taken by him to the Attorney-General together with a certificate signed by him.[6] He was also required to send a copy of the certificate to the Chief Police Officer. Despite the Government's efforts to amend the law relating to inquests of death, the role of the Coroner, and procedural routines, the factors affecting the level of registration and the transmission of findings to higher authorities were not well established until the turn of the century. As the population, economy and wealth of the city expanded at that time, so did the level of administrative efficiency of the medical and legal services attached to the Coroner's Court. Hastening this development was the incidence of the death rate, which rose dramatically between 1900 and 1905, and the Coroner and other officials concerned with identifying and recording it were soon given proper facilities for post-mortem investigations.

Inquests and inquiries of death were held either at the mortuary of the General Hospital or Tan Tock Seng Paupers' Hospital, or on the spot in rickshaw lodging-houses, brothels, markets, parks and latrines, by the roadside, river, and sea-shore, and in the vicinity of the harbour itself. The depositions taken by the Coroner, particularly those relating to inquests of homicide and suicide, have enabled the author to identify the faces of the 'other Chinese', the streets and addresses where they lived, the places they habitually frequented in work, solitude and pleasure, and the manner of death.

The intrinsic value of such testimony for historical study depends to a large extent on the investigative talent of the coroner. The taking of first-class depositions was a skill which not all coroners possessed. Taking depositions meant not only probing for the facts but constantly searching for the true motives of a puller, his friends and enemies, asking additional questions, following up discrepancies in the testimony, encouraging frankness on the part of a witness to clarify baffling information, a surprise revelation, or evidence which otherwise would not be forthcoming. To do this with precision and care the coroner had to have a real understanding of the social and cultural circumstance of the rickshaw coolies and be backed up by an exceptional interpreter and pathologist.

Inquests often involved a one-sided dialogue with the Coroner. His questions were based on the reports of police officers who had already visited the scene of the death and reported the results of their observations and inquiries. Despite skilful handling of an inquest it is evident from the depositions that coroners were not always able to obtain precise information, especially on motive. In some cases the coolies could not be induced to speak freely at all either out of grief or of fear, even by an officer speaking fluent Chinese. When the person making the deposition was prepared to cooperate, however, by providing a terse description of their daily life, information was divulged on the wider context of the workaday existence of rickshawmen. The depositions of inquests of death are a catalogue of human episodes that help to detail and explain common bonds of love, friendship, sex, the family, and work that united ordinary Chinese men and women of Singapore, and of the physical and emotional isolation experienced when these bonds were severed by forces beyond their control. It is also in such testimony that one learns about the rickshaw and the unexpected uses of its component parts; the surprising data tells us its wheel was used as a suicide device; its removable wicker seat as a weapon for self-defence; and its tarpaulin hood, as a shroud.[7]

The technique of collective biography has been used to compile information on the social and economic characteristics of rickshawmen from their inquests of death in order to identify and reach a sector of the Singapore population whose outlook and experiences have not been adequately represented. The specific advantage claimed for this approach is that it offers a means of reconciling an interest in the ordinary people of Singapore with an understanding of the urban world in which they lived. The historian need not renounce the human element in history in pursuit of structure and process. The simplicity of this technique for organizing and interpreting the inquest data has allowed the author to strip away the colonial rhetoric from certain parts of the written record of all its pretentiousness and mythic resonance. An attempt has been made to take the theme of immigrant labour, colonialism, and the city down to a human scale to a matter of mundane detail and complexity of meaning that happened to rickshawmen.

Many of the conditions the author was encountering in the inquests had not been written about because the rickshawmen had not left as enduring evidence of their lives except in death, as had the *towkay* (big businessmen) and Europeans who dominated their past. Through a collective biography of the rickshawmen in death, the material and moral circumstance of the underside of Singapore is presented in stark detail. The rickshawmen's elemental family tended to break down in the face of the nightmare attempt to scrape a living in the Singapore streets. Witness the death of Sim Kwee Geok, the 35-year-old wife of rickshawman Lim Jin San. After quarrelling with her husband over financial matters, and depressed by the recent death of her infant child, she drank liquid caustic soda while six months pregnant.[8] The meaning of such deaths was the key to unlocking the door of the past to an understanding of the elemental family-men, women and work during the Depression in Singapore about which the author knew nothing. There is a humbling sense of having lived with death and found, in its shadows, what really mattered to these men and women in misfortune. For them death was no mere statistic. Death was the inability to return to China to fulfil filial obligations, the failure to remit money to kin, the knowledge of leprosy and fear of separation from a loved one, the common plight of diseases like pulmonary tuberculosis, and the inevitable outcome of relentless labour that sapped men of their tragic strength. This source offered, paradoxically, the best means of attempting to resurrect Singapore life as lived.

However, it should again be stressed that generalizations regarding the experience of rickshaw coolies cannot be based wholly on the detailed reports of these depositions. For this evidence to be used to advantage it must be supplemented by information from oral testimony, literary description, and the Singapore in photographs and pictures. Until recently the few elderly rickshaw pullers left in Singapore had buried their experiences and memories, answering silence with silence. Nobody had interviewed them about childhood, village China, migration and becoming a rickshaw puller. The Archives and Oral History Department of the Singapore Government has begun a special project on the collection of early social history to fill this gap in living memory. In the course of this original work interviewers have recorded the reminiscences of people whose occupations are vanishing; among them were several rickshaw pullers turned trishaw riders in their early seventies, who migrated to Singapore during the 1930s.[9] The silence enveloping old men like Koh Teong Koo, Tan Ai Mai and Ng Kar Eng has been broken. Their memories were so impacted that some of their own friends had never heard their stories about rickshaw pulling until somebody had finally asked them.

Alongside the oral history, there exists in the literary documentation on Singapore and China a social history of rickshawmen. In these accounts, mostly fiction, there is an authentic description of experience that can lift the silence from the historical record about the setting and description of their life as pullers. It will be attempted here, through the medium of social description from the fiction, to expose aspects of experience and psychological insight of Chinese society and rickshaw pulling that cannot otherwise be known.[10] The rickshaw, with 'its distinctiveness, its visible social implications and its mesmerizing movement',[11] was also usually noted in reminiscences and autobiographies of European travellers, writers, and officials when describing their experiences, the atmosphere of Singapore, and the people of different races who today are called 'Singaporeans'. The authors, often in sections on tourism and travel, gave pride of place to rickshaws as a principal means of transportation in Singapore life and, for the wary, the travails of using this contraption.

Finally, there exists an important photographic record of rickshaws in Singapore. Intrepid photographers with unwieldy equipment and glass-plate negatives were already taking photographs of excellent quality at the time rickshaws were first introduced into Singapore in the early 1880s. It is their images of bygone Chinese society that remain to haunt Singapore in the present and bear witness to the past of the rickshaw puller. The most important photographs for this study were found in the photograph collections of the National Archives and Record Centre, the photo files of newspapers, and in books, periodicals, and magazines such as *British Malaya*.[12]

Before discussing their significance as a source, it is necessary to draw attention to problems involved in the use and interpretation of photographs of rickshawmen. In some respects no medium was less appropriate for recording how rickshawmen ordinarily acted than the early camera. The stillness required of the puller was singularly unsuited to capture the motion of a rickshaw, and the strength and strain involved in pulling it. Later photographers simply roamed the streets of Singapore with Brownie box cameras in hand seeking the exotic East, an ethnographic oddity, or to promote the tourist trade. These photographers frequently turned rickshaw pullers along with street hawkers and beggars into caricatured specimens for 'artistic effect', or for the fashionable genre of magazine pictures and picture postcards of the time. On the other hand, especially in the Singapore of the 1930s, the sensitive photographer could not get it all in—the damp nocturnal world of the cubicle, limbs deadened by pain, and the worn, weather-beaten faces of the men. While the results of photographers like Julius Friend were not responsible for distorting reality at that time, they often could not capture its essence. The poverty and despair defied translation.

Nevertheless, a 'reading' of the photographic record of Singapore is essential to tell the story of the rickshawmen. A thoughtful analysis of photographs can provide compelling information on a decisive moment in time and reveal in the process something about the behaviour of rickshaw coolies, the physical details of rickshaws themselves, and the characteristic environment of the men who pulled them. In this context, the images of these still photos, this moment rather than that, are a means of seeming to outwit time.

With these photographs we can delve into all corners of Singapore to develop a sense of the city the rickshaw pullers knew; filthy, bustling, chaotic, swarming with rickshaws, at major street corners, idly parked outside the Raffles Hotel, and in motion along the Esplanade and Collyer Quay from dawn to dusk. Just as significant is the immediate impression created of the kinds of work represented in the ordinary everyday life of the city, which ranged from the street vendors, a *singkeh* eating at a stall, a Chinese scribe engrossed in his work in the five-footway, to *poh sam* women (women who mend clothes) plying their needles industriously in a side alley. The rickshaw puller is there too, frozen in motion amidst the confused pattern of traffic, and so are the images of doomed older men capsulized in a rare moment of well-earned rest, sleeping in their rickshaws at twilight. Old Singapore, unchanged in many respects for over eighty years, is almost gone now and can be found only in these photographs with their fugitive images of rickshawmen—only their images remain as an element of the past in the city's present.

The author has pointed to the need for new directions in historical writing about the overseas Chinese in South-East Asia under colonial rule. There is scope for a whole range of studies of Chinese labouring-class men and women in the city that would not only answer questions about the relationship of immigrants, work-place and work in a colonial setting, but also have direct implications for history-writing and theory. A historical account of what the experience of Singapore rickshaw coolies has been would not in itself explain why their experiences have taken that form. History can only illuminate the past if it is given explanatory power through the development of theory. The task of developing the relationship between history and theory to understand the dynamics of change and social structure in order to deal more creatively with questions of immigration, labour, and colonialism in a city like Singapore need not be left to the demographers, sociologists and anthropologists.

The approach the writer wishes to pursue combines close attention to a specific period with a desire for a theory of historical transformation to place the rickshaw coolie in circumstance. In time, he has confined himself to that of late nineteenth- and twentieth-century colonial capitalism. Within this limited framework the author situates his enquiry 'in as local a setting as possible',[13] in order to reach the underside of Singapore to map its dimensions, to explore the big sectors and little crannies, to understand how the society of which the rickshawmen were a part worked, to describe on a minute scale what has not yet been described in the manner of the ethnographer. Raymond Firth used the term 'micro-sociology' in 1938 to describe such an approach, 'much of the anthropologist's work [and I would add historian's of urban social history in this case] has lain hitherto in what may be called micro-sociology—the study of small groups or small units in larger groups; of how relationships operate on a small scale, in personal terms . . . '.[14] Microdynamism not only marks a fundamental change in the way one describes the urban colonial past of Singapore, but also makes it possible for us to grasp in a coherent pattern the economic, social and psychological manifestations of urban life on the rickshawmen. The historiographical implications of this kind of approach dealing with the experience of an overseas Chinese community at a particular moment in time, as if under a microscope, is 'to enlarge upon the ways in which one's forbears have made a difference in history'.[15] To create such a history is to understand a totality of social relations, and the historian must range widely to match new questions to new knowledge.

The author emphasized earlier that the nature of the historical sources is decisive in determining the answers to the questions the historian starts with. The experience of the rickshawmen and their kin can be rediscovered in a source like the Coroner's Records, through oral interviews and in contemporary official reports and statistical analyses. It is the gaps in the everyday life of the pullers and their perceptions of that experience that must be filled in and redefined against a backdrop of world events—the rhythm of boom and slump, a world depression, and the impact of war and peace. The historiographical thrust is on the recovery of experience in a Chinese immigrant community; consequently a fundamental change occurs in the way Singapore's past is understood, in the shift in emphasis from 'places' to 'faces', in being able to see the society of the rickshawmen from within, and in a related concern with the quality of life. This study of rickshaw coolies is meant to present historical issues as they appeared to actors who have been hidden from history, and in such a way that reality can no longer be kept at bay. It must be categorically stated though that the main purpose of such historical writing is not to canonize the rickshawmen. The author has already laid stress on the methodological importance of working outward and upward, from the categories of the rickshawmen and events in their lives, to illustrate underlying social processes. His need then is to build facts about the overseas Chinese past in Singapore into a new historical analysis of what ought to be studied in a 'coolie town'—the life-cycle of labourers, the material deprivation under which they worked, and transactions of everyday life.

1. Maurice Freedman, *The Study of Chinese Society. Essays by Maurice Freedman* (Stanford: Stanford University Press, 1979), p. 161. While 'people's history' has been neglected, it is important to note what attempts have been made to present accounts of lower-class life in Singapore by other writers. On the formation of an immigrant society in Singapore, see C. M. Turnbull, *The Straits Settlements 1826–1867: Indian Presidency to Crown Colony* (Singapore: Oxford University Press, 1972); especially important for understanding the relationship between the mercantile class and the rest of Chinese society in nineteenth-century Singapore and Malaya is Lee Poh Ping's *Chinese Society in Nineteenth Century Singapore* (Kuala Lumpur: Oxford University Press, 1978), and Carl Trocki's *Prince of Pirates: The Temenggongs and the Development of Johore and Singapore 1784–1885* (Singapore: Singapore University Press, 1979). For information on a diverse range of topics pertaining to Singapore Chinese society and culture spanning more than a century, see J. D. Vaughan, *The Manners and Customs of the Chinese of the Straits Settlements* (Kuala Lumpur: Oxford University Press, 1978); and Barrington Kaye, *Upper Nankin Street Singapore. A Sociological Study of Chinese Households Living in a Densely Populated Area* (Singapore: University of Malaya Press, 1960).

2. Invariably works dealing with the *Kapitan* neglect any real consideration of how they actually got their money. See Michael Godley, *The Mandarin–Capitalists from Nanyang: Overseas Chinese Enterprise in the Modernization of China 1893–1911* (Cambridge: Cambridge University Press, 1981); Lea E. Williams, 'Chinese Leadership in Early British

Singapore', *Asian Studies*, 2, 2 (1964), pp. 170–9; Wong Choon San, *A Gallery of Chinese Kapitans* (Singapore, 1964); Yen Ching-Hwang, 'Ching's Sale of Honours and the Chinese Leadership in Singapore and Malaya (1877–1912)', *Journal of Southeast Asian Studies* (September 1970), pp. 20–32; Yong Ching Fatt, 'A Preliminary Study of Chinese Leadership in Singapore 1900–41', *Journal of Southeast Asian History* (September 1968), pp. 258–85; Yong Ching Fatt, 'Chinese Leadership in Nineteenth Century Singapore', *Journal of the Island Society* (Hsin-she Hsiieh-pao), I (1967), pp. 1-18.

3. Patrick O'Farrell, 'Oral History: Facts and Fiction', *Quadrant* (November 1979), pp. 7–8.

4. See Sydney Gamble, *Peking: A Social Survey Conducted under the Auspices of the Princeton University Center in China and the Peking Young Men's Christian Association* (New York: Doran, 1921); Sydney Gamble, *How Chinese Families Live in Peking* (New York: Funk and Wagnalls, 1933); 'Economic Study of the Peking Ricsha Puller', *China Economic Monthly*, 3, 6 (June 1926), pp. 253–65.

5. Saw Swee Hock, 'Population Trends in Singapore, 1819–1967', *Journal of Southeast Asian History*, Vol. 10, No. 1 (1969), p. 36.

6. Charles Goodricke Garrad, *The Acts and Ordinances of the Legislative Council of the Straits Settlements from the 1st April 1867 to 7th March 1898*, 2 vols. (London: Eyre and Spottiswoode, 1898). See Ordinance VII of 1884.

7. See SCII of Ling Ah Thui, No. 516, 30/12/24; of Tan Ah Siang, No. 71, 16/2/34; and of Ee Kin San, No. 497, 9/9/26.

8. See SCII of Sim Kwee Geok, No. 619, 11/12/29. Prosopography or collective biography has developed over the last two decades into one of the most valuable techniques for writing about the lives of ordinary people. The method works best with a readily defined, fairly small group, in a set period of time, usually not more than a century. The data is often drawn from a wide variety of sources that complement one another. On method and examples of this research technique, see Lawrence Stone, 'Prosopography', in *The Past and the Present* (London: Routledge and Kegan Paul, 1981); James Lockhart, *The Men of Cajamarca: A Social and Biographical Study of the First Conquerors of Peru* (Austin: University of Texas, 1972); Paul D. Escott, *Slavery Remembered. A Record of Twentieth Century Slave Narratives* (Chapel Hill: The University of North Carolina Press, 1979). On the significance of prosopography as a technique for writing South-East Asian social history, see James Francis Warren, *The Sulu Zone 1768–1898 The Dynamics of External Trade, Slavery and Ethnicity in the Transformation of a Southeast Asian Maritime State* (Singapore: Singapore University Press, 1981), pp. 237–51.

9. Personal communication, Miss Tan Beng Luan, Archives and Oral History Department, 28 April 1982.

10. I am thinking particularly of the historiographic importance of Lao She's novel, *Lo-T'o Hsiang Tzu*, which conveys the tragic quality of the life of the poor in Peking in the 1920s. The author's critical observations of Chinese society, based on first-hand experience, are told through the story of Hsiang Tzu, a strong young rickshaw boy from the country, whose sole ambition is to earn enough money to buy his own rickshaw. The novel depicts through the unsettling life of a typical man of the Peking masses, the terrible poverty and human motives responsible for Hsiang Tzu's moral and physical decline, until in the end all that is left is a shell of a man—a worn-out old hireling. That 'handsome, ambitious dreamer of fine dreams, selfish, individualistic, sturdy, great Hsiang Tzu', had become 'that degenerate, selfish, unlucky offspring of society's diseased womb, a ghost caught in individualism's blind alley'.

The kind of social misery experienced in the life of Hsiang Tzu as a rickshawman, compounded by ill-luck, insecurity, and his own unwarranted self-confidence, was always present in the lives of those who became rickshaw pullers in Singapore. The conditions of his life with its hunger, poverty, despair, his almost hopeless struggle for his hard-earned rickshaw, and his ultimate corruption and fall agrees with historical documentation based on the experience of Singapore's rickshawmen.

Lao She, *Rickshaw* (the novel *Lo-T'o Hsiang Tzu*), translated by Jean M. James (Honolulu: The University Press of Hawaii, 1979), p. 249; for a fine portrayal of the life and circumstance of Lao She set against the background of revolutionary change in China see Jonathan D. Spence, *The Gate of Heavenly Peace* (New York: The Viking Press, 1981), pp. 265–9, 316–19, 347–51.

11. UNNAYAN in association with T. H. Thomas, *Rickshaws in Calcutta* (Calcutta: UNNAYAN, 1981), p. 17.

12. Valuable photographs can turn up in the oddest places; a photo of rickshawmen standing in front of the Raffles Hotel was found among the personal papers of Reg Harrison, a prominent Perth hotelier, who briefly visited Singapore and the island of Java as part of a trade delegation in 1921, by Ms Wendy Brady, a Murdoch honours student, in the course of her research on women's work in the hotel, catering and restaurant industries in Western Australia. The photograph is in bundle No. 3 of PR. 549411-4 in the Battye Library, Perth, Western Australia.

13. Raphael Samuel (ed.), *People's History and Socialist Theory* (London: Routledge and Kegan Paul, 1981), p. 414.

14. Freedman, *The Study of Chinese Society*, p. 388; Samuel, *People's History*, p. 413.

15. Donald K. Emmerson, 'Issues in Southeast Asian History: Room for Interpretation—A Review Article', *Journal of Asian Studies*, Vol. XL, No. 1 (November 1980), p. 67.

2 On Leaving China

THE rickshaw was invented in Japan in 1869.[1] Originally called 'jinrickshaw' from the characters meaning 'man-powered carriage', the 'jin' was dropped from the term at the turn of the century and 'rickshaw' came into general use.[2] The rickshaw became a modern form of transport throughout Asia in the late nineteenth and early twentieth centuries. The rickshaw combined new technology—superior Western-styled wheels—with cheap, seemingly indefatigable Asian labour. The two-wheeled wooden carriage was an unquestionable improvement over the Chinese-invented wheelbarrow, the sedan chair, and animal-drawn vehicles. It is, after all, easier to pull a passenger along at rapid pace than to carry or push him over a distance. Rickshaws, which required only one man, superseded sedan chairs, which required the labour of at least two, except in China's mountain resorts and hilly Hong Kong. The comfort and speed of the ride improved, but the objectionable condition under which coolies had toiled since earliest times still remained—the rickshaw engine was a human one.

The rickshaw spread across Asia and became the most popular way of getting around for most Asians. It soon was a familiar sight in the larger cities such as Yokohama, Peking, Shanghai, Rangoon, and Calcutta. The rickshaw first made its appearance in Peking in 1886 and twelve years later appeared on the streets for public hire.[3] It was introduced into Calcutta by members of its Chinese community for carriage of goods around 1900. They came into use for passenger service in 1914, and 'Chinese rickshawalas awaiting custom at the roadside were a familiar part of the Chowringhee scene'.[4] Rickshaws also found their way to South Africa where they became part of the urban landscape in Durban for many years.

The rickshaw was tried out for public transport in Singapore in 1880. The first consignment came from Shanghai but they were imported from Japan the following year.[5] They proved to be an immediate success. The unheralded arrival of the rickshaw marked the beginning of a noticeable change in the traffic on Singapore's streets. Within a year of its advent, over a thousand of these two-wheeled vehicles were plying for hire in the city. The gharry had been synonymous with the street lore of Singapore. Carriages and horses had held sway for more than forty years. No more.

The gharry drivers resented the introduction of these 'manpower carriages'. In 1881 they struck, demanding that rickshaws should not be licensed for hire.[6] The strike proved in vain as the hackney carriage was to go the way of the sedan chair. Gharries were virtually extinct by the first decade of the twentieth century. From then the rickshaw reigned supreme in Singapore street life—until it too was ultimately replaced by motorized transport.

The rickshaw not only provided mass transport, it created new employment in Singapore. The majority of *singkeh* back in 1881 came from the lowest stratum of Chinese society in China without skills or capital. Their sole hope was a reputation that preceded them for hard work, endurance and thrift, and they were in steady demand as construction workers, twakow (lighter) coolies, stevedores, and coal loaders. But jobless men in China soon learned from kin, a father or an uncle in Singapore, about the two-wheeled wooden carriages, the number of coolies already involved in the rickshaw trade, and the money to be earned from the new profession. Regarded as little more than peasants with little hope of a future, they too wanted to be rickshaw pullers.

Between 1880 and 1940 millions left the two adjacent provinces of Fukien and Kwangtung in south-eastern China by sea, bound for the *Nanyang*.[7] Among these men, mostly under indenture, leaving from Swatow, Amoy, and Hong Kong on bat-winged junks and tramp steamers for Singapore, were represented all the major dialect groups. There were Cantonese, Hokkiens, Teochius, and Hainanese, as well as a far smaller proportion of Hengwah and Hockchew speakers who were to supply much of the labour required for the expansion of the rickshaw enterprise.

Many of these peasants were driven out by periodic poor harvests, flood-caused famines in all parts of South China, and by the rising price of rice.[8] They were also forced out by local conditions of over-population and the policies of landlords. For many survival hinged on escape from the impoverished domestic economy. Understandably, a multitude of *singkeh* left Fukien and Kwangtung in search of better prospects. They were indigent, barely knowing the written characters of their own language, but they carried with them the compass of culture, an iron will, and a burning ambition. Their dream was one of hard work, a decent livelihood, and a return in some comfort to home and hearth in China.

But not every one who emigrated did so because of local conditions. Colonial enterprise in South-East Asia also went far towards determining the number of *singkeh* who emigrated. Peasants were lured from south-eastern China by the development and expansion of colonial capitalism in rural agricultural enterprises, and in the public works, trade and finance sectors of the port cities. Sure of better paid employment, *singkeh* joined other Chinese migrants to mine tin in Perak, to open up the tobacco plantations of neighbouring North Sumatra, to pioneer rubber-smallholding in Sarawak, as well as to pull rickshaws in Singapore, where life was said to be better.[9]

Potential *singkeh*, poor, leaving their villages to women's care, came in their thousands on foot, by cart, or by river sampan to a sea-port where a passage to the *Nanyang* was sought. Huge profits were to be made in the traffic of importing coolies, commonly referred to as the 'pig business'. In the control and regulation of this immigration, the secret societies were heavily involved.[10] Few Chinese peasants could afford to pay their own passage. Recruitment agents of each major society in Singapore or independent labour brokers competed to offer the peasant or labourer the starting sum while they waited to sail. The total cost of a credit-ticket was about $33–38; the indebted immigrant usually took three years to repay the price of the assisted passage after it was transferred from the broker to a Singapore employer such as a rickshaw owner.[11] Other men were more fortunate as they came from families or sending villages where individuals of enterprise and wealth were willing to back their crossing.

Between 1881 and 1913, when colonial government reform was sought for labour contracts, 37,000–103,000 men a year sailed from Hong Kong to Singapore.[12] No other port, including Swatow and Amoy, ever exceeded 70,000 a year. Hong Kong was the starting point for the scheduled voyages of the passenger steamers and sailing vessels of firms like Syme Muir and Co. and Jardine and Matheson and Co., and principal port of call for competing German, Danish and Dutch sailing lines. There were also junks going to the *Nanyang*, from harbours small and large all along the China coast.[13]

Singkeh were not always well cared for on the voyage. Photographs show how small some of those ships were that made regular passages in the South China Sea with emigrants. Passengers were herded like cattle across a sea without the solace of kinship, in crowded, squalid, and unsanitary living spaces on board ship. Besides the appalling shipboard conditions there was the added terror of the unfamiliar, frequently being storm battered on voyages of several weeks' duration.[14]

On arrival in Singapore the new labourer was disposed of by secret society recruiters to an employer who spoke his own dialect. Dialect was one of the most important factors in establishing employment and a sense of place. Communication was the necessary prerequisite towards the kind of community the newcomer had known in China; Hokkien mixed with Hokkien, Teochiu hired Teochiu, Cantonese *singkeh* followed Cantonese *towkay*, and so forth. Recruitment conducted along speech-dialect lines meant that the stream of new immigrants had little say with regard to choice of occupation.[15] If a Hengwah *towkay* happened to be a rickshaw owner then *ipso facto* the Hengwah *singkeh* became a rickshaw puller.

The absence of the family, a pivotal force in traditional Chinese society, was the other significant factor in the experience of greenhorns[16] as they institutionalized their lives in Singapore. The major secret societies, the Ghee Hin, Ghee Hok and Hai San, which were often based on residential and occupational principles, not only found a place for newcomers in the economic system, they also bridged the gulf between the traditional territorial and kinship systems that these men left behind in China and the preponderantly all-male society they were forced to fashion in its place. The Singapore societies, as quasi-kinship organizations with secret swearing-in ceremonies, oaths and rituals, provided financial assistance to the ill and destitute, protected the monopoly of occupations of its members from all walks of life, including rickshaw pulling, and organized funerals. The secret society was one of the few elements of stability for coolies in a colonial plural society.[17] Its importance within the Chinese community was reflected in its membership rolls. In 1881, when the male population of Singapore numbered 72,571, secret society membership totalled 33,103. Significantly, despite the impoverished circumstance of the mass of Chinese labourers, more than half the members on the societies' books had paid their subscriptions.[18]

Politically, the secret societies proved too effective from a colonial point of view in controlling and regulating the affairs of the Chinese and in bringing about unity of all Chinese in relations with the British and the Malay or Indian communities. In this setting of an emergent coolie town, with the Chinese fragmented into various groups by speech and/or locality/origin, the wealthy headmen of these societies were actually the central arm of the British government. They represented themselves to the colonial administration as being the only ones able to maintain primary loyalties, mobilize labour, distribute opium, keep the peace, or avert a strike, and to the coolies that only they could give age-old security and effectively demand redress from British official abuses. And 'it is no doubt true that the *singkeh* were unaware of the existence of any other institution of government in the Straits Settlements'.[19] It was this unyielding insularity of coolies, as a result of secret society activity, from the wider society and non-Chinese which led to hostility between the societies and the British. By the late 1880s, as work drew more and more *singkeh* to the city, the Singapore authorities felt that the growth of the societies posed a real and grave threat to government. They were perceived as being too secret and too powerful to be utilized any longer as an instrument of indirect rule. The British declared the secret societies illegal in 1890[20] and established in their place an official Chinese Protectorate to regulate the immigration of *singkeh*, work, and custom, to look after the welfare of the Chinese in Singapore, and to keep them 'quiet, orderly and contented'.[21]

Immigration from China increased and most dramatically in the first decade of the twentieth century. Secret societies, no longer in control of immigration, and banned, became very secret indeed—criminal-like. This being so, the solitary newcomer wanting to pull a rickshaw sometimes went straight to the network of kinship-type voluntary associations that sprang up in Singapore after 1890. As was the case with the secret societies these associations cannot be understood without reference to the permanence of social ties and social structure in traditional China, especially the value placed on lineage and the family as an effective organizational force in Chinese society.[22]

The voluntary associations were organized on the basis of a common surname, a fictive kinship, dialect group, or area or origin, from neighbouring village to distant county or prefecture. Linguistic differences and alignments and recruitment on the basis of surname by clan associations fostered mock kinship, claimed loyalties, and established a framework of social and cultural life—a place of residence, a job, reliance on men of wealth and power—for *singkeh* from Fukien and Kwangtung.[23] It was the dialect and surname associations' resources which brought some semblance of strength and mutual aid to the society. In a non-kin environment, without family or lineage support, the immigrant associations were a lynchpin.[24]

The associations created ritual and secular solidarity among members by providing 'kinsmen' and 'descendants' for festivities and ancestor worship, and mourners for funerals.[25] Traditional anniversaries were ritually celebrated with dinners and visits, financial assistance was ensured to those in need, disputes arbitrated, and bereavement and death looked after.[26] Clan associations were also used to tackle a broad range of other problems. The newly arrived member from China facing problems of housing and work injustices quite naturally sought clan association help. However, against the background of several generations of immigration by China-born men deprived of family and marriage, the voluntary associations were not a sovereign remedy.[27] Yet, bonds of artificial kinship did provide a measure of stability in an urban overseas world without kin.

The immigration of *singkeh* stamped an indelible image on Singapore. It was a coolie town, with a heterogeneous Chinese work-force, a disproportionate ratio of males to females, and an abnormal age structure. Between 1871 and 1931 the rate of increase in the Singapore Chinese population due to migration was dramatic.

TABLE 2.1

Distribution of Chinese in Singapore, 1871–1931

Year	*No. of Chinese in Singapore*	*Percentage of Chinese in Total Population of Singapore*	*Total Population*
1871	54,572	57.6	94,816
1881	86,766	63.0	137,722
1891	121,908	67.1	181,602
1901	164,041	72.3	226,842
1911	219,577	72.4	303,321
1921	315,151	75.3	418,358
1931	418,640	75.1	557,745

Source: Reworked from Saw Swee Hock, 'The Changing Population Structure in Singapore during 1824–1962', *Malayan Economic Review*, Vol. 9, No. 1 (1964), p. 93.

At the turn of the century Chinese males constituted over 72 per cent of the total population of Singapore. Most of these men either were single or had left their wives and children behind. Aged between 15 and 59,[28] and alone, indebted, and jobless on arrival, they accounted for almost all the able-bodied men of the working population. There were few women (except for prostitutes), children, or old men among the Singapore Chinese in this period. A far more noticeable feature of this population in the early part of the century was the rate of return to China. *Singkeh* had come to do manual labour, to build, but not to stay. In the late 1890s only about 10 per cent of the Singapore Chinese were locally born.[29] The average length of time spent in the city by those who immigrated was about seven years. Later, when conditions were more favourable compared to those in China, especially in the 1920s, an increasing number of this immigrant transient community would settle in Singapore. For some the rickshaw was the answer to their sojourning dreams in China. The dream, if it were to come true, meant pulling one of these vehicles. If they had not gone to Singapore, the city of their hope, they imagined, they would still be suffering, or possibly have died, as a result of the effects of chronic depressions which swept from the densely populated villages to the ports and coast of south-eastern China.

1. John K. Fairbank, Edwin O. Reischauer, and Albert M. Craig, *East Asia. Tradition and Transformation* (London: George Allen and Unwin, 1973), pp. 524–5; 'Economic Study of the Peking Ricsha Puller', *China Economic Monthly*, 3, 6 (June 1926), p. 253.

2. The invention of the rickshaw has been credited to at least three different men: an American missionary named Jonothan Gable; Akiha Daisuki; and an out-of-work samurai called Yousouke Tzumi. Rickshaws were first called '*jin-riki-shaw*', which literally means 'man-power carriages'. Phonetically the word is derived from the Chinese '*jin*' for 'man', '*lek*' meaning 'energy' or 'strength', and '*sha*', carriage. In Hokkien the word 'rickshaw' is '*kan-cha*' (pull carriage). *Malay Mail*, 27 April 1965.

3. 'Economic Study of the Peking Ricsha Puller', p. 253.

4. UNNAYAN in association with T. H. Thomas, *Rickshaws in Calcutta* (Calcutta: UNNAYAN, 1981), p. 1.

5. *Singapore Free Press*, 19 February 1935.

6. Ibid.; W. E. Makepeace, R. St. J. Braddell, and G. C. Brooke (eds.), *One Hundred Years of Singapore* (London: John Murray, 1921), pp. 331–2.

7. See Joyce Ee, 'Chinese Migration of Singapore, 1896–1941', *Journal of Southeast Asian History*, 2 (1961), pp. 33–51; R. N. Jackson, *Immigrant Labour and the Development of Malaya, 1786–1920* (Kuala Lumpur: Government Press, 1961); Ta Chen, *Emigrant Communities in South China. A Study of Overseas Migration and Its Influence on Standards of Living and Social Change* (New York: Secretariat, Institute of Pacific Relations, 1940); Psia C. Campbell, *Chinese Coolie Emigration to Countries Within the British Empire* (London: 1923).

8. SSAR CP, 1910, p. 173; SSAR CP, 1911, p. 173; Ee, op. cit., p. 34.

9. See *Report of the Commissioners Appointed to Enquire into the State of Labour in the Straits Settlements and Protected Native States with Appendices and Papers in Continuation* (Singapore: Government Printing Office, 1891); W. L. Blythe, 'Historical Sketch of Chinese Labour in Malaya', *Journal of the Malayan Branch of the Royal Asiatic Society*, XX, 1 (1947), pp. 64–114.

10. *Report of the Commissioners Appointed to Enquire into the State of Labour in the Straits Settlements*, pp. 8–14; Mak Lau Fong, *The Sociology of Secret Societies. A Study of Chinese Secret Societies in Singapore and Peninsular Malaysia* (Kuala Lumpur: Oxford University Press, 1981), p. 22; Maurice Freedman, *The Study of Chinese Society. Essays by Maurice Freedman* (Stanford: Stanford University Press, 1979), pp. 73, 82.

11. *Report of the Commissioners Appointed to Enquire into the State of Labour in the Straits Settlements*, p. 10; Mak, op. cit., p. 46; Ee, op. cit., pp. 41–2.

12. The figures have been rounded off. The exact number of Chinese immigrants leaving Hong Kong for Singapore was 37,347 in 1881 and 102,997 in 1913. See SSGG, 1881, Table B, p. 323; and SSAR CP, 1913, Table A, p. 52.

13. Many emigrants still relied on the traditional mode of emigration from South China to the *Nanyang* during the transition period from sailing junks to steam navigation at the end of the nineteenth century. The bows of the Amoy junks were painted green, while those from Swatow were varnished red. Hence, the emigrant ships were popularly called the Green junks and the Red junks. Ta Chen, op. cit., p. 261.

14. Ibid., p. 262; Ee, op. cit., p. 33; and SSAR, 1884, p. C147, 'Passenger Ship Amendment Bill'.

15. Mak, op. cit., p. 45; Freedman, *The Study of Chinese Society*, p. 174.

16. The language of Maurice Freedman. Ibid., p. 72.

17. On the history and analysis of secret societies see W. L. Blythe, *The Impact of the Chinese Secret Societies in Malaya: A Historical Study* (London: Oxford University Press, 1969); M. L. Wynne, *Triad and Tabut* (Singapore: Government Printing Office, 1941); Maurice Freedman, 'Immigrants and Associations: Chinese in 19th Century Singapore', *Comparative Studies in Society and History*, Vol. 3, No. 1 (1960), pp. 25–48; Fei-Ling Davis, *Primitive Revolutionaries of China. A Study of Secret Societies in the Late Nineteenth Century* (Hong Kong: Heinemann Books, 1977); and Mak, op. cit. For the larger context of secret societies see Mak's book which generally supersedes the work of Blythe and Wynne who were British officials cum historians. Mak, however, is unsuccessful in his attempt to wed sociological theory to the historical study of Singapore's Chinese society for the period from the late nineteenth century to 1940.

18. Freedman, *The Study of Chinese Society*, p. 68.

19. Campbell, op. cit., p. 8.

20. SSAR, 1889, p. 295; SSAR, 1890, p. 518.

21. Copy of a Minute by Mr Pickering, Protector of Chinese, in N. 111 Sir F. Weld to Edward Stanhope, 10 January 1887, CO 273/143.

22. Freedman, *The Study of Chinese Society*, pp. 74–8.

23. Hugh D. R. Baker, *Chinese Family and Kinship* (London: The Macmillan Press, 1979), pp. 164–5.

24. Freedman, *The Study of Chinese Society*, p. 74.

25. Ibid., pp. 74–83; Yen Ching-Hwang, 'Early Chinese Clan Organizations in Singapore and Malaya, 1819–1911', *Journal of Southeast Asian Studies*, 12, No. 1 (1981), pp. 65–7, 75–6.

26. Baker, op. cit., p. 170; Freedman, *The Study of Chinese Society*, pp. 76, 135–6.

27. Yen, 'Early Chinese Clan Organizations', pp. 75–6; Freedman, *The Study of Chinese Society*, pp. 136, 183; Baker, op. cit., p. 171.

28. Saw Swee Hock, 'Population Trends in Singapore, 1819–1967', *Journal of Southeast Asian History*, Vol. 10, No. 1 (1969), p. 44.

29. Freedman, *The Study of Chinese Society*, pp. 61–2.

3 The Owners

THE owners of rickshaws usually came from the same area or dialect group in China as their pullers. Owners were primarily Hengwah, Hockchia, and Hokkien in this century, though earlier, most were Cantonese.[1] But other dialect groups also accounted for the purchase and maintenance of some of the thousands of rickshaws in operation in Singapore. The vast majority of owners were men. But women's names occasionally stood in the register of the Rickshaw Department as 'owner' of a numbered rickshaw, usually as wives of owners or widows. Ong Sam Moi, a Hengwah mother of seven children, owned one rickshaw as a side investment; she regularly hired it out to Chor Seng, a Hengwah, aged about 35 years, who lived in the next house.[2] In another instance, Kim Moh, a Hockcha rickshaw coolie, suffering from malaria and amoebic dysentery, collapsed while pulling rickshaw no. 7276. It belonged to one Cheah Pin Soo of Park Road, a widow, and rickshaw owner.[3]

The thousand or so owners of rickshaws in Singapore, during the period prior to the restriction in 1928, were mostly men of small capital. Owners normally possessed from one to twenty rickshaws.[4] For example, Koh Teng Hai and Ng Chi, a Hokkien and Hengwah respectively, both owned a rickshaw apiece—the former in 1912 and the latter in 1926;[5] earlier, in 1902, Tay Choon, of 380 Victoria Street, was the possessor of 14 registered rickshaws,[6] while Wong Song Song, a Hockchia owner at 147 New Market Road, also had 14 rickshaws in operation in 1929.[7] For most ownership of rickshaws was their sole source of income. Some, however, like the elderly Hockchia, Yeong Song Oo, combined rickshaw ownership with another small business—running a coffee-shop.[8]

Others, only some of whom are listed in Appendix 1, including Chee Kee Teng, a Hockchew owner of 7 rickshaws, ran rickshaw coolie lodging-houses between 1902 and 1939 in Victoria Street, Queen Street, Angullia Road, and Duxton Road, to bring in additional income. Some of them while still in Fukien and Kwangtung had chosen to start their lives over again in Singapore as rickshaw owners. Wee Siong, a Hengwah hawker in China, deliberately changed his life in mid-stream when he came to Singapore at the age of 40 to become a rickshaw owner. He prospered. By 1924 he owned more than 10 rickshaws and a rickshaw depot that housed twenty-eight coolies.[9]

On the face of the evidence few appear to have come up through the ranks the hard way as pullers. But there were exceptions, particularly among those men who had just enough capital to start in Singapore with their own rickshaw. A number of them went on to own 15 or 20 and retire from pulling.[10] Advancement from puller to owner was possible in the early years, if the coolie could make enough money to buy several rickshaws and start hiring them out. The exceptional career of Lee Choon is a case in point. A Hockchia, he was born in China and 21 years old when he started his life as a rickshaw coolie in Singapore in 1893. He pulled a rickshaw for one year. Lee Choon was frugal, never smoked opium, and made enough money in that year to start in business as a rickshaw owner. By 1924, when he was 52 years of age, he had been back to China twice, and was the registered owner of about 50 rickshaws.[11] Similarly, another Hockchia, Ting Pek Kia, at 36 years of age, already owned 12 rickshaws only seven years after coming from China in 1923.[12]

There were few owners who pulled themselves. Those who did so were men with limited assets—individuals such as Ng Ah Chan or Tay Choon. Ng Ah Chan, a Hengwah father of seven children, had two rickshaws. He worked one of them and the other was taken out for hire by Hengwah Chinese.[13] Tay Choon kept 14 rickshaws for hire, but only two were his own property; the remaining twelve belonged to other men but were registered in his name. He pulled a rickshaw himself.[14]

The big-time entrepreneurs who owned scores of rickshaws represented less than 5 per cent of owners, with a typical size fleet being 50 vehicles of the first class, often new, single-passenger, rubber-tyred. Normally, their rickshaws were in great demand by the coolies who pulled them. Business was profitable, even during the Depression, for the likes of Ho Kee Leong who owned 41 rickshaws and Seak Gin Gin, a Hockchew of New Market Road, who simply informed the Coroner in 1934 that he had 'many rickshaws'.[15]

Estimating the size of fleets, however, is a tricky business. Actual ownership of rickshaws was not necessarily reflected in their registration. An 'owner' meant the person whose name stood in the register as the possessor of a licensed rickshaw. The name entered on the register had to be that of an individual; names of firms, shops, joint partners or of trustees or agents could not be entered.[16] From the start individuals took advantage of the City's efforts to regulate the rickshaw trade. The large registered operators, most of whom were Hockchia and Hengwah and had secret society connections, were not always bona fide rickshaw owners. They had induced men to register their vehicles in their name to avoid the difficulties of dealing directly with the Rickshaw Department.[17]

In 1882 a municipal tax was fixed at the nominal sum of $1 a year, the idea being that rickshaw pullers could be encouraged to acquire each his own vehicle and pull it himself.[18] This proved a complete delusion. The tax rose, and within a decade cash security was also required to register a vehicle with the newly formed Rickshaw Department. It was a farce to think, as some officials did, that poor owners could grasp the registration system. They could neither understand the ordinance nor obtain the necessary security and were forced to fall back on the brokers. Nor could they rid themselves of the belief, enveloped within the confines of a hierarchical Chinese world, that they could approach the Registrar, a 'red-haired devil', directly and have their vehicles registered without graft.[19]

Every person obtaining a rickshaw licence had to pay security on a regressive scale according to the number of rickshaws owned (see Table 3.1). A broker could for $200 stand security for 100 rickshaws whereas the owner of a single rickshaw had to find security for $25. It was obviously cheaper to register a single rickshaw in someone else's name.[20] Yeo Ah Moey could not supply the required security. He owned rickshaw no. 8839, which was pulled by a Hengwah man, Teng Ah Yeok, who lived opposite him in Angullia Road. Yeo Ah Moey only told the Police, after they informed him that his puller was dead, that the rickshaw was not registered in his name.[21] Owners who could not get the security were forced to register under a broker's name in extortionate circumstances.[22] Though the cost of each licence for four months was $4, the broker charged between $7.50 and $9.00 per licence, besides a $1 fee for registering in his name. When a rickshaw was impounded an additional sum of 35–50 cents was paid to the broker for appearing in answer to the Registrar's summons.[23]

TABLE 3.1
Security Required for Licensing Rickshaws

No. of Rickshaws	*Security Required ($)*
1–5	25
6–10	50
11–50	100
51–100	200
101–150	250
151–200	300
above 200	3.00 per rickshaw

Source: SMAR JD, 1897, Appendix J, p. 35.

Thus the broker, or '*siong thau*'—the 'photograph head'—charged the real owners for registering the 25, 50, or 100 rickshaws under his name, and for appearing before the Registrar.[24] One such man was Wee Siong, the Hengwah who owned more than 10 rickshaws himself; the rest—numbering over 500—belonged to other pullers.[25] Another *siong thau*, Koh Chye, who was instrumental in organizing the rickshaw strike of 1897, signed before the Inspector of Prisons a statement saying to whom the rickshaws registered in his name really belonged, and 28 rickshaws were transferred to twenty different men.[26]

Aside from the cost of security, problems of lack of parking space and residence forced many into the hands of the *siong thau*. Ong Ee was a rickshaw owner living at 85 Bencoolen Street. His vehicles were all registered in Tee Tye's name as he had no place to keep them.[27] Place of residence was also a significant factor as men were sometimes obliged to register their rickshaws under the name of the headman of their lodging-house.[28]

It was not easy for the rickshaw coolie to become a bona fide owner.[29] Few were ever able to obtain sufficient funds for the purchase of a rickshaw, and to still eke out a living withstanding the liabilities with which they were saddled to meet the requisite expenditure. Perhaps two pullers in a hundred owned their rickshaws. The rest of the rickshaw-men—there were 20,000 coolies registered in 1902[30]—rented on a shift basis. Almost all rickshaw owners in Singapore rented their vehicles for half a day. It was the owners' responsibility to keep the rickshaws clean and in a fit state to ply for hire.

At dawn it was a common sight all over Singapore to behold the rent capitalists busily getting their rickshaws ready to let out on hire for the day to anyone who would pay the necessary amount. In Pitt Street at about 5 a.m., Ling King Chew, a Hockchia rickshaw owner, was distracted from washing a rickshaw outside his house, when he heard his small child crying.[31] In the early hours of the morning on Rochore Canal Road, Daniel Ross Cowie, a police inspector, noted that House 66 was a rickshaw coolie house as were most houses in that locality. Rickshaws were lined up three deep on the right hand side of the road, the shafts of one under the body of the other, constituting an obstruction of 12–14 feet. He made enquiries there and found that it was common practice for rickshaws to be washed by owners on the opposite side of the road near the canal, every morning.[32]

One can actually experience at close up this ritualistic daybreak activity

of owners tending their rickshaws by 'reading' a picture postcard entitled 'Jinrikisha Station' (see page 24). The scene is Sago Lane in Chinatown, *circa* 1910. It has rained and the area is relatively deserted. The rain-hoods have been put up on the rickshaws flanking both sides of the street. As one puller draws away on the puddle-soaked street with shafts held high, others stand or squat near by chatting. In the left foreground an owner or puller leans down to clean the mudguard of his rickshaw. Its rain-soaked hood lies on the ground in a heap beside the shafts. In the left corner another man stands between the shafts at work. Further down the street a man bends over to check a wheel, while across the road, on the upper right hand side of the street, a coolie wearing a conical-shaped straw hat inspects the hood on a rickshaw.

In yet another part of town, 60 to 70 rickshaws about two deep were stored on the side of New Market Road with their shafts pointing to the five-footway. On 6 June 1929 Lee Lak Tee went there to hire a rickshaw from Wong Song Song. About ten people were in front of the rickshaw agency; some were cleaning their rickshaws, while others were sitting, playing cards. Lee spoke to the owner and asked for a rickshaw. Wong Song Song replied that his usual rickshaw was not there but he could have another one which he was wiping off. The puller then sat down on the floor-board of a rickshaw, but not the one he intended to hire. While he waited the owner and his wife prepared the rickshaw, polishing the brass plates, one on one side behind the left wheel, and the other on the other side at the back, behind the right wheel. When a rickshaw was turned over to a puller like Lee Lak Tee, a licence and a badge were supplied to be returned along with the vehicle at the end of the hire period.[33]

Rickshaws were let out on two shifts. The day puller went out at 6 a.m. and returned between 2 p.m. and 3 p.m. Night pullers worked a series of shifts, the most common being 2 p.m. to midnight and 5 p.m. to 3 a.m., providing service throughout the city, but especially in the brothel districts and the vicinity of the harbour, till sun up. Goh Chwee Kaye, a rickshaw owner at 86 Bencoolen Street, described the way he rented out rickshaws: 'My custom in dealing with pullers is to let the vehicle to them from the afternoon of one day till the following morning at daylight. On the morning when they return the rikisha to me they pay me ten cents.'[34] The owners themselves, their wives or kin rented out the rickshaws at shift time. In Angullia Road in 1924, Tan Kin stepped out of the house at 6 a.m. to have a meal, leaving his wife in charge of the rickshaws. He returned home half an hour later to find rickshaw no. 2638 had been hired out by his wife to a Hengwah man named Ah Leng. Ah Leng pulled a rickshaw belonging to a neighbour and this was the first time he had taken out one of their vehicles.[35] Owners, who were thoroughly familiar with their pullers' hiring habits, were available at any time of the day or night for renting. Tay Ah Sui regularly hired rickshaw no. 4534 at 7 p.m., his usual hour. The owner, Tan Ah Keong, always delivered the vehicle to Tay Ah Sui himself.[36]

The testimony of owners and rickshawmen at inquests into the deaths of pullers inadvertently explains why some pullers chose their shifts, and what the relationship amounted to between an owner and puller, and a coolie and a rickshaw. Most men who pulled in the daytime were old hands and, equally important, they did not smoke opium. Opium was a significant factor in determining choice of time to hire a rickshaw. Owners preferred to let out their rickshaws in the daytime to non-smokers. The inexperienced, weak, elderly or those who smoked opium pulled at night.[37] Jin Aw had been a puller only two years. He frequented the New Bridge Road area only in the evening.[38] The somewhat less experienced Tan Kim Pong, who lived near the Roman Catholic church in Queen Street, was also a night puller from 2 p.m. till 9 a.m.[39]

Coolies who smoked liked to pull in the morning up to 11 o'clock and late in the evening. They did not like to be out in the middle of the day. Smokers had to earn money in the morning to buy *chandu*, prepared opium. After smoking they wanted to take a short rest. After being let alone during the hottest part of the day, they came out again in the evening.[40] Those who worked later till dawn were often not skilful enough to work in the daytime or the early evening. Let us look for a brief moment at a night puller prowling for passengers. Tan Poh Whye described his movements on 17 June 1934, '... a little past 1 a.m. I was pulling my empty rikisha along Bencoolen Street going towards Kampong Kapur, going home. I had been out since 5 p.m. and earned $1. I was a bit tired ... I was in between the shafts pulling.'[41] Unlike Tan Poh Whye there were many night pullers who, due to opium smoking, were not fit and lacked physical strength to run. Naturally, they earned less. For example, Lee Hoong, a Cantonese rickshaw puller, stated that his friend, Leong Lam, who lived with him at Hokkien Street, was an opium smoker, and pulled his rickshaw only at night. This fact was corroborated by Kuah Swee Kim, a Hokkien rickshaw owner at 55 Sago Lane, who did not know Leong Lam's name, although he regularly pulled rickshaw no. 7671 at night, usually from 5 p.m. till 3 a.m. The owner added that the puller's body was very thin as he smoked.[42]

In some situations rickshaw coolies pulled both day and night. There were many cases where passengers made a monthly contract with a coolie to hire a rickshaw to pull only them. The indifference of some of these private masters, as to where their rickshaws were kept during the night when not required by them, allowed the coolies to keep possession of them. The temptation to use them at night time, especially if they had families to support, was great.[43]

Many coolies religiously went at certain hours to hire their vehicles. Ng Kar Eng felt he was fortunate; rickshaw pulling was very good business in the morning as there were more people: 'I only worked half a day, I started out early in the morning, working very hard. I went out about 4 or 5 a.m., and came back at about 2 p.m., and passed the rickshaw over to someone else who worked the afternoon shift to make a living.'[44] Tan Sam Ong was in the habit of hiring a rickshaw from an agency in Bencoolen Street every afternoon at about 4.30 p.m.;[45] Ong Oh Kaw, a strong young Hockchia night puller of 29 years of age, hired a rickshaw at 3 p.m. every day.[46] Tan Uh Kit, a Hockchew aged 46, stated that his elder brother, Tan Nah Nai, who lived with him and was also a rickshaw puller, usually went out with a rickshaw at 6 a.m.[47] Brothers sometimes rented the same rickshaw and pulled by turns. Teo Kow Seng, an elder brother, and a Hengwah aged 48 years, pulled in the mornings and Teo Kut Seng, the younger brother, who lived in the same house at 228 Victoria Street, pulled in the afternoons.[48] Regulars often conducted their business with the owners on a first-name basis.

Along with the rickshawman's routine preference for a particular hiring time, there was also sometimes a tendency going back for months, and in some cases, even years, to rent from an owner who was from the same speech group or locality in China, and as a matter of course choosing a customary rickshaw. Kim Moh always engaged rickshaw no. 7276 from the widow, Cheah Pin Soo. He had been pulling the rickshaw every day for more than a month, and generally took it out at about 6 a.m.[49] Goh Chwee Kaye had known Tan Sam Ong, a puller who seldom worked in the day, for fourteen or fifteen months. He always took the same rickshaw, no. 4564. Tan Sam Ong got into debt, owing 80 cents. But Goh Chwee Kaye gave him credit on account of the hire of the vehicle because he was an 'old customer'.[50] On the other hand, Teng Poh had hired rickshaws from Leow Choon Seng for only three to four months.[51] Similarly, Lim Ah Phong, a 21-year-old Hockcha owner of eleven rickshaws for hire, rented no. 3681 to a Cantonese named Ah Kai. He had hired it for four months in a row.[52] A rickshaw was often rented as a matter of course when men were neighbours. Rickshaw no. 8839 was pulled regularly by a Hengwah man, Teng Ah Yeok, who lived opposite the owner, Yeo Ah Moey, in Angullia Road.[53]

But not all pullers were as constant about the rickshaw they hired or, for that matter, the owner who employed them. Koh Loh Tee did not always pull the same rickshaw. On the night of the accident he was pulling a rickshaw, but he didn't know the number.[54] Toh Poo told the Coroner, 'I usually hire from Ch'ing Choon of Duxton Road, I often change the ricksha.'[55] Teo Mak, who often hired rickshaws from Lye Sah in Bencoolen Street, when questioned over the assault of another puller, could not give the number of the rickshaw he had used: 'The rickshaw that I was pulling on the 15th September was from Lye Sah. I don't know its number. I gave it up at 10 p.m. that day. It was a no. 2 ricksha with iron wheels.'[56]

An almost insurmountable problem to contend with for owners was to instill in the casual puller a sense of care and responsibility towards maintenance of a rented rickshaw, and their method of pulling it. Take the case of Tay Tow Kiat, for example. His new rickshaw bought for cash two weeks earlier fell into the Singapore River. Goh Lye Boh, the Teochiu puller, whom he had not seen since he left with his rickshaw and the mishap occurred, absconded.[57] Owners such as Tay Tow Kiat had reason to be concerned about the welfare of their vehicles when confronted by irresponsible pullers: 'His ardor for buying one had already cooled and he was quite careless with rented rickshaws. A rickshaw was only a rickshaw. Pull one and you can figure that making enough to look after yourself and pay the rental fee takes care of everything.'[58]

When the rickshaw owners were sufficiently well acquainted with the coolies, especially regulars and 'old hands' who lived in their boarding houses or close by and pulled their rickshaws, to comment not only on the idiosyncracies of their hiring habits but on their character and personality too, and hence by inference on their relationship with them, it is not surprising to see them stress those qualities they deemed as both necessary and desirable in the making of a good puller, qualities that cost them next to nothing but immeasurably enhanced their authority, and profits from renting rickshaws, namely, cooperation and reliability, good health and physical strength, and common sense, and being careful with money. Leow Choon Seng described Teng Poh, who was assaulted as a result of a disagreement over a fare by two Malays, as a well-behaved and quiet man; he never knew him to be sick.[59] According to Goh Chwee Kaye, the puller, Tan Sam Ong, whom he had known for more than a year, was a hard-working and steady man of 20 to 25 years of age.[60] Tay Choon was quick to point out to the Coroner that Ong Oh Kaw was strong and young. He then continued, saying that the Hockchia night puller '... was a careful man who took care of his money and did not gamble, and always paid for his ricksha. He spent about 17 cents daily in [*sic*] chandu ... a good man, and not given to fighting'.[61]

The pullers had to pay a disproportionate amount of their earnings to the owners. A rickshawman paid from 30 to 60 cents in 1906 for his vehicle, for a period covering 12–15 hours.[62] For a minimum of several hours, the rate was still 50 per cent of the rent. Ong Ah Chew willingly paid this high return to an owner in 1902. On the afternoon of 15 June, at 3 p.m., he hired rickshaw no. 4635 from the Hockchia owner, Tay Choon. The puller and his brother, Ong Oh Kaw, left the rickshaw agency together. Ong Ah Chew brought back his rickshaw just after 7 p.m., and went out of the owner's house in Victoria Street where he lived, leaving the rickshaw behind. He paid 11 cents for those few hours.[63] Rickshaws were often let twice in the course of twenty-four hours; sometimes whole-day bargain rents were paid for older, cheaper rickshaws by brothers, kinsmen, or clansmen together.

Before the introduction of the first-class rickshaw in 1904 rental rates were calculated by the day, but after that time the quality of the rickshaw was also taken into consideration. Prior to 1897 the price paid for a rickshaw was 25 cents for day and 20 cents for night.[64] Between 1897 and 1904 prices paid for hire dropped to 10 cents for day and 9 cents for night.[65] Thereafter hire prices of rickshaws varied by district and according to quality. The rates between 1904 and 1916 are set out in Table 3.2.[66]

Within three years coolies were paying twice as much to rent a first-

TABLE 3.2
Rickshaw Rental Rates, 1904–1916

Year	*First Class*	*Second Class*
1904	—	18 to 36 cents per day
1905	50 to 60 cents per day	18 to 38 cents per day
1906	50 to 60 cents per day	15 to 32 cents per day
1907	50 to 60 cents per day	22 to 28 cents per day
1908	45 to 60 cents per day	20 to 28 cents per day
1916	50 to 60 cents per day	15 to 32 cents per day

class rickshaw as a second-class one. Thereafter the first class half-day rent was higher than the second class whole-day rent. But as the risks of pulling in the dark grew with increased traffic a rickshawman had to pay more for a vehicle at night. In 1924 able-bodied coolies grossed about $1 a day. Rickshaw hire then was 20 cents during the day and 25 to 30 cents after dark.[67] The day pullers had to return their vehicles punctually by 2 p.m., and the night men before 6 a.m., or they had to pay double to the owner.

Some coolies hired by the month, paying for first-class vehicles $12–15 and second-class, $4–7.[68] The explanation for this practice was that they could either pull themselves, and hope to save a little on the rent normally paid, and not be as beholden to the owner, or hire it out to whomever they pleased. Koh Ah Nea did this on occasion. On 15 July 1912, he gave Lim Tee Wah his rented rickshaw to pull. Lim Tee Wah left the house at 52 Victoria Street where he lived with Koh Ah Nee at about 3 p.m., and returned with it around midnight.[69]

Nobody helped the men to purchase their own rickshaws. The cost of a new rickshaw was equivalent to the rent paid to an owner for the hire of his rickshaw for a year. The rickshawman in Singapore never took home more than 60 per cent of his daily earnings in the best of times, while in slump periods he made next to nothing. He was the classic example of the traditional principle 'to him that hath shall be given, from him that hath not shall be taken away even that which he hath'.

The sweat and suffering of these hard-worked coolies made fortunes for the owners. For men inspired by profit, the rickshaw was a lucrative investment: the return on capital was as much as 100 per cent per annum. To prove that the rickshaw business did pay, and was a source of great wealth depending on fleet size, let us examine the expenditure and income of an owner in 1892 (see Table 3.3). Allowance has been made in this annual account for repairs, which covered depreciation of worn parts, a nightwatchman, as rickshaw theft was common, and only 24 days for each month. An owner could recoup his original capital in one year and still have his rickshaws for at least three more years with ordinary care.[70] There was often no charge for overnight garaging as owners frequently stored the vehicles in compact tiers in front of the agency

TABLE 3.3

The Expenditure and Income of an Owner in 1892

Income of 20 second-class rickshaws for 1 year	*Expenditure*	*Income*	*Profit*
24 hrs × 24 days × 12 months		1,440	
Expenditure for 1 year—initial investment			
Cost of 20 new second-class rickshaws at $25.00 each	500		
Cost of 20 pairs of lamps at $1.60 per pair	32		
	532		
Expense for licensing and maintenance of 20 second-class rickshaws for 1 year			
Licences at $12 each	240		
Rent at 30 cents per month	72		
Repairs at $16.20 per rickshaw	324		
Wages of one overseer at $10 per month	120		
Interest on $532 at 12%	64		
	820	1,440	620

house or on an adjacent site or found space for them on the ground floor of rickshaw lodging-houses. Rent, however, was an unavoidable factor for some of them.[71]

The figures represent a net profit of $620, or a return of 100 per cent on investment per annum. No account has been taken of broker's commissions, secret society fines, payments to *samseng* (thugs), and other 'squeezes' which owners were ready to satisfy. When rickshaw owning did not pay these were the channels which absorbed the profits. But few of the informal sector trades in Singapore paid so well as rickshaw owning. The fact that out of 6,946 rickshaws running on the streets in 1901, 2,796 were new Japanese ones, costing approximately $50 each, proves that handsome profits were made.[72] By 1919 the daily takings of the pullers were estimated to be over $20,000, and an indication that the

TABLE 3.4

The Number of Rickshaws Purchased per Annum, and Their Cost, 1917–1919

Year	*Number of New Rickshaws*	*Purchase Price per Rickshaw*	*Total Investment*
1917	2,455	130	319,150
1918	2,489	150	373,350
1919	1,116	165	184,140

rickshaw trade was as lucrative as ever is shown by the number of new vehicles purchased every year.[73] (See Table 3.4.)

The rental system made owners rich, and pullers hard-driven, exploited and poor. As long as the ownership of rickshaws was concentrated in the hands of rent capitalists, there was no means for the puller to increase earnings, to save, or to purchase a rickshaw, except to run harder and longer. Pulling like that could kill. The two elements—the high rental fee and restricted ownership—were a sign of the inequality of their life and death, and of the undue influence and power of rent capital in regulating the social relations of Chinese coolies in a colonial society.

1. SMAR JD, 1898, p. 102.
2. SCII of Ng Ah Mee, No. 551, 4/12/34.
3. SCII of Kim Moh, No. 297, 31/7/23.
4. SMAR JD, 1901, p. 130.
5. SCII of Chew Ah Tong, No. 170, 31/10/12; and of Khoon Cheang, No. 400, 22/8/26.
6. SCII of Ong Oh Kaw, No. 116, 16/8/02.
7. SCII of Wong Song Song, No. 263, 6/6/29.
8. SCII of Yeong Song Huay, No. 88, 18/3/38.
9. BMOC, p. c-45.
10. The evidence of Mr Hooper, SSOC, p. 28.
11. BMOC, p. c-47.
12. SCII of Ting Pek Kia, No. 309, 18/6/30.
13. SCII of Ng Ah Mee, No. 551, 4/12/34.
14. SCII of Ong Oh Kaw, No. 116, 16/8/02.
15. SCII of Chng Sim Geok, No. 231, 30/4/31; and of Mah Huat, No. 505, 16/11/34.
16. SMAR JD, 1897, Appendix J, p. 31.
17. SMAR JD, 1892, pp. 19–20; SMAR JD, 1904, p. 2; SMAR JD, 1906, p. 2.
18. SMAR JD, 1901, p. 137.
19. SMAR JD, 1906, p. 2.
20. SMAR JD, 1897, Appendix J, p. 35.
21. SCII of Teng Ah Yeok, No. 99, 23/2/25.
22. SMAR JD, 1897, Appendix J, p. 33.
23. SMAR JD, 1892, pp. 19–20. The amount coolies paid varied in different combinations in time. They were charged as much as $8–10 a rickshaw for procuring licences. The cost of registering in the broker's name dropped to 50 cents. At the turn of the century, 12–20 cents was demanded for appearing before the Registrar when their rickshaws were impounded; they were formerly charged upward of 30 cents and $1 respectively.
24. BMOC, evidence of David Beatty, Secretary for Chinese Affairs Settlements, p. c-45.
25. BMOC, evidence of Wee Siong, p. c–45.
26. SMAR JD, 1897, Appendix J, pp. 26–7.
27. SCII of Goh Chye Keh, No. 281, 30/10/20.
28. SSOC, evidence of Mr Hooper, Registrar of Rickshaw Bureau, p. 29.
29. SMAR JD, 1890.
30. SMAR JD, 1902, p. 30.
31. SCII of Wong Huat San, No. 606, 30/10/31.
32. SCII of Moy Kee Ah, No. 228, 25/4/27.
33. SCII of Wong Song Song, No. 263, 6/6/29.
34. SCII of Tan Sam Ong, No. 95, 6/7/02.
35. SCII of Ah Leng, No. 233, 24/6/24.
36. SCII of Tay Ah Sui, No. 241, 27/12/09.
37. SSOC, p. 163.

38. SCII of Ling Ah Ngong, No. 1, 3/1/26.
39. SCII of Choi Bak Lee, No. 192, 27/4/25.
40. BMOC, p. c-46.
41. SCII of George Buxton, No. 28, 5/2/34.
42. SCII of Leong Lam, No. 385, 20/10/30.
43. In 1904 a coolie could go to the Municipal Office, pay a tax for a private carriage and avoid the regulations and penalties of the Jinrikisha Ordinance. The law was clear on the point and required any rickshaw let or used for hire, whether by the hour, day or month, to be licensed and registered, and any owner or puller failing to do so was liable to a fine of $50 and the rickshaw could be seized and forfeited. Permits were granted free of charge to any coolie who brought a letter certifying he was engaged at certain hours, which was to prevent coolies from being stopped for refusing hire, and their regular passengers being put to inconvenience. SMAR JD, 1904, p. 3; SMAR JD, 1905, p. 3.
44. Interview with Ng Kar Eng, AOHD, Reel 3.
45. SCII of Tan Sam Ong, No. 95, 6/7/02.
46. SCII of Ong Oh Kaw, No. 116, 16/8/02.
47. SCII of Tan Nah Nai, No. 210, 14/4/38.
48. SCII of Teo Kow Seng, No. 436, 3/9/29.
49. SCII of Kim Moh, No. 297, 31/7/23.
50. SCII of Tan Sam Ong, No. 95, 6/7/02.
51. SCII of Teng Poh, No. 170, 1/8/10.
52. SCII of Ah Kai, No. 220, 18/5/34.
53. SCII of Teng Ah Yeok, No. 99, 23/2/25.
54. SCII of Fatimah, No. 205, 21/4/31.
55. SCII of Ong Kuah, No. 2, 5/1/10.
56. SCII of Teng Lam Pee, No. 164, 16/9/08.
57. SCII of Ng Pang Suah, No. 431, 28/10/22.
58. Lao She, *Rickshaw* (the novel *Lo-T'o Hsiang Tzu*), translated by Jean M. James (Honolulu: The University Press of Hawaii, 1979), p, 214.
59. SCII of Teng Poh, No. 170, 1/8/10.
60. SCII of Tan Sam Ong, No. 95, 6/7/02.
61. SCII Of Ong Oh Kaw, No. 116, 16/8/02.
62. SMAR JD, 1906, p. 2
63. SCII of Ong Oh Kaw, No. 116, 16/8/02.
64. SMAR JD, 1897, Appendix J, p. 21.
65. Ibid.
66. See SMAR JD, 1904, p. 2; SMAR JD, 1905, p. 2; SMAR JD, 1906, p. 2; SMAR JD, 1907, p. 2; SMAR JD, 1908, p. 2; SMAR JD, 1916, p. 16.
67. BMOC, p. c-47.
68. SMAR JD, 1907, p. 2; SMAR JD, 1908, p. 2.
69. SCII of William Grey Nixon, No. 94, 22/7/12.
70. SMAR JD, 1892, pp. 20–1.
71. Ibid.; the $16.20 for repairs when itemized on a quarterly basis included: hood, $2; cushion, 30 cents; back cushion, 40 cents; carpet, 20 cents; varnishing, painting, and general repairs, $2.50; the cost of maintaining an ordinary $70 rickshaw over five years in China during the 1920s was as follows: 'The expenses of repairing in the first is only about $2. In the second year the tyres have to be changed; a new pair costs $12. Some $3 is needed in repairs. The seat must be replaced in the third year, costing $12 or $13. But tyres and inner tubes are changed in the fourth year, the total expenses amounting to $20. In the fifth year more repairs are needed, costing $5 or $6. The total cost in five years is therefore about $130.'
72. SMAR JD, 1901, p. 130.
73. SMAR JD, 1919, p. 1-E.

4 The Pullers

In Singapore the legal definition of a rickshaw puller was a man who for the time being drew or pushed a rickshaw or was in charge of it in any street, road or public place or in the walks or paths or any private grounds or premises.[1] It is necessary to stress again, briefly, what motivated these men in choosing a life that was no better in certain respects than that of a beast of burden. Most rickshawmen had been peasants in Fukien and Kwangtung. The pattern of their lives in village China was shaped by mud, rice, and an old system of proprietary landowning. The life of the tenant farmer was locked in an endless struggle with nature—in planting and harvesting padi, digging canals and dikes, embanking rivers—and with landlords and enemies.

Local catastrophe, which was not always foreseen, also swept away the earth's promise. Calamity struck. Disasters in south-eastern China included endemic calamities, such as a certain famine, and periodical calamities, such as floods caused by rivers which might easily have been embanked before the monsoon. The exceptional misfortune thrown up at the end of the nineteenth century in South China might have been partially avoided by a prudent administration. However, it was a time when China was at a stage of transition from feudalism to capitalism and the astounding nature of this experience, which had assumed the proportions of a national mishap by the 1920s, engendered civil war, famine, epidemics, and forced emigration.

Hengwah and Hockchia peasants had little hope of ever owning land. The selection of rickshaw pulling was not necessarily a personal choice. The economic and political conditions in Fukien and Kwangtung provinces compelled these men to go far afield in preference to slow starvation in their homeland. Too poor to stay home, to marry, and multiply, they left.

Important assistance to potential migrants in search of jobs was given by *kheh thau*, returned rickshawmen, but at a price. Annually, they collected in their native villages or other suitable recruiting grounds in South China, a number of friends and relatives. These old hands took the *singkeh* to the port of embarkation, but they could get them no further without assistance. Thus, they went to a Chinese agent who supplied the funds, making of course his profit, to send the *singkeh* to Singapore as 'credit-ticket' passengers.[2] The scene of their arrival is recounted in this description:

> Slowly the coolies came down the several gangways on to the wharfside, carrying their bundles and boxes—rolls of bedding, pieces of furniture, baskets of clothes or food or other indescribable odds and ends so beloved of emigrants. Some had nothing but the clothes on their backs. All manner of men looking lost, anxious or apathetic. All seeking work in a foreign land unlike anything they had as yet seen. There were few old hands among these hundreds of 'new guests'.[3]

Voluntary associations found jobs for these Chinese immigrants to get them started, provided them with accommodation, and also extended credit.

A distinctive feature of this emigration of rickshawmen was the absence of women. There were no formal families and lineages, and thus, no customary coherence, nor customary stability. Emigration saw the widespread emergence of non-kin institutions rooted in the social structure of late nineteenth-century Chinese society in Singapore. Secret societies and voluntary associations were shot through by fragments of families and lineages, but possessing the closest of blood ties—brother–brother, father–son, and uncle–nephew. What is remarkable is that kinship established the pattern of emigration of rickshawmen linking kin, a predominance of immigrants from the same area in China, and surnames to extra-familial social organizations, work, and residence. Hengwah and Hockchia kindred followed one another forming a chain, pushed from behind by wretched conditions in China and drawn ahead by the remarkable economic activity of colonial Singapore, eventually linked to jobs as rickshaw pullers.[4]

These ephemeral groups, missing links in the chain of migration, suddenly become visible in an 'historical instance': the moment when persons at an inquest identified the deceased and gave his relation to the next of kin, and occupation. Out of 83 inquests into the death of rickshaw pullers between 1902 and 1938, 20 persons identified themselves as being either an elder or a younger brother of the deceased, and almost all of them pulled rickshaws; cousins and relations, including nephews and uncles, accounted for 15 individuals, and again, 'rickshaw puller' was their common occupation; among the closest of kinship ties there were 4 wives, 3 sons, and a daughter; 8 clansmen, mostly rickshaw pullers, came to view their deceased friends; while the remaining 32 persons were random individuals, non-kin, but frequently fellow pullers or tenants, and rickshaw owners from the same locality, or speech/dialect and surname group in China.[5] There is no doubt whatsoever that men who pulled and owned rickshaws were related by kinship or affinity. For example, Tee Chew Kim, a Hokkien rickshawman aged 43 years, living at 8 Craig Road, went to the General Hospital mortuary and identified the body of his brother, Tee Yeok Choon, a rickshaw puller, who was two years younger and had lived with him.[6] The testimony of a Hengwah son, Ong Ah Chan, was important in an inquest situation in restoring his father's name to posterity: 'The deceased was my father. He was a Hengwah aged 39 years. His name was Ong Ah Siew not Ong Ang Chong. He was also a rickshaw puller and lived at the same address.'[7]

The act of reporting a suicide could also provide systematic information on the relationship between kinship, surname, and occupation. Choo Liang San, an elder brother, made a report at Kandang Kerbau Police Station between 7 a.m. and 8 a.m. on 3 October 1908, stating that at 4.15 a.m., he and Choo Twa Ang, another rickshaw puller, had cut down the hanging body of Choo Tang Giak, his brother, who was by then dead and stiff.[8] The majority of these men, momentarily united in the 'death house', shared a common origin, experience of migration, and work, and lived at the same address or at least near by in the same district of Singapore.

This emigration was encouraged by kinfolk, friends, and employers. Through the kinship pattern of migration, group after group from villages in Kwangtung and Fukien provinces replaced one another, usually at intervals of 5–7 years. Tay Choon, a rickshaw owner, stated that Ong Ah Chew was the elder brother of the deceased puller, Ong Oh Kaw. He continued by noting that they had the same grandfather and then said, 'we all come from the same village north of Amoy. He also lived at my house no. 380 Victoria Street and hired my ricksha.'[9] The paths of men from the same village were apt to cross on tragic, as well as festive, occasions, as in the experience of Tay Ah Kin: 'I am a private ricksha puller engaged by Ong Soon Tee. The deceased, Tay Ah Sui, whose body I have today seen and identified in the mortuary is no relation of mine, but comes from the same village in China.'[10]

These networks of weak family ties and affinity, criss-crossing South China and stretching as far south as Singapore, were a reservoir of energy, sympathy and misery among those who followed the same route to be pullers; on the other hand, thankfulness, exploitation, and greed characterized employers and officials alike looking for periodic replacement of cheap labour to pull the rickshaws to keep pace with Singapore's growth and prosperity. There is some evidence pointing to the extent to which kinship, labour, and capital were blood-related. Kong Ah Fo, a rickshawman, lived at 99 Weld Road along with his brother, Ong Kow Koon, and a cousin named Ong Ah Choon. The latter pulled a rickshaw that he hired from his relative, Tay Liam, a rickshaw owner living at 56 Rochore Canal Road.[11] Similarly, Ch'ng Soi Bak Chew, a Hokkien puller aged 45 who was found dead beside his rickshaw by a Malay fireman, remained unidentified until one Ch'ng Choon, the deceased's cousin and an owner in Duxton Road, claimed his vehicle.[12]

The credit-ticket system, based on cash advances and a period of indenture, in combination with native place and dialect, tended to determine choice of occupation. But not all immigrants relied on the conventional means of labour organization and recruitment—of brokers, secret societies and clan associations organized on the basis of sub-communal divisions—to secure initial employment. Some found job security by relying on kindred on the spot who provided them with a fund of information on rickshaw pulling and found them employment. One elderly Teochiu migrant recalled:

> I came with three other of my friends after writing to some relations . . . they told me that I would find work . . . , if I am tough and hard working. By pulling rickshaws I can make a living and by the end of the year can return after making over $100. We left our village for Shauto (Swatow) and from there took a steamer, the 'Sea King', to Singapore. The fare was $19. When we reached Singapore, some government officials came aboard to check our tickets. Those who had tickets were allowed to land.[13]

The significance of this fact of kin-folk suggesting an occupation, part of the role of elder brothers, fathers, and uncles in economic life, is that the activity of rickshaw pulling was inextricably bound up with personal economic, social and political values and affiliations among the Chinese in Singapore, that began with kinship and emigration, defined work, and the limits of success.

To a European, a rickshawman was a 'Chinese', but to a coolie nothing was more familiar than their regional origin. A puller was a Cantonese, a Hokkien from the Amoy prefecture of Fukien province, a Hakka, or Kheh as the Hakkas were called in Singapore by adoption of the Hokkien pronunciation of their name, a Teochiu, from the Swatow prefecture of Fukien province, or a Foochowman—Hockchia or Hengwah.[14] At the beginning of this century a puller could identify the place of origin of the numerous men in the rickshaw trade by their speech, residence, place of worship, and where they plied for hire.

Most of the pullers were Hokkien and Cantonese before the abolition of the secret societies in 1890.[15] But within the short space of eight years the Hockchew and Hengwah increased rapidly. Their cheap labour was driving the Hokkien, Cantonese and others out of the trade.[16] Described as being 'dreadfully ignorant' by officials, they came without families from eight different districts in and around Foochow, and from the prefecture of Hengwah. It is difficult to learn from the inquests exactly where they came from in China. Pullers would tell the coroner their name, but not their place of birth. Seah Seh Gan was an exception. He told the Coroner, 'I was born in the district of Gai Ah, Hockchia, China.'[17]

By 1902 the number of coolies engaged in rickshaw pulling establish that the Foochow communities exercised jurisdiction over much of the economy and organization of the rickshaw trade. Of an estimated 22,000 rickshawmen, nearly 15,000 were 'Foochow' belonging to the Hengwah, Hockchia, and Hwee An groups who spoke different dialects of Foochow and Hokkien.[18] The Hengwahs and Hockchias formed the largest proportion. Most of them came direct from China from Fukien province through Amoy.[19] Low Ngiong Ing vividly remembers these men from the days of his youth in early modern Singapore:

> The neighbourhood [Lower Victoria Street] was dirty and noisy, but full of life. Most of the rickshaw pullers were Hockchias and Hingwhas, hailing from two adjoining counties south of Foochow. The Foochow dialect was understood by most of them, though they had their own patois which, like my own, sounded uncouth in finicky Foochow ears.[20]

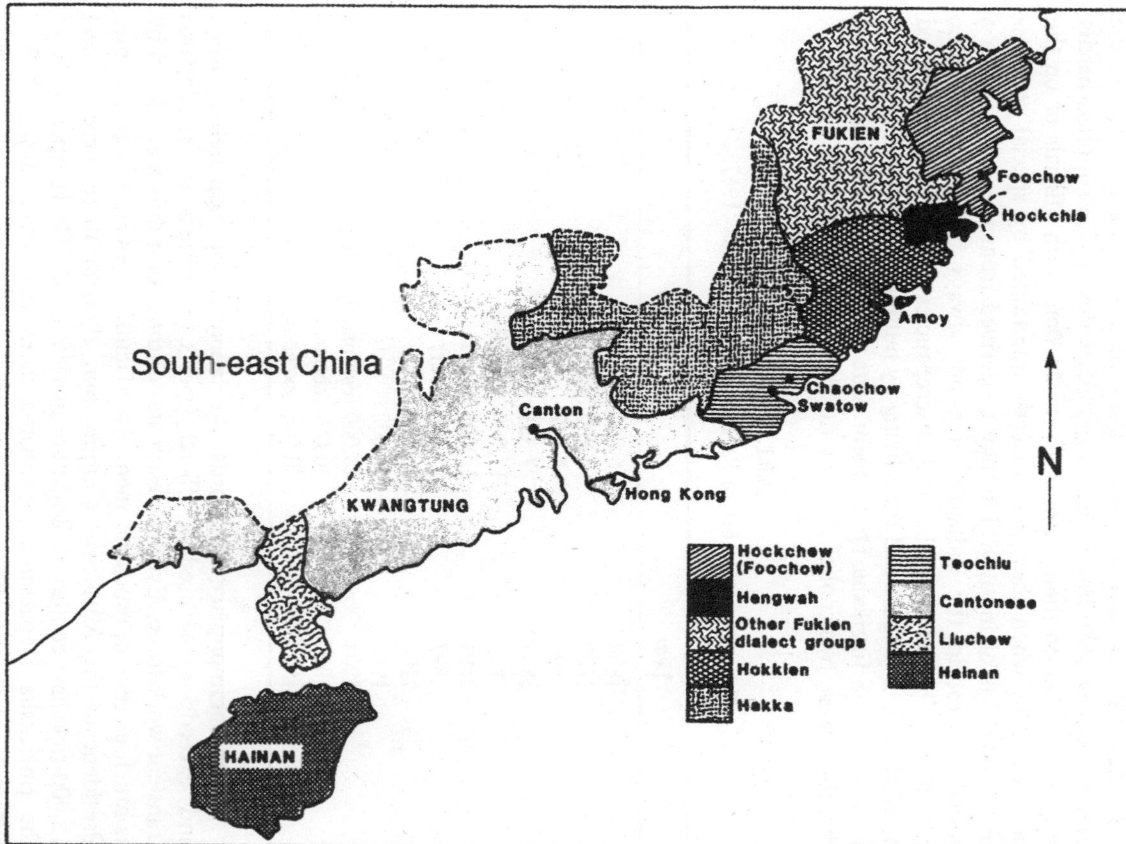

Map 1 The Provinces of Kwangtung and Fukien Showing Approximate Places of Origin of Different Dialect Groups

In 1924, Wee Siong, the 62-year-old Hengwah rickshaw owner and *siong thau*, told members of the British Malayan Opium Commission that Hengwahs and Hockchias formed the bulk of the rickshaw coolies in Singapore. This transformation in the population, which at times included sizeable Cantonese and Hokkien elements, had occurred since he first came in 1894.[21]

Estimates of the number of rickshaw pullers plying for hire on the streets between 1880 and 1940 vary. Pullers themselves supplied hardly any information on their numbers in discussions with officials or on the rare occasions when they were directly questioned by special commissions or boards of inquiry. The figures derived from the owners with a vested interest in the industry were not always based on the same calculus as that of officials, and discrepancies exist in the estimated number of men who earned their living by pulling rickshaws. The official statistics of the Jinriksha Department were calculated on the assumption that there were two coolies to every rickshaw, and often three by 1918.[22]

TABLE 4.1[23]

Estimated Number of Rickshaw Coolies, 1888–1917

Year	*Number*
1888	5,046
1889	5,000 (approximately)
1890	5,877
1891	7,331
1893	11,000–12,000
1894	12,000 (over)
1897	15,000 (over)
1900	20,000
1902	22,000
1904	20,000 (estimated to be over)
1908	20,000 (about)
1917	20,000 (exceeds)

It was commonplace for words like 'about', 'approximately', 'over', and 'exceeds' to be used in official reports to estimate the size of this transient work-force. Even the estimates of those best informed varied by as much as several thousand men. Alex Gentle, the Coroner and former President of the Municipal Commission, thought there were at least 15,000 rickshaw coolies in Singapore in 1908, while Mr Hooper, head of the Jinricksha Department, estimated there were over 20,000.[24] Any reduction in the number was often attributed to fewer coolies arriving from China. In 1918 there were still over 20,000 but the numbers were coming down.[25] The coolies were not emigrating from China in the same numbers as they had ten years earlier, owing to expensive passage, low exchange value of Singapore currency, and the high cost of living. Nevertheless, by 1921, the number of rickshaws on the streets had increased from 8,022 to 9,244.[26] All the pullers were still China-born with practically no Singapore-born coming into this kind of work.[27] Even during the 1930s the vast majority of them still started fresh from China.

The age distribution of the rickshawmen, which was a principal demographic feature of this emigration, was to have a marked effect on the character of the Chinese community, and upon the city itself. As to age, the only accurate statistics available come from the Coroner's Records. Here I have to begin by saying that even the best estimates with regard to age structure and employment are somewhat skewed by death. Because development in this distribution cannot be estimated with any certainty, one is unable to pinpoint the age at which they came and began to pull rickshaws and the length of time they pursued this occupation. We also are unable to say when they returned to China, but conclusive evidence does exist on age levels and death in employment. One thing is for certain: rickshaw pulling was an occupation for neither the faint-hearted nor the elderly. The work called for physically strong men, and preferably young, when they were still in the prime of their life. The following table shows the age structure of 102 rickshawmen.

TABLE 4.2[28]

Age Distribution of 102 Rickshawmen, 1902–1939

Age	*Number*	*Age*	*Number*
11–20	2	41–50	28
21–30	30	51–60	9
31–40	32	61–over	1

Their age at the time of their death ranged from 19 to 61 years old, but the work experience overwhelmingly represented was that of manhood, the period between 20 and 50 years of age. Sixty-one per cent were between 21 and 40, a time for hard work. There were also 27 per cent between 41 and 50. Significantly only 3 per cent were under the age of 20, and 10 per cent above the age of 51, with one man, Lim Phua Sim, an elderly Hengwah puller, over 61 years of age.[29] The largest groups were in the age spread between 21 and 30 (30) and 31 to 40 (32); there were few youths between 16 and 20 years of age. The sharp decrease in the numbers above the age of 50 is dramatic. Age was a sign to step outside the shafts before it was too late. When men entered their fifties rickshaw pulling took its toll on the body in a relentless way, even upon the toughest streetwise pullers. The choice was simple. They had to stop or die. The age structure that is disclosed is conspicuous for the absence of the categories 'youth' and 'old age'. It reveals rickshaw pulling as a tough job indeed, physically demanding, requiring a man to go to his limit: a job that could and did kill in accordance with age, but especially as one grew older. Supporting evidence concerning age distribution of rickshawmen in Singapore was supplied by pullers themselves in 1924.

The average age of the coolies questioned, whether opium smokers or not, was 37, with the range varying from 22 to 57.[30]

Single and transient, most rickshawmen lived in crowded two- and three-storey tenement houses. As mentioned earlier, the occupation of rickshaw pulling rested on the principles of kinship, speech and/or locality/origin. Residence was no exception. Rickshaw pullers of particular sub-ethnic groups congregated along certain streets next to one another, lodging-house by lodging-house. These areas where the men lived, from several weeks to a number of years, were dominated by a distinctive character that was Foochow or Hokkien and not, for example, Cantonese, and there were numerous signs on a street to symbolize this, and to evoke the residents' way of life, from temples to dialect associations or the name of the street itself and its derivation, and a cacophony of daily sights and sounds all orchestrated in the dialect of its inhabitants.[31]

A combination of sources will aid us in locating these streets and the men who lived and worked in and around them. Again, the Coroner's Inquests and Inquiries provide systematic information, in this case, on the names of streets, the number of the coolie lodging-house, where a rickshawman was living, indications of length of residence, and even rent paid. A second source and form of municipal intervention, a 1902 list of coolie lodging-houses in which water meters were installed, enables one to 'discover' on which streets pullers were most apt to congregate, in order to be near potential employment. Finally, there is a list of lodging-houses occupied by rickshaw coolies in 1918 that shows the 'piling up' effect of pullers in tenements on particular streets, and the problem of severe rent increases faced by these men.[32] From the inquests and inquiries it is clear that rickshawmen lived all over Singapore, wherever in fact their services were required. But certain streets in several downtown areas were identified with rickshaw housing: New Market Road, Park Road, Rochore Road, Queen Street, Johore Road, Ophir Road, Victoria Street, and Angullia Road.[33] The density of lodging-houses on these streets remained high. In 1902 water meters had been installed in 7 lodging-houses in Johore Road, 11 in Queen Street, and 15 in Victoria Street.[34] By examining 104 inquests of rickshawmen with regard to language and origin a pattern of loyalty, kinship and occupation emerges, which renders a street with an identity based on one of the two provinces in south-eastern China, Fukien (Hokkien) or Kwangtung (Canton), and representing at least eight 'ethnic' groups with varying dialects.[35]

One of the most striking examples, with 15 cases, is Victoria Street, with Hockchia, Hockchew, Hengwah and Hokkien pullers, all co-residing to form a little pot-pourri of Fukien province.[36] Low Ngiong Ing remembered the segregated housing in the lower end of Victoria Street in the 1920s, 'where most of the rickshaw pullers were Hockchias and Hingwhas, hailing from two adjoining counties south of Foochow'.[37] The atmosphere and population of Angullia Road was similar. On the other hand, a street such as Duxton Road was wholly dominated by Hokkiens,

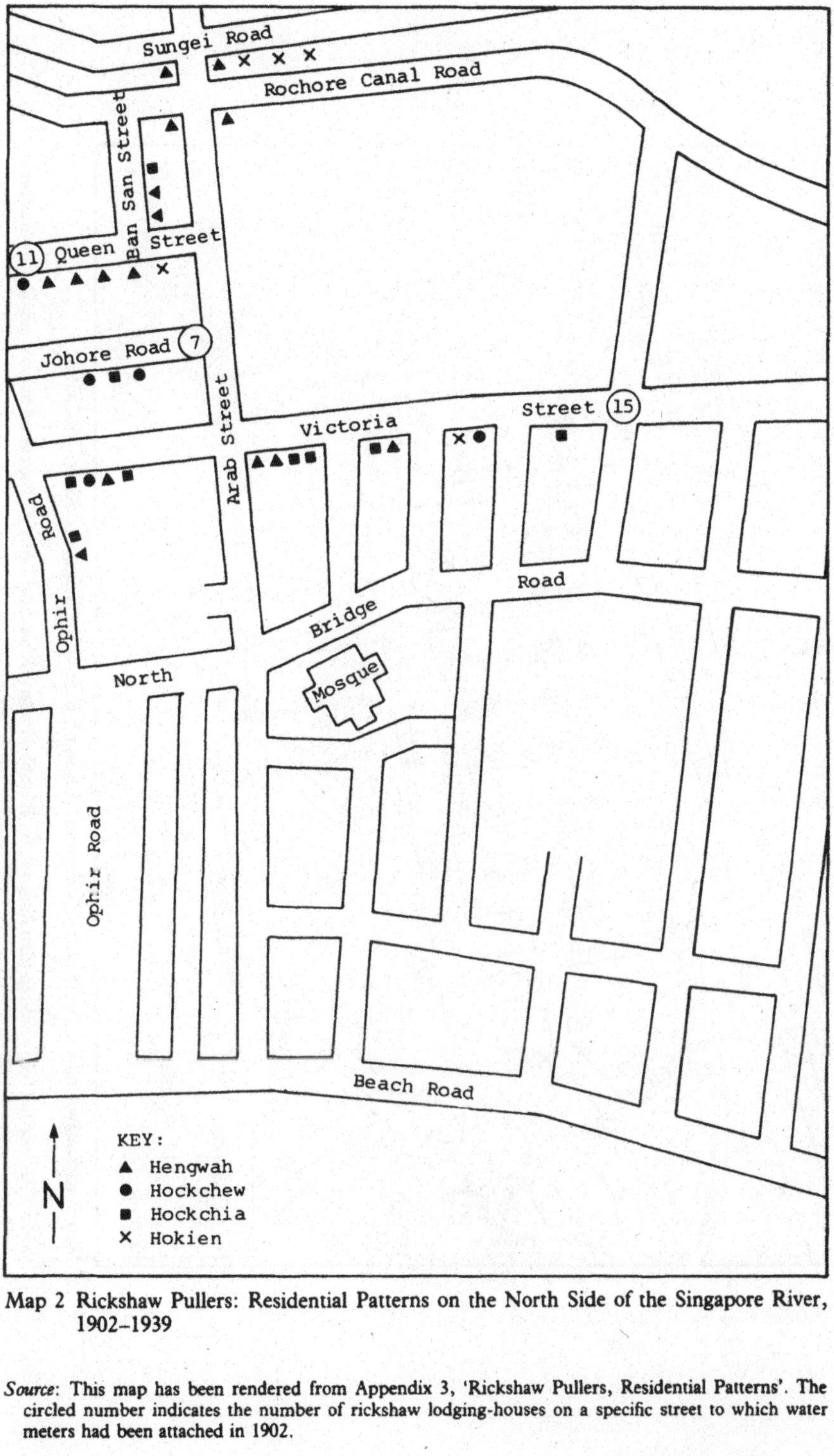

Map 2 Rickshaw Pullers: Residential Patterns on the North Side of the Singapore River, 1902–1939

Source: This map has been rendered from Appendix 3, 'Rickshaw Pullers, Residential Patterns'. The circled number indicates the number of rickshaw lodging-houses on a specific street to which water meters had been attached in 1902.

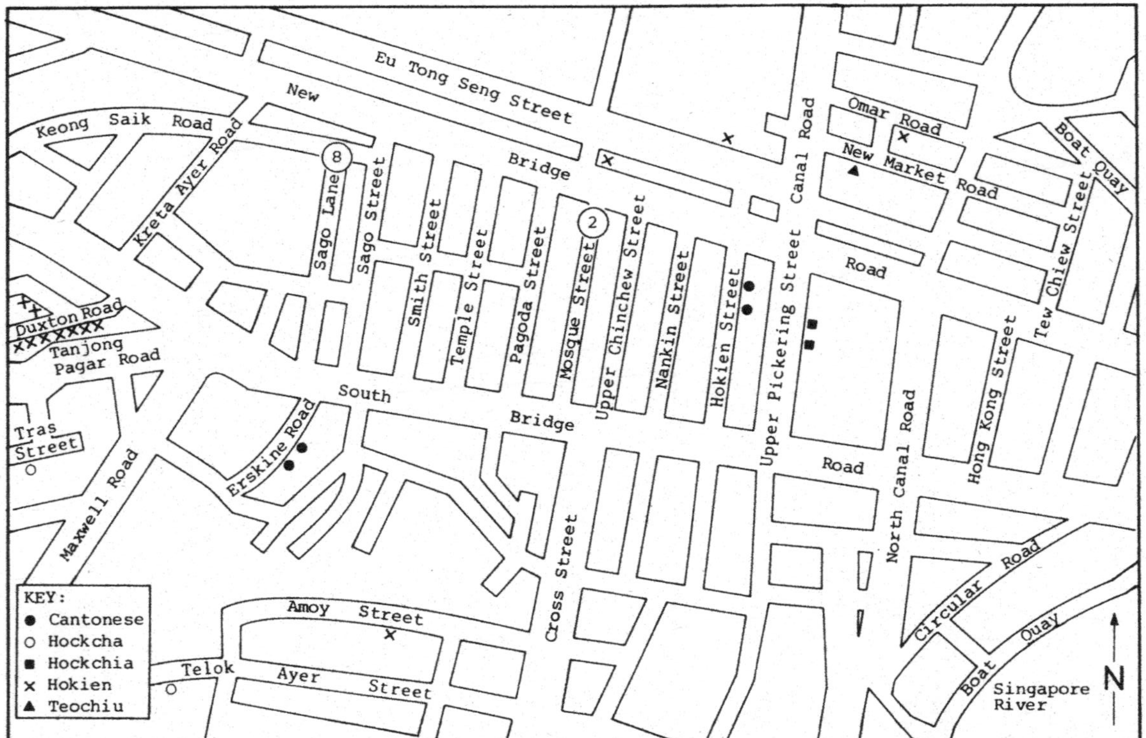

Map 3 Rickshaw Pullers: Residential Patterns on the South Side of the Singapore River, 1902–1939

Source: This map has been rendered from Appendix 3, 'Rickshaw Pullers, Residential Patterns. The circled number indicates the number of rickshaw lodging-houses on a specific street mentioned in various sources.

TABLE 4.3
Rickshaw Pullers: Residential Patterns, 1902–1939

Street	*Total*	*Hockchia*	*Hockchew*	*Hengwah*	*Hokkien*	*Cantonese*	*Unknown*
Park Road	5	3			2		
Craig Road	2				2		
Queen Street	6		1	4	1		
Victoria Street	15	6	2	4	1		2
Angullia Road	5	3		2			
Rochore Road	5			2	3		
Duxton Road	7				7		
Total	45	12	3	12	16		2

Source: This table has been compiled from Appendix 3, 'Rickshaw Coolies: Residential Patterns, 1902–1939'.

while Queen Street was mainly the home of Hengwah coolies.[38]

The number of men in these houses, who dossed down in shifts, varied in 1918 from as few as 15 at 96 Queen Street to the severe overcrowding of 124 Victoria Street with 175 occupants, with the average ranging between 35 and 60 along Johore Road, Bencoolen Street, and New Market Road.[39] The number of men in the two houses on Mosque Street listed in 1918 as occupied by rickshaw coolies, Nos. 36 and 41, were high, 80 and 85 respectively; at 96 Bencoolen Street, a big compound house, crowding began to approach the unbearable with 110 coolies.[40] As high as these figures are, they do not represent a considerable increase on pre-war densities for areas such as Kreta Ayer. It seemed reasonable as early as 1904 to situate the new 'commodius and substantially built' rickshaw station at Kreta Ayer (which is now being renovated as a maternity and child-care centre) in that 'crowded part of town, where so many jinricksha owners and pullers live'.[41] By 1918 there was no more housing in the area. The pullers did not want to go far out of the city. Mr Hooper, appearing before the Housing Commission Inquiry that year, testified that Duxton Road and Craig Road near Kreta Ayer were 'very crowded, and the vicinity of Peoples Park'.[42] Manassah Lane, off Park Road, was described by him as a 'dreadful place'. Certainly more lodging-houses were required. All around Muar Road and Angullia Road the crowding was extremely bad. The head of the Rickshaw Department finished his testimony on a sombre note saying that 'the houses in the [rickshaw] coolie districts are filled and overcrowded'.[43]

Many of these lodging-houses were either owned or rented by rickshaw proprietors. Nearly forty-five years later Ng Kar Eng could still remember where he went to hire his rickshaw as a young hopeful: 'Yes, the rickshaw belonged to the owner of the house where I stayed. There were only three or four rickshaws left then [1937].... They were used by some men to make a living, while some younger men used trishaws.'[44] The pullers were nearly always under an obligation to reside in the lodging-house of their employer. There they lived in cramped dormitories with friends and strangers, so as to defray the cost of rent. Men like Tay Choon, Ling Hee Lye, and Tan Ah Keong all housed the men and provided rickshaws. Tay Choon of 380 Victoria Street, where so many rickshaw coolies lived, described what it meant to live at his house, when he identified the body of Ong Oh Kaw: '... he had lodged at my house, that is he kept his box there, his bed was there and he bathed there and slept there. He took his food outside.'[45] While accommodation did not necessarily include board, it was noted in Ling Hee Lye's case that he was an eating-house keeper in Johore Road, who stored rickshaws on his premises; the pullers lodged upstairs, and generally ate downstairs.[46] When a puller kept his box at a house, which contained all his worldly possessions, including his clothes and clogs, perhaps a tattered letter or two, a photograph of a young mother and son in China, a small teapot, a talisman, or an opium pipe, he was not considered a temporary lodger. Tan Ah Keong, living at 43 Bain Street, described one of his men as follows: 'He has hired from me regularly for about three months ... [and] lived and kept his box in my lodging house at 42 Bain Street'.[47]

The length of time rickshawmen lived in a particular lodging varied, and there was continuous turnover. If the atmosphere was supportive, however, and that depended on the presence or absence of kin and current relations with the owner/landlord, a man could stay for years. Lui Ah Pek had been a tenant of Hwe Ah Tat's, who kept lodgers at Spottiswoode Park Road, for more than a year.[48] The puller, Tan Ah Foo, described a friend of five years, as having lived with him in his lodging-house for the past three years.[49] For these men, who regularly rented the rickshaws of their landlords, the lodging-house cum agency was a home away from home. They thought of it in this way:

> Ordinarily, there were about twenty men living at the agency. They either sat around talking or were dead asleep after putting away their rickshaws.... He had always regarded the Jen Ho Agency as his home. On private jobs his masters changed frequently, and when working the streets his passengers changed with every trip. This was the only place he was allowed to stay and there was always someone to chat with.[50]

On the other hand, the youthful Hockchia, Ong Oh Kaw, had lodged at Tay Choon's house for only four months.[51] It was the owners/landlords who referred to the period of residence of rickshawmen in lodging-houses: Lim Tiew stayed for 1½ months; Tay Ah Sui, about 3 months; Ong Cha Bah, 2 months; Yau Chin Swee, at least 6 months; Ng Liew, also 6 months; Ong Teck Cheng, a few months; and Low Nong Nong, for a month.[52] The more general practice was for coolies to live in a tenement for shorter periods. There are enough examples in the inquests of deceased pullers to show that men were continuously on the move, living in different lodging-houses, perhaps along the same street, or area, and shifting two or even three times a year.

Differences in rent tended to be justified by the location and extent of overcrowding. The rents were higher in the downtown area or on its fringe than anywhere else. Pullers shared cramped quarters because the acute piling up minimized rent in the compound houses, and enabled them to live close to where they worked. It serves a purpose here to compare the rents before the First World War to those in 1918 in several lodging-houses already mentioned. The fifteen rickshawmen living at 96 Queen Street paid on average $1.13 per month in 1914; four years later the rent had risen to $1.60.[53] In the larger lodging-houses like 96 Bencoolen Street, with 110 tenants, and 124 Victoria Street with 175 tenants, the monthly rents were 45 and 42 cents respectively in 1914, and 64 cents in 1918.[54] Rents seem to have remained at these levels during the 1920s; Yau Chin Swee, who had been living for six months at 96 Sungei Road, paid $1.60 per month to his landlord in 1924.[55] The following year the Hokkien rickshaw puller Hoh Oon's rent at 49 Duxton Road was fixed at $1.00 per month.[56] There is also some evidence that rent sometimes included the cost of the provision of a certain amount of *chandu* daily to pullers who smoked opium. In cases of extreme addiction, coolies were known to have taken up residence in opium shops. In one such instance, Lim Tiew rented a wooden bunk at the back of the opium shop at 109 Albert Street with board and *chandu* for $8 a month.[57]

Rickshawmen who were married constituted a small percentage of the total and lived in lodging-houses with heterogeneous populations. A report on the sanitary condition of Singapore in 1907 catalogues the household composition of the sixty-four residents living in a three-storey tenement house at 20–3 Sago Lane, a street in an overcrowded part of Chinatown.[58] The rents ranged from $1.50 to $4.50 per month. The report tells of a rickshaw puller and his family occupying cubicle no. 6 on the first floor with an area of 80 square feet. The married man paid $2.80 a month to Lim Ah Keng, the sub-tenant, who slept in the passage. The occupations of the other tenants on the first floor included a seamstress, a tailor, and a revenue officer who paid $4.50 per month rent, while a prostitute and her child lived directly above the family on the second floor.[59] Under such circumstances, saving on rent was difficult, as families could not crowd into cramped dormitory quarters in the big compound houses, nor sleep in shifts, to reduce payment.

The average daily earnings of a rickshawman in 1893 was 40 cents.[60] That was his gross earnings without deducting the 8–10 cents he paid for the hire of his rickshaw. By 1908 an experienced puller grossed between $1.70 and $2.00 per day, while the wages of an ordinary coolie was 50 cents a day, a labourer in the tin mines earned 70 cents, and $1 a day was the most a coal coolie ever received.[61] Rickshaw coolies' net earnings stabilized at about $1 a day by 1924, but the inexperienced and opium addicts were fortunate if they could net 40 cents.[62] These men with low incomes could not always afford to pay for the rickshaw and take care of themselves. Every effort was made to bring such parties together at the Rickshaw Department and a compromise reached, so that the puller could be given a fresh start.[63] Sometimes the attempt was successful. But not all coolies owing for rickshaw hire were so fortunate: '... unmarried men ... had to pay promptly for using the rickshaws. Anyone who couldn't pay up and tried to beg off would be thrown out the door like a broken teapot and have his bedroll confiscated.'[64] A good puller made as much as $2 in 1924. That was gross; from this must be deducted the rent of the rickshaw—20 cents during the day and 30 cents at night.[65] For the remainder of the decade and the 1930s rickshaw coolies averaged $1 a day; on a very good day they could possibly earn up to $1.50.[66] While Lim Jin San was working his earnings were about 80 cents a day in 1929;[67] night pullers averaged a little more. The night puller Tan Poh Whye, who had been out since 5 p.m. on 17 February 1934, had earned $1 at the time of his brush with death in the early hours of the morning.[68]

In 1897 a ride in a rickshaw cost only 6 cents for one mile. Providing one did not travel more than 10 miles one could go almost anywhere within the municipal limits of Singapore for an additional 2½ cents per mile. Between the hours of 9 p.m. and 5 a.m. there was an extra charge of one cent for every ½ mile.[69] The customer was entitled to detain the rickshaw for up to half an hour at work, home, the coffee house, or a brothel, but for every half hour during which the rickshaw was detained beyond the first one an additional sum of 5 cents was charged.[70] The law required that no puller could go more than 10 miles on a trip in one day, or remain engaged for more than 8 hours at a time, nor was he entitled to claim as payment for any distance drawn within municipal limits, or any time detained in one day, more than 80 cents.[71]

Fares were payable according to distance unless the customer initially expressed his intention to reckon by time.[72] In the absence of any special agreement no puller was required to draw his rickshaw a greater distance than 3 miles without a rest not exceeding 10 minutes. Rickshaw fares by time rose if there were more than two persons. Two children under 10 years of age counted as one adult. In 1898 the schedule of fares payable by time was as in Table 4.4.[73] Three years later steps were taken to simplify the fares schedule by introducing one charge of 6 cents a mile and 3 cents for every additional half mile. The rate was the same by day and night. As for time, in the municipal area, pullers could charge for one hour, 20 cents, and for every quarter of an hour, 5 cents.[74]

Despite rates being fixed, the rickshaw fare was apt to rise at certain times of the year, and in certain circumstances. The unexpected windfall usually came from generous foreigners—tourists, soldiers, and sailors—visiting briefly, attracted by the 'city lights'. But for Singaporeans the fares changed with the onset of wet weather. Rickshaw fares climbed

TABLE 4.4
Schedule of Fares, 1898

Fares by Time	*1 or 2 Persons*	*3 or 4 Persons*
For every hour or part thereof	$0.60	$0.75
For half a day or five hours	$1.50	$2.20
For a whole day consisting of nine hours	$2.50	$3.00
For every hour or part of an hour after the fifth or ninth hour	$0.30	$0.40

sharply with sudden torrential downpours. The heavy rains could cause considerable inconvenience to thousands of people left stranded in the downtown areas by daytime floods. The rickshaw, which was easier to handle in floodwaters than other modes of transport, helped to maintain the aura of satorial elegance and prestige of European officials dressed in white high-necked suits and polished black shoes by saving them the embarrassment and humiliation of having to tramp home in the red laterite mud of Singapore in the rain. They obviously did not relish such a prospect and paid the higher rates: 'Operation in a foot of water is hazardous but financially rewarding for pullers; a tripling of fares compensates the danger of stepping into an open drain.'[75] Rickshaws undoubtedly served useful purposes too during several tram strikes in Singapore and in those instances when dependence upon them increased, so did the fare.

Because rickshaw rides were cheap, the pullers' monthly income was fairly low as well, according to the Hockchia rickshaw owner, Lee Choon.[76] The rickshaw hire was 20 cents during the day and 25–30 cents during the night, which did not leave the puller very much.[77] A rickshaw coolie made about $1 a day (or $24 a month) in 1924. He had to buy food out of that, for which a puller spent about 30 cents a day. That left him 40–50 cents to buy clothes, send money to China, pay the prostitute, and buy opium, if he smoked. However, few pullers made more than $20 a month. Since the cost of living was from $12 to $14 a month, the puller could count on $6–8 clear to either remit or fritter away on opium, daughters of joy, and gambling.[78]

Because rickshaw pulling was a low-income labour-surplus occupation, some men attempted to hold down a second job. They worked as labourers, shop coolies, and made every effort to become a principal tenant in a lodging-house with free room. Low Nong Nong, a Hockchew rickshaw puller, was sometimes employed as a building coolie;[79] Khoon Cheang, a 30-year-old Hengwah, worked as a lamp repairer at Chop Hock Kee Chan, No. 110–1 Queen Street, and pulled a rickshaw at night. Described as a 'strong, quiet, hardworker', he usually got his rickshaw from Ng Chi, who pulled the vehicle during the day and rented it out to Khoon Cheang at night.[80] Some rickshawmen who got work as principal tenants included Lee Mia Mia, a 39-year-old Hockchia, who was in charge at 85 Maude Road,[81] and Woon Chin Huat, also Hockchia, who stated to the Coroner, 'I am a rickshaw puller. I am also principal tenant of 35 Queen Street. I have been the principal tenant since the 8th moon last year. I did not see the deceased on the day of his death. I was out [presumably pulling a rickshaw] from 6 a.m. till about 5.30 p.m.'[82]

The pattern of a puller's monthly income was complex because it rested not only on what people were paid, but on personal circumstances: good health and the number of trips averaged a day, whether the wife was working, the owner and job security, how many children. A wage which was a luxury for a 19-year-old Hengwah, Ong Teck Cheng,[83] living with clansmen in a rickshaw coolie lodging-house, or for a married couple who were both working with no family, was penury for a young man like Lim Ong[84] whose wife had to stay at home to look after two young children.

Because the rickshaw trade was labour-intensive with a low capital overhead per vehicle, the owners made a much better living out of rickshaws than their pullers. The rickshawman's income could improve only by getting rid of the rental, that is, if he owned his own rickshaw or shared the purchase of one with a group of pullers on an instalment basis. They knew this alone was the way to better their financial condition: to get beyond the worry of the rental fee, and keep whatever they earned:

> A similar rickshaw could be easily got for one hundred if the lacquer and brass work were slightly defective. So in all probability he only needed a hundred dollars to buy a rickshaw. Suddenly he thought, if I could save ten cents a day I'd have one hundred dollars in just one thousand days. He couldn't figure out how many years were in one thousand days but, he decided then and there, one thousand days were all right. Even ten thousand days were all right. He just had to buy a rickshaw. . . . His hope came much closer that way. He did not smoke, did not drink, did not gamble, wasn't addicted to anything, and had no family burdens. All he needed to do was grit his teeth and he wouldn't fail. He swore an oath to himself: in one year and a half he would have his own rickshaw or else.[85]

1. SMAR JD, 1897, Appendix J, p. 31.
2. *Report of the Commissioners Appointed to Enquire into the State of Labour in the Straits Settlements and Protected Native States with Appendices and Papers in Continuation* (Singapore: Government Printing Office, 1891), p. 31.
3. Rene Henry de Solminihac Onreat, *Singapore, A Police Background* (London: Dorothy Crisp and Company, 1947), p. 145.
4. See Appendix 2, compiled from Coroner's Inquests and Inquiries, 1902–38.
5. Ibid.
6. SCII of Tee Yeok Choon, No. 568, 28/9/37.
7. SCII of Ong Ah Siew, No. 664, 1/12/31.
8. CCVS of Choo Tang Giak, No. 67, 31/10/08
9. SCII of Ong Oh Kaw, No. 116, 16/8/02.
10. SCII of Tay Ah Sui, No. 241, 27/12/09.
11. SCII of Ong Ah Choon, No. 46, 23/2/20.

12. CCVS of Ch'ng Soi Bak Chew, No. 289, 30/11/34.

13. Choong Mui Hong, 'Migration from Kuo-cho-leow, Chao-yong, Kwantung, to Hale Street, Ipoh, Perak', unpublished course paper, Universiti Sains Malaysia, 1979, in Paul H. Kratoska, 'Rice Cultivation and the Ethnic Division of Labour in British Malaya', *Comparative Studies in Society and History*, Vol. 24, No. 2 (1982), p. 290.

14. On the general significance of locating where, when, why, and how particular villages within the total population of south-eastern China sent forth their men year after year, see Maurice Freedman, *The Study of Chinese Society. Essays by Maurice Freedman* (Stanford: Stanford University Press, 1979), pp. 393–4.

15. SSOC, evidence of Mr Hooper, p. 26.

16. SMAR JD, 1898, p. 102.

17. SCII of Tan Bah Bee, No. 71, 16/2/34; the author had hoped to find specific information on origin, and the pattern of migration for at least the 1930s in applications for a licence to pull a rickshaw (it was required by then) and applications for the licensing of rickshaws. His efforts proved in vain: 'I regret to inform you that we do not have any more records pertaining to rickshaws in our office'. Personal communication, Registry of Vehicles, Singapore, 15/4/82.

18. SMAR JD, 1902, p. 30.

19. SSOC, evidence of Mr Goodland, pp. 30–1.

20. Low Ngiong Ing, *Chinese Jetsam on a Tropical Shore* (Singapore: Eastern Universities Press, 1974), p. 73.

21. BMOC, statement of Wee Siong, p. C-45.

22. HCR, evidence of Mr Hooper, p. B91.

23. The estimates have been compiled from the annual reports of the Jinriksha Department. See SMAR JD for the years 1888, 1889, 1890, 1891, 1893, 1894, 1897, 1900, 1902, 1904, 1908, 1917.

24. SSOC, evidence of Alex Gentle, p. 326; evidence of Mr Hooper, p. 26.

25. HCR, evidence of Mr Hooper, p. B91.

26. SMAR JD, 1919, p. 2-E.

27. BMOC, p. B-28.

28. This table was compiled from data in Appendix 3, 'Rickshaw Coolies: Residential Patterns'. An even more age-specific breakdown into groups is as follows: 11–15, 0; 16–20, 3; 21–25, 12; 26–30, 18; 31–35, 11; 36–40, 21; 41–45, 14; 46–50, 14; 51–55, 7; 56–60, 2; 61–65, 1; above 66, 0.

29. SCII of Lim Phua Sim, No. 597, 2/12/33.

30. BMOC, p. B-29.

31. Mak Lau Fong, *The Sociology of Secret Societies. A Study of Chinese Secret Societies in Singapore and Peninsular Malaysia* (Kuala Lumpur: Oxford University Press, 1981), pp. 29, 60; Freedman, *The Study of Chinese Society*, p. 174.

32. See Appendix 3, compiled from the Coroner's Inquests and Inquiries, 1902–39; SMAR, 1901, Appendix A, 'List of Brothels, Coolie Lodging Houses and Private Houses to which Meters Have Been Attached, with Statement of Receipts Before and After Introduction of Meters', pp. 1–19; HCR, 'List of Houses Occupied by Rikisha Coolies', p. C-12.

33. Ibid.

34. SMAR, 1901, Appendix A, 'List of Brothels, Coolie Lodging Houses and Private Houses to which Meters Have Been Attached', pp. 17–18.

35. Appendix 3, 'Rickshaw Coolies: Residential Patterns'.

36. Ibid.

37. Low, *Chinese Jetsam on a Tropical Shore*, p. 73.

38. Appendix 3, 'Rickshaw Coolies: Residential Patterns'.

39. HCR, 'List of Houses Occupied by Rikisha Coolies', p. C-12; evidence of Mr Hooper, p. B-90.

40. HCR, evidence of Mr Hooper, p. B-90.

41. SMAR JD, 1904, p. 3.

42. HCR, evidence of Mr Hooper, p. B-90.

43. Ibid.

44. Interview with Ng Kar Eng, AOHD, Reel 3.
45. SCII of Ong Oh Kaw, No. 116, 16/8/02.
46. SCII of Tan Yeng Eng, No. 53, 1/4/07.
47. SCII of Tay Ah Sui, No. 241, 27/12/09.
48. SCII of Lui Ah Pek, No. 165, 18/9/08.
49. SCII of Chew Yong, No. 133, 2/7/11.
50. Lao She, *Rickshaw* (the novel *Lo-T'o Hsiang Tzu*), translated by Jean M. James (Honolulu: The University Press of Hawaii, 1979), p. 35.
51. SCII of Ong Oh Kaw, No. 116, 16/8/02.
52. See Appendix 3, 'Rickshaw Coolies: Residential Patterns'.
53. HCR, 'List of Houses Occupied by Rikisha Coolies', p. C-12.
54. Ibid.
55. Appendix 3, 'Rickshaw Coolies: Residential Patterns'.
56. Ibid.
57. SCII of Lim Tiew, No. 180, 8/11/07.
58. W. J. Simpson, *Report on the Sanitary Condition of Singapore* (London: Waterloo and Sons Ltd., 1907), pp. 17–24.
59. Ibid.
60. BMOC, evidence of Lee Choon, p. C-47.
61. SSOC, pp. 32, 279.
62. BMOC, pp. B-29, C-47.
63. SMAR JD, 1923, p. 2-B.
64. Lao She, op. cit., p. 33.
65. BMOC, p. B-29.
66. BMOC, evidence of Wee Siong, p. C-45.
67. SCII of Sim Kwee Geok, No. 619, 13/12/29.
68. SCII of George Buxton, No. 28, 5/2/34.
69. SMAR JD, 1897, Appendix J, p. 35.
70. Ibid.
71. Ibid.
72. SMAR JD, 1898, Appendix M, p. 59.
73. Ibid.
74. SMAR JD, 1901, Appendix A-III, p. 9.
75. UNNAYAN, in association with T. H. Thomas, *Rickshaws in Calcutta* (Calcutta: UNNAYAN, 1981), p. 17.
76. BMOC, evidence of Lee Choon, p. C-47.
77. Ibid.
78. HCR, evidence of Mr Hooper, p. B-91.
79. SCII of Low Nong Nong, No. 597, 18/10/38.
80. SCII of Khoon Cheang, No. 400, 23/8/26.
81. SCII of unknown Chinese, 14/6/34.
82. SCII of unknown Chinese, No. 49, 20/1/36.
83. SCII of Ong Teck Cheng, No. 174, 4/4/29.
84. SCII of Wee Choon Beoh, No. 612, 17/11/30.
85. Lao She, op. cit., p. 8.

5 Rickshaws

THE rickshaw was a small, light, hooded cart with springs and large-diameter wheels drawn by a man running between the shafts. The hood could be quickly raised or lowered against the weather. There were also front and side curtains and an apron to shelter the passenger from downpour. Rickshaws were pulled with their tops down except when a customer wished to be sheltered from either excessive rain or heat or to travel incognito. Prostitutes, for example, usually preferred to travel with the hood up. The rickshaw was described in *The Century Dictionary* in 1899 as a vehicle 'not unlike a Hansom cab, without the seat for the driver—there being no horse to drive'.[1] The rickshaw offered cheap effective transportation for the ordinary people of Singapore. It was manoeuvrable, comfortable, and moderately fast. Singapore was a city of pedestrians when rickshaws first came on the scene. Horses and riders still had priority over other traffic in the streets. Horses and carriages were for the rich, as were motor cars in the new century, but the rickshaw proved popular and was ideal for getting about safely over short distances, especially in the maze of crowded streets in Chinatown.

The rickshaws of Singapore were different from those of Hong Kong and China. Hong Kong roads were steep and rickshaws, because they were hard to pull uphill, were made for one passenger. The larger Singapore version had two seats for two, but they often conveyed entire families on Singapore's flat roads. Hence, ordinary Chinese—young and old, rich and poor—used the iron-tyred, 'double seated' rickshaw for all sorts of purposes. Low Ngiong Ing recollects the 'double seater' in the family drama of a Foochow childhood in Singapore more than 60 years ago: 'My first memory of Singapore is that of sitting in a rickshaw, a jinrikisha to be exact, a Japanese concoction which means "carriage moved by human strength", a contraption I was seeing for the first time. My aunt and my mother sat on the seat, my sister and I on the floor. The rapid motion made my aunt vomit.'[2] Parents with more than one child often sent them to school by double-seated rickshaw. The world of Tan Ah Nya's schooldays unfolds as he describes a rickshaw trip on Bukit Timah Road on a fateful day in 1928:

There were five of us in one rickshaw. I was the eldest one other ages [were] eight, seven, six and five. I sat on the seat and so did two others and the other two were on our laps. The hood was up, but not the apron [it] was not raining then. We were passing the trench in the middle of the road.... My house was very near where the accident happened. The puller did not know where we lived but I had told him the second mile.[3]

Larger rickshaws were used almost exclusively by the elderly on family errands or outings. Cho Beng Huat, a 69-year-old Hokkien widow, regularly engaged a rickshaw at Mandalay Road. On 10 February 1937, Sin Ah Mai, a Cantonese maid servant aged 17, got into the rickshaw with Cho Beng Huat's 2-year-old granddaughter. The elderly widow daily visited her son at Sim's Avenue.[4] The design of double-seated rickshaws meant they were difficult to pull, given heavier loads, and therefore slower, rarely travelling at more than 3 miles per hour. They were cheaper, though, than the single-passenger rickshaws.

The new first-class rickshaws appeared on Singapore streets for the first time in January 1904. They were designed for speed and comfort, fitted with English wooden furniture, Indian rubber-cushion-tyre wheels, with a single seat. Their popularity was immediate. Mr Hooper stated they were 'likely to increase in number, the fares are good and they are in great demand'.[5] In contrast to the public response the syndicate that introduced them experienced some financial difficulty at first. To overcome the difficulty of hiring them out they established an exclusive franchise (a farm) with one man, who gave security and paid the syndicate 75 cents a day for each rickshaw. The 144 new rickshaws were then hired to different pullers. The business was a money maker; more first-class rickshaws were already plying for hire by the end of the year.[6]

The quality of the second-class, double-seaters remained the same, except that with an increase in single-seated rickshaws coolies soon learned there was no advantage in pulling two passengers in a double rickshaw, when they could claim the same fare for pulling one in a single-seater. The pullers were finding the fares so profitable that everybody expected rapid increases in the numbers of single-seated rickshaws.[7] As was expected their numbers had shot up markedly by 1906. In that year there were 1,226 first-class, rubber-tyred, and 6,138 second-class, iron-tyred rickshaws running on the streets.[8] Newspaper advertisements provide evidence of attempts to satisfy the burgeoning demand. These smart-looking rickshaws had become very popular indeed by 1906:

Rikishaws! Rikishaws! Rikishaws! The very, very best kind of Rikishaws just unpacked. The undersigned beg to inform their numerous constituents and the public in general that they have just received several kinds of Rikishaws from the best manufacturer in Japan, fitted with ordinary or India rubber cushion tyre wheels. All rikishas guaranteed. Single or double seated rikishaws, fitted with English steel electro silver-plated, ball-bearing India rubber-cushion tyre wheels, with plain black colour and best velvet cushion.... Early inspection solicited. Price very very cheap.[9]

On flat stretches the double-seater could hold its own but the balance of advantage rested with the single-seater rickshaw in the start–stop conditions of inner-city movements and traffic, and in their hill-climbing ability.

The double-seater was reduced in size after 1913. Parliament and the Colonial Office focused attention on the problem of pulling double rickshaws in 1911, particularly the strain it entailed, and the incidence of mortality among coolies battling to eke out an existence with the double-seater.[10] The marked superiority of the first-class rickshaw over the double-seater suddenly became the focus of considerable controversy and criticism when the Governor, Sir Arthur Young, sought the gradual abolition of the double rickshaw over a three-year period as a result of Colonial Office pressure. The problem was highlighted by an active press campaign spearheaded by the *Straits Times* advocating that the Government abolish the double rickshaw on the basis of humanitarian principle. Its views were summarized in a grim editorial which viewed rickshaw pulling as 'the deadliest occupation in the East, the most degrading for human beings to pursue, and it is noteworthy that there is hardly any race under the sun except the Chinese which will serve as beasts of burden and cast away life with almost brutal disregard of its dignity and sanctity'.[11]

The records of the Legislative Council Proceedings detail the various stages of the double rickshaw debate as the wrangle dragged on for three years, through a winding series of suggested amendment changes. The twists and turns at every stage emerge; the Attorney-General argued that abolition would remove the deadly pressure on the puller, explaining that:

> ... the reason for abolishing is humanitarian. It is considered that the strain caused to a puller drawing a ricksha with two passengers in it is more than he can sustain without injury to his health; and that, therefore, the men who are engaged in this employment ought not to be permitted to pursue this means of earning a livelihood longer than is necessary for the institution on our streets of this class of vehicle to become gradually inexistent.[12]

There was opposition. Mr Tan Jiak Kim, an important unofficial representing the Chinese community in Council, argued that the Government was interfering unduly at the grass-roots level. He felt that by tackling double rickshaws on humanitarian grounds, hardship would be caused to poorer sections of the Chinese community. In his opinion the Government was strangling their means of transport, and hindering the puller's work. The proposed legislation on double rickshaws had a marked effect on licensing between 1911 and 1913 as their numbers steadily declined.[13] In the end a compromise was reached. No rickshaw which exceeded an inside width of 2 feet could be licensed; the width of the seating accommodation of the single rickshaw measured 1 foot 9 inches.[14]

The Governor, who voted with the minority against the measure, was of the opinion that the clause as it was originally drafted should have been allowed to stand, prohibiting the use of any but 'single' rickshaws. The Governor was right. The compromise proved perfectly futile. The reduction of the interior width of the rickshaw by 3½ inches did not make it impracticable for two adults to sit in it, nor did it prevent a woman and several small children using a rickshaw together. The cramming effect of the new double rickshaw, which was a compromise between the old 'double-seater' and the single rickshaw, was aptly written about in 1926 by a European traveller:

> The rickshaw needs little description, though here in Singapore they have a peculiar carriage which is really meant for one and actually will hold two with a squash. They are different from the Hong Kong or Bangkok rickshaws, which certainly only hold one, and they are not nearly as wide as those in Kuala Lumpur and other towns, which are specially built for two.[15]

In 1881 rickshaws were manufactured in Japan and imported into Singapore, but as their numbers grew locally manufactured rickshaws also appeared on the scene. The quality of the early Japanese rickshaws with iron-rimmed wheels was bad. The owners complained of the increases in the price of the inferior Japanese imports, which had gone up steadily from $25 to $38 between 1881 and 1894.[16] The import trade was entirely in the hands of the High Street Chinese dealers. The business was lucrative and British officials were both astonished and concerned that it did not attract the attention of some European firms. The Rickshaw Department was anxious to encourage competition in the hope of a better class of rickshaw being imported. The manufacturers in Japan were quick to point out though that up till 1894 the demand from Singapore was chiefly for third-class rickshaws. These cheap vehicles were not used in Japan, but only produced for export.[17] To remedy this difficulty and get a better class of rickshaw, Mr Hooper recommended in 1894, that the Municipal Commissioners should advertise for tenders for the supply of 1,000 rickshaws, delivery to be spread over twelve months, of a type to be selected and approved by the Commissioners. From enquiries he had made, Mr Hooper had little doubt that rickshaws of a better quality could be obtained at a lower cost and readily retailed to the owners.[18]

Owners frequently repaired their vehicles themselves to pass registration, and as the years passed continued to tinker with them, complaining that inspection was severe and repairs always wanted. Bad rickshaws were not uncommon among many of local manufacture that were presented for registration. The bodies of these vehicles were built chiefly of pine wood and were heavier than those imported, and the varnish was also inferior to that used in Japan.[19] In 1897, Song Bin was the bona fide owner of over fifty rickshaws but every one of them was made in Singapore out of old packing cases, and cost under $20 to manufacture.[20] When produced for licensing Song Bin's vehicles were well got up but did not stand up any length of time to the wear and tear of Singapore street life. Consequently, they needed constant repairs; springs collapsed and axles bent and snapped under heavy loads on the bad road surfaces, aprons and hoods tore into pieces in rainy, windy weather, while seat upholstery was liable to be stained or gashed—a drawback to carrying baskets full of filthy creatures, great and small, with beaks and claws. The practice of using rickshaws for the conveyance of 'objectionable' articles was to be hardly checked, despite all the efforts of the Rickshaw Department.

For the passengers' sake constant efforts were made to get owners to improve the appearance, comfort, and cleanliness of the cheaper rickshaws, especially the locally manufactured variety. The hoods and aprons supplied from Japan, which were substandard and did not last any length of time in the tropical climate of Singapore, received singular attention.[21] The time came in 1890, when Song Bin and other owners like him were required to have the back and seat cushions of their rickshaws covered with black American cloth and the insides of the hoods lined with it instead of the red baize cloth formerly used which so readily became dirty and attracted vermin. Firm insistence on the use of quality American cloth for the apron stemmed from the unfortunate experiences of those who had to use rickshaws during rainy weather. The red dye of the lining of the soaked rotten material was liable to come off on the clothing of unlucky passengers: 'A rikisha is not hired for the purpose of having the passenger's clothes dyed against his will, and the registrar is only doing his duty for the protection of the public in seeing that no unfit material is used for the purpose indicated.'[22] But so long as rickshaws were permitted to be used for the transport of pigs, goats, poultry, fish, manure, buckets of indigo, dye, and hog-wash, as well as diseased cadavers, it was clear that they could not always be kept clean and in a fit state for passenger traffic. The durable new cloth still had to be changed every four months to insure that hoods, cushions, and aprons were kept clean.[23]

Improved lamps of English manufacture were also introduced in place of the old defective local and Japanese ones. Between 1893 and 1896 the trade in lamps, which was in the hands of the Rickshaw Department, realized $13,454 in sales.[24] The following year the Department relinquished its hold on the lamp trade and a Chinese retailer secured the tender. A further change was suggested in 1917 because of the motor-car danger at night. To reduce the risk of hit-and-run accidents, suitable cheap tail-lights were recommended—lamps which could be attached to the axle and were clearly visible from behind—but rear reflector signs for the axles of rickshaws were not made a compulsory fitting until 1939.[25] Some further efforts were made as late as 1925 to insist on rickshaws being kept in better condition than hitherto had been the case, and some improvements can be noted. The red rear glass of the lamps was increased in size, and a back clip for holding the seat cover in position to prevent it obscuring the licence number plate was fitted.[26]

The greatest difficulty for the owners was, however, maintaining the rickshaws at the standard at which they were passed by the Registrar as fit to ply for hire. The licence ran for a period of four months, after which the rickshaw was again produced for inspection and condemned if unfit. Owners argued that compelling them to produce their rickshaws for inspection every four months created a hardship. The inspection was too severe.[27] A man with a bad rickshaw was refused a licence. Such owners often would not take 'no' for an answer and brought the same dilapidated rickshaw day after day to the registration yard, stating they had been trying for weeks to get a licence but neglecting to inform officials of the reason for their refusal. These owners simply thought anything that could hold together should be passed.

Owners conspired, especially before the turn of the century, against whoever's lot it was to examine their rickshaws. Bribery, imitation numbers, thefts of number plates and of rickshaws were rife.[28] The tricks resorted to, to cheat when licensing inferior rickshaws included bribing police constables and peons at the rickshaw yard, swapping metal and wooden components by secretly changing the wheels, wheel guards, hood apron, lamps and cushions, and imitating, altering, defacing or obliterating the numbers and marks branded on the carriage for the purpose of identification. Some owners even had the audacity to produce somebody else's new rickshaw, stolen of course, slightly altered, and minus its licence plate.[29]

The difficulty of maintaining a fair standard of cleanliness and fitness was experienced by the understaffed Rickshaw Department throughout the 1890s. Examination and impounding of vehicles was wholesale. In 1896 alone, over 29,000 rickshaws were impounded and their owners summoned before the Registrar.[30] Number plates had to be continually removed by the Registrar from broken-down rickshaws or those with bad fittings, in batches of from 50 to 150, every four months, which then had to be repaired afterwards, and sent again for inspection and licensing. The assistance of the public in reporting the number of any rickshaw found using bad fittings was repeatedly requested but was not forthcoming to any extent. Each year up to 1939 several hundred licences were cancelled, the rickshaws worn out, beyond repair; some of them were even cancelled at the owner's request.[31]

But in the case of the vast majority of the rickshaws presented for inspection little fault could be found even after the closest scrutiny. Though every possible precaution was taken by branding and marking the body, wheels, metal wheel guards, hoods (inside and out) and waterproof apron of the rickshaws, for the purposes of identification, the return of prosecutions showed that it was a never-ending struggle between a small department endeavouring to enforce the provisions of the Rickshaw Ordinance and a large body of owners who displayed considerable ingenuity in evading the requirements of the law to obtain a licence.

Owners gradually realized, however, that it was more expensive to be tinkering with cheap vehicles in a condition unfit for public use than to buy new rickshaws; repairs were not as likely to be required during the period for which they were licensed, not so much time was apt to be lost around the registration yard or in court, nor the licence number detained. There was a considerable increase in the total of new Japanese rickshaws registered in 1897, numbering 1,518. The following year, no less than 3,550 rickshaws were imported and registered.[32] Owners were also beginning to keep their rickshaws in better condition but this was the result of constant vigilance of the staff of the Rickshaw Department. Thousands of rickshaws were being impounded annually by the peons for being on the streets in a broken or unfit condition to ply for hire. Their number plates were removed and returned only when the necessary repairs, chiefly to hoods and aprons, were done.[33]

The quality of the rickshaws remained the same until the Registrar of Vehicles received a petition from a Chinese syndicate in November 1902, requesting that increased fares be charged for rickshaws of better quality with rubber-tyred wheels. The alteration in the by-laws and schedule of fares to enable higher rates to be charged for the better-quality rickshaws, and for those with rubber tyres to be registered as first-class, was sanctioned by the Governor in 1903, and the vehicles were ordered that August by the syndicate.[34] Owing to delays in delivery from Japan the first lot did not arrive and start to ply on the streets until January 1904. They were an improvement and in great demand.[35]

The normal life expectancy of a rickshaw was five years, providing it was regularly repaired. In the first year expenses for repairing these light wooden vehicles were nominal. In the second year the tyres had to be changed; the seat had to be refurbished or replaced in the third year; and new tyres and inner tubes were required in the fourth year. In the final year more repairs were carried out.[36] Accidents were a constant cause of concern and serious hardship to pullers. In case of damage incurred to rickshaws while on the streets, it was customary, at least in China, for the owner to pay the expenses for the repair of the wooden parts, while the puller had to attend to the more expensive iron fittings—axles, huge spoked wheels, springs, mudguards and so forth.[37] Pullers rarely had serious accidents before the advent of the motor vehicle, but unexpected mishaps occurred: tyres were worn out, hoods and aprons subject to banging and scraping were easily damaged, as was the upholstery and shell of the vehicle. When a rickshawman was having a bad time in his fight for survival he paid between a third and a half of his daily earnings to the repairers to maintain his rickshaw:

> In the midst of these confused thoughts he would forget his customary caution; the tyre would run over bits of brass or broken pottery and blow out, and all he could do then was quit for the day. Sometimes he ran into pedestrians, which was even worse. The limit was reached when the rickshaw had its top ripped off because he was in a hurry to get through a crowd.[38]

Accidents involving old axles requiring the skill of the blacksmith to repair, which bent and broke on Singapore's poorly surfaced roads, were often serious. Soo Kah Joon, a Hokkien coolie employed in a shop in Cross Street, went to visit a friend; he used a rickshaw, and just as he arrived at his friend's lodging the axle and wheel of the rickshaw snapped and he was thrown onto the road, injuring his head.[39]

Rickshaws were maintained and repaired in ground-floor shops and alleyways of buildings in the rickshaw districts. The small-scale workshops, usually located on the premises of large rickshaw owners, were staffed by wheelwrights, blacksmiths, painters, joiners, and upholsterers. The tools of their trade along with spare parts of old and new rickshaws littered the floor and spilled out on to the verandah pavement. The art of manufacturing spare metal and wooden parts to replace broken or unfit components was already highly developed by the time the first-class rickshaw appeared. Let us momentarily approach one such workshop at 11 Larut Road in 1928. We can hear distant banging and filing sounds coming from the front of the shop. Tools all around, Ng Cheng Moh squats on the five-footway of his house repairing a vehicle.[40] Craftsmen like him were capable of transforming a wreck into a 'new' rebuilt rickshaw. It was commonplace for a repairman to be a kinsman of an owner. Yeong Song Oo, a coffee-shopkeeper and rickshaw owner, employed his Hockchia cousin Yeong Song Huay to repair rickshaws.[41] Not surprisingly, some repairers were also owners. Ho Kee Leong, who lived at 22 Choon Guan Street and owned 41 rickshaws, rented the front part of his house to Ng Chong, a rickshaw repairman and owner, who kept his own rickshaws in a fit state, and turned out the odd 'new' one.[42]

Although the rickshaw was central to the work and life of Hengwah, Hockchia and Hockchew immigrants and ownership of one was their ray of hope, the investment required to become an owner remained beyond the means of most of the men. The market value of the Japanese-made rickshaw rose from $38 at the end of the nineteenth century to $90 in 1917. In that year the cost of new vehicles jumped from $90 to $160 for first-class and from $45 to $75 for second-class.[43] The dramatic rise was due to the war and high freight rates prevailing, but the price never came down again to pre-war levels. By 1921 the cost of new Japanese rickshaws had risen to $180 and in consequence rickshaws were being made locally but, as was the case in the past, these proved inferior to those imported.[44] The difference in the cost of a new and used rickshaw was astonishing as it depreciated rapidly in value over five years: 'Rikisha For Sail [*sic*], Second-Hand, in good condition with lamps and hood. $20. Apply RIKSHA.'[45] But there were not many advertisements of this sort in newspapers; instead rickshaws were routinely stolen. The higher the price of rickshaws rose the more numerous the police reports were of rickshaw theft.[46] For the puller the price of a rickshaw was equivalent to three trips to China in 1894, or one-third of the cost of a 'Raleigh' high-grade bicycle, with cushion tyres and gear case in first-class condition in 1901, or the entire annual wage of a rickshawman in 1917.[47]

1. *The Century Dictionary* (London: The Times, 1899).

2. Low Ngiong Ing, *Chinese Jetsam on a Tropical Shore* (Singapore: Eastern Universities Press, 1974), p. 102.

3. SCII of Lee Ah Liang, No. 59, 22/1/28.
4. SCII of Koh Kong Cheng, No. 99, 10/2/37.
5. SMAR JD, 1904, p. 2.
6. Ibid.
7. Ibid.
8. SMAR JD, 1907, p. 1.
9. *Straits Echo*, 9 September 1905.
10. No.109, Sir Arthur Young to Lewis Harcourt, 13 March 1913, CO 273/395.
11. Song Ong Siang, *One Hundred Years' History of the Chinese in Singapore* (London: John Murray, 1902; reprinted Kuala Lumpur: University of Malaya Press, 1967, and Singapore: Oxford University Press, 1984), p. 484.
12. Ibid.
13. SMAR JD, 1912, p. 7.
14. Ibid.
15. R. H. J. Sydney, *Malay Land* (London: Cecil Palmer, 1926), p. 26.
16. SMAR JD, 1894, p. 30.
17. Ibid.
18. Ibid.
19. SMAR JD, 1891, p. 15.
20. SMAR JD, 1897, Appendix J, p. 27.
21. SMAR JD, 1897, p. 24; *Singapore Free Press*, 1 August 1897.
22. Ibid.
23. SMAR JD, 1897, p. 24.
24. The amounts per year were: $5,284.20—1893; $2,403.90—1894; $3,235.62—1895; $2,531—1896; see SMAR JD, 1893–1896.
25. SMAR JD, 1917, p. 8; SMAR JD, 1939, p. B-5.
26. SMAR JD, 1925, p. B-4.
27. SMAR JD, 1893; SMAR JD, 1897, Appendix J, p. 24.
28. SMAR JD, 1901, p. B-7.
29. SMAR JD, 1897, Appendix J, p. 33; for example, in 1891 there were 85 cases against owners for using false plates on their rickshaws. On 9 November a rickshaw was impounded in Bali Lane with number plates painted blue in imitation of those issued by the Registrar. On 11 and 12 November arrests for a similar offence were made in New Bridge Road and North Bridge Road. SMAR JD, 1891, p. 15.
30. SMAR JD, 1897, Appendix J, p. 26.
31. In 1902, 2,448 were cancelled; by 1917 the number had dropped to 334. SMAR JD, 1902, p. 158; SMAR JD, 1917, p. 8.
32. SMAR JD, 1897; SMAR JD, 1898, p. 102.
33. SMAR JD, 1804, p. 2.
34. SMAR JD, 1902, p. 160.
35. SMAR JD, 1903, p. 2.
36. 'Economic Study of the Peking Ricsha Puller', *China Economic Monthly*, 3, 6 (June 1926), pp. 257–8.
37. Ibid.
38. Lao She, *Rickshaw* (the novel *Lo T'o Hsiang Tzu*), translated by Jean M. James (Honolulu: The University Press of Hawaii, 1979), pp. 8–9.
39. SCII of Soo Kah Joon, No. 40, 13/2/20.
40. SCII of See Hong Bee, No. 588, 10/10/28.
41. SCII of Yeong Song Huay, No. 88, 18/3/38.
42. SCII of Chng Sim Geok, No. 231, 30/4/31.
43. SMAR JD, 1917, p. 8.
44. SMAR JD, 1921, p. 1-B.
45. *Singapore Free Press*, 19 January 1897.
46. SMAR JD, 1904, p. 3.
47. The price of a passage ticket to China was between $12 and $14; for the bicycle advertisement see *Singapore Free Press*, 15 September 1897 and 24 October 1901; the wage figure is calculated on the average of a dollar a day.

6 Rickshaws in Singapore

A re-visitor would have seen great change in the appearance of the streets of Singapore between 1881 and 1931. In the decade the rickshaw appeared traffic comprised bullock-carts, gharries, and steam trams. Traffic control was difficult because there were no traffic police yet and there were only five-footways in front of buildings with no pavements on long stretches of road outside the city. Pedestrians swarmed. But by the early 1930s street traffic was thoroughly mechanical, faster, more congested, and obviously more dangerous. There were no gharries left and a bullock-cart was a rare sight. Omnibuses and trolley buses replaced electric trams in the main parts of the city, and swiftly moving motor cars and lorries had spread rapidly. There were still plenty of rickshaws but the downward trend had begun. Their numbers would dwindle until there were less than 4,000 licensed rickshaws for hire in 1939.

The advent of the rickshaw witnessed a keen but short-lived competition between the gharry owners and pullers. It was all over by 1892. The stinging competition of the rickshaws pressed hard on the syces and the pullers had superseded them inside a decade. A total of 557 gharry licences were issued in 1892; this figure is significant because 1,075 carriages were registered in 1883.[1] While the number of hackney carriages continued to decline there was a steady increase in the number of rickshaws. Table 6.1 shows this ascendancy.[2]

Since the population, trade and industry of the city were expanding no constraint was placed on the number of rickshaws registered, because the

TABLE 6.1

The Number of Hackney Carriages and Rickshaws on the Streets, 1883–1916

Year	*Number of Hackney Carriages*	*Average Number of Rickshaws Running on the Streets*
1883	1,075	2,000 or less
1892	682	3,991
1897	582	5,839
1902	533	7,209
1907	409	7,397
1912	382	8,931
1916	215	8,270

TABLE 6.2
The Total Number of Licensed Rickshaws, 1887–1939

Year	*Total No. of Rickshaws*	*First Class*	*Second Class*
1887	3,000		
1888	2,500		
1889	2,500 approx.		
1890	3,396		
1891	3,755		
1892	3,991	16	3,975
1893	13,041	41	13,000
1894	14,659	29	14,630
1895	16,453	30	16,423
1896	17,915	19	17,896
1897	17,518	31	17,487
1898	17,330	42	17,288
1899	18,805	162	18,643
1900	19,414	253	19,161
1901	21,381	297	21,084
1902	22,629	380	22,249
1903	20,433	167	20,266
1904	21,696	213	21,483
1905	19,541	473	19,068
1906	20,879	1,532	19,347
1907	22,009	3,212	18,797
1908	21,838		
1909	23,128	3,676	19,452
1910	23,128		
1911	26,072		
1912			
1913	24,359	6,896	17,463
1914	24,853	7,475	17,378
1915	21,934	8,039	13,895
1916			
1917	26,183	13,479	12,704
1918	24,922	19,847	5,075
1919	24,339	23,745	594
1920	23,673	23,640	33
1921	27,669	27,663	6
1922	29,646	29,646	0
1923	29,037	29,037	
1924	28,786	28,786	
1925			
1926			
1927			
1928	16,872	16,872	
1929	7,622	7,622	
1930	6,764	6,764	

(continued)

TABLE 6.2 (*continued*)

Year	*Total No. of Rickshaws*	*First Class*	*Second Class*
1931	5,635	5,635	
1932	4,615	4,615	
1933	4,062	4,062	
1934	3,908	3,908	
1935	3,891	3,891	
1936	3,707	3,707	
1937	3,704	3,704	
1938	3,586	3,586	
1939	3,693	3,693	

supply of these vehicles had not reached the limit of profitable employment. During 1901 there were on average 6,976 rickshaws plying on the streets. A total of 1,368 persons were registered as owners and the number of coolies in the trade was estimated at about 20,000.[3] The data in Table 6.2, based on the number of rickshaws licensed each year by the bureau, trace the growth and development of the rickshaw trade.[4] Decreases in the number of licences taken out during a given year and the number of new vehicles bought was due to the scarcity of coolies coming from China, government efforts to limit the number of rickshaws, and increased competition from motorized transport.

The number of first-class rickshaws with rubber tyres steadily increased but there was a drop in the overall number brought forward for registration in 1905. This decrease was due to rumours that it was the intention of the government to reduce by one half the number of rickshaws for hire when the tramcars began running. Consequently many owners were afraid to buy new ones as they feared difficulty in obtaining licences.[5] In spite of the tramway, 20,879 licences for rickshaws were issued the following year, being 1,338 more than 1905.[6] The number of first-class vehicles, which pullers paid up to 60 cents a day to hire, was increasing. By 1907, thousands of pullers drew these rickshaws right across the city and back again each day:

> Rickshas ply day and night to the number of 20,000 drawn by an almost naked army of Chinese pullers. There is not a single man of any other nationality doing this really hard work. Old fashioned gharries, with their lively Sumatran ponies in [the] charge of Tamil and Malay drivers, are still in considerable demand. Electric trams are much in evidence, and will be more patronized when they are extended to meet the needs of the travelling public. Few walk nowadays, as all but the fairly well-to-do did until the rickshaws came, just a little more than twenty years ago.[7]

A marked decrease in the number of rickshaws on the streets was recorded in 1913. The legislation proposed at the beginning of the year to abolish double rickshaws had deterred owners from buying new vehicles.

However, the first-class rickshaws increased by nearly 50 per cent. The average number of rickshaws running during the year was 8,299 against 8,931 in 1913, with the greatest number being 9,207 during the Chinese New Year.[8] The decrease in the number of rickshaws on the streets was noticeable. It was attributed, too, to fewer *singkeh* arriving from China due to quarantine, and this fact caused a further reduction.

With the outbreak of the First World War and restriction on Chinese immigration for a part of the year, the number of rickshaws continued to fall. Significantly, the number of first-class vehicles was more than one-third of the total, showing a progressive growth year by year. For comparison let us look at the number of rickshaws running during the Chinese New Year between 1912 and 1914, and the average number running during the year.[9]

TABLE 6.3
The Average Number of Rickshaws Running during the Year and at Chinese New Year, 1912–1914

Type of Rickshaw	*The Chinese New Year*			*Average No. Running*		
	1912	*1913*	*1914*	*1912*	*1913*	*1914*
First-class (rubber tyres)	1,888	2,055	2,972	1,542	1,724	2,237
Second-class (iron tyres)	7,582	7,152	5,862	7,259	7,207	6,062
Total	9,470	9,207	8,834	8,801	8,931	8,299

The increase in the first-class is noticeable. The falling off in second-class rickshaws was due to the stoppage of Chinese immigration. Once the restrictions were removed their numbers were again going up in 1915.[10]

On the western side of the river in Chinatown and in the main old high density housing areas on the other side of Singapore, rickshaws had become an indispensable part of the commercial and social life of the city. In 1917, a twelve-hour survey at six main bridges in Singapore recorded 72,772 crossings of rickshaws.[11] Rubber-tyred rickshaws continued to increase. In July 1917, 9,297 were in use, and for the first time at the end of the year exceeded the number of iron-tyres.[12] The sudden decrease in second-class rickshaws was hard on ordinary people, mostly Chinese, as it added to their expenses for transport. The rate of hire of first-class rickshaws was more than the iron-tyred vehicles, but the old double rickshaw vanishing also often meant that two rickshaws had to be engaged now instead of one. In 1918 the Registrar wrote that the iron-tyred rickshaw was 'rapidly disappearing and will soon cease to exist'.[13] At the time he wrote that out of nearly 9,000 licensed rickshaws only 700 were second-class. The iron-tyred rickshaw, which conveyed two passengers for 6 cents a mile, ceased to exist in 1919. Suddenly it had become a thing of the past. Six years earlier it had been predicted that if the size of the vehicle was reduced either a larger number of rickshaws would be required or it would lead to the pullers being in such demand that they would insist on higher fares. Rickshaws decreased and rickshaw fares (as paid though not sanctioned) increased. Pullers became more independent, and at times even insolent, causing many complaints.[14]

But by the late 1920s the tables had been turned on the pullers as trolley buses and light motor buses began to supersede rickshaws. This rapid transit, plus a period of compulsory reduction of rickshaws, saw the progressive decline begin. Also, never before had there been so many motor cars on the streets, often moving and always fast paced; there were over 7,300 in 1930.[15] The downturn in rickshaws was particularly evident when comparing the traffic flow passing over the city's bridges in different periods.[16]

TABLE 6.4

Traffic Passing over the City's Bridges, 1917, 1923, and 1930

	Anderson Bridge			*Institution Bridge*		
	1917	*1923*	*1930*	*1917*	*1923*	*1930*
Tramcars for 1917 and 1923	181	178				
Trolley buses for 1930			1,309			
Heavy motor buses		10	278		15	6
Light motor buses		167	228		190	238
Rickshaws	2,741	2,101	1,666	8,599	6,960	3,226

In 1939 there were only 3,750 rickshaws left.[17]

The amount of traffic in Singapore grew in direct proportion to the size of the town, the population, its wealth, and its business in the latter part of the nineteenth century. Rickshaws were a significant part of that growth. The economic and social conditions that had created employment in rickshaw pulling also gave birth to the rapid spread of through traffic in the narrow secondary streets. Officially, the traffic was felt to be an unavoidable necessity; at its worst, a necessary evil, at its best, a sign of progress, but never a blessing. The streets in the heart of the city became less quiet and less safe, even, according to the Senior Medical Officer, for the hospitalized:

> The noises in the vicinity of the [General] hospital mentioned in my predecessors' reports still continue, these being most noticeable round the maternity block, sisters' quarters and 1st class wards and arise from the traffic on the road passing between these buildings. I consider this road should be closed by a gate, the constant ... passage of rikishas, motors and carts interferes considerably with the

sleep of the nurses engaged on night duty, and is a source of danger and annoyance to patients in a critical condition.[18]

There were no traffic regulations or road signs, nor was there a hierarchy among road users. In old photographs and illustrations, such as 'The Padang, Singapore, circa 1905–10',[19] Singapore traffic was difficult with private carriages, hack gharries, bullock-carts, rickshaws, tramcars, hawkers carrying heavy loads in baskets, hand carts and push carts, pedestrians, and motor-car drivers, all jostling for right of way. On these streets jammed with traffic, the motor vehicles sounded their horns at the pullers, the pullers shouted at the pedestrians, and the pedestrians tended to ignore both. The result was a cacophonous nightmare and traffic that was unsafe at any speed. Vehicles could park almost anywhere, and a great deal still had to be done in the essential matter of framing rules and regulations to keep vehicles on one side of the road!

As rickshaws increased there was ample opportunity for conflict between pullers, police constables and peons over the interpretation of certain traffic rules. These regulations, printed in English, were not well understood nor kept by the pullers. The rapid spread of rickshaws caused confusion in Singapore streets and in these difficult conditions arrests were made and fines inflicted on coolies who were 'utterly careless about the rules of the road, and caused endless problems to traffic'.[20] Not surprisingly, accidents occurred, in one of which the Governor was alleged to have had a narrow escape from injury.[21] On closer examination, however, the problem of the rickshaw's contribution to the city's traffic accident toll was not so simple. The role of the rickshaw as a 'danger' and a 'nuisance' was exaggerated. If anything, the emergence of motor cars was to highlight all too well, just the opposite: the pullers' lack of safety on the streets, even when showing their lights at night.[22]

Singapore's traffic congestion was shocking by the 1920s. Notwithstanding the competition of omnibuses the average number of rickshaws running on the streets exceeded 10,000 in 1922.[23] Rickshaws and slow traffic were meant to keep to the left side of the road. The traffic situation was at its worst—noisy and deadly—at rush hours, dawn and dusk:

We will suppose that one has arrived in Singapore in the early hours of the morning has waded through the gesticulating and frantic crowd [of rickshaw pullers] at Tank Road Station, and has finally got into a hired car (so they call taxi cabs here), and been driven to one's hotel. After a bath and a change comes breakfast, and then maybe one has a few moments by the window to look therefrom onto the city below.... Let me try to tell you what can be seen.... Bullock carts slowly plodding on their way—their drivers quite oblivious to the passage of time; a few gharries pulled by rather small and not very fast ponies; rickshaw pullers—running fast; and a stream of motor cars. This makes up the visible traffic, but in the distance one can hear the constant drumming of the tram. One is bound to be amazed when first seeing Singapore at the enormous amount of motor traffic in the city. During the early morning hours, when business men and government officials are proceeding to work, the stream of motor cars down the roads leading into the city is continuous and apparently never likely to stop. Traffic on the side roads is often held up for a considerable time while these streams of motor cars, of every make, and of swiftly moving motor cycles, dash past.[24]

Rickshaws did swerve out into the main carriageway without warning, at peak periods. Motorists had to be constantly on guard. The danger to traffic of pullers crawling about with empty rickshaws as they lost more and more of their passengers to the cheaper mini-buses was real and it was a difficult problem to know how to deal with them. As mechanical progress began to impinge on their future, the risks rickshawmen were prepared to take on the streets increased. In 1922 out of 4,396 pullers brought before the Court, 2,788 were charged with loitering, obstruction or endangering traffic.[25] Pullers did wander about from side to side, but often in search of fares, and not with 'blissful indifference to their own danger or that of others'.[26] This latter was a commonly held view among Europeans, which of course provided a rationale for gradually removing them from the streets altogether. The pullers were streetwise for the most part, possessing a modicum of road sense, but their rickshaws were now empty more often than not, driving some towards a fatal error of judgement.

On the other hand, in a city where there were such differences in the speed of the vehicles, and where most thoroughfares needed widening, too often motor-car drivers were careless, even reckless, travelling at high speeds:

Everyone appears to own a car in Singapore—be they European, Eurasian, Chinese, Indian, Malay or Javanese. The tally of the Malay and Chinese operated taxis and buses must run into four figures or more. Motor lorries, private and public cars and buses, horses or bullock-drawn carts, man-hauled trucks, electric trams, the thousands of Chinese hauled jinrikishas, and a vast multitude of bicycles flood the streets.... In Raffles Square, during working hours, a solid mass of cars is parked, and in the vicinity of the hotels and clubs, or other popular resorts, there are long lines of other parked motors. Singapore has acute traffic problems ... the greatest problem of all is to drive about the city without running down a wandering Chinese pedestrian, ricksha or cyclist.[27]

The 1920s and 1930s were years of unprecedented death on the roads of Singapore. The tragic problem of traffic accidents is underscored in the hard evidence of inquests and inquiries in the years from 1920 to 1938 when the Coroner was preoccupied with the not infrequent deaths of rickshaw pullers and others at the hands of speeding motorists.[28]

The difficulties to be contended with by the traffic police and by the rickshawmen were great as there were few towns in the world that had such a variegated traffic. The police gave constant attention to the improvement of traffic control. Complaints were made by police on the spot against pullers, mostly for loitering and for misinterpreting the traffic signals. Despite numerous requests from public bodies and private individuals—an indication of the ever-present danger on the roads—it was not possible for traffic police to be stationed in all parts of Singapore.[29] Pullers commonly died on stretches of road where there was no traffic control and no street lights, frequently on the outskirts of the city. Drastic reforms aimed at the relief of traffic congestion in the inner city and the reduction of the mounting death toll were contained in the Trimmer-Traffic Committee Report of 1938. Holding that many accidents were due to excessive speed, the Committee proposed a speed limit of 30 miles an hour, for almost the whole town area. The proposal was not greeted with approval everywhere, but the rickshawmen momentarily felt thankful.

One of the touchiest problems with regard to traffic congestion was over the parking of rickshaws. Rickshaws were also considered to be a 'nuisance' when not operating on the streets. The vehicles, especially at night, could be found parked on both sides of the streets in the rickshaw quarters, but rarely on busy roads. The practice of parking rickshaws overnight in this manner was illegal but the municipal authorities and police did not press the rickshaw owners before the 1920s. With the coming of the motor car and truck, however, they were systematically harassed by the police and municipal authorities, who felt their rickshaws occupied too much street space, and obstructed the flow of traffic and commercial life in certain areas. Stationary rickshaws did occupy space along Singapore streets but mainly in the rickshaw districts. Hence, the accusations directed against owners about the space requirements for their vehicles and traffic congestion were ill-founded. Authorities overestimated the amount of street space occupied by stationary rickshaws, and more importantly, refused to recognize that most parking was on secondary streets in Chinese quarters and not on main thoroughfares.

Rickshaws were transformed into 'space hogs' by officials when motor cars and trucks refused to avoid the secondary streets and backlanes. Standing rickshaws parked close together in tiers next to the edge of the five-footway occupied less space than a row of motor cars. But owners of motor cars and trucks, pre-eminent symbols of status and wealth in Singapore, clamoured for more parking bays and garages in the inner city. The pullers were in deep trouble with the police over 'no parking' by 1923:

> The difficulties of controlling traffic in Singapore are great principally due to the fact that the streets are clogged with 'crawling' rickshaws and the great increase of motor buses and motor car traffic in narrow streets had led to a congestion which seems almost inevitable until the slow moving traffic is reduced in number and parking facilities are afforded for taxi cabs. . . . Another great difficulty which has to be overcome is provision of spaces for unemployed rickshaws at night. As it is, there are probably ten times as many rickshaws licensed as there is space to store them away when unemployed, the result is that in certain portions of the town many of the streets are packed with empty rickshaws which are left out all night. This problem . . . is at present engaging the closest attention of the municipality and of the police.[30]

By then there was not enough space for through traffic in the rickshaw areas. The change from ox-drawn wagons to motorized vehicles resulted in faster delivery of goods but it also brought sudden tragedy and mishap to the narrow streets, lined with rickshaws. On 6 June 1929, a five-ton motor water tanker, about three-fourths full at the time, went through Upper Cross Street and turned into New Market Road,

> We then opened up the water tap and started watering the left side of the road. At the place of the accident about ten people were sitting some of them were cleaning their rickshas and others sitting playing cards. They were sitting on the road.... There were about sixty to seventy rickshas all stored there. The rickshas [were] about two deep.[31]

The driver had watered this road frequently during the last month and a half at about the same time each day: once in the morning and once in the afternoon. 'I think the accident happened because he was not a competent driver. He was going zig-zag before he reached Park Road. Many rickshas park on the roadside there.' Kee Cheong, whose husband owned fourteen rickshaws, then described what happened next in a flash:

> I was standing on the road outside the other ricksha, i.e. on the opposite side of the two rickshas to Park Road. Lak Tee was sitting on the footboard of the ricksha that was slightly damaged. He was waiting to take away that ricksha for hire. My husband was standing close to me on the same side of the ricksha ... I did not see the lorry coming and the first I knew was when I was knocked down ... I remember when I was in a sitting position on the road. I was in front of the lorry. My husband was dead and Lak Tee appeared to be still alive. My husband was lying on the ground near me, near the left wheel.[32]

In another incident, in which the driver was not at fault, a Hengwah child, Moy Kee Ah, aged 8 and recently arrived from China, was accidentally killed by a motor lorry in a Rochore Road congested with rickshaws. She was fatally injured through the action of an unknown Chinese woman who ordered the child to cross the road, ignoring the traffic. Kumarasamy, the driver, gave this account to the Coroner:

> I was driving my lorry along Rochore Canal Road.... At a point opposite Angullia Road I noticed an obstruction of rickshaws. They were washing the rickshaws. I slowed down and sounded my horn three times. I then saw a child playing on my left side of the road. On the opposite side of the road was a woman. The woman called the child—waving her right hand. The child began to cross the road right in front of my lorry. I swerved to the right and applied my brakes. The child knocked her head against the side of the lorry near the rear wheels. The child fell on the ground. I stopped my lorry and picked up the child and was about to put her on the lorry when the above woman took her from me. A crowd collected and were threatening. I went to Kandang Kerbau Police Station, and informed the Police.[33]

A police officer described the scene of the accident. He found out that house No. 66 was a rickshaw coolie house, as were most of the other houses in that locality. There were rickshaws three deep on the right side of the road in front of the house, constituting an obstruction of 12–14 feet. He also learned from the residents that it was a common practice to wash the rickshaws on the opposite side of the road near the canal.[34]

Obviously, there was not enough space for through traffic in such areas and for the rickshaws too, any longer. Rickshaws were being discouraged from plying on major roads, and literally forced off their own streets. But nothing was done to make motorized traffic avoid the rickshaw areas after 1920, despite the fact that cars and trucks caused most of the accidents and traffic congestion on Singapore's roads.

Until the rickshaw came the largest share of traffic took place on foot. Rickshaws quickly became a feature of life on the move in Singapore because they offered convenient service and cheap fares to the public at large. Trams and taxis plied the wide avenues but elsewhere motorized transport was apt to give way to the ubiquitous rickshaw. One only had to step outside and a rickshaw was bound to be nearby, often within hailing distance. Getting around the inner city fast by rickshaw, especially off the wider avenues, was no problem, particularly on journeys of up to 2 miles. The rickshaw was without equal if one wanted to visit the alleys, side-lanes, shops, and brothels, and do it inexpensively. One can only admire the skill and dexterity with which the pullers wound their way through the traffic in the narrow streets of Chinatown to the patron's final destination. For many, particularly prostitutes and their clients, the rickshaw provided door-to-door service. Rickshaws also ran day and night. Singapore never suffered from a chronic shortage of rickshaws after dark:

> It was about one. Men and women were now sleeping everywhere, but the rickshaw pullers were still labouring. Many of them passed carrying white men, apparently towards the docks. In some of the rickshas I saw Chinese, wearing black suits. Several of the Europeans travelled in twos, which suggested they were casual visitors . . . who were taking the precaution of not missing their ship through any Chicagoism. Nearly all rickshas came from one direction. . . . No motor cars passed.[35]

The rickshaw was convenient low-cost transportation for Singapore. The coolie class were the principal users of rickshaws precisely because of their 'low fares, brisk motion, and ready availability',[36] advantages which trams, hire cars, and other modern forms of transport could not provide.

Rickshaw trips were generally short, ranging from several hundred yards up to two miles in distance. It was used by officials commuting to work, by parents sending children to and from school, and by Chinese men travelling to associations, clubs and brothels. Longer trips could entail carrying a cloth hawker on a huckstering round through neighbourhood areas lasting the most part of a day, Japanese sailors on a joy ride with a stop to visit the *Karayuki-san* of Malay or Trengganu Street before returning them to the docks again, and Europeans on rickshaw journeys round the clubs and bars. For example, Captain A. H. Tilly used Lee Ngang's rickshaw for almost 4 hours. When he eventually arrived at his house in Anson Road, he got out of the rickshaw in a drunken state and paid the puller 5 cents. The rickshaw trip was long, the transport cheap. For 5 cents, the pilot went, at about 4.30 p.m., in a rickshaw—'no. 4 name unknown to me'—to

. . . the Rendevous Tavern, opposite to the Chinese burial ground. Then I went to Smith Street to a spirit shop, as I know a Chinaman who is an interpreter in the Police Court, and had a whiskey and tonic. After finishing the same, I went to the Prince of Wales Hotel and had two glasses of beer there. Then I proceeded home by Tanjong Pagar Road (it being the nearest road to my house) and then came into Anson Road. I went along the said road towards Fort Palmer as my house is just at the foot of the above mentioned place. Then I stopped the ricksha coolie, and paid him. . . .[37]

According to the schedule of the rates of hire in 1897 no puller was required to draw his rickshaw more than 3 miles without a rest, or 10 miles in a single day or to remain engaged by a patron for more than 8 hours at a time.[38] However, rickshawmen recalled at inquests making longer trips non-stop, between 4 and 7 miles; sometimes they had to take fares even further away from Singapore in sweltering heat for hours on end as far as Tao Payoh, Bedok and beyond—from 10 to 14 miles. Sometimes, they collapsed in the process and died.

Rickshaws were the most popular way to commute to work, make the social rounds, and get around the markets. Such trips accounted for approximately nine-tenths of the total in 1900. There was variation though in trip-use and the time of day across the city. Rickshaws were used predominantly by Europeans and Asians to travel to office areas and places of business, and by children to schools in the early hours of the morning and mid-afternoon. Socializing was more common in the evening and the brothel areas supplied many of the patrons then:

It is possible to find times and locations where ninety per cent of rickshaws that pass carry school children, others where commuters dominate others where almost every vehicle bears over 60 kg of goods accompanied by one or two riders. The two shift system of vehicle renting causes sudden flows of empty vehicles at times like 3 p.m. . . .[39]

A rickshaw often carried Teo Way Yong's 11-year-old daughter to the market to visit her at 10.30 a.m. and returned her at 4 p.m. to her uncle's house at 45 Anson Road, and the puller on at least one occasion did not hesitate to give her a running commentary as they whizzed along.[40] Rickshaws were hired by travellers arriving by rail from the Federated Malay States at all hours. A photograph of the station at Tank Road shows nearly 20 rickshaws neatly lined up next to one another; the station clock showed the time to be nearly 5 p.m. (Plate 4). The railway station was so far from the business centre and the Raffles Hotel that any train passenger had to take a rickshaw[41] to his destination. The same strategy applied in getting to the station, too. On the night of 27 September 1937, Kong Ah Foon, a young Cantonese bride, rode in a rickshaw going to the railway station; her sister-in-law was returning to Penang and everybody turned out to see her off. Kong's rickshaw was one of three occupied by members of her family:

The rickshaw hood was closed down. Our rickshaw was the last of three rickshaws, our rickshaw being about fifty feet behind the next rickshaw. The other two rickshaws had crossed the road to go to the railway station and our rickshaw was crossing the road . . . the rickshaw puller stopped a little while before he commenced to cross the road. . . .[42]

Rickshaws also dropped fares at the races on the weekends. Once having left the precincts of the race course, pullers were not permitted to re-enter, except by special written permission of the Chief Police Officer.[43] And on special occasions, such as royal visits, rickshaws were used as a way to see the most overcrowded and exotic parts of the city. In April 1901, the Duke and Duchess of Cornwall and York visited Singapore:

I saw the procession of rickshaws round Chinatown on the Sunday evening from a shop in Kling Street (now Chulia Street). The owner of the shop was a very big dealer, and all the import men in the place seemed to be congregated there, and we were regaled with a large quantity of liquid refreshment while waiting. Kling Street was completely 'paved' with Turkey red cloth, while there was a complete 'ceiling' of the same cloth stretching from housetop to housetop across the whole length of the street. The Chinese dealers knew how to do things properly in those days. The rickshaw pullers were clothed in scarlet running pants and scarlet coats for the occasion. I remember that the Duke looked quite at home in his rickshaw, and the Duchess sat up very stiffly, and seemed most uncomfortable, as if she expected to be thrown out at any moment.[44]

The concentration of poor people in certain sections of the city and the high rate of morbidity and mortality within those areas meant that messages about accidents and the carriage of the ill and deceased were possible only because of the 'long legs of the rickshaw puller'.[45] Public rickshaws provided the sole ambulance service to Singapore's inhabitants for many years. The removal of smallpox patients was done in two rickshaws especially set aside for the purpose; they were kept at the rickshaw depot, avoiding the necessity of having to use public rickshaws for such a dangerous task.[46] In 1896 four more rickshaw ambulances were obtained at a time when fear of epidemic was prevalent.[47] For rickshawmen, mercy trips to and from the hospital entailed responsibility and risk, and the possibility, too, of a windfall for services rendered; it was known that few pullers wished to accompany plague victims:

The year [1900] under review was the unhealthiest since 1896. . . . One case of bubonic plague was reported. It was landed on Christmas Day. The patient was found in Ellenborough market and was sent to the hospital at the instance of a fortune teller who predicted a great fortune to the rickisha puller who should take him there.[48]

A motorized ambulance ordered from Europe arrived in 1913. The vehicle suffered a shortage of spare parts and on occasion those being taken to hospital had to push. However, it proved useful to officials in other ways, conveying police reinforcements to points where they were needed. The Singapore municipality ultimately decided to convert the ambulance into a prison van.[49] Besides this 'modern' ambulance, and stretchers kept at all police stations, Singapore possessed 9 wheeled hand ambulances and 11 carts for removal of corpses within the municipality. In practice, however, it was more expeditous to convey individuals to hospital in rickshaws though this was not in every case beneficial to the injured person.[50]

The medical evidence in the Coroner's Records demonstrates that an injured person's chances of recovery were reduced by the absence of an efficient ambulance service in Singapore. This was only too obvious in instances where individuals were being propelled along a street to a hospital in a rickshaw irrespective of their condition. Take the case of an unknown Teochiu Chinese found lying in Tanjong Pagar Road, dying. This injured man was conveyed in a rickshaw to the police station at Kreta Ayer and from there, sitting in a rickshaw, to the General Hospital where he died the same day: death was due to internal haemorrhage and shock from a ruptured spleen. The Coroner wrote a note on the necessity of proper ambulance facilities for this class of case:

> I am informed that the condition of the deceased was 'apalling' when he reached hospital. Apart from other considerations there can be no two opinions that the transfer of a gravely injured person in an unsuitable vehicle in which the sitting position is enforced either kills on the road to the hospital, prepares the way for a fatal ending on the operating table, or so increases the shock from which the patient is already suffering that he passes out soon after the operation.[51]

Rickshaws could inadvertently endanger the lives of the seriously ill, but in the absence of an ambulance service worthy of its name, the public rickshaw was readily available, and pullers did save people from outright death—labourers injured on building sites, victims of tenement fires, potential suicides, perishing beggars, and fellow clansmen who suddenly fell down between the shafts.[52]

But much of a puller's day could be occupied with moving goods rather than people: small pieces of porcelain ware for export, loads of vegetables for a quarter-mile run to the market, baskets of chicken and ducks for evening shoppers. Ng Kar Eng earned his living carrying fish, vegetables, and sundries at the Beach Road Market:

> At that time [1938] . . . businessmen used to go to the Beach Road Market on that side where the big bazaar was situated. Some small bazaar people went to the headquarters in the Beach Road Market side to bid for fish and vegetables, and then sold it on the small bazaar side. So I used to go to that side of the market to carry the vegetables and fish, to wait for customers over there, to make a living. If the businessmen were carrying fish and vegetables, I charged a bit more, otherwise after I carried them, the water from the fish, as the ice had invariably melted, was all over my rickshaw. I had to clean and wash it, that is why I charged more; if it was vegetables or sundries, a little less.[53]

Moving unaccompanied goods was both profitable and enjoyable since the rate charged was higher and the pace somewhat slower. Pulling people about at the normal gait was a constant race, a heavy burden, particularly when carrying both passenger and goods. Hawkers frequently carried their wares in rickshaws. Guan Ek Cheong, an iced-drink hawker at the Anglo-American School, regularly patronized rickshaws loaded with his 'goods'—buckets, glasses, sugar, and lemons.[54] Food and drink featured as accompanied goods in many rickshaw trips. Lee Aik, a 64-year-old partially blind hawker, was on his way back from delivering food and basins to about sixty entertainers of the Teochiu Sai Yong Hong Company performing a *wayang* (opera) near Beach Road, when he was thrown out of the rickshaw in a traffic accident. Ong Geok Swee, the rickshaw puller, stated:

> I pull ricksha no. 5988, a hired one not my own.... I was on my way from Beach Road Market to High Street after the actors had finished their food. The deceased carried a bucket with dirty cups, chop sticks, spoons and dishes and got into my ricksha. He told me to take him to High Street. I do not know his place.... There was a heavy tin box on the road which the deceased had been carrying with him in the ricksha. Its contents were scattered over the road mostly over the bloodstains....[55]

Each part of the city had its principal users and trip purposes. The rickshaw was there—available, flexible, and cheap, catering to a particular section of the population and its needs: office-workers, schoolchildren, prostitutes, travellers, racing fans, hawkers, and the sick or injured.

Power and work were central preoccupations of Singapore as a coolie town. In the nineteenth century the new power was steam. Along with the steam engine Singapore sought a more basic source of energy: manpower, coolies. Singapore was transformed by the spread of steam and later electrical energy in combination with the use of a tramway system to develop and integrate the various activities of the city. Yet, at the time the Singapore Tramway Company started in 1882, another form of public transport made its debut in open-competition with the mechanical 'juggernauts'—the man-powered rickshaw.

The tramway lines ran from New Harbour to Collyer Quay and as far east as Rochore. In 1905 the trams switched to electricity. The company obtained from the municipality a 35-year concession for the installation of electric tramways, and to use electric power supplied by them to supplement the existing system of lighting the streets by gas.[56] When the electric trams began running the rickshaw coolies were openly hostile: several attempts were made to derail trams, to damage the permanent way, and threats were made against the life and property of the manager, Mr Koh Seck Tian, who had to be provided with special security for several weeks.[57] The antagonism subsided though as quickly as it had flared up. Ironically, the establishment of the tramway stimulated rickshaw traffic instead of having the opposite effect. This was the first time in the world an electric tramway had to contend with a well-established rickshaw service. The trams had to meet in daily competition numerous rickshaws and instead of the trams running the rickshaws off the streets, as was the outcome predicted by some, the rickshaws continued to increase in number.[58]

Although the authorized fare was 6 cents for the first mile and 5 cents per mile thereafter, the labouring classes found no difficulty in bargaining for lower rates. Indeed few except Europeans paid the full fare.

At this rate per mile the ubiquitous rikisha is ready to carry two persons with their bundles, picking them up at their door and conveying them to their destination through narrow town lanes or even over rough country tracks. It is obvious that natives, especially if they are accompanied by women and children find the humble rikisha better suited to their wants than tram cars going from point to point and charging probably one penny a mile for each person.[59]

The fares collected did not cover running costs and the trams were never able to compete over short distances in the central part of the city, where the population was greatest. The cars started to take passengers on longer hauls on Serangoon Road in July 1905 but the fares charged were too high, compared with rickshaws carrying two passengers, to attract Chinese, Tamils and Malays, and in October a reduced scale was introduced. The company still did not carry enough passengers.[60] The falling off was ascribed to bad times rather than the stiff competition of the rickshaws. On the whole, the experience of the new tramways in Singapore was unfortunate. The main streets were too narrow and a double line of rails interfered with ordinary traffic. Rickshaws proved, as they had earlier, formidable competition. It remained to be seen whether the trams could be run profitably at the cheaper fares they were forced to charge by 1907.

Most people could not get into town just in a tram. Commuters from Serangoon Road had to stop at the Raffles, and then get a rickshaw down town. Because the trams could not come right through it was a disadvantage; other people also on the edge of the city had to take a rickshaw after leaving the tram at Bras Basah Road, or else change trams. The presence of the trams helped rather than hindered the rickshaw coolies, as more short journeys were made by passengers after leaving the trams than was the case formerly.[61] In 1916, 29,879 licences for rickshaws were issued.[62]

The effects of the tramways, however, in insuring the expansion of the town, was to be seen in Geylang District, where many building sites for houses were being developed. The trams went out to the Geylang area, which was about the only place where there was any cheap land available, and it was all taken up.[63] In 1913 the increase in passengers was marked, especially on the Geylang route, indicating the spread of the town in that direction for residences of labourers. By 1919, the tramways, which had been running for 14 years, had developed the neighbourhood along Serangoon Road and in Geylang.[64]

Despite some success the problem of the tramways in extending the suburbs was vexing. The condition of the sixty electric tramcars, which every year were examined and licensed to carry passengers, left much to be desired. Many were described as 'rather shabby and very noisy. Drivers and conductors are also of an inferior class.'[65] There were other objections too. Each year a significant number of Singaporeans were the victims of tram accidents. For example, 23 accidents were reported in 1908 of which three proved fatal.[66] Many of them were caused by passengers jumping off the cars while in motion. That was the way Ling Kong King, a 29-year-old Hockchia rickshaw puller, died. Ling Nong Noey, a clansman and hawker, remembered that the deceased, who was suffering from bronco-pneumonia, fell off the car in North Bridge Road at the junction of Arab Street when it had not quite stopped.[67]

The trams could not provide cheap, efficient, fast mechanical transport for a population on its way to half a million. They only ran on certain routes; and, of course, trams damaged the roads. The Municipal Engineer in particular did not like them, and was opposed to their further spread in any direction, suggesting motor buses or trackless trams as a paying alternative:

> If you had trackless trams, the cost of adding another route is very little, or if you adopt a certain route and then find it would be better to substitute another route for it, you waste very little money. It is simply a matter of removing the standards and the overhead wire, and they could all be used again. They do not cut up the road at all. They can pass other vehicles just as well as can a motor bus. They have a lot of them in Yorkshire, in Bradford and Leeds. They are run by the municipality there.[68]

The Municipal Commissioners considered the suggestions in favour of trackless trams, but were not prepared to recommend that system.

Many could do without the tram railed system with its noise, the standards in the centre of the road, and the difficulty of taking corners in narrow streets built in rectangular blocks. But the rickshaw was indispensable. That revelation was bad news for the tramway company, but not for the coolies who pulled rickshaws. Faced with a growing loss of passengers to rickshaws and private mini-buses, the money-losing, inefficient, and somewhat antiquated tramway was unable to get back on the track by the mid-1920s.

Singapore was behind the times and desperately in need of cheap rapid transport. The trams reflected little credit on the city. The state of the trams and the permanent way was bad by the end of the First World War, the noise was deafening, and the cars were overcrowded.[69] It was the service of mini-buses with bright blue bodies and red mudguards which successfully carried the public during the worst period of the tram system.[70] The complaints of overcrowding and discomfort suffered by passengers travelling in tramcars diminished when the mini-buses began plying the same routes. Both motor cars and omnibuses increased in number and the practice of converting Ford car chassis into seven-seater omnibuses, running on regular routes developed quickly. The success of the undertaking created rivals. The conversion of light lorries into omnibuses, stimulated by the absence of rubber to be hauled and the inadequacy of the trams, was a noteworthy feature of 1920.[71] But the number of these heavy buses decreased after 1922 in face of competition from the smaller seven-seaters which had become popular, and having pneumatic tyres did far less damage to the roads.[72]

The rates of the mini-buses were cheaper than those charged by either the trams or rickshaws. They were an economical means of transport, as fares were considerably less than the legal rate of 5 cents allowed by the schedule: an altogether satisfactory development from the public's standpoint.[73] The buses '... go softly past on balloon tyres. Quite a flash of beauty has been added to our scene.'[74] Notwithstanding the competition of the mini-bus the average number of rickshaws on the streets exceeded 10,000 during 1923. The figures for the previous three years were similar: 8,022 in 1920, 9,244 in 1921, and 10,021 in 1922.[75]

Trolley buses were introduced into Singapore in 1925. Before their coming electric tramcars had been the only large-scale public transport in the city for 20 years, and prior to that, steam trams. Sixteen miles of tram tracks were scrapped when the trolley buses and omnibuses came into operation and the fleet of sixty electric trams was broken up. The Singapore Traction Company was a municipal enterprise, and controlled transport within municipal limits. One advantage of the new service was that vehicles could be transferred at any time from one route to another. Another was that motor buses permitted experiments being made with new routes, and at little expense if they failed, especially when it appeared that a bus service could possibly develop an outlying district.[76] During 1933 many of the seven-seater buses ceased to operate owing to the failure of owners to put on adequate schedules. The Singapore Traction Company took over runs like the Finlayson Green–Paya Lebar and Tanjong Pagar–Geylang routes, adding more than fifty new buses to their existing services by the end of 1935.[77]

In that year there were ten regular bus concerns besides the Singapore Traction Company that maintained a satisfactory service on various routes.[78] These mosquito bus companies, which operated routes to the outlying districts, provided an important service to a city with an expanding population, and next to no space left in town. It must be remembered that the exodus of the poorer population to the outer suburbs was a necessity. Rents increased, driving them out, further away from the work-place, and therefore requiring a cheaper and quicker service than the rickshaw could offer. The buses were popular with the travelling public, running on definite schedules on a properly organized basis with an accelerated service during peak hours. More modern buses were built, routes extended, extra services to Tengah and Changi introduced, and the fleets of certain companies increased to cope with the extra night traffic.[79]

The buses proved to be a far more difficult opposition than the trams for the rickshawmen. As early as 1925, when the Singapore Traction Company was being set up, it was predicted that buses would take the place of rickshaws, 'which vehicles, from every point of view, should be discouraged as much as possible'.[80] By 1931 pullers were finding it increasingly difficult to obtain fares and loitering around bus stops, in North and South Bridge Roads, Collyer Quay and Raffles Place, was on the increase, as also was the carrying of forbidden articles. Passengers being scarce, pullers such as Ng Kar Eng hung around markets and carried loads of raw meat and fresh fish to make ends meet.[81]

Nevertheless buses still did not cater to a certain percentage of the travelling public's need. There was a sufficient demand for quick transport in the town itself to warrant a properly managed system of taxi-cabs in competition with rickshaws. The year 1933 saw the introduction of light saloon-type taxis seating up to four passengers.[82] They were an instant success with the public for short trips. A European writer observed this new form of public transport at its separate stand accommodation: 'There is a row of yellow taxis, stumpy two seater Fords, whose Malay syces in white uniforms and black songkohs [*songkok*, a pointed velvet cap] sit on heels and chat or sleep behind their wheels waiting for a fare.'[83] Jerome Caminada, the foreign news editor of *The Times* in London, recalled these taxis and rickshaws in his memories of the first time he saw Singapore in 1935; the rickshaws were gradually being wiped out in the inner-city area and the cab was playing a key role:

> I brought a sun-helmet with me myself, and wore it once. I put it on for my first rickshaw ride, and it fell off somehow at the back. Never again did it appear. I realised at the time that the sun-helmet was doomed, but it did not occur to me that the rickshaw was too. We used it now and then, though it had no chance against the taxi. Small maneuverable taxis roamed the island in those days ... and I can hear now the swift change of gears as they approached a corner.[84]

The speed of passenger transport also increased at the rickshaw's expense by adopting tricycles for passenger carriage. The cycle rickshaw or trishaw was almost twice as fast as the hand rickshaw on flat ground, and like other mechanical transport benefited from public works programmes building and extending metalled roads all around the city in the 1930s. The heavier trishaw was at a severe disadvantage though compared to the rickshaw on steep inclines and in the congested alleys and narrow lanes of Chinatown where there was constant stop–start traffic. The earliest trishaws appeared on the streets of Singapore in 1914 when a syndicate took out licences for fifteen 'pedal rickshaws' to ply for hire; the fares were the same as for first-class rickshaws. Crude in appearance, they were not terribly up to date, consisting of chairs welded on tricycle frames, and pedalled by Chinese coolies wearing a uniform. The trishaws had only been on the streets several weeks when they were all sold and sent to Java.[85] The novelty was over and they were inconspicuous for almost twenty years. Serious interest in trishaws was rekindled in the mid-1930s; the numbers increasing as rickshaws declined until 6,163 trishaws were registered at the end of 1936.[86] By-laws were introduced in September of that year limiting the number of trishaws to be licensed to 7,000 in the interests of traffic safety.[87] The trishaw, despite this unflattering description, held its own against buses and taxi-cabs at a time when the rickshaw's future was hanging in the balance:

> The way we happened to buy a car so soon was that we took a ride in a trishaw. A trishaw is a rickshaw attached to a bicycle (that's what I said), and there in one

handy little contraption is combined the worst of two worlds. The driver rides the bicycle and the passengers ride a little green sidecar with a frilled hood on red spokes. A trishaw may have such accessories as shiny brass rails, chintz cushions, and model-train curtains, but it never has springs, and you can record every cobble of the road using your spine as pedometer. In traffic it is a worse menace than an ox cart, since trishaw-drivers think faster than oxen and can do terrible things more unexpectedly. But we didn't know any of this. This particular afternoon we were down in the Chinese quarter on an errand. There were no taxis in sight, but there were plenty of trishaws and the haute monde of the district seemed to be bucking them with great aplomb, so the cosmopolitan Brittons hailed one too and climbed in. Or we tried too. I could just fit my head under the awning with the frill over my face, but Frank wasn't so lucky. He sat swayback with his shoulders braced outside the awning and his head somewhere up in the sky, and as our entourage jerked past, merchants stopped eating rice at the doors of their shop, hawkers stopped hawking, card games on the pavement were abandoned, and everyone just enjoyed us. We got out at Raffles Place, flagged a taxi, drove to Orchard Road, and bought a car.[88]

Mechanical transport brought changes and problems to the city, government, inhabitants, and rickshaw pullers. Horse-traffic days were gone. The traffic on the roads was modern, noisy, polluting, and dangerous to life and limb. Lorries thundered past on their way to Tanjong Pagar, to the barges lining the Singapore River, or building sites on the outskirts of town. Buses, cars, and trishaws continually jockeyed for right of way with pedestrians and rickshaws. The streets were congested, the pace fast, priority being given to mass transport. Rickshaws, now considered to be a public 'nuisance' or 'traffic hazard', were being excluded from the streets. Rickshaw traffic, however, was neither noisy nor reckless, and it was pollution-free. Nor was the rickshaw's usefulness ever seriously in doubt, even at this late stage:

So far as rickshaws are concerned you may note every type of passenger, from the shrouded Malay ladies who travel in a rickshaw closed in from the public gaze, to the European sitting behind a smartly stepping, blue coated Chinese who can really run. We are gradually abolishing the rickshaw in the city, but it is a vehicle that is still used by rich and poor of every nationality; occasionally by a family party; and occasionally as an aid to house removing![89]

The position of the rickshaw puller on the eve of the Pacific War is worthy of consideration here. The rickshaw continued to hang on in competition with motor traffic but its fate had been sealed. Hastening its extinction was the rapid progress that had been made in the field of mechanical transport, and a deliberate policy of restriction. Trishaws, motor cycles, hire cars, and motor buses were the rickshaw's rivals, and they were rivals that showed no mercy: 'They are out to hound and oust the ricksha off the streets, and against these ingenious contrivances of iron and steel, how much longer can the ricksha's propelling agent of flesh and blood and bone withstand.'[90] Time was short.

1. SMAR JD, 1893, p. 21.
2. SMAR JD, 1917, p. 5.
3. SMAR JD, 1901, p. 20.
4. The table is compiled from figures in the Annual Reports on the registration of rickshaws between 1887 and 1939.
5. SMAR JD, 1905, p. 5.
6. SMAR JD, 1906, p. 6.
7. Reverend J. A. Bethune Cook, *Sunny Singapore. An Account of the Place and Its People, with a Sketch of the Results of Missionary Work* (London: Elliot Hock, 1907), pp. 33–4.
8. SMAR JD, 1913, p. 7.
9. SMAR JD, 1914, p. 2.
10. SMAR JD, 1915, p. 1.
11. W. E. Makepeace, G. C. Brooke and R. St. J. Braddell (eds.), *One Hundred Years of Singapore* (London: John Murray, 1921), pp. 332–3.
12. SMAR JD, 1917, p. 8.
13. SMAR JD, 1918, p. 5.
14. SMAR JD, 1919, p. 1-E.
15. SMAR JD, 1931, p. 5-B.
16. SMAR JD, 1930, p. 28-F.
17. SMAR JD, 1939, p. 2-B.
18. SSAR, Report by Dr Fry, Senior Medical Officer in Charge, 1911, p. 531.
19. This painting can be seen in the National Museum, Singapore.
20. SSAR, Annual Report on Straits Settlement Police Force and on the State of Crime, 1884, p. C-186.
21. SSAR, Annual Report on Straits Settlement Police Force and on the State of Crime, 1892, p. 289.
22. See Appendix 8, 'Rickshaw Coolies: Traffic Accidents'.
23. SMAR JD, 1922, p. 1-B.
24. R. H. J. Sydney, *Malay Land* (London: Cecil Palmer, 1926), pp. 25–6.
25. SMAR JD, 1922, p. 5-B.
26. Robert W. Foran, *Malayan Symphony* (London: Hutchinson, 1935), p. 33.
27. Ibid.
28. See Appendix 8.
29. SSAR, Annual Report on Straits Settlement Police Force and on the State of Crime, 1924, p. 344.
30. SSAR, Annual Report on Straits Settlement Police Force and on the State of Crime, 1923, p. 399.
31. SCII of Wong Song Song, No. 263, 6/6/29.
32. Ibid.
33. SCII of Moy Kee Ah, No. 228, 25/4/27.
34. Ibid.
35. George Bilainkin, *Hail, Penang! Being the Narrative of Comedies and Tragedies in a Tropical Outpost, among Europeans, Chinese, Malays, and Indians* (London: Sampson Low, Marston and Company Ltd., 1932), pp. 37–8.
36. UNNAYAN in association with T. H. Thomas, *Rickshaws in Calcutta* (Calcutta: UNNAYAN, 1981), p. 46.
37. SCII of Captain Tilly, No. 135, 17/7/1895.
38. SMAR JD, 1897, Appendix J, pp. 34–5.
39. UNNAYAN, op. cit., pp. 9–10.
40. SCII of Teo Way Yong, 22/4/32.
41. HCR, p. A-37.
42. SCII of Tee Yeok Choon, No. 568, 28/9/37.
43. *Singapore Free Press*, 22 October 1901.
44. Edwin A. Brown, *Indiscreet Memories* (London: Kelly and Walsh, 1936), p. 55–6.
45. The language of Ida Pruitt: *Old Madam Yin. A Memoir of Peking Life 1926–1938*

(Stanford: Stanford University Press, 1979), p. 121.

46. SMAR JD, 1894, p. 9.

47. SMAR JD, 1896, p. 91.

48. SMAR JD, 1900, p. 7.

49. SSAR, Annual Report on Straits Settlement Police Force and on the State of Crime, 1914, p. 232.

50. Ibid.

51. SCII of unknown adult male Chinese, 25/6/27.

52. See SCII of Wong Ah Quai, No. 185, 11/7/20; of Lee Peng, No. 33, 3/2/20; of Ng Kum Moy, No. 41, 10/3/05; of Yuen Khoe Thian, No. 126, 26/8/04; of unknown male adult Chinese, No. 300, 25/7/22.

53. Interview with Ng Kar Eng, AOHD, Reel 3.

54. SCII, No. 226, 15/6/24.

55. SCII of Lee Aik, No. 503, 7/9/31.

56. SSAR, 1901, p. 32.

57. SSAR, Annual Report on the Straits Settlement Police Force and on the State of Crime, 1905, p. 169; A. Wright and H. Cartwright (eds.), *Twentieth Century Impressions of British Malaya: Its History, People, Commerce, Industries and Resources* (London: Lloyds Greater Publishing Co. Ltd., 1908), p. 705.

58. SMAR JD, 1907, p. 12.

59. SMAR JD, 1898, p. 16.

60. SMAR JD, 1905, p. 3.

61. SMAR JD, 1911, p. 6.

62. SMAR JD, 1916, p. 16.

63. SMAR JD, 1915, p. 7.

64. HCR, p. A-37; evidence of Mr F. J. Hallifax, p. B-23.

65. SMAR JD, 1914, p. 7.

66. SMAR JD, 1908, p. 3.

67. SCII of Ling Kong King, No. 380, 15/7/30.

68. HCR, evidence of Mr B. Ball, p. B-62.

69. SMAR JD, 1913, pp. 5–6.

70. SMAR JD, 1923, p. 5.

71. SMAR JD, 1920, p. 6.

72. SMAR JD, 1922, p. 2-B.

73. Ibid.

74. Richard Sidney, 'From a Singapore Verandah', *British Malaya* (November 1935), p. 170.

75. SMAR JD, 1922, p. 1-B.

76. HCR, p. A-37.

77. SMAR JD, 1933, p. 7-B.

78. SMAR JD, 1935, p. 5-B; the majority of the companies were organized on a partnership basis, the buses were operated by the individual owners who paid a percentage of the profits into the company funds in order to maintain the organization. The following companies had established a regular service in the different parts of the municipality: the Green Bus Company, 35 registered buses; the Keppel Bus Company, 35; the Soon Lee Bus Company, 5; the Ngo Hock Bus Company, 5; the Katong–Bedok Bus Service, 12; the Changgi Motor Bus Service, 15; the Ponggol Bus Service, 3; the Payar-Lebar Bus Service, 7; the Selatar Motor Bus Company, 20; the Singapore Blue Bus Company, 7.

79. SMAR JD, 1939, p. B-6.

80. SMAR JD, 1925, p. 2-B.

81. SMAR JD, 1931, p. 8-B.

82. SMAR JD, 1933, p. 7-B.

83. R. C. H. McKie, *This Was Singapore* (London, 1950), p. 44.

84. Jerome Caminada, 'Topee and Rickshaw—Both were Doomed', *Straits Times Annual* (1975), p. 124.

85. SMAR JD, 1914, p. 30.

86. SMAR JD, 1936, p. 5.
87. Ibid.
88. Nancy Pence Britton, *East of the Sun* (Blackwood, 1956), pp. 32–3.
89. Sidney, op. cit., p. 170.
90. *Malaya Tribune*, 16 January 1931.

7 The Rickshaw Department

BEFORE the advent of the rickshaw the Singapore Municipality was only concerned with how many carriages, horses, and ponies should be licensed and collecting taxes on them. In 1880 the first rickshaws arrived. Initially, the Commissioners aimed at placing the little understood vehicles under the Hackney Carriage Ordinance of 1882. It soon became apparent to officials though that the Hackney Carriage Ordinance was inadequate for this purpose, lacking provisions against the abuses already associated with rickshaw ownership, licensing, and taxation. The idea in officials' minds that pullers would be attracted by the nominal tax of $1 a year to each acquire his own rickshaw and stick to it as a living, selecting another industrious coolie to be his substitute when ill or indisposed, proved almost completely false. Instead, the trade quickly fell into the hands of rent capitalists who let out the rickshaws for daily hire, and furnished the Registrar's armlet badge, which was given to any presentable applicant, to serve as his warrant for plying as a rickshaw coolie on the streets of Singapore.[1]

The licensing of hackney carriages and rickshaws was under the jurisdiction of the Police Department but it was handed over to the Municipal Commissioners in 1888. There were then 1,000 hackney carriages and 1,800 rickshaws, and the issue of the best way to deal with the question of traffic was already under discussion.[2] At the end of January 1888 registration of rickshaws was commenced, and virtually completed by the middle of April. The services of the police were lent to the Municipality to conduct the work until satisfactory arrangements were made for the new Department. On 1 June, Inspector Emile Goodlands, who spoke Hokkien and a little Foochow, was appointed by the Municipality to the task of supervising 3,000 rickshaws, and twice that number of pullers.[3] During the course of the year a strip of ground, situated at the base of Fort Canning, was also made available by the Government to the city; it was at once converted into an enclosure where the work of inspection and registration of rickshaws could be conducted properly.[4]

It was evident that amendment to existing law was needed by 1889. On the introduction of the Hackney Carriage Extension Ordinance of 1882 little was known about rickshaws, and it was not anticipated that the trade in them would increase to such an enormous extent, and so quickly. The work of registering and continuously supervising 3,000 rickshaws and 6,000 coolies, whose owners displayed extraordinary ingenuity in their attempts to evade the licensing requirements, was no easy task, more especially when it had to be done with an inadequate, inefficient, and somewhat corrupt staff. Because the component parts of the rickshaw such as the body, wheels, wood, and apron could be removed and others substituted in the course of minutes, it was a matter of great difficulty to maintain them at the standard at which they were passed by the Registrar as fit to ply for hire on the streets.[5]

The problems surrounding the issuing of licences led to calls for legislation to be enacted giving the Registrar powers to deal with offenders committing a breach of the Ordinance. Too much time, which could be ill-afforded, was involved in issuing summons and attending the Police Courts to conduct the prosecution.[6] The relative immunity enjoyed by the owners could not last. The multiplication of rickshaws and coolies confirmed legislation was essential to deal with them. In 1891 a Municipal Committee was appointed to devise a scheme for the control of rickshaws. A report followed, recommending that a Rickshaw Department be established and controlled by a Registrar with a sufficient staff of inspectors and Malay peons for day and night work, that there be no limit on the number of rickshaws registered, and no licences required to act as pullers, but the owners were to be responsible for producing pullers when called upon to do so. The tax of $1 a year was to be increased to $12. The unofficial Chinese members protested on grounds that the tax increase was excessive and detrimental to the interest of both the puller and the Colony.[7]

The Committee felt that the annual $1 tax levied on rickshaws under the provision of the Extension Ordinance was too low. In Hong Kong the tax fixed on a rickshaw was $36 per annum and in Shanghai $18–24.[8] The tax was increased from $1 to $12 a year in 1892. The raising of the fee had engaged the Governor's attention, and he made his report to the Colonial Office at once:

> The license fee of twelve dollars is the maximum. It includes the cost of branding the numbers, plates and other expenses. I do not know whether the Municipal Commissioners in any of the Settlements propose to exact the maximum fee, but I expect that they will do so for the first few years in order to cover somewhat the heavy outlay in providing the necessary establishment and buildings. But, however that may be, I am strongly of the opinion that the maximum fee is not too high. So high a fee will, of course, tend to reduce the number of Jinrikishas, and this is urgently needed. The state of the streets in Singapore at the present time is a scandal, and a source of danger to the public. Neither Police nor Municipal Officers can keep under proper control the Jinrikisha traffic at the present time, owing to the large number, six or seven thousand, of ignorant coolies engaged in it . . . I shall hope that an increased fee which may be charged under the Ordinance will bring out a reform not only as regards the class of vehicles, but also in the class of men who are employed as pullers.[9]

The Chinese newspaper, *Lat Pau*, had argued that the legislation could not help pullers to become owners, urging a reconsideration of the decision to increase the licence fee:

> Major McCallum's proposal to increase the license fee on jinrikishas next year appears innocuous but in fact affects all the rickshaw coolies for the rickshaw owners will certainly raise the rate of hire on their rickshaws whereas the rickshaw coolies, unable to make the passengers pay a higher fare for fear of losing a good customer, will be made to suffer. . . .[10]

It was thought that the new tax would reduce the number of licensed rickshaws. But the boom in Singapore during those years created new openings for the rickshaw and coolies to pull them. The unexpected happened; instead of a reduction in number, rickshaws steadily increased until in 1901 there were over 7,000 on the overcrowded streets.[11]

The untried Ordinance came into operation in the latter half of 1892 and the owners and public watched and waited with curiosity, not knowing what was going to happen next. The Malay peons worked hard to control irregularities occurring among pullers and the number of cases they brought before the Registrar in the first four months, 2,131, speaks for itself.[12] It was originally proposed to employ a hundred peons, but the number was reduced for fiscal reasons to sixty. This ceiling was to prove inadequate to check cases of loitering and obstruction. The men were stationed at three depots, which were open from 4.00 a.m. till midnight; they were 4 hours on duty, 4 hours off duty, and 4 hours on reserve. The Fort Canning Office was suitable for the new system of work and could store over 400 rickshaws. The space was vital for keeping the rickshaws impounded for street offences and during the registration.[13] It was necessary for the work of branding, fixing plates, receiving into the store and delivering vehicles, to employ Chinese coolies on regular pay and to engage outside men when the pressure required more.

Experience soon showed where the loopholes were in the new Ordinance. First, the Registrar was an officer of the Municipality and the punishment he could inflict on owners amounted to the equivalent of a small fine. The Registrar had no power to make the owner keep his vehicles up to the standard at which they were passed once every four months. If an owner considered himself badly treated he would appeal to the Protector of Chinese, who could assist him in getting his case considered by the Municipal Commissioners, who had power over the performance of the Registrar's duties. Secondly, impounding rickshaws for offences committed by pullers was lawful only by detaining the rickshaw at the time, not by subsequent proof of evidence; and finally, to enforce this provision required an army of peons. Obviously too, the security clause pressed hardest on the small owner. In his first annual report Mr Hooper was already asking for personal power to suspend the licences of rickshaws which were not kept clean and in a proper state of repair, because many from the time they were licensed were put out day and night and never maintained.[14]

The quality of the rickshaws certainly improved in cleanliness and strength, due to the Registrar's unrelenting pressure on owners to maintain them. There was a great deal too that still had to be done regarding pullers who ignored all rules of the road. '... the coolies in their behaviour and dress leave much to be desired, and street obstruction is still the rule rather than the exception, it is likely that these faults will gradually be lessened, as the coolies find out what a paying thing it is to own a jinrikisha and a better class of man is attracted to the work.'[15]

Notwithstanding these problems, municipal officials wanted to believe that the Ordinance had worked. The 'rickshaw problem' was solved, pending keeping the vehicles in good condition. Within the short spell of five years, however, it was acknowledged that the Rickshaw Ordinance of 1892 had proved a failure. Instead of restraining the number of licensed rickshaws, they multiplied under it to a point far beyond the needs of the city. Owing too to the scarcity of Foochow interpreters, the pullers could only be reached through the owners and it was impossible for officials to know what garbled accounts of the instructions and explanations given by the Department were communicated to them.[16]

There was also the *siong thau*. During these years efforts were made to break their power and to get the real owners to register in their own names. The sway of the brokers was set back by the introduction of security bonds to be signed, but keeping check on 1,432 bonds by 1897, when the men were constantly changing addresses and returning to China, was impossible. The security system had to be abolished and power given to the Registrar to seize an owner's rickshaw for certain offences.[17] The rickshaw trade was controlled in part by fleet owners and by *siong thau* with some men filling both roles. The broker handled all aspects of vehicle licence application, squeezing the small owner, which was the cause of much discontent among rickshawmen. Until 1897 the ownership of rickshaws was steadily becoming less profitable because there was no relaxation of the standard which was required to pass them before being licensed. The owners and *siong thau* endeavoured to lessen the chances for their filthy and defective vehicles to be impounded by using every trick in the book, but to no avail. So bad were many of the rickshaws that sooner or later they were confiscated. In addition to this, there was corruption amongst the street peons and subordinates in the registration office, who, if they were not bribed, were apt to be 'rough, oppressive, and abusive'.[18]

The *siong thau* resisted all efforts of the Registrar to get the Ordinance changed to curtail their wealth, influence and authority in the rickshaw trade. The ownership and licensing of rickshaws was within their province, not the Registrar's; the line between role and responsibility was sharp, clearly drawn in their minds. They put the issue of licensing and inspection to the test in January 1897. The determination of these men to defy the regulations, coupled with the fear of impending legislation, and the desire to coerce the Registrar into registering rickshaws that were too filthy or dilapidated for public use, led to the rickshaw strike of 1897. The 'strike' was really a lock-out since owners and not pullers were behind it. It was organized by Hockchew and Hengwah owners and brokers who resided on the north side of the river in the neighbourhood of Victoria Street, Queen Street, and Rochore Road. They had been attracting the notice of the Department for the bad condition of the vehicles sent in for registration and for being obstinate in their refusal to repair them, sending back time after time unserviceable rickshaws which the Registrar and his staff would not pass.[19]

This faction prevailed on the trade to join them in a strike, partly by threats of intimidation and violence, and in the hope that the demonstration would result in the Rickshaw Department being more lenient, and street peons being less zealous in impounding 'loiterers'. The 'rickshaw problem' was brought to public notice, much to the chagrin of the Municipal Commissioners, by the onset of the well-organized strike. It commenced on the morning of 8 January and lasted four days during which time the owners refused to allow their rickshaws to ply for hire, leaving over 15,000 pullers idle, kicking their heels.

Mr Hooper first realized that something was amiss when not a single rickshaw had been brought to his office to be registered for two days, and on 7 January he reported this strange occurrence to the Police and also to the Protector of Chinese. That night a leaflet was circulated amongst the pullers stating that rickshaws found on the streets the next day would be destroyed, and that during the ensuing three days if they went out with a rickshaw it would be at their own risk. The next morning there was not a rickshaw on a street or road throughout the island.[20] An eerie silence reigned. Then the first and most important act of defiance occurred when twelve pullers attacked the rickshaw branch office in Beach Road. The men, armed with piles, rammed the door and broke all the windows. The militant pullers were dispersed, however, by the prompt action of the police who had been placed on alert to prevent serious disturbance.[21] They were arrested on the spot and charged with unlawful assembly, and bail was fixed at $250 each. In the same Court, later in the day, three other coolies were charged with breaking up a rickshaw, and Koh Chye, the suspected instigator and a big-time Hockchew rickshaw owner and *siong thau*, was arrested and charged with inciting to riot in Victoria Street.[22] This was a dangerous situation, but the prompt action of the police in arresting Koh Chye nipped a riot in the bud. It forced some of the owners to discuss terms with the police for the release of Koh Chye, stating that they would bring their rickshaws out if the authorities released the prisoner. But there was to be no horse-trading. Thirty rickshaw pullers were arrested on Saturday (9 January) and Sunday in connection with the strike, and though little brawling took place there were large, boisterous crowds to disperse. Stone-throwing by pullers and the use of abusive language was common and, in one separate incident, a group of sixteen pullers attacked a gharry in Victoria Street. After that syces were frightened, and the hack gharries did not venture out for fear of being attacked by the strikers.[23]

The situation was critical. The Acting Head of Government, J. A.

Swettenham, proclaimed the city to be under martial law. On Saturday afternoon the police received copies of the Proclamation in Chinese which were posted on placards all over the city.[24] The response was swift as a wall poster campaign began that aroused much interest. The Proclamations posted on the Police Court gates were found with Chinese notices pasted over them, stating that both the owners and pullers had grievances which had not been redressed. Other large Chinese placards to the same effect were found in Almeida Street, in addition to a pen-and-ink pictorial poster, which graphically illustrated to an illiterate public, the complaints of the rickshawmen against the peons. It consisted of three pictures, 'the first representing a rikisha peon beating some unfortunate coolie until the blood comes out of his mouth, the second a rikisha peon extorting a bribe by force, and the third the apathy of the much hated peon, who is represented, arms folded, coolly watching some frenzied puller commit suicide by taking a header into the sea.'[25]

A special committee was appointed by the Municipal Commissioners in an emergency session on 8 January to inquire into and report on the causes of the strike. The Committee held six meetings; two were held at Mr Hooper's Rickshaw Registration Office (8 and 13 January), Kandang Kerbau, to question a number of the influential rickshaw owners.[26] At the first meeting especially, they were loud in their condemnation of the Department. The complaints were that inspection of rickshaws was too severe, the pullers received no punishment when their rickshaws were impounded for street offences, and there were too many peons.[27] As a result of the initial discussion some owners promised to send out their rickshaws. But few actually broke the strike the next morning. Despite the concerted efforts of the authorities to persuade rickshaws to go out the attitude of owners was the same—their vehicles remained housed and the pullers remained idle. The Inspector-General of Police and the Protector of Chinese applied pressure in the Kampong Glam area to induce rickshaws to work, but they failed. Mr Hooper also met with no success. For several days he had been inquiring into the grievances and attempting to effect a settlement. He was soon convinced that the strike was a blatant attempt by the owners to force the hand of the Commissioners and the Registrar, and compel them to pass rickshaws which were unfit for public use. But there was no vacillation on the part of the Commissioners in supporting Mr Hooper's stand that the rickshaws must meet acceptable standards of safety, comfort, and convenience.[28]

Newspapers reassured the public that the strike would end no later than the third day, the period fixed by Koh Chye and others in their circular. It was estimated that the owners were losing $3,000 a day.[29] On 11 January owners on the west side of the river proposed that their pullers return to work subject to the provision of police security, and the condition that the men not be forced to cross the river into the disaffected areas. Policemen were immediately turned out to patrol the streets, and the Malay peons were armed with truncheons; every bridge from the mouth of the river up to the Kim Seng Bridge was assigned a detachment of police, both to prevent strikers from coming from Kampong Glam and to inform passengers why the rickshaws were not to cross the river. A number of rickshaws did go beyond the pale throwing caution to the wind, but the pullers, who were very nervous, managed to steer clear of the Rochore Road and Kampong Glam districts. Others were less fortunate. In the afternoon, two rickshaws, which started off without a police escort in the direction of Rochore Road, ran straight into the lion's mouth. The pullers were attacked, and their rickshaws smashed up. The police patrols went out again the following morning, some made the rounds of Kampong Glam, while others were stationed on the opposite side of the river.[30] Traffic built up on the west bank, enough rickshaws having returned to work to meet the public need, but on the Kampong Glam side the owners still refused to allow their vehicles to come out. But the following morning the rickshaw strike was all over, as suddenly as it had begun. It had practically ended the previous night when the Kampong Glam owners acknowledged defeat by sending out a few rickshaws that evening and the rest the following morning. Once traffic was re-established on the opposite side of the river, it was only a matter of hours before the owners ended the strike. Solidarity was forfeited as they kept in mind the approach of Chinese New Year. Lost fares had to be recouped.[31]

The town returned to normal in the aftermath of the strike, or did it? Beyond a few rickshaws smashed, a few syces assaulted, little damage was done, and little rioting took place. The strike had petered out because of the firm stand taken by the Government.[32] This was the official position. Others held less salutary views. Confidence in the Commissioners was lost because of the way they dealt with the strike. Right from the start it had caused inconvenience to a public accustomed to using rickshaws. The hardship caused to Europeans spawned incidents such as English clerks going to the Cricket Club in a bullock-cart followed by a procession of laughing spectators.[33] A comical occurrence, perhaps, but nevertheless, deadly serious in terms of the ideology of colonial rule. The British had a clear idea about how they should behave in public. An Englishman did not ride in an ox-cart, and be jeered at, in his role as the servant of imperialism. More importantly, in his mind's eye, the idle pullers were a large alien force, a disquieting presence in the midst of the European population of Singapore. He feared the assemblage of 16,000 rickshawmen who symbolized the persistence of poverty and coolie labour with its direct connection to Singapore's growth and future development.

The most dangerous area was Chinatown, a city in itself, with an unknown number of pullers, who were poor, prone to strike, indistinguishable from criminals, living in the lodging-houses of Victoria Street, Rochore Road, Angullia Road and elsewhere, and divorced from all forms of social control. The antagonism and anxiety that surfaced as a result of the strike within the European community was real. The Commissioners were hard pressed to refute public accusations that the owners and pullers were criminals. The call for solidarity and force, loud and clear, came from the unofficial European community living in Singapore. Their views were presented in letters to the editors of city newspapers:

If the rikisha contractors imagine that they are free to intimidate and coerce a public officer, acting with a just regard to the public interest, it is the business of the Government to convince them of their great mistake, and, more than that, to put it out of their power to again exercise such a force as lies to their hand for the coercion of a municipal department, the injury of the public, and the serious imperiling [*sic*] of public order, of property, and of life. These rikisha owners are the masters and dictators of a force of Chinese coolies amounting, it is believed, to 15,000 men. As we have seen today, by co-operation some of these rikisha contractors can throw at an hour's notice thousand's [*sic*] of men into the streets, inspiring them with the hints needful to direct their coercion against the owners of hackney carriages.... Fortunately the law places in the hands of the Government a weapon which though it should be used cautiously where there is some doubt of criminality, it should be used mercilessly where there is none—namely, the power of deportation. This weapon is all the more appropriately used in the case of apparently respectable Chinese who secretly instigate disorder and yet stand aloof disclaiming any connection therewith.... We therefore trust to hear that ... the colony will rid itself of them expeditiously in the proper way.[34]

Another writer the same day made the point more succinctly:

The interests at stake are too big for the ordinary operation of a Penal Code. The offence is one against society at large and the very celerity with which a dangerous mob can be organised should be the measure of the speed and efficacy of the punishment to be administered. When we find devils in possession we have excellent authority to cast them off.[35]

And the following day:

The Government should be on the alert over this rikisha lock out. The owners are using a continuously mobilized force of 15,000 men to exercise an immoral pressure on a Municipal Department. At present all is quiet but the Empty Belly is 'She Who Must Be Obeyed'. Who is to answer, but the owners, for what these men at any moment may be prompted to do? Still you deal with the criminal as you find him. And we think that the sooner triangles are rigged up in front of all the police stations with a bunch of rattans hung up handy, the better for all concerned. In case of street disorders far better the rattan in early profusion than a bullet at the last extremity. A hundred coolies with well scarified hinterlands are wonderfully effective as Gospellers of Peace and Good Order. We want a chance of doing this. A little convincing is wanted in some Asiatic quarters. We can guess pretty well what William Maxwell would do should the need arise. It is almost a pity it hasn't for we should put our authorities to the touchstone, and reread to the mob the most precious of all lessons.[36]

The strike had provoked panic. The punishment had to be as severe as the language that expressed the fear.

The Government took firm measures to allay the European outcry. Koh Chye was deported, on a warrant from the Deputy Governor, for his part in the strike.[37] But conditions remained on edge until the end of the year. In July police learned that a secret society was being formed amongst the Hockchew rickshawmen. It was difficult to get information on its activities, but in late September, when rumours began circulating about possible riots, evidence was obtained linking one Tan Kee Chuan with the society and he was immediately deported.[38] In the beginning of October the symptoms of unease spilled out into the streets again owing to a tax rise on rickshaws, current devaluation of copper currency, and the closing of contaminated wells in lodging-houses where pullers congregated. There was a great deal of discontent among Chinese coolies and wall placards boldly called for a *gadoh besar*, general riot, offering a reward of $500 for each head of a European official or member of Council.[39] The police and authorities prepared for all emergencies in answer to the manifesto. In the Chinese quarters, especially the rickshaw districts, there was an unusual stillness. The streets were deserted; shops and houses were closed, in many cases boarded up; and the customary flare of lanterns and lamplight in Chinatown was exchanged for darkness. The signs of an impending struggle were evident even to the casual observer. No riot took place, but the placards caused consternation to the public, as the rickshaw coolies refused to ply for hire on the evening of 3 October, and for several hours the following morning. In November, Koh Chye slipped into Singapore, but before any organizing was done, he was arrested and again deported.[40] There were no further incidents. The year 1897 had been remarkable for the strike in January among the rickshaw owners and *siong thau* accompanied by threats of rioting towards the end of the year. The Government had restored order. But the prestige of the Municipal Commissioners had been tarnished and the conviction of the community's inherent superiority shaken. The Hengwah and Hockchew owners, on the other hand, had gained little from the strike, except experience, and the prospect of a more stringent ordinance that would grant the Registrar far greater power to prosecute them in future.

The Ordinance of 1892 had come into force when 3,991 rickshaws were registered in the names of 378 owners. At the time of the strike there were 6,761 rickshaws registered in the names of over 1,400 owners. The law stated that for certain offences the owners were liable to have their licences suspended. The pullers were unlicensed and not subject to punishment by the Registrar; the owners were responsible for their conduct. During the four years since the Ordinance's introduction, Mr Hooper had frequently drawn the Commissioners' attention to the need for amendments and the different complaints of both owners and pullers. But pressure of work—Singapore was expanding rapidly—had made it impossible for the Commissioners to address the question of an amended Ordinance. The strike had now brought the serious matter of a new system for licence, control and regulation to the Commissioners' doorstep. If the public had just grounds for criticism of their handling of the strike, and for their fear, they could only be allayed by entrusting the

Registrar with more power. The time was ripe for a consolidating Ordinance because the Government promised favourable consideration of any recommendations brought forward by the Municipality.[41] The Bill to amend the Rickshaw Ordinance of 1892 was introduced early in 1899 and was the subject of several reports and much discussion and debate in the Legislative Council. It was finally passed on 3 January 1900 and came into force in May of that year.[42]

The Commissioners started with the 'owner' as the first link in the chain; the labour of registering an army of pullers would have proved an impossible task. The example of the Chinese ports was followed. No licence was required to act as a puller: the law insisted only on physical capacity, proper dress, cleanliness, and correct behaviour of the men. The onus was on the owner. He had to apply in writing on official forms; he had to provide security for his appearance when called on, $3–5 per rickshaw; he had to be photographed to prevent impersonation; and the photographs were to be filed in the Registry and one copy given to the owner and another attached to a schedule of his numbered rickshaws.[43] The registered owner was to be responsible for 'street offences' committed by the puller, so long as the latter was in charge of the rickshaw. The owner could summarily be punished by the Registrar, impounding his rickshaw and suspending the licence for a period up to one month. An owner found altering the registration marks or changing wheels, or other component parts, of a vehicle was subject to having his licence suspended for four months. An owner, whose rickshaws were impounded, now had to bring civil action against the Registrar to recover them, as he could no longer rely on the good offices of the Chinese Protectorate to intercede.[44] The owner's liability and the summary power of suspension and impounding conferred on the Registrar by the new Ordinance were the backbone of the scheme and without these enactments no improvements could be expected.

The examination of rickshaws prior to licensing was to be carried out under the personal supervision of the Registrar and his associates. A consolidated tax of $4 every four months to cover the fee for registration, branding, plates, and other expenses was to be paid by the owner for each vehicle at the time of registration, to the municipal fund. For the purpose of recovering property alleged to have been lost or stolen the Registrar could now also exercise the right of search given to police officers.

Under the new system rickshaw owners invariably produced the pullers when required by the Registrar, and experience soon showed it was to work more effectively than schemes licensing the puller.[45] Offending pullers brought before the Registrar could be sent by him under arrest for summary trial before a magistrate. Although the new Ordinance had been successful in securing the cooperation of owners, the *siong thau* were still rife. They were kept in check only by constant vigilance. In 1904, rickshaws were registered in the names of 1,029 owners, most of whom were *siong thau*. The vehicles were not their property, but were registered in their names for the convenience of the real owners who continued to pay brokers for this service. All attempts to get the owners to register in their proper names had failed. The abuse remained.[46] The brokers, however, with many rickshaws registered in their names, could always be found and seldom failed to produce a coolie when wanted. Hence, the Department tended to turn a blind eye to the *siong thau*, so long as they cooperated in making the system of the registered owner work successfully.[47]

Mr Hooper's efforts in the aftermath of the strike, not only were crowned with success in securing almost all the amendments needed, he also gained approval for the construction of new headquarters. The multi-storey building, completed in 1899 at a cost of $34,000, fronted on Middle Road and Prinsep Street, and in the quadrangle were placed the inspection shed, quarters for syces, and stables. On the ground floor accommodation was provided for impounded and unlicensed rickshaws; and on the first floor were the Registrar's Court and offices, and quarters for the inspectors and peons. The imposing building was designed for the task of enforcing the new Ordinance.[48] All examination and licensing of rickshaws was now carried out there. The new tax was levied on the likes of the Hockchia owner, Ting Pek Kia of New Market Road, who went every four months with Ling Kee Tou, a friend living in the same thoroughfare and also a Hockchia rickshaw owner, to the Rickshaw depot to have their vehicles tested. They usually arrived there at 7.30 a.m. and their rickshaws were placed in the yard. It was raining heavily one morning so rather than wait around after leaving the rickshaws for inspection, they went to a coffee-shop opposite the headquarters.[49] A branch station was also opened by Mr Hooper at Neil Road, enabling the Department to dispense with the hired houses it occupied at Beach Road and South Bridge Road.[50]

The magisterial powers conferred on the Registrar to deal summarily with offences regarding the condition of rickshaws or of the men employed as pullers, with respect to strength, fitness, cleanliness and dress, facilitated the working of the new law, and relieved the Police Courts.[51] The regulation of rickshaw traffic became essentially the duty of the Rickshaw Department. Under the old Municipal Ordinance the Police had power to make by-laws for traffic but it was purposely omitted in the amended Rickshaw Ordinance and rickshaw traffic control was left in the hands of Mr Hooper's Court and a staff of Malay peons.[52]

The Registrar's Court proved a convenience with respect to rickshaw cases. It afforded the public an easy method of laying charges before a magistrate who had jurisdiction over pullers away from the rush and unpleasant surroundings of the Police Courts.[53] It was not seen as strange that Mr Hooper was both prosecutor and judge except by the pullers. The cases before him for offences under the Ordinance frequently resulted in conviction, with perhaps 10 per cent of persons either being acquitted or cautioned and discharged. The cases for the most part were 'street' offences; charges of a more serious nature were exceptional.

Pullers became the substantial contributors to the special Court and were a source of wealth to the public authorities.

The central arm of the Court was the Malay peon. The rickshaw peons were on duty day and night to deal with rickshaws and pullers. Their duties were distinct from police constables', enforcing certain regulations and by-laws that it was felt the police could not be expected to handle. They could impound a rickshaw if it was unlicensed and plying for hire, if the licence had expired, if broken or in an unfit condition to ply, for using false or defaced number plates, for not having proper fittings or lamps, or for carrying forbidden articles, and if the puller was physically unfit or in rags.[54] At any time about 70 per cent of the peons were available for street duty, divided into three sections to canvass different parts of the city; the remainder were engaged in station tasks with Chinese clerks to assist in interpreting.[55]

Problems developed. There were not enough experienced men for street duty at any one time to regulate the traffic of thousands of rickshaws. There was turnover with new men joining the force throughout the 1890s. As soon as some of them began to learn the work, they gave a month's notice and left. As a result novices who did not understand their duties were constantly on the streets causing the pullers no end of trouble, demanding bribes, threatening violence, arresting them for any misdemeanour under the by-laws, or the Rickshaw Ordinance.[56]

Bribes were paid. The money was generally forked over through a third party. Sometimes a rickshaw coolie collected it from other pullers and the money was exacted by the peon when off duty, making it difficult to prosecute the offender.[57] In 1894, however, four peons were arraigned for extortion; one case was dismissed and three were sentenced to imprisonment. Interestingly, in a similar case five years later a magistrate discharged the peons but punished the puller who was their accomplice in an extortion racket at Johnston's Pier, to enable his particular dialect group to monopolize the rickshaw stand.[58] The Europeans in the Department, who were familiar with the nuances of the traffic rules, were disgusted at the disgraceful conduct of peons towards pullers, but they regarded both as having no moral fibre whatsoever: 'The peons . . . are not free from the faults of their class. Constantly tempted with petty bribes by owners and pullers of rickshaws, it is no wonder if they sometimes prove unfaithful.'[59] And, the following year:

> No doubt there is some exaggeration; but no one who knows the character and habits of the men concerned, both pullers and peons, can doubt that where a bribe is offered to escape impounding for some petty offence a Malay peon, whose wages are eight to ten dollars a month, will often take it, if he thinks he will escape detection. The utmost vigilance on the part of the Registrar and his officers have failed to do more than keep in check this inveterate bad habit which permeates all the lower classes in the East.[60]

The Department argued that the coolies were to blame to a large extent; they refused to come forward and when the Department prosecuted a peon it was difficult to get a conviction. But when pullers did come forward the Department was reluctant to take measures against peons for fear of the consequence on staffing and recruitment. In 1902 a peon was convicted of extorting 6 cents from a rickshaw coolie and sentenced to six months' imprisonment. The severity of the sentence caused consternation amongst the peons and nine deserted out of fear that it could happen to them too.[61]

With few exceptions the conduct of the peons was unsatisfactory. In his annual report for 1893, the Registrar recommended that the peons should be engaged on a contract for one year and be liable to punishment for deserting.[62] But nothing was done to strengthen his hand. The result was that although 195 peons had joined since 1892, there were just 54 by 1895; only 10 of them had been among the original batch, while the rest were recruits.[63] The following year only six of the original peons were left. Mr Hooper wanted to abolish them, and save the Department further embarrassment and expense, provided arrangements could be made to employ men under the Police Force Ordinance to do the work. The high rate of desertion during the 1890s was due to a large extent to the peons having to work without proper authority. They had no power of arrest and pullers who abused them often went unpunished.[64] They were placed in an unenviable position too as passengers and the general public did not realize they had no control over private rickshaws and were reprimanded by people on this account.

A salary increase in 1897, supplemented by a rice allowance, induced more men to come forward. Peons began to join the service on a yearly basis, but of the 352 who had been employed since September 1892, there remained only 4 men who had joined then, 3 in 1893, 3 in 1894, 6 in 1895 and 8 in 1896, which explained the large number of new, untrained peons on duty on the streets.[65] Even with the new measures few peons still remained beyond a year. However, fewer men deserted and more joined after 1900 with the introduction of a provident fund. There was not as much bitter feeling displayed against the peons by the pullers and owners as in previous years because the supervision was less strict and in accordance with policy the number of rickshaws had been reduced. Fewer complaints were received, but new and inexperienced peons were always employed on street duty.

Many of the regulations in the new Ordinance were ill-defined from the pullers' point of view. They did not always know if they were loitering in certain areas and at certain times of the day, causing 'obstruction', or pulling a rickshaw in an unfit condition, or carrying forbidden articles. Rickshaw coolies complained that peons impounded their rickshaws for no reason. This complaint arose from coolies who could not understand that 'crawling' about with an empty rickshaw and getting in the way of traffic was an offence. In nineteen out of twenty cases they pleaded, 'I was doing nothing wrong. If I don't walk about and look for fares how can I get food?'[66] The impression in their minds was generally that their rickshaw had been impounded because they had no copper coins to tempt the street peon. Some residents seemed to sympathize with the rickshawmen's plight, and street-level officials including police constables and bus conductors occasionally looked the other way at minor violations. Peons rarely did. Thus it is not surprising to find in those days that nearly all traffic offences dealt with rickshaw control and were committed by rickshaw pullers.

For such offences rickshaw could be stopped by a peon and the puller compelled to take it to the registration office; or the vehicle could be shut up at the nearest police station and a report forwarded to the Registrar. The complaint was then enquired into by the Registrar, who could impound the rickshaw in the municipal yard pending enquiry, or suspend the licence for a period of up to one month from the date of the offence. The puller was not detained but in the event of the rickshaw being impounded he was furnished with a receipt for it, on which was noted the offence. The same was served by the Registrar on the owner at his given address, calling on him to surrender his licence for the impounded vehicle.[67]

The punishment of rickshaw coolies by fines had the effect of making their earnings somewhat precarious. Pullers who had committed offences no doubt offered bribes to peons to release them; some were never charged. Others, being poor, could not pay the bribes, and avoid arrest. The result was that some were afraid to work in certain parts of the city out of fear of meeting just such a fate. The thing that shows up in the cases against rickshaws tried before the Registrar between 1893 and 1897 is the random power of peons over pullers, and its timing. For the slightest offence lots of rickshaw coolies had their vehicles seized: 5,277 for wearing 'bad' clothes in 1896 against 455 in 1893; 311 in 1897 for appearing tired and unfit; and hundreds every year for carrying forbidden articles like vegetables, poultry, and fish to and from the markets, or wooden crates and other more unwieldly items to the godowns and wharfs.[68] These men might be familiar with the traffic rules but they could not prevent the peons suddenly taking it into their heads to enforce a particular rule, say for example, forbidding pullers to loiter in quest of fares, or to halt with empty vehicles. When such a rampage began the puller had to watch out. Coolies were liable to be arrested returning to a rickshaw stand after taking a fare to a destination, or while waiting outside a premise, market, or brothel for a customer. Such a crusade by the peons in 1895–6 resulted in over 30,000 cases of loitering and obstruction.[69]

The main thoroughfares of Singapore were wide. There were not any signs for 'parking' and 'no parking' for rickshaws in the city yet; railed stands were just appearing. The pullers parked wherever they could, taking their chances. There was no sense, or justice, in arresting a rickshawman because he had nobody in his rickshaw and was walking along the road, or if he was pulled up at the roadside. Obstructions had to be removed in crowded streets, and peons had to interfere when traffic was congested, but even on the broad thoroughfares there was little consideration for the rickshawman.

In his Annual Reports in years as far apart as 1909 and 1922 the

Registrar notes the difficulty of dealing with pullers 'crawling' about, endangering traffic. He complained that the passengers themselves had to have a grounding in elementary traffic rules, apparently with some justification:

> Very few serious offences come before me but the nuisance and danger of empty rikishas crawling about the streets looking for fares is as bad as ever. I can only repeat that so long as people will persist in engaging passing rikishas, the crawlers get more fares and will continue to roam about the streets to the danger of traffic. Passengers are also to blame for stopping in the middle of the road to get in or alight from rikishas, instead of making the pullers draw up to the side of the curbstone out of the way of the traffic. In a community such as exists in Singapore it is very difficult to get any cooperation from the public and without such help it is hopeless to expect ignorant coolies to conform to ordinary rules of the road.[70]

Most cases heard by the Registrar were of a minor sort. The most troublesome were soliciting passengers, disturbing people on the street, and loitering and obstruction. Rickshaw stands were erected as early as 1893 in a number of places, and new ones were subsequently built, especially just after the turn of the century, but the difficulty experienced by the peons was to make the puller remain, when not engaged, at these stands.[71] The coolies simply did not consider it an offence to wander about in search of fares. The public encouraged them by engaging passing rickshaws, seldom hailing one at the stand; consequently 'crawlers' got more fares. The Registrar failed to point out though, the inconvenience caused to the public having to take rickshaws from the stands, blaming the multitude instead of the regulations, for encouraging pullers to commit such offences.

Nor could the Department prevent the employment of *singkeh* and unfit coolies, but the Ordinance gave the Registrar power to reject a puller who was physically weak. An owner could employ any coolie he could find. Serious accidents, with fatal results, happened to men who could not pull a rickshaw or were too weak to do it properly. Among the worst cases of all were opium sots and those addicted to morphia.[72] Many complaints referred to the emaciated, filthy appearance and disorderly conduct of these pullers, especially at night outside clubs, hotels, and brothels: 'The coolies have learnt they have nothing to fear and willfully solicit passengers in a persistent manner, whether required or not. The crawlers, who wander vaguely about the streets ignoring all rules of the road can only be dealt with by making it an offence to employ *singkehs*.'[73] In his 1890s reports Mr Hooper urged on the Commissioners the necessity of legislating for better pullers. Nothing was done: 'I cannot report any improvement in the class of pullers employed and the commendations made in my reports for the past five years I repeat in the hope that someday they may be adopted.'[74] By 1897 he was disheartened. Street traffic was difficult to keep under control; it was due in part to many of these coolies being *singkeh* fresh from China, and being ignorant of Malay and the rules of the road, such as loitering, plying on the wrong side of the street, and pulling a rickshaw without proper lights at night.

The peons brought in thousands of cases. Licences were suspended. Table 7.1, which gives the cases tried before Mr Hooper of offences committed by pullers, indicates an alarming increase up to 1902. It shows 29,601 rickshaws impounded in 1896 for various offences; in 21,833 cases the licences were suspended by the Registrar for different periods, 1,206 were discharged, and in 6,562 cases the number plates were returned to the owners, since the licences were about to expire. It is not surprising that with more peons the number of cases of rickshaws impounded further increased.

Once the new Ordinance came into force Mr Hooper looked for a greater number of arrests amongst the pullers. The fact that they were liable to be locked up and fined bore good results. The power given the Registrar of instituting prosecutions and causing refractory pullers to be arrested, and taken for summary trial before a magistrate, also had a salutary effect.[75] An amending Ordinance was introduced in 1902, granting the Registrar further summary powers, including authority to deal with cases of bilking, and making it an offence for owners to employ unfit coolies (cripples, and those suffering from sores or skin complaints).[76] However, the Ordinance was brought into force too suddenly to enable the Commissioners to allow proper notice to the owners and pullers.[77]

An additional complication was the untimely loss due to ill-health of the Department's head interpreter who had knowledge of the Foochow dialects. His absence was felt by Mr Hooper who spoke little Chinese. It was necessary for the Department to have qualified Foochow interpreters on hand when the amending Rickshaw Ordinance was introduced. In 1902 there were 15,000 pullers belonging to the Hengwah, Hockchew, Hockchia, and Hwee Wah speech groups. In the absence of interpreters to explain the requirements of the law, the Registrar had to depend on the owners, who were men who knew some Hokkien, but there was the danger of not knowing in what way the regulations were interpreted by them to their coolies in dialect. Unbelievably, the Government had only one Foochow interpreter for the Supreme Court, Police Courts, and Chinese Protectorate and could not lend a hand to the Rickshaw Department. Ironically, Mr Hooper had been asked on several occasions by the Courts to assist them by sending one of his interpreters who could speak some Foochow.[78] The next year a Foochow interpreter was engaged but problems had already arisen.[79]

Friction was unavoidable. The pullers had been allowed to go scot-free for over ten years. Now they were responsible for their offences. The amending Ordinance was liable to be abused and in many cases it was found next to impossible to prove to the puller what offence he had committed. When he appeared, for example, in answer to a summons from Mr Hooper, charged with pulling an unlicensed rickshaw, knowingly supplied by an owner, that was filthy looking, the problem was a difficult one. When brought before the Rickshaw Court for cutting

TABLE 7.1

Rickshaw Cases Tried before the Registrar, 1893–1907

Charge	*1893*	*1894*	*1895*	*1896*	*1897*	*1898*	*1899*	*1900*	*1901*	*1902*	*1903*	*1904*	*1905*	*1906*	*1907*
Coolie physically weak	26	22	102	244	311	767	693	362	892	471	93	170	221	202	446
Bad clothes	455	1,609	3,796	5,277	2,452	1,962	3,032	3,282	1,537	1,567		57	15	3	32
Unlicensed jinrikisha	3												32	9	4
Changing fittings	19	148	34	199	59	67	142	82	81	37	13	18	21	15	48
No lamps, bad lamps	93	306	344	161	329	616	632	299	237	402	285	330	426	513	550
Fouling jinrikisha	209	158	636	379	345	452	643	496	589	308					
Interfering with traffic		171	441	627	421	324	329	431	447	728	272	100	255	142	248
Loitering and obstruction	5,343	5,866	12,355	18,354	8,553	6,542	6,765	7,353	10,435	13,525	2,337	2,509	2,454	2,637	3,985
Soliciting passengers in a disorderly manner	218	1,086	2,393	3,702	1,604	1,477	1,342	1,844	2,315	1,259	182	761	856	858	1,115
Demanding more than the legal fare	19	26	23	33	42	51	63	34	37	63	59	87	84	35	46
Behaving rudely to passengers	47	46	28	30	26	76	56	65	72	83	144	167	175	130	191
Leaving fare before completion of engagement	27	32	69	58	88	121	149	108	136	167	257	232	202	93	92
Unwieldly articles (and forbidden articles)	558	263	340	354	338	237	277	296	432	257	99	80	105	57	51
Sundry offences	240	128	57	9	18	18	57	114	149	225	143	220	197	132	429
Refusing hire without a reasonable excuse				174	153	230	239	312	335	564	659	544	474	247	136
Using criminal force on pullers											81	123	109	68	72
Refusing to pay rikisha fare											104	164	230	160	133
Licences suspended (convicted)	6,933	9,589	19,788	28,395	13,233	11,405	11,993	13,630	16,436	18,069	3,847	5,138	5,002	3,906	6,236
Cautioned and discharged	450	272	830	1,206	1,506	1,535	2,426	1,448	1,258	1,581	881	424	854	1,385	1,337
Total	7,383	9,861	20,618	29,601	14,739	12,940	14,419	15,078	17,694	19,650	4,728	5,562	5,856	5,291	7,573

Source: This table has been compiled from SMAR JD, 1893–1907. Return showing the cases against jinrikishas tried before the Registrar, Deputy Registrar, and Acting Deputy Registrar during the years 1893 to 1907.

corners the puller invariably said the passenger told him to turn, the same applied to crawling, when pullers claimed to dash across the road only if called by a passenger.

More forcible measures were taken to reduce rickshaws on the streets once the motor car and bus arrived in Singapore. The traffic in Singapore streets, taking for example the two main streets North and South Bridge Roads and New Bridge Road which run parallel through the city, was an endless stream of people walking and at times almost running, keeping pace with rickshaws, and all busy. The increase in traffic jams and street accidents in Singapore as motor transport competed for space on the roads led to a call for public rickshaw stands within the municipality. By 1914 a Singapore traffic jam was a lurching, heart-stopping, deafening amalgam of taxis, trucks, trams, and—it seemed—all of the city's thousands of rickshaws. Europeans tended to drive more aggressively in Singapore than on the Continent. Rickshaws kept to the left side of the pavement and the puller was likely to be hit if he veered out or went against the traffic. The basic rule of the road was that the streets belonged to motor vehicles, which operated as if rickshaws did not exist: 'Rickshaws plunged and dodged in the maelstrom of traffic, their lowered hoods shaking and fluttering like the tails of angry peacocks. One shot under our wheels, and presently reappeared on the far side of the street, where its puller stopped to shout gutteral [*sic*] abuse at my grinning driver.'[80]

Recommendations were introduced for licensed stands with iron railing to prevent obstruction and traffic congestion at the mouth of roads. Rickshaws would be obliged to enter at one end and leave at the other, forcing pullers to go by turn and preventing them from rushing at passengers.[81] At some important spots like the Raffles and Straits Hotels an experimental system of railed-in stands was erected.[82] Soon iron-railed stands were adopted in all busy thoroughfares. Congestion caused by rickshaws in the business district was reduced in the 1920s by the construction of a series of railed-in stands in Battery Road and Collyer Quay.[83]

But in a real sense the stands were not public, and as such, contributed to the traffic problem. Itinerant pullers could not park their rickshaws at a stand if they happened to be in another neighbourhood, perhaps wanting to rest and grab a fare before returning to familiar territory. The rickshaw stands that cropped up around Singapore were monopolized by different speech/dialect groups. For example, the Hockchias controlled River Valley Road and the Tank Road Railway Station; Europe Hotel (outside) and Raffles Hotel were also controlled by the Hockchias, and Orchard Road and the Europe Hotel by the Hengwahs. Some stands were more lucrative than others, being situated in better locations for making money and avoiding traffic. Speech, age, skill and strength all mattered in determining who could work the most profitable stands, particularly those in front of Singapore's best hotels, where wealthy transient foreigners, who were apt to overcharge, stayed. The Department did not realize that competition at the stands often ruled out the inarticulate, weak and elderly. Some pullers avoided the stands for this reason and in the eyes of the peons became 'crawlers':

> His way of stammering and then blurting out his words hindered him when shouting out his price and competing for passengers with the other pullers. He couldn't get the better of all those fast talkers. He was aware that he had this shortcoming so he hardly ever went to a rickshaw stand. He waited for customers where there were no other rickshaws. In these out-of-the way places he could discuss fees calmly.[84]

With the development of Singapore's modern transport system the rickshaw became in the Department's eyes an anachronism. The Department's policy shifted from control and regulation to restriction and abolition in the period from 1924 to 1939. Rickshaws were no longer simply restricted to stands, and discouraged from using the main roads, they began to disappear from Singapore streets. The gradual banning of rickshaws was argued for on principles of efficiency, administrative order, and the 'inhumanity' of the trade.[85] By the late 1920s officials predicted that the rickshaw was on the way out. Singapore was a 'modern' city, a trading and financial powerhouse with powerful old firms, financial institutions, thousands of little businesses, and full of fast-moving vehicles. Rickshaws, symbolically, were an unpleasant reminder of constant poverty, and the straining and sweating Chinese labour behind it all. People were in a hurry and the rickshaw no longer held a special place.

The Department passed more and more legislation tightening control over rickshaws. In June 1924 officials stopped licensing new rickshaws. The object was to radically reduce the number in Singapore which the Commissioners felt was in excess of the needs of the city.[86] With a view to further reductions, and improving the standard as a result, the Department offered one new rickshaw to be licensed for every two old ones scrapped. That was in 1926. Owners refused for the most part, feeling it was an attempt to abolish the rickshaw and deprive them of a means of earning a livelihood.[87] Their assumption was correct. The year 1926 was the first time the Registrar felt the question of a reduction of licensed rickshaws should be tackled openly. Road space in the city was at a premium. With the increasing popularity of buses the pullers had been forced to quit outlying districts resulting in the city becoming even more overcrowded with rickshaws.[88] The 'rickshaw problem' seemed insoluble except by abolition. The progressive diminution began with a 15 per cent reduction from July 1928, followed by a smaller contraction in 1929.[89] The owners were notified of the steps towards compulsory reduction, as Singapore modernized with a vengeance, placing in jeopardy the employment of rickshawmen estimated to be as high as 25,000–30,000.[90]

The enforced decrease in rickshaws saw their place taken, despite bad times, by a rapid, cheap form of public transport—an adequate supply of motor buses. But it would still be some time before the rickshaw disappeared in spite of the fact that, by then, they were the slowest form of local transport, and a 'big thorn in the side of the traffic authorities'.[91] A further reduction of 15 per cent was made during 1930, but it had no effect in the city, the decrease was more noticeable in the 'country' districts. Rickshaws continued to be a source of bother to traffic control, particularly at busy street corners and intersections, where they waited on the chance of obtaining fares getting out of buses, and at night outside cinemas, cabarets and brothels.[92] In accordance with the Department's policy and the wishes of the Municipal Commissioners another thousand licences were cancelled the following year. At the same time taxi stands were being provided in all parts of the city indicated by notice boards, and new bus routes were being approved.[93] The total number of licences was down to 5,000 at the close of 1932. By the end of the decade it was no longer necessary to cancel public licences. There were less than 4,000 rickshaws left. The Department's policy to mark time and let the rickshaw die a slow death during Depression years proved effective.

In this discussion of the origins and working of the Rickshaw Department it only remains to show just how much money was made from the registration and licensing of rickshaws, and the regulation of pullers and traffic in Singapore under the Registrar's administration of the Ordinance, through his special Court. The amount of the registration tax, $12 a year or $1 a month, was the lowest sum acceptable to the Commissioners that would leave a margin over the Department's working expenses and make a contribution to the municipal revenue.[94] The receipts of the revamped Department in 1900 amounted to $80,589, almost all from the tax on rickshaws, as compared with $78,300 the previous year. The expense of running the Department was estimated at $38,000, which left a considerable profit to be credited to the municipal fund.[95] The following year in the final report of the audit of thc municipal accounts the total revenue was $120,000 over the budget estimate, the largest excesses being in assessments on houses, tax on rickshaws and fines, and private supply of water.[96] Table 7.2 shows that between 1893 and 1907 the Department's profit margin from the tax on rickshaws was never less than $31,000 and as much as $50,000 in 1902. The gross revenue of 1907, amounting to $159,424, was a record, exceeding the revenue of 1906 by $16,468. The Department's expenditures came to only $44,712![97] Likewise, as the cases heard before the Registrar increased, resulting in thousands of convictions, the fines increased in proportion, totalling thousands of dollars. Scores of pullers too poor to pay were committed to prison. For example, in 1907 alone, rickshaw fines accounted for $11,300.[98]

The Department had initially encouraged the rickshaw on the roads of Singapore, scheduling registration and licensing, capturing the will and strength of the immigrant puller, collecting fines, making money out of the centre of the coolie's interests—the rickshaw. The Department's measures and fines against the rickshawmen made the city richer, but the puller's world of work pulsed with hunger, poverty, rush, and death.

TABLE 7.2

The Rickshaw Department's Profit Margin, 1893–1907

Year	*Number of Licensed Rickshaws*	*Number of Cases against Rickshaws Tried before the Registrar*	*The Tax on Rickshaws ($)*	*Rickshaw Department Expenditure ($)*	*Profit Margin ($)*
1893	13,041	7,383	52,164	16,983	35,181
1894	14,659	9,861	58,636	12,549	46,087
1895	16,453	20,618	65,812	17,532	48,280
1896	17,915	29,601	71,660	32,664	38,996
1897	17,518	14,739	70,072	35,588	34,484
1898	17,330	12,940	69,230	36,992	32,238
1899	18,905	14,419	75,220		
1900	19,414	15,078	77,656	38,379	39,277
1901	21,381	17,694	85,524	41,963	43,561
1902	22,629	19,650	91,375	40,886	50,489
1903	20,433	4,814	81,732	44,508	37,224
1904	21,696	6,236	86,784	46,799	39,985
1905	19,541	6,248	78,164	46,557	31,607
1906	20,870	5,367	83,480	43,865	39,615
1907	22,009	7,779	88,036	44,712	43,324

Then, in that furious time that stood between the two wars, rickshaws and the men who pulled them were pencilled into the margins of Singapore's future. The puller's mad chase after a vision of a life with hope that enabled him to endure almost anything in Singapore was halted by a deliberate policy of abolition.

1. SMAR JD, 1897, Appendix J, p. 28.
2. SMAR JD, 1917, p. 5.
3. SMAR, 1888.
4. Ibid.
5. SMAR, 1889, p. 5.
6. Ibid.
7. SMAR, 1890.
8. Ibid.
9. No. 252, Sir C. Smith to The Lord Knutsford, 7 June 1892, CO 273/181.
10. *Lat Pau*, 26 November 1889, in Chen Mong Hock, *The Early Chinese Newspapers of Singapore, 1881–1902* (Singapore: University of Malaya Press, 1967), p. 45.
11. SMAR JD, 1901, p. 137.
12. SMAR JD, 1892, p. 12.
13. Ibid.
14. Ibid., p. 6.
15. Ibid.
16. SMAR JD, 1897, Appendix J, p. 25.
17. Ibid., p. 22.
18. Ibid., p. 24.
19. Ibid.
20. *Singapore Free Press*, 8 January 1897.
21. SMAR JD, 1897, Appendix J, pp. 23–4.
22. *Singapore Free Press*, 9 January 1897.
23. *Singapore Free Press*, 11 January 1897.
24. Ibid.
25. Ibid.
26. SMAR JD, 1897, Appendix J, p. 23.
27. *Singapore Free Press*, 8 January 1897.
28. Ibid.
29. *Singapore Free Press*, 9 January 1897.
30. *Singapore Free Press*, 11 January 1897.
31. *Singapore Free Press*, 12 January 1897.
32. SSAR, 1897, p. 11.
33. *Singapore Free Press*, 9 January 1897.
34. *Singapore Free Press*, 8 January 1897.
35. Ibid.
36. *Singapore Free Press*, 9 January 1897.
37. *Singapore Free Press*, 12 January 1897; SMAR JD, 1897, p. 95.
38. SMAR JD, 1897, p. 96.
39. SMAR, 1897, p. 12.
40. SMAR JD, 1897, Appendix J, p. 95.
41. SMAR JD, 1897, p. 12.
42. SMAR JD, 1899, p. 17.
43. SMAR JD, 1897, Appendix J, p. 29.
44. Ibid.
45. SMAR JD, 1908, p. 2; SMAR JD, 1918, p. 2.

46. SMAR JD, 1904, p. 2.
47. SMAR JD, 1907, p. 2.
48. SMAR JD, 1898, p. 55.
49. SCII of Ting Pek Kia, No. 309, 18/6/30.
50. SMAR JD, 1899, p. 17.
51. SMAR JD, 1897, Appendix J, p. 31.
52. SMAR JD, 1917.
53. *Singapore Free Press*, 5 January 1927.
54. SMAR JD, 1922, p. 4-B.
55. SMAR JD, 1907, p. 4.
56. SMAR JD, 1895, p. 68; SMAR JD, 1897, p. 96.
57. SMAR JD, 1898, p. 102.
58. SMAR JD, 1899, p. 64.
59. SMAR JD, 1896, pp. 3–4.
60. SMAR JD, 1897, Appendix J, pp. 24–5.
61. SMAR JD, 1902, p. 161.
62. SMAR JD, 1893, p. 22.
63. SMAR JD, 1895, p. 69.
64. SMAR JD, 1897, p. 96.
65. SMAR JD, 1898, p. 102; SMAR JD, 1897, p. 96.
66. SMAR JD, 1897, Appendix J, p. 22.
67. SMAR JD, 1897, Appendix J, p. 33.
68. See Table 7.1.
69. See Table 7.1 and SMAR JD, 1896, p. 96.
70. SMAR JD, 1909, p. 6.
71. SMAR JD, 1893, p. 21.
72. SSOC, Mr Hooper's evidence, pp. 26–7.
73. SMAR JD, 1895, p. 67.
74. SMAR JD, 1897, p. 95.
75. SMAR JD, 1900, p. 98.
76. SMAR JD, 1902, p. 159.
77. Ibid, p. 30.
78. Ibid., p. 161.
79. SMAR JD, 1903; p. 15.
80. A. Dixon, *Singapore Patrol* (London, 1935), p. 30.
81. SMAR JD, 1898, p. 102.
82. SMAR JD, 1901, p. 21.
83. SMAR JD, 1923, p. 2-B.
84. Lao She, *Rickshaw* (the novel *Lo T'o Hsiang Tzu*), translated by Jean M. James (Honolulu: The University Press of Hawaii, 1979), p. 6.
85. The same arguments have been used for banning rickshaws in Calcutta in recent times. UNNAYAN in association with T. H. Thomas, *Rickshaws in Calcutta* (Calcutta: UNNAYAN, 1981), pp. 49–50.
86. SMAR JD, 1924, p. 1-B.
87. SMAR JD, 1926, p. 3-B.
88. Ibid.
89. SMAR JD, 1927, p. 6-B.
90. Ibid.
91. SMAR JD, 1929, p. 4-B.
92. SMAR JD, 1930, p. 7-B.
93. SMAR JD, 1931, p. 7-B.
94. SMAR JD, 1897, Appendix J, pp. 29–30.
95. SMAR JD, 1900, p. 14.
96. SMAR JD, 1901, Appendix D, p. 27.
97. SMAR JD, 1907, p. 12.
98. SMAR JD, 1908, p. 1.

8 Strikes

SINGAPORE faced four major rickshaw strikes in the twentieth century: in 1903, 1919–20, 1935, and 1938. The anatomy of each of these strikes is somewhat different, but rent capital, public authority, and the world economy were all distinctive factors, in differing combinations. The Rickshaw Ordinance of 1900, the advent of Mr Hooper's special Court in 1903, the anti-Japanese boycott of 1919–20, and the struggle over rickshaw rates during the 1930s all enter the picture. Events suggest that the Government and Rickshaw Department's efforts to consolidate authority over owners, control traffic and regulate the puller fomented the strikes of 1901 and 1903.

The strike of 1901 was a more telling example of the struggle between public authority and rent capital in the rickshaw trade than that of 1897. Mr Hooper's annual reports since 1892 had drawn the Commissioners' attention to the coolies employed in the trade and the difficulties of enforcing the traffic rules.[1] He was opposed to licensing the puller. Making the owner responsible for the puller had worked. Ideally, rickshaw owners, rent capitalists who owned blocks of 50 to several hundred vehicles, were meant to teach their pullers the 'rules of the road', and that empty rickshaws were to return to the nearest 'stand' instead of crawling about in traffic. When a puller committed an offence such as loitering, the rickshaw was impounded, but there was nothing to prevent him from hiring another. The suspension of the licence did not affect the puller, only the bona fide owner.[2]

The Registrar complained of the difficulty in getting interest taken in the needs of his Department. Year after year passed without attention being paid to his recommendations. He had advocated making it an offence (under Section 38 of the Ordinance) for an owner to employ a *singkeh*, who could speak neither Malay nor a common dialect of Chinese, or was ignorant of the traffic rules.[3] The instruction of the pullers had to be forced on the owners, who alone could speak the dialects, in the hope that the Department's requirements could be explained, and the coolies taught. Another recommendation unheeded was that it should be an offence to employ an 'undesirable' coolie, covering the deaf, near-blind, deformed, emaciated, and those suffering from skin diseases. For such offences the owner was to be held responsible for employing an unfit puller.[4]

The overcrowded state of the streets was a danger. The thoroughfares, day and night, were thronged by 9,000–10,000 rickshaws. The rickshaws had to be reduced but not by creating a monopoly in the trade. Contradictions emerged in municipal policy and planning. The Report of the Committee appointed in 1891 had reached the unanimous conclusion that in future 'there shall be no limit to the number of rickshaws registered'.[5] The decision had been arrived at ten years earlier; the municipal position had altered on limiting rickshaws but the Registrar was opposed to it. He did not want to adopt a system that gave exclusive control to a handful of owners and *siong thau*. Far better, in his opinion, that power be given to the Commissioners to once again increase the tax. In Hong Kong the tax was $3 a month. If Singapore owners had to pay a similar amount rickshaw numbers would certainly diminish, and it could be expected, too, that the owners would be careful in selecting the coolies they employed, as the punishment would be heavier on them when their licences were suspended or cancelled. Public attention was drawn conspicuously to the lack of regulations for controlling rickshaw traffic, because of an accident on the Esplanade Road involving the Governor's carriage. The Governor reported the puller who had run into his trap, nearly causing a serious mishap.[6] The unnerving incident convinced Swettenham of the need to enforce the new regulations in a stringent manner. He felt the police ought to assist the peons to regulate rickshaw traffic, and under the Rickshaw Ordinance, in Section 38, they had the power to do so.[7]

The owners were intent on getting the Ordinance of 1900 changed whereby they were held responsible for the offences of the coolies they employed. The peons and police were particularly active in 1901, especially in the months following His Excellency's accident, with over 16,400 licences suspended; more than 10,400 cases involved loitering and obstruction. At the end of August a petition signed by 47 registered Hockchia and Hengwah owners was received asking the Commissioners to amend the law, withdrawing sections of the Ordinance that made the owner responsible for offences committed by a puller and liable to pay fines imposed. The petition was considered at the Commissioners' meeting on 28 August, and rejected out of hand. The sections in question, deliberately introduced after the strike of 1897 with the owners in mind, were considered vital to the working of the Ordinance. No steps were taken to alter them. The petitioners were informed accordingly.

This rebuff, in combination with the action the Governor was about to take, caused the strike. In September the police, acting under a directive from the Governor, took measures into their own hands to control rickshaw traffic. The Inspector-General of Police personally called on Mr Hooper to inform him that the Governor had instructed him to crack down on rickshaws. He told the Registrar to inform the owners that action would commence the following week.[8] The Government, however, had not informed the Commissioners of the heavy-handed step it was about to take. There could be no public outcry or vacillation, or sympathy for the owners out of fear of a strike. The situation of the irresponsible puller and the traffic congestion in the streets had continued too long. One hundred and twenty owners were assembled at Mr Hooper's office the following day and informed of the intention of the Government.[9] The head of the Rickshaw Department told them plainly to employ pullers who 'knew something of the rules of the road, sufficient at any rate, to enable them to understand that when a policeman put up his hand, it was a signal for them to stop'.[10] Mr Hooper sent the Inspector-General of Police a memorandum reporting what he had stated to the owners:

> I explained to them the dangers to traffic of employing *singkehs* and pullers who refused to keep on the left side of the road, wander about the roads in the way of traffic, interfere with carriages by cutting across in front of horses, rush furiously around corners or across a road to pick up passengers, and refused to stop or proceed cautiously when a policeman holds up his hand, will, in future, commencing on Monday, be dealt with by the police. I have cautioned the owners that if they employ undesirable pullers who commit the above offences, they will be held responsible, not only in having their rickshaws suspended, but that the law will be enforced and pullers who are arrested and convicted before a magistrate, that they [the owners] will be held liable ... to pay the fines ... under penalty of having their jinrikishas seized, until all requirements have been complied with.[11]

However, in dealing with the owners and the question of enforcement of the laws regulating rickshaw traffic, care was not taken to give ample notice to the Chinese community. The Governor's drastic step, so suddenly introduced, would throw out of work 20,000 coolies, and bring back a flood of lingering fears of the strike of 1897.

Early on Monday, 21 October, the strike came. It was organized by the Hengwah and Hockchia owners in Queen Street, Victoria Street and adjacent thoroughfares.[12] Rumours had been spread by them and secret society *samseng* (thugs) that police intended to levy a fine of $5 apiece on all pullers. *Samseng* pullers went on strike at once and incited others to do likewise, circulating the tale among as many coolies as possible in the Pearl's Hill area. The news soon spread over Kampong Glam, and later to the Kreta Ayer and Tanjong Pagar districts. By threatening to smash any licensed rickshaw seen out, pullers were frightened into returning home. That morning the inner courtyard and verandahs of the rickshaw stations were filled, the pullers congregating in groups, expressing their fear of *samseng* and refusing to work.[13] Singapore was paralysed again.

Samseng roamed the streets stoning pedestrians, bicycles, and hackney carriages. Incidents were reported in Tanjong Pagar Road and in New Bridge Road and, as the day wore on and the strike spread, police were ordered to carry pistols.[14] The tension and inconvenience to the public which faced Singaporeans in the strike of 1897, returned. John Littles and Robinsons was besieged by Europeans anxious to purchase hand guns.[15] The word went around again, in the same way, that the pullers were a danger. The European alarm was understandable. Pedestrians were jeered at and pelted with stones in Sago Street, Smith Street, and

Neil Road, and in other parts of town. Gharry drivers were threatened with destruction of their vehicles, and one hack gharry that came out was surrounded by a Chinese crowd and stoned in Cecil Street. Another was smashed up in Robinson Road.[16] In Sago Street a large-scale confrontation broke out between the police and several hundred pullers. Bricks and stones rained down on passing carriages from the lodging-house, No. 99, with entrances in Sago Street and New Bridge Road. Sikh reinforcements arrived, shots were fired, the house charged, and 40 rickshawmen were arrested and marched to the Central Police Station. Among the prisoners arraigned was one of the leaders, a hunchback of an 'unprepossessing appearance.'[17] The pullers did not want peace. It was not quiet after dark. Pedestrians, peons, and rickshaw officials were chased at night and stoned in Victoria Street, Johore Road, and Rochore Road.[18] Again, the Sikhs turned out. The crowds of pullers were charged and dispersed several times, only to fade away and reappear on the verandahs of another street corner, shouting '*pah, pah*'. Stones were thrown well into the night in defiance. And all the time, there was the ominous spectre of reserves of hundreds of dissatisfied rickshaw pullers squatting or standing on the verandahs, and in the streets, especially in the neighbourhood of Pearl's Hill, Pagoda Street, and Almeida Street. Others were jam-packed with empty rickshaws.

The next day it rained. The pullers refused to work. Europeans had to 'trudge dismally to the office again' as the rain poured down in torrents. Violent scenes were experienced in Malay Street, Sago Street, Craig Road, Duxton Road, and Rochore Road and Europeans were warned to give those areas a wide berth.[19] The discomfort caused by the strike was widely felt. Residents living in Tanglin, in the roads leading to Orchard Road, were unable to find rickshaws at the usual hour:

> Orchard Road presented a remarkable sight, being free from wheeled traffic, with the exception of a few carriages and here and there a single private rickshaw, whilst at intervals armed Sikhs were stationed, and the countenances of the disappointed ones was woeful in the extreme, as they viewed with envious eyes the few lucky ones in carriages pass and then made up their minds to 'tramp it'. To heighten the discomfort of the unwilling pedestrians, it was windy and inclined to be wet, but the mail was in and office had to be reached and so the majority reconciled themselves to foot it all the way into town.[20]

In the torrential downpour it proved impossible for Europeans to maintain a semblance of respect as they attempted to negotiate the puddles of red laterite mud passing for streets:

> It was a curious sight last night to watch the weary workers returning home, afoot.... The natives seemed to enjoy the novelty immensely and felt quite exalted to be trudging in the company of the *orang putehs* [whites]. Every available carriage, hack carriage, palanquin, trap and dog cart seemed to have been called into requisition, and of course, bicycles in all stages of existence saw light once more, but still many were forced to and they walked, but with unwillingness and muttering opinions on the perversity of things in general, not

loud, but deep.... This morning dawned gloomy and soon the rain came and with it the countenances of a good many would-be cyclists must have fallen considerably.... At the time when it was usual to make a start for office, rain was still falling and the roads were in a very sloppy condition.[21]

There was still no transport the next day. The coolies absolutely refused to pull. At that time three-fourths of the Europeans relied on the rickshaw to get back and forth to the office, and for the rest of Singapore's population it was the only form of public transport. But it was not just the business routine of Empire that was upset. Pleasure was, too. There were no rickshaws to attend the races and visit the brothels. While the strike was affecting everybody, it seemed to adversely affect 'Harmstons', a visiting circus, more than most entertainment.[22] Would-be circus goers could not get a rickshaw, and 'shanks mare' was the only alternative, after bicycles, to reach the Big Top along deserted streets. One European, describing his life in a personal memoir, recounted the seriousness of the strike and his society's dependence on the rickshaw to a 1930s audience bent on abolishing it:

The strike was well arranged, and was complete. With the exception of a few private rickshaws, there were none out on the streets at all. Residents in these days can hardly understand what this meant to the inhabitants of thirty years ago. They [rickshaws] were almost the only means of transport. Private carriages and public gharries—the latter expensive—were the only other methods before the trams and buses came in. The day the strike occurred was windy, with patches of rain. The mail was in that morning, and the offices had to be reached somehow, and there was nothing to be done but to 'hoof' it. So away went the male portion of the population, carrying Chinese umbrellas and the inevitable tiffin basket, hoping against hope that someone would pass in a horse vehicle and give them a lift. Imagine it, you who roll easily to office today in your saloon cars, imagine your predecessors trudging along Orchard and Grange Roads, their white boots covered with ... red mud—a mud which stained!—and send a little prayer of thanks to Mr Austin and Mr Morris and their friends who have delivered you for ever from such experiences as we had then![23]

Public fear of the owners and the possible creation of a coolie 'army' was expressed again in the newspaper editorials, as was the case in 1897; so did the calls for mass deportation:

It cannot be too carefully borne in mind that the only persons to blame are certain rikisha owners, who deliberately persuaded or coerced other owners to prohibit their coolies from going out with their vehicles for hire. That is to say that by the acts of these Chinese speculators in the rikisha business thirty thousand of the most ignorant of the Chinese coolie class were thrown idle for three days. And idle hands proverbially find mischief ready for them to do. Practically, it was not a strike: it was rather a lock out.... This 'strike' has shown what an excellent thing that provision is that makes the owner liable for the acts of his servants, the rikisha coolie [*sic*]. And the fact that two of these owners are now under arrest, with a possibility of deportation, is a ... significant hint of what, on another occasion may befall a very large proportion of the 1,400 rikisha owners who practically command an army corps of 30,000 Chinese coolies. But the owners who will be in peril of deportation in any future strike, if due to their incitement, will be the big men who own perhaps a couple of hundred rikishas. It is a good thing for the government to hold such men as hostages for order in the hollow of its hand.[24]

Much of what was written again came from those with a concern for 'showing them', for striking terror into the hearts of the owners and pullers:

What must be rubbed into the rikisha owners is that they are responsible for the conduct of the coolies in this case. But the mere incitement to strike, which has been the work of the owners, should be visited on them pitilessly. *Pour encourager les autres*, the deportation of twenty five or fifty, would be the best thing in the world. . . . Deportation, wholesale, is the weapon to hold over these blackguards. Mongolian secret combination is very easy. It is the duty of the Executive to make it proportionally perilous.[25]

Several owners stated to the Commissioners that if Section 36 of the Ordinance was withdrawn the rickshaws would return at once. This was the crux of the matter. The owners did not want to be responsible for the actions of the pullers. The municipal officials expressed no sympathy for the owners, giving their support to the Governor. After a frightful two days of 'irrational' and 'unjust' behaviour of pullers in which European men and women were pelted with stones, and of destruction of carriages, rickshaws and other property, the Government put a decisive end to the irreconcilable claims. The rickshaw owners were summoned to Government House.[26] The papers carried several versions of what transpired between the Governor and the owners. According to Mr Hooper, Swettenham hardly discussed the matter, simply pointing out to the Chinese who controlled the rickshaw trade that they were on British soil. They were expected to act accordingly, and were liable for their actions before the law. He was frank, threatening immediate deportation. In one account it was stated that the Governor

Left the Towkays waiting at Government House for about an hour, sending in biscuits and drinks to them. When he did appear, he talked to them affably about the weather, etc., and said it was very nice of them to call and see him. After a short while he excused himself, saying that he was very busy, and just as he was leaving the room, turned to them and said: 'Oh, by the way, gentlemen, there is a rikisha strike on in town. There is also a boat leaving for China tomorrow. If that strike is not stopped before the ship leaves, you will be on it. Good morning.'[27]

The three-day strike ended the next morning. The Governor's will and power was in this instance stronger than either the owners' or the Chinese community. The secret societies and the underworld of Singapore, as the strike had shown, were still an important barrier to British government. But the liberty the societies, owners, and *samseng* had enjoyed before 1890 were to have no parallels in the new century. The societies were ever present, formidable, hidden, but nevertheless, still only mere shadows of their former selves.

The Government was prepared to act against the owners. Prominent men were detained under the Banishment Ordinance. Among the rickshaw owners arrested on banishment warrants was Lee Chong Hing, the principal *towkay* amongst the Hengwah, who was deported to China for three years.[28] The police were active after the strike, reporting 5,697 rickshaws, mainly for obstruction and loitering. The cases were dealt with by magistrates and licences suspended in 5,185 cases. Fines of up to $20 were inflicted, which the owners had to pay.[29] But this method of policing the pullers was less than satisfactory. It was expensive, and in human terms the police could not maintain the dragnet on rickshaw traffic year-round. The public clamoured for registering and licensing the puller, but the Rickshaw Department opposed it. The system of rickshaw traffic regulation had to be altered. The public wanted the fledgling Department, instead of the police, to deal with the rickshawmen.[30] So did the owners responsible for the strike. An amendment to the Rickshaw Ordinance which enabled pullers to be dealt with by the Registrar was introduced in 1902. It conferred on him powers of a Police Court to hear charges against pullers under the Ordinance.

It was a peculiar irony that the strike of 1901 created the opening for the Rickshaw Department to develop effective power against the puller, by granting far more autonomy to the owner. Undoubtedly, the pullers now found the ground cut from beneath their feet. And two at least, who had been terrorized more than others by the experience, still believed they might be decapitated, months afterwards:

> Some curious repercussions of the strike kept cropping up, however, from time to time. One Sunday night I had been to dinner at the Salzman's as usual, and a sister from the hospital was there, too, and I offered to escort her home. We left Salzman's house in St Thomas' Walk in rikishas, and when we came to the junction of Kim Seng and River Valley Roads and made to turn down the former, the pullers put down the shafts and refused to budge. No amount of argument would get them to go down Kim Seng Road, and eventually I made out the reason. It was that the Governor had offered a price of one hundred dollars for the head of a rikisha coolie cut off in that thoroughfare![31]

When the owners began their three-day strike against the Department it did not seem a safe bet that the confusion and inconvenience would force the government to meet their demands. But in the ensuing months Europeans found out something the rickshaw *towkay* and coolies knew: they could not do without the rickshaw. The streets remained overcrowded, dangerous. Commuters continued to be caught in rickshaw traffic jams. The new Rickshaw Court was meant to cut to the marrow of the dilemma in the hope of supplying a solution to the 'rickshaw problem'. As was to be shown in the statistics of Mr Hooper's Court, the pullers knew they were about to be locked in a struggle with peons over capitulation and defiance on the streets. British authority, discipline, and punishment did not command their respect, despite the owners having succumbed. A singular lesson emerged from 1897 and 1901 in the puller's mind: the first step was to strike.

The Amending Ordinance was introduced in January of 1903 making it an offence for owners to employ unfit coolies, and conferring on the Registrar power to deal with traffic offences.[32] The Ordinance was brought into force before the Commissioners were able to give proper notice to the pullers and owners.[33] The rickshawmen wanted the amended Ordinance withdrawn. Loud objection to the first sentences of Mr Hooper's Traffic Court were made, as owners willingly produced culpable men. *Samseng* pullers began to circulate through the rickshaw districts stirring, threatening strike.

This strike was due not only to the stiff penalties handed out by the new Court, but to the fear of lawful restraint the puller would be subjected to under the Ordinance—a hamstringing process that began in 1890 with the secret societies through which the Government hoped to end the autonomy of groups like rickshaw pullers. Rickshawmen were being arrested for what they felt were trivial offences, and being locked up for the night or having to find bail. As in 1901 the strike was started in the neighbourhood of Victoria Street by coolies belonging to the Hengwah and Hockchew communities. It lasted seven days, the 15th to the 21st of January 1903.[34] *Samseng* intimidation and threat prevented coolies less sympathetic from turning out. Rickshaw traffic ground to a halt. There were no confrontations, stone-throwing or jeering as in the past, simply passive resistance. The pullers refused to go out and work. The 'Black Maria', the police wagon, made the rounds of the rickshaw depots, and pullers were summarily picked up.[35]

The inconvenience to the public was great during the seven days the strike lasted, and worse afterwards:

> The jinrikisha strike is clearly within the memory of all of us, indeed the traces or results of it are still to be seen as soon as it begins to get dusk, when to get one of these cheap and handy conveyances which have really become quite a necessity to most of us, would require the assistance of a police constable or else one has to foot it home as best as he can.[36]

Although the strike was over, the public was no nearer to a solution of the problems connected with rickshaws and rickshaw pullers than before the establishment of the special court. One thing was for certain though; there were fewer rickshaws running on the streets than before the strike and the inconvenience experienced by weary, hungry would-be passengers wishing to return home at the end of the day was keenly felt. It was calculated that there were 3,000 less rickshaws plying for hire. Rickshaw owners, who experienced losses as their vehicles were kept idle and steady pullers and lodgers sought employment elsewhere, joined petty traders, small shopkeepers, and the general public in a chorus of complaint against the Court:

> When one considers the fact that a special magistrate, and a special court have been appointed . . . for the sole benefit of ricksha pullers it is no longer surprising that these pullers should have had the good sense to look out for employment in other spheres, and decline to be constantly subjected to the ever mischievous eyes

of specially appointed constables and others, whose one duty in life seems to be to have these poor coolies before their big Tuan, there and then to be taught the law of the road, not gratis but at a cost ranging from $2 to $15 or $20. The fact that there is now a scarcity of rickshas bears out my contention that the law affecting these people has been too hard and exacting and if we want these people to come back to their work, as we undoubtedly do want, from the repeated complaints we hear on all sides of their scarcity, I think the authorities ought to make their lives more tolerable for them. I know that to many people this sounds like 'coming down' and 'giving way' but call it what they may, there is no gainsaving the fact . . . that if things are not adjusted better for them, we shall feel the inconvenience more and more. It is true that the tramway is soon coming, but judging from past experiences, I am sure that there are still many people who prefer the more independent ride in a ricksha than in a congested tramcar.[37]

There was a sustained campaign by the press carrying articles and representations demanding the Rickshaw Department become less severe, both in court and in its methods of testing rickshaws:

The Jinrikisha Department periodically publishes reports of its work and glories in the fact that it has been able to bring under its fining influences more ricksha pullers and owners than hitherto. This is all very well from a magisterial and business point of view, but I think one is apt to run away with one's zeal in this matter . . . let the rejoicing registrar and his myrmidons bear in mind that what is *fun* with them is *fine* with the ricksha people! . . . I think it is right to say that the ricksha people deserve more pity than blame, and that for them, it can be truly said that they have been more sinned against than sinning.[38]

Once again, contradictions had arisen over policy and practice both within and between the Government and the public over rickshaws. The strike had occurred shortly after the doors of Mr Hooper's Court opened. More effective control over the puller had been put into the hands of the Registrar. It was beyond question that once the institution was established, an institution specifically called for by the public to sort out Singapore's rickshaw traffic, the pullers had a difficult time on the streets. But the general public soon realized that they could not have it both ways; if they wanted a full complement of rickshaws out for hire, then the vigilance of the Court and its peons had to be relaxed. In point of fact, they had to live with the ubiquitous traffic jams and the quirks of the 'irresponsible' puller. The climate of opinion was hostile towards the Rickshaw Department and it yielded, acknowledging the criticism. The amended Ordinance worked more smoothly in 1904, and thereafter.[39]

The ability to strike, and to offer their labour as coolies to other employers in the face of unreasonable authority, prevented the pullers' absolute subordination to the law. Public transport was a problem in Singapore. Rickshaws were indispensable. The public and authorities recognized this as a fact after the strike. The puller without a rickshaw was destitute, dependent on the owner and the public for his livelihood. But there was veiled strength in numbers. Solidarity emerged among the pullers. The collective act of putting down the shafts had seriously upset the tenor of Singapore economy and society. A legacy of the week-long strike was a strengthening of the pullers' sense of independence and injustice. For it was at this time, just after the strike, that rickshaw coolies introduced the practice of walking outside the shafts, refusing a fare.[40]

This new sense of unity and collective action of pullers came more sharply into focus in the inter-war period over the issues of nationalism and the commitment of the overseas Chinese, the post-war commercial development of Singapore, and the world depression of the 1930s. The immediate post-war strikes of 1919 and 1920 had two principal aspects. First, the conflict over Shantung involving China and Japan. Secondly, the prosperity of Singapore resulting from high trade levels in the marketing and distributing of primary products like sugar, copra, rubber, and tin. It was a cruel irony for the puller that prosperity gave rise to the bad years with problems of acute overcrowding in the inner city, soaring rents, rice shortages, and falling fares. The immensity of the problem faced by the men, especially those with families, was to be made apparent.

The hostility in China over Shantung affected the rickshawmen of Singapore because their rickshaws were manufactured in Japan. Despite being a community divided according to dialect, lineage and place of origin in China, the Chinese in Singapore were united in their view on Shantung of the Japanese as aggressors motivated by imperialism. In the middle of June 1919 anti-Japanese posters and Chinese writing on walls suddenly cropped up around the city forecasting a boycott of Japanese goods.[41] The Chinese were told there were to be demonstrations and they were exhorted to take personal initiatives to assist in forcing the Japanese community in Singapore into an untenable position. Rickshaw pullers were badly off in 1919. Nevertheless, they began to refuse Japanese passengers in the spirit of the wall-poster campaign as the boycott got underway. Pullers who did not understand the situation unfolding, or for some reason believed in modern China, and who had to live on what was given to them by fares like the Japanese, came in for rough treatment from other rickshawmen for having wheeled them around.[42] For these enforcers, 'patriotism' was not a mere pose—a pathetic, blind personal commitment; rather their actions were part of an important process of Chinese political thinking and action—the boycott movement in China. This dialogue across seas was meant to jeopardize the Japanese world of Singapore, and thereby show that the overseas Chinese were against the retention of Shantung by Japan. It was also aimed at rattling the British, whose colony was unable to do without Japanese goods and textiles, as British and European wares could not be supplied at a price within the means of the Chinese labourer.[43]

The anti-Japanese demonstrations in support of the boycott included several courses of action: (1) Japanese shophouses were to be looted and their goods destroyed; (2) Japanese brothels were to be attacked; (3) Chinese shops were to be raided for Japanese goods, and got ridden of by smashing or burning; (4) Chinese street hawkers and other vendors were to be relieved of their Japanese wares; and (5) Chinese were to throw out all sorts of Japanese odds and ends, everything from cooking utensils and clocks, to bedding and private rickshaws, consigning them to be broken up or devoured by the flames about to light up the streets.[44] The boycott began in Rochore Road at 8 o'clock on a Thursday night, 19 June, as more than a thousand Chinese assembled. Then the destruction started in earnest. They started with Chinese shopkeepers. The *towkay* had been warned of what they could expect. Most of them threw their stocks of Japanese goods in the street and saved the demonstrators the trouble of breaking and entering their shophouses, but force was used when *towkay* objected. Likewise most householders voluntarily threw goods from windows of lodging-houses on to the streets, particularly in the vicinity of South Bridge Road and Upper Hokkien Street.[45] Combustible goods were put to the match while non-inflammable items, such as earthenware crocks, had a chop stamped on them to forbid future use. The fronts of shops and coolie lodging-houses were lit up as the streets of Chinatown became one continuous string of bonfires of household utensils, straw hats of the type rickshaw pullers wore, and other goods manufactured in Japan or made locally by Japanese. The next day also was devoted to the wholesale burning of Japanese goods. The following morning most of the shops along High Street, North Bridge Road, and South Bridge Road kept their shutters up. Only a few Chinese shops opened to supply rice to a hungry city. The Government declared martial law on Saturday, but the majority of shop owners did not take down their shutters. Despite a prohibition on the burning of goods, Japanese articles continued to be thrown out and consumed, including rickshaws.[46]

The docks were still. Coal coolies went on strike, too. The Japanese ships in port were deserted. The odd sense of quiet surrounding the neighbourhood of Keppel Harbour stood in marked contrast to the violence that erupted in parts of the city identified with the Japanese community, and where some of the ugliest scenes of the boycott campaign occurred.[47] Japanese shops which suffered the most damage were situated in out-of-the-way spots, the demonstrators leaving the long line of shops down North Bridge Road, where the Japanese presence was strong, unscathed. In that area the Japanese had shut and barricaded their storefronts and armed themselves with poles, knives, and pistols; the power of the Chinese would be put to the real test.[48] Instead, punishment was inflicted on the Japanese brothel quarter centring on Malay and Malabar Streets. It was the scene of some of the worst demonstrations as more than a thousand Chinese coolies, including rickshaw pullers, armed with fighting staffs, lead piping, daggers and bludgeons, surged through the quarter so familiar to them. They vindictively ensured that the *Karayuki-san*, to whom they brought fares and visited themselves, paid the price for taking their hard earned money, and, perhaps, for having given them venereal disease, but especially for being Japanese, and not just with empty words. They encouraged one another in smashing the numbered lanterns hanging over the entrances to the brothels, as others looked on shouting their approval as flower-pots and benches along with anything else they could get hold of was ripped out or turned over. The trail of destruction led to several Japanese drug stores in this part of town that were broken into, the display cases smashed, and the patent medicines destroyed, strewn all over the road. Another medicine shop on Rochore Road was gutted by fire. The vengeance did not end until several coolies were shot dead by the civil guard in a street clash.[49]

It was against this background of anti-Japanese demonstrations that the rickshaw pullers protested. As in 1903, they did not openly advocate violence. They took advantage of the opportunity to inconvenience the public by refusing to turn out on the night of 19 June.[50] For two days they did not budge. In a simple but effective act of resistance thousands of Japanese straw hats that the pullers wore were discarded, left at the corner of Market and Cecil Streets in a huge pile for everybody to see.[51] They went on strike because most of the rickshaws were manufactured in Japan. Many rickshaws were destroyed as an expression of the men's bitter political feeling. In one part of Singapore the twisted remnants of fifty were plainly visible. Piles of rickshaw debris were not an uncommon sight in front of lodging-houses.[52] Sometimes the pullers stood by and watched as others brought their vehicles to an 'inglorious end', and sometimes they joined in the pyromania wilfully, showing the crowd the Japanese trademarks, helping to destroy the means of their own livelihood for China's sake and out of hatred of Japan.

The Rickshaw Department sent for over 40 owners on Friday and requested them to send out their men. They refused on the grounds that the more radical element amongst the pullers would smash and burn any vehicles that turned out. In the early hours on Saturday Dr Lim Boon Keng, a prominent member of the Legislative Council, Mr Hooper and the police went to various districts where the pullers lived and spoke to them. They advised them to take to the shafts. There were a few rickshaws out and about in the outlying districts that morning but none in town. Late in the day the same delegation, but this time also accompanied by prominent members of the Chinese Chamber of Commerce, made the rounds of the rickshaw depots again, in an effort to persuade the pullers to return to work. The coolies' excuse was that if they turned out, they were not only liable to be attacked, but their rickshaws also would be reduced to ashes. The Registrar told them they would be protected by martial law.[53] Each man was losing a dollar per day, and the hard reality of this fact, coupled with prevailing high rents and the cost of rice, which affected them seriously, forced the rickshaw coolies to resume work the following day.

They had made their point, convincingly. Military were posted everywhere, with heavy patrolling done in the rickshaw neighbourhoods around Victoria Street, Middle Road and Rochore Road, where some of the worst fracas had occurred over the previous nights. The rickshaw question had been solved, but only under the barrel of a gun, by a city living in the grip of martial law. Few rickshaws were idle the following week. Japanese were found riding in them, but pullers only accepted them reluctantly, as the military continued to occupy their districts and patrol the city.[54] As a parting act of solidarity in defence of China against Japanese aggression, owners brought financial pressure to bear by not importing rickshaws after the boycott, cancelling pending orders by cable. Rickshaw deals with Japan were lucrative as the registration statistics of the Rickshaw Department revealed, with more than 3,000 rickshaws ordered in 1918 alone, at $150 each.[55] This act which drove the Chinese to cancel rickshaw orders after failing to obtain the ear of the Government who sympathized with the Japanese, proved costly to the puller, who had put Japanese 'imperialism' and British arms to the test. Patriotism and manipulation of resentment towards Japan came more easily at the end of 1919 than purchasing rice, paying the rent, or hiring a rickshaw, let alone buying one. Such feelings and politics advanced none of these needs of the puller. At the same time Singapore was about to enter a period of sustained prosperity based on high trade levels in primary products. It was not to benefit the rickshawmen.

Strike fever remained high among the pullers the rest of the year. In the aftermath of the anti-Japanese boycott owners demanded more for hiring out rickshaws as fewer were available, and because Japanese rickshaw accessories suddenly cost more.[56] Housing rents were rising too. In 1919 Singapore was fast becoming a major centre for trade in primary products, but it was strapped for warehouse space. Something had to give. The boarding houses for pullers were rapidly stripped and turned into godowns for bulk storage of rice, copra, and sugar. Not only were owners demanding more for hiring out rickshaws, but housing rents were also rising, even while pullers were being evicted from their lodgings near the waterfront. The Hengwah men of Tanjong Pagar were the first to put down the shafts. They were considered by the British to be the most truculent group among the pullers. They lived in one of the most dangerous districts, an area where their tenement houses were being confiscated in the interests of the commercial growth of Singapore.[57] The Hengwah confronted City Hall, demanding that the Commissioners double the rickshaw fare. But before the sanction for increased fares could be obtained notices were posted on the walls of rickshaw depots in Rochore Road, Muar Road, Victoria Street and Bain Street calling for a strike and a fare of 15 cents per mile.

> Notice to inform our relatives and others that as things are getting dearer day by day and we the rikisha pullers find it very difficult to cope with the present high cost of living. The pullers of Kampong Glam and town sections have held a meeting and are now able to state that the fares from the 14 February 1920 would be raised to fifteen cents per mile. On the 13th instant pullers of both Kampong Glam and town are not to ply for hire. In conclusion we appeal for unity.[58]

The rickshawmen wanted immediate action. But the Municipal Commissioners, caught somewhat off guard by the radical nature of the demand, were not prepared to sit in conclave on such short notice. They wanted at least a day to deliberate, and to have the last say on the matter. The psychology of the moment demanded time, for the sake of prestige. Their procrastination was a mistake. The lightning strike began on 13 February, the notices ordering the pullers not to ply for hire. For three days the majority of the public was inconvenienced by heavy downpours which held people up for work and dispelled the argument of some municipal officials that 'walking was always conducive to health'.[59]

Striking pullers stopped others from plying for hire, on main thoroughfares and in the rickshaw districts themselves. Quite a number of assaults were reported in the Rochore section alone which the strikers had sealed off. There were not more than a hundred rickshaws operating in the Rochore, Kampong Kapor, and Tanjong Pagar neighbourhoods, pulled only by desperate men, opium smokers.[60] Another notice was posted the next day in the various depots, calling for rickshawmen to stand firm, to unite and to continue the strike:

> This is to notify one and all that the reason we did not go out for hire yesterday (Friday) was due to the Municipality not raising the rikisha fares. Those pullers who are not ashamed of themselves and go out to hire today (Saturday) will be assaulted and their rikishas damaged. We would not care, what nationality their passengers are. We ask our people not to create any disturbance, but to wait and not go out for hire till the fares are raised and lastly we plead for unity.[61]

Once again streets like Rochore Road, Victoria Street, and Bencoolen Street came under police guard in case of threat, intimidation and violence to the public by striking pullers. With the exception of privately owned rickshaws, the rickshawmen had been enjoined to keep off the roadways and they did. Singapore's streets looked strangely empty without them:

> The roads were noticeable yesterday for the dearth of rikishas upon which so many depend for bringing them to work and which enable others to carry out their daily round of duties in town. Although there was the usual number of motor cars about, yet the streets did not wear their wanted busy aspect, as when the two-wheeled, man drawn conveyance plied about for hire or carried passengers, the men between the shafts racing with one another and shouting to people to get out of the way. One also missed the long queues in Raffles Place, outside Johnston's Pier, and round the fountain in Raffles Square, and was led to think that it was either a Sunday or some holiday but that the offices were open. The news of the men coming out [striking] was in the air the previous evening but not so widespread as to warn people to get away early the next morning in order to foot it and be in at business time.[62]

Public feeling was hostile towards the pullers for striking on the same day their demand had been put to the Commissioners.[63] There had been no period of grace—no time to arbitrate, all sense of decorum was lost, and the Commissioners could not avoid looking foolish. The pullers' lightning-like action alienated what little public support there had been in favour of raising the rate before the strike. An angry community recognized much to its chagrin that Singapore did not run an efficient tram service through all parts of the town so people could go about their business. Instead Singapore was dependent on the rickshaw coolie.

The question of increasing the fare was brought up at the Commissioners' meeting on the afternoon of 13 February and it was decided to allow a step-up from 5 to 7 cents for every half mile. However, the Commissioners insisted on the pullers' unconditional return to work, after which the terms would be announced. By recommending the fare for the mile be raised from 10 to 14 cents the pullers' demand had been met, but the status-conscious Commissioners, who could not afford to be laughed at, refused to inform the public of their decision straight away.[64] The strike continued much to the dismay of the man in the street. The Commissioners refused to convey the impression that they had yielded to the terms as a result of the strike, fearing pullers would take advantage of the precedent in the future.

Outside the chambers of the municipal building, Mr Hooper, the Registrar of Rickshaws, was at pains to counter a general view of the rickshaw puller as poverty-stricken and an object of humanitarian pity. He gave some hypothetical figures on the earnings of men who had regular work at night pulling rickshaws in the brothel quarters to 'open the eyes of those who talk ignorantly'.[65] But there was ample evidence in current reports and boards of inquiry that a puller's monthly earnings were significantly lower and progressively declining in real terms, despite gross takings at the rate of $1.50–2.00 per day. The strike bore testimony to that harsh fact—a dwindling income and standard of living. It was left up to Mr Hooper (who had more experience than anybody with pullers' protests and demonstrations) and several prominent owners to deliver the terms and obtain a return to work. Then, and only then, could the lines of the Commissioners' recommendations be announced. The 'government's' position was explained to the strikers by him and the numbers of rickshaws gradually increased on the roads over the course of the next couple of days. The pullers began to sense the reality of the situation. Within a week the last few who held out—not surprisingly, coming from the dock area where the strike had first begun—had again taken to the shafts. The deadlock had been broken. The rickshaw strike was over.[66] The pullers had won, but the clearcut settlement had to be presented without humiliation. The tacit recommendation of the Commissioners for increased fares was approved by the Governor in Council on 3 March.[67]

Almost at once there was a feeling among the public that the new schedule of fares would not work in practice. Nearly all Singaporeans arranged the cost before they started their trip, and often with reference to the prescribed rates. It was clear that if the new fares were adhered to rickshaw coolies would get less for obvious trips. For example, the following set of fares was provided to the *Singapore Free Press* to support this point[68] (see Table 8.1). In the past, it had been understood that people generally paid more than the regulation rate for such journeys, especially to the harbour. In the wake of the strike problems did proliferate over payment of the legal fare as pullers were prone to haggle with passengers about rates; some on receiving the set amount became insolent, sometimes even threatening passengers with bodily harm. Regulating the new scale of fares from the police standpoint was an impossible task. As a sequel to the strike, in September the fares were reduced by the Governor from 7 to 6 cents per half mile, to prevent an almost daily stream of incidents over the charges.[69] This measure plus competition from increased number of rickshaws plying the streets quelled the resentment of some pullers towards the public over fares, at least for the time being. The rise in the number of rickshaws running to 9,244 in 1921 resulted from the slump in employment on estates.[70] The rickshawmen's brethren from the Malay hinterland, frequently undernourished and impoverished, were willing to work for less, to survive. A year after the strike the pullers received a cent less than before for hiring, but they were not the real losers. The strike of 1920 had revealed to the authorities that the rickshaw coolies, who had been well organized, knew the value of the strike weapon and were prepared to use it on a moment's notice. Pullers united into a powerful force had wielded it successfully on this occasion against the city fathers. Coming together from all parts of the city, speaking different dialects and originating from different parts of Kwangtung and Fukien provinces, but all sharing a common purpose, the pullers acted to change their overcrowded, unhygienic, destitute condition under colonial rule. To be unafraid to strike against British authority and the *towkay* was an explicit political act. It was a powerful message. And it was to be adopted on a wider scale by rickshawmen in the depression-ridden 1930s to combat colonial authority and rent capital, in an effort to save themselves.

TABLE 8.1

A Set of Rickshaw Fares for Travel within the Municipal Limits, 1920

	New Fare	*Fare Paid under the Old Rate*
GPO to Tanglin Club (2¼ miles)	35¢	50¢
GPO to Tanjong Pagar (1½ miles)	24¢	50¢
GPO to West Wharf (2¼ miles)	35¢	75¢
GPO to Nassin Road	39¢	60¢

With admirable clarity the 1930s demonstrated the ways in which the growing deprivation of the rickshawmen was further aggravated by the policies of a government bent on abolishing rickshaws in the interests of the motor car. The question of control and eventual abolition first came up in 1927 when the Commissioners decided that unfit pullers and *singkeh* should be removed from the roads to prevent traffic congestion, and in the interests of safety. It was hardly coincidental that these men were also considered by Europeans to be eyesores on the streets. In 1928 the reduction of rickshaws by a stipulated percentage every year had begun, but not all pullers had time to seek another occupation before the force of the slump hit Singapore.[71] By 1931 there were no opportunities except hawking for out-of-work pullers. By 1935 this weeding-out process had already resulted in a drop from 9,000 to 4,000 vehicles for public hire.[72]

This ceiling on the number of rickshaw licences created a semi-monopoly in the industry. Competition was constrained more than ever before. Large fleet owners and *siong thau* banded against the rickshawmen to obtain the coveted licences. They therefore were in a position to charge higher rates for their vehicles. When the number was 9,000 a rickshaw cost $70 but in 1935 it was $160.[73] Half of this was the actual cost of the rickshaw and the other half was a quasi-monopoly value which the Government's reduction never intended to create. The owners were using the corner as a pretext to 'squeeze' the pullers, arguing the rates had to be raised to cover increased costs and overheads of their vehicles. According to a circular issued by the owners, the rates of hire in February 1935 were as follows: from 6 a.m. to 2 p.m., 20 cents; 6 a.m. to 3 p.m., 25 cents; 6 a.m. to 5 p.m., 35 cents; 2 p.m. to midnight, 25 cents; 5 p.m. to midnight, 15 cents; and 6 a.m. to midnight, 40 cents.[74] The fare hike was also justified in other ways. There was an increase in pullers, while at the same time the number of rickshaws was declining, many of the men were unemployed coolies from Johore, and there was competition for the rickshaws. There were also more opportunities for exploitation.

By then the pullers, who were frustrated and poor, knew how to express themselves. They knew how to reach the authorities and rickshaw capitalists with whom they were constantly struggling. Rickshaw coolies were dissatisfied with the conditions of an agreement between the owners and the Commissioners that enabled the *towkay* to reintroduce pre-slump rates for rickshaw hire. They took their grievances to the streets. Without any notice Hokkien rickshawmen in the Duxton Road area struck against the high rates on 19 February and the strike spread towards Tanjong Pagar and then throughout the entire city.[75] Other pullers followed and downed shafts. They would not be ridden over roughshod. Rickshaws stood idle in large blocs in front of lodging-houses around the city and the pullers stood about in groups discussing the situation, sizing up the growth of the strike, and their strength and unity. In the public mind the strike was due solely to the owners raising the rates but the fact could not be ignored that the *towkay* had formed an association creating a further hardship for pullers. 'Under the circumstances', continued a circular distributed by the rickshawmen just before the strike, '. . . we must all oppose, otherwise we will die of starvation. Wake up, wake up, our friends, we must fight against the owners who have adopted an increased rate, and we must go against government for assisting the owners.'[76] These men had developed the will to struggle, constantly, if need be, but the British had no intention of allowing their proto-political consciousness and resistance, which was part of an anti-colonial and anti-feudal struggle dating back to 1903, to become a revolutionary force. Sikh police patrolled the streets in the neighbourhoods most affected by the strike in an effort to prevent violence, and crowds from forming. Rickshaw coolies were arrested and protection provided to owners.

The strike ended on 22 February, four days after it had begun, when the owners agreed to reduce the rates by 5 cents. Thousands of pullers immediately turned out to ply for hire.[77] The strike of 1935 was revealing. The owners and pullers were now worlds apart. The rickshawmen had been very articulate, and very clear about what they wanted. The strike was much more than a disagreement over fares, it was unquestionably a class struggle. Pullers themselves, in a sense, characterized their conflict this way in circulars, wall posters, and illustrations going back to almost the turn of the century. The strike was based on the fact of an unequal distribution of power and wealth coupled with deliberate policies by the Colonial Government on the limitation of licences which, taken together, created a desperate situation for rickshawmen.

In an expected sequel to the strike the Commissioners considered further reductions of rickshaws.[78] The inconvenience caused by the strike was by no means as great as in the past as most of the public, except the poor, and rich school-aged children, had managed without them. Alternative modes of public transport, notably buses, had absorbed the lion's share of the rickshaw business. The strike also cleared the streets temporarily of rickshaws to the benefit of motorized traffic. This sudden change of affairs was not lost on the driving public who took advantage of the opening the strike had created to raise the question of total extinction. The rickshaw in Singapore was 'like a famous English king . . . [and] is an unconscionable time-a-dying'.[79] But the numbers did not drop below the 4,000 mark before 1939 which meant one more generation of rickshaw travel. The authorities, however, refused to assist the pullers to establish a provident fund on their behalf in face of the reductions. The Government felt the owners should take on the responsibility, but failed to punish them when they did not act. Owners were derelict in their duty with regard to welfare to pullers, and it caused hardship in the late 1930s. Despite the 5-cent reduction in rates, an estimated 10,000–12,000 pullers remained exploited—many without work, and increasingly without hope.

The picture that emerged between 1935 and 1938 was of a tangled web of circumstance in which neither the Government nor the *towkay* wanted to break through to improve the situation of the pullers. The city's problems grew deeper. The state of the Singapore labour market was a nasty shock and the rickshaw coolies were at the despairing end of that market. Therefore, they were prepared to stand up to the British and the owners in an even more militant way than they had in 1935. The need then, as severe as it was, did not compare with the urgency now. If there was ever a time for the pullers to use their power, it was 1938. A pattern of ugly violence had emerged within Singapore itself by then, and hard-core rickshawmen were working to inflict a grievous setback on the owners in order to secure a decent wage. The tactics ranged from wildcat strikes to intimidation and violence against those who refused to go along.

On 4 October 1938 rickshaw coolies struck to obtain lower rates of hire from owners. A settlement was not reached until 15 November; it was the longest, most bitterly fought, and the last strike of the rickshawmen.[80] They were paying 20 cents to the owners, referred to as 'profiteering proprietors', for half a day, from 6 a.m. to 2 p.m., or 2 p.m. to 6 a.m.[81] Unauthoritative reports had been made in the press that the owners intended to raise the half-day rate per rickshaw. In connection with these allegations 150 pullers marched into the Chinese Protectorate on 3 October and confronted Mr Rea, the Assistant Controller of Chinese Labour, laying their complaints before him. Militant representatives, who ran an office in Tanjong Pagar, sought his assistance, stating that owners were hiring out rickshaws at rates varying from 20 to 35 cents a half-day. He immediately summoned representatives of the Rickshaw Owners' Association and set the matter squarely before them, but refused to intercede directly on the pullers' behalf.[82] To leave the burden of settlement of the fare dispute to an unofficial agency, the Rickshaw Owners' Association, suited the Government well. Mr Rea avoided, or so he thought, the possibility of a good deal of extra work being thrown on his staff, and at the same time he could disclaim direct responsibility for any embarrassing incidents that might arise out of failure to reach a speedy resolution. Once the matter was handed over to the owners' association the fate of 7,000–8,000 pullers hung on their decision.

By 11.30 a.m. the next day more than a thousand rickshaw coolies had gathered on the steps outside the Protectorate as well as inside the building on a promise that the dispute would receive due consideration that morning. The significance of the impending meeting was signified by rickshaws parked three abreast in long rows stretching down the road from the Protectorate for over 500 yards.[83] Again, the pullers sent their representatives to the Protectorate office to gain support in asking owners not to increase the hire charges, but in vain. The owners made speeches assuring the men that the half-day rent would not rise. They argued that the dispute had not been caused by their proposal to raise the rent from 40 to 75 cents, rather it was the result of a misunderstanding over contributions by pullers to the China Relief Fund.[84] Modern China desperately needed the capital of its overseas subjects to stem the tide of Japanese invasion. All overseas Chinese were expected to come to the aid of their beleaguered homeland. According to the owners, representatives of the fund approached pullers asking them to contribute 50 cents each per month to the fund. Previously, the owners had paid a cent per day from the rent of each rickshaw. Now, on top of that, the pullers had to give, too. The owners also stated that there had been a steady reduction in the rent of rickshaws. The charge had been 80 cents per day before

1929. From 1929 to 1932 it dipped to 65 cents per day, and in 1934 it was reduced to 45 cents. The charge had been left at 40 cents per day since 1938. To further justify their claim that the pullers' demands were unwarranted the owners claimed that rickshaw upkeep, which included the $5 tax, was costing them $40 a quarter.[85]

The pullers rejected the owners' assurances out of hand, sticking to their original request to Mr Rea for a reduction of the rate to 10 cents per half-day. It was clear to all those present that the negotiations had failed. An impasse had been reached. This was the signal the pullers had been waiting for to take concerted action. The failure of the negotiations triggered the lightning strike of 1938. Pandemonium broke loose outside the Chinese Protectorate when news of the outcome of the deliberations reached the ears of the crowd. A thousand pullers rushed down the steps and out of the building waving their fists, calling for a strike, and smashing to pieces three rickshaws that just happened at that moment to be passing by on Havelock Road.[86]

Rickshaws were called off the streets and by dusk there were hardly any available. Rickshaws still plying for hire were stopped and the coolies told to down shafts. The pullers stood by stoically as their passengers were told by the strikers to get out of the rickshaws and walk, and they did.[87] The owners were badly hit by the strike, as can be seen from events that occurred just prior to the outbreak of a spate of the worst demonstrations of the inter-war years. Once again, the crucible of conflict was the Protectorate itself where, two days later (6 October) some 4,000 pullers arrived,[88] marching four abreast with the precision of trained soldiers—a frightening spectre to Europeans peering out of office windows, especially those officials of a new generation still too young to remember the events of 1903. The rickshawmen poured through the main entrance storming in on Mr Rea, calling on him to either reconsider their demands or send them back to China, as soon as possible. They wanted him to pay their passages. Representatives of the owners' association were called in but they refused to reduce the rate. However, community pressure from the Hokkien Advisory Board forced the owners to make a small concession by cutting the rent per day by 2 cents. This made the charge 38 instead of 40 cents. The angry pullers demanded passage to China.[89]

The discussion broke up acrimoniously with no decision having been taken. Police had to disperse the thousands of rickshaw coolies with baton charges as they milled about, throwing bottles and stones at the owners filing out of the building in the aftermath of the meeting. They were sent home under police escort as pullers jeered at them, threatening to smash their rickshaws.[90] There were indications of worse to come as personal threats were made against the owners, their families, and property. Later that same day violent demonstrations began as hundreds of pullers besieged various owners' houses in Market Street and Park Road, hurling bottles and stones in defiance. The police quickly moved in to disperse them.[91] While this strike was to have its greatest impact on

Chinatown and in the rickshaw districts, it was even more unwelcome outside those areas when it came closer to European establishments and homes, to create frightening demonstrations in streets and areas used only to the inconvenience of traffic jams. When hundreds of pullers attempted to march to the Chinese Consulate-General the following morning and caused alarm in the vicinity of Orchard Road, the police moved to break up the crowd.[92]

On the night of 9 October Muar and Ophir Roads were the scenes of general turmoil against owners and the streets were littered with broken glass from bottles used during the fray. More than a dozen rickshaws were dumped into Rochore Canal before Sikh constables appeared on the scene armed with *kandar* sticks (truncheons). Some of their number were set upon by angry pullers. Out of necessity police were forced into guarding the area.[93] All sorts of incidents began to take place simultaneously. In another part of town a group of fifteen hungry pullers rushed into the shop of Lim Ah Tu, the husband of a female rickshaw owner, demanding rice and threatening to harm the couple if it were not given to them. Lim Ah Tu's wife produced a bag of flour to placate the intruders.[94] Similarly, a gang of seven pullers was alleged to have demanded cash from the wife of a rickshaw owner, threatening to burn their rickshaws.[95]

Frantic efforts were made by the Chinese Chamber of Commerce to reconcile the owners and destitute pullers before the situation got out of hand completely. Europeans feared that the belligerent stance of the pullers was potentially contagious. The strike, from their point of view, was capable of growing into a more militant labour cause. It could spread to other disaffected groups such as coal loaders, tram workers, and stevedores, as coolies, their eyes turned to the immediate past, awakened a 'sleeping giant', rising out of the depths of Chinatown, to challenge the colonial authority and prosperity of Singapore. The four principal Foochow Chinese associations in Singapore, the Foochow Huay Kuan, the Hockchia Huay Kuan, the Hui Ann Huay Kuan and the Hengwah Community Guild, offered to establish an arbitration board to settle the dispute.[96] A circular from the Chinese Chamber of Commerce to coordinate the scheme asked both owners and pullers to remember the crisis that China was going through, and stressed that concessions had to be made by both sides. Negotiations began. At a marathon meeting at the Southern Hotel between representatives of the pullers, the owners and the four associations a unanimous decision was reached on a series of points: the rate was to be reduced to 35 cents for a full day; owners could not refuse their rickshaws to pullers who participated in the strike, and the pullers must return to work at once. However, once back at their respective headquarters, disagreements surfaced between the two factions of rickshawmen, the Hockchew and Hengwah, over outright acceptance or rejection of the package. All hopes of an early end to the strike were dashed.[97] One of the underlying reasons for the failure of other Singapore coolies, including some Hokkien groups of pullers, to rally behind the rickshaw coolies in 1938 was the heterogeneity of Singapore Chinese society with its numerous speech-groups and surname 'clanship' ties, each with a distinctive version of culture deriving from South-east China. Cultural differences among these communities reflected a lack of solidarity which surfaced behind closed doors and affected their strategy with respect to the strike. Ho Bee Swee, an elderly clan leader from Duxton Road, pointed to clan resistance to the strike as a root cause of the failure of Singapore's coolie class to unite:

> From what I saw of the rickshaw pullers from south of the river around Duxton Road, those who supported the strike were few, very few. The reason for this being that most of the Hokien pullers were clan oriented. That is why so few responded to the efforts of the labor organisers north of the Singapore River. On the other side of the river, the rickshawmen were united; the rickshaw owners were even afraid to venture out on the street for fear of being attacked. But south of the river, in the Duxton Road area, on this side, it was completely different. As I have just said, the reason why those of us in Duxton Road did not aggressively support the strike was because of our clan relationships. That is why the response from this side [of the river] was not ideal. Rickshaw pullers from north of the river wanted desperately to recruit people from Duxton Road for the strike but there was no way for them to do this because of the clan relationships. The growing militancy and organisations of the rickshawmen north of the river was perceived as a sort of threat to the clans and as such made them unacceptable to enter our territory to recruit for the strike.[98]

Certainly from the vantage point of the streets, where the militancy of strikers like the Hockchew puller Low Nong Nong was running high, little hope could be held out for an early settlement. He was employed as a builder's labourer and as a rickshaw puller. The Hockchew coolie had not pulled a rickshaw during the strike, and had last hired one about fifteen days before it started.[99] Low Nong Nong died a week after the Southern Hotel meeting, on the afternoon of 17 October, in a clash between police and a large crowd of rickshawmen at the junction of Arab Street and Victoria Street.[100] Unemployed, hungry, and desperately in need of money, he had visited Seah Toon Tan, a Hockchew friend, that morning. He borrowed a dollar from him and left his house in Geylang at about 9 a.m., without ever having discussed the strike.[101] The trouble leading up to his death began when a crowd attempted to restrain a Hengwah puller, Low Ah Law, who had ventured along Arab Street with his rickshaw. At the junction of Victoria Street he was assaulted by a Hockchew crowd. He dropped the shafts and fled for his life, only to be attacked again further down the street.[102] A graphic description of how the strikers attacked him was given in the Coroner's Court by Low Ah Law himself, at the inquest into the death of the rickshaw puller, Low Nong Nong:

> On the morning of the 17th of October 1938 I took my rickshaw out for hire and was in Arab Street about eleven a.m. I was badly assaulted there. I don't know who assaulted me. I became unconscious. I do not know what kind of people assaulted me. About ten persons assaulted me ... I do not know why I was

assaulted . . . I did not know that rickshaw pullers are on strike . . . I am in fear but cannot explain. I went to the Registrar of Vehicles office on the morning of 17th October and seven of us were released to pull rickshaws. I was attacked because I was pulling a rickshaw.[103]

Obviously, he was still very frightened, and not telling the whole truth.

Police had barely arrived in the nick of time to rescue Low Ah Law and arrest one of the assailants. At once a new crowd of around 400 began to take shape to rescue the captured puller. Some were armed with fighting sticks, rickshaw shafts, bottles and bricks, and among them was Low Nong Nong. A clash ensued with the police. Shouts of '*pah, mata, pah*' ('strike, police, strike') rent the air as the crowd of pullers slowly closed in, injuring several constables with wooden clogs, poles, and stones they hurled at them. The situation was desperate with police injured and rickshaws wrecked all over the adjacent streets, until reinforcements arrived. Strong-arm measures were used to control and eventually disperse the crowd. Low Nong Nong was found dying from a fractured skull, face down on the side of the street emptied of his comrades.[104] His death sent reverberations through the rickshaw districts, making pullers more determined than ever to force the owners to come to an agreement on their terms. His funeral the same day was an unnerving, demonstrable display of strength and solidarity. Three thousand men solemnly followed the lorry bearing his coffin to Bukit Brown Cemetery to a pauper's grave, and, as the police anxiously stood by and watched, one of the longest funeral processions in Singapore's recent history, stretching from Wajang Satu to Newton Circus, passed.[105]

The strike did not. Special police began to patrol this district, traditionally considered a hotbed of unrest, in which so many owners and pullers lived. Measures also had to be taken to safeguard the remaining rickshaws in Singapore. Thousands of them were rounded up and impounded at the premises of the Registrar of Vehicles in Middle Road because of rumours that strikers intended to burn them. The confiscated rickshaws were placed in the custody of a 'riot squad' of 40 Sikh constables armed with batons and circular rattan shields for crowd control. The vehicles were dismantled by the owners and stacked up in piles of wheels, springs, and bodies.[106]

Two days after Low Nong Nong's death a delegation of seven pullers, representing the 8,000 rickshawmen in Singapore, held a press conference to answer claims made by the owners discrediting their efforts. In this war of words the rickshawmen refuted the owners' assertion that maintenance was costing them $41 quarterly. It was ridiculous. The pullers stated that maximum cost of rickshaw upkeep was $10 a quarter. The chief bone of contention was something else—the proposed 5 cents a day each man was to contribute to the China Relief Fund. Most owners were now prepared to reduce the rate to 35 cents; 5 cents of it would be contributed by them to the Relief Fund. The pullers, however, insisted on 30 cents, and that they should pay the 5 cents themselves. Both sides were thinking ahead to a time when the Relief Fund would cease, hoping to pocket the 5-cent contribution.[107] The delegation argued that owners, especially large ones with up to 950 rickshaws, would still make a substantial profit, renting at 30 cents a day. The daily take would be $285, an amount well in excess of maintenance and other costs.[108] On the other hand, it was claimed that pullers averaged only 65 cents a day, and had to pay 40 cents hire. The delegation also called for compensation to be paid to Low Nong Nong's kindred.

The 30 cents proposal was formally made to the owners through representatives of the Chinese association. The rickshawmen made it clear to the mediators that if the owners agreed to the rate, they would donate the 5 cents difference to the China Relief Fund, and some 3,750 rickshaws would return to the streets. If these terms were accepted, each puller would contribute 75 cents on the basis of one shift per day instead of the 50 cents originally proposed. Many owners, who had lost an estimated $14,000 during the first week of the strike, were now prepared, in the aftermath of Low Nong Nong's death and the wholesale destruction of hundreds of rickshaws, to come to the table and abide by the terms. But five big-time *towkay*, who owned the majority of rickshaws, still refused to accept the proposal, knowing that the pullers had made it clear to the public that they were ready to turn out, but on their terms.[109]

The protracted nature of the strike was taking its toll on the pullers, many of whom were destitute and starving. The longer it lasted the more destructive was its impact on them—the young, old, and opium smokers. Some of those most adversely affected resolved their plight by stealing or begging. Pullers swiped rickshaws in a desperate effort to earn some quick money by plying on the sly. Hoo Chew pleaded guilty to the charge of theft of Hoo Teck Hin's rickshaw, conjuring up a vision of hunger: 'Owing to the strike I have no money for food. I went to find Hoo Teck Hin but he was not at his home. I was starving so I took his rickshaw away to ply for hire and earn a few cents.'[110] Low Puah, one of fifteen rickshaw pullers who broke into Lim Ah Tu's shop, claimed that he too '. . . was starving because of the strike. I asked for rice but was given a sack of flour.'[111] Gangs of hungry pullers roamed the streets as the weeks progressed; one party of thirty stopped all passing taxis at the third mile, Serangoon Road, begging the drivers for money for food.[112]

Others, already among the lowest of the low, and facing financial crisis, especially those with families, chose to return to war-torn China. The Government offered free passage to destinations near Amoy and Foochow, hoping to defuse the strike and rid itself of some militant elements. Hundreds accepted. Their way of life had become too precarious. They felt they would be better off 'fighting for the fatherland' than starving in Singapore.[113] Immigration officers printed the chop of the Assistant Controller of Labour on the forearm of 700 rickshaw pullers, as a mark of identification to be repatriated, who then gathered with all their worldly possessions near the immigration depot to say goodbye to friends and relatives before boarding the steamer *Hong Siang* bound for Hong Kong, Swatow and Amoy.[114] A further batch of 800 unemployed pullers availed themselves of the Government's offer a month later. They left for China on the KPM steamer *Cremer* with their wives and children, who totalled 117. Besides his passage each man received three Straits dollars to cover his fare from Swatow or Amoy to his village, but no financial assistance was provided for accompanying family.[115] The trip home began a foreboding journey as a deck passenger —a return that was to be too fast into an equally doubtful world:

> There was a rush yesterday morning for the best places on the deck of the Cremer, and claims were staked out quickly with matting and luggage. The luggage taken back to China by the men was as startling in quantity as it was in variety. On top of one basket was three bottles of Brillantine. In the afternoon the men returned to the ship with their tickets and were closely scrutinized as they walked in single file up the gangway. As each man stepped aboard, the 'chop' of the Immigration Department, placed there the previous day when it had been proved he was a genuinely destitute rickshaw puller, was cancelled with another 'chop'.... On board, each man was given another ticket, and the three dollars. As he moved to the place he had secured in the morning he found that some enterprising person had placed a bundle of five tracts on each place. A few of the pullers were accompanied by wives and children, whose passages were also provided.... Most were alone, as they had left their wives in China.... The men will find it virtually impossible to return ... as the competition for quota tickets from China is so keen that each ticket is worth 300 dollars Chinese.[116]

For the 7,000 pullers who remained in Singapore there was no discernible improvement. The situation remained one of hostility and dearth of opportunity. The attempt of the Chinese Chamber of Commerce to mediate the dispute had failed by the end of October. The Chamber withdrew from any further discussions after the owners insisted on a fee of 35 cents as a basis of agreement. The pullers offered to pay 32 cents to break the deadlock, but the offer was rejected.[117] Renewed agitation occurred in the Rochore district, with rickshaws continuing to be smashed up there. Police vans and Sikh riot squads patrolled the troubled spot in an effort to prevent violence from flaring up again on the same scale as in the previous four weeks.

A successful effort to end the strike was finally made by Mr Ch'ng Sen Jin, son of the large fleet owner, Mr Ch'ng Soh Lan. Through his initiative 50 rickshaws were on the city streets on 12 November, while small numbers of them began to appear independently in the outlying districts.[118] On that weekend an understanding was reached with the pullers over hire charges; the new fixed rate, which was to include the relief contribution, was 35 cents a day. About 90 rickshaws, out of Singapore's 3,750 which had not been seen on the roads since the beginning of October, resumed work over the weekend. Hundreds of damaged rickshaws were also released by the Rickshaw Department. These shattered vehicles were taken by their owners to Queen Street, Victoria Street, Rochore Road, Duxton Road and other districts without incident.[119] The owners' first task was to restore their rickshaws, as this was the source of their wealth, and then their pride.

The 1938 rickshaw strike, which began on 4 October and lasted till 14 November, was the longest of its kind. Yet, despite its success, it seemed in the end only to hasten the cry for the abolition of rickshaws. During the five weeks that both sides stubbornly held out, a large section of the travelling public suffered, particularly the elderly and children, who had to walk to school for a change. But Singapore was learning to do without rickshaws. The strike led to a big increase in the number of bicycles registered, which only pushed along the demise of the rickshaw.

Unlike past strikes the small community of Europeans did not appear to be seriously affected by or even care about the absence of rickshaw transportation by then. But the question of the strike action of the rickshawmen was an altogether different matter. The Europeans on the whole did not have any sympathy or respect whatsoever for the pullers and their cause. They were just coolies, disobedient coolies, who had defied Crown law and, once again, disturbed the city's overall peace and prosperity. Although the pullers had organized themselves, albeit on a temporary basis, into a Rickshawmen's Association to seek redress for owner exploitation, they were unable to draw such cases to the attention of the authorities, who refused to take the issue seriously, except in regard to the use of the strike.

The pullers had stopped work because of owner exploitation, hard times, and the issue of the manipulation of the monthly donation to the China Relief Fund and had expected the Chinese public to rally to their cause. But the mass of Chinese in Singapore remained apathetic, even hostile at times, refusing to support them openly. The Government condemned the stoppage; the owners refused to sit down and negotiate a prompt settlement. The owners relied on time, once all hope of a quick resolution had faded, intending to starve the pullers into submission. They were backed by the force of colonial law, for the police constantly assisted by patrolling affected areas, protecting their rickshaws, and arresting strikers. The Government and owner opposition did not diminish the pullers' strength or resolution, but magnified it.

Despite a massive display of support and sacrifice from fellow pullers, the rickshawmen had little reason for optimism. Throughout the strike, arbitration by various individuals and groups failed. The pullers lost tens of thousands of dollars, and many were reduced to hunger and destitution and were forced to take advantage of the government offer of repatriation. Furthermore, as a result of the policies of rickshaw abolitionists, the vast majority of vehicles remained firmly in the hands of a small number of *towkay*. Finally, and perhaps, most importantly, the rickshaw strike did not succeed in reaching beyond the confines of puller politics and community to touch the concerns of other Chinese coolies in a joint struggle to confront the power and prejudice of a colonial system that was overwhelming them. In the end Singapore was saved the 'humiliation' of a general strike generated by the coolies' struggle against oppression and injustice. The pullers did obtain considerable reduction in the rates of hire for their rickshaws, but the 1938 strike did not change anything else—the owners endured.

1. SMAR JD, 1901, p. 130.
2. Ibid.
3. Ibid., p. 138.
4. Ibid.
5. Ibid., p. 137.
6. Ibid., p. 130; Edwin A. Brown, *Indiscreet Memories* (London: Kelly and Walsh, 1936), pp. 72–3.
7. SMAR JD, 1901, p. 130.
8. *Singapore Free Press*, 21 October 1901.
9. SMAR JD, 1901, p. 130.
10. *Singapore Free Press*, 21 October 1901.
11. *Singapore Free Press*, 24 October 1901.
12. SMAR JD, 1901, p. 130.
13. Ibid., p. 131; *Singapore Free Press*, 26 October 1901.
14. *Singapore Free Press*, 21 October 1901.
15. Brown, op. cit., pp. 72–3.
16. *Singapore Free Press*, 21 October 1901.
17. *Singapore Free Press*, 23 October 1901.
18. Ibid.
19. Ibid.
20. *Singapore Free Press*, 21 October 1901.
21. *Singapore Free Press*, 23 October 1901.
22. Ibid.
23. Brown, op. cit., pp. 70–2.
24. *Singapore Free Press*, 24 October 1901.
25. *Singapore Free Press*, 21 October 1901.
26. *Singapore Free Press*, 23 October 1901.
27. Brown, op. cit., pp. 73–4.
28. SMAR JD, 1901, p. 131.
29. Ibid.
30. *Singapore Free Press*, 26 October 1901.
31. Brown, op. cit., p. 75.
32. SMAR JD, 1902, p. 30.
33. Ibid.
34. SMAR JD, 1903, p. 1.
35. *The Straits Chinese Magazine*, Vol. VII, No. 1 (1903), p. 25.
36. Ibid.
37. Ibid.
38. Ibid.
39. SMAR JD, 1904, p. 1.
40. *The Straits Chinese Magazine*, Vol. VII, No. 2 (1903), pp. 69–70.
41. *Singapore Free Press*, 19 June 1919.
42. Ibid.
43. *Singapore Free Press*, 23 June 1919.
44. *Singapore Free Press*, 21 June 1919.
45. Ibid.
46. *Singapore Free Press*, 23 June 1919.
47. Ibid.
48. Ibid.
49. *Singapore Free Press*, 21 June 1919.
50. SMAR JD, 1919, p. 2-E.
51. *Singapore Free Press*, 23 June 1919.
52. *Singapore Free Press*, 21 June 1919.
53. *Singapore Free Press*, 23 June 1919.
54. Ibid.
55. *Singapore Free Press*, 16 February 1920.
56. Ibid.

57. *Singapore Free Press*, 18 February 1920.
58. *Singapore Free Press*, 16 February 1920.
59. *Singapore Free Press*, 17 February 1920.
60. *Singapore Free Press*, 16 February 1920.
61. Ibid.
62. *Singapore Free Press*, 14 February 1920.
63. *Singapore Free Press*, 16 February 1920.
64. Ibid.
65. *Singapore Free Press*, 18 February 1920.
66. *Singapore Free Press*, 19 February 1920.
67. SMAR JD, 1921, p. 5.
68. *Singapore Free Press*, 19 February 1920.
69. SMAR JD, 1921, p. 5.
70. Ibid.
71. *Singapore Free Press*, 23 February 1935.
72. Ibid.
73. Ibid.
74. Ibid.
75. SMAR JD, 1935, p. 5-B; *Singapore Free Press*, 20 February 1935.
76. *Singapore Free Press*, 23 February 1935.
77. *Singapore Free Press*, 22 February 1935.
78. *Singapore Free Press*, 25 March 1935.
79. Ibid.
80. SMAR JD, 1938, p. 20.
81. *Singapore Free Press*, 5 October 1938.
82. Ibid.
83. *Singapore Free Press*, 6 October 1938.
84. *Singapore Free Press*, 5 October 1938.
85. *Malaya Tribune*, 8 October 1938.
86. *Singapore Free Press*, 5 October 1938.
87. Ibid.
88. *Malaya Tribune*, 8 October 1938.
89. Ibid.
90. Ibid.; *Singapore Free Press*, 8 October 1935.
91. *Singapore Free Press*, 8 October 1935.
92. Ibid.
93. *Malaya Tribune*, 10 October 1938.
94. *Singapore Free Press*, 18 October 1938.
95. *Singapore Free Press*, 21 October 1938.
96. *Singapore Free Press*, 11 October 1938.
97. *Malaya Tribune*, 12 October 1938.
98. Interview with Ho Bee Swee, AOHD, Reels 12 and 13.
99. SCII of Low Nong Nong, No. 597, 18/10/38.
100. Ibid.; *Singapore Free Press*, 18 October 1938.
101. SCII of Low Nong Nong, No. 597, 18/10/38.
102. *Singapore Free Press*, 19 October 1938.
103. SCII of Low Nong Nong, No. 597, 18/10/38.
104. *Singapore Free Press*, 19 and 28 October 1938.
105. Ibid.
106. *Singapore Free Press*, 21 October 1938.
107. *Singapore Free Press*, 12 October 1938.
108. *Singapore Free Press*, 21 October 1938.
109. *Singapore Free Press*, 19 October 1938.
110. *Singapore Free Press*, 4 November 1938.
111. *Singapore Free Press*, 13 and 18 October 1938.
112. *Malaya Tribune*, 12 November 1938.

113. *Singapore Free Press*, 7 October 1938.
114. *Malaya Tribune*, 25 October 1938.
115. *Singapore Free Press*, 11 November 1938.
116. Ibid.
117. *Singapore Free Press*, 10 November 1938.
118. *Malaya Tribune*, 12 November 1938.
119. *Malaya Tribune*, 14 November 1938.

Jiksha Statio

Part II

The Rickshawmen of Singapore: The Structure of Life

9 To be a Rickshaw Coolie

SINGAPORE was a path to prosperity in the minds of Hengwah and Hockchew emigrants at the end of the nineteenth century. Knowledge of success brought back by *kheh thau* and kin from the *Nanyang* perpetuated the belief among peasants that the 'progress' of Singapore could provide a job; perhaps even an opportunity for fame and fortune. They had no chance at all in their villages. Poverty was rife. Life was bitter. The landlords refused to give them the means of subsistence—land. Nor did they always provide the rice they needed in a time of trouble. The crux of the matter was the peasants worked too hard and for too little. For an unemployed youth who had no family, no roots, Singapore was even a fine city to starve in: 'Even starving here was better than starving in the country. There were things to look at, sounds to listen to, colour and voices everywhere. All you needed was to be willing to sell your strength. There was so much money . . . it couldn't be counted.'[1] In such circumstances lineages or even whole villages could not avoid sending their men to work the astonishing wave of economic development that swept up Singapore in the last years of the nineteenth century. The spectre of starvation in China and the pull of the Singapore dream was the basis of most decisions to emigrate. The goal of the men who left was clear: to return to those who remained behind, with dignity and wealth to buy land. Hengwah and Hockchew immigrants, who came to Singapore in search of success, were assisted by secret societies, voluntary associations and kin who already lived in the city, to get a job.

Peasants constituted the largest percentage of rickshawmen. But many emigrants had no occupation before they came to Singapore. To earn a livelihood as a rickshaw coolie was the first choice of the jobless rural migrant. Pulling rickshaws called for a minimum of special skills; it only required coordination, physical strength, and stamina. Those who had no vocation chose rickshaw pulling because it afforded a reliable, low daily income. Payment was immediate and in cash: '. . . he earned his keep by selling strength in one day labour jobs after another. But he realised before long that pulling a rickshaw was the easiest way of all to earn money.'[2] Hawking, on the other hand, could not always guarantee a subsistence. It was an occupation that initially involved problems of capital expenditure, or credits and debts:

> Be a street vendor? All he had for capital was five dollars. And besides, the carrying pole had to be bought before hand [*sic*]. And what kind of goods

> brought in enough to live on anyway? Pull a rickshaw and you could make thirty or forty cents easy but you need capital to be a street vendor and there was no guarantee you'd be able to clear enough money to pay for three meals. Wait until he'd eaten up his capital and then go pull a rickshaw? But wasn't that the same as pulling down your pants to fart and a waste of five dollars? He couldn't piddle this five dollars away in pennies and dimes—it was his very last hope![3]

Young *singkeh* did not treat rickshaw pulling as a last resort.

Technology, problems of urban growth and mass transport created a new occupation in Singapore. Since most *singkeh* were neither skilled nor educated, they made no bones about settling into the city to pull rickshaws. A good many, however, became rickshawmen not through misfortune or chance. It was rather by vocation. As brothers, fathers and sons of sojourning families they followed in the footsteps of kindred, clansmen, and thousands of others. They were only too glad to place themselves within the lower stratum of Hengwah and Hockchia society to pull a rickshaw through Singapore's streets. There is a strong sense of occupational continuity among the men of these dialect groups. Once they started pulling rickshaws as a profession they rarely gave it up. The rickshaw they drew became the symbol of their lives and destiny. It was perceived by them and others as a cause of happiness, misery, alienation and death.

Ng Kar Eng became a rickshaw puller because he did not have friends who did anything else. There was no other way; his mate was a rickshaw puller, so he had to earn his living in the same manner. 'That's how it was,' Kar Eng reminisced of the 1930s. At first he did not know how to pull a rickshaw. His friend taught him: 'I understood what he told me. Initially, he took me to particular places, he showed me for several days the Pearl's Hill area, the streets, the street names, he also showed me how to run, so I learnt.'[4] The elderly puller paused, and then explained in detail about the skill involved in learning to pull a rickshaw:

> He taught me how to turn when pulling the rickshaw, for example, how to maintain control going uphill; and how to go downhill by slowing down. If going uphill, get a tighter grip so that it won't roll back; coming downhill I have to keep a secure footing, in order not to crash; if I want to turn, I can't do a sharp turn, when I am approaching the turn, I should slow down.[5]

The learning effort caused extreme physical discomfort and pain to the body. The suffering of the novice was so hard for most of them. *Singkeh* like Ng Kar Eng ran about until their arms, chest and legs ached. There was that humiliating moment when their lungs became starved of oxygen. Short of breath, sweat-soaked, they walked along the laterite roads in search of shade and a breath of fresh air, hoping the pain would subside. Some felt strengthened by learning how to breathe properly, and were made tougher and more self-confident. Even when hardening themselves to the early experience of pulling, it took weeks or even months before the aches and pain disappeared. But for some, especially the frail, the torment never went away completely. Some coolies were philosophical about their own suffering:

> He decided to pull a rickshaw, so he set out to get one to pull. First he rented a battered one and practised. He did not make any money the first day. He didn't do too badly the second day but then he had to spend the next two days lying down; his ankles had swelled up like gourds and he couldn't lift his feet. He endured it. He didn't care how much it hurt. He knew it was unavoidable, a stage of rickshaw pulling he must experience. He would be unable to run fearlessly unless he had been through it.[6]

Learning the technique of rickshaw pulling was as difficult a task as getting the necessary physical strength and stamina. Neophytes often had to perfect it while running on bad road surfaces down congested streets in Singapore. They had to find out how to hold the shafts—high, medium or low—and steer while stopping or turning, in order to minimize jolting of passenger or goods. To pull at any speed without caution was full of danger. The greenhorn had to develop an awareness of both, when and how to pull people and loads about at a dog trot, the rickshawman's normal gait, or at a faster pace, and when to slow down, or suddenly stop. Hills were particularly ominous for the newcomer. The extra effort involved in pulling a heavy load up a steep hill was frequently accompanied by physical strain and, in some cases, even heart attack for those who threw caution to the wind and refused to slow down. The rickshaw had a high centre of gravity.[7] Let us move beyond description and see what happens when an inexperienced puller loses control of the balance and steering of his vehicle on a steep incline. In November 1922, Ng Pang Suah, an elderly Teochiu shopkeeper, was riding in a rickshaw going along Lorong 3, Geylang Road. On the first and fifteenth days of each month for the past ten years, since he first came to Singapore, Ng Pang Suah had gone to the Teochiu 'Bat Tai Miew' in Geylang to worship. People always got out of their rickshaws at a bridge and walked across to reach the temple but the shopkeeper, being an elderly, heavy man, did not want to do so. He insisted on the puller going over the old, broken wooden bridge about 1½ miles in from Geylang Road. It was too steep. The rickshawman got near the top and lost control. The rickshaw ran backwards and went over the side into the river. The puller managed to swim to the shore and disappeared; the old man barely got out of the water only to die shortly afterwards; and the brand new rickshaw was carried away by the tide.[8] Here is the rickshawman as he so often was depicted by Europeans—the unthinking coolie conditioned to carry out orders. It was a risky thing to try and cross the bridge in a rickshaw, let alone one with a heavy passenger. The status of the old *towkay* made the coolie try to pull him across it. But the young puller was more vulnerable for other reasons. He lacked good judgement and without the strength and experience he could not brake suddenly and thus prevent the accident from having occurred.

A coolie's technique with a rickshaw was a source of interest and concern to fellow pullers, and often to potential customers, especially Europeans. Some had natural ability when it came to rickshaw pulling:

> He got his stride right after three weeks of work. He knew his way of running really looked good. The way a rickshaw man ran was proof of his ability and qualifications. That splay footed fellow, flopping his feet down onto the ground like a pair of rush leaf fans, is undoubtedly a beginner fresh from the village. That man with his head sunk way down and his feet scraping the ground, who puts on a show of running but isn't moving much faster than he walks, is one of the fellows over fifty. The ones who have all the experience they need but not much strength have another method. They push their chests way out and hold their stomachs way in. They raise their knees high. They stretch their necks and heads forward when they move. They look like they are running with all their might, but in fact they aren't a bit faster than anyone else. They rely on exaggerated gestures to maintain their dignity. Hsiang Tzu certainly never chose to conduct himself in any of these ways. His legs were long, his stride was long, his torso was firm. There was scarcely a sound when he set out. His stride seemed to expand and contract. The rickshaw shafts did not wobble, which made the passenger feel secure and comfortable. Tell him to stop and no matter how fast he was going at the time, he'd be standing still in two more light steps. His strength seemed to permeate every part of the rickshaw. He ran with his back bent forward, his hands gripping the shafts lightly; he was energetic, smooth in his motions, precise. He didn't appear to be in a hurry and yet he ran very fast, but without jeopardising anyone.[9]

Ida Pruitt speaks directly about the skills of rickshaw pullers and travelling in rickshaws in the Peking of the 1920s:

> They were, or considered themselves to be, the aristocrats of the unskilled labour of the city, and put on airs. And never, if more than two or three of these were in a group, could they resist the urge to race, to show off their strength and dexterity, and also their style of running. They also loved to turn corners. They seemed to feel that the more corners they turned, the shorter the distance; but I was sure they loved the sensation of control given them by turning the corners neatly and at as great a speed as they could, still keeping both wheels on the ground, or almost on the ground. I would not be surprised if among themselves this was one of the criteria by which they judged themselves. I often wondered how they could anticipate each other's actions quickly enough to avoid locking wheels or running the shafts of the rickshaws into each other's cars. Sometimes a rickshaw boy would leap into the air and swerve to one side when the rickshaw in front slowed suddenly, but I never saw a passenger spilled in any of these races, nor anyone hurt.[10]

Rickshawmen were usually quick to make a distinction between a skilful and an unskilful puller to the Coroner as the risk of accidents increased with the advent of motorized public transport and private cars. Tay Ah Choo described Toh Ah Soh, his 24-year-old Hengwah cousin, who was run over and killed by a tram, as 'not a very good puller'.[11]

The work was hard and the climate made a rickshaw coolie's life even more unbearable. His face was covered with choking red dust in the hot, dry months and splattered with water and mud during the monsoon.

Many new pullers first saw Singapore in the South-west monsoon, when the city was under assault from an old adversary—the weather. Singapore's red laterite dust was at its peak, hot breezes swirling the fine soil from the city streets on to the rickshawmen. The red powder stung their skin, clogged their throats, and penetrated the windows and doors of the tenement houses where they lived. A red haze hung over much of the city at this time of the year; day after day, convoys of rickshaws whirling down the streets, just yards in front of one another, vanished in the red dust by mid-afternoon. Through the grit, Singaporeans watched poker-faced pullers running home, bowed and choking on the dust. Some with long *towchang* (queues) had developed red streaks along their plaited hair. The dust raised by the whirling motion of the rickshaw's wheels and the padding of the puller's feet caused discomfort to passengers too:

> ... enough dust climbed into the air to make those of us in the back rickshaws see as through a gauze veil. Lao Tai Tai coughed the dust out of her throat. "They like to race, but it is dangerous, especially for one as old as I am," and she looked slightly apprehensive. A spill on the ground was not the kind of excitement she wished.[12]

John Cuylenburg, whose career spanned more than half a century as a medical practitioner, was impressed as a child by these filthy roads: 'Singapore about 1902 was quite undeveloped, with roads radiating from the business centre for about two miles. These roads were of laterite, and red dust was the order of the day everywhere, especially on warm days.'[13]

When the sun was overhead at midday, the heat was devastating. For new men trying to earn a living by the sweat of their brow, this time of day was not favourable towards them. Their time was early evening and at night after the sun had gone down. But not all the untried spared themselves. They could not afford to be idle, and face the prospect of hunger or indebtedness. Some, sweat-soaked and edgy, followed old hands on the dusty roads for hours on end in search of fares. Cuylenburg reminds us, though, that the laterite roads at the beginning of the century were not what they are now: '... shady trees lined them everywhere, so that the tired, ricksha-puller had some shelter whilst he waited patiently for a fare. One of the most beautiful thoroughfares was Beach Road, with its well spaced and blooming flame-of-the-forest trees.'[14] The strongest and most experienced went further afield and continued to pull, albeit slowly, through the scorching heat of the noonday sun on roads where there was no shade. On such days the work seemed more distasteful and exhausting, even for these men:

> Dogs crawled along with their red tongues dragging. The nostrils of horses ... flared out. The street vendors didn't dare yell and the asphalt pavements began to melt. It was so bad it seemed the sun would even melt the brass shop signs. The streets were very quiet, except for monotonous banging and clanging from the metal working shops which annoyed people. Rickshaw pullers were well aware that they wouldn't eat if they didn't get a move on, but they, too, were reluctant

to look for business. Some parked their rickshaws in a shady place, put the top up, and took a nap in the rickshaw. Some burrowed into teashops and drank tea. Others didn't take their rickshaws out at all; they just went out and looked around to see if there was any possibility of working. Those who were out working lost face quite willingly, even if they were the most prepossessing of fellows. They didn't dare run and just shuffled along with their heads down. Every well became their lucky star. It didn't matter how far they'd gone—when they saw a well they hurried over to it. They'd just take a long drink at the trough along with the horses ... if there wasn't any freshly drawn water. And there were those who, coming down with cholera ..., just went on and on until they collapsed and never stood up again.[15]

Sometimes, too, pullers collapsed fatally, from over-exposure to the sun. This is what happened to the Hokkien rickshawman, Ong Keng, on 3 August 1912. He was found prostrate next to his rickshaw dying from sunstroke in Macao Street. A Malay constable placed the coolie, who was breathing with difficulty and had a high fever, in his rickshaw to die, just as the sun set.[16] Ong Keng and others had to recognize a simple truth against their hopes for tomorrow: one cannot stop the sun.

The air was fresh during the monsoon. But the laterite clay turned into mud in the rainy season. The old picturesque roads and narrower streets leading into and out of Singapore became impassable. Roadways in outlying villages disintegrated, washing away in the wet:

Geylang and Kallang roads were then in very poor condition, with huge holes that had to be negotiated carefully by rickshas, gharries and old-fashioned motor cars, the springs of the last very often cracking up under the strain. In fact, about 1921 when I began private practice, it took me about forty-five minutes to get to Katong in my second hand two seater motor car![17]

Singapore was a filthy place at this time of the year without proper street paving and sidewalks. Old photographs and pictorial postcards present the rickshaw puller standing in ankle-deep water in the heart of town or negotiating torrents of mud to get across a kampong track at the edge of the city.[18] Torrential rain that went on for days was an arch-adversary:

Everybody was alarmed and frantic as if some great disaster loomed. Rickshaw pullers hurriedly put up rain covers, shopkeepers scurried to take down their signs, street vendors scrambled around stowing away their goods and mats, and pedestrians rushed by.... There was yet another flash, white and clear and right overhead. The fast falling rain drops came with it and forced the dust to leap upward, giving the ground a rainish look of its own. Many huge drops pelted Hsiang Tzu on the back and he shivered twice ... the dust flew in all directions, and the rain fell in sheets. Wind, earth and rain were all mixed up together ... there wasn't a dry spot on him and his hair was wet under his straw hat. The water on the ground covered his feet. It was already hard to walk. The rain above pelted his head and back, swept across his face, and wrapped around his loins. He couldn't lift his head, couldn't open his eyes, couldn't breathe, and couldn't move forward. He was forced to stand in the middle of all that water without knowing where the road was or what front, back, left, and right were. All he was conscious of was the water that chilled him to the bone and sloshed over him. He was aware of nothing except a great vague hotness in his heart and the sound of rain in his ears. He wanted to put the rickshaw down but didn't know where to put it. He thought about running but the water held his feet. He could only keep moving, pulling the rickshaw with his head down one step at a time and more dead than alive. The passenger seemed to have died right there in the rickshaw. He let the rickshaw man risk his life in the rain without saying a word ... when he looked at how dripping wet he was, he knew he'd only get the shivers if he stopped. He ground his teeth and, paying no attention to whether the water was deep or shallow, began to run. He hadn't been running long when another flash came close behind another darkening of the sky and rain blurred his vision again.[19]

The danger from tropical thunderstorms was especially great for rickshaw coolies; in rainy weather they usually ran with their heads down, and when passengers wanted to guide them it was hard if the hood and apron were up. The problem of how best to deal with wet weather was a difficult one for them. Furthermore, reckless driving, roadside parking bans, and traffic congestion combined with the rain to make their lives even more perilous. During the rainy months the roads became slick and wet, particularly those that were being covered with tar to accommodate motor vehicles. From 1914 onwards the Coroner's Records show cars, trucks, and trolley buses skidding out of control on slippery road surfaces and knocking down and killing several rickshaw pullers every year. The Coroner, F. G. Bourne, in handing down his findings of the inquest into the death of the Hengwah puller Ling Kheng Teh in 1928, appended the following rider on the hazardous condition of the city's roads in wet weather:

The accident would appear to have been principally due to the slippery surface of the road at the time. In August 1927, there was a fatal accident at practically the same place which was attributed to the polished and greasy surface of the road. There is no doubt that some of the polished surfaces of certain thickly crowded streets while excellent when dry become extremely dangerous directly when their surfaces become wet.[20]

The rain was also dangerous because it was never far away from illness. Some could not afford to stop and seek refuge; they had to support themselves, to put by money to return to China or satisfy their craving for opium. They knowingly risked their health time and again. This was the complexity of the problem posed by the rain; how to remain hale and hearty pulling a rickshaw, while the rain poured down on the weakest, exhausting or even killing:

The greatest loss of all resulted from the sickness brought on by the rainwater. All of them, young and old, were out in the streets looking for a deal all day and the furious rain of summer could pelt down on their heads at any time. They all sold their strength to make a living and were always covered with sweat. . . . The children got sick and there was no money for medicine. A spell of rain ... sprinkled death onto many of the poor children in the city. The adults got sick and that was even worse. Poets chant about the lotus 'pearls' and double rainbows that come after rain but poor people suffer from hunger when the wage earners are sick. . . . The rain falls on the rich and on the poor, falls on the just and on the unjust. But the truth is that the rain is not even handed at all because it falls on an inequitable world.[21]

While there were only trams, a few buses, and a limited number of motor cars in Singapore, the prime mover was still manpower, not motorpower. The serious business of life, the hauling of passengers to the central business district, markets or schools and to the brothels was done by the rickshaw coolie. Commodities, manufactured and agricultural, also moved from producer to consumer in rickshaws; pullers hauled huge jars to market, carting fish, fruits, vegetables and other goods. This reality forced the rickshawman to recognize, once he stepped between the shafts, that his physical strength—in other words, his own lungs, chest and legs—was his most precious possession. His body, and its state of fitness or neglect, was the key to winning or losing his fortune. Rickshawmen had to have the capacity to undergo prolonged strain. Loads of several hundred pounds had to be pulled all over Singapore each day. Ng Kar Eng knew one had to be physically strong: 'If you can't pull, then there's no way. You must have strength, without strength, there's no way.'[22]

Pullers were required by law to travel with reasonable speed and yet, at the same time, manoeuvre their heavily loaded vehicles with care, prevailing over traffic in the way, and in all conditions.[23] The strength and stamina of the Singapore rickshaw coolie could be quite extraordinary:

The account I wrote at the time goes into details about that ride, but it is sufficient here to say that we left the village at 6.20 p.m., and I was home in Zetland House at 7.15, having done the journey of over eleven miles, including the climb up the hill at Bukit Timah, in five minutes under the hour, without changing rickshaws or pullers! Believe me, pullers were pullers in those days.[24]

The Reverend Cook also remembered the staying power of certain men who were capable of travelling uncommon distances, and in the short space of several hours:

With a good puller I have done the fourteen miles from Kranji to Singapore in a little more than two hours, and that once with a man who had just arrived from Singapore with two Malays a quarter of an hour before. He only rested to have a drink of rice-water and a rub down. Had he been an opium smoker, he would have crawled for a few miles till he could get rid of his fare into another rickshaw.[25]

There were limits to what most pullers could endure. When it came to this type of trip, novices were excluded. They learned to pull heavier loads over much shorter distances. Nor could all of them run at an even pace without swaying a little, when pulling an excessive load, or climbing up hills.

The rickshawmen of Singapore were divided not only by place of origin and speech but also according to physical strength and age. Their gait, and the powerful figure that went with it, was responsible for the reputation of the top-ranking rickshawmen:

> Those who are young and strong and springy of leg rent good-looking rickshaws and work all day. They take their rickshaws out when they feel like it and quit when they feel like it. They begin their day by going to wait at rickshaw stands or the residences of the wealthy. They specialise in waiting for a customer who wants a fast trip.... The members of this band of brothers generally have two hopes; either to be hired full time, or to buy a rickshaw....[26]

But there were those who did not have the stamina. They were either too young or too old, or in poor physical condition. These coolies were invariably left out of groups that gathered at the best spots in Singapore:

> It is not easy for those who are over forty and under twenty to find a place.... Their rickshaws are rickety. All they can do is start out very early, hoping that they can earn the rickshaw rental and their expenses for one day.... Their rickshaws and they run very slowly. They work long hours on the road and come out short on fares. They are the ones who haul goods at the melon market, fruit market, and vegetable market. They don't make much but there's no need to run faster either.[27]

Opium smokers were among the worst off in this respect, and they came in for some of the toughest criticism from their comrades for lacking stamina but refusing to get out of the business. Say Kong, who came to Singapore in 1903 when he was 32 years old, could pull a rickshaw 10 miles and told a member of the Opium Commission that he could draw him to Kranji and back. However, he went on to reveal that he had taken to pulling at night, unlike in the past.[28] It was too hot during the day. Say Kong, an opium smoker, did not like the heat. But without opium men like him could not pull. Rickshaw coolies who were heavily addicted were unable to work for a single moment once the time came to have their pipe. They often insisted on leaving their passengers on the spot, as they began to experience withdrawal symptoms. Some even went so far as to say that they did not care about the fare. They simply had to stop and have their opium.[29] The Rickshaw Department received many complaints of this sort.[30] The craving came with some once, with others twice, per day. After three years of opium smoking a man could still pull a rickshaw, although few wished to travel in it. The worst cases could take an hour to cover less than a mile. The Reverend Cook commented on the decrepitude of such pullers in 1907:

> I should like such to have had some of my experiences of opium smokers, both in their own homes and in business. When caught in a heavy tropical downpour, woe betide you if you have a broken down opium-smoker to pull your rickshaw! On such occasions, for many a year we used to sigh for the long promised railway.[31]

The length of time a coolie could pull a rickshaw depended on the state of his health, the age he started his career and personal circumstance. In

1908 the Government found it difficult to ascertain how long a man could remain a rickshaw puller in Singapore. Mr Hooper stated some had been pulling for 10 years.[32] Some others had the calling for 15 or 16 years but this period was far above the average length of time, unless they went to China and came back.[33] There were even some older men who had been in Singapore longer. One official knew a non-opium smoker who had been pulling rickshaws for over 20 years. It is quite likely though that most lasted only 5 or 6 years and then returned to China. Significantly, enquiries in 1924 disclosed that the average length of time opium smokers had been plying their trade was 9½ years.[34] Most could not afford to go back to China to rest and recuperate. Nevertheless one remarkable old man aged 55 proved a hardy individual could last long, and still smoke opium! He told the Opium Commission that he had been a puller for 30 years; he was an inveterate opium smoker and had been back to China four times to convalesce, was married, spent about half of his earnings on opium and swallowed *chandu* or *chandu* dross.[35]

In an occupation where strength counted for so much the Colonial Government, through the watchful eye of the Rickshaw Department, paid attention to the physical characteristics and appearance of the pullers. Rickshaw coolies were required to be physically fit by colonial law. Owners sorely in need of labour, as Singapore expanded and rickshaws became the vogue, were in the habit of employing raw *singkeh* and boys, who were too weak and too young, to be rickshaw pullers. This practice had become commonplace by 1900 and was always a danger to the puller.[36] Many of these underaged youth did not have the necessary degree of physical depth and were broken on the wheel: 'Very few of those under twenty—and some start at eleven or twelve—became handsome rickshawmen when older. It is very difficult for them to grow up healthy and strong because of the deprivation they suffer as children.'[37] If a coolie could not pull a rickshaw properly because of age or unfit condition, he was liable to be confronted by either an irate passenger, or a peon on the spot, arrested, and tried before the Registrar for being 'physically weak', or 'ragged and dirty' in appearance. Eight hundred and ninety-two men were charged in 1901 alone for 'weakness', while thousands of others were found guilty of wearing 'bad clothes' annually.[38] A rickshawman to be judged on the basis of physical appearance 'sickly', 'broken-down', 'feeble' or 'decrepit' could spend his last cents in court. But he could rarely afford to reject his ambition and vocation, and give up for want of physical stamina. As long as he remained a rickshaw coolie his life and work were locked in the strength of his body, no matter how frail.

These laws provide not only a guide to the way the Rickshaw Department responded to rickshaw pulling as hard work, but also insight into how Europeans sought to deal with an occupation and the thousands of Chinese around them learning it, as they strove to establish 'modern' Singapore. The physical characteristics associated with pulling a rickshaw improperly were not only punishable before the law but perceived by

Europeans to signify a moral danger. This was particularly felt to be the case with regard to opium smokers. They were considered to lack moral fibre and self-restraint, and to be unclean, in short, disease-ridden—an outright moral if not physical danger to the welfare of the passenger and the community at large.

This obsession with the rickshawman's feeble constitution is most apparent in the language used by owners and coroners to identify them and describe the causes of their death. There are few owners' testimonies which do not have some physiological reference on the poor state of the deceased puller's health or physical condition. Lim Ah Phong, a 21-year-old Hockcha owner, stated that 'Ah Kai was an old man, a chandu-smoker, not a bright person, of poor physique'.[39] Ng Liew, a Hokkien rickshaw puller, was kicked to death by an unknown Malay in Jalan Besar on 1 October 1924. The following was noted in the finding: 'Ng Liew was weak and emaciated and that the injuries were not such as would cause the death of any normal healthy man.'[40]

It is the terse 'body language' of the Certificate of Coroner's Views that explicitly links the regulation of the rickshaw trade, and a set of rules that made it an offence for a puller to be weak, to a vocabulary of death used in post-mortem investigations of rickshaw coolies. The similarity of usage of this legal and medical vocabulary, although by no means a coincidence, is nevertheless striking. The Registrar and Coroner had little to do with each other directly. Still they thought in the same 'body language' regarding the rickshawmen with all that it implied, to regulate and describe them as a separate group in life and death. The language of the views recite the physical characteristics of men who could no longer be legally fined by Mr Hooper's Court for being short of breath and dizzy on a hillside, or pose a symbolic danger to Europeans in Singapore, because of their inequality of strength. Let us look for a moment at just a few cases between 1906 and 1910. Some of the men have no names. In 1906, the Coroner described Hok Keh Sing as 'a cooly who sometimes pulled a rikisha, somewhat thin'; Yong Kee Sia, 'rather thin, but no signs of disease'; Ong Ah Peh, 'spare'; in 1907, Toh Luat, 'an unhealthy man'; Ling Kee Kee, 'emaciated, feeble'; in 1908, Hoh Monh, 'once a rikisha puller, latterly sick'; unknown, 'feeble, dirty'; Choo Tang Giok, 'somewhat thin'; in 1910, unknown, 'about 25, looks sickly'.[41]

The physical characteristics and technique of the rickshaw coolie were never emphasized so strongly as in the years 1929–35. The 'rubber revolution' that converted more than two-thirds of the cultivable land of the Malay States into a vast rubber garden, collapsed at the onset of the world depression with dire consequences for Singapore:

> Rapid advances in ... commerce and industry took place after the Great War and the prosperity of Singapore seemed assured, when suddenly the Great Depression of 1929 shook our very foundations. It shattered all our hopes. A period of unprecedented unemployment stalked the land, and the repercussions of the Slump in America and Europe were felt here. It was only then that we realised how unsafe it was to have 'all our eggs in one basket'—in tin and rubber![42]

Unemployed Chinese from the peninsula flocked into the city in their thousands to work the rickshaws. Their obvious inexperience was often accompanied by weak hearts and other physical shortcomings. The years of working in tin mines and rubber estates had left their mark. This state of affairs was highlighted in the Annual Report of the Rickshaw Department for 1930: 'The physique of the majority of the pullers is poor, and their traffic sense practically nil. It seems that only the very lowest type seek this form of employment now.'[43]

The development of Singapore required the recruitment of Chinese labour. Hidden behind the high trade profits, the motivating force of this City's colonial policy, was constant pressure to treat the quality of the rickshawman as a commodity, and subject his health and physical appearance to strict regulation under the law. The Colonial Government and a municipal administration were in need of mass transport. *Towkay* were in need of labour to pull rickshaws in the boom years. Here was where the path to prosperity started for the young, strong *singkeh*. Some found out how to pull rickshaws without jolting, around the narrow congested streets of Chinatown, running miles on dusty or rain-swept laterite roads on the outskirts of the city, learning to concentrate their breath and release their body's strength at will. The men who accomplished this technique learned to pull rickshaws, kept their health, and usually avoided the summons of the Rickshaw Court.

But the Singapore of the Depression, 'the Clapham Junction of the Eastern Seas', as Europeans referred to it, attracted only grizzled non-professionals and hapless near-neophytes:

> They never expected to have anything to do with pulling rickshaws. But when faced with a choice between living and dying, they'd had to grab the shafts of a rickshaw. They were ... workmen who had lost their jobs. When the time came when they had nothing left to sell or pawn, they gritted their teeth, held back their tears, and set out on this death-bound road. Their best years are already gone and now the poor food they eat becomes the blood and sweat that drips on the pavement. They have no strength, no experience, and no friends. Even among their co-workers they are alone.... They'll get a fare and then beg for 'understanding and pardon'.[44]

Rickshaw pulling was strenuous work. Thus, it is all the more ironic, that the physique of the rickshawman, which Colonial officials of the 1930s described as being very weak and typical of all coolies, became an important pretext to legitimate efforts to abolish rickshaws.

1. Lao She, *Rickshaw* (the novel *Lo-T'o Hsiang Tzu*), translated by Jean M. James (Honolulu: The University Press of Hawaii, 1979), p. 31.
2. Ibid., p. 4.
3. Ibid., pp. 107–8.
4. Interview with Ng Kar Eng, AOHD, Reel 2.
5. Ibid.
6. Lao She, op. cit., p. 6.
7. UNNAYAN in association with T. H. Thomas, *Rickshaws in Calcutta* (Calcutta: UNNAYAN, 1981), p. 37.
8. SCII of Ng Pang Suah, No. 431, 28/10/22.
9. Lao She, op. cit., p. 7.
10. Ida Pruitt, *Old Madam Yin. A Memoir of Peking Life 1926–1938* (Stanford: Stanford University Press, 1979), pp. 114–15.
11. SCII of Toh Ah Soh, No. 183, 18/4/25.
12. Pruitt, op. cit., p. 115.
13. John Cuylenburg, *Singapore through Sunshine and Shadow* (Singapore: Heinemann, 1982), p. 3.
14. Ibid., p. 5.
15. Lao She, op. cit., pp. 176–7.
16. CCVS of Ong Keng, No. 5, 4/8/12.
17. Cuylenburg, op. cit., p. 19.
18. See, for example, postcard no. 323 in *Singapore Retrospect through Postcards: 1900–1930* (Singapore: Sin Chew Jit Poh: Archives and Oral History Department, 1982), p. 125.
19. Lao She, op. cit., pp. 180–1.
20. SCII of Ling Kheng Teh, No. 52, 18/1/28.
21. Lao She, op. cit., p. 19.
22. Interview with Ng Kar Eng, AOHD, Reel 2.
23. SMAR JD, 1897, Appendix J, p. 37.
24. Edwin A. Brown, *Indiscreet Memories* (London: Kelly and Walsh, 1936), p. 70.
25. Reverend J. A. Bethune Cook, *Sunny Singapore. An Account of the Place and Its People, with a Sketch of the Results of Missionary Work* (London: Elliot Hock, 1907), p. 81.
26. Lao She, op. cit., p. 1.
27. Ibid.
28. SSOC, evidence of Say Kong, p. 265.
29. Ibid., evidence of Mr Hooper, pp. 27–8.
30. The following figures have been compiled from the return of cases against rickshawmen brought before the Registrar for leaving a fare before completion of engagement between 1893 and 1907:

1893—27	1901—136
1894—32	1902—164
1895—69	1903—257
1896—58	1904—232
1897—88	1905—202
1898—121	1906—93
1899—149	1907—92
1900—108	

31. Cook, op. cit., p. 81.
32. SSOC, evidence of Mr Hooper, p. 28.
33. Ibid., evidence of Mr Goodlands, p. 31.
34. BMOC, p. B-28. A table included in an important survey of 1,000 rickshaw pullers in Peking shows that over 80 per cent of the men pulled a rickshaw for less than 10 years. Very few reached 25 years.

Number of Years They Have Pulled	*Number of Men*
less than one year	107
1– 5 years	509
6–10 years	231
11–15 years	86
16–20 years	46
21–25 years	18
26–30 years	1
more than 30 years	2
Total	1,000

Source: 'Economic Study of the Peking Ricsha Puller', *China Economic Monthly*, 3, 6 (June 1926), p. 255, Table III.

35. BMOC, p. B-28.

36. SMAR JD, 1898, p. 102.

37. Lao She, op. cit., p. 2.

38. See cases tried before the Registrar, Deputy Registrar, and Acting Registrar in the years 1893–1907 in SMAR JD, 1893–1907.

39. SCII of Ah Kai, No. 220, 18/5/34.

40. SCII of Ng Liew, No. 386, 3/10/24.

41. CCVS of Hok Keh Sing, No. 70, 14/2/06; of Yong Kee Sia, No. 95, 19/2/06; of Ong Ah Peh, No. 166, 28/3/06; of Toh Luat, No. 47, 25/4/07; of Ling Kee Kee, No. 45, 25/5/07; of Hoh Monh, No. 53, 23/5/08; of unknown, No. 57, 23/9/08; of Choo Tang Giok, No. 67, 31/10/08; and of unknown, No. 33, 20/8/10.

42. Cuylenburg, op. cit., pp. 52–3.

43. SMAR JD, 1930, p. 7-B.

44. Lao She, op. cit., p. 2.

10 The Puller and the Public

THE rickshaw puller was a man of a hundred faces. Shopkeepers, colonial officials, businessmen, housewives, schoolchildren, sailors, tourists, pedlars, and prostitutes all turned to him whenever they wanted a ride to work, to school, to the brothels, to a rendezvous, to dispatch goods, to do the shopping, or convey a sick friend to hospital. Cheap public transport was absolutely necessary for the humdrum, pleasures and alarms of Singapore's life. That was why rickshaw pullers always seemed to have so many roles to play in the life and circumstance of the people they pulled every day. A private puller was apt to be a jack of all trades to a family, business or clan association, while a public puller usually acted as a guide and helped a visitor find a hotel, restaurant, place to shop, or even a pretty girl. He could be a good samaritan, a pimp, a witness to the dark underside of the city's life, and readily fall victim to it. Interaction between the puller and public was complex, sometimes dangerous. Seemingly chance transactions of life take on new significance, having a lot to say about the relations between a puller and customer, as thousands of men and rickshaws moved through the crowded city in search of a destination, a fare, the next meal or a dream of reunion in China. The visual record and archival evidence prove that rickshaw coolies were omnipresent on the joyous excursions of life and in moments of sudden danger and tragedy.

Coolies who pulled private rickshaws, which were rented by the month or owned outright, considered themselves more fortunate than public pullers. They were well fed and received more in earnings. It was not unusual though for a private puller to be given all kinds of tasks from sun up to sun down around the house or shop when not on the street. He might sweep out the courtyard, run an errand for a family member, chop vegetables for a large dinner and mahjong party, draw water from the well, or clean out the latrines. In the sometimes frenetic world of prominent Chinese traders and leaders, a private rickshaw puller could not refuse to help out in the daily business affairs and ordinary household life, even when overworked:

> Hsiang Tzu almost fainted after his first day at work. The senior wife had to be taken to the markets to shop for food first thing in the morning. The young masters and mistresses had to be taken to school as soon as Hsiang Tzu and Mrs Yang returned. Their schools were all different; some went to elementary school,

some to primary school, some to kindergarten. They came in all ages and didn't look alike but they were equally obnoxious, particularly when riding in the rickshaw.... Mr Yang had to be taken to his office after the children had been delivered. Then Hsiang Tzu had to rush back to take the junior wife to the Tung An market and to visit friends and relations. And when he'd brought her back, he had to collect the children, bring them home for lunch, and take them back to school again. Hsiang Tzu thought he could get his own lunch after delivering the scholars but the senior wife sang her tune, ordering him to haul water. Although their drinking water was delivered, water for washing was hauled in by the rickshaw man. This job was not one of the regular duties of a rickshaw man, but Hsiang Tzu thought he'd better go along with it. He said nothing and filled the stone cistern. Then the junior wife ordered him to go out and buy some things as soon as he put down the water buckets and was about to get his lunch.[1]

Taking the children of various wives of an upper-class family to school was a primary responsibility of the private puller. It was a common belief and family concern that it was dangerous for a young child to walk and risk an accident, getting lost, or abduction.[2] School-age children, especially the youngest, were entrusted to the care of a private puller who watched out for their safety. For decades, several thousand Chinese children travelled through the streets of Singapore each day in their own rickshaw to school. Within the confines of this old way of life mothers like Chao Seah Neo waited daily for their children to come home. She had engaged the 27-year-old Hockchia puller Kow Wuh, a popular figure in Cornwall Street where she lived, to take her young daughter and another girl from next door to school. Sadly, while watching Kow Wuh return from school with her daughter on 6 May 1930, she saw him stabbed to death as he ran up the street to rescue a shouting Hockchia puller assaulted by a gang of Malays, just minutes after delivering her child home safely.[3] Felix Chia presents a picture of his childhood in Singapore and opens a window on the life of a Baba (Straits Chinese) schoolboy who went out in a rickshaw every day. He allows Ah Thiang, his faithful puller who always waited as long as he wanted, to appear in the background of his existence again:

I remember Ah Thiang, who with his kind, used to line the street just outside my home, with some admiration and sympathy. The motor car had honked the last horse and carriage off the roads, and now it screeched its tyres at old Ah Thiang, the rickshaw puller. His weary but cheerful face always made me wonder at his forbearance, and soon it struck me that he was making the best of a bad bargain in life. He was but a little better than a beast of burden. He brought me to school and back, patiently waiting for me whenever I was detained in class, only because geometry confused me and algebra horrified me. He always helped me to carry my bag all the way to the rickshaw. For his sake I was glad when the rickshaws finally went off the streets.[4]

In Singapore private rickshaws were used by shopkeepers in dealings with customers and for the movement of goods. Pullers attached to shops had to be ready to pick up the shafts at a moment's notice. They played an important role in helping to initiate vital transactions, carrying urgent business messages at the *towkay*'s command or fetching an important customer at a cracking pace to his master's shop. Lee Hock How, who owned a 'remittance business' and spirits shop at 33 New Bridge Road, possessed his own rickshaw. Lim Choon Huat, who was paid $20 a month and his meals, was described by the shop-owner's 15-year-old son as 'our ricksha puller'. He was employed at the shop for anyone's use on shop business. Lee Hock How, the bill collector, did not usually use the rickshaw, preferring to walk. Koh Poh Soon, the manager of Chop Chye Hua Seng, the wine and spirits shop, generally rode in it.[5] Similarly, in a statement to the Coroner, Tee Choon Lye, the owner of rickshaw no. 6268, added that the deceased puller Ah Pee was 'a healthy man and had pulled for our chop for about one year. He lived at Victoria Street, but not on my premises'.[6] But we learn about Tan Moh Tee's full-time employment only because of the case of Kow Wuh's death. Tan Moh Tee pulled a rickshaw belonging to Song Kee, a sundry goods shopkeeper, who went to Cornwall Street on business at least twice a week. He always got out of the rickshaw and walked up the hilly street to spare Tan Moh Tee, who remained at the bottom. On 6 May 1930, he pulled his *towkay* there. But there was nothing he could do on that particular day to prevent Teong Choon from being stabbed to death, followed closely by Kow Wuh, the private puller of the widow, Chao Seah Neo.[7]

A private rickshaw was particularly useful to money collectors in dealing with customers all over Singapore. Leong Ah Thum, a Hakka clerk, used the rickshaw belonging to a money-collecting establishment at 81 Cross Street, to demand payment of bills and outstanding debts from hapless borrowers.[8] Pullers were also engaged by individuals on a steady basis, either for the entire day or a specific part of it, to take them to work or on their rounds in a business like hawking. Ong Teck Cheng was lucky. Only two months after he arrived from China, aged 19, he was given a steady customer to pull by a kinsman. Ong Kim Luan had pulled the Tamil cloth hawker, U Toomal Kheatomal, for three years, but when Ong Teck Cheng came he gave him this work. The *singkeh* pulled the cloth hawker and his enormous bundle of cloth for $1.50 per day from 9 a.m. till 5 p.m. He did this every day, despite his inexperience and slight frame; the Tamil referred to Ong Teck Cheng as 'Kechil' ['Small'].[9] The journey of a dhobi through the congested, torrid streets of Singapore could be simple compared to the routine tour of a cloth pedlar. Laundryman Yong Kee employed the 48-year-old Hengwah puller Low Leong to take him from his house to the General Hospital and back each day with bundles of cleaned and soiled linen.[10] Ng Kar Eng also used to take fishmongers on a similarly undeviating excursion to the Beach Road Market to bid for fish at 5 a.m. each morning: 'Some of the hawkers lived in Lavender Street, some in China Street, and some in Smith Street. At about 5 a.m. they used to ask me to take them there.' Ng Kar Eng did not go to their lodges. These small 'business people' used to come to the rickshaw agency at the crack of dawn seeking the young puller:[11]

He came himself early in the morning. After he asked me then I would take him there, it was like that. If the hawker lived in Lavender Street on that side, I would take him there. I would only take him there, I did not bring him back. When I took him for a single trip I charged him first, it was not done on a monthly basis unless a puller was taking school children; if I was carrying businessmen there was no monthly fare, the charge was always per trip.[12]

The pressures of work revealed that some customers hardly knew their private pullers at all, even though they met on a daily basis. Ng Cheow Ker, a hawker off Circular Road, recognized the 60-year-old rickshaw puller, Ng Pin, by sight, not by name. Ng Pin came every day at 9 a.m. to take the hawker to Ellenborough Market. The elderly rickshawman had done this for over a year and before that he used to pull Ng Cheow Ker's partner.[13] Ng Pin's experience cannot be considered uncommon. Private pullers did encounter a sense of distance and unwelcome from employers of the urban middle and upper classes who felt themselves to be 'better off'—they simply referred to the likes of Ng Pin as 'the coolie'.

Clerks and office staff also were taken in the morning from their houses and fetched home again each day. Puah Ah Low always took 16-year-old Irene Atlias to her work in the telephone office and brought her back to 72 Bukit Timah Road. Her mother used to pay him 40 cents per day. On 13 January 1921, Irene was on afternoon shift which meant that she left the house at 12.30 p.m. When she wanted to go the rickshaw was standing in front of the house as usual, but Puah Ah Low was nowhere in sight. He often went to a coffee-shop not far away and Irene's mother went to look for him. He was not there. She could not find 'the coolie' anywhere, so she got another rickshaw for her daughter. About 3 p.m. Puah Ah Low's body was discovered in the canal near the Atlias house. His hat and coat were lying on the grass bank. The 28-year-old Hengwah had apparently sought relief from the scorching heat while waiting for the young lady, and drowned accidentally.[14]

The fear that could surround pulling a customer on a steady basis in another district is not difficult to understand. Cursory contact and the desire to strike an immediate bargain caused pullers to fall prey to other rickshaw coolies in their 'fight' to survive. Evidence from the Coroner's inquest of Teo What Swee indicates that such fears were not exaggerated. He decided to take on a regular customer in a district usually monopolized by pullers of another dialect group. He was assaulted by two rickshawmen who later returned with others and stabbed him. Teo What Swee was taken to the General Hospital and made this statement before he died:

At 6.30 a.m. the 27th of November 1922 I was pulling a ricksha number not known along Everton Road with a Tamil clerk, name unknown, in the ricksha. I arrived at the clerk's house. I saw two rickshas, numbers unknown, pulled by two Hockchews. They were waiting in front of the clerk's house. I put my ricksha in front of the clerk's house, but the two Hockchews would not allow me to stay there. I told them I had arranged to pull the Tamil clerk every day.[15]

There were also men like the iced-drink merchant, Ng Pang Suah, who regularly went to the Teochiu temple in Geylang in the same rickshaw.[16] An old photographer's print tells us of such visits to Thian Hock Keng Temple, Telok Ayer Street, in 1900. Large numbers of pullers congregate around the steps of the main entrance to this well-known temple. Their rickshaws stand idle while their private patrons pray, at the same time other pullers are arriving with passengers intent on worshipping the goddess Ma-Cho-Pao, mother of the Heavenly Sages.[17]

Private pullers on average earned more than public rickshawmen. They paid no hire fee, and usually received their meals and/or a room as part of the contract. Lim Choon Huat was paid $20 a month, or 67 cents a day, and board; but Ong Teck Cheng received $1.50 per day from a Tamil cloth vendor without room and board. Puah Ah Low was paid 40 cents daily to pull Irene Atlias to work; he was free in non-contract hours to get as many fares as possible.[18] Private pullers also were apt to receive tips for running errands or when their *towkay* entertained, attended long dinner parties, or celebrated Chinese festivals.[19]

It was more difficult for the public rickshawman to lead a decent life. His relationship with his customer was bound to be different, as was what he received. There was greater distance, more uncertainty, and less empathy. Public rickshaws were hired out night and day to just about anybody or to convey goods. Leaving aside the problem of the variety of possible customers, it is obvious that of the factors involved, the time itself was invariably too short to foster any sense of familiarity with the person in the rickshaw. Interaction between the public puller and shop-keepers, visitors, officials and anybody else who needed transport, was far less than in the case of the private puller. It was based on contact that rarely lasted for more than a few minutes, up to a day at most. One feels nevertheless, that at least some rickshaw coolies developed in that brief span of time—the length of a journey—a sense of identity with them, if only out of fear, exhaustion, envy, or joy upon the receipt of a small windfall. They did not know their customers, yet some pullers could recognize them on the basis of physical size and appearance, from their clothes, or by the expression of their voice. The indelible impression that these strangers made was of their sheer physical bulk being a cause for distress, or as a drunken European, or a beautifully dressed *nonya* (Straits Chinese lady). Sometimes they were familiar people, even to the inexperienced puller.

Lim Ah Sui described the beginning of a dangerous journey and his two Baba passengers, who were thrust into the underworld of Singapore, and lived as criminals:

> I remember the 16th of July at 8 a.m. when I was in Upper Hokkien Street . . . a Chinese Baba, Ang Jiak Chuan, called me and I drew him to Telok Ayer Street where he went into a house. He came out of it with another Chinaman, a Baba, a thin man. . . . The second Baba had a basket and umbrella with him . . . [and] was

dressed in a black baju [shirt], [and] European shoes. I noticed the shoes when he came out of the first house in Telok Ayer Street. He had on red socks.[20]

In addition to crime, the craving for opium was apt to be strongest at night, especially for a puller like Koh Mia Siah. His passengers were less familiar to him on the evening of 10 February 1931 than in Lim Ah Sui's case. He remembered only their weight, due perhaps to the dream-like feeling of his euphoria from smoking. It was after 5 p.m. when he started out with his rickshaw. He returned home three hours later for food. Koh Mia Siah then smoked 25 cents' worth of *chandu*. He felt good but did not go to sleep. When he eventually came out on the street after 10 p.m., he got some passengers, 'some heavy and some light but [I] cannot remember how many. I was hoping to get further passengers after the lady.'[21]

Public pullers often remembered passengers who were drunk, obnoxious, or made a nuisance of themselves over directions or fares. Drunks were likely to be an unpleasant experience, even when unconscious. The Scotsman, Robert Laing, was seen staggering along Dunlop Street. He was put in a rickshaw by a police constable to be taken to hospital but died in the rickshaw. At the inquest the puller recalled how strongly the dead body smelt of alcohol.[22] On the other hand, Lim Tee Wah, who on the night of 15 July 1912 was given the rickshaw of Koh Ah Nea as a favour, suddenly found himself discussing the death of a complete stranger—a drunken European—with the Coroner. He denied emphatically ever having seen or pulled the deceased in his rickshaw. It was a case of mistaken identity. In his defence, the rickshaw coolie gave the complete trip details of his sole European passenger that afternoon. Additionally, he described himself, making it more difficult to implicate him directly in the death of the drunkard—one William Grey Nixon:

On the 15th July the previous witness [Koh Ah Nea] gave me his ricksha to pull; its number was 8968. I left the house at about 3 p.m. and returned about midnight. I know the High Street. At 9.30 that night I was on the south side of the river and was not in the High Street. The only European fare I had on that afternoon was about 4 o'clock when I picked him up near the Raffles Museum whence I took him to Selegie Road and thence to Thomson Road. I know the house I went to in the Thomson Road. I had no other European fare; nor had I any person drunk in my ricksha that night. I wear a que [*sic*] and have no bare patch at the back of my neck.[23]

In a different sort of case an old Hengwah puller, Ling Soh Kai, even mentioned the degree of drunkenness of the passengers he was pulling along Serangoon Road on a miserable November day: 'The road surface was slightly wet. It had been raining.... There were two passengers in the rickshaw. One was absolutely drunk, the other was half drunk.'[24]

Sometimes the moves that made sense to the drunks or criminals controlling the trip seemed frightening or worse to the puller. In the case of the two Baba offenders, Lim Ah Sui felt as though he was being forced to run against his will to the point of collapse. They harangued him to go faster:

I drew them both to the burial ground at Alexandra Road. There they both got out and took the basket and umbrella with them and went on the burial ground hill. In half an hour, Ang Jiak Chuan, returned and with him a Cantonese Chinaman, Ling Ah Phong. They were coming in a hurry and were panting. They came from the same hill as the two Baba had gone to. Ang Jiak Chuan and Ling Ah Phong got into my rickshaw and I drew them to town. I asked them where the second Baba was and they told me he was looking at a grave. They pressed me to go fast but I said I could not as I had a headache. They got out at Upper Hokkien Street and Ang Jiak Chuan paid me sixty cents.[25]

Sober Europeans hired only the best public pullers—strong, experienced men with muscular legs. Administrators and businessmen never walked about in the burning heat of the day if a rickshaw was handy, and when their women rode in the town proper they used one with the hood raised. The idea was widespread among pullers that to draw a European the ride had to be comfortable and swift. This view was reinforced by the fact that runners sometimes accompanied the rickshaws of *tuan besar* (Europeans of importance) to offer help 'pushing' on Singapore's steeper roads at the turn of the century:

Some of them preferred to go to office in Raffles Square or nearby by ricksha, and to show their superiority, they had in addition to the puller a runner behind, whose head emerged immediately behind the sitter. This runner also had his value in that he pushed the ricksha up the many hillocks which beset the roads—these hillocks have been flattened out by subsequent road construction.[26]

At certain times of the day, especially in the early hours of the morning, when the streets were still relatively quiet and empty, and when the air was cool, these rickshaw rides could be very pleasant: 'On the side of the Esplanade, now St Andrews Road, the trees were flowering ones, "Flame of the Forest" and other lovely trees predominating. I have seen times when we have driven along in our rickshaws to office over a veritable carpet of yellow and red flowers. A very beautiful sight.'[27] Public pullers who came across Europeans knew they had to be prepared for periods of intense hard running. Not surprisingly, rickshaw coolies with an opium habit rarely, if ever, earned a living by pulling them. The stigma involved, and the extra strength required, made it difficult for men such as Low Yah Cheong to work the hotels or other typical places where Europeans shopped or went sightseeing. This plain truth was not lost to Low Aik, a rickshaw owner, when speaking to the Coroner about Low Yah Cheong: 'On 14th July 1925 Low Yah Cheong took the ricksha out at 7 p.m. I don't know where he used to go. . . . He was an opium smoker. He swallowed opium dross—20 cents worth per day. He was only a moderate puller, no Europeans used him.'[28]

Pulling for Europeans could be lucrative. There was always the expectation that one might receive a fare far greater than the norm—unwittingly, or as an act of generosity. A good puller, especially around the hotels and those pulling 'joy riders' at night in the 1920s, was alleged to make as much as $5 a day and save at least $2, after paying expenses.[29] On the other hand, Coroner's evidence suggests that pulling for an abnormally long period and at a cracking pace on top could be fatal, no matter how young and strong. This work was doubly dangerous though because few Europeans had sympathy for the puller's needs in their haste to go about their business. Some felt pullers to be impervious to pain because they were Chinese, and compared their style of running and the tremendous physical effort involved with draught animals and machines:

> The coolies were rushing in a long line one behind the other. The perspiration was pouring from their sinewy bare backs. . . . The light little carriages rolled smoothly, the coolies trotted outstripping one another, like little horses playing for the sheer fun of it. . . . Briskly we turned in before a curious building: it was the hotel.[30]

At first Richard Sydney, author of *Malay Land*, a 1920s travelogue, had a twinge of conscience about being pulled in a rickshaw but his compunction soon disappeared:

> A fuller knowledge of this town makes it almost impossible to realise how difficult it was to find one's way about on first arrival here. The difficulty is that walking is almost taboo. If one has no car one travels by rickshaw. . . . The consequence is that one does not find one's way about on foot and so does not realise whither any road may lead. Travelling in a rickshaw for the first time is a never-to-be-forgotten experience. It seems almost inhuman to be pulled through the streets by a fellow man. This is more particularly so if your puller happens to be old and somewhat tired. There is, however, a charm about the rickshaw which one feels at first and soon forgets. To sit in these fairly comfortable small carriages and to glide along with a silent runner in front is to experience an entirely new means of locomotion. It is difficult to recapture the early thrill, though often when coming back from a long walk I have got into a rickshaw somewhere near the top of a hill and have then felt quite thrilled by the fast-moving puller who has made the rickshaw travel at a pace almost equal to that of a smartly stepping horse. The feeling of humanity very soon leaves one and the taking of a rickshaw becomes an ordinary event.[31]

The sense of distance and ambivalence in the use of euphemisms erased all feeling of compassion, allowing Europeans like Sydney to deny the reality of the act of being pulled around by a fellow human being. Few Westerners were in close and sympathetic touch with problems faced by pullers on the streets as they progressively lost their strength, and speed. Some reserved the same scorn and ridicule for them as they grew older and weaker as was cast on the opium smokers. Little pity generally was shown by European fares in the unequal competition for their custom. George Bilainkin, the editor of the *Straits Echo*, was an exception to the rule:

> I ran down the office stairs and stood facing two ricksha pullers. One was the elderly coolie who had been waiting outside for me every night at one or two o'clock, and the second was a much younger stronger fellow. I wished to be in

the hotel as quickly as I could—all alone—without anybody within hearing or sight. But I had not the spirit to disappoint the old man, so I sat impatiently in the carriage while he did his best to imitate a runner.[32]

The European women in pre-war Singapore led charmed lives. Most of them went accompanying husbands and families to enjoy the exoticism of the East and the social opportunities. They had servants to relieve them of most domestic responsibilities and took for granted the dinners and dancing at the Raffles Hotel. They made the social rounds and went on shopping sprees in European shops and the big stores situated in Raffles Place, Battery Road and Orchard Road, by rickshaw:

And now perhaps you would like to go out and see what the town itself has to offer you, and if you have not got a motor car then ring a bell and a rickshaw will come for you and you will get in. There will be no need to tell the man where to go, and unless you give him any direction he will make straight for the centre of town, which is Raffles Square : . . [which] contains shops which would not be a disgrace in London, and here one can buy almost anything one needs.[33]

Rupert Emerson, a gifted young American student of politics who went to Malaya to study 'Imperialism at high noon', found this colonial way of life in Singapore unsavory:

With the exception of very small areas devoted to the European stores and business houses and to the big hotels, one may walk for miles through the streets of Singapore . . . without ever laying eyes on a European or hearing a European word. Equally it is all too possible for Europeans and Americans to visit or even live in these cities and see little more of the oriental world than the sweating, but no doubt picturesque, back of the Chinese rickshaw 'boy' who pulls them around at a dog trot under the blazing sun from their hotel to the department store or office and back to the bar again. Just outside the [city], nestling comfortably among the shady trees of the hills, are the white villas of the British officials and the European and the wealthier Chinese businessmen.[34]

When not engaged in pulling *tuan* and *mem* (European women) some rickshaw pullers could be seen drawing stunningly clad *nonya* in the late afternoon to 'specialist' shops in Arab and High Streets for laces, sarongs, and foodstuffs.[35]

For the tourists, curiosity seekers, soldiers and sailors who flocked to Singapore, the rickshaw was the backbone of wheel traffic, and part of the port-city's 'oriental charm'. Steamers from Bangkok, Saigon, Java, Hong Kong and Australia anchored some distance off Johnston Pier in full view of the city. Their passengers and baggage were landed by launch. Waiting to meet them on arrival at the Pier were neatly stacked rows of public rickshaws. Patient muscular pullers moved back and forth along the wharf, hoping to dispatch arriving travellers to all parts of the city:

. . . I made a choice among a score of grinning rickshaw coolies and made a first test of the Malay I had acquired by diligent study on the steamer during my voyage from Australia. Much to my contentment I was correctly comprehended and a few minutes later I alighted at the fountains before the great statue of Sir Stamford Raffles—which stands, facing the sea ... in front of the Victoria Memorial Hall.[36]

European tourists wishing to shop, do some sightseeing or just experience the great deal of atmosphere Singapore offered were provided with hints on rickshaw travel in local guides. By 1931 hotel guests were advised not to hire a rickshaw for a journey of more than a mile. They were also given instructions on how to call a rickshaw: 'Panggil Kretah Hong Kong!' Some publications even had a glossary of terms with sufficient directions to enable the person to show the way in Malay to a rickshaw coolie.[37] Pullers were only too glad to offer advice to the *mem*, the curio-hunter or French sailor on what Singapore had to offer, from Malay silverware and Malacca canes which could be purchased in High Street, to superior quality jewels, laces, carvings, and silks. Eurasian and Japanese women were attractive to the European eye, but their services were more difficult to obtain.

Because of the language barrier, misunderstanding was bound to occur. Problems cropped up between pullers and European visitors over their intent, points of interest, and charges. Rickshaw drives could not be booked like seven-seater motor cars, with English-speaking guides. The resultant shouts, giving of orders and directions of the grand masters often were unintelligible to the pullers:

... the ricksha coolies still speak no known tongue. If you want to tell them where to go, you grunt hard then point; if you don't know where the place is, God help you, because the coolie won't. He'll run off somewhere where he thinks you may want to go and grin happily when he finds he's guessed wrong, after which he'll run off somewhere else and grin happily again, and so on until you and your temper are entirely lost. But please don't hit him or kick him as I too often see people doing.[38]

Misunderstanding also was created in the eye of the camera by insensitive Europeans who approached their pullers as one more curio Singapore offered to the traveller. Rickshawmen were posed as still-life subjects against backgrounds that excelled in scenic beauty, such as the primeval setting of the Botanical Gardens or facing the sea on the Esplanade. By the use of disguised settings the photographer distanced himself from the image of the straining, sweating rickshaw coolie. The resultant photograph prevented the person from facing the depth of his emotion—anxiety, guilt, pity—over having been pulled in a rickshaw by a toiling coolie. Instead, the exhausting life and the rickshaw ride became a pleasing sight to remember. Such photos robbed pullers of their humanity and, as objects of curiosity about a journey to the East, misrepresented what life they had. At least one coolie, though, drew the line when an unthinking passenger attempted to take a 'picturesque' photo of him. He took it as a sign of bad luck—an invasion of his soul: 'I came up here against a curious superstition, for my rickshaw-puller refused to have his photograph taken, lest I might enclose his soul in the body of my camera!'[39]

It was a fact though that not all their passengers were devoted to photography, bargain-hunting and sightseeing which, admittedly, Singapore provided for magnificently. Some wanted to get out of their hotels, barracks or warships amidst the smells and bustle of the living city and visit the red-light districts. In the days before the abolition of the brothels in 1927, one of Singapore's foremost industries was prostitution, and camera-slung tourists, wealthy Chinese, drunken sailors, and coolies were picked up by pullers catering to the brothel trade. Brothels were allowed in several sections of the city known as the 'district or quarter'. In 1898 the Chinese houses in Singapore were divided into public brothels, registered under the Contagious Disease Ordinance with the Chinese Protectorate, about 200 in number, with over 3,000 prostitutes, all Cantonese, and private or 'unregistered' brothels, about 150 in number, containing 600 prostitutes, chiefly Teochiu. Brothels and street prostitution were such a widespread phenomenon in Singapore because of its large bachelor migrant population.[40]

The rickshaw served many purposes. It was customary for Macao or Cantonese women and *Karayuki-san*, the Japanese call-girls of old Singapore, to ride to their assignations in curtained rickshaws. Some were even privately registered as 'brothel vehicles' for the use of the prostitutes and patrons. Numbers of these women, however, always lived outside the red-light districts, and the rickshaw coolies pimped for them, especially after 1927 when the public brothels were abolished.

Hundreds of pullers with exceptional knowledge of city life and a smattering of foreign words hung around the hotels, docks and European shops, specializing in well-off foreigners who came to Singapore on business or for pleasure. As soon as they stepped on shore, passengers landing at the wharves were liable to be met by a string of touts and rickshaw pullers calling out 'Malay Street'.[41] Tan Sam Ong, a young Cantonese puller, earned a decent income plying about the hotels and brothels in Kampong Glam, and took Europeans back and forth to the docks.[42] Pullers drew prostitute-hunting tourists, seeking amusement outside the confines of luxury hotels, dinners and dancing, through the streets of Chinatown for a glimpse of the night-life of Singapore. The rickshaw coolie ran along with his head down through the gaily lit districts past the lighted windows of houses of ill-fame until the lantern of a Japanese brothel with a large number painted on it came into view:

> On the night of the dinner I hailed a rickshaw and set off for Chinatown. My puller threaded his way through the dense crowds and hooting taxis and brought me at last to Trengganu Street, which is the Picadilly of Chinese Singapore. Presently he stopped before a shadowed doorway over which ... shone brightly the blue globe of a hanging lantern.[43]

In the late 1930s, Bruce Lockhart paid a nostalgic visit to Singapore and took one last rickshaw ride into yesteryear—a trip that invariably was meant to end in Malay Street:

My last night in Singapore I kept to myself. It was to be devoted to a return to the past. I should engage a rickisha puller, preferably one who could speak no known language, and the rest of the evening would be left to the whims of his mechanical jog-trot. . . . My rickisha puller was a scraggy, toothless old man. Like the harper in the *Lay of the Last Minstrel* he was admirably suited to perform the rites at the last rickisha ride that I shall ever take. For even if I ever return to the East, the rickisha will soon be a vehicle of the past . . . I had some difficulty in clambering into my seat. Perhaps I had lost the knack. . . . My puller spoke no Malay and no English. From his lips came a scream of unintelligible labiels. I waved an arm towards the night. With a grin he seized the shafts, and off we jogged. Twenty-five years ago we should have pulled up at a brothel, for your rickisha puller, even if he is inarticulate, knows instinctively the tastes of the tourist, and in those days Malay Street was the obvious destination of a European setting out alone at night.[44]

Each district had loyal clients. During the first part of the twentieth century Europeans—diplomats, officials, and planters—favoured the discreet Japanese women of Malay, Malabar and Trengganu Streets. Tourists, soldiers, and sailors also sought their sexual favours, as well as visiting the unregistered haunts of Malay and Eurasian women scattered in the sidelanes of the city. Brothels in China Street, Temple Street, Smith Street, and Tan Quee Lan Street were exclusively Chinese.[45] It was here that most of the pullers' time was spent, carrying Cantonese prostitutes to rendezvous with wealthy *towkay*, running errands for the women, and pulling their ordinary customers, the large migrant coolie population, no matter how drunk they might be, or poor. Rickshawmen were always eager to accept fares such as Kiong Whye who liked to smoke opium in the company of sing-song girls:

While I, Kiong Whye and Kiong Lam were smoking together [at No. 99 Duxton Road] Kiong Whye said that he was going to send for a girl the next night. He said he was going to send for Kum Chye. The next night (6/10/29) at about 7 p.m. I met Kiong Whye and Ah Ngan in Temple Street at the junction with New Bridge Road. Kiong Whye asked me to go to People's Park to have food. I went with him—just the three of us [in rickshaws]. After taking food we all went to smoke opium at Temple Street. Kiong Whye smoked. It was Kiong Whye's friend's place. While we were there . . . Kiong Whye proposed that we should all three go to Ah Ngan's place [No. 99 Duxton Road] and send for a girl. He proposed to send for Kum Chye to play on her harp. Eventually she came. Someone wrote a chit—I don't know whom—and sent for Kum Chye [by rickshaw]. She arrived before 11 p.m. with a harp and a maidservant Sam Sam. She played on the harp and sang three songs. She then remained there chatting till past 12 midnight. Then Kiong Whye took Kum Chye away. His Temple Street friend went with them. After about fifteen minutes Kiong Whye returned alone. About ten minutes later Kum Chye returned again. It started raining after Kum Chye's return. Kiong Whye had proposed to go out and take food but it began to rain and so he asked us to wait till the rain stopped. About 1 a.m. it stopped raining so we started off to People's Park in three rickshas. Kiong Whye and Kum Chye in the first ricksha, I and Mok Kuan in the second ricksha, and Ah Ngan was alone in the third rickshaw. We were at People's Park taking food till about 2 a.m.[46]

The peak hours for rickshaws in Chinatown were in the early evening when coolies would go to the brothels, and 11 p.m. to 1 p.m. when they returned home to their dormitory quarters in lodging-houses. Rush-hour passengers sometimes made an appointment to be picked up later on at a brothel. Lim Ah Sui, a rickshaw puller living at Havelock Road, recalled one such fare:

... They got out at Upper Hokkien Street and Ang Jiak Chuan paid me 60 cents. He told me to come and see him in a brothel Soon Lye Tong in Upper Cross Street which I did at 7 p.m. that night.... The prostitute with whom he was with in the brothel gave me Hong Kong ten dollars.... When I saw Ang Jiak Chuan in the brothel he was drunk. I should know the prostitute again.[47]

Chinese prostitutes also tended to move from one brothel to another by rickshaw to accommodate customers. Even when the trip was only a block or two away the women called for a rickshaw, as they were often beautifully dressed and wearing gold jewellery. These special trips of the puller and prostitute could be dangerous. The police could not prevent thieves from attacking rickshaws and assaulting and robbing the prostitutes. Incidents occurred with alarming regularity in broad daylight and brothel-keepers were known to carry whistles to make it more difficult to be set upon by ruffians. Ong Geok, a brothel-owner at 56 Jalan Sultan, was clear-headed enough to blow her whistle when a group of Chinese deliberately slowed her rickshaw down. She had hired it on 24 March 1919 at noon, and went for a ride with one of her prostitutes, a Hokkien girl named Puah Chee Lye. They travelled along Victoria Street towards Arab Street, but before they got there a Chinese man appeared suddenly and hung on to the back of the rickshaw by the hood. Then two other Chinese stepped up to the rickshaw, and quickly grabbed each shaft. When the women saw the thief holding onto the back of the rickshaw they shouted '*Tolong!*' ('Help!') Ong Geok got hold of her whistle and started blowing, but two of the men seized it, robbing her and Puah Chee Lye of their jewellery.[48] It was incidents like this that forced pullers to leave the profession after either having been wounded in self-defence or giving up their entire savings to repair a rickshaw damaged by rampaging thieves. One of the paradoxes of pulling prostitutes was that while it offered the opportunity for a relatively good income, social attitudes, public abuse of prostitutes, and criminal practice made it fraught with danger.

When they were not busy pulling their vehicles, the rickshawmen were free to avail themselves of the services of the Cantonese women. Their requests to smoke opium and have sex with the 'flower girls' of Tan Quee Lan Street were rarely turned down. The women were forced to submit to any client who could pay the fee. Particularly resented though was the high personal price coolies were often forced to pay for a moment of self-indulgence and sexual intimacy—infection with venereal disease.

In 1927 the red-light districts were closed down. Traffickers and brothel-keepers tried to carry on their business along other lines. Chinese and Japanese lodging-houses were used for brothels. The number of unlicensed lodging-houses was three times the number necessary for bona fide business. Their main concern was prostitution. Rickshaw coolies knew where these sly brothels were located. Every visitor brought by rickshaw was asked if he wanted a woman; the employees had lists of prostitutes and the rickshawmen were sent to fetch them. Girls on the streets also took their clients to lodging-houses in rickshaws. Street prostitutes were charged a percentage of their takings and rent was obtained for rooms for which otherwise there was no demand. The girls connected with the lodging-houses in the Depression years were Chinese, Eurasians, Tamils, Javanese, and Malays from the peninsula. The majority of them were young and lived with middle-aged women, often ex-prostitutes, who, as 'pocket mothers', had bought them from destitute parents.

When Japan invaded China, female refugees fled from Shanghai and Canton in their thousands to Singapore. To make a living they went on the streets, selling themselves for a few cents outside the lit-up gateway of 'The New World' amusement centre or under the shade of Flame of the Forest trees along the Esplanade. They were forced to choose between starvation and prostitution. In their choice of futures, the rickshaw puller was never far away. A European journalist vividly remembered the face of one of these street prostitutes, a Eurasian, who approached him at Dhoby Ghaut, a good place to make pick-ups from a rickshaw:

> Returning from the Worlds [Amusement Centre and Cabaret] we stop the car at the side of the Parade and half a dozen girls languidly leave their rickishas and sway across on high heels.... Some of the girls who wanted to come with us in the car were new arrivals who as yet had not learnt Malay, the language of Singapore. They were tragic question marks of war, forced, many of them, into this foul, frustrated life, usually with one end—the river. Frighteningly real people, yet in the shadows of the trees their mask faces and long thin bodies gave no impression of reality, of being flesh and blood. They were like those nameless people you see in the streets of any big city before dawn, shadows merging with shadows.... We were about to move when another girl, a Eurasian who had just drawn up in her ricksha, pushed the Chinese roughly aside, put a cracked gold slipper on the running board, and leant her elbows on the window edge. Her worn, flame-coloured silk dress rustled like tissue paper, her black dyed hair was coiled over her ears and she wore a small gold crucifix on her tawny throat. As she bent down and said 'Good Evening' in perfect English I got a photographic impression of a faded, lined face, a nose slightly hooked, a jutting chin, steady greyness of eyes with the light gone out of them, and memory jolted me like an electric shock. She was startlingly like an aunt of mine. I have never forgotten that face among the frustrated lives of the ricksha parade.[49]

At the end of every trip a fare had to be paid. The fare becomes relevant in the relationship between puller and public when deception or misunderstanding was present. Often it was the prostitute, tourist or *towkay* who held the upper hand when it came to settling the fare. The rickshaw coolie had no immediate recourse, other than pestering and physical intimidation, against bilking.[50] Passengers rarely paid the fare for which the puller was glad to work. It was notoriously common that full fares agreed to at the time of hiring were never paid up. However, as few foreigners could speak Chinese misunderstanding and disagreements over fares were bound to occur. Some pullers had no trouble until the time a European asked them a perfectly innocuous question about the fare in English. The coolie was apt to be exhausted and could not understand the stranger. Suddenly he was screaming obscenities at him—destroying him, until the curses gave way to heaving sighs and all he could do was yell through his sweat at the perplexed man to pay him and get out:

> He had never, when he was working so hard at selling his strength, asked for more than a fair price. Now he knew how valuable his sweat was and he'd reduce it by even one drop if he could. He didn't fool around when someone tried to take advantage of him. He'd just put the shafts down and refuse to take another step. He didn't care if it was a legal stopping place or not.[51]

Coolies often had cause for provocation and were disgracefully swindled by the public. Lee Ngang could not get one Captain Tilly, his drunken passenger, to pay him the proper fare, after a tavern crawl that lasted about four hours and included stops at places as far apart as a spirit shop in Smith Street, the Prince of Wales Hotel, and the Rendezvous Tavern opposite the Chinese cemetery. The rickshawman eventually arrived at the Captain's house in Anson Road at 8 p.m. The intoxicated man paid Lee Ngang 5 cents. He was not satisfied with what he had been given and asked for more. Captain Tilly said, 'No, No,' refusing to give him a 10-cent piece. It is not clear at this point whether the puller in desperation pushed him and he fell to the ground or whether Captain Tilly turned to leave and accidentally stepped into a drain and fell down under the influence of alcohol. In either case, Lee Ngang did not collect the rest of his fare.[52]

In a case with the exact opposite ending a Teochiu puller, who claimed to have been cheated by his juvenile passengers, accidentally fell down outside their house in Serangoon Road, and sustained injuries which resulted in his death. Lim Yew Liang, a 14-year-old Hokkien, had hired Mah Huat's rickshaw outside the City High School; he and his 12-year-old sister, named Baby Lim, who attended the French Convent, went home in the rickshaw. It rained heavily on the way much to Mah Huat's chagrin. Upon arriving at the house they were met by the female servant, Ah Siew, who opened the front door. Mah Huat had left his rickshaw at the roadside and followed them into the compound and up three steps to the porch. He had not been paid off at the roadside because it was raining. Lim called the rickshaw coolie and paid him 16 cents. Mah Huat took the money but protested it was not enough. The youth then described to the Coroner what happened next:

> I asked him how much he wanted. He spoke in Hokien dialect. He then used a filthy expression (Chebai). I told him not to use bad language. The female servant advised me to pay the rickisha puller some more money. I put my hand in my pocket to take out some money. While I was doing this the rickisha puller struck me once in the stomach with his fist. He then turned around quickly to run away. He had to run down three steps and when he got to the bottom he slipped and he fell backwards. He struck his head on the edge of the second step. After the rickshaw puller had fallen down he could not get up. He appeared to be unconscious. I carried him up the steps to a dry place under the porch. The servant helped me. I then went immediately to Rumah Miskin Police Station to report the matter. The rickisha puller ran away because he was afraid I would return the blow ... I have never paid more than sixteen cents for rickshaw fare from school to my house. I have never had trouble with rickisha pullers before.[53]

In Mah Huat's case a stingy youth, his own temper, and the weather combined to get the best of him. But pullers were bilked for a variety of other reasons too, often beyond their control: the size and anonymity of a crowd; an 'event' such as the sudden onset of a strike; an act of crime; or death as an indigent person passed away in the rickshaw. Waiting rickshawmen could experience difficulty in pinpointing their European patrons when first coming out of a theatre or the racecourse. At that moment a frantic dash usually took place to pick up passengers and an impatient, forgetful or ill-at-ease European was apt to get into the first rickshaw that 'dipped' to admit him: 'When I came out, I found my puller anxiously scanning the faces of the Europeans at the main exit. In the old days in Negri Sembilan he would not have cared if he had been bilked. He would have known where to find his man. Here in Singapore with its ten thousand whites such confidence would have been misplaced.'[54] In 1897, as the rickshaw strike commenced, and pullers downed shafts, a frightened, drunken sailor on the corner of Malay Street refused to pay his coolie because of the strike suddenly swirling around him. A fight broke out that ended with the sailor chasing the puller.[55] But Koh Loh Tee lost his fare under very different circumstances. It was not a mass event like a strike; there were no witnesses when the abduction of his passenger occurred, as he was far way from Malay Street out in the 'country'. Koh Loh Tee was bilked when the Cantonese woman he was pulling was forced into a car against her will. Nothing was said about his rickshaw fare as he watched the car drive off in the direction of Bras Basah Road with her sitting in the back of it. He subsequently asked the woman, when he accidentally met her on the street, to pay him but she refused to do so.[56]

Rickshaw coolies brought thousands of complaints to the Registrar over failure to pay proper fares. But this was only the tip of the iceberg. The exceedingly large number of cases reported in no way represented the actual number of rickshaw bilkings. Seldom could an offender be arrested on the spot. Unless this was done, the coolies' only hope was a summons, and then only if the police or Rickshaw Department had obtained the name and address, which, as a rule, was not easy. It seemed unfair, too, that a puller who had been bilked, had to pay 50 cents for a summons—half a day's wages—and lose valuable time at the Registrar's Court to recover his fare. Not surprisingly, only several hundred cases ever came before the Court.

In 1901 Mr Hooper provided figures to show the necessity for action to stop rickshaw coolies being bilked. During the year 3,790 reports regarding fares were received; in 2,636 instances the proper fare was recovered, and 114 persons were arrested, but in 1,154 cases pullers were cheated.[57] The Registrar felt it was vital to have special power to deal with these disquieting cases; additional rickshaw peons and police constables were needed to curb the excessive number of bilkings reported daily. Then, if a passenger refused to pay a fare or give a name and address, the person could be arrested on the spot and taken to the nearest police station and charged. The Government turned a deaf ear to his proposal, slashing expenditures wherever possible. The Rickshaw Department was told to make do with the staff at its disposal to combat bilking or any other complaints made by pullers or owners to the Registrar.

Bilking continued to be a source of much trouble to pullers and no fewer than 6,367 reports regarding fares were made in 1906.[58] In 2,635 cases the fares were recovered but in 3,732 instances the rickshawmen were bilked as it was impossible to trace the passengers. Over the next decade bilking remained as bad as ever; the number of reports of pullers having been cheated shows a slight downturn, but the improvement was illusory as the percentage of cases in which the fares could not be recovered actually rose![59] A lot of trouble continued to be experienced and as late as 1913 Mr Hooper was to write in a monthly report: 'The mean tricks resorted to to cheat coolies are astonishing and simple minded pullers will even be induced to hand over hard won earnings to passengers, who deposit sham jewellery or bogus parcels [in their rickshaws].'[60]

TABLE 10.1

The Number of Bilking Cases Reported and Untraced, 1901–1917

Year	*Number of Bilking Cases Reported*	*Number of Bilking Cases Untraced*	*Percentage of Cases Untraced*
1901	3,790	1,154	30
1902	3,735	1,425	38
1905	5,557	2,304	41
1906	6,367	3,732	59
1911	4,211	2,222	53
1913	3,400	1,800	53
1914	3,285	1,684	51
1917	3,145	1,411	45

On the other hand, pullers usually got much more than the proper fare, especially to the wharves and brothels, from seamen and other transients. Tourists and sailors were apt to be ignorant of the fares and susceptible to being overcharged. Altercations over fares was commonplace on the waterfront. It was for this reason that the Tanjong Pagar Dock Company erected a small information office at the Borneo wharf for the use of the Rickshaw Department in 1904. An inspector was placed on special duty to meet the mail steamers and assist passengers, informing them of the correct fares to pay, noting complaints and directing the pullers where to run.[61] Despite information kiosks and other precautionary measures some pullers bent on hitting the foreigner where it hurt most—the pocket-book—would protest no matter what was given. The coolie would insist on more while the passenger was apt to be 'beset by irritating doubts about whether it was artfulness or simple-mindedness that he had to deal with'[62] in paying for the trip.

When the number of rickshaws did not keep pace with public demand, pullers became very independent indeed, wilfully soliciting passengers, behaving in a disorderly manner, and asking several times the amount normally paid.[63]

> Nor was he polite to his passengers. When they told him to take them some place he'd go there and not one step further. When they told him to go to the head of a side street and then, when they got there told him to go down it, he'd do no such thing. The passenger would glare. . . . He knew that gentlemen wearing western suits were, for the most part, domineering and stingy. Fine. He was ready for them. Let them change their minds and he'd grab the sleeve of their fifty or sixty dollar suits and give them a grimy handprint at least! They'd have to pay up once they had a handprint bestowed upon them. They realized how strong that big hand was. Its grip made their scrawny arm hurt.[64]

In outlying areas complaints were received from time to time of the bad conduct of the pullers, especially at places like Kranji, where the coolies combined together to refuse hire unless at excessive rates.[65] In 1901 Mr Hooper had no jurisdiction to deal with these 'offenders' as they operated beyond the municipal limits, and it was left to the itinerant Malay police constable to proceed against pullers bent on bilking kampong folk. Some, however, had chosen not to be like their peers and always forcefully demand a larger amount from a foreigner or villager. They had no desire to have them in the palm of their hand: 'Pulling a rickshaw is really what you ought to do, so you do it. He was still free from the contagion of bad habits. He had never learned how to shake down a passenger for a higher fare, or overturn the rickshaw in the middle of the road, or sitting around all day waiting for a profitable deal.'[66]

The poor haggler and the general public were capable though of taking their revenge on the rickshaw coolie, and in ways far worse than bilking. In an overseas Chinese community where almost everyone was struggling to make ends meet, the city's personality reflected it. Rickshawmen accepted the need for wariness as the price they had to pay to work on the streets of Singapore. Coolies had to look out for cheats, but customers were not above using criminal force against them. Rickshaw pullers learned to shrug off an assault or knife murder—there were scores of them each year—and press on with life between the shafts. The Coroner's Records, police occurrence books, and newspapers are replete with examples of grievous crimes against rickshawmen. They were stabbed or beaten to death for refusing a fare, for not running fast enough, for pestering against underpayment, and for reasons unknown to the authorities. It was often against a background of misunderstanding, mistrust, fear, and anger that rickshawmen were murdered both in broad daylight and pitch darkness, at places all over the city including the congested streets of Chinatown, the sinister area on the waterfront, and on lonely tracks leading out of the city to country districts.

From the rickshaw coolie's side the rickshaw he pulled was a heavy burden. His life was dangerous drawing it around the city. Some passengers had bad habits when it came to rickshaw pullers, easy to acquire but difficult to get rid of. It was convenient to obtain a lift in a rickshaw without finding the small change, but so discomforting to one's sense of pride to be refused hire by a coolie, and then have to 'nurse one's wrath'. The practice of stepping outside the shafts was not recognized as a right of rickshaw coolies, except by a sympathetic few:

> We do not write as if we have had no personal experience of a momentary desire to thrash a ricksha coolie walking outside the shafts for refusing a fare, but we are fortunately able to understand to some extent 'the horrible voices' that he makes 'in a jargon of his own', and his explanation that he has just returned from a long distant journey in the country, or that he has been some hours without food and does not willingly refuse an addition to his daily income seems quite reasonable. The public is too apt to forget that the ricksha pullers are human beings capable of doing only a certain amount of work.[67]

But as the Coroner in 1921 knew, Ong Chew Kay, the public's victim, was just one in a macabre string of killings that could be traced as far back as 1902 (see Appendix 4). Ong Chew Kay, aged 24, was found by a Malay constable in Telok Ayer Street sitting in his rickshaw shaking all over and in a dazed condition. Kassim bin Ali spoke to the coolie and asked him what was the matter but got no reply. With the help of a nearby constable he got another rickshaw and took Ong Chew Kay to Telok Ayer station and from there to the General Hospital where he died on arrival. There would have been no explanation for his death, except that Lee Chye, an ice-water seller at the corner of Telok Ayer Street and MacCallum Street in front of the Ai Tong School, happened to see the crime committed in a flash, for no other reason than walking outside the shafts:

> About 11.45, 9th February, 1921 I was at my stall ... I saw a coolie pulling his ricksha along Telok Ayer Street going in the direction of the Chinese Temple. A

> Chinese Baba called him, he said he was too ill to pull. The Baba then said if you are too ill to pull why are you inside the shafts, [he] came outside of them. The Baba then struck him on his chest three or four times, the coolie struck back with his fist and broke the Baba's wrist watch. The coolie then stooped down to pick up his ricksha and then the Baba saw that his wrist watch was broken and kicked him in the stomach as he was stooping down. The puller then picked up his shafts and pulled his ricksha to the corner and then put down the shafts and sat on the footboard of the ricksha. Soon after two P.C.'s came and took him away in another ricksha and also took his ricksha to the station. The Baba went away before the P.C. came. The baba used to live at Chop Heng Cheng Joo no. 2 MacCallum Street but I have not seen him there since.[68]

The Coroner's files bring to light that arguing over fares was even more dangerous than refusing hire. The corpse of Tay Ah Sui, a young puller, lay in a pool of blood in the five-footway of Boustead and Company's Godown. He had been stabbed to death on the upper part of the chest. Near the body were found a metal tipped walking stick and coat, in the pocket and buttonhole of which hung a metal watch and chain with a small medal of Dutch origin. It took the Coroner more than a month to solve the mystery of his death, and then only because one of the assailants turned informer when finally apprehended by plainclothes detectives. Tay Ah Sui had demanded the fare for a ride during the evening rush hour to Malay Street. His insistence became a question of 'kill or be killed'. Two Malay coolies working as stevedores on the Tanjong Pagar wharf accidentally met in Tanjong Pagar Road opposite the Presbyterian church. Abdullah Adam, who was drunk, said to his friend, Abdullah bin Abdad bin Salleh, that he was going to Malay Street and asked him to come along. They got into Tay Ah Sui's rickshaw and travelled along South Bridge Road. Drunken Abdullah Adam wanted the puller to go faster and struck him several times on the back as if he were an animal, with a metal rod. Toh Poo, another rickshaw coolie, saw the affair but was not in time to prevent the young man from dying on the verandah:

> The taller man when he poked the puller with his stick said 'Meh Meh' which is Chinese for 'quickly'. I heard the puller say in Chinese 'I cannot go any faster'. Then the puller put down the shafts and the two dark men wanted to go away. The puller seized the taller man by the wrist and demanded his fare. The tall man did not pay anything, but drew a knife from his belt and stabbed the puller.

Tay Ah Sui fell on the edge of the road next to his rickshaw calling out '*Mata Mata*', but none came. The two men left in haste but did not run. Abdullah Adam mistakenly left his coat and the rod in the rickshaw—a tell-tale sign.[69]

Ordinarily one had to determine the price of a ride before climbing into a rickshaw. Many passengers chose not to honour the agreement, and haggle over it at the end of a trip. This was Leng Lock's misfortune. He did not report his attack, although he told his unsympathetic *towkay* in Victoria Street about it. He could not afford time off from work and still cover the cost of his rickshaw rental. After having been assaulted Leng Lock continued to pull a rickshaw for three days but then had to give it up due to injuries. While convalescing in Tan Tock Seng Hospital he recounted to a police inspector why he had been thrashed so violently:

> About ten days ago two Chinese engaged my rikisha in North Bridge Road and told me to pull them to Thompson Road. I pulled them to near the bridge in Thompson Road where they alighted. I then asked them for my fare they paid me ten cents. I asked them for twenty cents which they had agreed to pay. We had an argument and they took back the ten cents from me and one of them caught hold of me by my touchang and struck me with his fist on the ribs, the two men then ran away. I do not know where they ran to or . . . where they live. I do not know their names. Their nationality [*sic*] was Hokien. After I had been assaulted I returned home to my house and informed my Towkay about the assault but he did not do anything. I did not make a report in the police station, as I had no money to pay for rickshas.[70]

All too often being short-changed triggered an abusive argument that ended in the puller's death by means of a knife. The area around Tanjong Pagar was particularly sinister in this respect as the stevedores, coal coolies, and seamen were a hard moneyless bunch. Chee Moh Moh died in his rickshaw from stab wounds inflicted by three Chinese wharf coolies at about midnight on 26 December 1918. Ting Sam Mui, a stevedore, was eating in a lane behind Boustead Institute when he saw a Chinese coolie arrive in a rickshaw and pay the puller 30 cents. The puller said, 'Not enough,' and asked for more but was refused. The two men fought. The passenger ran into a house in the same street and came back with two other coolies: Chee Moh Moh was still there angrily shouting into the night, and then the three of them assaulted him with knives. Ting Sam Mui raised the alarm and chased after one of the assailants who shoved him aside and ran away. Ting Sam Mui picked himself up and then went to his work as he was late. While working on a steamer the next day he heard that a rickshaw coolie had been murdered.[71] In another incident cast in the same mould a wharfie employed by the Pacific Trading Company quarrelled with a rickshawman over a trip fare from Rochore to Synagogue Street; the dock coolie paid 15 cents, the puller demanded twenty. The coolie refused and they came to blows.[72]

In a desperate effort to recover fares pullers hung around entrances to public premises or chased after departing passengers following them right into shops. Ling Thye, a rickshawman, was having coffee at a shop in Orchard Road at about 8 a.m. when he noticed two Malays come into the cafe. They sipped coffee for about a quarter of an hour and then got up to go. As they were leaving a rickshaw puller, who had been standing at the door, asked them for payment. Chew Ah Fat, the coffee-shopkeeper, described what happened next:

> The Malay in the white baju, from whom he demanded money, refused to pay, and struck the puller one blow with his fist on the side. The Chinaman fell into

the drain and lay there. The Malays at once walked away quickly. The deceased lay about 10 minutes in the drain. Then I went and called a Municipal Overseer who got klings [Tamil migrants] to lift out the injured man.[73]

Ng Liew, an opium smoker, met a similar fate when his rickshaw with two Malay passengers stopped in front of a coffee-shop in Jalan Besar. One of the Malays handed him six cents but Ng Liew said it was not enough, having pulled them from Arab Street to Jalan Besar. The two men got down, came into the coffee-shop, and went out the back door, closely followed by the puller pestering for money. One of the Malays, whom he suspected was a government servant, turned and kicked him in the crotch. There was blood all over his white trousers. The principal tenant of his lodging-house advised him to report the matter as he became very sick. In Ng Liew's case his opium addiction was a contributing factor towards his violent death: 'He did not look fit to be a rickshaw puller as he looked too thin, but he said he was a puller'. The Surgeon's Report at Tan Tock Seng Hospital noted that '. . . the injuries were not sufficient to kill any normal healthy man. He was quite unfit to pull a rickshaw.'[74]

There were police stations scattered all around the city. Yet there was still fear of rickshaw coolies getting pushed around or killed by passengers, wharfies, or rival gangs of pullers. Rickshawmen knew the location of almost every police station—large or small—like the backs of their hands. When attacked, chances were they tried to get to the closest one in that part of town, especially at night. To our horror, wounded, dying rickshaw pullers wandered in the traffic congested streets of Singapore in search of a station alone, often ignored. For someone who had never seen it before, the sight of a blood-strewn puller was unnerving. 'But is he safe?', pedestrians and on-comers asked as they kept their distance or stepped gingerly to one side to let him pass. Ong Oh Kaw sensed this fear in the Singapore of 1902:

The night was not dark. There was moonlight, but none of the people in the street followed the wounded man to the station, nor did anyone come to say they had seen him. There were many people in the road coming and going, when the deceased was at the station door. I saw a good many Chinese and others looking but they kept at a distance. No one came to the station and said that there was an empty rikisha a few hundred yards off on the road. There were rikishas too going and coming along on the road but none of the pullers or passengers made any statements.[75]

It was often the Malay constable on night duty who came to the assistance of a stricken puller. Police constable Osman's prompt action while stationed at the Tanjong Pagar station was responsible for Tan Sam Ong's killer, a French sailor, not getting away:

On the morning of Sunday 6 July 1902 I went on duty at the station door at 2 a.m. and my watch extended till 6 a.m. Shortly after the clock had struck three there was a Chinaman came running to the door of the police station on the Keppel Road side. Just as he reached the corner of the entrance steps, he called out 'ayah' and fell down on his left side. I ran down the steps and found he was a Chinaman and was bleeding. I did not wait to do anything but went at once behind and called the Corporal. . . . The Corporal at once went and summoned Sergeant Hickney. I stayed by the wounded man. The Sergeant came in five or ten minutes and by that time the wounded man was dead. . . . We went towards Keppel Bridge no. 1. When we had gone about one hundred yards from the station we found an empty rikisha with its two lamps lighted. The shafts of the rikisha pointed towards town and it rested on the west side of Keppel Road. . . . The road was quite deserted when we were looking for traces of blood and . . . found the empty rikisha. We saw no one, no carts, no foot passengers nor anyone on the road. I believe there were rikishas that passed along Keppel Road as late as 2 a.m. that morning going towards Borneo wharf. . . . The spot where I arrested the accused was distant from Keppel Bridge no. 1 about 100 or 120 yards and was between the bridge and the Tanjong Pagar police station. When arrested the accused said a few words in French which I do not understand. He was very excited.[76]

Street violence which was a dominant feature of the puller's life led on occasion to police constables being seriously wounded, too. On the night of 14 June 1896, a Spaniard named Sison Lopes was arrested in Tanjong Pagar Road by Sikh constable Sultan Singh, for having assaulted a rickshaw coolie. While being apprehended he stabbed the constable several times.[77]

Owing to sub-communal rivalry and dialect difference, lack of employment, and mistaken identity, rickshawmen were subject to gang beatings and robbery, and all who happened to be around usually suffered. A group of six Hylams had a quarrel with a puller in a lane off River Valley Road. The coolie fled past Lee Yong Moi and Wong Cray Tee, who were sitting in their rickshaws next to each other in River Valley Road, waiting for hire. The angry bunch of Hylams burst out of the lane in a blind rage with fists flying. They repeatedly struck Lee Yong Moi, yelling they would make short work of any rickshaw coolie. Wong Cray Tee was kicked to the ground as he tried to escape. Altogether there were fifteen Hylams present when the assault occurred but it is not clear whether they all went on the rampage. The two coolies dragged themselves to the Middle Road Rickshaw Depot and made a report. Lee Yong Moi then returned home; he separated from Wong Cray Tee at Dhoby Ghaut where he saw him sitting in a rickshaw being pulled but drawing his own from behind. The next morning he saw Wong Cray Tee at 6 a.m. in his cubicle at 27 Park Road—he was dead. Amin Noordin was on duty at the Rickshaw Department, Middle Road, when the battered coolies came into the station. The attack was described in faltering Hockchia, which was translated into Malay, and reported as follows:

At 12.30 p.m. while we were at the junction of River Valley Road and Killiney Road waiting for fares ten Hylams came up and struck us with their fists. I, rikisha coolie no. 1407 fell down and bruised my elbows and had red marks on my sides. I, rikisha coolie no. 1284 had a swelling on the mouth. All the hylams [*sic*] then ran away.[78]

When gang muggings occurred in the workplace, fellow pullers were apt to abandon their friends in the face of danger, out of fear—fear of being stabbed to death and robbed with impunity. Ngo Mook Too remembered taking a fare to Kim Keat Road just outside the temple. It was a little past 10 p.m., after he had been paid and was on his way back to the main road, when a man asked him to stop. He halted. Next to the man who held him up were two other pullers sitting on the floorboards of their rickshaws. As soon as he stopped two other Chinese came out of the shadows from the side of the road and the man who had detained him produced a knife from his waist and attempted to stab him. The puller called out for the police and ran into the temple seeking refuge, where he stayed for five minutes still screaming at the top of his lungs 'police and help'. He eventually joined six people who had gathered outside, and one went with him to retrieve his rickshaw. It was intact. One rickshaw coolie and the man who had set upon him were gone, but the other rickshaw was still there. Ngo Mook Too described how he felt at that moment when he came upon the body of the other puller in the grass at the side of the road:

> He had been stabbed. There was blood on his trousers. I passed without putting down my rikisha. The lamps of this other rikisha were lit. My companion looked at the injured man who was struggling with his legs but making no noises. I was frightened. I went on. My companion was frightened and went back to the temple. I went straight home and did not call at any police station. I am recently from China. I do not know who my companion was, nor do I know the man who told me to stop. . . .[79]

The threat of violence and the fear it engendered persisted over a long period of time. It became almost axiomatic for pullers and the public to lose courage and initiative to prevent rickshawmen from falling into the hands of 'enemies on the streets'. Ong Oh Kaw was walking slowly. He may have walked for 300 yards after being stabbed. He stopped at the foot of the steps leading to the Havelock Road Police Station. He spoke first in Chinese and said, '*Noh Lang Hokkien pak gua*.' The Malay constable understood enough Chinese to know that this meant 'Two Hokkien Chinese have beaten me'. After saying this the wounded puller sat down on the steps speechless, groaning. The blood was flowing freely from a wound on the right side of his neck. Anyone who kept a moderately close eye on his passage to the station would have known he was in dire need of help. Fear itself made the public wary. No one on the street took any notice of him, despite the moonlight.[80]

Some pullers died for reasons only known to them at the hands of unknown assailants; Teng Ah Yeok, a 39-year-old Hengwah, was assaulted in Arab Street and his body found face downward in a drain.[81] Khoon Cheang, also Hengwah, collapsed between the shafts and fell forward on top of the cross-bar 25 yards from Rochore Police Station. He dropped down, got up again and then collapsed. Khoon Cheang, described as a strong, quiet, hard-working man with no kin in Singapore, and who did not smoke opium, had been assaulted by persons or some person unknown.[82] In yet another case, on 12 June 1895, Neu Cha, a Hokkien puller, took out a rickshaw from Tanjong Pagar Road to seek fares. At 6 p.m. the next morning the rickshaw was discovered behind a house attached to the barracks at Tanglin, and Neu Cha's body was found in the bath. He had been rendered unconscious by a blow and then thrown into the bath. No clues were obtained as to who was responsible for the murder.[83] Ang Ah Kow lived in the same rickshaw lodging as Ang Gua in Havelock Road. He actually managed, despite being close to death with a stomach wound, to get home. He died an hour later saying to Ang Gua, over and over again, that someone had beaten him up.[84] Even when circumstantial evidence existed it very often proved a hard task to sentence the perpetrators of such crimes. The body of one Oh Ah Kao, a Hockchia puller, was found in Kerbau Road. He had apparently been stabbed while in charge of his rickshaw. Inquiries cast suspicion on two Malays named Usuf and Itam but there was insufficient evidence to convict them.[85]

If an old puller walking along the street was called a bastard or worse he might ignore it. But the young could not. Men like Seah Seh Gan were not about to be abused and publicly humiliated without retaliating. Seah Seh Gan was just 26 years old, and had been in Singapore only three years, when he was attacked during Chinese New Year for refusing a fare. He was pulling his rickshaw along Kallang Road when Tan Bah Bee beckoned to him that he wanted to hire his rickshaw. He was accompanied by two other Chinese. Seah Seh Gan did not stop to take them. He shouted that his rickshaw was not for hire. Tan Bah Bee asked the puller why and began to abuse him and at the same time kicked his rickshaw. The rickshaw coolie stopped and returned the invective. Tan Bah Bee then approached Seah Seh Gan and punched him in the face with a clenched fist. He reeled under the blow and fell to the ground. Sensing grave danger, the puller rose to his feet as the three men encircled him but not before he ripped out the rattan seat of the rickshaw and hit Tan Bah Bee with it. He then began to scream for police assistance and the attackers fled.[86]

Pullers were expected to come to the aid of their passengers if they were either robbed or assaulted. The record shows that their enthusiasm for the welfare of their passengers was suspect. Frightened and unarmed, they often ran away seeking a private escape. In such moments, fear of rowdies tended to dominate over a sense of responsibility and concern for the passenger's well-being. In an unusual crime a European lady living at the Sea View Hotel was in a rickshaw when a Chinese snatched her purse. She attempted to strike him with her tennis racquet but her assailant drew a knife and slashed her hand. Six other Chinese then came up and robbed her of jewellery valued at $500. The puller, hopelessly outnumbered, stood by in helpless silence.[87] Most, however, ran away in fear of their lives. Teow Gow Teng was at the junction of Sago and Trengganu Streets, a rough spot in the brothel quarter, when two

Hylams who had just come up in another rickshaw engaged him. He overheard one of them say, 'I am going to Keppel Harbour'. Then both of them got into Teow Gow Teng's rickshaw but before he even had time to lift his shafts, three men rushed up and shouted '*Pah*'. He saw no assault as he ran away when he heard '*Pah*'. Sometime later he came back to the rickshaw and saw that one of the Hylams was wounded. He refused to pull him in his condition but relented at the behest of the crowd and took the bleeding man by rickshaw to the General Hospital.[88]

Tan Tong's passenger simply disappeared in a moment of fright as the coolie fled from his besieged rickshaw. A Japanese got into his vehicle at the sixth mile, Serangoon Road. On the way to the fifth mile someone grabbed hold of the rickshaw from behind, as they were going uphill, and the shafts shot up in the air. Tan Tong panicked and took to his heels. He drew a picture of how a man vanished from his rickshaw for the Coroner:

> After going a few paces I heard the Japanese shouting out 'Apa, Apa' so I returned to the spot. I found my ricksha there but everyone had disappeared. Then I pulled my ricksha home. I never saw the Japanese again. Don't know what happened to him. It was very dark at the time, too dark to see anybody. I don't know whether there was more than one person that stopped the ricksha or not.[89]

Sometimes the attack was too sudden for the puller to react, even if only to run away. Low Ah Su saw a Chinese man run towards him from the direction of the Sailors Institute where the road was particularly crowded. He shouted at him as he was afraid they would collide. Then there was a cry from behind, 'Oh Yoh'. He stopped, turned around and saw that one of his passengers had collapsed in the rickshaw. Low Ah Su told the police that:

> The assailant was Chinese but I cannot say what part of China he came from. I have not seen the man again. I would not recognise him if I saw him. Nothing at all was said. He just ran up and stabbed the deceased. I did not see where he disappeared to after that. The street was crowded. It all happened very quickly. I cannot say whether anyone else saw it.[90]

Times became harder as the Singapore economy sagged in the late 1920s, and the incidence of these attacks multiplied. An unemployed Teochiu confessed how he and his accomplices murdered and robbed in cold blood a Hokkien pork butcher, Goh Joo, in Upper Weld Road after his rickshaw puller ran off on him:

> Regarding the stabbing three of us went to the back of Guan Guan Hotel. There we waited on the five foot way of the house. One of the two men named Twa Koh told me we were waiting to rob a passer by. The other man's name was Tian Hock and he also said the same thing to me. Then a Chinese came up in a ricksha. Twa Koh caught hold of the man by the head and pulled him down from the rickshaw. The man struggled to get away. Tian Hock put both arms round him to stop him getting away. The man called out for help, whereupon Twa Koh

stabbed him with a knife in the chest. The man still struggled and I saw he was falling. Tian Hock then pushed him from behind. As he was falling down Tian Hock then stabbed him with [a] knife in the region of the buttocks. Whatever money the man had Twa Koh took away. After the stabbing we parted in different directions.[91]

On the other hand, rickshaw pullers, as good samaritans, were prepared to come to the aid of other late-night travellers, passers-by or comrades. Lim Chuan Neo was sitting on the five-footway of her house in Cornwall Street holding her grandchild. There were usually three or four rickshaws parked one beside the other with their backs towards her door. She knew two of the pullers by sight but not by name; Kow Wuh because she used his rickshaw and Teong Choon because he parked there every day. At 12.30 p.m. on 6 May 1930, a small Austin driven by Rik bin Awang came up the hill and drove over the shafts of Teong Choon's rickshaw. The coolie jumped up and cursed the driver. The car stopped further up. The driver, accompanied by five other Malays, then came down to Teong Choon, who was standing in front of the broken rickshaw, and began to strike him. The rickshawman fell down under the barrage of blows. At that moment Lim Chuan Neo saw Kow Wuh return with his rickshaw. He joined the fray to protect his friend and was stabbed to death. When the old woman saw the knifing she ran into the house—her grandchild was frightened. Another puller at the scene, Tan Moh Tee, did not consider it 'his affair'. Nevertheless, like Kow Wuh, he was attacked just the same:

Kow Wuh went up to the accused [Rik bin Awang] and told them not to strike Teong Choon, he spoke in Hokien. Koh Wuh [*sic*] was also struck and fell down. Then Chin Tee went to lift up Koh Wuh [*sic*]. As Chin Tee was lifting up Koh Wuh [*sic*] he was stabbed in his stomach by Rik bin Awang with a knife about four inches long. . . . When Chin Tee was stabbed I was five or six paces away. As I was lifting Chin Tee up I was stabbed twice on my left hand and arm by Rik bin Awang. I was actually lifting up Chin Tee when I was stabbed. I let go of him. Then I fell down and don't remember anymore . . . I did not think they would stab me as I had not taken any part in the affair. It was Teong Choon's affair. Kow Wuh only wanted to assist Teong Choon. Chin Tee was only lifting Kow Wuh up. I did not think they would attack me as I was not taking any part in the fight.[92]

In a different kind of case Nyeng Hiah Long recounted how he went to the aid of the 8-year-old daughter of his cousin. She accidentally stepped in front of a lorry, giving the driver no chance to avoid hitting her. He was standing at the junction of Rochore Road and Queen Street. Two Chinese ladies had just engaged his rickshaw:

I lifted up the shafts of my rickshaw and then looked along Queen Street towards Arab Street. A lorry came from behind and passed me going along Queen Street towards Arab Street at a fast speed. I saw a woman holding a child by its hand walking along the street. They were about thirty yards ahead of me. The lorry bumped into the child and knocked it on to the ground. The woman also bent down towards the ground. I put down my rikisha shafts, left my passengers, and went to the spot.

The driver was stopped from running away by an angry crowd of Chinese bystanders. Nyeng Hiah Long ran to get a police constable and the driver was escorted to the station.[93] Another emergency involved Tee Haw, who was standing on the five-footway of his lodging in New Bridge Road, when he saw a motor cycle going towards Sepoy Lines. The motor cycle had nearly reached his house when it hit 62-year-old Lee Kew Moi who was walking along the side of the road on her way home from market. It spun out of control, and struck her from behind. The puller ran to the spot, called a rickshaw, and picked up the elderly female Hockchia who lived in the same house as he.[94]

The records disclose that a rickshawman such as Leng Ah Pok could not turn his back on a comrade bent on committing suicide. He attempted to save the puller's life when the occasion arose. Leng Ah Pok was passing a barber shop in Albert Street with his rickshaw when he heard the sound of someone panting as if in pain, but did not see anyone in the shop:

> The noise was quite loud. I entered the shop to see what was the matter. In a room behind the shop I saw the deceased lying on a raised platform. He was bleeding from his face. I asked him what was the matter but he did not reply. He made a gesture with his right hand which I understood to mean that I was not to interfere but go away. I did not see any wounds. I only saw blood flowing from his face and feet. I went away immediately. I went to look for the barber who I knew had gone for food at that time. I found him near the market. I told him what I had seen. I went with him to the shop. . . .[95]

Medical trips, however, which entailed additional responsibilities and risks were an altogether different matter from the puller's point of view. The relation between a puller and his gravely ill passenger was subject to a different set of considerations, from the choice to act on the spur of the moment to help someone out. Pullers wanted to be reassured that they would be paid for delivering an indigent person to hospital. When providing ambulance service they ran the risk of breaking the law if the passenger died in the rickshaw; they could be charged with an offence either for conveying a forbidden article, a corpse, or for dumping it when the first opportunity presented itself. Further, it was generally acknowledged that this creaky form of transport could endanger the lives of the seriously injured or kill outright. For these reasons rickshawmen were far more reluctant to render assistance to the gravely ill than to pedestrians in crisis, whom they chanced upon in the course of their rounds. Nevertheless, the rickshaw was the only form of ambulance service worthy of its name in Singapore for emergencies and accidents in the streets as late as 1920.

Pullers conveyed accident victims such as tenants, from lodging-houses that were so rotten they collapsed on them burying them alive amongst the debris; coolies, from building sites when industrial mishaps occurred;

prostitutes, from a burning brothel in Smith Street; drunken lodgers, from the kerbside who fell out of windows, and many others to hospital.[96] Invariably some died on the way and the puller at a minimum lost his fare. Tan Kim Kew was drawing his rickshaw along Tanjong Pagar Road when Koh Ah Sam called and placed a Chinese man who was seriously ill in his vehicle. He told the puller to carry on and sat in the rickshaw beside the sick man. He pulled the two men as far as North Bridge Road, opposite the Malay Cemetery, when the man died. His companion jumped out of the rickshaw, paying no fare. Tan Kim Kew left the rickshaw with the corpse and chased after Koh Ah Sam but to no avail. By pure chance, he later saw him loitering opposite the Kreta Ayer Rickshaw Station and reported him.[97]

Often when a crowd was on hand, a puller had to comply with their wishes irrespective of the passenger's condition. Chan Kay Swee happened to be near Elgin Bridge when people in a crowd there called him and wanted to place a Chinese man, who was only half conscious, in his rickshaw. He refused, but the bystanders remonstrated against his decision, saying they were all Chinese and that the man was wounded. The crowd then lifted the man into the rickshaw and told Chan Kay Swee to take him to Hokkien Street. The ailing man wanted to go to Kampong Glam, but afterwards agreed to go to Hokkien Street. A friend joined him there and the puller took them to the hospital.[98] Teo Eng also received less than he was promised to convey an assault victim to Tan Tock Seng Hospital. He too tried to refuse. Teo Eng was in MacPherson Road at about 3.30 in the afternoon when Teo Ah Kay called his rickshaw. The passenger placed in it was in a bad way and could not walk. Teo Ah Kay sat with the dying man and told Teo Eng to pull to the Rumah Miskin Police Station. But when he got as far as the gate of Tan Tock Seng Hospital, the man died. They proceeded on to the station. The police then sent the puller back to the hospital with the corpse. The following day he complained to them that: 'The men who put the sick man in my ricksha, did not tell me he had been assaulted. I refused to take him, but the people in the road compelled me to take him. They only paid me thirty cents yesterday and they told me they would give me some more today.'[99]

A crowd of a different sort insisted that Yeet Ah Why carry the unconscious body of an unknown malaria-ridden man, from People's Park to the hospital. He had been called by a group of paupers and a woman, Loy Ah See, who said she would pay the fare. It was an empty promise. The rickshaw coolie pulled the moribund man as far as New Bridge Road. There a police constable ordered him to take his passenger to Sepoy Lines Police Station before continuing to the hospital. For Yeet Ah Why it was an unforgettable experience. Calamity had struck. Not only was he bilked but ten days later he still suffered under the misapprehension that he had been arrested because the constable had taken him to the station.[100]

Assault victims frequently died in rickshaws; Teo Yong, a Hokkien mee hawker, was returning home with his basket, which contained plates, cups, a lamp and stool, when he was set upon by two persons and stabbed. He was put in a rickshaw and died on the way to hospital.[101] Tan Ah Yam, a Teochiu vegetable hawker, also died from knife wounds while on his way to the Central Police Station in a rickshaw.[102] Similarly, Wan Chee, the Cantonese mistress of Wan Fook, died on the way while accompanied by a child who was said to be her daughter.[103]

Drunks and beggars were picked up on the streets by police and placed in rickshaws, only to die in transit to the station. One such report from the wharf area reads: 'The deceased was found by P.C. 318 wandering about in Anson Road. He fell into a drain. He was arrested for being drunk taken to Tanjong Pagar Station and charged. The same morning about 6.30 a.m. he was sent off to Sepoy Lines Station in a ricksha and died on the way.'[104] An unknown beggar was found dying in a rickshaw by police. Ng Kow Poey was resting at Jalan Sultan when the constable spotted him. He had been in North Bridge Road plying for hire; suddenly four Chinese, out of a crowd of about twenty, hailed him. An old man was lying on the road. Kwang Seong, a clerk in Chop Kee Whatt just across the way, identified the man as a beggar:

> A crowd collected. I went to see and saw three people, one of them, a ricksha puller lift him up and put him in the rickshaw. The injured man was a beggar and had been there sometime begging. We used to give him food every day. He was ill and could only walk with the aid of a stick. I don't know what made him fall down.

The police constable escorted Ng Kow Poey to Rochore Station. The beggar was dead by the time they reached there.[105] Another unknown Chinese man who 'seemed to be a pauper or vagrant' was found lying on the road near the post of the rickshaw stand in Hong Kong Street. He was emaciated and speechless, but not dead. No puller had found it in himself to take him to the hospital free of charge. Instead, he was covered with a mat and left to lie there; the callous neighbours round about, including pullers, would tell nothing about him to the police. He was placed in Go Oh Ah's rickshaw with a police constable and sent to Tan Tock Seng Hospital but the man proved dead on arrival.[106]

The practice of dumping bodies was common, and increased in the late 1920s. An unknown male Chinese who was very ill attempted to reach hospital in a rickshaw pulled by Tay Choon Choon. On the way his passenger died. Tay Choon Choon dumped the corpse on the side of Said Alwi Road. He was apprehended and charged with depositing a dead body on a public road, cautioned and discharged.[107] The authorities, and the Coroner in particular by 1927, felt something had to be done to curb the growing practice of dumping cadavers. It was against the law and costly to the city:

> In the first place the practice is illegal; it is conducive to crime; and it is a public nuisance of a particularly offensive kind. It is a grave waste of time in the Hospital and police force—two services already overworked and barely sufficient

for the legitimate requirements of Singapore. One or more dead bodies are dumped by ignorant and irresponsible individuals almost everyday; and if the time paid for and lost by the state in this manner could be costed against the work entailed the result would be surprising.[108]

Lim Boh's case was a classic example. In desperation he threw the body of his dead passenger, Ah Low, into the Kallang River, but only after nobody would claim it. Unfortunately for him, the body landed on rocks and mud at the foot of one of the pillars of the bridge. The tide was out at the time and it was plainly visible. Chia Siew Koon, a tramway inspector, was in a tram going across the Kallang Bridge when he saw a puller start over the bridge in the direction of Geylang. He watched him stop the rickshaw on the bridge, pull the dead man out of the vehicle and, with a furtive glance, push him through the railing into the river—the final transaction between a puller and the public. Chia Siew Koon got down from the tram, chased and caught Lim Boh, and then brought him to Rochore Police Station. He asked Lim Boh why he had done it but the puller refused to answer. It was later learned that Ah Low had been unemployed and had gone to inquire about a job at the Tan Kah Kee Rubber Factory. He had a fever and collapsed in front of the factory. Ram Pasad Rai, a watchman at the works, takes up the story: he was in his house when he heard people say that a rickshaw coolie had placed a dead man on the footway of one of the coolie lines. The puller wanted to leave the corpse there, but the inmates refused. The watchman told him he must take the body to a police station. Lim Boh then put it back into the rickshaw and went off towards Geylang, but once on the bridge close by he threw the body into the river. Ram Pasard Rai gave chase but could not run fast enough to catch him. He was too old. Lim Boh admitted he was at fault in discarding the body but emphatically denied having dumped it into the Kallang River:

I pulled a Hockchia man from Ellenborough Market up to Geylang. On my way back with an empty ricksha, I reached near Tan Kah Kee's coolie house, someone called me, I went there. One Chinese was supporting another Chinese. They both got into my ricksha. One of them seemed to be ill. They told me to go to the Hospital. I got as far as Lavender Street, about half way. Then one of the men called to me to put down the ricksha. I stopped and one man got out and ran to a vegetable garden belonging to a Cantonese. I chased after him but I lost sight of him. I returned to my ricksha and found that the other man was dead. I did not want to leave a dead man on the roadside, so I took him back to the house where I had first got him from. When I reached the house I told the inmates of the house that I had got the dead man from their house, but they denied that he belonged to their house. So I had to pull my ricksha and the dead man away. When about half way across the bridge I stopped my ricksha and placed the deceased on the roadside at the edge of the bridge. I then went on towards Geylang not towards Duxton Road. The tramway inspector caught me at Lorong 3. I had not run there only walked. He took me to the police station. I cannot say how the body came to be there. . . . I made a mistake in leaving the body on the roadside.[109]

1. Lao She, *Rickshaw* (the novel *Lo-T'o Hsiang Tzu*), translated by Jean M. James (Honolulu: The University Press of Hawaii, 1979), pp. 43–4.
2. UNNAYAN, in association with T. H. Thomas, *Rickshaws in Calcutta* (Calcutta: UNNAYAN, 1981), p. 6.
3. SCII of Kow Wuh, No. 220, 7/5/30.
4. Felix Chia, *The Babas* (Singapore: Times Books International, 1980), p. 181.
5. SCII of Lim Choon Huat, No. 664, 15/12/32.
6. SCII of Ting Lam Pee, No. 164, 16/9/08.
7. SCII of Kow Wuh, No. 220, 7/5/30.
8. SCII of Leong Ah Thum, No. 22, 22/1/16.
9. SCII of Ong Teck Cheng, No. 174, 22/1/29.
10. SCII of Low Leong, No. 399, 14/8/27.
11. Interview with Ng Kar Eng, AOHD, Reel 4.
12. Ibid.
13. SCII of Ng Pin, No. 393, 6/10/22.
14. SCII of Puah Ah Low, No. 18, 13/1/21.
15. SCII of Teo What Swee, No. 428, 28/10/22.
16. SCII of Ng Pang Suah, No. 431, 28/10/22.
17. See postcard no. 81 in *Singapore Retrospect through Postcards: 1900–1930* (Singapore: Sin Chew Jit Poh: Archives and Oral History Department, 1982), p. 41.
18. SCII of Lim Choon Huat, No. 664, 15/12/32; of Ong Teck Cheng, No. 174, 22/1/29; of Puah Ah Low, No. 18, 13/1/21.
19. 'Economic Study of the Peking Ricsha Puller', *China Economic Monthly*, 3, 6 (June 1926), p. 255.
20. SCII of Tan Guan Sui, No. 153, 7/9/97.
21. SCII, No. 2, 10/2/31.
22. SCII of Robert Laing, No. 617, 25/12/25.
23. SCII of William Grey Nixon, No. 94, 22/7/12.
24. SCII of Ling Soh Kai, No. 597, 9/10/37.
25. SCII of Tan Guan Sui, No. 153, 7/9/97.
26. John Cuylenburg, *Singapore through Sunshine and Shadow* (Singapore: Heinemann, 1982), p. 4.
27. Edwin A. Brown, *Indiscreet Memories* (London: Kelly and Walsh, 1936), p. 4.
28. SCII of Low Yah Cheong, No. 329, 16/7/25.
29. *Singapore Free Press*, 18 February 1920.
30. Ladislao Székely, *Tropic Fever. The Adventures of a Planter in Sumatra* (Kuala Lumpur: Oxford University Press, 1979), pp. 30–1.
31. R. H. J. Sydney, *Malay Land* (London: Cecil Palmer, 1926), p. 30.
32. George Bilainkin, *Hail Penang! Being the Narrative of Comedies and Tragedies in a Tropical Outpost, among Europeans, Chinese, Malays and Indians* (London: Sampson Low, Marston and Co. Ltd., 1932), p. 43.
33. Sydney, op. cit., p. 30.
34. Rupert Emerson, *Malaysia* (Kuala Lumpur: University of Malaya Press, 1966), p. 23.
35. Chia, op. cit., p. 181.
36. Ambrose Platt, *Magical Malaya* (Melbourne: Robertson and Mullen Ltd., 1931), p. 41.
37. Ibid., see Appendices A and B, pp. 270 and 275.
38. Roland Braddell, *The Lights of Singapore* (London: Methuen, 1934; reprinted Kuala Lumpur: Oxford University Press, 1982), p. 41.
39. Sydney, op. cit., p. 19.
40. Enclosure in no. 227 Acting Governor Sir J. H. Swettenham to Mr Chamberlain, 5 August 1898, CO 882/6.
41. Enclosure no. 6 in Confidential Sir Arthur Young to Walter Lord, 13 July 1917, CO 273/457.
42. SCII of Tan Sam Ong, No. 95, 6/7/02.

43. A. Dixon, *Singapore Patrol* (London, 1935), p. 116.
44. Bruce Lockhart, *Return to Malaya* (New York: G. P. Putnam and Son, 1936), pp. 126–7.
45. Enclosure no. 227 Acting Governor Sir J. H. Swettenham to Mr Chamberlain, 5 August 1898, CO 882/6.
46. SCII of Kiong Whye, No. 328, 5/10/29.
47. SCII of Tan Guan Sui, No. 153, 7/9/97.
48. SCII of Abdùl Rahman Bansir, No. 76, 24/3/19.
49. R. C. H. McKie, *This Was Singapore* (London, 1950), p. 104.
50. UNNAYAN, op. cit., p. 26.
51. Lao She, op. cit., pp. 212–13.
52. SCII of Captain A. H. Tilly, No. 135, 17/7/95.
53. SCII of Mah Huat, No. 505. 16/11/34.
54. Lockhart, op. cit., pp. 127–8.
55. Song Ong Siang, *One Hundred Years of the Chinese in Singapore* (London: John Murray, 1902; reprinted Kuala Lumpur: University of Malaya Press, 1967, and Singapore: Oxford University Press, 1984), p. 300.
56. SCII of Fatimah, No. 205, 21/4/31.
57. SMAR JD, 1901, p. B-2.
58. SMAR JD, 1906, p. 5.
59. The statistics in the table have been compiled from annual reports of the Rickshaw Department for the following years: 1901, 1902, 1905, 1906, 1911, 1913, 1914, and 1917.
60. SMAR JD, 1913, p. 3.
61. SMAR JD, 1904, p. 3.
62. V. G. Kiernan, *The Lords of Human Kind. European Attitudes to the Outside World in the Imperial Age* (London: 1972), p. 155.
63. SMAR JD, 1919, p. 1-E.
64. Lao She, op. cit., p. 213.
65. SMAR JD, 1901, p. 132.
66. Lao She, op. cit., p. 189.
67. *The Straits Chinese Magazine*, Vol. VII, No. 2 (1903), pp. 69–70.
68. SCII of Ong Chew Kay, No. 55, 10/2/21.
69. SCII of Tay Ah Sui, No. 2, 5/1/10.
70. SCII of Leng Lock, No. 30, 12/4/03.
71. SCII of Chee Moh Moh, No. 343, 27/12/18.
72. SCII, No. 293, 13/3/22.
73. SCII of Teng Poh, No. 170, 1/8/10.
74. SCII of Ng Liew, No. 386, 3/10/24.
75. SCII of Ong Oh Kaw, No. 116, 16/8/02.
76. SCII of Tan Sam Ong, No. 95, 6/7/02.
77. SSAR, 1896, p. 54.
78. SCII of Wong Cray Tee, No. 36, 7/3/15.
79. SCII of Ling Ah Teng, No. 69, 12/4/17.
80. SCII of Ong Oh Kaw, No. 116, 16/8/02.
81. SCII of Teng Ah Yeok, No. 99, 23/2/25.
82. SCII of Khoon Cheang, No. 400, 23/8/26.
83. SSAR, 1895, p. 36.
84. SCII of Ang Ah Kow, No. 109, 26/5/96.
85. SSAR, 1893, p. 254.
86. SCII of Tan Bah Bee, No. 71, 16/2/34.
87. SSAR, 1914, p. 239.
88. SCII of Soon Say Ann, No. 85, 13/4/19.
89. SCII of an unknown male Japanese, No. 144, 10/4/23.
90. SCII of Soh Yiam Hiang, 23/5/28.
91. SCII of Goh Joo, 4/5/28.
92. SCII of Kow Wuh, No. 220, 7/5/30.

93. SCII of Nyeng Tong Moi, 25/6/34.

94. SCII of Lee Kew Moi, No. 278, 8/6/26.

95. SCII of Teng Lau Ting, No. 247, 24/4/36.

96. See the following cases: SCII of the hawker, Wong Ah Quai, No. 185, 11/7/20; of the carpenter, Lee Kheng, No. 33, 3/2/20; of the prostitute, Ng Kum Moy, No. 41, 10/3/05; of the drunkard, Yuen Koy Thian, No. 126, 26/8/04.

97. SCII of Liong Choo Koh, No. 84, 2/6/07.

98. SCII of an unknown Chinese, No. 2, 5/1/10.

99. SCII of Teo Teck Seng, No. 83, 1/6/07.

100. SCII of unknown male Chinese, No. 112, 20/7/07.

101. SCII of Teo Yang, No. 221, 3/6/21.

102. SCII of Tan Ah Yam, No. 18, 17/1/21.

103. SCII of Wan Chee, No. 36, 4/2/20.

104. SCII of Beng Seng, No. 356, 29/12/20.

105. SCII of unknown male Chinese, No. 300, 25/7/22.

106. SCII of unknown male Chinese, No. 58, 20/4/02.

107. SCII of unknown male Chinese, No. 495, 4/11/27.

108. Ibid.

109. SCII of Ah Low, No. 438, 13/9/25.

11 A Sense of Time and Place

WHAT was the 'time of the rickshaw coolie' like in Singapore? The special time of the rickshaw puller must be measured both in terms of the process of pulling a rickshaw, and the 'time of Singapore' with its natural rhythms of life and work.[1] There was no minute of the day or night when the rickshawman could look along the street and say the city was sleeping. Each district had its particular activity or speciality, and 'special time'. How could the city sleep when there were hundreds of thousands of Chinese within its boundaries all jostling for survival. Everything in Singapore was busy from dawn to dusk, and well into the night—the bureaux and banks, markets and shopping centres, countless brothels and opium shops, and the hospital and morgue.

The measurement of time was inextricably bound up with the cycle of the puller's work and domestic responsibilities. His timepiece was the 'rickshaw clock'; the hiring and maintenance of a rickshaw on a shift basis, and the search for fares comprised the passage of time through the day and night for the puller. It was the sequence of these tasks which suggested that rickshaw coolies knew very well the time of day, and how time passed in the course of a typical day—a time to congregate at the Railway Station to assist travellers arriving by express train from Penang and Kuala Lumpur, a time to rest away from the burning sun and maddening crowd, a time to visit Johnston's Pier to meet the passenger steamers, a time for a pipe of opium as the craving began, a time to go to Malay Street for the rush hour, and a time to quit due to illness.[2] The 'natural' work rhythm of rickshaw pullers was related specifically to the different work-situations where labouring from dawn to dusk was commonplace. Night shift-work was 'natural' in Singapore as the population, trade economy, and harbour facilities expanded in this century. This was most apparent before dawn among the faceless coolies on the docks coaling steamers, and in the myriad godowns, shadows loading and unloading sugar, copra and rubber, as well as disappearing into eating-houses, cabarets, brothels and other businesses linked to entertainment and pleasure.[3]

For rickshawmen there was no weekly division of time made use of by colonial officials to administer the city. Sunday was not a day off for the rickshaw coolie in Singapore. When they did not turn out on the day of the week observed by Christians as a day of rest and worship it was noticed by those conscious of the 'time of the church': 'On Saturday the day before, ... there was a row between Hengwah and Hockcha rickshaw coolies. Rickshaw coolies were not pulling their rickshaws on Sunday as usual.'[4] Dividing the days into weeks was irrelevant. Rickshawmen worked year round except to stop and observe certain festivals and holidays, including Chinese New Year, the Ch'ing-ming festival (visiting ancestral graves), and the Moon Festival (the Mid-autumn celebration).[5] Instead, there was a longer monthly division of time based on the Chinese lunar calendar. Pullers used the term 'moon' to mark off periods of time in a year. The notion of a 'month' or part thereof and 'days' was used to describe the passage of time, especially the recent past, rather than 'weeks'. Rickshaw coolies spoke of becoming ill ten days ago, or having an accident at the beginning of the first moon last year, or of a brother having died in the middle of the twelfth moon of the year before. Interpreters in the police stations, courts, and at the mortuary, however, were inclined to record and translate the 'time' expressed in the statements of rickshawmen into an exact division of time—'15 February 1912'—that corresponded to the dictates of the official form, and that was observed by the English—'the time of the ruling class'.

Normally short periods of time were measured in terms of doing things. For example, motion as a measure—the time it took to pull a passenger from Kranji to the Central Post Office; and consumption as a measure—the time it took to smoke a pipe of opium, drink a cup of tea, or eat a bowl of rice. A rickshaw puller expressed this familiar sense of time related to his work cycle to Roland Braddell, a prominent lawyer and author of the 1930s bestseller, *The Lights of Singapore*: 'Time does not mean much to the Asiatic, and he has his own way of reckoning. I once asked a rickshaw coolie how long he had been waiting, and he replied, "two and a half cigarettes", which was about as graphic a description of time as I have yet met.'[6] Time was also measured in other ways, according to how long men had been in the trade or whether they smoked opium. Experienced, strong men, usually in their mid- to late thirties, pulled during the busiest time of the day, and left the quiet hours in the afternoon to inexperienced young lads.[7] Rickshaw coolies who smoked opium liked to come out early in the morning and late in the evening. They did not like to crawl about in the busy hot hours in the middle of the day. It was the worst possible time for them from the standpoint of their drug habit.[8]

The division of the rickshawman's time of work into night and day was 'natural' in relation to other occupations in a city like Singapore, emerging as a coolie town and the financial and administrative hub of an expanding network of trade and empire. The implications of having to work at night, though, were biologically abnormal. The difficulty of obtaining rest and sleep in the daytime in the midst of the noises of the city and the roar of the traffic was unsettling.[9] Seldom could an exhausted man expect to find a moment of extreme quietness away from the intense noise and bustle of the day. This problem was compounded for coolies with families and small children, confined within a cramped, ill-ventilated cubicle. Yes, opium could be smoked with pleasure in the morning, if only to drown out the incessant sounds of the street, but even a visit to the brothel was apt to be less rewarding as the prostitutes also found their best customers at night. They preferred to sleep off their exhaustion and rest during the first half of the day.

The puller when plying for hire could accept or reject patronage. He could use the time of his labour to advantage and not waste it.[10] The value of time was synonymous with money. The number of fares and hours of work meant success or failure in paying the hire fare, purchasing a meal or packet of *chandu*, and not simply establishing a more exhaustive routine. Most of them knew that a rickshaw coolie ran on his stomach:

> A rickshaw was only a rickshaw. Pull one and you can figure that making enough to look after yourself and pay the rental fee takes care of everything. You don't have to hand over a rental fee if you don't work, so there's no need to work if you have enough money on hand to eat for a day. That's all the relationship between a man and a rickshaw amounts to.[11]

Rickshawmen recognized that it was physically impossible to work around the clock all the time. They were not machines and even the best had to rest sometimes. There was a time to recoup strength. Pullers had to have a number of days off each month. The willingness to work to the limit of physical exhaustion to pay for opium or a prostitute, to meet a gambling debt, or routinely remit money to China, could kill them otherwise.[12]

The nature of rickshaw pulling meant that the puller's work routine was distinct from other coolies' by its irregularity; there were periods of intense hard work, perhaps followed by hours of 'passing the time', sitting on the floorboard of a rickshaw shooting the breeze with fellow pullers, or sipping tea and smoking cigarettes under the shade of Flame of the Forest trees in Raffles Square.[13] Mr Hooper wrote the following about the number of hours a day a puller worked: 'The puller is his own master and does not carry anyone if he does not choose to. He does not work the whole day, but only a few hours.'[14] Not surprisingly, rickshawmen were regarded as being slackers of sorts, despite their capacity for hard work when things got busy around the city. They were accustomed to the work schedule of their day being somewhat elastic—punctuated with trips, rest breaks, more trips, and mealtimes. Their sense of time was also affected by the weather; pullers tended to shorten the hottest part of the working day with a timely nap in the rickshaw, or just head home in the face of a cold, hard, ankle-deep downpour.

For the personal and domestic routine of the rickshaw coolie's passage of time there is far less information than for the work situation. Pullers starting out with a rickshaw either first thing in the morning or evening tended to have a snack at a hawker's stall, and then eat a heavier meal later, after they had pulled several passengers, made some money, and worked up an appetite in the process. Ng Kar Eng recounted at what time he customarily stopped to have his meal:

My lodging house used to be near the Beach Road Market. I usually went out at about 3 a.m., and at about 8 to 9 a.m. I went back to the kongsi for my meal. Sometimes, at home, I had congee for breakfast. After I finished eating ... I went back out [on the street], until between 1 and 2 p.m., then I finished [my work] for the day, and went home.[15]

Koh Mia Siah, a bachelor, often started out with his rickshaw some time past 5.00 p.m. and returned home around 8 to 9 p.m. for his meal, hungry. He then smoked opium for several hours before coming out again.[16] Kwang Ah Lee, who was married, was in the habit of leaving about 5.30 a.m. to ply for hire. At that time of the morning his wife was still asleep. He regularly came home at 9.00 a.m. for a mid-morning meal and to see her.[17] Rickshawmen washed and bathed following a hard day's work, often coming home soaked in perspiration and grime. It was the first thing they did upon entering the damp, dark lodging-house except when the craving for opium was too strong. Men like Tan Geok Heng established a routine of returning at 3.00 p.m. and going upstairs straight away to shower and change before sitting down to supper and a well-deserved rest.[18]

Some pullers, especially those with regular clients, had fixed time commitments and were accustomed to schedules. They pulled at a particular pace, and delivered their passengers to their destinations punctually. Being able to operate on a schedule was one of the hallmarks of a good private puller, especially those employed to convey businessmen to work during rush hour, to get children to school on time and bring them home safely, and to move prostitutes from a brothel to a restaurant or lodging with as little fuss as possible. In 1938, one such puller was Ling Mong; he used to pick up a passenger every day near the old racecourse just after dawn, at 6.00 a.m., and take him to Lavender Street where he boarded a bus.[19]

Space—geographical, sociological, cultural—in Singapore was linked to what rickshaw coolies saw and did during the course of their work cycle every day. Singapore at the turn of the century was still a relatively compact city; the urban sprawl of the new town and 'country districts' was only just beginning then. This 'space' contained, among other aspects, a temporal dimension. The rickshaw puller's perception of the city was built up over months and years into a kind of shorthand, 'a notation of space', replete with minute details on morphology and change in the urban landscape and its relation to their work situation. Rickshaw pulling was an occupation that facilitated journeying right across this social space of Singapore. Pullers did not always confine themselves to working in one part of the city; sometimes they traversed it, and the back and beyond. Singapore, in a very real sense, was an open directory to the puller complete with signposts and landmarks—prominent and innocuous—to guide him round about the city. Rickshawmen developed an acute sense of place and were capable of reading the city like a book. Not only did they rely on such knowledge of the workplace for their livelihood, but their very lives could depend on it. When an accident or assault occurred, they had to fall back on their sense of place or convey it to somebody else to confirm the location of the nearest police station or hospital.

Direction was signified in terms of travelling to town or away from town. The streets in Singapore for the most part obediently ran parallel or perpendicular to the main thoroughfares—North Bridge Road, South Bridge Road, and New Bridge Road—in a nearly perfect checkerboard. The other method was to indicate whether one was north or south of the Singapore River.[20] A puller did not just go from Temple Street to St. Andrew's Cathedral; he crossed from one side of the river to the other—a cultural ecological divide, separating the physical presence of Chinatown and all that it implied from the banking and administrative heart of Singapore run by Europeans. Singapore's obsession with the compass was very much alive in those days, and not just on board ship, as rickshaw pullers would ask passengers if they wanted to go north or south. During stages in a journey passengers also were expected to help navigate, indicating a wish to turn north or south (not left or right) at corners. Koh Ah Nea mentioned that, 'I was on the south side of the river and was not in the High Street'; while Ong Geok Swee who was on his way from Beach Road Market to High Street told the Coroner, 'I was on the market side of Beach Road coming towards town pulling an empty rickshaw'; Ting Kin Seng spoke of coming 'along Havelock Road from town, i.e. from the direction of the [Chinese] Protectorate'; while Low Ah Su described a journey of his as follows: 'I was passing the Manila Show in Anson Road when two Teochew Chinese came and engaged my rickshaw. They both got in my rickshaw and I started off towards town.'[21]

Pullers described a journey not only in terms of its orientation—'towards town' or 'away from town'—but also in terms of streets traversed en route to the destination. Landmarks, usually in the form of buildings, were referred to as a form of 'notation in space' to describe stages of the journey. This remarkable sense of place often was conveyed when rickshawmen were working a particular area and an 'event' suddenly occurred such as an accident or homicide. It was then that pullers demonstrated their extraordinary knowledge of the location of buildings and places, and in a hurry. Tan Moh Tee said, 'I sometimes go to this place (Cornwall Street) near the Ho Ho Biscuit Factory, once or twice a week but not daily'; Teong Seong Chak was sitting in his rickshaw waiting for hire 'in North Bridge Road opposite the Cathedral and near the Stamford Road Bridge'; Lim Chow Tow came out of an opium shop and went to buy cigarettes at a stall when he saw the accident: 'I was on the same side of the road as Fraser and Neaves Aerated Water Factory. The girl came from the opposite side of the road, coming towards me'; Ling Mong picked up his passenger on the morning of the mishap 'near the old racecourse'.[22]

What is also at work here in the puller's visual perception of the landscape is a somewhat unsophisticated form of urban *fung shui* (geomancy—adapting buildings and graves to the landscape).[23] For the rickshaw coolie, space in Singapore was bounded by philosophical and cultural elements contained in the mystical ecology of *fung shui*. In Singapore, rather than in the rural landscape of South China, pullers did distinguish between buildings and parts of the city as either *Yin*, dwellings and places of darkness and unease, or *Yang*, as dwellings and/or places of light and peace. Some spots on the landscape were closely associated with power and fortune in their minds. When conducting people around the Havelock Road area pullers invariably mentioned the Chinese Protectorate, 'that grey awesome squat building' where, since 1911, the Chinese Protector or '*Tai Jin*' (the 'Great Man') sat in judgment and had the final say on all matters affecting the welfare and future of the rickshaw coolies.[24] Rickshaw stands scattered about the fronts of the best hotels were lucrative points and considered to be favourable in the eyes of the pullers along with the Singapore Cricket Club and the Tanglin Club, Singapore's suburban Elysium, where there was dancing on Friday evenings. Molteni's two ice-cream shops in Victoria Street and Dhoby Ghaut did a roaring trade and 'rickshaws ... could be seen outside these shops not only on moonlight nights but also at all times from sunset to midnight'.[25]

Rickshaw pullers also knew other places around the city, though, that were unfavourable; dangerous sites that could affect them adversely. *Yin* surroundings made them ill at ease, if not very frightened at times. Tanjong Pagar, for example, was an outward sign of the material prosperity of the city, and proof of the success of Singapore's free-port status, and its claim to be the gateway of the East. However, to a puller bringing a stranger back to the wharves in the early hours of the morning it was an unquiet place dominated by shadows, poorly lit streets, and death. Experienced coolies must have responded to grafting peons and secret society bullies in the same manner. They knew which streets were permissible to work on year in and year out, which markets and stands were forbidden and dangerous, and where the brutal peon or *samseng* might be waiting to swoop down and confiscate their licence or intimidate them to pay a bribe. This happened to newcomers who guessed wrongly about the *Yin* present in particular streets and dwellings. The role of secret societies in disrupting native-place ties in such spots and effects of extortion, violence, and fear were well known from one generation to the next of rickshawmen. Let us enter into the *Yin* world of the Beach Road Market of the late 1930s, a pot-pourri of Fukien and Hengwah, as seen through the eyes of the elderly Hockchia, Ng Kar Eng: 'In the beginning when I first went [to the market in 1938] I was asked to give protection money. I was not familiar with the person who demanded it; once I had become known, he didn't ask. I told him then that I had certain native place people "protecting" me. Then he didn't dare take it.' Listen to the rickshawman explain in more detail about the indefinable presence of *samseng* on his side of the fish and meat market where the native place of the majority was Hengwah; among the collection of shops and stalls on the opposite side that sold almost any vegetable under the sun, they were mostly 'Fukien people':

> The Beach Road Market had secret societies, their hooligans came to our side of the market to make trouble. They used to say, "you can't stop here, or you can't park there". They didn't allow us to remain around the market. They didn't allow you to make a living. This situation existed. If you wanted to stop at the market to earn a living, you had to give them so much a month. They came to collect it, like that.

Although Ng Kar Eng was looking for a steady place to work, he refused to pay after a while. An incredible conversation unfolds as he relates how the hooligans tried to get down to the needs of an ordinary coolie like himself, and deprive him. He told the *samseng*:

> I am earning a living. I am a labourer. What reason do you have to extort money from me? The samseng would say, "you're making a living here, this place is mine, you must give me 'protection money'.
>
> As I was a newcomer I asked some of those who came from the same native-place as I to go and see him. They told him "you can't do this. If you persist, your people will not be allowed to come to our places. We will not let them make a living". After that they didn't dare take money like that.

But if a puller did not have someone from his own sub-community protecting him a *samseng* could do almost anything to the stream of rickshaws that filled the road outside the market. 'If you didn't give [a bribe], he could give your rickshaw a deliberate jolt. If you left your rickshaw over on the old bazaar side, he would dump out the fish and vegetables from the client's basket, damage the seats, using a knife to cut the cushion. He did this to "*Kacau*"—to make trouble.'[26] Rickshawmen did work certain parts of the city in groups both in the interests of company and safety. These work areas were explicitly defined as off limits to other speech-dialect groups and were the persistent focus of territorial strife between tightly knit cliques of pullers. Small peer groups divided up the city and handfuls of rickshawmen could regularly be found occupying a particular place, huddling together. When a puller had an uneasy feeling about the landscape and the influence it could exert on him, European passengers were apt to be utterly shocked:

> ... when we came to the junction of Kim Seng and River Valley roads and made to turn down the former, the pullers put down the shafts and refused to budge. No amount of argument would get them to go down Kim Seng Road, and eventually I made out the reason. It was that the Governor had offered a price of $100 for the head of a rickshaw coolie cut off in that thoroughfare! And so we had to walk, and an eerie and evil smelling walk it was! No lamps, and swamp on either side until we got to Havelock Road, where we got another Rickshaw.[27]

Rickshaw stands were an obvious place where coolies came and went, as frequently as every few minutes during rush hour, bringing news of the city to relate to fellow pullers. Information and gossip was also exchanged between rickshawmen while staring out to sea along Collyer

Quay from the floorboards of their vehicles, standing on the platform of the Tank Road Railway Station waiting for the trains of the Federated Malay States Railway to arrive, watching the *tuan besar* turn up on the Tanjong Pagar wharf on mail day, or while 'sipping hot coffee with hot buns from a Bengali hawker, or gulping down icewater, sweetened with doubtful syrup at half a cent a glass' under the umbrella of shade trees in Raffles Square.[28] Rickshaw coolies appeared in the same place—at the hotel, wharf, railroad station, a particular street corner, or quiet out-of-the-way spot near the water—on the dot every day. A holiday was a luxury most could ill afford and only sickness would deter them from keeping their daily appointment. Teo Kut Seng described the orientation of his elder brother's sense of place as follows: 'He pulled in the mornings and I pulled in the afternoons.... He usually goes to Lavender Street near the Gas works. No regular customer, just waits there for hire.'[29] The rickshaw owner Tay Choon in relating the workaday routine of Ong Oh Kaw made the point that he was not aware of him having 'any special place or district where he plied for hire. He had no regular time of stopping work and bringing home his rickisha but was seldom out later than 1.00 a.m.'[30] Ch'ng Jit Sing, a Hokkien rickshawman, with three other pullers with the same surname, was in the habit of plying for hire in the Telok Ayer Basin. They often could be seen sitting on their rickshaws, all stationary in a row, facing the sea. At such places rickshawmen like Ch'ng Jit Sing, Ch'ng Hay Koo, Ch'ng Ah Swee, and Ch'ng Tan Hock, were always talking over things they had either seen in the city or overheard at a clan meal or news they had received from their villages in China.[31] Pullers who gathered at the same spot every day tended to blend into the landscape and were considered a part of the local 'community' by neighbours. The elderly wife of Koh See Ho resting with her grandchild in the door of 34 Cornwall Street knew two of the rickshaw coolies by sight always sitting in front of her house; she knew Teong Choon because he parked his rickshaw there every day while the youthful Kow Wuh was a popular figure in the neighbourhood.[32] Tan Moh Tee, a private puller, also knew the three Hockchia coolies who congregated in Cornwall Street as he sat with them whenever his *towkay* visited the area, usually twice a week: 'I know the names of the other three pullers as we associate with each other at this very place'.[33]

1. For important works that deal with the concepts of time, space, work, and history see Emmanuel Le Roy Ladurie, *Montaillou Cathars and Catholics in a French Village 1294–1324* (London: Penguin Books, 1980), pp. 277–87; J. Le Goff, 'Au Moyen Age, temps de l'Eglise et temps due marchand', *Annales: Economies Societies Civilisations*, 15 (1960), pp. 417–33; E. P. Thompson, 'Time, Work-Discipline and Industrial Capitalism', in M. W. Flinn and T. C. Smout (eds.), *Essays in Social History* (Oxford: Clarendon Press, 1974), pp. 39–77; and Georges Condaminas, *L'Spqce Social a' propos de l'Asie du Sud-Est* (Paris: Flamarion, 1980).

2. See Thompson, op. cit., p. 42, on the specific notations of time related to particular work situations.

3. Ibid., p. 76.

4. SCII of Lau Ah Chiew, No. 370, 17/9/23.

5. Yen Ching-Hwang, 'Early Chinese Clan Organizations in Singapore and Malaya, 1819–1911', *Journal of Southeast Asian Studies*, 12, No. 1 (1981), p. 80.

6. Roland Braddell, *The Lights of Singapore* (London: Methuen, 1934; reprinted Kuala Lumpur: Oxford University Press, 1982), p. 41.

7. UNNAYAN in association with T.H. Thomas, *Rickshaws in Calcutta* (Calcutta: UNNAYAN, 1981), p. 22.

8. BMOC, p. C46.

9. On the biologically abnormal aspects of working at night see Louis Chevalier, *Labouring Classes and Dangerous Classes in Paris during the First Half of the Nineteenth Century* (London: Routledge and Kegan Paul, 1973), p. 304.

10. See Thompson, op. cit., p. 43, on the distinction and the value placed on the difference between an employer's time and one's 'own' time.

11. Lao She, *Rickshaw* (the novel *Lo-T'o Hsiang Tzu*), translated by Jean M. James (Honolulu: The University Press of Hawaii, 1979), p. 214.

12. In a survey of 1,000 Peking rickshaw pullers in the 1920s about 95 per cent of the men remained with their rickshaws in the streets between 8 and 12 hours; they only pulled fares on an average for 4 hours. An average of three days per month were spent in resting but approximately 13 per cent of the pullers had no holidays at all. 'Economic Study of the Peking Ricsha Puller', *China Economic Monthly*, 3, 6 (June 1926), p. 256.

13. On elastic time schedules see Thompson, op. cit., pp. 50, 64–6.

14. *Singapore Free Press*, 16/2/20.

15. Interview with Ng Kar Eng, AOHD, Reel 4.

16. SCII, No. 2, 10/2/31.

17. SCII of Teng Ah Poh, No. 392, 10/7/36.

18. SCII of Lim Cheng, No. 415, 22/8/29.

19. SCII of Koh Kim Seng, No. 87, 1/4/38.

20. On space and how distance was measured and described see Le Roy Ladurie, op. cit., pp. 282–3.

21. SCII of William Grey Nixon, No. 94, 22/7/1912; of Lee Aik, No. 503, 7/9/31; of Ling Ah Liew, No. 360, 29/6/31; and of Soh Yiam Hiang, 23/5/28.

22. SCII of Kow Wuh, No. 220, 7/5/30; SCII of an unknown Chinese woman, No. 288, 31/5/28; SCII of a Chinese girl, 22/4/32; of Koh Kim Seng, No. 87, 1/4/38.

23. For a detailed discussion of geomancy and *fung shui* see Maurice Freedman, *The Study of Chinese Society. Essays by Maurice Freedman* (Stanford: Stanford University Press, 1979), pp. 192, 201, 318.

24. Yap Pheng Geck, *Scholar, Banker, Gentleman Soldier. The Reminiscences of Dr Yap Pheng Geck* (Singapore: Times Books International, 1982), p. III.

25. John Cuylenburg, *Singapore through Sunshine and Shadow* (Singapore: Heinemann, 1982), p. 27.

26. Interview with Ng Kar Eng, AOHD, Reel 4.

27. Edwin A. Brown, *Indiscreet Memories* (London: Kelly and Walsh, 1936), p. 75.

28. Cuylenburg provides much interesting information on the Singapore landscape at the turn of the century. See Cuylenburg, op. cit., pp. 5–6, 20, 25, and 28–9.

29. SCII of Teo Kow Seng, No. 436, 3/9/29.

30. SCII of Ong Oh Kaw, No. 116, 16/8/02.

31. SCII of Ch'ng Hay Koo, No. 530, 8/9/37.

32. SCII of Kow Wuh, No. 220, 7/5/30.

33. Ibid.

12 A Crisis of Habitability

THE rickshaw coolie's economic power and his health grew out of a full bowl of rice. Rickshawmen eating out night or day took their place in queues to wait for a bench or stool, or for a bowl and chopsticks at one of Singapore's outdoor hawker stalls, where the food was likely to be as wholesome and plentiful as in the special eating-houses, and economical.[1] The eating-houses provided a fuller service and a place where pullers could rub shoulders with one another, enjoy a satisfying meal of several courses, and linger over tea and talk, while the stalls were places where a coolie went to be fed cheaply, quickly, and generally in silence. All meals were prepared in front of him at his table or as he squat on the ground beside the road next to a Chinese food-hawker with his heavy pole and baskets. But patronizing the stalls had its dangers too. Streetside hawkers such as those who sold *tofu* (beancurd) soup to tempt the palate of the rickshawman were licensed and subject to municipal by-laws in a colonial society, where cleanliness was strictly enforced. Nevertheless, it was common for stall-keepers and food hawkers to wash crockery in open drains which ran on either side of most Singapore roads. Nor were there printed warnings set into the table-tops or on the sides of the stalls stating that the food was considered unhealthy by the authorities, possibly spreading gastro-intestinal diseases such as diarrhoea and typhoid fever.

The vast majority of rickshawmen buying local fare came from congested areas in Chinatown and Rochore Road within five to ten minutes' walking distance of the hawkers. The Hockchia and Hockchew controlled most night stalls in Singapore and they were found principally in Queen Street and the Johore Road district.[2] Their customers were mostly rickshaw pullers. Hockchia hawkers also roamed the streets and set up wherever rickshaw coolies congregated to sell really cheap Chinese dishes and drink. There was no extravaganza but all of a sudden the facilities were there to enjoy a meal—a perambulating stall, the *maa mee* (noodle) seller, and the savoury smell of sweetmeats. On the docks, in Raffles Square, near the Railway Station one could always see the itinerant Chinese hawker with his cooking pots, lowering his pole to cater to the appetites of hungry rickshawmen: 'Presently my nostrils caught the heavy reek of curried food. Chinese hawkers, with baskets of cakes and sweetmeats slung from their carrying poles, moved at a mincing but urgent trot towards the quay side.'[3]

The stalls remained open night and day in shifts. With these hours coolies in Singapore were well served. A certain freedom was possible when it came to fitting eating into the work schedule of the likes of rickshaw pullers, coal coolies, stevedores and others, allowing the choice, for instance, to a rickshaw coolie to deliberately forgo a meal earlier in the evening knowing that he could have his dinner on the street not far from home or work later on when he was apt to be hungry and solvent, just as pullers often went out on the street to have a meal not far from their lodging-house first thing in the morning. At 6.00 a.m., Ting Oh Tee, a Hockchia living at 32 Park Road, usually left the house to 'take food'.[4] Ong Ah Puan, another Hockchia puller, residing in Queen Street, last saw his brother alive having his routine breakfast in a coffee-shop in Victoria Street;[5] Tan Nah Nai, who lived with his brother and was also a rickshaw coolie, frequently set out at 6.00 a.m. without lamps on his rickshaw as it was bright enough by then, for his early morning tea;[6] while Ling Lai Kee, a Hockchia, began his day on 15 June 1939 at a coffee stall not far from the Chinese Protectorate:

On the 15th June 1939 at 6.00 a.m. I was sitting at a coffee stall standing almost opposite the junction of Keng Cheow Street and Cummings Street. Another man, Ting Ah Lai, was also seated at the coffee stall. We were the only customers at the stall. I was sitting on the side of the stall farthest away from the junction. . . . The lamp of the stall was alight.[7]

It was common for pullers to be given some credit in the early hours of the morning and to pay at the end of the shift for their meal. Rickshawmen like Teo Kow Seng were granted credit regularly. Teng Pin Hua sold cakes on the five-footway of No. 228 Victoria Street where Teo Kow Seng lived. When he left his lodging at 4.30 a.m. with a rickshaw, he always stopped at Teng Pin Hua's stall and bought 6 cents' worth of cakes to be paid for later that morning. He ate them there and then set out for his favourite spot, Lavender Street near the gas works.[8] Lee Ah Lak was a hawker who sold cakes around the clock in front of a rickshaw lodging-house in Sungei Road where he lived downstairs. He was not as fortunate as Teng Pin Hua as the credit he extended was not always recoverable. Project yourself into the emaciated body of Yau Chin Swee, aged 34, a Hokkien rickshaw puller who was to ultimately commit suicide. He had been out of work for sometime due to illness. According to his fellow lodgers he frequently talked nonsense about cakes made of clay. He bought his sweets from Lee Ah Lak, the cakeseller, who lodged in the rickshaw house. Yau Chin Swee owed the hawker money and when the latter did not want to extend any more credit to him, the puller was overheard by his comrades to have said he did not want his cakes anyway as 'they were made of clay'. There may be an explanation for his suicide; however, nothing is mentioned about it in the Coroner's Inquest beyond a brief reference to recurrent illness. But when Lee Ah Lak speaks the relationship between a street hawker and a rickshawman is recounted:

I knew Chin Swee. A ricksha puller and [he] lived upstairs in 96 Sungai Road. I have known him for about three months. He used to buy cakes from me. He still owes me thirty or forty cents. I have asked him to pay me but he seemed to be mad and laughed at me and called out the name of a Chinese God, but did not pay. I took him to be mad and never expected to get my money from him. He used to help himself sometimes to cakes but as he was poor and also a little mad I did not stop him. I don't know if he had any friends. I never heard anybody asking for him.[9]

The sympathetic bond linking hawkers as clansmen and 'street people' to rickshawmen made them helpful in other ways as well. After the humiliation of a protracted illness rickshaw coolies in need of quick money knew they could go to a foodstall-keeper not only for a charitable meal but also to get a loan. Lim Chip Moey came down with a fever for a fortnight after which he borrowed 30 cents, the cost of the rickshaw rental, from his friend, a cakeseller named Lim Ah Long.[10]

Living cheaply in the rickshaw quarter, though, meant not all coolies ate out regularly. Rickshaw pullers lived communally and the lodging-houses usually contained a common kitchen at the rear of the building. They prepared meals for themselves or took it in turns on a roster basis; breakfast was rarely eaten in the house but a hearty meal of rice and vegetables was often prepared in the afternoon and evening. Wonderful smells wafted through the front doors of Victoria Street as scallions, lots of sesame oil, fried mixed vegetables, garlic, and cabbage were combined by the sure hands of men such as Tan Tee Kim, for other lodgers.[11] Considering the overcrowding and the difficult conditions of the kitchen area in rickshaw houses, it is surprising how few cooking accidents occurred. Tan Tee Kim experienced one in 1896. He was cooking on a one-burner charcoal stove, and stooped to transfer rice and mixed vegetables to old, chipped, earthenware plates. There was no counter, so when Tan Tee Kim turned to lay the crockery on the floor, he accidentally overturned the cooking pot.[12]

Rickshaw work was physically exhausting. The puller's diet was not always sufficient for good health. Although rickshawmen were hearty eaters, there were few, if any, fat or ungainly figures among them. Normally, when times were good, pullers ate decently. It was noted by doctors in Tan Tock Seng Hospital that 90 per cent of opium patients were rickshaw coolies and they were better fed than the average patient.[13] The staple foods were rice, prepared as a porridge, *congee*, or fried with bits of pork or vegetables, and Chinese *mee*, a sort of noodle, which in a few minutes expert hawkers cooked for hungry coolies into an appetizing mixture of pork, prawns, various vegetables and *mee* that was as colourful to look at as it was delicious. A chief source of protein was *tofu*, soya bean cakes, made to rejuvenate the strength of a puller who stopped for a timely snack: 'He rested for some time and then crossed the bridge and bought a bowl of bean curd from a street vendor. Warmed by the scalding hot snow-white bean curd, the vinegar, soy sauce, chili pepper oil, and scallion tips gave off an absolutely wonderful smell. . . . He took a mouthful. The bean curd opened a path in his body.'[14] Rice porridge was the favourite meal rickshawmen ate when they rubbed shoulders with one another in the early hours of the morning at food stalls in the streets of their quarters. While bland compared to *tofu* soup or hot spicy curry the inexpensive porridge still tempted the appetite, and it often turned up in post-mortem examinations. Let us look for a moment at a few cases in 1938–9: Tien Sang Kwai's stomach contained a large quantity of *congee*; the content of an unknown puller's stomach was partly digested porridge; while the stomach cavity of Ting Choon Moy had a small amount of 'porridgy substance'.[15]

To the Chinese cooking is an art, and in Singapore rickshawmen knew some of the best food was cooked and eaten in the street. Pullers would go out of their way to share the pleasure of a simple meal with a neighbour. Yew Tua Mui, a Hengwah puller resident in Prinsep Street, knew the barber, Teng Hong Chew Kiah, who had a shop near where he lived. Yew Tua Mui often went to his shop at about midday: 'When I arrived there he was attending a customer. I told him I was on my way to take my food. He ask [*sic*] me to wait for him. I waited for a short while. We went out together. We went to the market for food.'[16] On auspicious occasions rickshawmen would pool their resources to enjoy an extraordinary meal in the company of their friends but in the rickshaw house rather than on the street. One rickshawman, Ong Seng Hong, measured time and friendship in terms of the small pleasures of life derived from a special 'feast' with friends, a meal that might add virtue, cure their ailments, make them capable of better work. Chua Kiong was one of five pullers at 34 Muar Road who partook of this rich repast. They all contributed towards the food, paying 30 cents each, an amount equivalent to the rickshaw rental for one day. Ong Seng Hong went to the local market and bought two chickens, some *samsu* (Chinese rice wine), and vermicelli. The sense of informality and enjoyment surrounding the preparation and sharing of the meal was highlighted by Chua Kiong's experience:

> We all helped to prepare the meal. The two chickens were boiled in ordinary water until cooked and then ten cents worth of samsoo was poured into the remaining liquid (only about ⅓ of a cup). The vermicelli was mixed with the chicken and samsoo. The five of us then sat down and ate it. That was between 12 and 1 p.m. (I took no rice). I then went out and enjoyed myself. I did not know there was any durian there, also I do not like it....
>
> I felt no ill effects from the meal. We finished up the meal and I would have eaten more had there been some.... We all ate about the same amount. I very rarely take samsoo. I don't know whether the deceased (Ong Seng Hong) used to drink samsoo but he did not earn enough to buy much samsoo. He did not smoke opium. This was the first time I had a meal of chicken mixed with samsoo.[17]

On the other hand, Chua Sin Chin, who left to gamble at a neighbour's house afterwards, was used to socializing in this fashion with friends. 'I often have a meal like this with various people and it is always prepared in the same way. I did not have any durian as I do not like it.'[18]

Food cost less at home, even compared to the inexpensive meals eaten outside, except on occasions like the one above when men came together to celebrate within the confines of lodging-houses. While the average per capita monthly food expenditure was higher when rickshawmen ate out, there were many who were loath to take the time to cook at home, as the time and money saved by being the cook had to be balanced against time lost in real wages from pulling the rickshaw. Approximately 25–40 per cent of the puller's daily income was spent on food. Because rickshawmen often earned irregular incomes they tended to live on a day-to-day basis. Thus pullers were forced to buy foodstuffs in small quantities from fresh food hawkers who lived close by. Their low incomes forced them to purchase primarily rice and vegetables. Obviously, for many, except the really poor among them, it made sense to pay a little extra to eat a regular meal with a bit of meat or fish at a stall where the hawker could also extend credit to his customers.

It was difficult enough to work so hard, but to go hungry on top was a reality of life for rickshawmen in Singapore by the 1920s. A few cents really counted at the turn of the century. At that time a puller could eat well and still pay his rickshaw hire:

> A cup of coffee with milk was three cents in a coffee shop and two cents from a hawker.... On the five-footway, satay twice the size of that sold today and better in quality sold at two cents a stick; Kui-teow [a kind of noodle made from rice flour] cost three cents for a large plateful. A big cupful of Hokkien mee, sufficient to satisfy one for a day, cost ten cents.[19]

However, by 1918 the wages of rickshawmen had fallen at least 20 per cent behind the increased cost of living. This was particularly noticeable with regard to the pattern of purchasing and consumption of food. The rise in the cost of food, mostly condiments (soya sauce, sesame oil, vinegar) or preserved food from China, was tremendous. Salted cabbage, for instance, which was one of the main vegetables, increased from 50 cents to nearly $3 per kg.[20] As a consequence of falling wages, rising prices of basic necessities, and acceptance of lower nutritional levels, many of the pullers classified as offenders for being 'physically weak', 'decrepit' or 'ragged and dirty', were, in fact, suffering from malnutrition—a condition that was virtually non-existent among them two decades earlier. It was for these really poor coolies, who found it difficult to muster the strength day after day to earn enough to get a reasonable meal, that some wealthy Babas used to place pots of tea at the edge of the five-footway in front of their houses.

> Two bowls, one filled with water and the other containing empty Chinese teacups, gave the weary rickshaw-pullers ... the opportunity of refreshing themselves with a drink whenever they walked past the homes of those Babas. The bowl of water was for them to wash the cups after they had their drink. This gesture of offering relief to hardship suffered by the less fortunate stemmed from the advice given to the Babas by priests, in whom they had great faith.[21]

Just occasionally though, an innocent drink or meal could end in accidental death. The daily expense for food no longer mattered to Seow See, a young Hokkien puller who was found lying dead in Telok Ayer Street near the food stalls where he was said to have had a meal the night before. The verdict was ptomaine poisoning.[22] A fish bone, about an inch long, from a hawker's fare was found embedded in a bloodclot near the ulcerated portion of the oesophagus of the puller, See Hong Yen.[23] Tragically, Ong Seng Hong, who partook of a meal of chicken prepared with Chinese liquor and afterwards ate some durian, was later found dead from alcohol poisoning on his bed.[24]

Rickshaw pullers owned little in the way of material possessions. It was an important strategy of transient single labourers not to have superfluous things that could tie them down. If one visited the cubicle of a puller one might see a sleeping mat, red blanket, teapot, a cracked dish or two, possibly an opium pipe and one or two changes of clothes lying about. That was all. As birds of passage with no home of their own, except when they returned briefly to China, rickshawmen had a different sense of wealth and of the meaning of objects from permanent residents. They did not accumulate needless possessions. Owning furniture such as a bed hindered them in moving from one part of Singapore to another in search of a better *towkay*, boarding house, or place to work. The only thing worth acquiring that signified wealth, mobility and security was a rickshaw. All their worldly effects were carried in a long pillow box with a rounded top which every Chinese immigrant in those days owned.[25]

Clothing at the beginning of the twentieth century comprised a pair of running shorts, a hat, and sometimes a loose open shirt. In 1900 pullers were prone to run on the streets naked from the waist up. Dress became an essential item of expenditure when laws were passed requiring rickshaw coolies to wear certain types of clothes so as not to offend unduly the sensibilities of the public. The clothing to be worn by pullers of each class of rickshaw was prescribed in the by-laws.[26] Between 1894 and 1902 thousands of cases against rickshaw coolies for wearing 'bad clothes' were brought before the Registrar. A study of old photographs shows that pullers were forced to be more clothes-conscious and dressed somewhat differently by 1914. They retained their traditional garb—tight-fitting 'coolie blue' shorts or black baggy pants and straw hats—adding the loose-fitting coat-shirt to cover up the strain, sweat and nakedness. There was no way to identify one puller from the next, except by dialect and the shape of their hats.

> But the puller himself is the interesting person. At first we can see little difference between one puller and another. All seem to have bare feet and to be wearing either black or blue shorts, with a short coat, sometimes with sleeves and sometimes without. Their head-covering is usually a basket hat, fairly wide in the brim and going to a point in the middle—cone shaped. Some have evidently still got their pigtails and these they wear done up tightly with a piece of wood through them, though most wear their hair cut short except for the heavy black bunch that hangs over the elastic strap at the back of their head which keeps the

hat on. Now look a little more closely and see if all the hats appear to be alike. After a while you will discover that many of the hats, though cone shaped, do not have sharp points, but are rounded at the top. You will also see that some of the round knobs are wide and some are much narrower. Each type of hat indicates a different clan of Chinese, and the hats themselves are alone worth a careful study. In Singapore also we shall find many rickshaw-pullers wearing ordinary felt-hats—very old and battered—and also many who wear Japanese straws; it is therefore difficult to tell what clan these pullers belong [to].[27]

Ng Kar Eng described the apparel of the Singapore rickshaw puller of the 1930s in detail:

The rickshaw pullers mostly wore blue clothing, some of it was dyed blue, some green, mostly blue. The Amoy people's material, like those clothing worn by refugees, was most common [among rickshawmen]. Pullers mostly wore shorts, it was difficult to run with long trousers. The vast majority wore shorts, blue shorts mostly; this way the shorts would not get dirty.[28]

He then proceeded to talk about the ubiquitous straw hat: 'We had to wear a hat, a straw one. Hainan hats were not worn so much. Some pullers also wore the old-fashioned wide-brim straw rain hats, and gathered up their queue, others also wore large hats made from split bamboo. Without hats it was very hot, it was unbearable.'[29] Besides the hat, the rickshawman also had a piece of cloth, something like a sweat rag: 'Some took towels, tied to this side [of the rickshaw shaft], some wrapped the towel on their head, and some tied it to their wrist, to wipe their sweat with.'[30]

It was difficult to run in shoes, especially when a man first started pulling. Most went barefoot. Ng Kar Eng was no exception when it came to not wearing shoes:

No, I did not wear those straw sandals. It depended on whether you could get used to wearing them. If you could not get used to it the first time, you would never know how to run properly . . . I remember some wore rubber sandals, the tubes of tyres; when the tubes were damaged, they [the pullers] made rubber sandals out of them, some wore these, but generally speaking no shoes were worn; to pull with those rubber sandals was not comfortable that is why most of us went barefoot. Initially, when I first started to pull rickshaws, the roads were not as good then, it used to be tarred roads, and the tar used to melt under the sun, sometimes your feet ran over the burning tar, with the fierce sun shining . . . the tar stuck to the feet, and you got blisters. Later on the soles of your feet were not affected in the same way because the skin became tough and hard. It was better in rainy weather because the road was harder, and it was easier to run; the hot weather was more difficult on one's feet, the road was soft, the tar got soft and melted, it stuck to rubber, stuck to the tyre, sometimes stuck to my feet, a bit tough.[31]

Rickshawmen ran barefoot or in straw or rubber sandals but when not working they gave their tired feet a well-deserved rest 'in wooden clogs, very cool, very comfortable, and very cheap, at ten cents a pair'.[32]

A puller went to the tailor for all rickshawmen in his quarter, who also made the rounds of the houses from time to time, took orders and later delivered the finished apparel:

It took a total of two dollars and twenty cents to get properly turned out. A jacket and trousers of fine looking unbleached rough cloth cost one dollar, black cloth shoes were eighty cents, cotton socks were fifteen cents, and a straw hat cost twenty-five cents. He gave the tattered things he took off to a rag picker in exchange for the usual two boxes of matches.[33]

Although most rickshaw coolies in Singapore dressed in blue or black cotton outfits, some non-conformists wore white pants, checked shirts and Panama hats or pith helmets. A few were even willing to wear clothing with advertisements sewn on if it meant a free coat:

Attempts were made by one or two advertising firms to introduce a system of advertising by providing the pullers with free coats to the back of which the advertisement was attached. The pullers appreciated the coats immensely, but were extremely callous as to the fate of the advertisements, with the result that as an advertising medium, the experiment has not proved entirely successful.[34]

The documentation in the Coroner's Records provides some detail on the matter of dress. The Coroner mentioned items of clothing only when identification of a corpse was in doubt; the only recognizable fact being that the deceased was a coolie and had physically worked hard. Clothes, under such circumstances, were a singularly important clue in helping to identify the origin and occupation of an 'unknown' Chinese who had been run over, assaulted, or dumped outside as a cholera victim.[35] The 'coolie blue' or black shorts and a red blanket in the 'language of clothing' corresponded to the dress of a rickshaw coolie. The items found in the pullers' clothing also told the Coroner something about their destitution; the contents of the pockets invariably yielded paltry amounts. Let us momentarily examine this documentation in cloth for 1911 when cholera was rife in the rickshaw quarters. The clothing at least still signified their occupation in that terrifying moment when pullers lost their identity as their comrades abandoned them unceremoniously in the streets out of fear of disease and death.[36]

TABLE 12.1

Coroner's Inquests and the Language of Clothing

Name	*Date*	*Dialect Group*	*Age*	*Apparel and Possessions*
Unknown	7/10/11	Hokkien	45	Blue coat and pants
Unknown	7/10/11	Hockchia	35	Blue clothes/red blanket
Unknown	15/10/11	Hockchia	37	Blue clothes, red blanket, mat and water vessel
Unknown	24/10/11	Hockchia	30	Blue clothes/mat
Unknown	24/10/11	Hockchia	20	Red blanket
Unknown	29/11/11	Hockchia	40	Blue clothes/reddish mat

Food and clothing became more expensive and difficult to obtain by the 1920s, as was housing. Singapore, with its free-port status, was presented as a model of administrative and economic success for other colonial powers and the rest of the region, yet the vast majority of its Chinese inhabitants including the rickshaw pullers lived in dire poverty. The large rickshaw houses used by the pullers ought to have been called 'Dickensian'. Upward of 30,000 men lived in these lodgings during the 1920s, most of which had neither running water nor toilets. According to official Municipal figures, each Chinese resident had only a tiny amount of living space. The area of some cage-like cubicles or rooms was as low as 60 square feet per man. Some rickshawmen slept on the five-footway or in the alleyway at the back. They preferred that to soaring rents and the grimness of accommodation for their kind. Most of the tenement houses were dreadful, decrepit, and dangerous by the first decade of this century. A large proportion of the buildings had been erected before 1860.

The municipal regulations were ignored by owners and landlords, some of whom also ran rickshaw agencies on the same premise or nearby. They drew large rents from these houses. Many owners angered and displeased their tenants by not making necessary repairs. In most of the lodging-houses there were no hygiene or safety standards. Fire precautions, in the older buildings particularly, were non-existent; only one stairwell as a fire escape for 100–120 men in a tumbledown three-storey building. Occasionally the attention of the authorities was drawn to these derelict houses. They were visited by municipal officials and found to be absolutely unfit for habitation but the buildings were rarely closed. Some of the properties had been in a rotten filthy condition for so long they were incapable of renovation, short of being condemned, demolished, and rebuilt.

Beauty, the aesthetic of the city, became a class thing. It was a privilege reserved for European officials and wealthy *towkay* who lived in rambling house compounds with landscaped gardens. Their mansions were far from the slums of the pullers, and their places of work in downtown Singapore to which they commuted in rickshaws. Let us penetrate into the recesses of Chinatown enclosed in its own bleak privacy in the 1920s and pay special attention to the housing conditions of rickshaw pullers. Rickshaw lodging-houses had one or more large rooms; the average number was two to three, the highest being six to nine rooms in a building. The men slept in wooden beds fixed to the wall in tiers, on canvas or straw cots in the centre of the room, and on the floor in the passageway. The lodging-houses were characterized by intensive use of shared bed 'space' which was rented out in some instances for 8- to 12-hour periods. In the biggest compound houses where there were 130 or more occupants, if a coolie wanted to move about the room he had to literally walk over the bodies of fellow pullers. This was the case when Low Ngiong Ing was a boy.

1 A rickshaw coolie sitting on the floorboard of his rickshaw, smoking an opium pipe. Attached to the floorboard was the mount for the box-shaped coconut-oil lamps, while stamped on the tarpaulin flap was the registration number.

2 The central passage of the lower floor of a tenement house. This photograph was taken with a magnesium flash in 1907.

3 A rickshaw coolie dressed in traditional garb—tight-fitting shorts, a coat-shirt, and the ubiquitous straw hat. Most pullers went barefoot and this man was no exception to the rule. (*Courtesy of the Singapore National Archives and Records Centre*)

4 Rickshaws were hired by travellers arriving by rail from the Federated Malay States at all hours. A postcard of the station at Tank Road shows nearly twenty rickshaws lined up next to one another with rain-proof hoods raised and lowered; the station clock showed the time to be nearly 5 p.m. (*Courtesy of the Singapore National Archives and Records Centre*)

5 By the first decade of the twentieth century rickshaws had become an indispensable part of the commercial life of Singapore. Here rickshaws flank the Hongkong and Shanghai Bank on three sides. (*Courtesy of the Archives and Oral History Department, Paul Yap's Collection*)

6 Moving unaccompanied goods, such as fruit, was both profitable and enjoyable since the rate charged was often higher and the pace somewhat slower.

7 Rickshaw coolies running past the bronze statue of Sir Thomas Stamford Raffles in front of the Victoria Memorial Hall. (*Courtesy of the Archives and Oral History Department, Paul Yap's Collection*)

8 Raffles Place, by the 1930s, was one enormous parking lot filled to capacity with saloon-type taxi-cabs. The rickshaw was gradually being wiped out by then and the taxi-cab was playing a key role in the process. (*Courtesy of the Archives and Oral History Department, Paul Yap's Collection*)

9 Rickshaw stands were an obvious place where pullers came and went, bringing news to relate to fellow pullers. At this particular stand situated next to a food stall, four out of the six parked rickshaws are unattended. (*Courtesy of the Archives and Oral History Department, Paul Yap's Collection*)

10 Rickshaw stands in front of the best hotels in Singapore were considered to be lucrative spots to work. This photo captures the daily activity of the rickshaw pullers around the Raffles Hotel in 1921. (*Courtesy of the Battye Archives, State Government Library of Western Australia*)

11 A row of rickshaws stretching towards infinity along Collyer Quay in the early 1930s.

12 During the rickshaw strike in 1938 thousands of vehicles were impounded for safe keeping at the premises of the Registrar of Vehicles in Middle Road because of fear that striking coolies intended to destroy them.

13 Before the turn of the century over 18,000 rickshaws were in use in Singapore. The two rickshaws in the foreground were the old-fashioned iron-tyred double rickshaws.

14 To reduce the risk of hit-and-run accidents at night, a rear reflector sign which could be attached to the axle was first recommended in 1917, but it was not made a compulsory fitting until 1939.

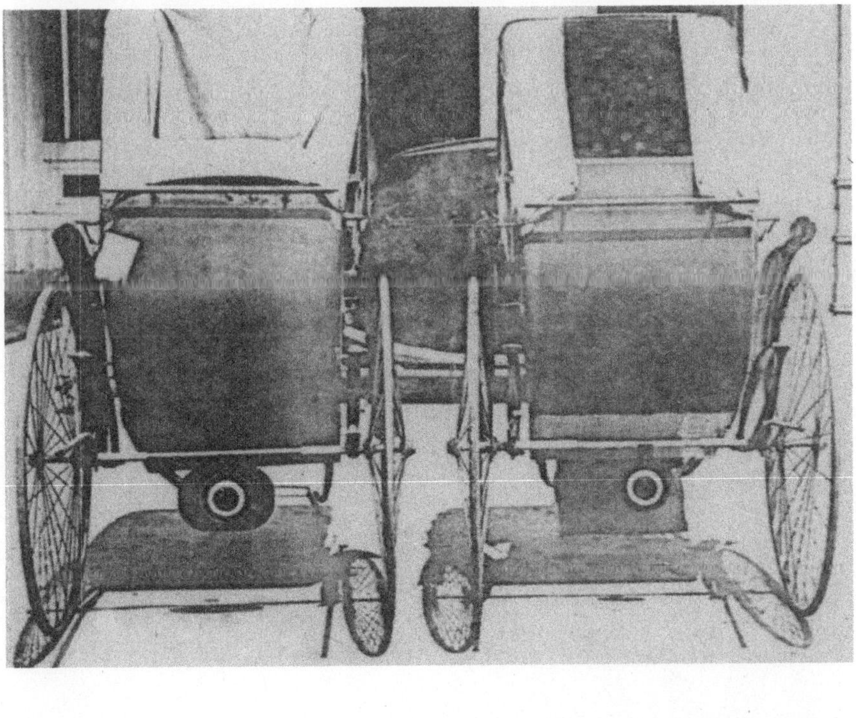

15 The amount of rickshaw traffic grew in direct proportion to the size of the town, and its population. Here, South Bridge Road is jammed with rickshaws on both sides of the tram tracks in the vicinity of Temple Street. (*Courtesy of the Archives and Oral History Department, Paul Yap's Collection*)

16 South Bridge Road in 1911. The traffic on this thoroughfare was difficult with bullock-carts, rickshaws, hawkers, cyclists and pedestrians all jostling for right of way.

17 A typical traffic scene in New Market Road in the mid-1930s. The motor cars and lorries tend to dominate the space on the left side of the street, forcing the rickshaw puller to veer out into the path of oncoming traffic.

18 In the inter-war years the number of licensed motor cars on the road rose sharply from a few hundred to thousands. One of the most popular motor cars of this era was the Austin-tourer.

19 In some respects, no medium was less appropriate for recording accurately the movement of a rickshaw puller, than the early camera. Here two rickshawmen are caught in full stride in front of the Thian Hock Keng Temple, Telok Ayer Street.

20 The local police station near the junction of Pasir Panjang and Clementi Roads. The Chinese woman and child appear to have been posed in the rickshaw for the photograph. (*Courtesy of the Archives and Oral History Department, Paul Yap's Collection*)

21 A posed photograph/postcard. Written on the postcard, dated 27 April 1908, was the following: 'These rickshaws are very pleasant to ride in—the Chinaman runs almost as fast as a horse.' (*Courtesy of the Archives and Oral History Department, Paul Yap's Collection*)

22 Photographs of this type turned rickshawmen into caricatured specimens for the fashionable genre of magazine pictures and picture postcards associated with imperial tourism. (*Courtesy of the Archives and Oral History Department, Paul Yap's Collection*)

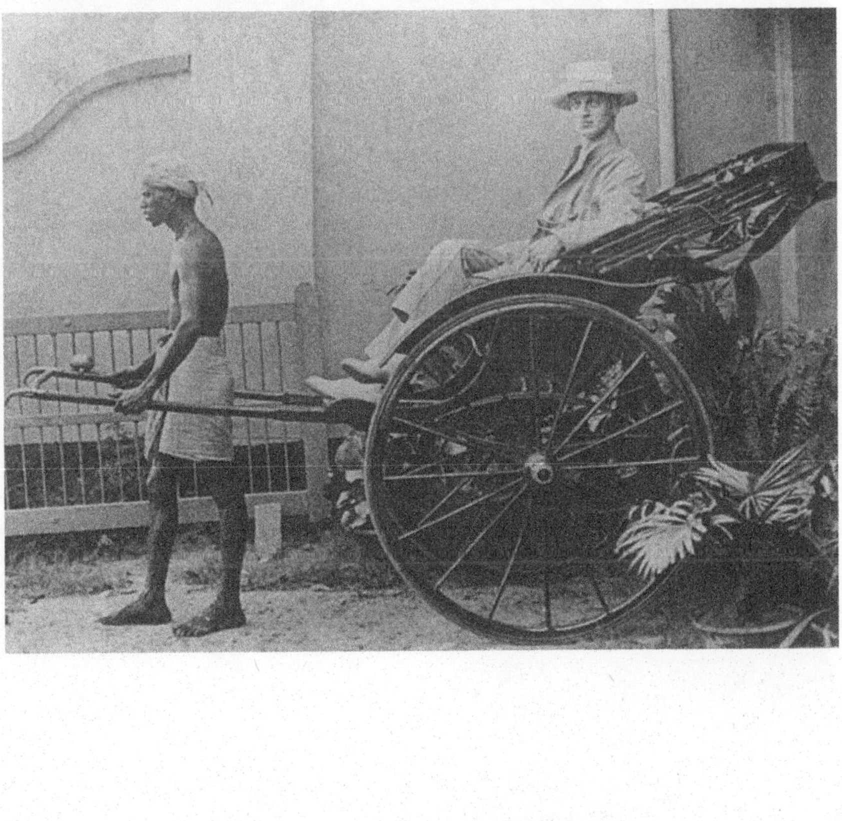

23 & 24 Photographs of the type which turned rickshawmen into caricatured specimens for the fashionable genre of magazine pictures and picture postcards associated with imperial tourism. (*Courtesy of the Archives and Oral History Department, Paul Yap's Collection*)

25 A posed photograph of a Malay passenger with umbrella seated in a first-class rickshaw, *circa* 1914. (*Courtesy of National University of Singapore Library, Rare Photographs Collection*)

26 The rickshaw was without equal for visiting the side-lanes, shops and brothels. In 1938 French marines bound for Indo-China went sightseeing in rickshaws.

27 A streetside hawker and rickshaw coolie near the Read Bridge, early 1900s. (*Courtesy of the Singapore National Archives and Records Centre*)

28 The average consumption of prepared opium by rickshaw coolies was high even when compared with Chinese coolies working on railroad construction or the docks.

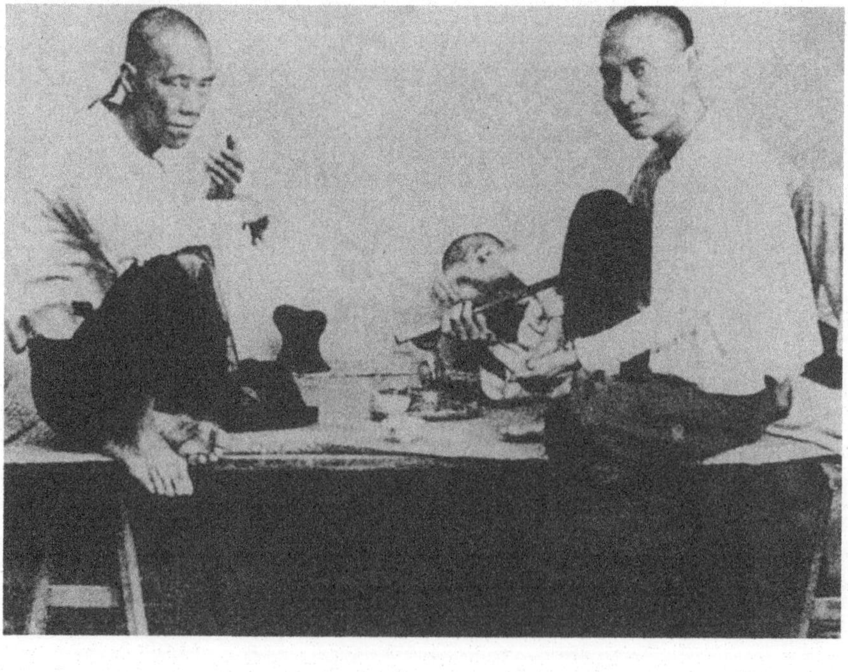

29 Prostitution was such a widespread phenomenon in Singapore because of its large bachelor migrant population. A number of brothels and eating-houses were located in Sago Street in 1910 when this photograph was taken. (*Courtesy of the Archives and Oral History Department*)

30 An older rickshawman observing a rare moment of respite, sitting in his rickshaw in a suburban country lane. (*Courtesy of the Archives and Oral History Department, Paul Yap's Collection*)

31 The end of an era, Singapore, December 1941. A heart-broken Chinese mother mourning her child's death amidst the twisted wreckage of rickshaws after a Japanese bombing raid. (*Courtesy of the Australian War Memorial*)

32 The rickshaw keeping pace with its successor, the trishaw, on a rainy Bras Basah Road in 1947. (*Courtesy of the Singapore National Archives and Records Centre*)

Our home was in lower Victoria Street. It was a slum in which the rickshaw-pullers pullullated. Most of them had left their families in China hoping to make money quickly and return. They dossed in tiers, tier above tier, the higher two feet above the lower so that there must have been at least three tiers on each wall. The middle space was left as a passageway in the daytime and littered with canvas camp-beds at night.[37]

The *pang keng*, or common room, was frequently rented by pullers of the same dialect group, especially when the landlord also happened to run the rickshaw agency. Each man paid a certain amount per month towards the rent. The room served as a meeting hall, the mess, and as a dormitory—the living, eating, and sleeping quarters of the rickshaw coolie all wrapped up in a single room. Some rickshawmen slept in the *pang keng* regularly, while others preferred clear nights and fresh air or the 'all night smoking shops—these keep their belongings there and use the place as a sort of club'.[38] Generally, most pullers went to bed confined to dark, crammed upper floors of lodging-houses. The front of the first floor was used usually for repair and storage of rickshaws while the *towkay* lived at the back.

Sometimes, when space was at a premium, men slept three ways in a room—on the wooden tiers, on the floor, and on cots—or even, for the poorest, on the same bed with another puller. Tang Neo Kong, a rickshaw owner living at 21 Omar Road, explained that several of his boarders slept on one large bench. The hammock-like bench was on a rope swing which was attached to the ceiling! At both ends of this suspended platform were beds and in the centre was a table. The men kept their matting, clothing, and opium tray on it. To get up to the platform bed there were two ladders, one on each side.[39] In Peking in the 1920s rickshaw firms accommodated on average 10.5 men in each room, although one case was found where 16 men were living together.[40] By 1921 living space in Singapore was at such a premium that 16 men living in one room was common. Let us look at an extreme example of overcrowding in a *pang keng*. Ting Chong Soon described his first-floor dormitory at 22 Tras Street:

There were eighteen or nineteen of us living in the same room. Some of them were hockchews the remainder were hockchas, Ong Mah Tee was one of them. There is a staircase at the front end of the room, a door at the back end, sleeping benches alongside both sides of the room and another sleeping bench down the centre of the room. I sleep on the end of the centre bench near the staircase. My brother (the deceased) used to sleep under the window at the back of the room. Ong Mah Tee slept on the bench alongside the wall (the right hand side facing the street) quite close to my place. Ong Mah Tee and the accused shared the same sleeping platform.[41]

Each man paid 80 cents for a space to sleep whether he shared it with another coolie or not. The tenants in this case were also required to have their own wooden platforms.

In an effort to obtain living space rickshawmen were forced to accept severe overcrowding—an overcrowding that would have been considered intolerable even by the lax colonial standards of a few years earlier—and 'pile up' in dark, poorly ventilated buildings. There were few uncrowded rooms in the slums of Chinatown. Those pullers fortunate enough to find them had to be prepared to pay a much higher rent than for the cramped quarters of the big rickshaw houses. Yau Chin Swee knew the rickshaw coolies of Singapore were facing a great social problem of urban overcrowding. He had been a tenant at No. 96 Sungei Road for six months in 1924, and had always lived in the same room, the top left one looking at the house from the canal. There were six other pullers with Chin Swee in the room, and each paid the principal tenant $1.60 per month for the privilege to sleep on a trestle bed with straw matting and have some elbow room to spare.[42]

The severe overcrowding saw people take in desperate lodgers to make a little money. They were usually bachelors, who were apt to be clansmen and opium smokers. The opium shop of Lim Yam at 109 Albert Street was home to Lim Tiew for about a month and a half before he killed himself. The rickshaw coolie had been sick for over a month and could not work. He suffered from venereal disease. Rent for him included a daily ration of *chandu*:

> He had lodged in my house for a month and a half. . . . He suffered from swelled legs and swelled testicles. I never heard him threaten to kill himself. He had no money and could not pay his rent. He owes me eight dollars rent. I was not pressing him for payment. I allowed him his food and about thirty five cents worth of chandu a day. I include all that in the eight dollars.[43]

Another addict, Teng Lau Ting, who was to commit suicide right next door at 108 Albert Street, had a similar arrangement in 1936. Teng Hong Chew Kiah, a barber, gave the following details on the 'sleeping space' in his shop at the inquest.

> I am Hengwah Chinese . . . I have a small [barber] shop containing two chairs at 108, Albert Street. I sleep on a canvas bed in a small room behind the shop. There is a door leading from the shop to the room. There is another door in the backroom. This door opens out to the courtyard. There is also a window in the backroom. This window also opens out to the courtyard. Another side of the room is made of wire netting and a few planks. In the room was a sleeping bench fixed up about six feet from the floor. Besides myself Teng Lau Ting occupied the back room. He was a Hengwah Chinese, over forty years old. He was a rickshaw puller and a clansman of mine. He slept on the sleeping bench. No one else slept in that room.[44]

A principal cause of the shortage of housing by 1918 was the proliferation of cubicles in most public lodging-houses in Chinatown, and elsewhere. Property owners found it more profitable to subdivide their tenements than to construct new housing. Large houses were subdivided into a honeycomb of temporary single rooms, or cubicles with a communal kitchen and a common living area. There were wooden cubicles built out of tea boxes and cloth ones constructed from canvas sacks.[45] This resulted in the worst sort of overcrowding imaginable.[46] Because of the demand, a poor rickshawman could not afford to pay more than a share of the rent of a lodging-house cubicle. The rent varied between $10 and $15 a month depending on the locality. Some rickshawmen did not even have a share of a cubicle; they occupied 'bunk space' in the narrow corridors of the lodging-houses. Some ended up occupying these 'spaces' for years. Married rickshawmen needed either a room or cubicle to themselves, or several for their families. On the rare occasions when the Health Department pulled cubicles down they were put up again as fast as they were demolished, because family men could not get on without them.[47]

The lives of the rickshaw coolies and their families were bounded by the cubicles they lived in. The interior of the cubicles became their whole world: a small world of gloom in which the dust settled heavily, the air became stale, and the light dim, even in the middle of the day. We know from turn-of-the-century photographs of the interiors of lodging-houses showing cubicles that they were simply furnished. In one spartan-like cubicle,

> dark, confined, insanitary, and without comfort—[in which] may live a family of seven or more persons. Many of them sleep on the floor, often under the bed. Their possessions are in boxes, placed on shelves to leave the floor free for sleeping. Their food, including the remains of their last meal, is kept in tiny cupboards, which hang from the rafters. Their clothes hung on the walls, or from racks.[48]

There were no windows and no means of light in many of the cubicles. The lodging-house floors were densely packed, the heat and humidity almost unbearable at times, and visibility was rarely more than a few steps along the narrow passage before stepping out into the full glare of the blinding sun or the sting of driving rain.

In the slums of the rickshaw quarter men often returned from a hard day's work, washed up, and ate. They then drifted outside onto the five-footway to chat, gamble, smoke opium, or tinker with their rickshaw. Coolies often strolled through the streets on sultry summer nights, when they were dotted with card players and families escaping their stifling cubicles. One especially hot night several pullers joked with some of the gamblers who squatted on the pavement, playing hand after hand until it was cool enough to go to sleep in the cubicle. The cubicle, oven-like in the dry season, turned dank in the wet months and was liable to be tainted with mildew and infested with cockroaches. In Victoria Street and the seedy area around it, there was an air of transience and decay by 1918. Here and there buildings were near collapse and the roofs were shored up with sheets of rusty corrugated iron.

> Some had roofs that leaked like sprinkling cans and got everything inside soaking wet. They were busy moving things outside next to the cook stove to dry or hanging them on window sills in the sun. They had huddled in their rooms while

the rain was falling; rooms that might, when the moment came, collapse and bury them alive. They left their fate to Heaven. After the rain they tried to figure out how to repair their losses.

Although a heavy rain might lower the price of a pound of rice by half a cent, still, their losses were so great that such a trifling drop in price could not make them up. They paid their rent but no one ever came to repair the place unless the dilapidation was so bad that no one could possibly live there. In that case, two masons would come along and fix up the wall haphazardly with mortar and broken bricks, preparing it for its next collapse. If the rent wasn't paid the whole family would be thrown out and have its goods confiscated. The walls were cracking, the roof might fall in and kill someone, and no one cared. A place like this was all their tiny income could afford. It was tumbledown (and) dangerous.[49]

Within the cell-like atmosphere rickshaw coolies and their families struggled to bring some sense of quality to their lives and make their cubicle surroundings more tolerable. There was a simple poignancy about the potted flowers and herbs with which they decorated the window ledges and doors of those miserable lodging-houses.

Overcrowding was to become a major reason for the breakup of some rickshawmen's families, and a cause of their children suffering from tuberculosis and other infectious diseases. This was to be the brutal reality faced by Tah Moon Heng who lived with his wife and 11-year-old son in a small, dark cubicle at the rear of a house in Tiwary Street.[50] The lack of space also strained Lim Ong's family ties:

I returned from pulling my ricksha at about 1 a.m. 26th day of Chinese 9th moon. I saw my wife sleeping with my children. I sleep in the outside room usually . . . I did not sleep in the same room with my wife because the room is too small and I have two small children. I went to sleep soon after taking food [as] I was too tired. I had been up since 2 p.m. the previous [afternoon].[51]

The Government was to blame for the fate of these men and their families. Colonial authorities felt it was not possible to legislate against cubicle overcrowding because it would require a very large staff and considerable expense. Drastic measures would have to be taken to deal with it, and authority given to health officers to tear down cubicles and relocate tenants.[52] The Commissioners had legal power to remove any partition which had been erected without approval. The section, however, was a dead letter. Summonses and serving of notices had proved a waste of time in the past. The Municipal Commissioners gave up trying to deal with cubicles. Experience in 1918 had shown that it was useless to pull them down as the authorities had nothing to replace them with, and because necessity knew no law, as desperately poor rickshawmen put them up again.[53] Despite positive recommendations of the Emergency Housing Commission Report of 1918, calling for cubicles to be dealt with systematically, the dark, cramped room portrayed in Dr W. J. Simpson's celebrated report of 1907 on housing in Singapore did not disappear from Chinatown.

The problem of overcrowding and worsening housing conditions for rickshaw coolies shows up in the accident statistics in the Coroner's Records. It is not surprising that pullers did die, and sometimes horribly, in buildings in which the densities were far too high, and which were fraught with structural and design problems; the arrangement of the staircases and windows was dangerous and they were badly provided with amenities like tap water and wells. Occasionally a rickshaw coolie thought in a more forbidden moment that for some of them their world would end in flames. For the dead pullers at 260-E Victoria Street, it ended in fire during the Chinese New Year of 1896. The house was gutted in an inferno. Rickshawman Say Ah Seo, found in Middle Road suffering from second degree burns, made a statement in the General Hospital. He had returned with his rickshaw at 10 p.m. and went upstairs to sleep. During the night he woke up to white heat, a mass of flames, and the smell and sound of burning rotten timbers cracking: 'During the night I got up feeling my body burnt and I went downstairs and passing through the burnt room the fire was raging. I fell down. I remembered no more till I was in hospital.'[54] Toh Kee, who was severely burned, also returned at the same time as Say Ah Seo, and had gotten up in the middle of the night too, ablaze. He ran to the front of the room in a panic, only to collapse. Someone dragged him out. He remembered seeing the lifeless bodies of three coolies who had managed to get outside but expired soon afterwards from smoke inhalation as well as two others who perished from third degree burns. Ang Boo, a rickshaw puller who lived in Havelock Road, heard his brother had been fatally burnt in the conflagration. He ran to the blazing house: 'I found him lying at the side of the road near the burned house. I took him to hospital in a ricksha. He was badly burnt. He told me he was lying in his room upstairs and heard as if something had fallen. He got up and found the place on fire. As he escaped, he was burnt. He said he thought he would die.'[55] What Ang Boo's brother heard was the paraffin lamp explode as it fell on the floor shooting flames in all directions and, in that instant, Soo Neah Choo's clothes went up as he ran from the sheet of fire. It spread to the kitchen, a big tin of kerosene close by went up in a roar scorching Tan Tee Kim in the midst of cooking. It had been his turn on the roster.[56]

In an identical accident Tan Ah Tong was asleep in a lodging-house in Queen Street, when the kerosene lamp which hung over his head, burst, pouring glass and flaming oil over most of his body and legs. His brother, who was lucky to escape without injury and took him to the hospital, described what happened:

> He was burnt by the fall over him of a kerosene lamp which was hanging over his bed. I was lying on the next bed at the time about four or five feet away. The lamp burst. It was a glass lamp and half filled with kerosene. It was about 5 a.m. I don't know why it burst. I brought my brother to hospital here. The lamp belonged to the people of the house the Towkay. The lamp burst. It did not fall from the hook.[57]

Nobody could explain why the lamp exploded. Yat Kin, a clansman and puller, who was in the opposite end of the room at the time, offered several plausible reasons for the unfortunate accident: 'The lamp seemed to be in good order. I don't know why it burst, perhaps it was dirty or the oil may have been bad.'[58] In the case of Teng Ah Mui's death from extensive burns there was no mystery as to why the lamp had broken. She was the young wife of Lim Chong, a Queen Street rickshaw owner, and on 14 April 1913, he was upstairs with her, sitting by the side of the bed, over which was a lighted hanging kerosene lamp. One of his rickshaw coolies named Chai Kwai Kwai went out to buy tobacco. He soon returned hotly pursued by Ong Ah Choon, who followed him right up the stairs; the angry *singkeh* threw a stone at the puller but it hit the bedroom lamp instead. The oil holder shattered and the kerosene fell in a cascade on Lim Chong's wife, setting her alight. The stone-throwing coolie ran off as the terrified husband desperately tried to beat out the flames enveloping his wife with his bare hands.[59] On the other hand, despite being sane and conscious, Lam Ah Long died without being able to explain how he was consumed because it was Chinese New Year, and no interpreter was available. The pattern of the burns, and the time of year, with upstairs rooms of rickshaw houses especially crowded with men gambling and generally having a good time, point in the direction of an accidental lamp fire:

> The deceased, named Lam Ah Long, was brought to hospital by the police on 13th February [1907] at 6.50 p.m. He was suffering from extensive burns to the trunk, of the buttocks and of both arms and both legs. He was suffering much from shock and was in great pain. He died at 12.45 a.m. on the 15th. Death was due to exhaustion following burns. Being the Chinese New Year, no interpreter was present when I interviewed the patient, and I could not learn how he was burned.[60]

Falls in lodging-houses were also a serious problem. Men slipped and fell to their death while repairing leaks in the roof, or while hanging out or collecting the wash;[61] Ling Poo Kiang, aged 55, was living in a packed house in Queen Street when he accidentally fell to his death. He was stretching over a window on the first floor when he lost his balance and fell into the well, a height of about 15 feet;[62] Lim Tiang Soo, a young man, had been drying some clothes on the terrace of his lodging in New Market Road. He went to pick them up and in the process got on the surrounding parapet; his foot slipped and he fell a distance of 12 feet into the basement below,[63] fracturing his spine. He never ran again.

The renting of cubicles to rickshaw coolies was handled by a 'principal tenant' who lived on the premises and paid the owner/landlord the rickshawmen's rent each month. The more coolies a principal tenant put into a house the more he made. The cubicle dwellers could, in turn, rent out their 'spaces' to other lodgers. As a rule coolies paid between 60 and 80 cents a month. If a rickshaw was housed inside, the landlord charged $1 a month for it, but only 20 cents if it was outside in the yard, or under the verandah.[64] The majority of rickshaw houses were let out in this fashion, and a real cause for high rents in the houses themselves was the fact that the landlord had to get his profit, the principal tenant had to get his profit, and very likely another tenant had to get his profit too.[65]

The principal tenant was usually termed the 'headman'. He was responsible for the rent and collected it monthly from the coolies. It was common for headmen to rent a lodging-house and sublet whole floors to tenants. In some cases tenants were making as much as $20 or $25 a month on rent.[66] But, of course, they had all the risks; the gamble of pullers absconding, the worry of not being able to get enough tenants, and the hazard of collecting the rent. In these lodgings, the total rent paid by the rickshaw pullers was much greater than the actual amount the owner of the house received. Men like the Hockchia puller Lee Mia Mia living at 85 Maude Street and Goh Pan at 437 Havelock Road got a room rent free and made between $5 and $10 a month.[67] Goh Pan described how the system worked in his house: 'I am the principal tenant of house 437 Havelock Road. I sleep on a platform near the front door. Sometimes I sleep in the back room, ground floor. The top floor is sub-let to Tan Tow. I collect rent from sub-tenants on the ground floor. Tan Tow collects rent from sub-tenants on the top floor.'[68] Not all principal tenants lived on the premises. Yew Ah Choon, a rickshaw coolie, was the headman of 22 Tras Street but lived in a coffee-shop on Telok Blangah Road. His friend Wang Ngue Soh, a cigarette seller, lived at 22 Tras Street, and looked after the lodging-house. Yew Ah Choon visited the house five times a week and the tenants paid their rent of 80 cents each either to him or to the cigarette hawker.[69] Hoh Oon, whose responsibility it was to collect a share of the rent at 79 Duxton Road, was, at one and the same time, a fellow rickshaw coolie, kindred, and clansman of his tenants. Hoh Buay told the Coroner: 'I knew ... Hoh Oon since childhood. He lived on the same floor at No. 79, in the same room. The deceased was the man to whom we paid our rent. Each man paid 1/– per month. Hoh Oon paid the Towkay $12.20 for the floor. [There were] thirteen of us living on the floor.'[70] Hoh Tian Sze added that Hoh Oon was also a clansman of his and they had lived in the same room together.

The difference in the amount of rent rickshawmen paid before the First World War and after was dramatic. The effect of changes between 1919 and 1921, in the use of buildings from residential to shophouse and godown (warehouse), was to concentrate more and more men in less space. Thus for the years 1908, 1918, and 1921, a house in China Street had 20, 42, and 65 tenants and another in Macao Street 20, 27, and 49 respectively. Between 1908 and 1918 the rent increased by 40 per cent while in 1923 it was 135 per cent higher than in 1908.[71] The neighbourhood around the rickshaw quarters, where thousands of pullers found cheap drab housing, served as a suitable setting for life-and-death struggle over payment of rent. Sometimes coolies could not part with more than a certain amount of income, or simply refused to pay rent on the date due. Hoh Choon Bok, a Hokkien rickshaw coolie, was pulling in North Bridge Road 'on the 11th day of the 3rd Moon [4 April 1925]' when another rickshawman told him there had been a fight amongst the 'Hohs' in Duxton Road. He went home straight away and placed his rickshaw on the roadside at 72 Duxton Road. He then proceeded to No. 79 and found a dead man lying on the footway. It was Hoh Oon. He had been stabbed by Hoh Giong Toh, a relation and a rickshaw coolie who lived at 79 Duxton Road. They had quarrelled over the payment of rent: 'I was not present ... nor did I see the stabbing but Hoh Buay told me about it. The deceased and Hoh Giong Toh were on good terms but occasionally Hoh Oon abused Hoh Giong Toh for gambling. The stabbing took place about 10 p.m. 3/4/25.'[72] Hoh Buay, a close friend of Hoh Oon's, gave a vivid account of the tragic rent dispute:

> I know Hoh Giong Toh, he also lived in the same room. About 9 p.m. 3.4.25 I was asleep on my bed. Hoh Giong Toh was standing. They had a quarrel about 8 p.m. before I went to sleep. Hoh Oon and Giong Toh quarrelled. Hoh Oon was angry and scolded Giong Toh. Saying, 'You have money for gambling and money for women but no money for rent'. Giong Toh replied 'I have no money'. Giong Toh was displeased and abused Hoh Oon. They were going to fight so I separated them. Then Hoh Oon went downstairs and I went to sleep.... After a little while I heard shouts from downstairs that Hoh Oon had been stabbed by Giong Toh. Giong Toh had gone then. I then went downstairs on the footway. I saw Hoh Oon being supported by two or three men on the footway of the next house No. 80. I saw Hoh Oon bleeding from a stab wound on his chest. He was still alive but unable to speak. We dragged him to the footway of his own house in order to take him inside. The people at No. 80 grumbled and told us to wash the blood away. We did so. This happened soon after 9 p.m.—about 10 p.m. I did not go to the Police and report the matter ... as the deceased was not my relative. Deceased still lying on the footway. No Police there. [The] Place [was] in darkness when I returned so I was afraid to go in and went to another house to sleep. [I] cannot say whether the other coolies were still there or had run away. Hoh Giong Toh has disappeared and I have never seen him since.[73]

There it is, an authentic bit of frank conversation of sixty-one years ago, dissecting the motives of two coolies caught in a heated altercation over default of rent, gambling, and women; it also shows with candour the puller's fear of the police, the detachment and lack of sympathy of neighbours, and the organized flight from the house in the face of sudden and dramatic death.

Rent collectors had a particularly difficult time with rickshaw pullers who smoked opium or injected morphia. In houses in Victoria Street where many of the men were using morphia and ruining themselves, they could not pay the rent. The collectors told the Opium Commission in 1908 that the rickshawmen on morphia could not pull rickshaws and thus earn money.[74] When addicted pullers became too ill to work, principal tenants were apt to turn them out. Ng Siah Lee, a 26-year-old Hengwah, had been ill with tuberculosis for three years. He could not pay the rent and was evicted. He slept in the five-footway in Arab Street until he died.[75] To be poor and sick was to be isolated, both in material and social terms.

Absentee landlords who owned many of the lodging-houses were Arabs. They put the rents up as a rule on acquiring a new property and kept the houses in bad condition, only repairing them when forced to do so by the Municipality. The housing problem, like the plight of the rickshaw coolie, and the inflation, was not going to go away. The landlords showed no lack of resources in exploiting the housing shortage, and 'gouging' their principal tenants too. When coolies could not pay the rent they absconded, leaving behind empty cubicles and an indebted principal tenant. Ching Chye Leng had rented 82–1 Duxton Road and turned it into a rickshaw pullers' house. The landlord, an Arab, demanded two months' back rent from him in 1929. He was unable to pay, and suicided. His Cantonese widow explained why there was no way out of his financial entanglements except by 'squeezing' his dwindling number of tenants:

> He was a Hokien. We have been married for twelve years and have two children. The deceased formerly worked on board a steamer supplying food for passengers. For the last 5 or 6 years he had not done any work and was living on the profits he made by renting no. 82–1 Duxton Road. He rented this for $100 per month and got about $150 to $160 per month from sub-tenants when it was all rented. Recently it has not been all sub-let, and he was owing $200, two months rent, at the time of his death. The landlord pressed very strongly for payment. My husband was unable to pay. He promised that he would try and borrow the money and pay on Wednesday 11th day of 1st Moon (20.2.29). He was not able to borrow the money, and so could not keep his promise to pay.... My husband hanged himself, and I think it was because he was worried and ashamed that he could not pay the rent.[76]

To remedy the overcrowding, and obstruction caused by rickshaws being left on 'public roads' outside coolie houses, as early as 1911 it was proposed to build model houses especially designed to accommodate rickshaw coolies and their vehicles. The plan, however, suggested rather foolishly, that rickshaws should be parked on the ground floor and the coolies live overhead; a rough estimate to build such a house to hold 200 rickshaws and 400 coolies was $35,000 in 1911.[77] Considering there were over 9,000 rickshaws and 20,000 coolies at that time the expense made the scheme prohibitive. It was an undeniable fact that there were not enough dwellings to meet the demand by 1918 and houses suitable for rickshaw coolies were not being built. But when Mr Hooper was questioned by members of the Housing Commission in 1918 on the subject of rickshaw lodging, he still felt the 1911 plan was not a paying proposition.[78] The Registrar ironically noted that the Municipality had intended shortly after 1910 to measure up all the rickshaw houses, and put in large letters on the wall the number of coolies who were allowed to occupy each room, but it was never done.[79]

Rickshaw coolies could not get living quarters at reasonable rents. Colonial medical officers also knew if the congestion were relieved the mortality rate would be lowered, but European municipal officials, with the exception of Mr Braddell, could not have cared less. Many of the pullers were too destitute to live anywhere else. They were still being paid at the same rate in 1918 as several years earlier. Dr G. A. Finlayson stated before the Housing Commission, 'I am in favour of increasing the [rickshaw] rates. They are the only class that have not been allowed to increase their rates and I think it is very hard.'[80] The municipality was not prepared to invest in rickshaw quarters to reduce cramping pressure on buildings in town. It would have had to offer cheap rents to compete with other lodgings. This, despite the fact that pullers contributed sizeable amounts to municipal coffers in taxes and fines each year. Dr Lim Boon Keng noted this while sparring with one of the commissioners:[81]

Dr Lim Boon Keng:

> You should treat these rikisha people very fairly. I think they are entitled to that, from the amount that they pay to the municipality. Instead of municipal policemen and watchmen getting palaces, these coolies might be given decent sanitary lines. It would be for the benefit of the town. Then they would go, and they would pay a fair rent. At present, I think, they pay too much.

Commissioner:

> That would get rid of the rikisha coolies. There are other classes in Chinatown who still overcrowd, so that after you had done that there would still be many houses overcrowded, would there not?

Dr Lim Boon Keng:

> Have coolie lines. These houses are overcrowded because the coolies live on the premises. If coolies could get reasonable quarters at a reasonable rate, a little outside, they would go.

Three principal arguments were put forward by the Government as an excuse against providing necessary accommodation. First, rickshaw coolies were stereotyped as 'notoriously undesirable tenants owing to the filthy mess they make of houses'.[82] According to Mr Hooper it was only by paying *high rents* that owners were willing to let their houses to them. Secondly, it was considered common for them 'to flit' and landlords had difficulty in recovering their rent. Finally, a basic problem in providing rickshaw housing was the amount of space the men needed for their vehicles. Ultimately, in 1928, an experimental building was erected for 114 pullers and their vehicles at Said Alwi Road, Jalan Besar; the building constructed of *kapoh* timber with a Chinese tile roof with baths and latrines was set on high piles, providing ample space underneath it for rickshaws.[83] The experiment was short-lived. The coolies were turned out after only four months, because the building was 'so persistently misused by the occupants'.[84]

It was a plain fact throughout the 1920s and 1930s that there was not enough lodging to house the number of rickshaw pullers. The supply of housing did not nearly approach the demand in the inter-war years, and thus there was no way to reduce the landlord's ability to force the men to pay exorbitant rents. Neither the private sector nor the Colonial Government was prepared to shoulder the expense of increased residential construction to ease the situation for the rickshaw coolies. The immensity of the problem and the cost were all too apparent to the Colonial Government: it simply said 'no'. In the 1930s the Government studiously ignored the housing problem and the vexed question of inordinate rents. This urban overcrowding of Singapore was largely a British failure. When the Japanese Imperial Army occupied the city in February 1942, Chinatown was more than half a million people jammed into tiny cubicles in lodging-houses that had not seen improvement in over seventy years, many would not bear inspection and renovation and all needed it.

There was a considerable amount of building, though, in this period. The trend of both public and private ambition, and of capital, lay in quite a different direction. It was easier and more profitable in Singapore to construct quarters for government servants and the employees of big firms, and monumental buildings like the Post Office in 1928, the massive Municipal Building (later City Hall) in 1929, and Clifford Pier, than 'to clean it [up], easier to embellish its face than sound its depths'.[85] These major construction projects were undertaken in the interest of the trade and colonial administration of Singapore, creating an illusion of accelerated prosperity and the image of a showcase city. At the same time, the speculation in essentials of life to rickshaw pullers—food and shelter—was not subject to strict control. This contradiction involving prosperity and poverty remained hidden, deliberately buried in the illusion of an economic miracle. As one American, who had been there before, wrote in 1929: 'Its [*sic*] marvelous how you have progressed. Why, I hardly know the place.'[86]

1. For an in-depth discussion of the role and problem of the hawker in Singapore in the 1920s and 1930s, see: *Committee Appointed to Investigate the Hawker Question in Singapore* Report 1932, or RCAIH.

2. Statement of Mr Edwin Tongue, RCAIH, 18/8/31, p. 17.

3. A. Dixon, *Singapore Patrol* (London, 1935), p. 26.

4. SCII of Gian Yeow Sun, No. 319, 17/7/35.

5. SCII of Ong Kwee Tiam, No. 584, 5/10/37.

6. SCII of Tan Nah Nai, No. 210, 14/4/38.

7. SCII of Chee Hang Kee, No. 354, 21/6/39.

8. SCII of Teo Kow Seng, No. 436, 3/9/29.

9. SCII of Yau Chin Swee, No. 236, 26/6/24.

10. SCII of Chew Ah Teng, No. 170, 1/11/12.

11. SCII of Ong Hu, Tan Que Ku, Say Ah Seo, Nu Mah Yah, 21/2/1896.

12. Ibid.

13. SSAR, 1925, Health Report, p. 635.

14. Lao She, *Rickshaw* (the novel *Lo-T'o Hsiang Tzu*), translated by Jean M. James (Honolulu: The University Press of Hawaii, 1979), pp. 31–2.

15. SCCV of Tien Sang Kwai, No. 57, 28/8/38; of unknown, No. 31, 20/2/39; of Ting Choon Moy, No. 154, 25/8/39.

16. SCII of Teng Lau Ting, No. 247, 24/4/36.

17. SCII of Ong Seng Hong, No. 410, 20/8/33.

18. Ibid.

19. John Cuylenburg, *Singapore through Sunshine and Shadow* (Singapore: Heinemann, 1982), p. 48. In the late 1930s Ng Kar Eng lived in a lodging-house, and cooked his own meals in the *kongsi*: 'At that time I ... cooked my own meals at home. To drink coffee outside then cost thirty to forty cents a day. For drinks outside, it also cost about thirty to forty cents. For coffee and beverages, thirty to forty cents was sufficient for a day's work.' Interview with Ng Kar Eng, AOHD, Reel 4.

20. HCR, statement of Dr Lim Boon Keng, p. B154.

21. Felix Chia, *The Babas* (Singapore: Times Books International, 1980), p. 23.

22. SCCV of Seow See, No. 24, 19/5/15.

23. SCCV of See Hong Yen, No. 30, 24/1/15.

24. SCII of Ong Seng Hong, No. 410, 20/8/33.

25. W. L. Blythe, *The Impact of Chinese Secret Societies in Malaya: A Historical Study* (London: Oxford University Press, 1969), p. 243.

26. SMAR JD, 1897, Appendix J, p. 31.

27. R. H. J. Sydney, *Malay Land* (London: Cecil Palmer, 1926), p. 26.

28. Interview with Ng Kar Eng, AOHD, Reel 3.

29. Ibid.

30. Ibid.

31. Ibid.

32. Low Ngiong Ing, *Chinese Jetsam on a Tropical Shore* (Singapore: Eastern Universities Press, 1974), p. 122.

33. Lao She, op. cit., p. 30.

34. SMAR JD, 1927, p. 6-B.

35. For an important discussion of the 'language of clothing' see Richard Cobb, *Death in Paris 1795–1801* (London: Oxford University Press, 1978), pp. 21, 38, 71–83.

36. The table is compiled from the following cases: SCCV, No. 27, 7/1/11; No. 29, 7/10/11; No. 64, 15/10/11; No. 79, 24/10/11; No. 81, 24/10/11; No. 91, 29/10/11.

37. Low, op. cit., p. 73.

38. Blythe, *The Impact of Chinese Secret Societies in Malaya*, p. 305.

39. SCII of Koh Lek, No. 59, 25/4/13.

40. 'Economic Study of the Peking Ricksha Puller', *China Economic Monthly*, 3, 6 (June 1926), p. 263.

41. SCII of Tan Chew, No. 78, 26/2/21.

42. SCII of Yau Chin Swee, No. 236, 26/6/24.

43. SCII of Lim Tiew, No. 180, 8/11/07.

44. SCII of Teng Lau Ting, No. 247, 24/4/36.

45. HCR, statement of Mr J. R. Glennie, p. B113.

46. HCR, p. A-3.

47. HCR, statements of Mr T. O. Mayhew, p. B-71; and Mr J. R. Glennie, pp. B112–113.

48. Barrington Kaye, *Upper Nankin Street, Singapore. A Sociological Study of Chinese Households Living in a Densely Populated Area* (Singapore: University of Malaya Press, 1960), p. 2.

49. Lao She, op. cit., p. 182.

50. SCII of Ler Cho Wing, No. 303, 10/7/35.

51. SCII of Wee Choon Beoh, No. 612, 17/11/30.

52. HCR, statement of Mr T. O. Mayhew, p. B-71.

53. HCR, p. A-33.

54. SCII of Ong Hu, Ten Qua Ku, Say Ah Seo, Nu Mah Yah, 21/2/96.

55. Ibid.

56. Ibid.

57. SCII of Tan Ah Tong, No. 54, 4/4/05.

58. Ibid.

59. SCII of Teng Ah Mui, No. 56, 18/4/13.

60. SCII of Lam Ah Long, No. 30, 15/2/07.

61. See the following cases: SCII of Ong Ah Siew, No. 664, 1/12/31; and of Yeong Song Huay, No. 88, 18/3/38.
62. SCII of Ling Poo Kiang, No. 58, 17/4/10.
63. SCII of Lim Tiang Soo, No. 179, 7/11/13.
64. HCR, statement of Mr W. Hooper, p. B90.
65. HCR, statement of Mr Hallifax, p. B11.
66. HCR, statement of Mr T. O. Mayhew, p. B71.
67. SCII of unknown Chinese, 14/6/34.
68. SCII of Sia Sen Hert, No. 354, 21/6/39.
69. SCII of Tan Chew Moi, No. 78, 26/2/21.
70. SCII of Hoh Oon, No. 162, 4/4/25.
71. No. 57, Report of a Committee Appointed to Consider the Alleged Shortage of Houses, 3 September 1923, in CO 275/109.
72. SCII of Hoh Oon, No. 162, 4/4/25.
73. Ibid.
74. SSOC, p. 162.
75. SCII of Ng Siah Lee, No. 614, 3/11/31.
76. SCII of Ching Chye Leng, No. 67, 21/2/29.
77. HCR, statement of Mr W. Hooper, p. B89.
78. Ibid.
79. HCR, statement of Mr T. O. Mayhew, p. B72.
80. HCR, statement of Dr G. A. Finlayson, p. B153.
81. HCR, statement of Dr Lim Boon Keng, pp. B152–153.
82. Letter from Mr W. Hooper to President Singapore Housing Commission, 14/11/17, p. C11; and statement of Mr Hooper, pp. B90–91.
83. SMAR, Annual Report of Municipal Architects Department 1924, p. 23-G.
84. SMAR JD, 1928, p. 10.
85. Louis Chevalier, *Labouring Classes and Dangerous Classes in Paris during the First Half of the Nineteenth Century* (London: Routledge and Kegan Paul, 1973), p. 200.
86. F. M. Luscombe, *Singapore 1819–1930* (Singapore, 1930), p. 66.

13 Marriage and the Elemental Family

KINSHIP and quasi-kinship organizations bound together rickshawmen in Singapore. They were almost to a man bachelors. Most of them came from Kwangtung and Fukien provinces as indigent youth in search of a new life. Family pressure and poverty pushed them out. Singapore as the road of possibility had led them into the city. The rickshaw opened up other opportunities for work employment than the ones they might have chosen on barges, in coal bunkers of tramp steamers, inside godowns or on the scaffolding of construction sites in a mushrooming city. They had no intention of staying. It was the ideal pattern of circular migration: 'men go abroad, earn, remit money, and return'.[1] It is the posed photograph depicted on the odd postcard and in travel accounts that speak of the general nature of this exodus of young men going abroad to pull rickshaws in Singapore. Look at this photograph of a youthful puller for a moment. He is kneeling between the shafts of his immaculately set out rickshaw, wearing his best work shorts, his hair combed for the occasion with his straw hat inconspicuously tucked away between the floorboard and the wheel, and looking straight into the eye of the camera.

A rare picture as a sojourning youth that would be sent to someone dear in China.

It was normal for rickshaw coolies to return to China with savings and experience every six to ten years. Opium smokers made fewer trips. Their links with kin were often left to run down or fall apart at the expense of their habit as they failed to earn a living. When a young puller had accumulated enough money he could return to his village, take a wife, wait a year and procreate a first child. He then returned to Singapore after the birth of his offspring to work in a male-dominated society for another decade. Overseas marriages with a China-born girl were arranged either by kin in China or voluntary associations in Singapore and young coolies were packed off to the provinces to marry China-born brides who were considered to be far more submissive than local women.[2] The following Hockchia pullers are examples of men who had wives and families in China. They would tell the Coroner about them in passing at an inquest. They did not mention their names nor where they lived: Ee Ang Ang was married 'but his wife and son aged three years are in China'. He had been back once within the past three years to see his family;[3] Teng Ah Poh came to Singapore in 1911 at the age of 43, and had been married for some time with a wife and child in China.[4] The sojourning cycle of going to and fro repeated itself, at least up to the age of 40. The few who brought their wives with them to Singapore before the 1920s were exceptions. One such Hockchia man to do so was Ling Ee Ngoh who married his wife in China when she was seventeen in 1912.[5]

Despite the pervasive pattern of a bachelor society with village links in China between 10 and 15 per cent of rickshaw pullers had families in Singapore by the 1920s. This development of domestic affairs, of hearth and home, marriage and children was a new and altogether different matter among rickshaw coolies. A few pioneers of sorts, like Ling Ee Ngoh, brought their China-born wives as early as 1912; he and others like him began the painfully slow process of creating a household society in Chinatown. Other men though chose to break with tradition and married locally. They remained and settled down to raise a family, instead of returning to China. These elemental families were developed on rather short notice—a decade or two at most—from the 1920s onwards, and faced serious demographic and social problems right from the start. They were the exact opposite of the large, extended family in China, often consisting of just a young puller, his wife, and their children, and on occasion, the odd relation—a widowed grandmother or a newly arrived nephew.[6] The converging path of his vocation and domestic life, as a rickshawman, husband and possibly father, could easily end in old age alone with a spouse, or as a poverty-stricken widow. If a rickshaw coolie fathered more than one child there was bound to be privation. This was a normal married life providing misadventure, disease or death did not cut him short. Lying behind such 'events' was the failure of the elemental household to bind together rickshawmen and their families on principles of kinship long established in Chinese society.

Most pullers had no faith in the elemental family. They had no intention of marrying and held fast to the idea that to do so was an irrevocable mistake: 'He realised that the entire course of a rickshaw puller's life was described in two words: tough luck! A rickshaw puller, and only a rickshaw puller, had better never put a foot wrong or get involved with a woman. Get stuck like that and you've made a mistake as big as the sky.'[7]

For historians concentrating on the lives and circumstance of coolies, the family and family life must be an integral part of their studies. Notably, the effort must be made to break the silence regarding women. The history of ordinary Chinese women in a city like Singapore must consider what for many was their most important role in life: the role of wife and mother. The Coroner's Records provide a unique perspective on the inner workings of family life among rickshaw coolies. While the records are broken up into unconnected cases and episodes, patterns nevertheless can be discerned to help us understand the household shape and size and the social realities of daily life dealing with in-laws, children, personal problems and marital stresses for the period between the wars. They can reveal a great deal about specific relationships within the family between, say, a mother and infant, a wife and brother, an uncle and nephew, as well as those between the husband and wife themselves. Often in the course of describing these relationships, specific information which helps to explain the character and development of the family emerges, for example, on child-spacing and mortality. An abnormally large number of cases of assault, traffic accidents, and suicide took place between 1918 and 1939.[8] The data show that in this period when the rickshawmen had few resources beyond their own physical strength and experience, money-lenders, pawnshops, and the charity of friends and associations, changes in personal and family circumstance could create disaster. Large families, widowhood, accidents, ill-health, or personal habits such as opium smoking, gambling, or poor budgeting could quickly force married rickshawmen below the poverty line with no hope of recovery.

The tendency to establish elemental families and settle permanently in Singapore came about because large numbers of single Chinese women started to flood into the city from war-torn China and because the Chinese and British authorities began to adopt a more relaxed attitude toward female immigration. A gradual change in the character of the rickshaw coolie's society began to take place with the coming of more women. Fate in the form of wives represented a break with the sojourning past, with China, and what remained of 'village China' in Victoria Street, Queen Street, and other like neighbourhoods. For some pullers of this generation there was no longer any reason to go back despite improved transportation. But there was also a more immediate, deeper, and even more profound break with village ties and clansmen in the local rickshaw houses: a married couple could not live in the *pang keng* of a rickshaw house—force of circumstance required them to find a cubicle elsewhere. A different pattern of living arrangement went along with being married that increased physical and social isolation. Cubicle-living forced couples to be more highly individualized and privatized in their dealings with other tenants along a corridor.

In these low-status families interpersonal relationships were different from those in the traditional extended family. The structure of these new households was characterized by a striking lack of convention and a 'poverty and powerlessness'.[9] A rickshawman as a father was not a strong patriarch because he had few if any resources at his disposal. He could not hope to have more than one son grow to manhood, yet there was no way he could make his grown son stay with him as in China. Brothers who married had to stand by their families and could not lend support to one another in face of crushing poverty and hard work. The demography and economy of rickshaw families insured that they remained elemental in structure, small-scale in size, low in status, and therefore weak.

Rickshawmen in Singapore were generally in their early twenties when they married. Similarly their wives were in the spring of life, married between the ages of 16 and 20; Ler Cho Wing was a 17-year-old Hengwah maiden when she met and married Tah Moon Heng, an enterprising Hengwah rickshaw coolie, two years her senior.[10] The difference in age between a husband and wife in an occupation where men wasted away by forty, was usually four to five years at most. But some rickshaw coolies deliberately exercised self-restraint on early marriage, remaining single until at least their late twenties, and then marrying young adolescents, opening up a disproportionate gap in the marriage age between husband and wife. Ting Oh Tee was married at 29 years of age to Gian Yeow Sun, just turning eighteen,[11] while Kwang Ah Lee married Teng Ah Poh in 1927, when he was 30 and she 20.[12] In an extreme case involving twenty years' difference in age, Chong Swee Lin suddenly became the widow of Koh Kim Chwee at 18 years of age and a mother; she was married when she was 16 years old to a fully adult man, an opium smoker, whom she described as 'a good husband'.[13]

The attitude of married rickshaw coolies and their spouses towards birth control and family size was of crucial importance to their way of life. Rickshaw pullers and their wives faced economic crisis in the Depression, were themselves victims isolated in private cubicles, and did not generally desire large families. After marriage some form of contraception was deemed socially acceptable and necessary. Tragically, a rickshaw household rich in children was a household ruined, for the father could not possibly hope to feed all of them and bring them up. Nevertheless, the value of children, especially sons, was felt to be an important asset; sons who could provide an income and support for parents in illness or old age. However, there is little evidence to suggest that the elemental family was larger than six or seven souls, and was reduced in the case of childless couples to one, when either a husband or wife was left in the aftermath of a traffic accident or suicide, as a widow. Such households could also from time to time include a related person, a grandmother who child-minded but did not necessarily contribute to the household budget, and the occasional guest, a nephew or person with the same surname and coming from the same village, just arrived in Singapore. Ting Oh Tee, a 30-year-old Hockchia puller, and his wife Gian Yeow Sun, a 19-year-old Hockchia bride, were childless. They married at the height of the Depression on the '28th day of the 9th moon last year [1934]'. To help make ends meet Gian Yeow Sun made cakes and was prepared to risk selling them in the streets in the face of a government campaign to remove itinerant food hawkers from certain parts of the city. Ting Oh Tee informed the Coroner they were unable to have children yet.[14] In a similar circumstance Kwang Ah Lee had been married to Teng Ah Poh for nine years. They lived together in a cubicle at 94 Sungei Road without any children.[15]

The elemental family was apt to be at its greatest extension when a man was able to pull his own rickshaw for 10–15 years without mishap. Yap Seah Hing married late at 36 and pulled his rickshaw for fifteen years before being run over, during which time he managed to raise four children.[16] It was more difficult though for Ng Ah Chan, a 46-year-old Hengwah who owned two rickshaws and plied for hire. He had been married thirteen years and had seven children, but only three of them, a girl aged 9 and two boys aged 5 and 3, lived with their parents because of the shortage of housing space.[17]

The small number of children in the families of rickshaw coolies was also the result of the high rate of mortality among infants and pre-school age children. Living in the cubicles of the tenement houses of Chinatown had a terrible effect on newly born Chinese children. The constant need for children to be brought out into the daylight for a breath of fresh air obviously would have helped to reduce infant mortality. Tragedy's alien face was a weary young rickshaw mother. Many of them were malnourished and cubicle-bound from morning to night, especially if they already had one child at the breast. Early marriage and early death of children were very much a part of Sim Kwee Geok's life. She had married in Singapore when she was 20, and lived with her husband until her death at which time she was six months pregnant. She had been pregnant the year before, too, but her new-born child lived only a few days.[18] Children like Sim Kwee Geok's suffered in the dark, cramped oven-like cubicles and the horror of malnutrition and infection were a brutal reality for them. Chinese infant mortality hovered well above a level considered normal for Singapore in the inter-war years. The cause of death of Chinese infants was usually linked to some form of gastro-intestinal disease or beri-beri.[19]

Infants were a source of great joy and sorrow to their young mothers. Chinese wives of rickshaw coolies fell into states of deep depression sometimes lasting for months after having lost a child, particularly a son. Within the solitary world of their cubicles mothers divided up their day between household chores and their offspring; breast-feeding them, rocking them in a hammock-cradle, and carrying them about in their arms. If their child suddenly died there was still the expectation that they could have another one, a string of children if necessary, to overcome the heavy infant mortality. But not all mothers had the necessary strength and will-power to confront death year after year. Weary, grief-stricken, bereft of courage, alone, some lost heart. Wong Huat San was like a volcano, whose eruption was the more devastating for having been so long suppressed. Her grief over the death of her child was so great that she killed herself. At the time of her suicide she was seven months pregnant and lived in fear of losing this one, too. The way out of the terror that was gripping her was to hang herself with a rope: it was no ordinary rope, as she used to suspend the baby's cradle from it. Her husband, a rickshaw puller, expressed the tragic intensity of her love and sorrow tinged with shame that drove her beyond herself in 1931:

> This is the rope which she used. It was kept in my room. My wife was a Hockchia Chinese aged 31 years. [We were] married for about three years. One child aged three years—adopted—as my own child died. She was seven months pregnant and she was worried about it. She was depressed over the other child which only died in August [2 months earlier] this year. I slept with her that night and got up at 5 a.m. on 30/10/31 ... I think the reason for my wife hanging herself was because she was sorry over the death of her child.[20]

In another example from the Depression a mother's extreme affliction led her to suicide out of love for her deceased children. Her name was Ling Ah Moi. She was a Hockchia, 28 years of age, and the mother of two children, a son and a daughter. The daughter died in 1933 and her son passed away two years later. She ate irregularly during her son's illness, becoming weaker and weaker, and terminated her life shortly after his death, swallowing a glassful of caustic soda. Her pitiful state was betrayed in her husband's remarks: 'My wife was very upset about the death of her son.... She did not take her food regularly while her son was ill. I did not suspect she had taken caustic soda and thought she was ill from hunger.'[21]

Some rickshaw families were so poor that when a child died the parents could not afford to have the baby buried. The aftermath of early childhood death itself could create a crisis for couples like Woon Ho San and her husband, Ee San Moey, among some of Singapore's most needy people. After Woon Ho San's 6-month-old daughter ceased to live, she wrapped her in a discarded rickshaw apron, because she could not afford a coffin and proper burial. She had not heartlessly abandoned her dead child; rather, she reminded the Coroner of her poverty and powerlessness:

> The deceased was my daughter named Ee Kin San aged six months and ten days born in Singapore. My daughter had been ill for four days with boils on the head and fever. I had no money to buy medicine for her. She died on the second day of the 8th moon (8.9.26). Neither I or my husband reported the death. I waited till 3 a.m. (9.9.26) and then called a strange ricksha and took the dead child to some vacant ground at Kampong Kapor. I don't know the name of the road. The child was wrapped in a bundle and then in a ricksha apron. I don't know whose

ricksha apron it was. It was an old one, thrown away ... I only left the body on the roadside because I was too poor to bury her.[22]

Like their mothers, children also are apt to be left out of accounts dealing with ordinary Chinese society, even within the context of Chinese family and kinship. Ordinary Chinese children not only experienced a considerable morbidity and mortality, they suffered from the condescension of posterity as well. They rarely appeared in historical records on their own accord, except as a demographer's statistic to determine, for example, the frequency of births and deaths. Granted it is not easy to explore patterns of childhood in the rickshaw quarters without the assistance of living memory and the photographic record but even the official documents can be of some assistance on this score.

Young children spent almost all their time confined to the upper floor of lodging-houses in cubicles either playing with another sibling or as an only child tagging after their mother. When they were a little older, aged 4 or 5, playing moved outdoors to the back alleyway or verandah or as far away as the edge of a nearby canal. This sort of amusement involved discarded objects—trash, tin cans, sticks, and stones—and of course digging, a child's world set against a background of noise, bustle and a society under increasing pressure. There was little segregation and it was common for young boys and girls to play together in the five-footway itself. Naturally older children were expected to look after younger ones. Ng Ah Chan's house was near a canal not far from the Arab Street Bridge. His two sons used to play alongside the canal regularly, and his daughter, a 9-year-old, looked after them in an all too often unsympathetic environment on the street. The father did not think there was any danger in this arrangement.[23] If we could turn back the clock to understand the effect of Singapore's growth on early childhood—overcrowded buildings, narrow streets, traffic congestion—the importance of the five-footway and the kerb to children's play becomes self-evident. There was not much space for kids of elemental families in the cubicles and like their fathers, they spent a lot of time in the streets, especially if the head of the household had to sleep in the daytime. They had a lot to learn about street life and took their chances. Fatalities suffered by slum children offer systematic evidence of how dangerous this 'child's world' was at times. While playing, children were killed instantly when tenement houses under repair collapsed on them, when bullock-cart wheels knocked them down due to the carelessness of the drivers, or when they accidentally drowned in a canal.[24]

Just occasionally though their lives were punctuated by an event that was to always occupy a prominent place in their childhood memories such as a funeral, Chinese New Year, or a visit to a 'tiger performance' or circus. Chor Seng, a Hengwah bachelor, took the two sons of Ng Ah Chan, a Hengwah rickshaw owner next door, to see the circus. The mother, Ong Sam Moi, described her neighbour's unusual attachment for her children, and how dressed up they were for this special occasion:

A rickshaw puller named Chor Seng came to the five-footway of the house at about 8 p.m. on 3/12/34. He asked me if he could take the two elder children to see a tiger performance (circus at Tank Road). He loved my children very much and occasionally gave them money. I dressed up the two eldest children and allowed them to go with him. . . . He frequently played about with my children on the ground floor of the house. . . . Chor Seng frequently took my children out to buy them something. . . . When my son Ng Ah Mee went out with Chor Seng he was wearing a charm and a dog license round his neck. He had one ear-ring on the left ear, also a bangle and a chain on each ankle. He had a pair of silver bracelets.[25]

As a source of this kind of affection, grandmothers were favourites. Some came every day to visit their grandchildren, to help out, and maintain family relations. It was more usual, though, for an elderly widow to formally move into the cubicle with her son and his family. Ong Ah Toon's mother who was 71 years 'Chinese reckoning' lived with him. She was hale and hearty and could take care of herself: 'My mother's eyesight and hearing were good. She had bound feet but could walk well.'[26] Grandmothers provided needed assistance to younger mothers by cooking and child-minding, but their presence did not necessarily make for a serene atmosphere. An elderly woman's flight from the countryside of South China to Singapore in search of kin and a better life could strain family ties. As the younger generation became more impoverished, some married rickshawmen preferred not to have their mothers stay with them. The cubicles were too little, even for small extended, three-generation families. Overcrowding was a major reason behind the breakdown of traditional regard for the elderly. Cramped housing and the resultant change in attitude forced some grandparents to live alone. Often a sick elderly parent was too great a burden for rickshaw families to bear. On the death of a grandmother the breakup of the extended elemental family was complete.

In the elemental family the wife was apt to possess more strength of character as an individual than she might in the extended family, because relations were limited to husbands and wives and on occasion wives and mothers. She was the matriarch, and had sole responsibility for the activities and concerns of the family, that is, coordinating the domestic economy, housekeeping, and child-rearing. But these women, who were married to pullers during the 1920s, were cut off economically and legally from their own families. Once married a woman's interests were bound up entirely with her husband and his people. The working out of social ties within the elemental family often meant that a wife's sole source of security and hope for a future was her husband. Brides from China rarely lived out their lives among kin, except when their brothers or fathers were rickshaw pullers. It was a lonely way to spend a lifetime, isolated from most other members of the husband's household also living in China, and trapped in a cubicle with a young family to rear.

Since rickshaw pullers were among the lowest-paid workers in Singapore, frequently women worked until they had children. From the

Coroner's Records it is obvious too that their desire to work grew as their marriages were placed under increasing pressure during the Depression. Wives of rickshaw pullers faced a basic contradiction in Singapore at that time: their position was central to the social and economic survival of the family unit but they could not fulfil the social role of wife and mother and the economic role of worker at one and the same time within the framework of the elemental family. Rickshaw family units began to crumble under the strain because the woman's role as wife and mother had to be fulfilled at the expense of working to help meet the consumption needs of the family. Children meant an increase in the necessary labour within the home and an increase in household expenditure. The cost of living continued to climb while the families' existing income was at the mercy of currency fluctuations, and future capacity to earn waned.

Lack of cash to meet the total monthly expenses of families (even with the earnings of the wife), short of borrowing from friends or pawnshops, led to the breakdown of marriage and family life, and ultimately to despair and death. In the cases revealed in the Coroner's Records the collapse of the elemental family reached unquestionable intensity. In them husbands and wives share their grief, dreams, and nightmares, and allow the historian of society to weave a tapestry of the agony of the underside of Singapore in the 1920s and early 1930s. These are the voices of the dead, recounting the details of problems that were tearing their elemental families apart. Rickshaw pullers were very poor indeed between 1918 and 1921. Men were working for next to nothing, everything they needed—food, lodging, rickshaws—was too costly and in short supply; everything that is, except eligible illiterate women from China to marry. It was not an era in which a rickshawman could expect to provide a woman with a proper home and family, yet, at the very same time, events in China had initiated a period of unprecedented female immigration to Singapore which was not to come to an end until the Second World War. One puller knew that marriage could finish a rickshaw coolie and painted a dismal picture of the condition of married pullers at the end of 1920:

> But how could he take care of a family when he depended on pulling a rickshaw for his living. He knew about his long-suffering brothers in the mixed courtyards. The men pulled rickshaws, the women sewed, the children scavenged.... They gnawed on watermelon rinds dug out of garbage heaps ... and they all went to get handouts of rice gruel....'[27]

To have children was to be poor. Wee Choon Beoh and her husband Lim Ong were happy together, according to the tenants who lived opposite them in a lodging at 231 Waterloo Street, but they had children which placed them under increased stress: 'She was on very good terms with all the inmates of the house but she was poor and hardly had work. She was unable to work because she had to look after her own children.'[28] Once the children were born it was hard for Lim Ong to be as close to his wife as when they had lived together alone: 'I saw my wife sleeping with my children. I sleep in the outside room, usually I did not sleep with my wife . . . I did not sleep in the same room with my wife because the room is too small and I have two small children.'[29]

Under such circumstances some children were the innocent victims of pressures and strains placed on the family. They were neglected, abused or rejected by one or both parents. Cheap Dog's father symbolically thought of his young son and the rest of the family as deadly objects—bullets and a revolver—signifying a way of death, that was capable of inflicting terrible harm upon him: 'He had five children, two daughters and three sons—five little bullets which filled a gun aimed at himself. . . . Five children who looked like five terrible bullets, and their mother was none other than the gun itself. In addition, she was a bitch. So Cheap Dog's father believed.'[30] It was the rickshaw traffic accident that pulled the trigger. He felt bitter, and hopeless without his rickshaw:

> 'Papa, we're hungry!' cried the two oldest children running out from inside the house. 'I had a dream. I dreamed I was eating so many things! Beef-noodles, barbecue . . .'. Cheap Dog butted in, 'Damn you!' A hand was raised, poised to slap, but the child was swifter and stepped aside. 'Beef, beef and red chili . . .' continued Cheap Dog, tripping nonchalantly down the stairs. Cheap Dog's father then went into the front room, followed by his wife and the other children. It seemed to him as if something had flown past him—those five bullets which had exploded, as did his dreams. Suddenly he felt his heart sinking. He could not shoulder this burden any longer, and his eyes drooped to the ground. 'You must do something. We can starve, but how can we allow the children to go hungry?' The wife choked over her words.[31].

Married men had to work harder and try to save money. They had to put their bachelor past behind them, otherwise success would elude them. Married pullers could not indulge in old habits that made it impossible to own a rickshaw—the brothels, gambling, and opium smoking were out. By and large they did not accept their station in life and tried to make the most of it. In Singapore in the 1920s nobody seemed to be striving so determinedly against impossible odds for a magic formula that would raise one to ownership status as the married rickshaw coolies. By a twist of fate Lim Ong had married and lived with his wife in a single room. Now, more than ever before, he was in need of his own rickshaw:

> Becoming independent was not a simple matter at all. It took one year, two years, at least three or four years, and one drop of sweat, two drops of sweat, who knows how many millions of drops of sweat, until the struggle produced a rickshaw. By gritting his teeth through the wind and rain, depriving himself of good food and tea, he finally saved enough for the rickshaw. That rickshaw was the total result, the entire reward, of all his struggle and suffering. It was the equivalent of the campaign medals worn by a soldier who has gone through a hundred battles.[32]

The big problem for him was his rickshaw; once he got it he felt he had the world. 'As long as it was his own rickshaw he could earn sixty or seventy cents every day no matter what, and that was enough to get along on.'[33]

Let us now explore the inner workings of rickshaw families, beginning with authority and the family's need to budget. Lim Jin San placed his daily earnings in the cubicle for his wife's use. Sim Kwee Geok, his spouse, laboured as an earth-moving coolie as part of the total work contribution of the household. Lim Jin San described their financial arrangement this way: 'I gave her money for food and clothing but she also went to work to help contribute towards our living expenses. I did not force her to work. I usually earned about eighty cents per day and always placed it in the room for her use. . . .'[34] It cost them several dollars a month for lodging and at least $8–10 a month for food. Domestic authority in this rickshaw family was vested in the husband. He controlled the purse-strings. It would have been rare for a Chinese wife not to hand over her wages to her husband; Goh Ah Mie worked as a maidservant in a house at Telok Ayer Street belonging to one San Yong for $8 a month. She always turned her income over, but did not know where her husband kept his earnings.[35]

Poverty unleashed the violent demons of domestic discord. Marriages stretched thin and died in disputes over family expenses and actual expenditures. Lee Ah Toh, a Hengwah rickshaw coolie, heard his sister, Ler Cho Wing, arguing with her husband about money. He lived in the same building in an upstairs cubicle; occupying a small cubicle at the rear of the first floor were his sister, brother-in-law, and their 11-year-old son. Lee Ah Toh remonstrated with her and the matter was settled. He did not realize that his taking his brother-in-law's part against his sister would have fatal consequences. Her husband, Tah Moon Heng, then went out with Lee Ah Toh to a tea-shop opposite the lodging-house. By the time they came back three hours later Ler Cho Wing had hanged herself over 20 cents. She had become very depressed because of her husband's spendthrift behaviour. Obviously, the death was attributable to their poverty. Tah Moon Heng described the sequence of events leading up to his wife's suicide:

> On the 10th July 1935 at 5 p.m. I returned home after pulling my rickshaw for two hours. I went to our room. My wife was there. I found she had been paid one dollar being repayment of a loan to someone. I took twenty cents of this one dollar and bought a durian. . . . My wife scolded me for taking the money and threatened to throw the rest away. I went out again to a nearby teashop with my brother-in-law. I returned home again after 8 p.m. . . . that evening she accused me of spending money too freely.[36]

In a similar way Gian Yeow Sun's husband refused to let her work as a hawker and she became distraught. Her husband was concerned that she might be arrested for hawking without a licence. She stopped selling cakes a week before her death:

> We did not quarrel about it. I am in regular employment myself. I do not know of any other reason [apart from wanting to be a hawker] why my wife should

commit suicide. I gave her all my earnings. She enjoyed good health and behaved normally. She did not threaten to take her own life. She was quite happy and joked with me on the night before her death.[37]

The feeling of helplessness in not being able to make enough for family maintenance was most apparent among opium smokers. They were always in desperate need of money to support the family, on top of their habit. Low Oh, the widow of Chung Ah Hoot, explained her husband's suicide in their Duxton Road lodging-house this way: 'My husband was an opium smoker. He must have hanged himself because he did not earn enough money for opium and for food for all of us.'[38]

There was physical violence as well as emotional violence: the wounds that poverty, miscarriage, rejection inflicted on married women, and from which some never recovered. Marriages were wrecked out of non-communication and the desperate need of money and being cared for. Some men had not mastered their rages or their personal habits; nor had they overcome that numbness of soul that kept them from responding to a loved one, because of having lived for too many years alone in the all-male world of the rickshaw house. Women in elemental families, particularly those with a quarrelsome streak, could expect to be beaten occasionally. This behaviour was reinforced by the widely held belief within Chinese domestic life that women were felt to be harbingers of evil and misfortune. Disease, barrenness, and death could all be ascribed to a wife.[39] The solidarity that existed between a rickshaw puller and his wife could be shattered by constant rows over earnings and the management of debt, the children's needs, and the future of a relationship in which it was hard to make anything last at all, in face of a colonial policy of impoverishment.

Women who were beaten could not expect much assistance from family in reaching a settlement. Small fragmentary kinship units involving fathers, sons or brothers did not have sufficient authority to resolve serious marriage disputes. Marriages in which husbands battered their spouses sometimes ended with the wife drifting to another puller—one with a future tempting enough to hold her. Lim Mui Noh lived with the Hockchia rickshawman Wang Ah Tio but she was ill-treated by him when his real wife arrived from China. Her life became miserable and she left him with her daughter to live with Tin Kin Tee, another Hockchia puller.[40] Each year during the Depression couples separated, threatened separation or suicided because of marital discord over earnings and the way debt was managed. They knew at first hand the survival of the elemental family was at stake. Some of them felt demoralized, isolated, and powerless. Cheap Dog's mother was furious with her husband because he stupidly lost his rickshaw in a traffic accident:

'How rough you are! How I wish I'd never married a beast like you!' That, apparently, was his wife's verdict on him. 'When you arrive at the cross-roads, you have to be careful and look-out for oncoming cars. Now the rickshaw is smashed!' mourned his wife. 'If your stinking skeleton had also been smashed together with it, it would have been simpler!' the woman added.... He was bored. With his rickshaw smashed, his life now seemed to get flooded by waves of apathy. He did not hate the car that had smashed into him for he believed that this was the fate of poor people. But as far as his wife's scoldings were concerned, he would have protested, for he thought he was lucky not to have been smashed together with his rickshaw by that car.[41]

Sometimes the details of these marital conflicts were terrifying. In 1929, Sim Kwee Geok lived with her husband, Lim Jin San, in an upstairs cubicle in Kerbau Lane. He was a rickshaw coolie. At 5 a.m., on 11 December, they quarrelled because Lim Jin San refused to allow her to go to work as usual, hauling earth. His newly arrived nephew from China was feverish, and the husband insisted she stay home and look after him. She protested. A fight broke out. They abused each other a lot. According to the principal tenant the couple had quarrelled on previous occasions but not like this. Lim Jin San had hit her in the past when they had wrangles. Sim Kwee Geok's mother described her daughter's marriage shortly before she killed herself, out of a sense of humiliation:

The deceased was my daughter ... at the time of her death she was about six months pregnant.... Her marriage was a mistake as her husband was very selfish and always spent all the money he earned on himself so that she was compelled to work hard to get food and clothing for herself. Her husband did hit her at times when they quarreled. He was a good husband till he started gambling alot.[42]

Sim Kwee Geok's husband, though somewhat remorseful, attributed the misfortunate death to her, and denied the fact that he gambled:

It is not true that I am a regular gambler.... My nephew recently arrived from China and on 11/12/29 he was ill ... so I told my wife not to go to work that day but to remain at home and look after him. She was a bad tempered woman and said she was going to work. There was over a dollar there for food so that there was no need for her to go to work that day.... She hit me with a piece of firewood and I slapped her face twice. I did not hit her body as she was six months pregnant and I might have injured her.... She must have done it [swallowed liquid caustic soda] because I had quarreled with her and she was very angry with me. She was a bad tempered woman, but I am very sorry that she took her own life like this.[43]

The combination of being in the depths of the depression, pregnant, married to a gambler, and having to minister to a newly arrived kin in cramped quarters, on top of not being able to work proved to be too much for her. Sim Kwee Geok was at the bottom of the heap. She was outraged and her actions show us that husbands did not claim a monopoly on violence. Wives did strike back in resentment and self-defence.

Ordinarily, husbands dominated wives, being strict and at times heavy handed, regarding them as little more than sexual objects. Precious little can be learned about married women's feelings and illicit unions. However, conjugal silence is broken in rare instances in the Coroner's Records. We can note a number of young women who expressed their feelings about the rickshawmen in their lives and their relationships. Besides poverty and personal incompatibility, adultery also led to the breakup of marriages. The demographic characteristics of the rickshaw coolie population, the pitiful conditions of cubicle life, and a husband's poor treatment of a wife in need of care and love, were all reasons that drove women toward being unfaithful. Yeo Sin Kam Poh lived on 'fairly good' terms with her husband, Chew Ah Tong, at Victoria Street. She was formerly from the Poh Leong Kok Home and had been married for fifteen years. On 1 November 1912, the dead body of her Hokkien husband was found covered with stab wounds in Payah Lebar Road, half a mile from Geylang Police Station. Lim Chip Moey, the rickshaw coolie who pulled the assailants, described how her husband was silenced:

On the 31st of October last at 11 p.m. I had a fare from Weld Road to Serangoon Road and to McPherson Road. I put down my ricksha. My fare got down and told me to wait. This is near the corner of Payah Lebar Road and McPherson Road. He said he was going to see a friend. My fare was a Hengwha Chinese by name, Lee Low Chee. After waiting about fifteen or twenty minutes I heard cries of Police from Payah Lebar Road. The cries were 'Mata', 'Mata'. I heard the cries seven or eight times, but the first two cries were louder than the rest. About five or ten minutes after the cries Lee Low Chee came back with a man, a Hengwha Chinese, and shorter than Lee Low Chee. I asked him what the cries were about. He said, 'You are a ricksha puller why should you mind other people's business'. They went into my ricksha and just as I walked about two paces I heard the shorter man say to Lee Low Chee, 'Had I known you were going to make such cases I would not come for a hundred dollars'. As I was pulling the ricksha they were talking to each other and I could not understand what was said. On arrival back at Weld Road and near Jalan Besar, Lee Low Chee asked me to stop and I put down the shafts and they got out. Lee Low Chee then paid me eighty cents for the fare. Low Chee went towards Arab Street and the shorter man turned towards Rochore Canal Road . . . Lee Low Chee is a ricksha puller and used to go to Malabar and Malay Street with his ricksha to wait for fares, and I used to go there with my ricksha and so I knew him.[44]

Additional information was eventually obtained and a warrant was issued for the arrest of the Hengwah rickshaw puller, Lee Low Chee, who lived in Victoria Street. He was apparently on familiar terms with Yeo Sin Kam Poh and the two men had quarrelled. After the murder, Lee Low Chee managed to escape to China leaving nothing behind, except an empty coffin box under his sleeping bench. Yeo Sin Kam Poh was guarded in her statement to the police. She admitted only that she knew Lee Low Chee as her late husband's friend, that Chew Ah Tong had fought with him over her on one occasion, and ended by denying emphatically that she had ever been Lee Low Chee's mistress:

I know Lee Low Chee. He is a ricksha puller and he lives in Victoria Street. I do not know the number, I have not seen him since my husband's death. He was a friend of my husband. My husband met me on one occasion when I was talking to Lee Low Chee and my husband struck him. This was about two years ago. I do not know of any recent quarrel. They were friendly after the quarrel. He [Lee Low Chee] never asked me to be his mistress. I do not know where he is now.[45]

A far more tragic case involved the Hengwah rickshaw puller Chor Seng and a neighbour, a Hengwah mother, Ong Sam Moi. What is so striking in this instance is the repercussions of a possible extra-marital relationship upon the children. Ong Sam Moi had married at fifteen to a rickshaw puller Ng Ah Chan, who was eighteen years older than she. By the time she was 28 years old Ong Sam Moi had seven children, but only three lived with her. Chor Seng was a 31-year-old rickshaw coolie with a wife in China, when he met Ong Sam Moi next door to his lodging-house at 7 Weld Road and must have discovered how lonely he had been. She owned two rickshaws. Chor Seng began to take one out for hire, and paid her 20 to 30 cents for the use of it. Over those four years Ng Ah Chan did not know whether Chor Seng visited his house, in his absence; he was out daily from 5 a.m. to 5 p.m. plying for hire. Chor Seng was in the habit of coming to the house with presents for the children, and taking them out. He always got Ong Sam Moi's permission to do so. He never asked Ng Ah Chan. On 3 December 1934 Ng Ah Chan returned home as usual at 7 p.m. and did not go out again. He was tired, having been on the streets since dawn, and went to sleep. His wife was cooking downstairs and the three children were playing. Chor Seng was downstairs too but Ng Ah Chan did not speak to him. His wife had told him that Chor Seng was going to take their two sons to see the circus. Ng Ah Chan did not raise any objection. The next morning the body of Ah Mee, his 5-year-old son, was found near the canal at Sungei Road. The police were unable to trace the whereabouts of Chor Seng or the other son.[46]

The relationship between Chor Seng and Ong Sam Moi appears to have been close. Chor Seng worked for her, paying only when he had the cash. They were together for nearly four years and she bore a son, aged three, during that period. There is no way of confirming that Chor Seng was Ah Chow's father, but the possibility exists. Ong Sam Moi was married to Ng Ah Chan, and could not be expected to confess that she was the mother of Chor Seng's child. From Ong Sam Moi's statement it is clear there were a number of imponderables regarding her relationship with Chor Seng; they involved not only the children, but reached right across a vast distance to his village in China and his 'other wife' there. All that is certain is that whatever their relationship was it began cracking just before Chor Seng possibly threw Ah Mee into the canal and disappeared with Ah Chow:

> I have known Chor Seng three or four years. . . . He still owes me about four or five dollars. I did not quarrel with Chor Seng about a month ago. He frequently played about with my children on the ground floor of the house. He was not my lover. Ng Ah Chan is the father of the children. I do not know if Chor Seng divorced his wife in China. Chor Seng frequently took my children out to buy them something. . . . He did not have a wife with him. . . . As far as I know Chor Seng is his full name.[47]

Women who were either thrown out or left of their own accord in the Depression did form temporary unions with rickshawmen to survive.

These unions involving a 'followed' or *de facto* wife tend to highlight the extent to which people were driven beyond the law by the hard times and all too often on account of rivalry in sexual love. On the subject of jealousy and temporary unions one has to look no further than the death of the Hockchia rickshaw coolie Sia Sen Hert who was found by the police lying in Bolo Street with a knife wound of the chest. He had stayed the night with his *de facto* wife, a Teochiu woman named Chew Chui Lan, at 19 Fisher Street and was on his way home when he was stabbed to death. There was circumstantial evidence that his assailant was a Hokkien named Goh Geok Lim alias Mopeng who was also intimately acquainted with the woman.[48]

Sia Sen Hert described, in a statement to the police shortly before his death, his relationship with Chew Chui Lan, who had walked out on her husband fourteen months earlier. After she left him Chew Chui Lan rented a room at 19 Fisher Street and lived alone. She then met Sia Sen Hert, and he paid her for sexual favours. She was also seeing Mopeng at the same time, despite being kept by the rickshaw puller. She had visited Sia Sen Hert the night before he was murdered, asking him for money for maintenance. Later that same night he went and slept in her room. Chew Chui Lan, he stated,

> ... was my followed wife who is known to me by the name 'Ah Nee'. I have been keeping her for about seven or eight months. I used to give her between eight dollars to ten dollars a month. She lives by herself in a room in Fisher Street. I live separate in Bolo Street no. 8 a rickshaw coolie house. I only go to her room and sleep with her two or three times a week. My nights sleeping with her at her room are irregular ... I never even quarreled with my followed wife.[49]

Chew Chui Lan was frank in discussing her relationship and not at all perplexed over her sexual entanglement with the two men. What is so striking, as she described the seven or eight months with Sia Sen Hert with its tragic repercussions, is that she seems to have had little remorse. Chew Chui Lan distanced herself from the violence and her role in precipitating the crime in the first place:

> I am a Teochew Chinese, aged 34 years. I was legally married to Tan Cheng Ho. I left him about fourteen months ago. When I left him I rented a room at 19 Fisher Street and lived alone. I then met a Hockchia Chinese whose name I did not know. He was a rickshaw puller and lived in a ricksha kongsi house near People's Park in the same house as Seh Ah Moi. The rickshaw puller kept me. We met on the evening before he was taken to hospital.... He came and slept in my room. He left in the morning after 5 a.m. At 7 a.m. Seh Ah Moi came and told me that he had been assaulted ... I knew a Hockchia Chinese known as Mopeng who lived at the house of Goh Pan. I knew him for two or three months. Whenever he came and called me I went to his room and slept with him, probably two or three times a week. The night before the day when the Hockchia man was assaulted Mopeng came and called me to go to his room but I did not go because the Hockchia man was in my room then. I do not know if Mopeng knew the Hockchia man was there. Mopeng did not say anything two or three nights previously. Mopeng took me to the Great World and while there we met the

Hockchia man. They did not speak to each other but looked at each other. The Hockchia man walked away. Mopeng disappeared and I went back to my room with the Hockchia man. I do not know if the Hockchia man and Mopeng quarreled with each other at any time. The Hockchia man knew that I went to sleep with Mopeng but did not say anything about it. The Hockchia man and Mopeng first met each other on that night in the Great World as far as I know . . . I went to Mopeng's room in the morning when the Hockchia man was assaulted . . . I met him walking to and fro on the five footway of his house. He looked pale and frightened. I went there to ask him why he had called for me on the previous night. When I asked him he scolded me and said that I could go and die. He left me and went upstairs. I followed him into his room. He took two framed photographs of himself and went downstairs. I remained in his room for about five minutes. He did not return . . . I have not seen him since that morning.[50]

The same problems that were responsible for increased poverty and the collapse of elemental families by strangling the puller's traditional sources of income also led to suicide. The difficulties of poor wives were acute in a society where women were considered generally to be little better than 'pieces of meat put on the table for men to slice'. Inequality in the family combined with the wretched existence of living in a tenement cubicle with several small children and where all were likely to suffer serious illness drove women to commit suicide. Their acts must be interpreted usually as an outcry against the cruelties of Singapore life in the late 1920s and 1930s.

The striking impression the Coroner's Records convey of wives of rickshaw coolies who suicided between 1929 and 1936 is that they were young to middle-aged, ranging from 19 to 39, and reacting against abuse, rejection, or loss of a loved one. What an effect it makes especially in the revelation, pain, shock and indignation of the elemental family drama with its epidemiological aspects of suicide. The behaviour and feelings of the women betrayed their agitation, dependence, and isolation. Their suicide often was an 'appeal' to change a person such as their husband, or the more general circumstances of their lives in Singapore: an act meant to overcome a sense of helplessness and hopelessness.

This discussion has already touched on marital conflict and infidelity, the Depression and grief over loss of a child, and hostility in relations between in-laws, in which suicide resulted. Let us conclude this account of suicide and the elemental family with a story that emerges from the Coroner's inquests in the 1930s. It emphasizes the strain and burden of losing a parent in China, and how that 'event' was viewed at an intimate level in the midst of the Singapore Depression by a young woman. Wee Choon Beoh was faced with the failure of fulfilling her filial responsibility as a married daughter because she was destitute. She was the wife of a rickshaw coolie. Her mother died in China in 1930. She was unable to perform the rites of a filial daughter by sending money for her mother's funeral. Wee Choon Beoh had two young children and could not work. With the news of the death of her mother her life changed. She brooded in shame for ten lonely nights with a sad heart, and across her days was the shadow of her mother which not even the smiles of her children could block out. As a married daughter and the wife of a rickshaw coolie she had her own tragedy to come to terms with and she chose to learn her lesson in the most dire way possible. On 26 November 1930, Swee Ah Ham, the principal tenant at 231 Waterloo Street, was awakened when she heard Lim Ong shouting for help: 'help, quick, quick'. The woman rushed downstairs into a cubicle to the sight of Lim Ong holding his wife up: she was hanging from a beam. Swee Ah Ham helped the tearful puller untie the rope and lift his wife on to the bed. The reason for her suicide was straightforward as Lim Ong later explained:

> I returned from pulling my ricksha at about 1 a.m. 26th day of Chinese 9th moon. I saw my wife sleeping with my children.... She was then alright. She seemed quite normal. She had no trouble as far as I know previously. She has relations in China. About ten days before my wife had received a letter saying her mother was dead. This upset her as we had no money to send her. I saw her at the time she gave me food. She did not speak to me. This was during my absence in the bathroom, that she prepared the meal. When I returned she had gone to bed. She complained of nothing except having no money to send home to China. She had no enemies. I did not sleep in the same room with my wife because the room is too small and I have two small children. I went to sleep soon after taking food, I was too tired. I had been up since 2 p.m. the previous [afternoon]. I woke next morning between 4 and 5 a.m. It was nearly daylight. The crying of my child woke me. The first thing I did was to call my wife from her room. She did not answer the child was still crying the small one. There was no light in that room. I did not usually get up from bed so early. If the child did cry for food I would call my wife. On this occasion the child cried more than usual. I think the hunger made the child cry. When I called from the door I got [no] answer. I then went into the room without a light. I saw her in a standing position with the knees bent.... A rope was tied round the neck. The other was tied to [her] waist on a beam. As soon as I saw this I lifted her immediately and shouted for help. In response to my shout the chief tenant of the house came down—this is the woman (Swee Ah Ham). She helped me to revive my wife. She was not dead at the time. We were not successful ... I only know of this reason for the committing of suicide, her mother having died in China and not being able to send money to her relatives.[51]

The widowed father of two young children buried his wife himself.

Through the means of the rickshaw as their source of livelihood and the institution of marriage, men and women from China strove to create a better life in Singapore with families, but their future was foreclosed by colonial policy and practice and terminated in the Depression. The attempt must be made to view this crisis and resultant poverty not simply from a colonial developmental perspective, but rather from the point of view of the poor rickshaw coolies themselves, especially those who married and had families. Structural poverty was linked directly to colonial policy and practice and expressed itself predominantly in terms of inadequate food and housing, but also affected all areas of life, beginning with family circumstances and relationships between family members. This poverty led to the breakdown of elemental families, not only as a result of marital strain but also because of illness, or for cultural reasons, like Wee Choon Beoh's 'shame'. The rickshawmen and their families in the inter-war years could hardly take satisfaction for their individual efforts and suffering in the glory of Singapore's future. They were consumed trying to earn a living pulling a rickshaw in Singapore during the two decades of the great economic growth and crisis.

1. Maurice Freedman, *The Study of Chinese Society. Essays by Maurice Freedman* (Stanford: Stanford University Press, 1979).

2. Yen Ching-Hwang, 'Early Chinese Clan Organizations in Singapore and Malaya, 1819–1911', *Journal of Southeast Asian Studies*, 12, No. 1 (1981), p. 84.

3. SCII of Ee Ang Ang, No. 82, 9/2/27.

4. SCII of Teng Ah Poh, No. 15, 14/1/14.

5. SCII of Ngoh Ah Mui, No. 460, 18/9/29.

6. Freedman, *The Study of Chinese Society*, pp. 244–5; I have used the term 'elemental family', as a social category, to describe the suddenly changing fortunes of the 'nuclear family' or the 'extended family' of rickshaw coolies, especially in the period 1918–39. Depending on time, place and circumstance the 'elemental family' could either rapidly take the form of the 'nuclear family' or the 'extended family', because of factors pertaining to the migration cycle and personal events in the pullers' lives. The elemental family of rickshaw coolies is one area where social experience and psychological phenomena can best intersect accurately. It serves, as a social form, in its typicality and uniqueness, from the early 1920s as a mid-point between the life history of individual rickshaw pullers and the group history of a coolie occupation. By focusing on the dynamics of the 'elemental family' of the rickshaw pullers of Singapore, in the lens provided by the Coroner's records, social historians can examine the nuclear social and psychological relations from which all others spring. The inquests and inquiries record patterns of loving and hating, giving and receiving, and controlling and being controlled which are all trained for and played out in the Chinese family setting. Changes in these basic patterns, in turn, effected changes in the attitude, character and personality of members of the elemental family, and its very structure. This social category and source humanizes the rickshaw coolie's society at an intimate, unstereotypical level of ordinary household decisions and their impact on men and women, revealing complex conflicts and personal crises.

7. Lao She, *Rickshaw* (the novel *Lo-T'o Hsiang Tzu*), translated by Jean M. James (Honolulu: The University Press of Hawaii, 1979), p. 85.

8. See Appendices.

9. Freedman, *The Study of Chinese Society*, pp. 235–6.

10. SCII of Ler Cho Wing, No. 303, 10/7/35.

11. SCII of Gian Yeow Sun, No. 319, 17/7/35.

12. SCII of Teng Ah Poh, No. 392, 10/7/36.

13. SCII of Koh Kim Chwee, No. 677, 23/11/32.

14. SCII of Gian Yeow Sun, No. 319, 17/7/35.

15. SCII of Teng Ah Poh, No. 392, 10/7/36.

16. SCII of Yap Seah Hing, No. 1, 3/1/26.

17. SCII of Ng Ah Mee, No. 551, 4/12/34.

18. SCII of Sim Kwee Geok, No. 619, 11/12/29.

19. One of the great problems in dealing with beri-beri in the traditional diet of pregnant Chinese women was that, however willing the mothers were to consume unpolished rice, they were more often than not unable to do so because they could not purchase it within a reasonable distance of their homes and could not afford to pay bus fares in 1939 to the very few shops in the centre of town where it was sold. SMAR, 1938, p. 10; SMAR, 1939, p. D-55.

20. SCII of Wong Huat San, No. 606, 30/10/31.
21. SCII of Ling Ah Moi, No. 205, 6/4/36.
22. SCII of Ee Kin San, No. 497, 9/9/26.
23. SCII of Ng Ah Mee, No. 551, 4/12/34.
24. See *Singapore Free Press*, 5 January 1900; SCII of Lim Kwee Ping, No. 52, 3/4/05; of Ng Ah Mee, No. 551, 4/12/34.
25. SCII of Ng Ah Mee, No. 551, 4/12/34.
26. SCII of Ng Hai Noh, No. 582, 25/9/36.
27. Lao She, op. cit., p. 61.
28. SCII of Wee Choon Beoh, No. 612, 17/11/30.
29. Ibid.
30. Zeng Shanti, 'Life and Crime', in *Reunion and Other Stories*, trans. by Ly Singko (Singapore: Heinemann Asia, 1982), pp. 40–1.
31. Ibid., pp. 42–3.
32. Lao She, op. cit., pp. 3–4.
33. Ibid., p. 164.
34. SCII of Sim Kwee Geok, No. 619, 11/12/29.
35. SCII of Seah Wan Tan, No. 214, 16/9/14.
36. SCII of Ler Cho Wing, No. 303. 10/7/35.
37. SCII of Gian Yeow Sun, No. 319, 17/7/35.
38. SCII of Chung Ah Hoot, No. 703, 23/12/31.
39. Freedman, *The Study of Chinese Society*, p. 308.
40. SCII of Lim Mui Noh, No. 550, 14/9/28.
41. Zeng Shanti, op. cit., pp. 42–3.
42. SCII of Sim Kwee Geok, No. 619, 11/12/29.
43. Ibid.
44. SCII of Chew Ah Tong, No. 170, 1/11/12.
45. Ibid.
46. SCII of Ng Ah Mee, No. 551, 4/12/34.
47. Ibid.
48. SCII of Sia Sen Hert, No. 354, 21/6/39.
49. Ibid.
50. Ibid.
51. SCII of Wee Choon Beoh, No. 612, 17/11/30.

14 Leisure and the Four Evils

MOST rickshaw coolies saw no future in marriage. They realized it was impossible to have a family, and chose to live as bachelors. That is what it meant to pull a rickshaw in Singapore:

> Another one said, 'Now about your way of running. Isn't it a fact that it holds you back? Do you agree? Age does make a difference. I'm serious'. The tall one smiled slightly and shook his head. 'Well, it isn't all a matter of age, brothers! I'll tell you one thing you can be sure of. Guys in our line must not get married and that's the truth!' He lowered his voice a bit when he noticed that they were all listening. 'Get married and there's no rest for you night or day. You're just played out! Take a look at me. There isn't a trace of vitality left anywhere so I'd really better not run hard. I end up coughing when I grit my teeth and do it, and I feel just awful. There's no point talking about it. Guys in our line of work must be bachelors all their lives, damn it! Even those fucking sparrows can pair up but not us! And besides, after you get married there's one brat a year and now I have five of them! And all of them with their mouths open, waiting to eat. Rental fees are high, food is expensive, work is hard. Is there anything you can do? It's not as good as never marrying and rushing off to a cheap whorehouse when you can't stand it any longer. And if you get the clap, well, that's life! When a single man dies, he's dead and that's that. But get yourself this joy of a family and what with all those mouths, the old ones and the young ones, you still can't close your eyes when you die.[1]

Thousands of solitary men pulled rickshaws to a moronic rhythm of work, little or no leisure, and work for years on end. Apart from drawing a rickshaw, the single puller's life was 'empty', lacking the ordinary joys of family life, parenthood, and for some, even friendship. There was no limit to the amount of work a rickshaw coolie could do. His time and strength were his own affair. Still, it was precisely this concentration of energy that produced the abnormal will-power and stamina to pull a rickshaw year after year, alone.

What were the implications of the impact of living individually upon the behaviour, values, and feelings of the rickshawmen? Networks of lineal, economic, and emotional ties bound co-villagers together in native-place associations, and in rickshaw lodging-houses. The experiences of rickshaw pullers show though that while these ties were crucial in linking coolies to one another *en masse* at the level of the *pang keng*, they did not always unite them to each other, and to their material world. For many pullers in the lodging-houses it was not a case of being accepted or rejected by their workmates because the men who lived in the dormitories did not belong to tightly-knit cliques. Indeed, a great many of them did not know one another at all despite the fact that they belonged to the same surname and dialect groups. This seems to have been particularly so in the overcrowded environment of the big lodging-houses with rooms containing upward of twenty men. Social relationships also were impersonal because pullers worked different shifts and lived on different floors or parts thereof in the tenements. This is not to say that rickshaw coolies did not belong to small groups of kin or clansmen, but such clusters did not necessarily coincide with their co-lodgers.

Anonymity and a feeling of loneliness were characteristic of the bachelor's way of life and there is some evidence in the Coroner's reports to this effect. Men living in the solitude of the upper floors of the larger compound houses could rarely be identified by tenants in other parts of the building. Sometimes a puller could only be recognized on sight: 'I pull a ricksha belonging to Shong Shong who lived in the same house. The deceased was also a ricksha puller but I do not know his name nor where he lived nor did he pull a ricksha belonging to my house. I knew him by sight as he formerly lived in the same coolie house as I did.'[2] Greenhorns had to be educated in just how hard rickshaw coolies in the lodging-houses could get towards one another. At times their indifference took the best part of his youth away from a puller leaving him on the edge of the Singapore Chinese life that he desired so much to be part of. Such men survived by hardening themselves to their lack of identity and resources, becoming cold as ice. Tiang Seang accidentally trod on a mud-covered milk tin on South Bridge Road while running very fast. The puller, dying of tetanus, mentioned his one friend in the city: 'My foot got worse and my friend (named Ting In) took me to hospital the following day. It was purely an accident. This Ting In is my only friend in Singapore. I came from China about three years ago.'[3]

Living a solitary life far from family and village in China, the bachelor's whole world was reduced to memories and reminiscencing about the past, and men became homesick. Such discussions invariably revolved around images of China, of a family left behind, and talk of remitting money and, perhaps, someday owning a rickshaw. In lodging-house rooms worn photographs exchanged hands, and heated arguments flared up over women, over rights and obligations between kin, and over rents. The men with rare exception were illiterate. Consequently nearly all coolies in the rickshaw neighbourhoods could not read a letter from home without the assistance of a letter-writer. Letters from China usually began with the standard polite professional phrases but went on to urge the men to work hard, to be frugal, and above all, to avoid the attractions of the 'city lights'. Ling Ah Ngong stands out because he was able to read and write and therefore overcome the solitude, the sense of distance, and time on his own initiative: 'He did not smoke opium. He had good eyesight and could see to write letters at night time.'[4]

Work was compulsive for most rickshaw coolies. A more leisurely social life was constrained by absence of family and lack of cash. But occasionally there was free entertainment in the neighbourhood. *Wayang*-going was a common way to break down the wall between work and life. Men could actually get away from it all to unleash the frustrations of pulling a rickshaw and living alone. The streets in the rickshaw quarter were a stage when a Chinese *wayang*, or street opera, played to the delight of the coolies. Temple and native-place associations often arranged such open-air entertainment to celebrate a religious holiday. The operas ran for days with itinerant *wayang* troupes performing on makeshift stages from dusk to dawn. The surrounding streets became a hub of activity, alive with spectators socializing, filled with the sound of clashing cymbals and drums, and hawkers providing delicious fare along the five-footway.[5]

Social life was apt to be even livelier during the major festivals. Rickshawmen observed Chinese New Year, the Ch'ing-ming Festival, and the Moon Festival; the Ch'ing-ming Festival was the most serious, involving ancestral worship, pilgrimages to cemeteries, and a commemorative banquet. When men worked year round these holidays provided a welcome break and helped to reinforce personal ties and clan solidarity.[6] Naturally, Chinese New Year remained one of the great occasions for rickshawmen. They celebrated in the company of their comrades by going out on the town to opium dens and brothels, or buying a new outfit, perhaps having a photograph taken to send home, or riding round in a rickshaw: 'I have never seen on the face of anyone a look of sheer joy to surpass that which I have seen on the face of a puller being drawn in a rikisha by another puller for a friendly ride.'[7] To usher in the New Year squares of red paper were fixed to the rickshaws:

> Most of the shops were open but some houses still had closed gates. Above the front doors the paper bearing auspicious mottoes was still red but the gold paper ingots hanging there had been shredded by the wind. The street was very quiet. There were quite a few rickshaws out and their pullers were rather more energetic than usual. Most of them had new shoes and squares of red paper pasted on the backs of their rickshaws for good luck.[8]

There was considerable carousing in the streets at this time of the year, and children were not above playing pranks on the rickshaw coolies:

> Besides cracker-firing on Chinese New Year's Eve, 'dashing' crackers were on sale everywhere, and hawkers did a roaring business selling these to all and sundry. . . . All one had to do was to take a 'dashing' cracker out of the box and hurl it at any object. Contact brought a violent explosion with hardly any damage . . . whilst ricksha-pullers swore when youngsters in the seats behind them crashed 'dashing' crackers on their nether parts, telling the pullers to mai-mai-lah ('run-faster').[9]

The Chinese New Year festivities officially drew to a close for some pullers on the first full moon of the New Year, when they pulled resplendently dressed women of wealthy Chinese families around the Esplanade before thousands of onlookers:

> There were those who drove round in gaily decked rickshas, the pullers of which either wore new suits or were bare-bodied, as the case may be, but who added gaiety to the occasion by affixing large bright acetylene lamps to their rickshaws in place of the usual shabby oil and wick lamps. This procession of maidens with their chaperones started at dusk and carried on till about midnight, when the crowds would melt away from the padang [field].[10]

Besides *wayang*, festivals, and religious holidays, the art of living was maintained by pullers fulfilling their social obligations to a deceased companion. Death, from the point of view of the native-place association, demanded a set of social activities and obligations that stressed ancestral worship, strengthened social ties, and promoted clan solidarity. The personal and social relationships between two rickshawmen were expressed in the reciprocal rights and obligations associated with the mourning ritual as fictive kin.[11] The rickshaw coolies helped in the preparations for a simple burial and formed the funeral procession to a clan cemetery or the pauper's cemetery with its fixed grave plots.

Within rickshaw houses loneliness, work, and social life were mediated to a certain extent by the observance of ancestor worship, festivals, and ritual activities dealing with death and the cycle of burial. Friendships were based on lineage ties and quasi-kinship relationships fostered within the framework of native-place associations. These bonds of comradeship were important indeed but were subject to disruption as men moved about the city, returned to China, married, or died. It was in the spirit of friendship that a rickshaw coolie contributed towards the cost of a decent funeral for a comrade. He knew, in case he died without kin, the association and his fellow pullers would raise enough money to give him a proper burial. Nor did he wish to wind up at the end of an unfortunate life being labelled an 'unknown Chinese' by the Coroner, for want of friends:

> His solitude would, he feared, be unbearable if he didn't make some friends.... In the past, he had not known how to fulfill his social obligation when one of his friends had a family wedding or a birthday or a funeral. Now he'd put up his forty cent share too, or join in a pool to buy presents. Not only did he now contribute money. He also went in person to congratulate or to mourn, because now he understood that these affairs were not staged to waste money. They were necessary in order to fulfill the obligations involved in human relationships. There was sincere laughter and sincere weeping with people like these. They weren't making a lot of meaningless noise.[12]

Despite spartan living conditions and a government whose control reached into the most intimate aspects of the rickshawman's workaday life, the majority of them—even those most left alone—managed to pursue their passions. They found some solace in the four evils. The four evils were all known amongst the rickshaw coolies, and the four went together in Singapore. They were opium smoking, prostitution, drinking, and gambling. Opium accompanied the sojourner to the *Nanyang*. It was a devastating master, destroying the career of many pullers, but it also helped others to live in an unhygienic, overcrowded city, and endure the pain of pulling a rickshaw.

The Colonial Government up until 1911 leased the right to control and distribute opium to the highest bidder, a Chinese revenue farmer, at a fixed rent for a set number of years. It was a remarkable situation. The farms were a primary source of revenue to the Government yet it did not have to invest a cent. Furthermore, they were ideal for taxing a transient population as they were a form of indirect levy. The most profitable farms were linked to the so-called 'vices' of the immigrant labourers—opium and spirits. The revenue-farmer paid the government a monthly fee and sold opium and alcohol through agents to the rickshaw coolies at enormous profit.[13] The Government did not care about the health and welfare of the rickshawman except when he was between the shafts, and as long as the import of opium brought in considerable revenue, British officials encouraged the Chinese farmers who also cared only for their own gain. Networks of opium dens and spirit shops sprang up, controlled by the farmers with the assistance of secret societies.

Under these circumstances, the needs of the rickshaw coolie in Chinese society at the end of the nineteeth century must be considered. Most pullers, being single and with nowhere to spend their free time, were attracted to the opium dens, and brothels where the drug was smoked. Once the mistake was made it was difficult to rectify because the taste always lingered. The money earned with their sweat and blood was committed to flames. The system was invidious because to pay for opium the wages of the rickshaw coolie were 'recycled' with a proportion recovered by the farmer who also might have behind-the-scene interests in rickshaw rentals, coolie housing and the brothels.[14] But not just the rickshawmen were affected by the recycling of wages; all other 'hard labourers' were in the same dilemma.

The gap between public opinion and official policy towards opium use and addiction amongst the Chinese labouring class was wide and growing all the time. All indications were that opium abuse was developing at a frightening rate by 1908 due to its increased cost. In that year records of sales of *chandu*, prepared opium, were supplied to a commission of inquiry by the Secretary for Chinese Affairs; from the beginning of 1905 monthly returns of sales were available showing the pattern of consumption for ensuing years.[15] Daily consumption among rickshaw pullers was 6 *hoon* a day (35 grams). Opium was not cheap then as a 3-*hoon* packet, the most popular variety, cost 40 cents.[16] The average consumption of *chandu* by rickshawmen was high even compared to Chinese coolies working on railway construction. The amount varied amongst railroad workers but 3 *hoon* daily was normal; thus rickshaw pullers consumed twice as much *chandu* per day on average.[17] Ideally, the tendency was to reduce the amount with advancing age, as their strength and capacity to earn declined.

The lack of family comforts, the strenuous nature of their occupation, and the total absence of any healthy form of rest and recreation predisposed rickshawmen to smoke opium. Irrespective of whether the habit was started as 'a remedy for sickness', as 'an antidote to sorrow', 'for fun' or from 'bad example',[18] one thing is perfectly clear—opium smoking and its political economy must be situated within the circumstance of a mushrooming colonial city. For rickshawmen beginning opium smoking was part and parcel of a larger problem of living with the social and economic inequality of Singapore in the first decades of this century:

> Do you not think that these people who are most industrious, frugal, vigorous and the most fruitful nation on the earth are not capable of giving it up themselves? No, and for this reason, that the economic conditions are against it. They work too hard, have too long hours and have no comfortable home, and for those reasons they take these narcotics. It gives them a temporary soothing effect but the price paid is too great.[19]

A report into the use of opium by 175 destitute Chinese, then patients in Tan Tock Seng Hospital, showed that 40 per cent or 71 cases cited relief from fatigue or pleasure as their reason for starting the habit.[20] Opium helped pullers sustain great strain and fatigue for a time; the time, for example, it took to pull a European out to Kranji and back without delay. There was considerable debate, especially in medical and religious circles, as to whether opium did increase a puller's stamina, temporarily. There was no doubt in the other quarter. Rickshaw owners and coolies were adamant in their view that the majority amongst them could not do heavy pulling if deprived of opium.[21] This was most apt to be the case when a man habitually smoked. Such pullers experienced withdrawal symptoms every day and could not work without opium. However, as the amount of work they did became less because of the debilitating effects of the drug, the greater was the quantity required to satisfy the craving, so that they had to pull longer to purchase more opium. It was a vicious circle that was difficult to break out of.

There were no arguments though about its soothing effect, putting road-weary coolies under sedation quickly. Opium was considered an important sedative drug by pullers, as it helped them to get off to sleep especially those who worked at night and slept in the daytime. It also relieved them of exhausted feeling after the wear and tear of a strenuous day's work. By 1924 nearly all rickshaw coolies smoked opium because they could not stand the arduous strain of their calling without it. Relief from pain or illness was another reason given by Chinese labourers for beginning to smoke opium. Pain and rickshaw pulling were inextricably associated with one another. Besides common muscle strains and lacerations of the feet, many pullers suffering from dysentery or chronic appendicitis also took it as an analgesic for abdominal cramps or pelvic pain. The medicinal effects of opium as a panacea for many ailments was a widespread belief among rickshaw pullers and the use of it for therapy was recommended by *sinseh*, practitioners of Chinese medicine.[22] To the rickshaw coolies opium was one of the few readily accessible medicines about which they knew.

Besides crucial relief of suffering there were three illnesses for which a rickshaw puller believed opium exercised a beneficial effect. They used it for tuberculosis, malaria, and venereal disease—especially during the nocturnal agonies of syphilis—and at any time when there was excruciating pain.[23] In the process, many men became addicted and every lodging-house, especially those that were filthy and overcrowded, had its share of addicts. Men such as Say Kong through no fault of their own became inveterate smokers; he had been in Singapore for six years in 1908 when he was asked about the origins of his addiction. Say Kong had begun to smoke opium three years earlier because of an attack of malarial fever; he recovered, but could not rid himself of the habit.[24]

Only 2 per cent of the rickshaw coolies were opium smokers when they arrived in Singapore.[25] The Hockchia had the highest percentage acquiring the habit after landing—well over 90 per cent. Several estimates of the average number of smokers amongst rickshaw pullers were provided to the Opium Commission of 1908; they ranged between 30 and 40 per cent, or 7,000–8,500 men; different averages for other occupations ran from coal coolies at 40 per cent to gardeners at 5–10 per cent.[26] The actual number of smokers involved though was higher, perhaps as high as 80 per cent of all pullers if those who used opium only at intervals are included.[27] But the truth of the matter will never be known as the authorities did not make the effort to detect rickshawmen who smoked until they were visibly affected by the 'disease' and considered potentially a dangerous class of person—a menace to society. Once they had been in the city for some time the ordinary percentage of addicts amongst rickshaw pullers rose to over 10 per cent. On the basis of statistics compiled from the records of the Rickshaw Department addicts averaged 2,000–3,000 a year in the period 1900–30. Within that 10 per cent there was a hard core, about 5 per cent, comprising the worst cases: men totally unfit for work, opium sots.[28] They included pullers who took opium in other forms, such as by hypodermic injections, and those who swallowed *chandu* dross. Taking opium by the mouth did more harm to the coolie's health than smoking it, but it was practised widely after 1898 because dross was much cheaper.

In China, opium was beyond the means of Hengwah and Hockchia farmboys. They contracted the habit in Singapore because they earned more money there, and they were young bachelors with little or nothing to occupy their time. There is also evidence to show that the habit was acquired in pleasure-seeking, after being persuaded by friends to try opium in the brothels, as an aphrodisiac.[29] Tragically, the very same rickshaw coolie would later use it to ease the pain of venereal disease acquired in that initial moment of excitement and sexual arousal. Smoking opium with clients was a regular practice among Chinese prostitutes in Singapore. Brothels in which it was common were called in Chinese, 'flower smoking brothels'. There were large numbers of them in Kampong Glam, and in Tan Quee Lan Street and Fraser Street.[30] Almost every Cantonese prostitute had the implements for smoking opium, and when a rickshaw coolie called, especially among the 'flower girls' of Tan Quee Lan Street, he was entertained with *chandu*. Young pullers,

> . . . who have not yet fully attained manhood very easily contract the habit of opium smoking in brothels, because they hanker so ardently after the girl that they have to rely on smoking as their go between; and though they are not addicted to the drug, yet they will smoke away as far as their passion will carry them. Thus the prostitute relies on opium to fish for money, while opium relies on her to gain a greater sale. There is no road to ruin so bad as this. . . .[31]

Companions enticed pullers to go to the brothels in the beginning. They went in and the women prepared opium for them, they met old friends there and made new ones, and were induced to smoke. If all the *chandu* was consumed, the brothel keeper was always ready to send out servants for more.[32] The opium shops closed at 10 o'clock at night, but a puller could get opium up to 2 a.m. in the brothels. It was in these 'flower smoking brothels' that the rickshaw coolies acquired the habit for the most part, especially the Hockchias who seemed to smoke more than the Hengwahs and went to the brothels. Few frequented the public shops.

The majority of rickshaw coolies, though, smoked in their lodging-houses.[33] For reasons of economy the space allotted to each lodger was small indeed. In the overcrowded dormitory room there was no place to sit, talk or play a game of chance. The only place the coolies could go to were their beds; they would lie down there to pass the time in the restful position in which opium smoking must be practised, and as the habit was commonplace amongst other men around them, they also took it up. The older pullers at the turn of the century, were nearly all addicted and in their lodging-houses there would have been an opium lamp between the bunks generally serving two men, one on each side of it. In the big compound houses facilities were always provided. There were four or five beds set aside for every fifty men where opium could be smoked. Day pullers scarcely used these beds at all; the night pullers did,[34] and they were rarely empty. It took a man about fifteen minutes to have a smoke depending on the quantity, and afterwards he might doze off. Opium smoking in rickshaw houses varied amongst speech-dialect groups; the Hockchias tended to smoke in the houses, while the Hengwahs more often went out to the shops.[35]

Rickshaw houses were subject to inspections by municipal officials but the practice of smoking opium was not considered serious enough to warrant prohibition of its use on the premises. The reason for this restraint was the fear that legislative interference would drive the rickshaw coolies into less easily controlled tenements. City officials felt that suppression of opium usage in lodging-houses would do more harm than good to the city coffers, because rickshawmen were an important bloc of rate-payers.[36] Their deteriorating health and capacity to earn was of no consequence to the Commissioners' attitude on this matter. In the lodging-house at 96 Sungei Road the men smoked opium regularly. This is what See Koh, the principal tenant, saw when he entered Yau Chin Swee's *pang keng*:

> There was a sick man—Teng Boon Seng—asleep on the floor, some distance from Chin Swee. I am sure he was alseep as I had to kick him several times before he would wake up. There was no one else in the room. There was a chandu smoking set on the floor close to Boon Seng. This belongs to Boon Seng. I did not notice any empty chandu packet there. I thought he had been smoking opium.[37]

Within three years of tabling the massive report of the Opium Commission the Colonial Government had taken over the running of the opium farm and established its own monopoly. The Government reached its decision after weighing up the increasing costs involved in underwriting the farm system in its present form, and because of mounting international criticism concerning the social costs involved. The informal controls of the Chinese opium farmers were considered to be too complex and rigid to condone any longer. More importantly, by 1911 the authorities were capable of organizing and administering the importation, preparation, and distribution of opium on a scale unimaginable two decades earlier. The revenue from opium was to increase dramatically over the next decade.[38]

By 1923 there were 423 government-run shops where opium could be purchased over the counter, with the average number of Chinese customers per shop conservatively numbering 377.[39] The dark red public shops remained open from 6 a.m. to 10 p.m. It was the proprietor's responsibility to supply the opium-smoking pipes, lamps, oil, and other paraphernalia. The interior of the government shops where pullers congregated to smoke was absolutely stark; there was nothing in the room, except wooden benches for the men to stretch out on, and a wooden block for a pillow:

> The smoking room measured about sixty feet by twenty, and accommodated a hundred men without overcrowding. A shallow gully marked the centre of the dirty floor. Two wooden benches, six feet wide, were built one above the other against the side-walls, and ran the length of the building. These benches were neither screened from the room nor divided into cubicles, so that smokers lay in long rows, cheek by jowl, with their feet towards the gully.[40]

The public smoking houses were generally filthy with little overall air space.[41]

Not all coolies were permitted to smoke in lodging-houses. Some owners and landlords forbade the practice; for example, Wee Siong, the elderly Hengwah rickshaw owner, did not permit it in his house. If his coolies wanted to smoke opium they had to go to a shop or brothel.[42] Certain shops catered to particular speech-dialect groups. Kuay-Tiong, the Hokkien proprietor of Chop Hin Tai at No. 268 Victoria Street, could accommodate twelve men at a time as the premise was licensed for six lamps. His principal customers were Hockchia pullers who mostly came between the hours of 7 and 8 p.m.[43] Hockchews, it seems, went only to Hockchew shops; there were three of them to cater to their needs in the 1920s.[44] Not all pullers were enthusiastic about the government-run opium shops, though, because they were required to return the dross, the remnant of the *chandu*, to the person in charge. When they smoked in the houses there was the advantage of being able to keep the dross, which could be used by addicts. In a good month a proprietor might sell as many as 4,000 packets of opium.[45] It was sold either by the packet or in hermetically sealed tubes manufactured by the government factory in Singapore. Sales were higher in the first half of the year with the best time being Chinese New Year.

Rickshaw coolies were encouraged to take opium by a government bent on maintaining a migrant work-force. However, few Europeans involved had an inkling of the proportion of rickshaw pullers who spent their hard-earned income on the government monopoly:

> The rickshaw pullers of Singapore trot about the streets all day in a temperature of ninety degrees fahrenheit.... Yet nine out of ten pullers habitually smoke a few pipes of opium at the end of their day's work. As much opium as would fill a matchbox costs about a guinea, and the wage of a coolie seldom exceeds ten shillings a week; thus not more than one Chinese in a hundred can afford to smoke immoderately.[46]

Say Kong earned between 40 and 60 cents a day of which he spent 20–30 cents on opium. He had a very desperate life-style with two periods of withdrawal—at 8 a.m. and 5 p.m.—every day. He experienced a state of collapse with abdominal cramps and cold sweats without smoking two packets a day. When he had no money to buy opium, he borrowed it from friends: 'my friends are good friends and would help me'.[47] It was even more difficult for middle-aged smokers, 8–10 years older than Say Kong, who were addicted and out of cash. Their symptoms of deprivation included: '... shock, there is the grey, slightly livid, pinched face, slow feeble pulse, profuse sweating with cold extremities, salivation with mucous roles all over the chest, vomiting, abdominal pain, generally accompanied diarrhoea. The respirations are slow and sighing ... collapse is always imminent....'[48] Friends did refuse to give money to the likes of Goh Chye Keh as they got older. He was becoming an opium sot. But it was almost impossible for a hard-core addict to give it up. The opium-shop proprietor, Chu Sooh Poh, described Goh Chye Keh's daily routine:

> I don't know where he lived. He had been coming to my shop to smoke for about two months and spends most of his spare time there. Comes two or three times per day. [He spends] about one dollar per day. On the 29th October I saw him alive. He was at my shop as usual. He came there twice. The last time was between 6 and 7 p.m. Smoked one packet. Remained about one hour. Paid after he had smoked.[49]

In the case of a rickshaw coolie like Goh Chye Keh, he had reached the limit of his earnings, irrespective of food and lodging, to purchase the amount of *chandu* he needed. The next stop was starvation, theft, or suicide.[50]

At first opium was cheap. It got to be expensive when pullers fell into the habit, and larger quantities were required. When the habit took hold rickshaw coolies could spend as much as 80 per cent or more of their income on the drug. In the 1920s the net wages of pullers were about $1 per day, but some earned as little as 40 cents and others as much as $2. The per diem spent on opium varied according to the amount earned and the degree of addiction; on average it was about 60 per cent of the puller's wage. Rickshawmen customarily spent 80 cents a day (the equivalent of two packets) on opium, far less on food, and next to nothing on clothes. Opium became their major source of 'nourishment'. Consequently, they were often emaciated. Coal coolies, stevedores, twakowmen and other hard labourers were provided with food by their employers. Rickshawmen were provided with nothing and their slovenly appearance led to many being fined by Mr Hooper's Court on charges of being 'physically weak', 'ragged and dirty' or for wearing 'bad clothes'. The Courts made money off the rickshawmen too because of the government opium monopoly.

Opium consumption among rickshawmen varied with their earnings and the current retail price of the drug. The higher price charged for opium with the outbreak of war in 1914 reduced its consumption. The increase in price also was necessarily accompanied by an increase in rent and the price of rice, but the wages of rickshaw pullers remained frozen at the pre-war level, until the lightning strike of 1920. By that time the cost of opium to the puller was twice as much as in 1914.[51] The habitual smoker without enough to 'feed' his habit, swallowed dross. Swallowing *chandu* of variable quality was cheaper. The practice became prevalent and increased in direct proportion to the rising cost of opium and the pullers' declining standard of living. Rail-like thinness, amounting to emaciation, was the rule among coolies who chose the 'compromise' method of swallowing opium.[52] Those who did it excessively suffered severe abdominal pain accompanied by diarrhoea. Low Ah Cheong was one of them: he was described as a moderate puller, whom no European would use, swallowing 20 cents' worth of opium dross per day in 1925.[53] The rickshawmen lying on the hard benches of the government shops, puffed contentedly, hopelessly lost in their self-induced miasma in the recession-ridden Singapore of the 1920s. But when the state of benign stupefaction began to wear off, they anxiously scraped out the dross and kept part of it for their own use. The rest they bartered to the proprietor for just a little more opium. This is how they felt at such times:

> Under the pitiless sky a man with grief in his face and deep in thought is reclining on his bed where burns a solitary lamp. A noise from the opium pipe strikes his ear; with knitted eyebrows he does his best to scrape out the dross left at the bottom of the bowl. My old cravings return with tide-like regularity; my heart bears a pain limitless as the sea.[54]

Morphia-injecting was introduced as a cheap substitute for opium. The increased price of *chandu* in 1904, from $2.20 to $3.00 per tahil, caused sales to plummet by 32 per cent. Morphia-injecting came into prominence at this time as a habit, and its prevalence increased with progressive rises in the price of *chandu* over the next decade.[55] Rickshaw coolies thought the use of morphine by hypodermic injection was a cheaper, easier way of taking opium. Weary, trembling pullers found they could get relief much quicker. Physiologically, injected morphia acted rapidly on the puller's system, dispelling the feeling of being worn out. Sadly, they also believed the advertising of the pushers about morphia's power to cure the opium habit. The cost of an unadulterated injection was 5 cents. They rarely received the pure article. If a rickshawman got a good injection two would suffice in twenty-four hours, but pushers adulterated the morphine to such an extent that some had to have on average twenty injections a day. Their bodies were 'absolutely rotten' from hypodermic needles, their arms and legs covered with the marks of the syringe, a mass of sores and ulcerated scars.

Pullers went regularly to places in Victoria Street, and near Duxton Road in the slums of Kreta Ayer, were injected with morphia and walked back to their lodging-houses.[56] They woke later on and started all over again. That went on occasionally five, six, even ten times or more every twenty-four hours. It was a ritual without joy. The early injections were in search of pleasure and saving, all the rest to avoid resignation and pain. See Quah attributed his morphia habit to the escalating cost of *chandu* in 1908. He lived in Victoria Street, and injected himself. As a night puller he could go the distance for 7 miles, slowly. His nightly take varied between $1.00 and $1.50. He had smoked opium for five years, the amount progressively rising to 50 cents' worth per day. See Quah had taken opium originally because his teeth caused him much pain and discomfort. He gave up using it when he discovered morphine provided more immediate relief and cost less. His dosage cost 18 cents, and he took three morphia injections daily. At the beginning of 1908 when he started, he only used 10 cents' worth, finding a 5-cent dose was not enough to substitute for 50 cents' worth of opium. His body was already demanding twice as much morphine; the amount he injected morning, noon, and evening cost 6 cents per shot. Soon it would cost 10 cents each time. He lived in a shabby room with three other addicts: a Teochiu rag picker, a Hokkien whitewasher, and a Hylam dishwasher. Men like See Quah and his room-mates could not afford opium at prices current in 1908, but they could acquire morphia.[57] They got more satisfaction for less money, or so it seemed, but death was as close as a rusty needle. Kim, a 28-year-old Hokkien rickshaw coolie and a morphia injector, died from blood poisoning in 1908. His body was like a pincushion with almost no place left to inject except the eyeballs, his veins had all but collapsed, and yet his taste for morphia lingered, undiminished. He was found by a clansman from a nearby lodging-house in the five-footway at No. 65 Duxton Road 'covered with needle marks'.[58]

Rickshaw coolies looked upon the worst cases as some kind of bad joke, fate's nasty trick, but they did not consider their besotted companions to be of immoral character or criminals. Some coolies simply laughed at those who lacked the wisdom of the older non-smokers, and behaved as though opium would never harm them, thinking they would be forever young and strong. Drugs were part of the tragedy of their circumstance in Singapore, and recognized to be a general curse, but sometimes just a little too late. The British officials and English community at large, who were Victorian Britons ruling a quarter of the earth's surface through a powerful national *persona* and sense of self-esteem, had rather different ideas about opium swallowing, morphine addiction, and the moral character of rickshaw addicts. For them it was not just a bad national habit that accompanied the sojourning Chinese wherever they went. It was a compulsive disease. But with the medical view of addiction current at the end of the nineteenth century in Britain came the rotten; the social and cultural attitude of this policy was partly legalistic and penal and partly racialism. The opium that the British so resolutely sold as a tool of their economic policy opened up a miserable gap between the ruler, the public, and the addict.

The greatest cruelty was to deny in the conclusions of commissions and major reports that rickshawmen smoked opium excessively, and to argue as a result that the drug habit had done little harm to the welfare of their community.[59] At the climax of their powers, British servants were concerned that rickshaw coolies could no longer afford to purchase the *chandu* they needed, and thus resorted to 'compromise' methods, partly swallowing and partly smoking, ending in the practice of morphia-injecting. Yet it was the government-regulated price of *chandu* itself that drove pullers to adopt these practices. At the other end of the scale with a twinge of cruel irony, the Government argued persuasively against the tenets of the anti-opium society by criticizing these very practices. Their line of thinking was a muddle of motives and social attitudes that was never unanimous in its intention, except to avoid the abolition of opium smoking: 'We may without fear of contradiction postulate that the habit is an extravagant one and that it makes considerable inroads into the earnings of the poorer class. From this it is an easy step on the part of the prohibitionists to say that it must inevitably ruin the poor who indulge.'[60] The Government's argument was simple. If smoking shops were closed it might well result in rickshawmen and other coolies substituting the more harmful 'compromise' practices over which the authorities exercised far less control. In other words, rickshaw coolies were to be encouraged to smoke in the shops because it prevented excessive addiction, apart from the important unstated factor—it was a most lucrative source of revenue. Officials had no intention of abolishing government-run smoking shops. It was the Government's contention that they fulfilled a definite need for thousands of rickshaw coolies who otherwise would frequent brothels or lodging-houses to smoke.[61] The number of puller addicts continued to rise during the inter-war years. Addiction was reaching epidemic proportion by the 1930s and nobody, either the authorities or, indeed, the public, seemed to care any longer. At the same time the Government was concerned that opium smokers did not fill up pauper institutions, hospitals, and prisons during a trying period of trade recession and unemployment in the 1920s and 1930s.[62]

Rickshaw pullers who smoked habitually forfeited their health after a number of years. Loss of weight and appetite accompanied addiction. Then, they lacked strength to do their work on a daily basis. They made less, and spent most of it on opium. Tan Eu Moy died in the General Hospital racked with pulmonary tuberculosis and filled with opium. His was an example of a life lived in the twilight world of drug addiction as a rickshaw coolie. He was taken to the Hospital by a fellow lodger and rickshawman, Teng Ong Ock, when he became too ill to ever work again. Extremely emaciated, and on his last legs, Tan Eu Moy had been an opium smoker for over a decade, and had been in Singapore for twenty-two years, when he died in 1916 from tuberculosis and the adverse effects of opium smoking.[63] If addicted pullers became too sick to work for any length of time it could easily lead to a suicidal crisis. Addicts, who experienced constant pain and depression because of deprivation, the spectre of debt, and an official attitude of indifference towards their plight, tended to be chronically suicidal. The Coroner, Alex Gentle, explained to members of the Opium Commission why suicides were constantly occurring that were indirectly due to opium:

> A man is an opium smoker, he gets out of work, and cannot procure the drug, so he puts a rope around his neck and hangs himself to a tree.
>
> These are not suicides by opium? No, but the men have got into the opium habit, and not being able to indulge, they find themselves so miserable that they destroy themselves.
>
> Why do you say they commit suicide on account of opium? I suspect it, from the appearance of the corpse. They are probably very emaciated, and there are all the signs of the use of opium. The cause of death must be stated as suicide by hanging or mutilation, as the case may be, but I would note that the deceased appeared to be an opium victim.[64]

Not all Coroner's Records and medical returns, however, did take account of the condition brought about by opium addiction, only giving the immediate cause of death. Despite this drawback, the distinct impression left by these Records is that a significant number of addicted rickshaw coolies scarcely had the will to live.[65]

In an overwhelming male society of immigrant Chinese labourers prostitution was a basic phenomenon. Chinese and Japanese women in their thousands occupied hundreds of brothels lining streets near the rickshaw quarters to provide sex to a veritable army of pullers. There was a definite relationship between the number of prostitutes and the size of the coolie population; between the economic ascendancy of Singapore at the end of the nineteenth century and a notable increase in prostitution; and between the repeal of the Contagious Disease Ordinance in 1887 in

Singapore and the occupational distribution of venereal disease. What is most significant is the incidence of sexually transmitted diseases increased dramatically among rickshaw coolies and other hard labourers from the 1890s onwards and its tragic social significance is shown in the Coroner's Records by the phenomenon of suicide.

Rickshawmen regularly visited the brothels in Chin Hin Street, Fraser Street, Sago Street, Smith Street, Tan Quee Lan Street, and Upper Hokkien Street.[66] The women in these brothels were all Chinese, predominantly Cantonese and Teochiu. The Japanese *Karayuki-san* were found in Malay, Malabar and Trengganu Streets. The Cantonese 'flower girls' had the reputation of giving men what they wanted, more so than any other women. They won renown for being startlingly good prostitutes. They also had a reputation for being the worst spreaders of gonorrhoea and syphilis. It was not at all uncommon for a rickshaw coolie to develop a sexually transmitted disease after enjoying casual copulation with one of these prostitutes, and in turn infecting another woman when he visited a different brothel. Unlike the Japanese women, the majority of Chinese prostitutes were not examined on a regular basis after the repeal of the Contagious Disease Ordinance in 1887.

Gonorrhoea and syphilis were a constant danger for the unattached rickshaw coolie. Every rickshaw *pang keng* was affected sooner or later. All the medical evidence established the classical symptoms of gonococcal conjunctivitis (gonorrhoeal ophthalmia) when an outbreak of the disease occurred among a section of the puller population in July 1926. Several men went blind.[67] In the case of syphilis many coolies experienced damage to the heart which only manifested itself from ten to thirty years after they were infected in a brothel. This form of syphilis in its advanced stages was common among hard labourers like rickshaw pullers: 'If the heart was involved, the patient developed chest pain and shortness of breath. If the great vessels were involved he often had no symptoms, but was likely to drop dead suddenly when his aorta ruptured.'[68] Chew Ah Kow's heart was weak due to syphilis so much so that he had difficulty in breathing. He had to give up pulling his rickshaw because of pains in his legs and his problem breathing. He became a hawker and opened a small fruit stall in an attempt to make a living but the pain persisted, to such an extent that he tried to swallow a cup of liquid caustic soda.[69] Tan Peng Keng showed none of the symptoms of Chew Ah Kow in the process of his dying—no breathlessness, no swollen legs, no chest pains. He just suddenly staggered and crashed to the ground in a vacant lot in Lavender Street as his heart burst apart. Death was due to syphilis.[70]

The misery of being infected with venereal disease was so great that some rickshaw coolies took their lives. In those days, without adequate treatment of syphilis in its early stages, the horrible third phase was commonplace among both pullers and prostitutes, and their cries broke the stillness of the Singapore night. The most tragic, haunting examples are those of syphilitic rickshawmen living in a nocturnal world of sharp pain caused by ulcerating tumours, gut cramp and vomiting, and of gradual loss of memory, judgement and emotional control, until they could barely walk, and finally become bedridden and incontinent. One can enter into their consciousness and learn, without having to go through their miserable school, what it was like to have a sexually transmitted disease. Tan Say Tee's testicles were on fire and his heart ached. He had pulled a rickshaw for eight years and had nothing to show for it. He had no money and told Tan Toh Kang, his younger brother, three or four times that he wanted to die, repeating the Malay words '*ta boleh tahan*' ('can't bear it any longer') as he fanned his genitals against the maddening itch and pain. Tan Toh Kang found the body of his brother two days later floating in the sea near the mouth of Stamford Canal. Tan Say Tee had to rid himself of the unimaginable burning sensation. He went to seek the solace of the sea. Ill himself, Tan Toh Kang described his frantic efforts to find his brother, rightly fearing for his safety:

> I found the body of deceased about 9.30 a.m. today (23/9/03) in the sea near the Esplanade . . . I was looking for the deceased from 6.30 a.m. today because he had disappeared last night under peculiar circumstances. He had been ill for about three weeks of a skin disease in the testicles which the Malays call 'krak krak'. Last night about 6.30 he went and bought some Chinese medicine called 'kamchow' and 'hokleng'. I boiled this for him and he drank it. After that he lay down and went to sleep. I went to a wayang, and came back about 10.30 p.m. The other coolies in the room told me he had gone out about half an hour ago, and showed me the direction in which he had gone. I got into a rikisha and tried to follow him. I cannot tell what rikisha it was. I went round by Hill Street, and then round by Bencoolen Street, inquiring for my brother. I was anxious about my brother because he had told me his heart was hot, from the testicles up to the heart. I sometimes pull a rikisha for Tan Ang Kian. I have been sick and have not pulled for ten days. I got home about 11 p.m. having heard nothing . . . I went to bed till daylight. About 6.30 a.m. I went out again to search for my brother. I went on foot and in two rikishas. I could not find these rikishas again. I found [hired] them in Victoria Street. I went all along the beach from Robinson Quay to Esplanade, and about 9.30 a.m. I found my brother's corpse. I was in the company of Tan Ah Sim another rikisha puller from the same house when I found the body.[71]

Some men, scarred by syphilitic suffering, said nothing to fellow lodgers and endured the pain in silence. When the time came, and they could no longer grit their teeth and bear the nightmare feeling of gnawing and burning, they swiftly put an end to their agony. Leong Ah Keng, a 45-year-old puller, had been ill for weeks and could not work because he suffered from venereal disease. Ng Ah Ng, a rickshaw coolie living in the same lodging-house, was just outside the door when he heard Leong Ah Keng groaning. He looked in and saw him lying on his bed with his throat cut, a razor by his side.[72] Among the worst cases were men who habitually smoked and frequented the brothels. Lim Tiew had experienced all four evils in his lifetime and at 50 he lay gasping for breath on his bunk in the back of an opium shop; he had not worked for a month.

Lim Chau Tau, another rickshaw puller living in the opium shop, told the Coroner, 'I had often seen him like that before.' Goh Heng, a coolie in the shop, described the symptoms of a man who had developed the opium habit and a sexually transmitted disease in tandem:

The deceased is a ricksha puller, named Lim Tiew, who was a lodger in the house for about one and a half months. For the last month he was ill. His legs and testicles were swollen and he could not pull his ricksha or earn a living. He complained of pain in his stomach, and could not take his food. He smoked about thirty five cents worth of chandu everday. The shopkeeper gave him that. I last saw him alive about 10 p.m. 7th November. He was then lying on his bed smoking chandu. At about 6 a.m. today, I went to the latrine and there I saw the deceased hanging from the roof of the latrine by this rope, which he had put round his neck . . . his feet were about four inches from the floor . . . I don't know where the deceased could have got the rope.[73]

Rickshaw pullers spent far less on alcohol than opium. Drinking did not suit the temperament of road-weary pullers. Most preferred lying down to enjoy a pipe of opium, rather than indulge in alcohol. In 1924, 53 per cent of the rickshawmen interviewed in selected government opium shops admitted to swallowing *chandu*; only 6 per cent confessed to having drunk liquor.[74] Turning to the non-smokers the percentage was higher; 36 per cent stated they drank liquor and their earnings were comparable to opium smokers—$1 a day.[75] Lee Choon, a Hockchia rickshaw owner, confirmed that a minority drank arrack but most smoked opium.[76] Consumption of alcohol was limited primarily to Chinese liquor although a favourite mixture was concocted from brandy and samsu.[77] Drink was cheap compared to opium but a bottle of liquor could cause trouble in the confined quarters of the lodging-houses. Men generally drank outside in the company of other pullers, and on social occasions such as a clan banquet, or in brothels. A hard-up rickshawman took pleasure in a drink every now and then; after all opium was far more expensive a habit than an occasional indulgence in spirits:

Sometimes he almost felt envious when he watched the other men drinking, smoking opium, and running off to brothels. Ambition was useless. Why not enjoy what you had? They were right. Even if he didn't run off to a brothel, he ought to be able to have a few drinks when he felt like it. Cigarettes and liquor appealed to him right now. He knew you didn't have to spend too much on them and they were sure to comfort him. They would help him move ahead on his bitter road and let him forget the pain of the past at the same time.[78]

Gambling, like prostitution, was an inevitable fact of life in a migrant community bereft of family life comprised largely of restless adult men with time on their hands and money to burn. Public gambling was illegal, but suppression by Singapore authorities proved impossible.[79] Pullers met in small groups to play cards and dice behind closed doors. Chua Sin Chin, after helping to prepare an extravagant meal of chicken, vermicelli and samsu, 'went out for a gamble at a neighbour's house'.[80] Larger gatherings of ten or more men, usually from the same neighbourhood, converged on nearby gambling dens when they wanted to do something at night. Again, in this way, the rickshaw coolie's earnings were 'recycled'. They gambled away their income in houses owned by *towkay* who were also likely to have had interests in the next-door pawnshop, tenement housing, adjacent rickshaw agencies, and brothels.[81] In these gambling joints pullers freely staked their earnings against one another or the house in card games and games of chance like *Ho-Lan-Pai* and *Fan-Tan* and *Chap Ji-ki*, but it was seen as being an important part of their social life and a favourite pastime.

What motivated rickshawmen to gamble? What kept them going even when they lost their hard-earned cash and had to pawn their few possessions? Many pullers who gambled were optimistic about winning next time, hoping to recoup their losses and make enough to go home to China in some style and comfort. A pipe-dream for most, perhaps, but they knew the odds were against them living much beyond the age of forty. They were prepared to stake everything against the eventuality of a premature death. Few struck it rich. Many lost their savings and got stuck in Singapore for years on end. There were other pay-offs though for gamblers, apart from making a small fortune. For these lonely single men there was something else at work—the experience of gambling itself. Many rickshaw gamblers lived for the tension and excitement when they placed a bet and the charged atmosphere of the 'calls of people bellowing and singing out the winning numbers and Chinese characters in the game of Chap Ji Kee, Fan Tan and other noisy games'.[82] Lots of pullers would have liked to either cut down or stop gambling but they could not. They missed the excitement of trying their luck when the betting was running high, even if it meant losing heavily because the odds were consistently stacked against them by the house. The inveterate gambler no more had the will to stop gambling experience than the addict did to put down his opium pipe. But it is most important to understand the conditioning process that kept rickshawmen gambling, set against a background of an urban colonial city that offered little recreation, and even more importantly, at a level where it created financial, personal, legal and employment problems.

The British considered gambling another failure of Chinese national character: 'You know perfectly well the poor Chinese coolie is born to gamble.'[83] Rickshaw coolies were not only criminal, violent and addicted to opium, they also were born gamblers! Rickshaw owners, and many bachelors themselves, however, took a far less sympathetic view of gamblers than opium smokers. Everything could suddenly be lost, right down to the last cent, even the shirt off the puller's back, on the drop of a card or the roll of the dice, throwing an individual or a whole *pang keng* if they staked him, into a state of panic. Further, knife fights were liable to break out over gambling losses on the day set aside in rickshaw houses to collect rent. Money meant to be remitted to kin in China was never sent and trips to be taken home had to be postponed. The rickshaw owner Tay Choon was blunt when it came to gambling in describing the character of one of his pullers, a Hockchia named Ong Oh Kaw: 'He was a strong young man of about twenty nine. He was a careful man who take [*sic*] care of his money and did not gamble and always paid for his rikisha. He spent about seventeen cents daily in [*sic*] chandu.'[84]

The four evils individually and in combination prevented many hard-working pullers from fulfilling the 'inexorable duty of every son'[85]—the regular remittance of money to support destitute kin in their villages in China. Many coolies spent next to nothing on themselves, remitting most of their savings to dependants they had left behind. Some sent as much as $200 a year—a sum equivalent to the price of a new rickshaw.[86] Hoh Swee Kim, the sundry shopkeeper at 80 Duxton Road, was the man the 'Hohs' of that area relied upon for sending their monthly remittances. A puller like Hoh Giong Toh who lived next door could buy a money order from him to send to his family, or Hoh Swee Kim could take down an urgent letter from another neighbour detailing the circumstances of the murder of Hoh Oon by Hoh Giong Toh over default of rent, and the preparation of funeral arrangements.[87] There were many other nameless Hoh Swee Kim's living on all the main thoroughfares of the rickshaw quarters always ready to place their services at the pullers' disposal, to either remit money or write to a loved one, enclosing a recent photo. In some cases, though, these characters—professional remittance men—apparently swindled pullers of their savings. Lee Hock How ran a 'wine and spirits' shop and 'Chinese remittance business' on the same premise. Lim Choon Huat claimed he was robbed by the manager and clerk. He used to remit spare money to his uncle through the shop. At least $10 a month was sent. Lee Hock How asserted that the puller's money had been received in China and acknowledged. According to his account the total amount remitted was about $100. He accused Lim Choon Huat of having gone mad. Distraught over having been deceived, the puller suicided. In his dying deposition he stated: 'Yesterday, I was in Chop Chai Wa Sing. A clerk in the shop, Chu Eng Tong by name, and the manager Koh Teo, swindled me. I stabbed myself as I was so depressed.'[88]

In their first few years in Singapore, rickshaw coolies sent their earnings home at regular intervals. Being in a new land was no excuse for forgetting their past; the survival of the family depended on them pulling rickshaws. But as time passed and men began to smoke opium and visit the brothels out of loneliness, remittances were sent less frequently. The bond of loyalty linking rickshaw pullers to family and village in China began to fray, and then come apart as the years went by in Singapore. Men frittered the money away on opium, daughters of joy, alcohol, and gambling—money that their whole families depended on for income. When rickshawmen failed to remit money or answer stinging letters reprimanding them for their laxity, kin, mostly wives, wearied of waiting. Some finally left China to search for their brothers or husbands in Singapore, only to discover once having found them, that they had left a past at home a lot better than the present. The cause of the paradox was their brothers and husbands had become different men after long years of working alone in Singapore—they were addicted to opium, alcohol and gambling, and infected with venereal disease.

Considerable tragedy was tied to the failure to remit money. The weight of this filial obligation reaching across time and space from villages in Kwangtung and Fukien with laser-like precision to touch men in the rickshaw quarters threatened with disease, drug addiction, loss of employment or worse, sometimes proved too much for them to bear. Lim Kee Lee received a letter from his parents asking him to remit money; the year was 1923. He had no cash; times were especially hard in Singapore for rickshawmen. He worried, as his parents were in desperate need. Three days after receiving the letter Lim Kee Lee bought four packets of *chandu* and ate the contents. Lim Ah Tee, his younger brother, was on his way home at noon with the rickshaw, when he saw his elder brother standing by the side of the road eating the *chandu*. He pulled him home at once and called a doctor. He then rushed out to borrow some money. When he returned his brother was dead. Unfailing remittance was impossible for Lim Kee Lee in the midst of an economic recession but he could not bring himself to tell his destitute parents that. Nor could he bear the stigma of shame of having failed to fulfil the cardinal duty of every sojourning son. There was no hope left. Lim Ah Tee had to shoulder the burden of the future alone: 'I don't know why he did it. Our parents were asking for money and he had none to send them. I am only new here from China.'[89]

A rickshaw coolie was also considered a failure if he could not return to China as originally planned. Rickshawmen who were frugal and largely avoided the four evils, went back to China at intervals of 5–6 years; however, most opium smokers could not afford to go back.[90] The statements of rickshaw pullers taken by members of the Opium Commission support this fact: 59 per cent had been unable to return to China since arriving in Singapore; the remaining 41 per cent claimed to have been back to China at least once or twice, and one old man, who had pulled rickshaws for eighteen years, had gone back six times, while another, aged 55, who had been resident in Singapore for thirty years and spent half his earnings on opium, stated he had returned to China four times to recoup his health.[91]

The four evils were the sole recreation afforded to rickshaw coolies in Singapore. The paradox surrounding them was that they seemingly made what in most respects was a miserable life for the puller tolerable, even exciting, joyous on occasion, if only for a moment, or a few hours. But ultimately their health, ambition, sense of responsibility, and dreams were consumed by the opium, sexually transmitted diseases, alcohol and gambling 'fever'. The four evils also destroyed the bonds of reciprocity between generations that linked filial sons to elderly parents in China. Their parents, the ancestors, and the past were forgotten for the passion of the moment in a city that had slowly worn them down. The Colonial Government, on its part, was neither prepared to raise the puller's wages nor create a more beneficial environment with appropriate housing, suitable recreational facilities and open spaces as a substitute for the sole means they had at their disposal to rest and enjoy themselves.

1. Lao She, *Rickshaw* (the novel *Lo-T'o Hsiang Tzu*), translated by Jean M. James (Honolulu: The University Press of Hawaii, 1979), p. 154.
2. SCII of Ling Ah Liew, No. 360, 29/6/31.
3. SCII of Tiang Seang, No. 30, 6/4/04.
4. SCII of Ling Ah Ngong, No. 1, 3/1/26.
5. See the photos nos. 285 and 286 of Chinese street opera in *Singapore Retrospect through Postcards: 1900–1930* (Singapore: Sin Chew Jit Poh: Archives and Oral History Department, 1982), p. 112.
6. Yen Ching-Hwang, 'Early Chinese Clan Organizations in Singapore and Malaya, 1819–1911', *Journal of Southeast Asian Studies*, 12, No. 1 (1981), pp. 79–80.
7. Sir William Peel, 'Notes Covering His Colonial Service in Malaya, Singapore, and Hong Kong from 1897 to 1935' (typescript). Mss. Brit. Emp. S. 208, Rhodes House Library, Oxford, p. 134.
8. Lao She, op. cit., p. 142.
9. John Cuylenburg, *Singapore through Sunshine and Shadow* (Singapore: Heinemann, 1982), p. 12.
10. Ibid., p. 11.
11. Maurice Freedman, *The Study of Chinese Society. Essays by Maurice Freedman* (Stanford: Stanford University Press, 1979), p. 242; Yen, 'Early Chinese Clan Organizations', pp. 63, 80–1.
12. Lao She, op. cit., p. 201.
13. The general discussion of the role of the revenue farms relies heavily on the work of John Butcher. See 'The Demise of the Revenue Farm System in the Federated Malay States', *Modern Asian Studies*, Vol. 17, Part 3 (July 1983), pp. 387–412.
14. Ibid., pp. 395–6.
15. SSOC, p. 8.
16. BMOC, p. A-15.
17. Ibid.
18. SSOC, p. 11.
19. SSOC, p. 44.
20. BMOC, pp. B-20–21.
21. SSOC, p. 45; BMOC, p. B-28.
22. SSOC, p. 11.
23. BMOC, pp. B-96, 101; C-203.
24. SSOC, p. 265.
25. Evidence of Mr Goodland, SSOC, p. 31.
26. Ibid., p. 492.
27. Ibid., p. 26.
28. Ibid., p. 28.
29. Ibid., p. 31–2.
30. Ibid., p. 134.
31. 'A Joint Letter from the Chinese Chamber of Commerce Singapore and the Chiu Bu Anti-Opium Society Singapore', 17 January 1908; Appendix XCII, in SSOC, p. 185.
32. Evidence of Alex Gentle, Coroner, SSOC, p. 317.
33. SSOC, pp. 31, 33, 324; BMOC, p. C-48.
34. Ibid.
35. Ibid.
36. Ibid.
37. SCII of Yau Chin Swee, No. 236, 26/6/24.
38. Butcher, op. cit.

39. BMOC, p. A-25.
40. A. Dixon, *Singapore Patrol* (London, 1935), pp. 108–9.
41. BMOC, p. B-50.
42. Ibid., p. C-45.
43. SSOC, pp. 253–4.
44. Ibid., p. 263.
45. BMOC, p. C-115.
46. Dixon, op. cit., p. 110.
47. BMOC, p. 265.
48. Ibid., p. B-100.
49. SCII of Goh Chye Keh, No. 281, 30/10/20.
50. SSOC, p. 16.
51. BMOC, p. A-31.
52. Ibid., pp. A-40, B-29, C-201.
53. SCII of Low Ah Cheong, No. 325, 16/7/25.
54. Translation of a leaflet distributed by Mr Eu Tong Sen amongst his mining coolies at Kampar, Perak, in the Federated Malay States, Appendix LV, SSOC, p. 145.
55. SSOC, pp. 34, 41, 75.
56. Ibid., p. 322.
57. Ibid., p. 55.
58. CCVS of Kim (a Hokkien rickshaw puller), No. 64, 27/9/08.
59. SSOC, p. 15; BMOC, p. A-44.
60. BMOC, p. A-41.
61. BMOC, pp. C-14–15.
62. Ibid., p. A-41.
63. SCII of Tan Eu Moy, No. 130, 13/7/16.
64. SSOC, p. 328.
65. See Appendix 9, 'Rickshaw Coolies: Suicide'.
66. For just a partial listing of these brothels see SMAR, 1901, Appendix A, 'List of Brothels, Coolie Lodging Houses and Private Houses to which Meters Have Been Attached, with Statement of Receipts Before and After Introduction of Meters', pp. 1–19.
67. SSAR, 1926, Report of the Chinese Protectorate, p. 74.
68. Derek Llewellyn-Jones, *Sex and V.D.* (London: Faber and Faber, 1974), p. 65.
69. SCII of Chew Ah Kow, No. 86, 14/2/38.
70. SCII of Tan Peng Keng, No. 412, 7/10/21.
71. SCII of Tan Say Tee, No. 115, 23/9/03.
72. SCII of Leong Ah Keng, No. 459, 12/11/21.
73. SCII of Lim Tiew, No. 180, 8/11/07.
74. BMOC, p. B-29.
75. Ibid.
76. Ibid., p. B-20.
77. Letter from Dr Gilmore Ellis, 9/10/07, SSOC, p. 79.
78. Lao She, op. cit., p. 39.
79. Butcher, op. cit., p. 4.
80. SCII of Ong Seng Hong, No. 410, 20/8/33.
81. Butcher, op. cit., p. 6.
82. Yap Pheng Geck, *Scholar, Banker, Gentleman Soldier. The Reminiscences of Dr Yap Pheng Geck* (Singapore: Times Books International, 1982), p. 8.
83. Cited in Butcher, op. cit., p. 397.
84. SCII of Ong Oh Kow, No. 116, 16/8/02.
85. Yap, op. cit., p. 10.
86. Evidence of Mr Hooper, SSOC, p. 29.
87. SCII of Hoh Oon, No. 162, 4/4/25.
88. SCII of Lim Choon Huat, No. 664, 15/12/32.
89. SCII of Lim Kee Lee, No. 59. 11/2/23.
90. SSOC, p. 31.
91. BMOC, p. B-29.

15 Morbidity and the Environment

THE Singapore of the rickshaw coolie was decidedly unhealthy. The effects of endemic and epidemic diseases on the social and medical history of Singapore at the end of the nineteenth century were immense, because of changing patterns of migration and population densities, urbanization, water supply, and sewage disposal. Yet this dimension of the relationship between Chinese society, colonialism, and the city has not been adequately studied. The development of Singapore as a modern port and centre of trade and finance in the period from 1890 to 1930 resulted in increased shipping and communication, growth of plantations, mines and industries in Malaya, and a migration of labour descending on the city, which accentuated encounters with infectious diseases. Geography became destiny. Here, medical geography is important, to understand the rickshaw coolie, his environment, and disease in Singapore. The port-city was part of an Asian-wide network of steam shipping, human movement, and regional communication that constituted a single disease pool comprising the coastal cities of south-eastern China and Hong Kong.[1] Colonial authorities took strict measures to control the movement of Chinese migrant labour to prevent the spread of epidemic infection, particularly plague, from more populous areas of South China to Singapore. The passage of the Chinese Immigrant Ordinance in 1902 required coolie ships to carry a certified medical doctor and a quarantine station was established in the harbour to handle health problems arising out of the enormous flow of *singkeh*.[2] But once a Hockchia or Hengwah walked down the gangway as a greenhorn, he was laid wide open to disease infection and the frightening array of illnesses on the streets of Singapore.

The city's environment had a significant effect on the health and lifestyle of rickshawmen. The quality and quantity of water available, an inadequate supply of housing, and conditions of severe overcrowding, made Singapore dangerous to life. Water-borne, insect-borne and infectious person-to-person diseases were commonplace in the rickshaw quarters. As rickshaw population densities built up in that distinct period between the advent of the rickshaw and the world Depression, and as patterns of life suited to the spread of infectious diseases developed, certain maladies assumed greater importance. The history of the rickshaw puller's encounter with infectious diseases, and of changes in disease patterns, has not been recognized. The historian's task is to illustrate the effects of locality, climate, water supply, housing, diet and other factors on the incidence of disease among groups such as the rickshaw coolies. Levels and causes of death varied from one decade to the next and from one rickshaw neighbourhood to another but there is little evidence to suggest that the overall level of infectious disease deaths (intestinal and diarrhoeal, tuberculosis, cholera, and malaria) declined before the Pacific War. The intensification of disease among Chinese labourers became part of their inexorable movement of life towards a premature death: a death that was not, as stated on the Coroner's Certificate, due to a 'natural cause'; a death that was not a historical accident, and a death which for the most part a rickshaw coolie could not avoid. Certain diseases with patterns of unusual frequency of infection among pullers were social and historical products, the result of urban growth and colonial irresponsibility in areas of public health and disease prevention. Hence, levels of susceptibility or immunity to infection among pullers rose or fell according to changes in policy of control and treatment and the changing pattern of the disease.

The principal causes of death were intestinal and diarrhoeal diseases, pointing to the need for more effective control of water and sewage disposal; malaria, highlighting the necessity for more stringent measures and lack of quinine; and diseases of the pulmonary/circulatory system because of overwork, overcrowding, sex, and chronic malnutrition. In the rickshaw houses sickness announced itself every day with the rattling cough of the consumptive or the figure of a coolie squatting with diarrhoea over a filthy latrine; while many emerged each morning in wretched condition with a bout of fever. Besides malaria there were tuberculosis, worms and other intestinal ailments, and skin diseases to which their scrawny bodies were exposed in the 1920s and 1930s. A rickshaw coolie could not afford to lose his health to the city's harmful environment: 'He also worried about his health. He knew how a man who sold his strength for a living ought guard his body: his physique was everything. If he went on living like this he'd soon be nothing but a dried up skeleton. He'd still be just as tall but there'd be nothing left inside him at all. He began to shudder.'[3] To take away his health was like a cart without a horse. What do you have? A puller who cannot run, a weak puller without a rickshaw. A lot of rickshawmen came down with 'fever' but they knew the worst was yet to come and could not spare themselves. Pullers had to endure illness by putting what hurt out of mind and keep working. Lacking money, strength or political connection, the sick rickshaw pullers' living conditions were appalling even by Chinese hardened standards. The Colonial Government seemed unwilling to recognize there was a real and grave problem linking infectious diseases, urban growth, and sanitary arrangements, directly to death.

Singapore's water supply was precarious in the nineteenth century. The problem of the use and control of water became even more alarming as the coolie population rose dramatically in the first decade of the twentieth century.[4] In Singapore, excreta was traditionally collected by

Teochius for their market gardens, so at first, there was no incentive to develop a system of water management and sanitation similar to that introduced in Britain in the 1850s. It was the visitations of cholera, and high levels of morbidity and mortality from intestinal and diarrhoeal diseases amongst the Chinese, that belatedly forced municipal authorities to take steps for the construction of an adequate water and sewage system for the population as a whole. Until 1893 the city's supply of fresh water came from one pathetically small reservoir. There were no streams on the island to supply water for the growing population, including rickshaw coolies numbering over 20,000 in 1902. They all drew their water from courtyard wells situated towards the rear of the lodging-houses. Most were polluted. This ready supply of contaminated well water was to determine the pattern of certain infectious diseases amongst rickshawmen.[5]

Rainfall was a mixed blessing. The months of heavy showers helped to keep the drains and other sources of infection clean, and fill the cisterns, but cessation brought drought. The water levels in wells plummetted. When the bucket hit the bottom of a well in a rickshaw compound drinking water became very scarce. At that point, pullers were forced to get their water from rather filthy drains. Serious infections involving water soon spread. This was the norm at certain times of the year in Singapore. Without a proper waterworks there was sickness and suffering on a seasonal basis every year. In 1902 the drought was so grim as to warrant mention in the Governor's *Annual Report*: 'The prolonged drought in Singapore in August and September resulted in great scarcity of water. The municipality supply had to be carefully husbanded and for a time was cut off daily except at stated hours. Steps are being taken to improve the present reservoir and to develop the resources of the Kallang Basin.'[6]

The costs involved in providing an adequate water supply and sewage scheme were astronomical, and municipal officials wrangled among themselves and with the Colonial Office for years over how to find capital to finance this costly amenity as the city grew. In 1902 the Colonial Office sanctioned a loan of $2½ million to the municipality for the purpose of carrying out an extension of the waterworks scheme. Three years later the consumption of water in Singapore reached its maximum and the new works had not yet been completed. This was because by 1905 the total expenditure confronting the Commissioners had risen to $9 million. Colonial heads of Government were pressing for the completion of a comprehensive scheme for the future and were both embarrassed and concerned over the delays. The municipality persisted in postponing its accomplishment because of high cost overruns, choosing instead to construct it in stages over a much longer period of time. For the Government the urgent necessity of increasing the sanitary water supply was beyond question. Governor Sir John Anderson pressed the Colonial Office to allow the Municipal Commissioners to obtain the loan for the proposed scheme at cost price to expedite the project. There was an obvious contradiction emerging between Singapore's increasing prosperity as the centre for British imperial expansion in the region and its effects on the quality of life of the labouring Chinese, living in congested lodgings with inadequate water supply, and an inefficient system of sewage disposal. But, as officials rightly pointed out, it would be the rickshaw coolies rather than the city fathers or the Colonial Government who would indirectly bear the burden of the costly improvements:

> The general rates here and the charges for water are already comparatively high looking to the poverty of the great mass of the population. The sanitary condition of Singapore leaves much to be desired, and I am pressing on the Municipal Commissioners the necessity of taking steps for its improvement. Any such measures will not only add to the rates but also involve considerable outlay on the part of the individual ratepayers in so far as they will involve structural and other alterations in most of the houses inhabited by the labouring classes.[7]

It is against this background of procrastination, wrangling and failure to solve the problem of water supply, that attention must be turned to the wells themselves. Wells in Singapore were commonly used by rickshaw pullers, as late as the 1920s. They were still a source of infectious diseases, even more so, as overcrowding was greater than in previous decades. There were two types of wells in Singapore: deep wells located in lodging-houses in the city and shallow wells often found in outlying 'kampong' areas.[8] In the drought of 1902 a return of wells was made, listing 3,877 within the municipal limits; only 609 contained possibly potable water.[9] The situation was far worse three years later, when Dr G. A. Finlayson, the Government bacteriologist, in a report examining 105 wells found only five containing water safe to drink; the remainder were 'more or less diluted cesspools'.[10] Until the 1920s many lodging-houses did not have municipal water supply laid on. Well water was considered drinkable, and used for domestic purposes and cooking. Most deep wells were liable to contamination because they lacked a protective brick or cement lining, and on account of their proximity to latrines, and poor drainage.[11] The existing arrangements for removal of excreta and cleansing latrine buckets in rickshaw houses afforded ample opportunity for pollution of wells by excreta. The principal channels of contamination and infection were soakage from the drain or surface, and dipping night-soil buckets into the well to clean them.[12] Surveillance of wells by the Health Department was rare before 1918. A constant 'bacteriological watch' was impossible to maintain on hundreds of rickshaw houses from an administrative and financial standpoint.[13] Thus, despite improved methods for testing water for contamination, the majority of wells remained unchecked, and were a dangerous source of water-borne infections.

Nevertheless, by 1922 hundreds of wells in the inner city were being condemned. The public health campaign was part of an effort dating back to 1914, and it forced hard-pressed rickshaw coolies to either use public standpipes or pay higher rents with the installation of municipal taps in their houses. By then health officials felt no well should be kept open within municipal limits.[14] They were without exception liable to intermittent contamination due to overcrowding and related problems of drainage and sewage disposal. One official remarked: '... probably the most uneducated coolie would object to drink the sewage effluent flowing from our contact beds, but this is a purer and safer water to drink than that from the great majority of wells in the town limit.'[15] It was easier and less expensive to close them down on a wholesale basis than to sustain a constant watch against the spread of infectious diseases. There was little doubt that if the wells were filled up and municipal water was laid on instead in rickshaw houses, there would be an appreciable decline in the death rate from intestinal and diarrhoeal diseases and cholera. The cost of that policy was passed on to the rickshaw coolies in soaring rents, and at a time when housing was scarce and the cost of rice prohibitive.

The closure of wells and supply of filtered water was only a partial solution at best to eradicating the complicated circumstances giving rise to water-borne diseases. The sewage disposal problem and drainage remained untouched. The arterial–venous system of water supply and sewers constructed out of ceramic pipe that was commonplace throughout Britain by the end of the nineteenth century was not brought to Singapore.[16] Open surface brick drains and concrete culverts were constructed on a grid pattern running along each side of the street to carry off the water. In the late 1870s they varied in size from 1 foot wide by 1½ feet deep to 3½ feet wide and 5 feet deep.[17] In some places excreta was dumped in the drains, causing danger to public health. When the rainfall level was high the drains were kept well flushed, but in dry weather the exact opposite occurred. They filled up with filth.[18] The system could not be considered complete. The vast old network of mud drains needed to be abolished and a regular system of flushing introduced, which would be independent of rainfall.[19] Of course, drainage was considered to be a municipal matter rather than a government one. The whole issue of attempting to cope with sewage problems was constrained by costs. The spread of settlement made the obsolescent system hopelessly inadequate by 1886 for the requirements of an expanding Chinese population: 'Personal observations lead me to believe that typhoid, and other continual fevers are much more prevalent now than formerly, owing doubtless to the rapidly increasing population with which the improvements in sanitation do not keep pace.'[20]

The city was large, and growing rapidly, yet the municipal government chose not to face up to the costs of the introduction of a modern sewage system to maintain the health and comfort of the entire population, rather than just those in the European quarter. The lodging-houses were jammed up against one another back to back, and water escaped by a drain that ran through the house from back to front, connecting with a street drain at the front of the house. Most drainage, including urine at times, was washed out through a house drain covered with a loose board into the street. These house drains were rarely cleaned, and in older houses it was impossible to flush them out owing to cracks, and improper levels.[21] Much of the sewage from rickshaw houses passed into open drains lining the edges of the streets. Slop, dirty dishwater, and the washings of latrine pails were emptied into street drains. At certain times of the year, and in certain parts of the city, particularly in the overcrowded rickshaw districts, and in the vicinity of the prison, asylum and Hospital, the sight and smell of water in these drains was absolutely nauseating: 'The smell of faecal matter and urine is very strong in Singapore, not only in a large number of houses but also in the morning in the streets. When one considers what life must be like for a small child or a sick person in a cubicle in one of these houses, the wonder is, not that they die, but that they live.'[22]

Singapore's population was almost a half million by 1907 but sewage was still removed by means of manual labour. The latrines in rickshaw houses were emptied by a night-soil coolie who had to pass through the front door. This was a particularly obnoxious means of sewage disposal as reloading from latrine buckets to carts parked alongside the street, attracted flies and encouraged the dissemination of insect-borne diseases, apart from the horrible stench on still days.[23] Often the carriers' pails were leaky, creating an even worse hazard as they passed through the houses. On top of that the collectors were not above waking up rickshaw coolies as they clattered down the corridor to the foul-smelling latrines at the rear of the houses: 'The nuisance created during these operations has, on occasions, become so accentuated on sultry nights that it has awakened people from their sleep in buildings where they were being carried out.'[24] Sometimes delays were experienced in removal of night-soil which further exposed rickshawmen to risk of infection; buckets laden with the night-soil of more than a hundred men were left standing in close proximity to the kitchen which was also situated at the rear of the house, while the pathetic single toilet filled up and could not be used.

Death from 'bowel complaints' ranked right behind fevers of various kinds as the principal registered cause of death by 1890.[25] The level of deaths from intestinal and diarrhoeal diseases (amoebiasis and bacterial infections) remained particularly high between 1900 and 1910, with an average death rate of 5 per 1,000 of the population.[26] Burgeoning population in rickshaw districts meant increased danger of the spread of infectious diseases associated with overcrowding and poverty, of which typhoid or enteric fever was the most common. The actual number of cases of typhoid fever occurring in any one year was difficult to estimate. The labouring Chinese were not in the habit of seeking European medical assistance, and this fact, together with the system of death registration, made it almost impossible to estimate the number of deaths caused by the disease.[27] In connection with this problem of disease intelligence gathering, one thing is clear: rickshaw coolies consistently formed the bulk of notified typhoid victims classified by occupation. In 1907, for example, the disease showed no novel features in comparison with previous years except for a sudden increase in the number of reported cases in August. As usual, the Chinese suffered most—nearly 86 per cent of notified cases were Chinese, the ratio of males to females succumbing was about eight to one. Three-fourths of the men were in the prime of their life, between 20 and 45 years of age. Sadly, but most important, rickshaw coolies (111) comprised nearly a third of the total.[28]

The following year, out of those whose occupations were known, 67 per cent belonged to the coolie (85) or rickshaw coolie (67) class.[29] Most of these cases in the rickshaw community were spread by contact between the sick and the healthy, the puller looking after a diseased friend oftentimes being the next victim. Those attendant on sick friends were forced to change residences when they felt the premonitory signs. In 1909 the disease first appeared in the south side of the city amongst rickshawmen and was carried across the river by those who were turned out of their lodgings, and tried to escape discovery in the course of house-to-house inspections.[30] Whenever a case occurred in a new locality, the houses in the neighbourhood were searched, while in localities where experience had shown that typhoid was likely to be met with, such as in the rickshaw environs, the lodges were searched twice a day. About 1,200 lodging-houses were visited daily in 1909, in the hunt for carriers.[31]

The disease was active year round in Singapore. Again, in 1913, taking cases where residents could be traced, the first eight with one exception occurred between March and July on the north side of the river amongst rickshaw coolies. During August and September cases occurred equally on both sides, but from the beginning of October the majority occurred south of the river; the victims were mainly pullers and stevedores on the docks. This outbreak had none of the characteristics of water-borne or food-borne epidemics, and in all probability its persistence was due to personal contact between sick and healthy pullers.[32] The previous year, the annual medical report noted that the majority of typhoid cases seen in Singapore occurred amongst rickshaw coolies. Of the 53 admissions to the General Hospital in 1912, 34 were rickshawmen, and 9 out of the 11 cadavers showing typhoid ulcers at the public morgue were also pullers.[33] Colonial doctors stressed the need for an investigation of the phenomenon of 'carriers' amongst them but still felt that with 'this class of people a thorough examination was practically impossible'.[34] There were many rickshaw coolies who would not give physicians information as to where they lived out of misplaced fear that they might be required to pay for their hospital stay. It was obvious to all concerned that the need for an effective means of gathering disease intelligence was a necessary first step to thwart the incidence of typhoid fever. The health authorities had reason to be pessimistic. It was unlikely that rickshaw cases notified represented anywhere near all that occurred during a particular year. More than half of them were never seen by colonial medical personnel, preferring to consult a *sinseh*, and there had to be a sizeable number of unrecognized cases, all providing potential foci for dissemination of the disease with a proportion, after recovery, continuing to act as carriers.

Under these circumstances, even if prompt removal and destruction of garbage had occurred, the puller carrier would have still remained, in the absence of effective tracing techniques.

Besides the built-in environment of the city, climate was also a nemesis. One of the reasons why rickshaw coolies suffered premature death from typhoid fever and diarrhoeal diseases was a deceptively simple one—drinking of contaminated water. These diseases were a major cause of death among pullers in the hottest parts of the year, when rickshaw coolies tended to become severely dehydrated after running long distances. When a roasting, thirsty man stopped to rehydrate himself as the sweat poured off his body, by drinking from the bucket of a well, by cupping his hands at the edge of the river bank, or by having an ice-cold syrupy drink from an itinerant hawker, his body was laid open to agents which produced typhoid and diarrhoea. Ironically, the main reason why these diseases killed is because thirsty pullers drank the polluted water and, as a result, became severely dehydrated. Some rickshawmen preferred hot tea as a way to bolster their defence against typhoid fever, acute gastro-enteritis, and other miserable ills: 'Rickshaw men as imposing as he was would always go to a teahouse after a flying trip and drink the better tea with two lumps of white sugar in it to restore their spirits and cool off. When he had run so hard the sweat dripped from his earlobes and his chest felt on fire. . . . Gulping down two cups of good tea like that was really necessary.'[35] Sugar was critical in restoring the balance of glucose in the bloodstream, but many pullers could not afford cheap tea, let alone sugar. They preferred to risk drinking from the nearest well, stream or drainage ditch, after discharging a fare.

Let us briefly look at a series of cases in the Certificate of Coroner's Views for 1906 giving a picture of pullers literally 'dying of thirst' from typhoid fever and diarrhoeal diseases. Without sophisticated research into transmission of intestinal and diarrhoeal diseases yet underway, their deaths for purposes of administrative and medical convenience were placed within the broad disease classification 'Fever'. Not surprisingly, it was pointed out to the Government by Professor Simpson during his visit in 1907 that the death rate from diarrhoeal diseases, especially amoebic dysentery, as recorded in the Death Registers was grossly underestimated. It is only in records like the Certificate of Coroner's Views that the historian of Chinese society is apt to find even the barest of details necessary to begin to understand the actual pattern of these diseases and death among rickshaw coolies. Khoo Che had a run of 14 miles in February 1906; he drank cold water after the trip, came down with typhoid fever, and died eleven days later.[36] The following month, Ong Ha Peh, 48 years of age, 'had a hard run and was ill ever after'. He, too, had drunk water and did not leave his bed for five days before he died.[37] In almost identical circumstances, Chao Ah Chang took ill after running 7 miles and at the end of the trip, drank water on top of it.[38]

Intestinal and diarrhoeal diseases were incredibly painful, the sick puller not being able to walk for weeks sometimes after each recurrent bout. Rickshaw coolies hated the disease because it robbed them of their strength and savings:

> Actually, he was not in good shape. On top of that, he was greedy for all the fares he could get to make up the deficit that piled up during his illness, so in a few days he had a relapse and this time dysentery was added. He slapped his face in a rage at himself but it was no use. The skin on his belly seemed to be meeting his back bone when he bent over on the privy and still the flow went on. After a lot of trouble the dysentery finally stopped, but his legs were so weak that just squatting and standing up took all his strength. What was the use of saying he thought he'd go out and work? He had to rest for another month![39]

The pain that Leong Koh Long experienced was agonizing enough to drive him mad and during his delirium he slashed himself with a razor.[40] It was not easy for rickshawmen to regain their strength, stride, and pride in the fight against intestinal and diarrhoeal diseases. For many who could not get treatment the pain lingered, and the toll among rickshaw coolies who suddenly died from 'natural causes' on the street was not insignificant. Kim Moh, for example, was found lying on the road between the shafts of an empty rickshaw belonging to the female owner, Cheah Pin Soo, who identified his body for the Coroner. There were no marks of violence and the post-mortem revealed that death was due to chronic amoebic dysentery.[41]

Among all water-borne diseases rickshawmen encountered, in lodging-houses and on the streets, cholera was the most terrifying. The rapid, erratic nature of the disease as it cut a swath through a local neighbourhood, spreading from one lodging to the next side by side, suddenly skipping several, moving across the street to break out in another rickshaw house, only to fade away and reappear, fresh, in a totally different part of the city inhabited by pullers, and its lightning-like ability to kill, left coolies dismayed, in a state of crisis.[42] Again, the immutability of the weather was a major reason why pullers became cholera victims in the first place:

> They didn't dare run and just shuffled along with their heads down. Every well became their lucky star. It didn't matter how far they'd gone—when they saw a well they hurried over to it. They'd just take a long drink at the trough along with the horses ... if there wasn't any freshly drawn water. And there those who, coming down with cholera ... just went on and on until they collapsed and never stood up again.[43]

By virtue of occupation and environment there were always susceptible hosts in the rickshaw areas to harbour the pathogenic organism until a fresh outbreak flared up in lodging-houses among pullers who had no previous experience of cholera. Psychologically, cholera, as an epidemic disease, was most feared by rickshaw coolies because it was elusive, readily communicable, and lethal, defying all known principles of quarantine. It killed at random, in a rapid, violent manner, often within hours of the first signs of the illness. The symptoms of a puller dying from cholera were frightening to the eye:

> . . . radical dehydration meant that a victim shrank into a wizened caricature of his former self within a few hours, while ruptured capillaries discoloured the skin, turning it black and blue. The effect was to make mortality uniquely visible: patterns of bodily decay were exacerbated and accelerated, as in a time lapse motion picture, to remind all who saw it of death's ugly horror and inevitability.[44]

The Municipal Annual Reports provide evidence of its perigrinations through rickshaw neighbourhoods repeatedly held in the grip of this dreaded contagion. In 1906, the disease occurred in the first ten months of the year, but it was most prevalent in April and May when 118 bacteriologically confirmed cases occurred. Cholera was scattered throughout the city, but two districts in particular were especially affected, as had been the case in previous years—the neighbourhood of Tanjong Pagar, comprising Tanjong Pagar Road and docks, Raub Street, Krian Street and Anson Road, and the district at the upper end of Queen Street encompassing the following streets: Rochore Road, Queen Street, Muar Road, Angullia Road and Ban San Street. The first district contained coolies employed on the docks as stevedores, and the second had mostly rickshaw coolies.[45]

Usually it was houses occupied by rickshaw coolies that were affected by the outbreak and spread of the disease. Cholera seemed to single out densely packed rickshaw lodgings with their contaminated wells, inhabited by men with a way of making a living that exposed them to the disease every day after a long, hot run. By occupation, rickshaw houses consistently had a high distribution of confirmed deaths from the disease. The ricochet effect and the rapidity with which cholera killed had a traumatic effect on rickshawmen in a particular house, street or neighbourhood. The outbreak of cholera in a lodging-house created fear, sending a chill down everybody's spine of impending death, possibly brothers, fathers and sons dying simultaneously, horribly, and each man became frightened for his life. The reaction of feelings and emotions to its appearance in a house was liable to be a combination of anger, fear, and a looming sense of mass death. The response was swift. The lodgers shared a common concern to rid the house of its victim as soon as possible. There was no sense of rejection or guilt here. Frightened pullers acted on their pathogenetic knowledge of cholera, taking the only measures they knew in order to defend themselves and stay alive.

When a cholera death occurred in a lodging-house, as a rule, the body was dumped elsewhere, speedily. If several deaths occurred simultaneously or in quick succession as the epidemic rose, the men scattered. When the contagion subsided other rickshaw coolies came in, and the cycle repeated itself. It was rare that a rickshaw lodging was empty, even after a localized cholera epidemic.[46] The tragedy of having to dispose of a body in this manner meant the deceased frequently remained unidentified. The number of suspected cholera cases in the rickshaw quarters increased significantly in 1911 and 1914. The Certificate of Coroner's Views confirmed the pattern of dumping cases of suspected deaths from cholera, while also showing its nasty movement through a neighbourhood. In October 1911 Hokkien and Hockchia pullers in dreadful fear of being next to die dumped bodies of fellow lodgers, mostly 30–40 years of age, in Rochore Canal Road, Victoria Street, and Johore Road. The Views give evidence of the epidemic peaking in the second week of October and not spreading to Hengwah houses. In 1914, cholera raged around Johore Road from the end of April till the middle of May, and then became a major cause of death in Rochore Canal Road throughout June and July. As in 1911 it was predominantly Hokkien and Hockchia, aged 30–40, who were killed. The sanitation, housing, and water supply of the Hokkiens in these areas was amongst the worst in Singapore. In 1914, only forty-five rickshaw coolies dumped in the streets dead or dying of cholera were notified, so it appears from the Views that merely 40 per cent of confirmed cases were actually reported to the Coroner for investigation.[47] The others were dealt with by the Police and the Municipal Health Department in the course of their daily activities.

Diseased bodies were found by police constables on the beat—in a canal, on a verandah or by the edge of the road—often with some clue as a tell-tale sign of occupation, such as clothing, a red mat, or a broken rickshaw bar, and in one instance, the puller's pillow box into which the dead man had been unceremoniously stuffed. Municipal scavengers making early morning rounds cleaning the streets often reported suspected cholera victims who had been dumped. Just occasionally these acts of disposal were witnessed by other rickshaw coolies and reported. Lim Lye, who was resting on a verandah off Queen Street, watched two Chinese dump the corpse of a rickshaw puller, a cholera victim, on the verandah at about 2 a.m. in the morning. They had taken the body from No. 129–4 Queen Street which stood empty as all the pullers had cleared out.[48]

Ting Choon Moy was haggard, feverish, and on edge, suffering from a severe headache and body pains; he thought, 'Why me again?' He had come down with malaria, a nasty debilitating form. His nights were sweaty with high fever. He tried to think how he might get some Chinese *maleria medica* or quinine before the disease killed him. The puller had endured the fever seven days, and he could no longer walk.[49] He knew that a friend must get him medicine or take him to hospital; then perhaps the disease would spare him. Among infectious diseases endemic to Singapore, malaria was a principal killer. The public health problems created by malaria within the municipal limits of Singapore defied an effective medical breakthrough. The Colonial Government was not prepared to intervene on a systematic basis at the lodging-house level to eradicate the disease. It was considered too difficult and costly a task to be worth the effort. Instead of Chinatown, where the symptoms regularly appeared, public health officials concentrated their activities in the newer outlying areas on the edge of the city. These public health experiments involving malaria eradication had no immediate benefit for the pullers. They were left to their own devices when it came to defending themselves against the plasmodium which produced malaria and the bite of the blood-sucking anopheles mosquito, which conveyed the parasite, and swarmed around the filthy drains, wells, and spots for garbage disposal in the rickshaw quarters.

The Coroner's Views give evidence of rickshaw coolies like Ting Choon Moy being inflicted with malarial fever from a few days up to several weeks, sometimes longer, before dying. Let us look again at the year 1906, and peer into the rickshawmen's lodgings as they struggled with malarial infection. By pausing to do so, we can begin to understand just how difficult this disease was to cope with, alone, without the support of official health services, advice of *sinseh*, or sometimes a friend.

Goh Koh Boo was ill for one week before he died; Goh Eng had a fever for one month and in the last week the fever was so strong that he became delirious; Tan Ah Mui had been ill for only seven days when he passed away; Een Sang Hee, on the other hand, suffered intermittently and had been out of work for two months; Ong Lan Hi endured the fever for fifteen days before he died in a cubicle that he had lived in for only three months; Hok Keh Sing of 80 Duxton Road had been ill with intermittent fever for six months, provoking total debility; Siow Sin Sang of Tanjong Pagar Road succumbed after fifteen days; Goh Soh Soon also lasted fifteen days but was delirious from pain for three days before his death; Teng Ah Leng was afflicted with the malady for ten days and in the latter stages experienced delirium; Lou Tong Hout and Teng Bee both languished for a month watching their world crumble around them; and finally there was Ng Ah Mah, who was said to have been in a bad way—sick with malaria—for twelve days, eight of which were marked by crippling fever and delirium.[50]

Like cholera cases, the bodies of malaria victims were often dumped, though in smaller numbers, as the disease tended to kill endemically rather than epidemically. A neighbouring verandah was a favourite spot to dispose of a puller who died from malaria. A boarder in a lodging at 25 Bain Street discovered the body of an elderly Hockchia on the verandah of his house as he was leaving for work in the early hours of the morning. Malaria was the cause of death.[51] Far worse was for a man to have been dumped still alive with a semblance of his senses about him, knowing his fellow pullers had abandoned him to the jaws of death. This perhaps was the case of an unknown puller who rested all day on a verandah in Eng Bee Lane where he had been dumped by his friends. He died an isolated death in the late afternoon—the lonely end of a sojourning dream shattered by malaria so far away from home.[52]

Rather than concentrating on poor drainage, overcrowding and water supply, colonial health officials tended to gather evidence to suggest that even in areas where mosquitoes freely bred, much of the malaria was imported.[53] Imported yes, but only from one rickshaw neighbourhood to another, as pullers moved in and out all the time, along with the mosquitoes, who were ensured a ready welcome in the filthy tenements several blocks away or a few miles down the road. Disease and health were appalling in South China, but it was more likely malaria was exported to Fukien and Kwangtung along with venereal disease, than imported into Singapore. The neighbourhood around upper Queen Street, Kreta Ayer, Duxton Road, and Victoria Street—drab, filthy districts where many of Singapore's 20,000 rickshaw pullers found cheap housing—served as a suitably anonymous breeding ground for the malarial plasmodium.

The insanitary houses harboured another equally dreadful illness besides malaria—tuberculosis. Pulmonary tuberculosis, 'the disease of darkness', was unknown in Singapore before the end of the nineteenth century.[54] This new killer was the characteristic disease of the crowded vermin-ridden slums of the rickshaw coolies. The lodging-house had always been a disease-infected area. Life within its dark, damp cubicles had always been cheap, but tuberculosis was not only fatal, it could, unlike other infectious diseases, be passed directly from one puller to another without the necessity of an intermediate 'carrier', and the disease carried them off quickly.[55] Tuberculosis among rickshaw coolies was confined almost exclusively to the pulmonary form. It attacked pullers of all ages but was especially prevalent among older ones, and was a frequent cause of death after middle age. The major cause of infection was overcrowding. *The Gazetteer* descriptions of Singapore made only passing reference to the occurrence of tuberculosis in the city, and rarely said anything about how it propagated itself in those areas where there was severe overcrowding in inner city lodgings, where rickshaw coolies were likely to congregate, and where cramped quarters shared with kin and strangers facilitated the transmission of infection from one puller to another by coughing or sneezing. The colonial medical data repeatedly emphasized the fact that the high death rate among rickshawmen was associated with the irremediable housing conditions.[56] The *pang keng* and cubicles were conducive to the spread of the disease. When healthy pullers only lived in one room all the time, with very often a tuberculosis sufferer, it meant that sooner or later some of them were bound to be infected by tuberculosis, although it might not manifest itself then. The disease once present in a lodging-house tended to recur, some years proving worse than others, until it assumed the form of a localized epidemic. Tuberculosis was not treated as a notifiable disease and as a result many rickshaw houses where it spawned were never inspected or disinfected.[57] Again, the weather was harmful to rickshaw pullers with tuberculosis as they could not afford to leave their damp, hot cubicles for a drier, cooler climate once the symptoms appeared.

The death rate of 8 per thousand for tuberculosis and 11 per thousand for respiratory and tubercular diseases in 1907 was an ominous sign and drew attention to the congested housing of the pullers.[58] As early as 1893, in the Prison Hospital, the doctor had reported a rise in the number of cases of pulmonary tuberculosis. He was of the opinion that the disease was on the increase amongst the poorer population, and as proof stated that was the case amongst short-term prisoners who were 'ordinary people'.[59] There were other signs; between 1893 and 1907 the percentage of total admission of tuberculosis cases in the native ward of the General Hospital tripled.[60] The annual returns from Tan Tock Seng Paupers' Hospital, providing free treatment to rickshawmen, also show a steady rise in the 1890s in the number of tuberculosis cases admitted, indicating that the disease was being more frequently met with among the class from which the pullers came, than had been the case formerly.[61] In post-mortems in hospitals large numbers of coolies exhibited active tuberculosis of the lungs, and invariably died:

> Naturally, the coolie class are almost like the vagrant class at home, in which any acute disease is rapidly fatal. That is especially so in the case of the Chinese coolie. When he is taken by a disease like tuberculosis, he ceases to be an earning unit, and his nutrition becomes very much impaired. He cannot feed himself. In other words, you might say that once a coolie acquires tubercle he dies.[62]

The death rate rose as immigration increased. The year 1911 marked the end of a dramatic decade of migration from South-east China. It was also an unhealthy year; there were 2,907 deaths returned from tuberculosis, compared with 2,571 for 1910, and 2,659 in 1909.[63] On the eve of the Depression in 1928 tuberculosis (1,411) and pneumonia (1,806) together accounted for approximately 25 per cent of all notifiable deaths. What was so depressingly outstanding was the two infectious diseases taken together showed no sustained decline in the previous twenty years.[64] The following year of the chief causes of death, the pneumonias with 1,770 and tuberculosis with 1,500 again headed the list, constituting 26 per cent of total deaths.[65] In 1930 they accounted for just over 24 per cent of all deaths, and 25.9 per cent the next year despite the large number of vacant houses which should have helped to ease overcrowding.[66] However, the 'piling up' was far worse, as a consequence of the depressed state of the economy and the level of poverty present in Chinatown. The tendency was to give up tenancy in smaller houses and crowd into already cramped bigger lodgings so as to spread the rent burden over a greater number of individuals. Colonial officials reconciled themselves to these high death rates fully realizing they would not decline until the housing itself was eradicated: 'It [the cubicle problem] is altering but slowly for the better but until there is a radical improvement I am afraid we must expect a continued high mortality from the diseases in question.'[67] The census of 1931 showed the rickshaw areas more overcrowded than ever before, and these slums were, in the main, responsible for the continued high incidence of the disease, as the depression bit deeper:

> There were 567,433 persons then on the island, of whom 447,741 were located within the municipal limits, which means within the town proper; and that town was so thickly over-populated that it ran 14,000 persons to the acre. In one division of Chinatown over 18,000 persons were enumerated within the boundaries of an area under 30 acres, which works out at about one person to a

rectangular space of four feet by two feet! No wonder that public enemy number one is tuberculosis, despite the constant sunshine.[68]

The reason why rickshaw coolies acquired tubercles especially in the lungs was on account of the cubicle system and overcrowding. The Government knew the cause and remedy. Sanitary housing was the only lasting solution, but officials tended for many years in their reports to blame outsiders—decrepits finding their way into Singapore from elsewhere—for the death rate from tuberculosis.

Tuberculosis was fatal for the puller.[69] The ordinary experience was that a rickshaw coolie became so ill he was unable to work, and died gradually from starvation. While it is not possible to know the ratio of deaths from tuberculosis to all deaths for rickshawmen, it is possible to demonstrate that death from tuberculosis was linked directly to the puller's way of life. Again, the Certificate of Coroner's Views for 1906 will help us to understand the extent to which tuberculosis was responsible for deaths among rickshaw coolies. Listed here are a fraction of the men who never made it back to China, dying, their lungs screaming for air, holding on to their chests, as a paroxysm of coughing seized them: Quo Gen Hok 'always had a cough' but he died ten days after it became severe; Lee Teng was ill and out of work for over a month with tuberculosis and during the last fifteen days his cough became very bad, especially five days before his death; while Yong Kee Siah coughed for twenty days before finally dying in the early hours of the morning. What happened to these pullers happened to hundreds of others each year who have no names or occupation: they are buried in the annual statistics for tuberculosis admissions and deaths for the General Hospital, Tan Tock Seng Hospital, the Lunatic Asylum and Prisons.[70]

The disease drove some rickshaw coolies, like an unknown man in 1902, to a life of crime. In desperation he grabbed hold of Chua Hoon's rickshaw, shouting it was his; the two men struggled near Elgin Bridge for several minutes and then Chua Hoon shouted for the police. A constable arrived on the scene and found the seemingly insane coolie trying to get possession of the rickshaw. The anonymous puller, 'a very emaciated subject', was turned over to hospital authorities for examination. He was reported to be violent and apparently insane and for two weeks was kept in solitary confinement. On several occasions he cried out in fear and his health ran down. He had not been well before, suffering from tuberculosis, but having been abandoned in a dark cell drove him to the brink of madness. His official cause of death was listed as pulmonary tuberculosis.[71] Consumptive pullers died in sunlight too—beyond the walls of cubicles and cells—on the streets in fits of coughing, turning scarlet and vomiting blood as they dropped down between the shafts. A wasting disease like tuberculosis also separated men from one another in houses just when they needed the care most, in depression years. They were hard times. The disease drove a wedge in social relations and reciprocal obligations, as wasted, pale men were thrown out because they could not pay rent. Here was See Chin Siong's fate. He was a 26-year-old Hengwah, who had been ill with pulmonary tuberculosis for three years, and was unable to pull a rickshaw. He was turned out of his lodging-house at 23 years of age and forced to sleep on the five-footway in Arab Street. He died there at the height of the depression, shivering, with feverish eyes. A municipal refuse collector, Vythilingan, was on his rounds when he saw the dead puller lying on the five-footway with his mother bent over him, weeping. He spoke to her in Malay but she did not understand him, staying by her son's side until the police came.[72]

When a poor puller, such as See Chin Siong, had tuberculosis and could no longer earn a living, there was no place to go, except to Tan Tock Seng's. There was opium of course, which always occupied first place in the rickshaw coolie's mind as a remedy for the pain of tuberculosis, especially if accompanied by haemolysis.[73] Tuberculosis was to remain widespread because colonial and municipal authorities were not prepared to spend the enormous sums necessary to drive backlanes through Chinatown and develop parks and open spaces.[74] The Government knew if the population could be spread out the death rate from tuberculosis would drop. But the spreading of the population was far too drastic and costly a measure for the Government to contemplate in the 1930s. The colonial medical officials for their part, while advocating urban renewal, felt it was hopeless in the practical sphere to educate China-born Chinese by pamphlets and notices, to prevent the spread of tuberculosis.[75]

Pulling a rickshaw with two passengers for hours in temperatures of up to 100 °F could kill a puller. The strain was etched on Ling Ah Thui's face as he started back on the return leg of a 14-mile run from Kranji. Every muscle in his body ached under the scorching sun, as perspiration rolled down his face in beads, burning his eyes. He blinked. As he ran Ling Ah Thui felt a rickshaw coolie was lucky to reach the age of 40. Only last week, a fellow lodger fell down dead on a long run when his heart failed, weakened by a decade of tuberculosis, opium smoking, whoring, and a poor diet. He summed up the misfortune of his deceased friend in a Chinese saying: 'the legs of a bull would not go far on the heart of a chicken'. In considering diseases specific to occupations, there can be no doubt that those relating to the heart and circulatory system were more fatal to rickshaw pullers than any other coolies. In the absence of any special arrangement pullers were not required to draw rickshaws more than 3 miles without a rest of up to ten minutes, or 10 miles in any one day or remain engaged for more than eight hours at a time.[76] The weather, shortage of public transport, and private business all combined at times to compel a rickshawman to agree to take fares as far as Bukit Timah and Bedok, non-stop—14 miles' distance one way.

In some cases pullers fell down dead when their heart muscles failed on a long run because they were young, unfit or inexperienced. Ng Yeak looked strong but his body had only cosmetic value in attracting passengers like Saheran, as his heart was in a bad way. Saheran, a goldsmith working in Arab Street at Haji Asad's shop, described how Ng Yeak, a newly arrived puller from China in 1902, collapsed and died gasping for breath, after a long jog from one end of the city to the other:

About 8 a.m. today I wanted to go to the jail to see a friend who is soon to be released. I called the deceased and got into his rikisha in Arab Street. I was alone. We went by Victoria Street and New Bridge Road. The deceased did not pull strongly or run straight. I thought he was a new puller and did not urge him to go faster. I had no talk with him. After we had turned into Outram Road from New Bridge Road past the Sepoy Lines Police Station and nearly opposite the row of houses facing the Sikh Police Parade ground the puller stopped and quitted the shafts. He stepped on one side, the left side of the road. I thought he wanted to make water and said nothing. I did not speak to him. I did not push or pull him. He then leaned down over the rickshaw shafts and in a few minutes he seemed to be almost dead ... I walked back to the Sepoy Lines Station and reported to the P.C. at the door.[77]

Quan Lock, a rickshaw owner living in Victoria Street, saw Ng Yeak's corpse in the mortuary, and had this to say about the man who pulled his rickshaw:

I am no relation of his. I last saw him alive at 6 a.m. today when he came to my house and hired the rikisha. I don't know how he died. I have not got back the rikisha which is still at the Police Station. The deceased has newly come from China only a few days ago. He was in Singapore before but I did not know him then. This was the first day that I let a rikisha to him. He seemed to be in good health when he came to me this morning. I know nothing of his habits.[78]

It was not at all uncommon for an inexperienced puller to fall down dead in the street with a weak heart. Doctors who made post-mortem examinations often detected it. Seng Ah Beo, only recently arrived in Singapore, collapsed after pulling his rickshaw at the end of one day. There were no marks of violence on the body except a tattoo of a Chinese lady on a horse over his right arm. He was in shock and unable to speak when admitted to the General Hospital. His heart was enlarged, the beat slow, and it was unable to pump the blood around fast enough while he pulled the rickshaw.[79] Many pullers who collapsed due to cardiac arrest were suffering from opium addiction or syphilis. They were usually older, and carrying passengers at the time of their death. Not surprisingly, these men were often on an intermediate or long haul when they keeled over. Keng Ann was 40 years of age and an opium smoker in 1908 when he was hired by Peter Norbert and Racia Muntly at Kandang Kerbau to go to the sixth mile of Nousemy Road. At the second mile they stopped to refresh themselves at a tuckshop for about five minutes, and when they came out they found Keng Ann dead.[80] There were scores of such cases between 1906 and 1940; 39 per cent or 49 out of the 191 cases in the Coroner's Views dealt with some form of cardiac arrest. Teo Ay Soon, a 47-year-old Hockchia, fell with a passenger in his rickshaw in Neil Road on his way from Tiong Bahru; Ah Mua was pulling his rickshaw towards

Tanglin with two Japanese passengers when the pain in his heart became too great and he died; Koh Leong, 55 years old, collapsed when pulling two Europeans in Robinson Road; Kwan Moh Kia, a seemingly strong, well-fed Hockchia, had passed by a Tamil house on Bukit Timah Road going towards Kranji pulling two Macao women as fares. When he was just beyond the house Kwan Moh Kia dropped down between the shafts, on that March afternoon in 1906, when his aorta exploded like a roadworn tyre. Taju, a Tamil woman, said he never rose up again. The Macao women, dressed in dark cotton, abandoned Kwan Moh Kia, running off towards Almeida Road, and Taju could not say whether they were prostitutes.[81]

There were usually witnesses in daytime and in the busier parts of the city, when a puller suddenly collapsed from cardiac arrest, if his rickshaw was empty. This of course was not always the case on the fringes of the city, on long runs back to town empty-handed, and after dark. Ahmad, a constable, watched Chan Tee drop between the shafts, bruising his nose and forehead from the force of the fall, at the corner of Beach Road in 1908. The next year, Kamin, a Javanese syce, came upon an unknown puller in waste ground off Havelock Road at about 8.00 p.m.; the rickshawman was still alive, lying across the rickshaw bar which had broken as he suddenly collapsed on it with all his weight. Yap Chan Guan saw 48-year-old Ong Lee Kaw lose his breath and balance as his heart muscles failed to contract properly—the pain from the uncoordinated twitches spilled him into a drainage ditch on North Bridge Road. See Li Mui had the good fortune to fall dead right in front of Dr Brooke's office and the physician immediately dispatched his body to the mortuary.[82] It was the suddenness, acute pain and force of cardiac arrest that slammed the door of life in their faces. The door of See Ah Chong's life abruptly closed as he fell in between the shafts in Temple Street.[83] There was often no premonition. One minute a rickshaw coolie was alive and the next minute he was dead. Cheang Chin Hoe lost the incentive to push on further, and all of a sudden he fell over dead in Hill Street opposite the Waverly Hotel in full view of its guests.[84] Ng Cheng Moh, a rickshaw repairer, was working on the five-footway of his shop in Larut Road when unexpectedly Siah Hong Mee, a Hockchia, who was walking along the road with his empty rickshaw, sank down, rolled over twice, and died from a massive heart attack. It was, said the Coroner who performed the inquest, the kind of attack you would expect to see in older rickshaw coolies—men, say, of 40–55 years of age. Siah Hong Mee was 30 when he died. His heart was 'enlarged with all the heart chambers dilated and excess of fat in the heart muscles'.[85]

Just occasionally, pedestrians attempted to save a puller's life by administering first aid or notifying the police of the emergency. Often the rickshawman could not speak for himself, because of shock, loss of speech, or unconsciousness, and the samaritan had to talk for him. Isaac Elias was cycling along Orchard Road on a September afternoon in 1908 when he saw a crowd congregating near the Government House gates, and stopped to see what was happening. At the front of the crowd he found a rickshaw coolie lying on the ground writhing in pain, speechless, and obviously in need of emergency medical treatment, but neglected by onlookers. The youth ran and got some water from a hawker and threw it on his face as the puller began to lose consciousness, but could not revive him. He stood by helplessly and watched him die a few minutes later.[86] Passers-by reacted more quickly to Ah Long's cry for help. He was sitting in his rickshaw in New Bridge Road when he experienced a sudden heart attack and fell face downwards into a street drain 6 feet deep with a foot of water in it. Two Chinese detectives, who happened to be passing nearby, heard Ah Long call out for help and raced to the corner of Pagoda Street and New Bridge Road, where they found an unconscious rickshaw puller in a black coat and pants in the drain. They pulled him out and tried artificial resuscitation but his breath was short, so he was taken to the Government Hospital for emergency treatment, by rickshaw.[87]

Appendix 7 shows that in the case of more than half the men (26) the exact time of their death was not known; hence, the death was presumably unobserved, and eight pullers were never identified. These pullers whose deaths were either not witnessed or went unreported were found later, dead or dying, on street corners, in verandahs, or sitting in parked rickshaws. Sim Kay Say was found unconscious in the five-footway of Hill Street where he had collapsed on a verandah following cardiac failure due to syphilis. Although pulling a rickshaw might trim off excess weight, it did not strengthen the muscles of a heart weakened by venereal disease. It was 'enlarged considerably [with] much fat and flabby. All chambers were greatly dilated especially the right auricle. On the aorta were several large syphilitic plaques....'[88] At night, the stationary glow of burning rickshaw lamps was often the sign of a puller dying in the road from heart failure or as a result of a hit-and-run motor vehicle accident. An unknown puller was found dead at dawn between the shafts of his rickshaw with its lamps still burning, in Hassim Road. The Coroner had no idea when this puller, aged about 30, dropped between the shafts; '[he] seems to have fallen dead at midnight or morning'.[89] When the pain in their hearts drove coolies beyond themselves they slowly stopped and sat down in their rickshaw to die. In the Coroner's Views one can picture how disbelieving pullers learned that their hearts were not indestructible, as they expired without solace in the cradle of their work. The rickshaw owner Ng Mee was taken to 4½ mile on Barclay Road where he saw Ah Chew sitting in his rickshaw, dead.[90] The elderly Tien Sang Kwai was found sitting upright in his rickshaw by a police constable in Bernam Street—not unusual, except he too was stone dead.[91]

The coroners rarely felt it necessary to hold an inquest on such bodies because the pullers were considered to have died from 'natural causes'. In a very real sense the deaths of most of these men were complicated by the environment—by the changing character of urbanization, by opium and venereal disease—but the coroners, especially after 1918, rarely bothered mentioning that a puller smoked or had developed a sexually transmitted disease. These cases did not swell the coroner's returns of opium or venereal disease deaths. Rather, the 'natural cause' was 'aortic disease', 'acute dilation of the heart', 'morbus cordis', or 'heart failure'. The Coroner summed up 65-year-old Sim Chwee Kiat's death from heart failure this way:

That Sim Chwee Kiat, an adult male Hokien Chinese, aged 65 years, a rikisha puller, fell down dead in Serangoon Road on the 29th day of March 1934 at 8 a.m. That the death was reported to me and the body viewed by me. A post mortem examination was ordered. That I am satisfied from my view of the body and the medical officer's report of his post mortem examination that death was due to natural causes and that there are no suspicious circumstances connected therewith. No enquiry is therefore necessary. Death from Natural Causes.[92]

Most rickshawmen were either too poor or too ignorant to take advantage of the limited medical facilities, financed almost entirely by Chinese merchant–philanthropists. Without comfort and security of family, ailing rickshaw coolies looked to next of kin and clansmen for support. Some were bonded together by lineage in a relationship that would last forever, despite the presence of a great deal of illness and poverty. Singapore's economic development had beckoned them from China to pull rickshaws and live in some dark room in Victoria Street or Duxton Road, and that terrible loneliness of men confronting illness, indebtedness, and ultimately death fused many of them together, like brothers, even when they were not so. When a puller got sick, or suffered misfortune such as a traffic accident or an assault, his friends would maintain him for a time, usually giving what food they could spare.[93] The remarkable thing about such relationships was there was no self-pity. Some recovered. Others died—but not always comforted, and rarely with dignity. Thrown out, they went from door to door picking up a cup of rice or a few cents and at last toppled over dead as a 'vagrant' or 'beggar'. Chan Ah Tok suffered with swollen legs for over a month. His heart was failing. Despite the mounting health problems, income difficulties, and high level of dependence, the lodgers in his *pang keng* gave him medicine for a month but 'it did him no good'. So Chan Ah Tok, to relieve the pressure on his friends, asked to be taken to hospital. The task fell to Lok Ah Kow who was instructed at the Central Police Station to take his friend to Tan Tock Seng Hospital but Chan Ah Tok died in his comrade's rickshaw before reaching their destination.[94] In rather different circumstances, when Ang Ah Kow came home complaining that someone had beaten him to within an inch of his life, Ang Gua cared, watching over him until he passed away. He knew that Ang Ah Kow did not feel anything but lonely, stating 'he has no relations'.[95] Lee Tien had no kindred in Singapore either, but his clansmen at 24 Duxton Road knew what he had been through in Singapore and what he had endured in the previous two months since coming down with fever. They gave him medicine regularly and arranged his funeral among themselves when he died.[96] Some rickshawmen tried to support those less fortunate than themselves single-handedly by paying hospital fees or providing a small allowance for food. Among them was Lim Sing Soo; his brother, Lim Tiang Soo, fell from a tenement house while collecting drying clothes. He took him to the General Hospital and paid his expenses. Later his brother was removed to Tan Tock Seng Hospital by the police, as Lim Sing Soo had no money left to pay the fees.[97] Tan Moey Teng faced an increase in the cost of living in 1922 but he gave 10 cents daily to an elderly clansman, Tan Eng Song, to help him over the toil of the last years, and the bad dreams of a disconsolate opium smoker:

> The deceased was from the same village in China. His name was Tan Eng Song, a hockcha aged about 55 years. He ... had been unable to work for the last six months. He had been suffering with a bad cough and had got very thin. He was an opium smoker but could not get very much. I used to give him ten cents a day for food, but could not afford more. He slept downstairs. I slept upstairs. About twelve midnight on 24 May, 1922 when I returned home with my ricksha he was downstairs. I gave him ten cents and went upstairs to sleep. About 6 a.m. on 25 May, 1922 I came downstairs and went to the back to relieve myself. I found him hanging to a wooden partition there. He was dead ... I think he hung [*sic*] himself because he was old, ill and unable to work.[98]

Singapore, in the words of a senior army medical officer, was 'a nursery for disease' in 1872.[99] Rickshawmen were to live with disease-infectious death for more than half a century after he said that, and despite an unprecedented rise in the death rate from endemic diseases, like typhoid, cholera, malaria and tuberculosis, both the Colonial Government and municipal authorities refused to take steps to eradicate them. The authorities consistently chose alternatives that minimized costs with respect to housing, water supply, and waste disposal problems. Slum property retained its inflated value right through the Depression. As long as the Government was not prepared to pay market price for this class of property and buy over the slums for redevelopment, death from diseases caused by poverty and overcrowding, particularly tuberculosis and pneumonia, continued to take their toll among rickshaw coolies. The city's decision to cope with its environment in this way meant that a puller came home each day to a neighbourhood that lived in the shadow of death. He knew what his friends were going through in this cramped, filthy, disease-ridden place called a city—the sleepless nights with malarial fever, the fear of not being spared by cholera, the nights he lay awake because of the hacking cough of his tubercular clansmen coming through the dark from the floor below—but some nights he wondered amidst all this disease whether death would spare him. Yet, the truth of the matter was that, he did not seem to care any more. He knew the worst was coming. The environment of the city was gradually destroying him, too:

> Men have separated themselves from the animals but now drive their own kind back among the beasts. [He] remained in this ... city but he was being

transformed into an animal. Not a bit of it was his own fault. He had stopped thinking and, therefore, the human being in him was destroyed. He bore no responsibility for that all. He'd never hope again. He'd just sink blindly, stupidly, lower and lower, into a bottomless pit. He ate, he drank, he whored, he gambled, he cheated, and all because he had no heart left in him. Others had taken it from him. All that remained was his big frame and now he waited for it to burst open like an abscess. He was getting ready for the potter's field.[100]

1. On the notion of a disease pool and their transference by sea see William H. McNeill, *Plagues and Peoples* (London: Penguin Books, 1976), p. 105.

2. Joyce Ee, 'Chinese Migration to Singapore 1896–1941', *Journal of Southeast Asian History*, 2 (1961), pp. 45–6.

3. Lao She, *Rickshaw* (the novel *Lo-T'o Hsiang Tzu*), translated by Jean M. James (Honolulu: The University Press of Hawaii, 1979), p. 152.

4. On the problem of water supply for Singapore see Anson to the Earl of Kimberley, 6 November 1875, CO 273/51; Ord to the Earl of Kimberley, 5 October 1893, CO 273/70; Smith to the Earl of Derby, 23 March 1885, CO 273/133; Anderson to Alfred Lyttelton, 20 June 1905, CO 273/309; Anderson to Alfred Lyttelton, 21 September 1905, CO 273/310; C. M. Turnbull, *A History of Singapore 1819–1975* (Kuala Lumpur: Oxford University Press, 1977), p. 16.

5. SMAR HR, 1922, p. 46-D.

6. Annual Colonial Reports, Straits Settlements, 1902, p. 32.

7. Anderson to Alfred Lyttelton, 20 June 1905, CO 273/309.

8. SMAR HR, 1923, pp. 39–40D.

9. W. J. Simpson, *Report on the Sanitary Condition of Singapore* (London: Waterloo and Sons Ltd., 1907), pp. 46–7.

10. Ibid.

11. SMAR HR, 1923, p. 40D.

12. Simpson, op. cit., pp. 46–7.

13. Language of William McNeill in *Plagues and Peoples*, p. 252.

14. SMAR HR, 1922, p. 46-D.

15. SMAR HR, 1915, p. 13.

16. McNeill, op. cit., pp. 250–1.

17. On drainage construction see Municipal Commissioners to the Colonial Secretary, 22 April 1878, in n. 127 Robinson to Sir M. Hicks Beach, 6 May 1878, CO 273/93; Weld to the Earl of Granville, 5 August 1886, CO 273/4; Principal Civil Medical Officer to Colonial Secretary, 7 July 1886, in n. 251 Weld to the Earl of Granville, 5 August 1886, CO 273/140.

18. Simpson, op. cit., pp. 52–3.

19. Ibid.

20. Enclosure, The Principal Civil Medical Officer to the Colonial Secretary, 7 July 1886, in Sir F. Weld to the Earl of Granville, 3 August 1886, CO 273/140.

21. HCR, 1918, p. B-45.

22. HCR, 1918, Appendix I, p. A-63.

23. Simpson, op. cit., p. 50.

24. Ibid.

25. Ibid., pp. 10, 43; SSAR, 1890, p. 232.

26. SSAR, 1910.

27. SSAR, Annual Medical Report, 1889, p. 2.

28. SMAR HR, 1907, p. 2.

29. SMAR HR, 1908, p. 3.

30. SMAR HR, 1909, p. 4.

31. Ibid.

32. SMAR HR, 1913, p. 4.
33. SSAR, Annual Medical Report, 1912, p. 537.
34. Ibid.
35. Lao She, op. cit., p. 40.
36. CCVS of Khoo Che, No. 100, 20/2/06.
37. CCVS of Ong Ha Peh, No. 166, 28/3/06.
38. CCVS of Chao Ah Chang, No. 53, 13/6/06.
39. Lao She, op. cit., p. 186.
40. CCVS of Leong Koh Long, 8/9/11.
41. SCII of Kim Moh, No. 297, 31/7/23.
42. On the pattern of disease experience pertaining to cholera see McNeill, op. cit., p. 21.
43. Lao She, op. cit., pp. 176–7.
44. McNeill, op. cit., pp. 240–1.
45. SMAR HR, 1916.
46. HCR, evidence of Mr Hooper, p. B-89.
47. SMAR HR, 1914, p. 11.
48. CCVS of unknown Chinese, No. 20, 13/8/10.
49. CCVS of Ting Choon Moy, No. 154, 25/8/39; McNeill, op. cit., p. 89.
50. CCVS of Goh Koh Boo, No. 30, 7/1/06; of Tan Ah Mui, No. 110, 21/1/06; of Een Sang Hee, No. 155, 29/1/06; of Ong Lan Hi, No. 58, 11/2/06; of Hok Keh Sing, No. 70, 14/2/06; of Siow Sin Sang, No. 15, 3/3/06, of Goh Soh Soon, No. 34, 7/3/06; of Teng Ah Leng, No. 43, 8/3/06; of Lou Tong Hout, No. 55, 10/3/06; of Teng Bee, No. 101, 28/3/06; of Ng Ah Mah, No. 114, 22/6/06.
51. CCVS of unknown Chinese, No. 44, 28/6/07.
52. CCVS of unknown Chinese, No. 33, 20/8/10.
53. SMAR HR, 1928, p. 59-D.
54. HCR, p. A-7; SSOC, p. 690.
55. McNeill, op. cit., pp. 165–6.
56. HCR, evidence of Dr D. J. Galloway, p. B-80.
57. Duke of Devonshire to Sir L. Guillemard, 26 January 1924, CO 273/523.
58. Simpson, op. cit., pp. 10–11.
59. SSAR, Annual Medical Report, 1893, p. 4.
60. Simpson, op. cit., pp. 10–11.
61. SSAR, Annual Medical Report, 1894, p. 3.
62. HCR, evidence of Dr David Galloway, p. B-81.
63. Colonial Reports Straits Settlements, 1911, p. 25.
64. SMAR HR, 1928, pp. 59–60D.
65. SMAR HR, 1929, p. 58-D.
66. SMAR HR, 1931, pp. 50–51D.
67. SMAR HR, 1929, p. 58-D.
68. Roland Braddell, *Lights of Singapore* (London: Methuen, 1934; reprinted Kuala Lumpur: Oxford University Press, 1982), p. 42.
69. HCR, evidence of Dr D. Galloway, p. B-89.
70. CCVS of Quo Gen Hok, No. 130, 26/1/06; of Lee Teng, No. 150, 28/1/06; of Yong Kee Siah, No. 95, 19/2/06.
71. SCII of unknown Chinese, No. 142, 30/9/02.
72. SCII of See Chin Siong, No. 614, 3/11/31.
73. BMOC, p. B-101.
74. HCR, evidence of Dr D. Galloway, pp. B-80, 86; and page A-7; SMAR, 1935, p. 11.
75. HCR, evidence of Dr D. Galloway, p. B-83.
76. SMAR JD, 1897, Appendix J, p. 35; for references to average life expectancy see SSOC, pp. 26, 325.
77. SCII of Ng Yeak, No. 144, 1/10/1902.
78. Ibid.

79. CCVS of Seng Ah Beo, No. 12, 16/1/38.
80. CCVS of Keng Ann, No. 61, 21/1/08.
81. CCVS of Teo Ay Soon, No. 20, 15/4/20; of Ah Mua, No. 38, 22/5/16; of Koh Leong, No. 13, 21/2/24; and of Kwan Moh Kia, 28/3/06.
82. CCVS of Chan Tee, No. 65, 30/6/08; of unknown Chinese, No. 7, 2/4/09; of Ong Lee Kaw, No. 53, 23/5/09, of See Li Mui, No. 12, 7/9/10.
83. CCVS of See Ah Chong, No. 46, 30/8/14.
84. CCVS of Cheang Chin Hoe, No. 43, 27/6/17.
85. SCII of Siah Hong Mee, No. 558, 10/10/28.
86. SCII of Ting Lam Pee, No. 164, 16/9/08.
87. SCII of Ah Long, No. 233, of 24/6/24.
88. CCVS of Sim Kay Say, No. 30, of 23/9/17.
89. CCVS of unknown Chinese, No. 49, of 22/5/09.
90. SCII of To Ah Chew, No. 119, 6/7/97.
91. CCVS of Tien Sang Kwai, No. 172, 28/8/38.
92. CCVS of Sim Chwee Kiat, No. 74, 29/3/34.
93. SSOC, p. 324.
94. SCII of Chan Ah Tok, No. 53, 6/3/96.
95. SCII of Ang Ah Kow, No. 109, 26/5/96.
96. SCII of Lee Tien, No. 125, 20/7/97.
97. SCII of Lim Tiang Soo, No. 179, 7/11/13.
98. SCII of Tan Eng Song, No. 203, 25/5/22.
99. Turnbull, op. cit., p. 116.
100. Lao She, op. cit., p. 233.

16 A Murderous Vocation

DISEASE and death were central to the rickshaw coolie's way of life. Another aspect of death must be considered though in the period 1914–40 that placed an additional burden on the livelihood of the rickshaw puller. It was heralded by the birth of the motor car. The appearance of cars and other forms of motorized transport turned the streets of Singapore into an endless stream of fast-paced traffic in this century. Traffic jams and accidents became commonplace as rickshaws competed for space on city streets. Motorists drove much more aggressively than the horse-and-carriage set. Rickshawmen stuck to the left side of the road close to the drainage ditch and were likely to be run over if they veered out or went against traffic. A Singapore traffic jam was a long series of discordant sounds of trams, taxis, cars, buses, trucks, and—it seemed—all of the city's 12,000 rickshaws, lurching in fits and starts, accelerating, and suddenly screeching to a grinding heart-stopping halt as a rickshaw cut across the road. The basic rule of the road was that streets belonged to the motorist. They drove as if the rickshaw coolie did not exist, roaring into traffic heedless of traffic police, pedestrian crossings, and signals. Pedestrians, only slightly less daring, jaywalked, thinking they were still in the old horse-and-carriage era.

The scores of testimony from accident cases involving rickshawmen in the inter-war years, when the number of licensed motor cars on the road rose from a few hundred to thousands, reveals that rickshaw pulling had become an extremely dangerous vocation (see Appendix 8). The work took on a murderous quality with increased traffic, and the rickshaw coolie ran on the streets at risk of his life. The statistics in the Coroner's Records show that the death rate from traffic accidents increased every year from 1914 with several pullers being killed or maimed for life. Men who narrowly escaped death in an accident, but lost their health and job, faced the prospect of a hard life as a hawker or beggar, or starvation.

In this context the main reason for death or maiming was their working life, the most important factor being their occupation—rickshaw coolie. It was a physically strenuous calling that forced men to compete for space and custom against the motor car, a powerful machine. Here is the inextricable link in the relationship between occupation and mortality: 'When one sees that most of the workers who operate certain branches of industry do not live out more than half the span of an ordinary life, does it not seem that man is destined to find his destruction in the very causes of his existence?'[1] It is the pattern and evolution of the total number of confirmed deaths in the Coroner's Inquiries, forty, to which attention must be paid, because they single out rickshaw coolies as having a higher incidence of traffic deaths than any other occupational group in the city. These road deaths are important as a way of measuring violence and attitudes towards rickshaw pullers as a group. They not only disclose the material means by which violent and accidental death of rickshawmen was facilitated in the car, they also show that lying behind the façade of the car and motorist was the chief culprit—the idea of progress of empire and the corollary of the motor car as a symbol of status and wealth. The life of the car signifying all that was modern about colonial Singapore demanded that the rickshaw be removed from city streets. The history of traffic accidents of rickshaw coolies in the Coroner's Records sets the development and municipal administration of Singapore in a rather different perspective. The images of progress, power and prestige were signified in the motor car and in the lifestyle of Victorian Britons and wealthier Chinese, who were determined not to walk about Singapore. Motoring was quicker, more convenient, and most importantly for Europeans, tended to reinforce their sense of self-esteem. To own a car was to overawe most Singaporeans, and a way of sustaining one's confidence. Just as a rich red stained popular world maps at the turn of the century, spilling across five continents boldly signifying the British Empire, so traffic accidents created their unmistakable effect on the streets of Singapore, shedding the pullers' blood like imperial paint on the mercator projections.

In the years before the motor car the Coroner's Inquests show very few fatal rickshaw accidents on the streets, except the occasional mishap with a gharry or bullock-cart. However, the rickshaw coolie and syce were not always careful enough in the streets.[2] In 1905 a practical lesson in exercising control over a rickshaw on the street was taught to a Hokkien puller, Sua Bok Yong, when he collided with the horse and carriage of the Resident Councillor:

> Mrs. Birch, wife of the Hon. the Resident-Councillor, was being driven home in her carriage, progress was barred in Anson Road by a rickisha on the wrong side of the road. Notwithstanding the appeals of Mrs. Birch's syce, the puller refused to go to the proper side of the thoroughfare, the result being that the rickisha collided with the horse which was injured in the foot, while the rickisha capsized. Eventually Mrs. Birch had to alight from her carriage and proceed home in a rikisha, the horse being unable to complete the journey. The syce entered a charge against the offending Chinese of pulling his rikisha other than on the left side of the road.[3]

The puller was fined $10, the equivalent of one month's wage, or in lieu of payment two weeks in prison. Other coolies with bad habits were not so lucky. The negligence of Tan Twah Sah cost him his life when he cut across a bullock-cart at the level crossing for the railway at Havelock Road. When the crossing gate was raised, rickshaws and carts started to continue their journeys. The bullock-cart was on the left side of the road, while the puller with his empty rickshaw was on the right hand side of the road—the wrong side. As the vehicles began to move the rickshaw puller crossed over and the right wheel of the bullock-cart crashed against the shafts of the rickshaw; Tan Twah Sah fell and the wheel of the heavily laden cart passed over his body, crushing him to death.[4]

It was at places like level crossings, junctions and bridges that accidents with bullock-carts occurred. Part of the reason was, as a bullock-cart started or renewed a journey the bullock on one side was sometimes slower to move than that on the other side as they were whipped up, causing the cart to swerve abruptly. In the course of such accidents about half the fatalities were passengers. In one incident, a rickshaw coolie was pulling his rickshaw along Bukit Timah Road 'towards town'. He passed the bridge just beyond the Post Office as a bullock-cart, heavily laden with casks of concrete, came off it and turned so sharply that it collided with the rickshaw. The puller had no room on his left and no time to stop, as the right wheel of the cart crushed the shaft of the rickshaw. The woman who was inside was thrown forward on to the road in front of the cart which passed over her. She died on the spot. The puller, who was knocked down and wedged between the cart and his rickshaw, managed to prevent the bullock driver from whipping up his cattle and getting away.[5]

In accidents involving carts or other rickshaws, pullers felt fortunate to escape with only an abrasion or incised wound. But they could still be unlucky. Death took them by surprise, as a result of dirt embedded in the wound from a skidding or bone-crushing fall. Such wounds tended to be jagged and deep, and bled profusely or oozed, and if not attended to immediately, got infected. A low-grade infection from washing a wound in well water, though, could lead to lock-jaw, or tetanus. Rickshawmen learned from painful experience that the most insignificant wound could cause this agonizing disease, and once contracted they had little hope of recovery. While tetanus was almost incurable it was preventable by cleaning such wounds thoroughly with sterile water and antiseptic. Yet rickshaw coolies continued to die every year from this disease out of ignorance and because of their environment. Ho Hee died from this inexcusable disease as a result of a bullock-cart wheel going over his foot; five days after the accident he developed tetanus. Tah Pok, a Hokkien carpenter, happened to be standing near the Arab Street Mosque when he saw a bullock-cart coming towards him, from Rochore on its side of the road, laden with planks. He described how the cart caught Ho Hee completely off guard:

> I saw a ricksha standing at the side of the road, the puller standing between the shafts sideways looking towards the houses on his side. The wheel of the bullock cart went over the puller's heel. The puller had turned away from the house into the street a little so that he was sideways and the cart coming behind ran over his foot. (explains by pulling a ricksha outside the Court). I cannot say who was to blame but think the bullock cart man might have called out. The bullock cart was

not going too fast. The ricksha puller turned into the way of the cart and so was run over.[6]

Ho Seng, a rickshaw coolie and the younger brother of Ho Hee, heard that his brother had been hit by a bullock-cart. He went straight to the hospital but the injured man did not blame the bullock driver outright. He said, 'If I get better do nothing, if I die go to the station and have the man arrested.'[7] Tan Ah Chay also died of tetanus in less than two weeks as a result of a wound to the left foot in an accident with the wheel of a bullock-cart.[8]

The congested streets, rainy weather, and later on motor cars made rickshaw trips for the likes of Yap Ma Yam and Lee Kwong hazardous—trips that ended suddenly in collision with another rickshaw. Lee Kwong had two fares from South Bridge Road and went to Trengganu Street via Temple Street, and at the corner of the two streets he ran into Yap Ma Yam and his two fares. The passengers jumped down and the pullers picked themselves up off the road and began a fist-fight. When arrested, Lee Kwong in his defence said, 'there was little space to travel as vegetable sellers and their vegetables were on both sides of the road'.[9] When a more level-headed puller faced the same kind of incident, he often tried to handle it differently at first, irrespective of whether he was hurt or the rickshaw damaged:

Sometimes, when he wasn't paying attention, another rickshaw man would run into him and some damage would be done. He certainly did not jump up and down in a frenzy screaming at the man. Very coolly, he'd go back to his agency. If fifty cents was what he ought to pay for the damage, he'd pay twenty and that would be the end of it. If the boss didn't agree, well, all right, the final solution was generally to start a fight.[10]

Ch'ng Chuan, a 42-year-old Teochiu, was gored in the abdomen as a result of a collision between rickshaws. On 8 September 1921 he knocked on the door of his favourite haunt, Swee Kim Kam's opium-smoking shop in Rochore Canal Road. The proprietor opened it and asked him what he wanted. The coolie showed him the hole in his stomach with the intestine hanging out. He said he had smashed into another rickshaw and the metal tip of the shaft had lanced his stomach. The accident occurred in Stamford Road near the museum, and it had taken him two hours to reach the shop by foot. Swee Kim Kam escorted him to the Kandang Kerbau Police Station from where he was taken away to Tan Tock Seng Hospital. Ch'ng Chuan gave the following report of the freakish accident to a constable shortly before he died:

At 4.25 a.m. on 8th September, 1921 I was pulling my ricksha, number I do not know, from Rochore Canal Road on my way to Singapore. On reaching Stamford Road another ricksha came (number I don't know) from Stamford Road going in the direction of Kandang Kerbau, going fast. I also was going fast as it was just going to rain. The other ricksha and mine collided, ran into each other. The end of the shaft of the other ricksha entered the left side of my stomach and blood and gut came out. I fell down. The other ricksha ran away. I then got up and went home to Rochore Canal Road . . . Kim Kam, the proprietor of an opium shop . . . brought me to the Police Station. . . .[11]

Pullers, in order to avoid accidents with cars on streets packed with the motor vehicles at certain times of day, occasionally rammed into one another with their shafts. One or both of them sometimes died from the fatal impact. Low Siang Quay received a penetrating wound in the left thigh in a collision with another rickshaw. Tetanus set in afterwards from which he died. He had been pulling a Baba Chinese from Tanglin towards town. When he arrived at the junction of Stamford and Beach Roads a rickshaw tried to cut in front of him to go towards the Hotel Europe, as he wanted to go around the Esplanade. The right shaft of Yew Teng's rickshaw pierced his left leg. Low Siang Quay fell to his knees and the rickshaw capsized. At the same moment the shaft of his rickshaw struck Yew Teng in the groin. What Low Siang Quay neglected to mention in his account to the police was the sudden appearance behind him of a car travelling at high speed. He could not stop his rickshaw in time; nor could Yew Teng swerve because of a car behind him. The anatomy of this accident becomes clear only as a result of what Yew Teng added, drawing the danger of motor cars to the attention of the police. The pullers were destined to smack into one another, frozen in their stride out of fear of the cars:

I was pulling the ricksha with two Hokien Chinese in it, from Tanjong Pagar going to the Godown. When I arrived at De Souza Street I was going along on the left hand side at the edge of the road. A ricksha, number not known, came from the front. Then a motor car, number not known, came from behind that ricksha. The ricksha puller was frightened and ran into me and his shaft knocked me in the stomach. We both fell down. The passenger went away I don't know where.[12]

The rickshawman's nerves got used to all the usual noises of traffic, being able to detect the roar of cars and lorries as they shifted gears, turned corners, and tore down streets hooting their horns. Even the older-style rickshaw contributed noise to the sounds of the street: 'The rickshas had wheels with rims of iron which made a peculiar sound—these rims later gave way to solid rubber tyres, and I well remember the excitement caused by the earliest "rubber" wheels.'[13] But in the midst of this noise and bustle the bicycle was quiet, and despised by rickshaw coolies for its sound of silence. The cyclists as a lot were no better. To the middling European on a bicycle, or the Chinese cyclist and assistant clerk, it was a consolation to find someone like the rickshaw puller to look down on, and against whom they could unite with the wealthier, more powerful motorists—the *tuan besar* and *towkay*—who tended to look down on them. The rickshaw coolie felt that he and his comrades had to put up with too much from cyclists, especially Europeans, who considered themselves to be prima donnas.

Rickshaw pullers . . . found bicycles extremely obnoxious. Cars were hateful but they made a lot of noise and you avoid them well ahead of time. Bicyclists would squeeze through every opening they saw, wandering eastwards and wobbling westwards, and watching out for them made you dizzy. Furthermore, never tangle with them. If anything goes wrong the rickshaw puller is always to blame. No matter what, the police figure the rickshaw pullers are easier to handle than the riders of bicycles, so they always go after the rickshawman first.[14]

An illustration of the 'dangers of the uncontrollable rickshaw puller' occurred in Selegie Road in 1900 involving one Mr Thoburn; he was riding his bicycle 'quietly' when a puller collided with it and knocked him over, badly hurting him with the shafts. According to the newspaper account the puller was at fault as he tried to run away but no detailed information is given on how the accident occurred. In his own mind the rickshaw coolie probably felt that in the event of an accident the law and traffic rules would find him guilty. He attempted to bolt either for this reason or because he was in fact at fault.[15]

Accidents involving bicycles and rickshaws often proved fatal for the cyclist just as accidents between rickshaws and cars often were fatal for the puller. Lim Boon Seng, a clerk at Tanjong Pagar, came home saying that he had collided with a rickshaw while riding his bicycle. In the evening he complained of severe abdominal pain and was taken to the General Hospital but died before making a report.[16] There was no doubt though as to who was responsible for the death of a teenage Eurasian, Maximillian Aloysius Andrews, who was fond of cycling. He was cycling towards Tanglin along Orchard Road when he attempted to pass on the wrong side of a first-class rickshaw in front. The bicycle caught the left shaft of the rickshaw, causing a spill in which he fractured his skull. Mrs Kate Mitchell, a passenger in the rickshaw, was in a state of shock due to the cyclist's fatal mistake, but managed to pluck up sufficient courage to direct traffic away from the scene of the accident:

I remember about 6 p.m. on 22 October, 1918 I was in a first class ricksha with my little boy and we were going along Orchard Road towards Tanglin and my ricksha was traveling along the left centre of the road: when near the [Abrams] Horse Repository a bicycle from behind passed on the left of my ricksha, very close and as this bicycle came up my ricksha went more to its left and the cyclist collided with the ... ricksha; the cyclist fell flat on his back; I and my son were knocked out of the rick; the ricksha coolie was not really knocked over though he went on his knees. I got out of the ricksha and the cyclist, assisted by people was taken to the five footway. I was really too timid to go near the cyclist but I did my best to ease the traffic; after I saw the cyclist put into the horse repository I left for home.[17]

Cyclists could also set up accidents between cars, trucks, and rickshaws by suddenly swerving out in the path of oncoming traffic. To avoid a cyclist, who had without warning crossed his path in 1938, a lorry driver crashed into a rickshaw and another truck at the junction of Beach and Rochore Roads. In a sequel in the Criminal District Court the lorry driver pleaded guilty to the charges of reckless driving and driving with bad brakes; interestingly, the cyclist, despite his error of judgement which had set the train of events in motion, did not have to make an appeal.[18]

Rickshaw accidents required the conjunction of two kinds of agency, human and technological. Rickshaw casualties were related primarily to making a living in a colonial–capitalist economy; the rate rose steadily in this century and owed a great deal to new technology—motor cars and trucks—and new-found prosperity. Among the unending stream of imports handled by the stevedores working on wharves and in godowns, motor cars were prominent. Motor touring became popular and car rental services sprang up by the dozen and did a booming business hiring motor cars by the hour to Europeans or Chinese with little driving experience. The number of licensed motor cars increased enormously in the 1920s and developed a sinister reputation except among those who drove them, often with reckless abandon, 'through Chinese streets, swerving, braking, the horn continuously blaring at padding ricksha boys . . .'.[19]

The loss of life and limb to ordinary persons including rickshaw coolies showed a marked rise after 1912. Electric trams, motor cars, and lorries were responsible for the larger number of street accidents. In 1912, when the average number of rickshaws was 9,025, there were 157 persons injured in motor accidents; of these 48 were caused by cars and 39 by electric trams.[20] 'Islands' to control traffic were placed at key intersections and crowded corners, but difficulties of traffic direction were greater in Singapore than elsewhere. People preferred in many parts of town to walk in the street rather than on the narrow, uneven five-footways cluttered with shop goods and hawkers' stalls. The number of rickshaws, carts, and motor vehicles on streets adapted for pedestrian traffic accentuated not only the problem of the rickshaw but also that of the police who were supposed to direct it.[21] By the 1920s motor vehicles were killing '. . . one coolie or child on average each day, and render business in Battery Road a nerve racking nightmare, but we hear nothing regarding their abolition and little with reference to control of their tooting.'[22]

Traffic death on a large scale was a new phenomenon. It called for an entirely new solution in rickshaw safety and design, but it did not happen. Something as simple and innovative as a safety belt would have saved lives. From the point of view of design improvement the seat in the rickshaw was too open; this opening-out effect made it too easy for passengers to be jerked forward or thrown out of the rickshaw, often fatally, once accidents began with motor cars. A particularly dangerous situation was when a rickshaw, encountering another rickshaw, cyclist, pedestrian, or pile of debris in front, swerved out without warning, only to be hit from behind by fast traffic. What happened then was that the passenger was ejected from the rickshaw head first with great force. Hence, it is not surprising to find European travel guides of the 1920s warning prospective tourists of the dangers of rickshaw travel on roads filled with swiftly driven cars; in this whirlpool of traffic 'one is safe in a tram even from the motor buses, and much safer than in a rickshaw'.[23]

The increase in fatal accidents on Singapore roads in the 1920s did not serve to call attention to the real peril which existed for rickshawmen, although the city itself was developing an unenviable notoriety on account of road deaths. The streets were congested, many crowded with stalls and pedestrian shoppers, and accident figures show that the slow speed of the rickshaw did not compensate for its lack of safety in collisions. The roads had become dangerous, and the cause of the majority of accidents was the craze for speed. For most motorists there was no place on the road for rickshaws; they were expected to keep within the confines of the narrow space at the edge of the left lane designated for bicycles and other slow traffic:

> Taxis and car drivers shout at pullers of rickshaws parked by the roadside where they wish to park themselves: the pullers usually (if slowly) move out of their way. A lorry driver in a narrow alley expects any rickshaw he encounters to turn aside or retreat. Only where severe congestion has brought traffic to a standstill does the rickshaw puller show any boldness in his relations with drivers; elsewhere deference is the rule. Pedestrians by their massed presence can sometimes overawe the drivers of motor vehicles. Rickshaws seem very rarely to achieve this.[24]

As traffic fatalities peaked in the 1930s, it not only proved difficult to take precautions to minimize the danger, it was also difficult to secure convictions in reckless and drunk driving cases where serious charges had to be preferred, especially against Europeans.

Lee Ah Loi was pulling his rickshaw along Orchard Road when he was hit by a motor car driving towards town. His death was only a portent, an ill-omen of what was to come in the Coroner's Inquests; Lee Ah Loi was running on the left side of the crown of the road, and saw a motor car approaching 40 feet away in the centre of the road. He swerved to the left to avoid the car. The motor car then swerved to the right and Lee Ah Loi found himself for one horrific moment facing a head-on collision. The force of the impact drove him underneath the car and to the back of it; the smashed rickshaw and the passenger wound up on the hood of the car. Lee Ah Loi, who was considered a careful puller, died hard, moaning.[25] His case was the first numbing experience for the author of what was to become a familiar sight of pullers bleeding to death on the roads as a result of bad driving. Lim Hoon Keng, a young Hockcha puller engaged by the members of the Young Man's Friendly Society, was travelling along the Esplanade on a moonlit evening on the left side of the road, when a hired car with two Japanese passengers, going at a fast pace, ran into the rickshaw. The Malay driver did not blow his horn nor attempt to brake. Far worse, the car was on the wrong side of the road. Just moments before impact, Chua Choon Cheng, the passenger in the rickshaw, not believing his eyes, shouted to the driver of the oncoming car, '*Eh! apa lu tidor?*' ('Hey! Are you asleep?'); the next instant the tourer smashed into the rickshaw.[26]

Yang Chee Tee's rickshaw was run into head-on by a car on the wrong side of the road because half the width of New Bridge Road was under repairs up to and on a line with the centre of Upper Hokkien Street. At the junction of the two roads a motor car collided with the rickshaw, and overturned it. The two passengers were thrown out, injuring one of them fatally. Catherine Goh, the other passenger, described the accident:

> On the day of the accident I was in a ricksha with a female Eurasian: we were going towards Sepoy lines: when we arrived near the Chinese Protectorate on the left of the road about three feet from the drain I saw a motor car coming towards us: I told the puller that a motor car was coming and the puller said "We are near the drain", then suddenly the ricksha was turned over and we fell out: the motor car was travelling rapidly and I heard no horn blown. I then became unconscious after I regained consciousness I saw a crowd of people and one of them at my request came and assisted me: took me to a ricksha not the one I was in . . . at the time of the accident there was not much traffic. The motor car was coming along the wrong side of the road.[27]

Goh Chye Keh was run over at the junction of Hill and High Streets by a *towkay*'s son who did not have a licence and had driven his father's car only five times. He died because of having had the misfortune of being caught on the wrong side of the road by a carload of wealthy young Chinese joyriding after dark. They were speeding and the puller had no indication they were coming until it was too late as the car hit him coming out of nowhere:

> We went along the East Coast Road [in the 4 cylinder Buick], Grove Road, Kallang Road, as far as the new bridge, over the new bridge and then along via Jalan Sultan and into Beach Road, then along the Esplanade and round once then to Johnston's Pier, Collyer Quay to Tanjong Pagar, Cantonment Road, New Bridge Road as far as the bridge. We crossed the bridge. As we were crossing I put out my left hand as . . . we were going home . . . via River Valley Road. The accused sounded the horn. There was a ricksha on the left, coming along River Valley Road, the ricksha was coming towards us on our left . . . the river side on the wrong side of the road . . . when we were about two fathoms away from the ricksha he turned to his left and cut straight across in front of the car and then turned a bit more towards the direction of Tanglin. Then our car hit him. Our right front mudguard [fender] struck his right wheel and tipped the ricksha over on to its left side. There was no passenger in the ricksha. The puller was thrown out of the shafts onto the tram lines. . . . Our car stopped about five yards after striking the ricksha. . . . The truth is we stopped for a moment to see what had happened and then started off again.[28]

In a similar incident Ling Ah Ngong, an elderly married Hengwah, was killed by a motor car driven by Chow Seh Woo with a business friend and two singing girls as passengers. They went for a ride along Pasir Panjang Road. They reached New Bridge Road on their way back when a rickshaw only 3 yards in front of them began to cross towards the Chinese Protectorate. There were no cars ahead of them but several rickshaws were on their left; Chow Seh Woo braked hard to avoid hitting the rickshaw and the car swerved slowly to the right only to smash head-on into a rickshaw coming towards them on the opposite side of the road. The puller was struck dead. Jin Aw, who was pulling his rickshaw with two female passengers towards Kampong Glam, explains the dangers caused by such an accident. He too could not brake in time:

> I had two female passengers in my rickshaw. . . . We passed the junction of the street behind the [Chinese] Protectorate. Another ricksha was going along ahead of me. There were two passengers in the ricksha, men. . . . The other ricksha was two or three yards in front of me. There was a motor car coming from Kampong Glam direction going along straight on the left hand side of the road. The car was going fast. Then the motor car came across the road and ran into the front ricksha and stopped. The puller was knocked down by the motor car, and the passengers were on the road, one on each side of the car near the back and the puller was between the front wheels. My ricksha was overturned to the right. My passengers jumped out and ran away. My rickshaw knocked against the rickshaw in front. . . . [There is] generally a lot of traffic about 5.30 p.m. [but on] this day there was less than usual.[29]

The weather was a significant factor in causing accidents between rickshaws and motor vehicles. During the rainy months road surfaces remained slippery and wet and speeding vehicles, especially those with defective brakes, often could not stop in time to avoid an accident. Ling Kheng Teh was pulling along New Bridge Road when he was run over by a trolley bus coming from the opposite direction. The driver of the bus lost control and it skidded on the slick road. The Coroner noted that another fatal accident had occurred at the same spot several months earlier due to the oily surface and declared it an extremely dangerous place when it was wet.[30] Lee Ah Liang was also hit by a bus trying to pass his rickshaw on a slippery portion of Bukit Timah Road under repair. It had been raining. The road was muddy and Lee Ah Liang was running flat out at the time. His rickshaw was on the edge of the road when the bus, on almost reaching the end of the trench in the middle of it, skidded. There were five children in the rickshaw ranging in age from thirteen to five; Tan Ah Nye, the eldest, gave this account of the accident in the miserable conditions:

> There were five of us in one ricksha. I was the eldest one, other ages 8, 7, 6, and 5. I sat on the seat and so did two others and the other two were on our laps. The hood was up, but not the apron. . . . We were passing through the trench in the middle of the road. There was a motor bus following behind us. The driver was sounding his horn. Suddenly the motor bus knocked into the ricksha and we were all thrown out. It knocked against the right wheel of our ricksha. I and another were thrown out, my brother aged eight managed to hold on to the other two and then jumped out. The puller was bleeding from his cheeks. He was thrown down on his face. We all ran home quickly. My house was very near where the accident happened. The puller did not know where we lived but I had told him the 2nd mile. I had not spoken to him just before the accident. The puller was wobbling a little as the road was bad. . . . The middle of the road was dug up for sewerage works.[31]

An unknown driver dressed in a white suit set out from home on a rainy morning in August 1937 and headed in the direction of Geylang along

Victoria Street in the heart of the rickshaw district. It was between 8 and 9 a.m. and the street was slick. Meensha Singh, a young Sikh watchman, knew what happened to Lim Kim Cheok when a motor car, believed to be a baby Austin tourer, sideswiped his rickshaw:

I was standing on the five footway of 313 Victoria Street alone facing Geylang. I saw a ricksha empty, pulled by a Chinese puller going from Singapore direction towards Geylang, close to the drain on the left side of the road. It was raining slightly. The road was wet and slippery. I saw an old baby Austin car, tourer, coming from the direction of Singapore towards Geylang, a dark blue colour. The car travelled at normal speed. In passing the rickshaw the car appeared to swerve to its left and the left front portion of the car struck the rickshaw on the right wheel causing the rickshaw to swing round to its left across the drain and the puller was thrown violently on the five footway, landing heavily on his right side.... The car did not stop but continued along Victoria Street faster than before. There was a loud noise when the impact took place and the driver must have known he had struck the rickshaw. The driver was dressed in white. I did not get the number of the car as the car went too fast.... There was no other traffic on the road at the time of the accident. There was plenty of room on the road for the car to have passed the rickshaw.[32]

The Coroner's inquest recounted that Lim Kian Lye ran across the road in front of a taxi-cab. His rickshaw was so close there was no time for Ramasamy, the driver, to do anything. The puller suddenly turned back because a bus was coming from the opposite direction and the front of the cab struck the right side of the rickshaw. It overturned and was pushed along for some distance but Lim Kian Lye was left on the wet road. He had been running with his head down because of driving rain and may not have seen the bus when he decided to cut across the road. The taxi's brakes almost failed and it ran out of control, swerving to the right after the collision. The bus veered across the road to avoid hitting the cab. The puller never made it to the hospital alive. The driver, who suffered only minor injuries, explained to the Coroner just how bad the brakes were on the cab:

... I applied my brakes but the brakes were defective and I could not pull up in time so my car struck the right wheel of the ricksha ... I told the owner two days before the accident that one of my brakes was defective. The left brake. He said he would get it attended to in a few days. The thread of the screw was worn away.[33]

Rickshaws had wheels buckled, lamps shattered, frames bent, and shafts broken in collisions with trolley buses and lorries when they cut off rickshaws, tipped them over from behind, or forced them off the edge of the road, causing them to overbalance, and turn over. Tang Ah Kow was running towards Keppel Harbour wedged between two buses; he never heard the sound of the horn as the rear bus tried to pass him:

I was pulling ricksha 8127. A woman was in the ricksha.... The woman engaged me in Narces Street and wanted to go to Telok Blanga Road. I was pulling her along New Keppel Road towards Keppel Harbour ... just before getting to the entrance of Low Hill there were two buses—one in front of me and one behind, going in the same direction. The bus behind me in trying to pass me caught my right ricksha wheel. At the time my ricksha was on the left side of the road about a yard from the drain. The woman in the ricksha was thrown head first on to the road, my ricksha and I were knocked into the drain. My left arm was injured ... I was detained at Hospital for six days....[34]

Bus drivers rarely slowed down for one another let alone rickshaw coolies, even when they had the right of way. Ong Teck Cheng was pulling a Tamil, who hawked cloth, along Rochore Canal Road when a bus ploughed into him. U Toomal Kheatomal, the hawker, felt the bus driver was at fault:

We were going along Rochore Canal Road on our way to Prinsep Street on our way to High Street. We were going near our left hand side of the road. There were two cars came [*sic*] from behind us. And a bus coming toward us but some distance away. The puller held out his right hand to indicate that he was turning to his right into Prinsep Street, but the bus still came on. The puller got at right angles to the road and the front of the bus hit the end of the ricksha shafts, pushed the ricksha around and the puller fell down. The ricksha overturned backwards. One of my two bundles fell on either side of the ricksha. A crowd gathered and some of them carried the puller and put him into the bus. They said they were going to the station ... I think the bus driver was in the wrong, not the puller.[35]

Tang Ang Tee, a tea-stallkeeper, not far from the junction of Ophir Road and Queen Street, witnessed a collision in the middle of the crossroads between a rickshaw and a bus. The rickshaw came out of Ophir Road, while the bus was coming along Queen Street from the city, going very fast:

He just went straight into the ricksha. He swerved to the right to try and avoid the ricksha but struck the shafts of the ricksha and broke them. The puller was knocked over on to the road and laid there. When the bus stopped the puller was under the middle of the bus. The passenger was not thrown out of the ricksha but he jumped out and ran away.[36]

In another incident a bus was proceeding along a stretch of Kallang Road when the road was under repair, leaving tram-lines and the right side of the road for traffic. As the bus proceeded along the tram-lines it attempted to overtake another bus which had stopped in front of it, and just as it came out to pass, the driver saw a rickshaw at a standstill only a few yards in front of him. The bus barely managed to squeeze through but struck the right wheel of the rickshaw. It was thrown into the drain and the puller driven into the road. Low Neo, the Hengwah coolie, described what happened as the bus struck his rickshaw: 'I was on my left hand side of the road. A motor bus, number unknown, came from the direction of Gaylang, and struck me. I fell with my ricksha into the drain.'[37] Several mistakes were made in this accident by the bus driver: first, he chose to pass on an unsighted section of road under repair at an excessive speed; secondly, he did not use his horn to signal the fact he intended to pass; finally, and most importantly, the bus's foot brake was defective. The bus could not be stopped quickly, because part of the hand brake was also worn out and not much use as an emergency brake.[38]

Continuing the upward trend in road fatalities combinations of buses and trams ran over pullers and passengers, and in such instances death was instantaneous. In some cases both the driver and motorman showed lack of judgement. Che'Mat bin Haji Sahat had just crossed Elgin Bridge in North Bridge Road with his tram; rickshaws on his left were going in the same direction and at about the same speed. A bus approached the tram from behind, sounding its horn. The bus suddenly tried to pass on the wrong side of the road, and collided with one of the rickshaws as there was not enough space to squeeze by, throwing it up against the tram. The Chinese passenger was thrown clear. The puller was not so lucky, falling across the front of the tram.[39] In an equally horrific accident with the exact opposite ending, two female Cantonese were travelling in Ting Ee Noh's rickshaw along Serangoon Road, and either the rickshaw collided with the tram because of conflicting sets of instruction given by the women or the tram ran into it because of an error of judgement on the part of the motorman. The rickshaw was smashed and the two women were tumbled on to the rails in the direction of Serangoon. Another tramcar coming from the city happened to arrive at the same time, crushing the rickshaw and running over the women. This is how the two protagonists in this macabre street drama described their roles.[40]

First the puller, Ting Ee Noh:

> Two female Chinese got into my rickshaw in a lane off Serangoon Road. When we got to the main road, one of the two fares told me to go to town: I was then on the left hand side of the road, then the other fare told me to go to the opposite side of the road. I pulled towards the opposite side: a tram car going from Serangoon Road struck my ricksha ... another tram came up, the two women and the ricksha had just been upset and this tram collided and ran over the rickshaw and the two females ... it was getting dark....

Secondly, the motorman, Neinah:

> I was driving Tram Car No. 18 along Serangoon Road towards town and when I got near Kerbau Road I noticed a ricksha in front of me and going in the same direction but on my right. When I first saw the ricksha it was about twelve feet ahead of me. I sounded my gong and the ricksha turned sharp to the left, trying to cross in front of me. I applied my brake but the car struck the ricksha ... and it fell to the right....

Bad accidents with other large vehicles, notably lorries, often occurred on private roads around the wharves and warehouses of Tanjong Pagar, and in the vicinity of larger produce markets in the early hours of the morning.[41]

The risk of accidents was highest at junctions and major intersections at peak hours and at dusk. Rickshaws were vulnerable in such spots because their size and speed were handicaps when they had to turn, often from a stationary position in the middle of the road, against oncoming traffic on very wide thoroughfares. Appendix 8 shows what a decisive effect the layout of junctions had in creating a context for accidents involving rickshaws. Pullers often had to take calculated risks at these extra-wide intersections; the timing was critical, knowing just when to dash, cut or swerve, as was the time of day. It was always more difficult to negotiate big junctions at night when pullers were apt to be disoriented by the glare of oncoming lights and the blare of horns, or not see at all a car without lights until too late. Intersections were also dangerous because as rickshaws waited to turn on ill-lit streets motor cars and trucks often ploughed into the back of them.

Ng Pin, at the age of 60, was still pulling a rickshaw in 1922 when his luck ran out at the junction of Circular Road and New Bridge Road. The elderly puller, who was in good health and did not smoke opium, came out of Circular Road on the wrong side of the street, and cut into the traffic hoping to find a secure place in the flow of cars and trucks. Instead he ran smack into the rear of a fast-moving night-soil lorry.[42] See Piong, much younger and far less experienced than Ng Pin, was running along South Bridge Road from Tanjong Pagar with two passengers in his rickshaw. A car was coming from the opposite direction. He began to cut across the road to enter Cross Street when the car sounded its horn; the young puller panicked, and in his moment of equivocation the car ran him over. The only damage to the rickshaw was a broken shaft:

> I saw a rickshaw coming from the direction of Tanjong Pagar with two passengers in the rickshaw. The puller did not put out his hand but he turned towards Cross Street. There was a motor car coming along South Bridge Road.... The driver blew his horn two or three times. He was not going fast.... The rickshaw was going into Cross Street. When the puller heard the driver sound the horn he turned sharply towards Tanjong Pagar again. The motor by this time had just reached the back of the rickshaw. The puller let the shafts go up, then the hood which was down caught on the tank of the car. The shafts came down again and the puller fell down.... The puller hesitated when he heard the horn. The motor car was then about two fathoms away....[43]

Yip Ah Kim was pulling two church-going Eurasian passengers when he suddenly started to cross the junction to get into Ophir Road and ran smack into the front of a motor lorry. The passengers were quick to blame the puller for the accident, but they realized that they perhaps could not absolve themselves entirely. They gave him directions, saw the lorry coming, and issued the fatal instruction to make the turn. The rickshawman only did what he was told to do:

> I engaged a ricksha in Syed Alwee Road and both my wife and I got into the ricksha. We were on our way to Ophir Road to the church there. I think he knew the way but missed the turning and so went to Bencoolen St. Bridge. We crossed the bridge over Rochore Canal.... We went along Rochore Canal towards Ophir Road.... When approaching the junction I said, "ini jalan" (this is the street). I

was about ten feet from the corner of the junction of Ophir Road but we had to cross over the road in order to turn into Ophir Road. He started to turn and then I noticed a motor lorry coming toward us from the direction of Rochore so I called out to him "jaga lorry" (watch out, a lorry). The puller tried to stop his rickshaw but was hit by the lorry before he could do so.... The lorry was quite close when I said to the puller "ini jalan" so I expected him to wait till the lorry had passed but he started to cross at once and so I shouted "jaga lorry" ... I think the puller was to blame as he should have waited till the lorry had passed and not tried to cross in front of the lorry.[44]

Rickshaw coolies were very conscious of maintaining their stride and running straight ahead at all times. To wobble, even slightly, in traffic could prove fatal on main streets or bridges with a stream of cars and buses passing a yard away. Rickshawmen were most vulnerable if they happened to lose their concentration, and stride, or accidentally tripped. Their concentration had to be total: 'ordinarily when he pulled a rickshaw across this bridge he put all his vigor into his legs and dared not even glance to the left or right because he was afraid of tripping.'[45] Animals, particularly stray dogs and cats, darting in and out of traffic could shatter a puller's concentration and throw him off stride: 'my mother, I remember well, had an irish terrier that used to run between the ricksha wheels when she went shopping!'[46] One rickshaw coolie was tripped up in 1905, by a 20-foot python lying across Garden Road. The force of the collision threw the puller on his knees and the horrified fare fled, after having landed on the monstrous snake.[47] It was the blasting sound of a motor car horn from behind, though, and not a python that filled most pullers with terror and confusion and threw them off their pace. When motorists hit their horn they expected pullers to get out of the way quickly. In such frightening moments rickshaw coolies wondered if they were supposed to move to the right or left, and they knew what an enemy fear was if they did not react at all. If a puller froze on the spot in terror as a car bore down with its horn honking, he would be killed for not having been able to budge, before the driver would stop. Dolah bin Omar, a hired driver of the Straits Motor Garage, took a Baba Chinese and a Chinese woman to Pasir Panjang and returned via Holland Road, Middle Road, and North Bridge Road. On Beach Road he saw several rickshaws in front of his car:

I blew my horn four or five times and the rickshas cleared out of my way. I slowed down when I first saw the rickshas and kept on going slow behind a ricksha ... I saw the ricksha cut across the road from right to left in front of my car. He came right across me and immediately in front. I put down my brakes both foot and hand, hard and just then the man was struck and fell down.[48]

Low Leong fell while going down a hilly stretch on Grange Road as a motor car passed within inches of him sounding its horn, telling him to get off the road. He was so frightened that he instinctively ran towards the drain where he lost his footing, and fell striking the cross bar, fatally injuring himself.[49] But some rickshaw coolies were not like Low Leong, wondering if his heart would drop into his stomach, when he heard the piercing sound of a car horn. They learned to make the motorist come to terms with the varying moods of rickshaw traffic on Singapore streets. One of their favourite tricks was playing chicken, forcing the drivers to slow down; a lesson in patience and humility:

> He wasn't afraid of those motor cars that ran around all over the streets. A car would come at him head on, rolling up the dust on the street, but [he] wouldn't flinch. It didn't matter how the horn blasted at him. He didn't care how frenzied his passengers got. There was nothing the driver could do about it either; he would have to slow down. [He] would turn aside after the car slowed down in order to avoid eating the dust. He would use the same trick if the car was coming up behind him. He had it all figured out; cars did not dare injure people no matter what. Well then, why move over and bring along all that dust? All the cops cared about was keeping the road open for motor cars. Their sole fear was that the cars wouldn't go fast enough and wouldn't bring along enough dust.[50]

But there was one situation in which not even an exceptional puller could always slow down properly. Running downhill was when rickshaw coolies were most apt to make a fatal mistake if they broke stride or lost their balance and control even for a split second. Teng Ah Poh, a 46-year-old Hockchia, was literally flying down the right side of upper Wilkie Road as Mrs Jane Downe drove her car into it. Teng Ah Poh, who was pulling a passenger, could not stop because of the momentum already built up and the weight of the rickshaw hurtling him forward, and collided with the car, dying.[51] Chin Ah Ching died in the same way but the motorists did not stop and were apprehended only after his death. He had been running along the left side of Tanglin Road towards the junction coming down the incline, unknowingly set on a collision course. A motor car driven by one Khoo Boo Keng was proceeding up the hill. When about 5 yards apart the rickshaw suddenly swerved to the right towards the car as Chin Ah Ching lost his footing, and then in an effort to avoid it he desperately swerved back again to the left side, but did not get clear of the car, as the right front fender struck the right wheel of the rickshaw; the driver did not slow down to see what had taken place.[52] The Coroner, Frederick Bourne, in presenting statistics on road deaths involving rickshaw pullers, made special reference to this type of accident: 'one ricksha puller [in 1937] when coming down a steep slope lost control and died from his injuries'.[53]

The arrogance of motorists, the layout of streets, the rickshawman's fear or lack of good judgement added even more difficulties to the inherent dangers of night pulling. Singapore streets were as late as 1938, in the opinion of the Trimmer Traffic Committee, the worst lighted for a city of its size anywhere in Asia. Pleas in the Courts continually pointed to the poor light of gas incandescent lamps on the main roads as being to blame for many accidents. Before 1900, kerosene street lamps had to be lit by Tamil men who went around the city, climbing a ladder to light the wick of each lamp.[54] When the municipality purchased the gas works, and introduced welsback incandescent burners on some of the principal thoroughfares at the turn of the century, it was considered to be a modern step in city planning and 'greatly added to the appearance of the town at night'.[55] However, once one left the carnival brightness of the main thoroughfares, the rest of the city was plunged into pitch darkness except for gaily lit brothels and the odd lantern in eating-houses. The rickshawmen and tens of thousands of other Chinese were rate-payers, yet they were compelled to live in streets with little or no illumination. Even after the city expanded and motorized traffic reached the point where roads were heavily travelled night and day, the Municipal Commissioners were not prepared to incur any undue expenditure in schemes urging the replacement of gas on main roads with sodium-vapour electric lighting.

Consequently, rickshaws often could not be seen at night by vehicles overtaking and fatal accidents occurred. Every licensed rickshaw had to be furnished with a pair of regulation lamps supplied by the Registrar at cost. It was the puller's responsibility to supply the coconut oil for the wick lamps.[56] A rickshaw lamp filled with coconut oil would last about nine hours. The lamps, despite having a thick red glass plate at the back, tended to shine faintly from behind. The rickshaw owner Chow Kow Ern related how Teo Ah Lak came and hired his rickshaw, always lighting both lamps before leaving his house.[57] On the other hand, Tan Nah Nai, a 51-year-old Hockchew, usually went out with his rickshaw at 6 a.m. after the street lamps had been turned off, just before dawn. He pulled without lamps because he considered it bright enough not to need them.[58] In the early days, the odd, enterprising rickshaw coolie mounted carbide lamps on his vehicle and managed to charge three times the normal fare at night; the public felt they were safer at night in one of these rickshaws.[59]

The danger from motor vehicles in the dark, particularly the excessive speed at which cars were driven, led the Rickshaw Department to search for suitable cheap compulsory lamps which could be attached to axles and be clearly visible from behind. Because of many complaints that rickshaws could not be seen at night by oncoming motor vehicles, due to the position of the rickshaw lamps high up towards the front of the carriage, the colour of the vehicle's body, and the puller's clothes, frequently black, it was decided that from the beginning of 1918 lamps had to be fitted into sockets above the mudguards so that the red light should be visible from behind.[60] There was opposition as some officials were in favour of tail-lights being carried on rickshaws, but suitable reflector signs which could be attached to axles and clearly seen from behind were not entertained seriously again, until 1938.[61]

The constant movement of cars and lorries around unlit parts of Singapore, on rural stretches at the edges of the city, on roads passing through the rickshaw districts, or over bridges increased considerably the dangers to rickshaw coolies. One morning, just before sunrise, in 1927, Ling Kow Kay was struck from behind by a hit-and-run driver as he pulled his rickshaw along Balastier Road. He had left the lodging-house at 5 a.m. as usual, and his rickshaw had no lamps. From the marks on the road it appeared that the rickshaw and the puller were struck by an oncoming vehicle. It had endeavoured to stop because there were distinct skid marks on the road suggesting that the brakes had been suddenly jammed on just before the point of impact, as the puller came into view.[62] It happened over and over again, especially in the dark (see Appendix 8). Suddenly a car driven by a Swiss, with three other men as passengers, loomed around a bad bend in Meyer Road as they were going towards the Sea View Hotel, colliding fast with Low Yah Cheong's rickshaw. The 39-year-old opium smoker, who was described as a moderate puller, never knew what hit him. The motorists attributed the accident to the rickshaw being without lights on a dark stretch of the road. They did not see the rickshaw until they ran into it. The reason for this, perhaps, was that their car did not have headlamps other than small sidelamps fixed on the windscreen:

> We were going along the middle of the road and the rickshaw was a little more to the left. The ricksha was going along in the same direction as we were. We struck the rickshaw with the left mudguard of the car. I did not see the rickshaw until we collided with it. It [the car] had no lights. We had the small sidelights on. Mr. Leuthold stopped the car immediately. Then we saw the coolie just at the left of the car near the front wheel. We were going about eighteen miles per hour at the time. No other traffic on the road. . . .[63]

Lee Yew Kiah was riding in a ricksha along Beach Road when a speeding motor car ran into the back of it, throwing him out to his death. The road was under repair. Red lanterns had been left up, and it was very narrow there, only wide enough for two rickshaws to pass; no motor car could pass a rickshaw at this point. The clear lane, which the motorist avoided, was in the centre and on each side of it repairs were going on. A policeman beckoned the driver to stop but the car was going fast when it passed him: 'I shouted "tahan, tahan" the driver did not stop . . . and as the car turned . . . I saw the number behind. The number was 221.'[64] The beleaguered police periodically attempted to restore order on the streets at night, but nothing worked for long; when Singaporeans were in a hurry, red lamps, traffic cops, and lane markings meant nothing at all, as we learn from Yu No Po's last rickshaw trip. This 20-year-old Hokkien puller was travelling along Stamford Road in the direction of Orchard Road. When he arrived at the junction of Stamford and North Bridge Roads, a police constable who was directing traffic stopped his rickshaw and other vehicles. A Fiat motor car driven by Amat bin Asim then came up and ploughed into the back of the stationary rickshaw, throwing the puller to the ground. The two passengers were also hurled out of the rickshaw and rendered unconscious. Despite brakes, Amat bin Asim never stopped if he could swerve, never slowed down if he could pass. He was driving at a high speed just prior to the accident considering the traffic, locality, and above all, the fact that he did not have a licence to drive a Fiat car. The Coroner added the following observation on this case: 'The owner of car no. 4454 should have checked the accused for driving at an excessive speed. It is clearly an owner's duty to prevent his syce from committing this class of irregularity and if that fact was more fully realised in Singapore many lives would be saved.'[65]

In pitch blackness it was often difficult for motorists to notice the shadow form of rickshaw and puller suddenly looming out of the night. There was no iridescent clothing in those days, as nothing of that sort was required by the law to prevent pullers getting run over in the dark. In hit-and-run accidents the rickshaw coolie often died instantaneously or was left speechless, dying shortly afterwards from a fractured skull. These accidents often occurred when few people were present with the odd witness instinctively choosing to come to the aid of the puller rather than take down the number of the offending motor car as it escaped. Soo Ah Mui hired Teo Ah Lak's rickshaw at 4.30 in the morning near the New World Amusement Park. He did not know the Hengwah puller, who had a wife and two children in China, and who, according to his rickshaw owner, had good eyesight and hearing. The rickshaw travelled along the left side of the road a few feet from the drain. The Hylam cook was wide awake while sitting in the vehicle. One lamp was lit on the offside of the rickshaw. It was not raining and there was a little moonlight. There was dim light from the street lamps. Suddenly, something struck the rickshaw. Soo Ah Mui was flung out and knocked unconscious. This is what Francis Thomas, a school teacher at St. Andrew's School, discovered on his way home at 4.30 a.m. on Serangoon Road:

> I was driving my car .... along Serangoon Road coming from Lavender Street going towards Kandang Kerbau. When about two hundred yards beyond Lavender Street I noticed a stationary car standing on the opposite side with bonnet towards Lavender Street. I also noticed an overturned rickshaw standing more on the centre of the road but I cannot speak of its exact position as I did not stop. There were headlights alight on the car and they were either dimmed or they were side lights as they were not strong. After passing I thought of stopping and just then the other car drove off. I turned my car round and came up behind the rickshaw. I found the rickshaw puller lying on the road across the centre of the road and a passenger of the rickshaw (Soo Ah Mui) sitting on the road holding his head. The rickshaw puller was unconscious and breathing heavily. I took both parties in my car to Rumah Miskin Police Station. I got the impression that it was a small saloon car dark in colour. The car moved off in the direction of Lavender Street. I fancy that the windscreen of the car was broken.... On my return from the Police Station at about 5 a.m. I stopped at the scene again and learned from an English speaking person standing there that another car had collided with the rickshaw while it was lying overturned on the road. The rickshaw had definitely been moved quite a distance from the place where I found it.[66]

Tired pullers, barely able to keep their eyes open, walking between the shafts in the early hours of the morning, were sometimes ploughed into by Europeans coming back from a hard night on the town. George

Buxton was driving his car along Bencoolen Street at 1 a.m. on 17 January 1934, when he crashed into the back of a rickshaw being pulled by Tan Poh Whye along the left side of the road. There was no evidence to show what caused him to veer sharply to his left but it is clear that the puller was in no way to blame. Tan Poh Whye's report was taken in Tan Tock Seng Hospital:

I was pulling my empty ricksha along Bencoolen Street going towards Kempong Kapor i.e. going home. I had been out since 5 p.m. and earned about one dollar. I was a bit tired. The lamps were both alight. They are of the approved pattern with a red glass at the back. I was in between the shafts—pulling, the shafts were at ordinary level, not up in the air. I was going along the very edge of the road going straight. I heard the noise of a motor vehicle coming very fast but no horn. I did not bother to look around because I was at the side of the road and the car had all the remainder of the road to pass me in. No other traffic and no other people on the road. Suddenly the car crashed into the back of my ricksha and swung the shafts round to the left throwing me to the left near the drain and the left side of my face hit the drain and caused it to bleed and also hurt on both knees. I got up and went to the [Police] Station . . . I was a bit dazed and was in a hurry to get to the Police Station to go to Hospital but on the way I fainted, not actually fainted but had to keep stopping as I was dazed . . . I saw nothing on the road to cause the car to swerve.[67]

In a very similar incident four policemen returning from duty were walking along the left side of Grove Road when a passing car crashed into a rickshaw with no other traffic around. The red lamps at the back of the rickshaw could not be seen as they were very dim. The rickshaw was too far out into the centre of the road and the police felt if the puller, Leong Lam, had kept to the side, nothing would have happened:

We were walking on the left side of the road going towards Rochore. On arrival in front of the Jit Lin Rubber Factory I saw a rickshaw near the centre of the road. It was facing towards Katong. The puller was in the shafts holding chest up, his head was stooping and the rickshaw was stationary and the lights very dim. The road was not well lighted at this particular spot. The road is straight and wide at this spot. The puller was merely standing between the shafts as if half asleep. Just after passing the rickshaw I saw a motor car (a two seater) coming from town going towards Katong. Two Europeans were in the car. . . . The two headlights were burning. . . . Just after this car passed me I heard a crash, I turned around and saw the rickshaw which had been standing there was smashed and the car standing facing the middle of the road on the right side of the road . . . I rushed to the rickshaw and saw the puller lying on the road near the rickshaw . . . he was bleeding from the side of the mouth. He could not speak. . . .[68]

Under pressure to provide additional evidence, Vaughan Jones, the driver, wrote to his friend and passenger to get his version of what happened. The man's personal reply is extraordinary. It reveals an attitude towards the life of an ordinary Chinese, as cheap and unimportant. The letter is both callous and light-hearted as the author pushes the whole affair into the background of his mind; the puller is chastised rather than mourned because his death has proved to be a public embarrassment to Vaughan Jones. Despite the fact that a man had been run over and killed, it was still a 'topping weekend':

Very sorry that your letter hasn't been answered before but unfortunately there was no stamp on it and was left at the Post Office a couple of days until I went down to the village myself last evening. However I hope my evidence will not arrive too late. How confoundedly stupid of that old bloke to pass out, he didn't seem to be badly hurt when he got to the hospital. Must be rather rotten for you but I hope that the verdict will be a pure accident cause it couldn't have been avoided as far as I could judge. Hope to see you up here on Saturday week. Were trying out a couple of new people against the A.P.C. which I trust will give us that extra bit of thrust behind the scrum. Well cheerio and very many thanks for a topping weekend. I hope this unfortunate affair will blowover.[69]

It is not surprising to learn in a city that took a slap-on-the-wrist approach to drunk and reckless drivers who killed hundreds of people a year—the total traffic fatalities—that rickshaw coolies did not remain unscathed when they walked outside the shafts or were off work at home. Choi Bok Lee was crossing the road after having gone to the public latrine at Dhoby Ghaut junction when he was hit by a European couple without a driving licence, in their newly acquired two-seater Chevrolet.[70] Siah Goh Seng was on his way to town to buy goods for his family, after having pulled his rickshaw. He was knocked down at the corner of Geylang and Joo Chiat Roads at night by a taxi-cab.[71] The Trimmer Traffic campaign in 1938 to stiffen penalties for reckless driving came too late to protect these pullers and many of their comrades against people who drove dangerously or while under the influence of alcohol. In the Coroner's Records were the casualties: as the percentage of drivers increased between 1914 and 1940 and the percentage of motor vehicles on the road jumped, traffic fatalities and the fatality rate involving rickshaw coolies progressively rose. As late as 1937 a rickshaw puller's life was worth only $80. That was the value of the fine Tan Kong, a lorry driver, paid for causing the death of the 45-year-old Hengwah puller, Tan Moi Kah, by a rash act of driving.[72]

1. Louis Chevalier, *Labouring Classes and Dangerous Classes in Paris during the First Half of the Nineteenth Century* (London: Routledge and Kegan Paul, 1973), p. 340.
2. *Singapore Free Press*, 5 January 1900.
3. *Straits Echo*, 14 June 1905.
4. SCII of Tan Twah Sah, No. 175, 3/11/13.
5. SCII of Wan Chow Hoe, No. 167, 18/9/09.
6. SCII of Ho Hee, No. 128, 25/9/98.
7. Ibid.
8. CCVS of Tan Ah Chay, No. 60, 23/5/12.
9. SCII of Yap Ma Yam, No. 202, 13/9/17.
10. Lao She, *Rickshaw* (the novel *Lo-T'o Hsiang Tzu*), translated by Jean M James (Honolulu: The University Press of Hawaii, 1979), p. 214.

11. SCII of Ch'ng Chuan, No. 395, 30/9/21.
12. SCII of Low Siang Quay, No. 459, 16/11/22.
13. John Cuylenburg, *Singapore through Sunshine and Shadow* (Singapore: Heinemann, 1982), p. 7.
14. Lao She, op. cit., p. 99.
15. *Singapore Free Press*, 5 January 1900.
16. SCII of Lim Boon Seng, No. 38, 20/1/25.
17. SCII of Maximillian Aloysius Andrews, No. 284, 24/10/18.
18. *Singapore Free Press*, 19 October 1938.
19. R. C. H. McKie, *This Was Singapore* (London, 1950), p. 13.
20. SSAR, Report of the S. S. Police Force, 1912, p. 331.
21. SSAR, Report of the S. S. Police Force, 1913, pp. 223–4.
22. *Musings of J. S. M. R.*, p. 30.
23. R. H. J. Sydney, *Malay Land* (London: Cecil Palmer, 1926), p. 34.
24. UNNAYAN, in association with T. H. Thomas, *Rickshaws in Calcutta* (Calcutta: UNNAYAN, 1981), p. 47.
25. SCII of Lee Ah Loi, No. 183, 17/8/17.
26. SCII of Lim Hoon Keng, No. 164, 15/7/19.
27. SCII of Bibiana Rodrigues, No. 36, 23/2/17.
28. SCII of Goh Chye Keh, No. 281, 30/10/20.
29. SCII of Ling Ah Ngong, No. 1, 3/1/26.
30. SCII of Ling Kheng Teh, No. 52, 18/1/28.
31. SCII of Lee Ah Liang, No. 59, 22/1/28.
32. SCII of Lim Kim Cheok, No. 506, 27/8/37.
33. SCII of Lim Kian Lye, No. 38, 20/1/30.
34. SCII of unknown Chinese female, No. 221, 16/5/25.
35. SCII of Ong Teck Cheng, No. 174, 22/1/29.
36. SCII of Ee Ang Ang, No. 82, 9/2/27.
37. SCII of Low Neo, No. 266, 28/4/23.
38. Ibid.
39. SCII of Toh Ah Soh, No. 183, 18/4/25.
40. SCII of Ip Yeok Yeng, No. 109, 1/6/17.
41. For examples of deaths due to lorries see SCII of Hadji Omar, No. 115, 8/8/12; of Ong Ah Choon, No. 46, 23/2/20; of Teng Tong, No. 484, 15/12/23; of Tan Soo Ghee, 6/7/32.
42. SCII of Ng Pin, No. 393, 6/10/22.
43. SCII of See Piong, No. 209, 3/6/21.
44. SCII of Yip Ah Kim, No. 177, 13/4/33.
45. Lao She, op. cit., p. 83.
46. Cuylenburg, op. cit., p. 4.
47. *Straits Echo*, 21 July 1905.
48. SCII of unknown Chinese, No. 56A, 12/4/13.
49. SCII of Low Leong, No. 399, 14/8/27.
50. Lao She, op. cit., p. 213.
51. SCII of Teng Ah Poh, No. 15, 14/1/14.
52. SCII of Chin Ah Ching, No. 397, 11/10/23.
53. Frederick Bourne, H. M. Coroner, Singapore, to Colonial Secretary, Straits Settlements, 22 January 1934, in Mss. Ind. Ocn. S. 203, Rhodes House Library, Oxford, p. 11.
54. Cuylenburg, op. cit., p. 4.
55. Annual Colonial Reports, Straits Settlements, p. 31.
56. SMAR JD, 1897, Appendix J, p. 34.
57. SCII of Teo Ah Lak, No. 135, 4/3/39.
58. SCII of Tan Nah Nai, No. 210, 14/4/38.
59. Cuylenburg, op. cit., p. 4.
60. SMAR JD, 1917, p. 8; SMAR JD, 1925, pp. 4–13; pullers continued to mount or hang the large box-shaped coconut-oil lamps on the off-side of the rickshaw where there was

usually a space for it to be attached or mounted. Ng Kar Eng explained the problem of lamp installation to Ms Tan Beng Luan of the Archives and Oral History Department in 1981: 'So that was how rickshaw lamps were mounted, is that right? No, that is where the passenger's seats were, there is no space to attach it next to where the passenger sat. So the puller attached it on the horizontal crossbar in the front, connecting the shafts. Some did it this way. You cannot attach the lamp on the other side because it is where the passenger sits.' Interview with Ng Kar Eng, AOHD, Reel 3.

61. SMAR JD, 1939, pp. 5–6.
62. SCII of Ling Kow Kay, No. 174, 1/4/27.
63. SCII of Low Yah Cheong, No. 329, 16/7/25.
64. SCII of Lee Yew Kiah, No. 151, 30/9/13.
65. SCII of Yu No Po, No. 364, 27/7/27.
66. SCII of Teo Ah Lak, No. 135, 4/3/39.
67. SCII of George Buxton, No. 28, 5/2/34.
68. SCII of Leong Lam, No. 385A, 20/10/30.
69. Ibid.
70. SCII of Choi Bok Lee, No. 192, 27/4/25.
71. SCII of Siah Goh Seng, No. 702, 1/12/28.
72. SCII of Tan Moi Kah, No. 260, 24/4/37.

17 The Spiral of Failure

THE significance of suicide in Singapore was related to all aspects of the rickshaw coolie's life, the general features of colonial urbanization and institutions, and social change in the city between 1880 and 1940.[1] Especially important was the relationship between unemployment and suicide rates due to particular social and environmental factors such as illness, poverty, bachelor life, and marriage. Suicide was an indication of the grave social effect of the economic blight of the 1920s and 1930s on rickshawmen and their families; the increased admittance to pauper institutions, hospitals and prisons, drug abuse, lost income, and the collapse of the elemental family. These factors all tended to rise in periods when rickshaw coolies were unemployed, with a cumulative effect on Chinese society as a whole, creating extreme social problems. Rickshawmen could live on less, with next to nothing in their pockets. But losing their job was catastrophic. All pullers knew that basic truth: 'There is that Taoist saying: life is a sea of suffering; turn but your head and you see the shore. Once someone asked me what the shore was. Bitter and cynical, I told him that if he bought a dollar's worth of stout rope, and hanged himself he would know.'[2] Men despaired—and killed themselves in the hard times over loss of strength and unemployment.

The suicide cases in the Coroner's Inquiries (see Appendix 9) between 1903 and 1939, more particularly those between 1921 and 1936, which are some of the worst as regards the impact of unemployment, lead to chilling conclusions. The reason behind the incidence of suicide among rickshaw coolies in recession–depression times was directly tied to loss of their jobs. About half the suicides in Appendix 9 were men 35–45 years of age, and they were overwhelmingly single. Rickshawmen, especially middle-aged ones in the 35–40 age bracket, had a strong identification with their occupation and way of life. If they lost their job through illness, or through violent injury or accident, they frequently suffered loss of personal esteem, felt they were failures in the minds of their kindred, and had nothing to live for. The decision to kill themselves seems to have been preceded by just that loss of personal self-esteem and of self-identity.[3]

The statistics on suicide in the Coroner's Inquests and Inquiries (Appendix 9) are underestimated.[4] So too are the suicide cases which appear in the Coroner's Views and Dispositions (14 out of 190 between 1906 and 1940). Most of them did not have an inquest; these deaths, to the coroners, especially by the 1930s, were intentional, and no inquiry was necessary in their mind. Apart from the means arrived at by different coroners in the way they broke the data down so well or not on suicide, there remains the related issues of under-registration, the problem of categorization and bias inherent in the figures on 'suicide', and the operational terms of the medico-legal language, like 'cause', 'intention', 'sane', 'accidental', 'homicidal', and 'death'. The extent of under-registration of suicide in Singapore among rickshaw coolies was directly affected between 1883 and 1940 by the degree of professional medical training of the coroners and subordinate staff, the number of staff and 'man-hours' available to ascertain cause of death, the current standard of public health services, and the system of categorization of suicide. Gleaning statistics from colonial administrative and medical records on suicide in order to reconstruct an accurate count is difficult, and in some respects impossible; many instances of suicide were probably ascribed to illness or accident, particularly in the case of 'unknown' pullers, while almost all attempts to attempt suicide and attempted suicides remain unrecorded. Here, however, one can only assume a constant and fixed relationship, that is, an increase in the suicide rate among pullers led to an additional number of attempted suicides.

Certain ways of committing suicide made it more difficult to determine intentional death. This seems to have been particularly so in the case of a rickshawman eating opium, injecting morphia, dying in delirium of 'fever' or falling from the heights of a tenement building. The relationship between method and the attempt to end his life is not clear here. Suicides by drug overdose, deliberately leaping from three storeys up, or slashing one's face with a razor while delirious with fever are all almost impossible to distinguish from accidents or sub-intentional deaths involving drug poisoning, accidental loss of balance as the foot slips, and disease-infectious death from 'natural' causes. Coroners by tending to classify such deaths as 'accidental', 'by misadventure', 'natural' or, in rare instances, 'open', lowered the official suicide rate for rickshawmen, but by just how much is not clear. For example, Lui Ah Lak fell from the upstairs of Chop Lok Sing Lum, an eating-house, onto North Bridge Road at the end of January 1925, but the Coroner found no evidence, despite the man having been an unemployed opium smoker who had been ill for several months, to show whether the fall was either intentional or sub-intentional (i.e. suicidal) or unintentional (i.e. accidental): the verdict was 'open'.[5]

Some rickshawmen who 'died by their own hand', in a very real sense, were not committing suicide. They were not seeking death as much as a temporary escape from the embarrassment and horror of life in Singapore:

> That is to say, they do not, in their own minds, kill themselves or seek death. Instead of fleeing into a vaguely conceptualized 'death', they behave so as to escape from aspects of life. For some the concept of death, or final cessation of

being, does not enter into their thinking. They rather indulge in either a planned or a momentarily impulsive act—and termination of life is the result.[6]

However, the actions and motives of rickshawmen in bringing about their own demise were often socially construed as 'suicidal' from things said or observed by next of kin and clansmen, rickshaw owners, and strangers. Rickshaw coolies were illiterate on the whole and did not leave evidence such as suicide notes to clarify wish and motive, and spoken testimony by the victim about his 'intentions', if rescued in time, or just before dying, was rare. In the few recorded instances where rickshawmen were actually observed in the act of attempting to kill themselves, they consciously drove off their would-be saviours. Therefore most coroners in the absence of such evidence for rickshaw coolies tended to categorize the cause of death as suicide when there was an eyewitness, when a clear motive could be inferred from inquest testimony, or as a rule of thumb when the method was unequivocal—hanging, throat-cutting, or swallowing poison.

Despite a lack of statistics to plot suicide rates accurately, the historian of society can still pinpoint the occupations in the depression-lost job-situation to which high rates of suicide were tied in Singapore. At first glance, the number of notifiable cases of suicide among rickshaw pullers in Appendix 9 would appear to be demographically insignificant, affecting only several hundred living people at most, as compared to the massive statistics available on all deaths in the Colonial Records. To make that assumption, however, would be to commit a serious fallacy of factual significance. The few cases of suicide of rickshaw coolies can reveal much about the complexities of life and its patterns and about the social problems of thousands of pullers and tens of thousands of other poor Chinese who survived them. Their deaths were merely the tip of the iceberg and, as such, epitomized the plight of other Chinese who were hurting because of colonial and municipal policies of unemployment, high death rates from infectious diseases, and the withdrawal of most funds and support for social welfare. It is the unmistakable significance of statements of those who came to inquests of death labelled 'suicide' that rise above the illusion of the writing in Singapore's colonial/nationalist historical genre with unforgettable force. These rickshaw coolies, their families, friends and enemies displayed enough human frailties to make their circumstances all the more understandable—and the unimaginable terribly believable.[7] Their deaths should make one aware of the vital distinction between colonial Singapore's 'economic miracle' of the 1930s measured in terms of the growth of international and intra-regional trade and an increasing Gross National Product, and the social costs of living with the short-run effects of such an economic policy for the majority of Chinese by the 1930s.

In most cases of suicide of rickshaw coolies there is a complex of factors concerned with being squeezed out of work by debilitating illness, grinding poverty and inability to fulfil family and filial obligations, and loss of income due to accident, bad judgement in gambling, or cost of maintaining a drug habit. The goal of these men, and the society that sent them to the *Nanyang*, was to work hard pulling a rickshaw, amass money, remit it, and come home some day with enough savings to buy a small piece of land. However, when the precarious balance between the physical strength required to pull a rickshaw and the environment was upset, a man became ill, and his work routine collapsed. In the absence of family, or perhaps even friends to support him, the stark reality of the loss of work and the failure to achieve his goal became a powerful influence for self-destruction, especially during the economic crises of the 1920s and 1930s. In Ling Ah Thui's case he knew the precipitating factor in surrendering his will to live would be the loss of his job due to recurrent illness: 'On the fifteenth of September he decided to take the rickshaw out again. And if he got sick he vowed he'd jump in the river!'[8]

The ordeal of rickshawmen on the streets, and their motivation to attempt suicide as a result of peon brutality, was pressed home to the public in the form of an anonymously scribbled 'appeal' that could be seen and understood by all. The large pictorial poster was found on a wall in Almeida Street in 1897 and consisted of three pictures: the first showed a rickshaw peon beating a coolie until blood ran out of his mouth; the second represented a rickshaw peon extorting a bribe from a puller by force and intimidation; and the third signified the sadism and apathy of the rickshaw peon, who was depicted 'arms folded, coolly watching some frenzied puller commit suicide by taking a header into what is supposed to be the sea'.[9] Such a plea signified a desperate recourse for some rickshawmen caught between the turbulent politics of owners and the Registrar with his fledgling army of peons. In seeking redress for real grievances on the streets, some despaired of all hope of vindication. It was said that there was a direct connection between the third frame of the poster and an actual incident that had occurred a short time earlier:

> ... a ricksha coolie jumped into the sea off Beach Road, and gave no end of trouble to five men before he could be got out. He was charged with attempting to commit suicide, but the magistrate held that there had only been disorderly conduct and fined him two dollars. Nothing more was heard of the matter until some unknown pictorial genius attempted in this way to make capital out of the incident.[10]

The environment and advancing age—the years between 40 and 50—forced men to act old, stripping them of their strength and role in life, with consequent loss of purpose, economic independence, and physical well-being. Ageing was an important factor in the conscious demise of some pullers. Rickshawmen with families sometimes had to retire early because they were not well. They started to lose their health and so they left the streets. They began pulling rickshaws when they were 20 and their health went at 45. The rickshaw and the city shortened their lives. Pulling back and forth, back and forth, just pulling all those years, in poverty and pain. To be a rickshaw coolie, and to be old, was to despair. Yet in some cases it is difficult to identify and explain the internal (subjective) and external (objective) factors responsible for suicide: 'The widow is my grand-daughter . . . I have no idea why he took opium. He was not ill nor in debt so far as I know. He was a very quiet man. I doubt whether he was earning enough to support himself, wife and child.'[11] Koh Kim Chwee's suicide was every bit as harrowing as the suicides decimating the bachelors in the rickshaw quarters, and the testimony in the Coroner's inquest of this particular case works to convey a horror beyond the reach of words, of the breakup of the elemental family because of one reason—poverty. The Colonial Government's lack of adequate resources to provide housing and medical care for poverty-stricken families like Koh Kim Chwee's accelerated suicidal activity within families of married rickshaw pullers.

The details in the Coroner's inquests provide information on intention, the situation in which the rickshaw coolie found himself, and the result of action. Pullers crippled by tuberculosis through years of living in lodging-houses, opium addiction, and sexually transmitted diseases, knew they would never embark at the Singapore wharves to die in their ancestral village. They had not fulfilled their dream to make a fortune. With the onset of illness and age, there was no false hope that their way of life would get better. They had already lost their great expectations. They were alone for the most part, but they did not make enough and their feverish bodies and weak hearts bore testimony to the truth of this fact. The rickshaw had provided them with a livelihood in a city where life was said to be better. It was no longer possible for Ling Ah Thui's colleague Leong Ah Keng by 1921.[12] He and other rickshawmen like him took charge of their own fate.

In examining particular cases the explanation of motives and ideas of the men, that is, their thoughts and fears, are central to understanding the phenomenon of suicide among rickshaw coolies in colonial Singapore. The meaning of a particular suicidal act was often understood by other men who were not involved if it was directly related to loss of employment. This is understandable as most pullers, including the individual who committed suicide, experienced protracted illness, and a resultant loss of self-esteem and identity. But it is only within the context of the circumstance of their everyday lives in recession–depression times under colonial rule that suicide can be understood to be a socially meaningful act, and not simply an aberration of Chinese character: 'the Chinese are without exception, when suicidal, the most persistently suicidal of any of the numerous races with whom I have had dealings'.[13] Most rickshawmen killed themselves out of a sense of hopelessness, shame, and escape from pain. The circumstances of rickshaw coolies' lives as a result of illness, loneliness, and drug addiction generally meant the men had a high suicide potentiality; the characteristics of their occupation and the situation in which they found themselves made them more lethally suicidal than most 'hard labourers'.

It is possible from the Coroner's Inquests and Views to create in minute detail a profile of the typical rickshaw-puller suicide—age, time of the year, time of day, the place and chosen means of self-destruction, and motives. Of the 19 rickshawmen listed in Appendix 9, the largest group fell between 35 and 45 years of age, the youngest was a 27-year-old opium smoker, and the oldest aged 55, whose death was due to opium poisoning, was married with family. The incidence of suicide increased as they became older. The rise in suicide among pullers over 40 was sharp, and definitely higher than in most other coolie occupations. As rickshawmen became older the chances of killing themselves increased as they realized that there was no possibility of ever owning a rickshaw, and thus they were spiralling downhill in a narrowing circle of poverty and debt, waiting for the end.

The method chosen by a puller to kill himself was rarely arbitrary, and was influenced by his age, health, the intention to want to end his conscious life quickly or by sub-conscious factors such as neglect or mismanagement in the use of opium. Most found a stout piece of rope and resorted to hanging to end their lives.[14] The extent of under-registration is evident from just this handful of cases of hanging from the Coroner's views and dispositions between 1907 and 1914 which do not appear in Appendix 9; Hong Cha Bah had been out of work for five months. He was 45 years old when he hanged himself from a beam across the doorway of his bedroom; an unknown rickshaw puller, 40 years old, was found hanging from a hinge at the back of a lodging-house at No. 54 Aliwal Street. There was an empty rickshaw directly beneath the body which had been used as a step-ladder; Hoh Monh, aged 45, had been sick for some time, and could no longer pull his rickshaw. He was found hanging at the rear of the lodging-house by his nephew's wife; Ling Kee Kee's emaciated body was found hanging from a roof beam. His friends who identified him said the 35-year-old puller had suffered from dysentery; Tan Ah Moh was also 35 when he was found dead hanging in his lodging-house in Pasir Panjang Road, by a kinsman.[15] Asphyxiation by hanging was followed by opium poisoning, swallowing liquid detergent such as caustic soda, and throat-cutting with a knife or razor. It was an unquestionable fact that the availability of opium for purchase over the counter helped rickshawmen to hasten their demise, especially if they were in great pain, suffering from pulmonary tuberculosis or the latter stages of syphilis:

> Instances are known to me where young Chinese for a slight cause have obtained a large quantity of opium, not for smoking, for they were not opium smokers, but for consumption mixed with water with the intention to commit suicide. One may be morally certain without having sufficient evidence, or desiring to obtain it, that cases of the use of opium to terminate life and suffering at the same time in diseases, such as cancer, diseases of the liver, and pulmonary tuberculosis, are not infrequent.[16]

Intentional death by opium- or morphia-swallowing was chosen because it was one of the easiest ways to suicide, and this applied to caustic soda poisoning as well.[17] In the case of suicides by throat-cutting, the deaths were often sub-intentional; only men suffering in agony and delirium could muster the will-power to horribly mutilate their body in order to bring an end to the pain, but they killed themselves.[18] Drowning was much easier. The proximity of the ocean to his lodging-house made it simple for Tan Say Tee to walk into the water to drown himself and anaesthetize the burning feeling right in his loins from venereal disease.[19] Among the scores of bloated corpses found bobbing in Singapore waters each year, or quietly rotting on the colony's sandy foreshore, were other unknown pullers, without a brother to identify them, who had failed in their bid to exchange the poverty of Chinese villages for the 'bright lights' and prosperity of the city.

The particular place of the suicide was usually the lodging-house where the puller stayed. Hanging went unobserved in the early hours of the morning—generally between midnight and 6 a.m.— in the man's cubicle or the latrine at the rear of the house. They were favourite spots because a puller, bent on killing himself, could bolt the door of the cubicle or latrine from the inside so that his act of departure could neither be witnessed nor disturbed. Men who were too sick to get up to loop a piece of rope around a beam or walk to the rear of a lodging-house waited until the *pang keng* was empty and, unnoticed, they cut their throat or swallowed poison while lying on their bunks. The distribution of these suicides by time of the year shows that the period from June to February was when many of the deaths occurred, especially in the robust period of the north-east monsoon from October onward, when it rained for days on end. Although it is difficult to establish a positive relationship between suicide rates and climate and temperature, there seems to be little doubt that the damp-dark, oven-like conditions of cubicles drove disease-ridden men, with no hope of relief or release from their lodgings, in the direction of total self-destruction.

Let us end this account of suicide among rickshaw pullers in Singapore by looking more closely at several cases illustrating the problems of the aged rickshaw coolie who rarely had children and could not always find a welcome among kinsmen and clansmen. Older men came to feel helpless and unwanted when they were removed from the struggle to make a living on the streets. They had acquired experience with the coming of age but lost the strength so vitally necessary to do their job. The loss of vigour led to a loss of personal self-esteem. Ageing, and chronic diseases associated with the ageing process, had increased importance for the rickshawman because the chronic infections and internal pains sapped his strength, seriously hampering his ability to pull a rickshaw. The puller could not be blamed. It was a function of years and change in the environment of pulling a rickshaw. Alex Gentle, the Coroner for Singapore at the turn of the century, felt that no man should pull a rickshaw after 40 years of age:

I don't think it does harm to young men, who are active and whose bones are flexible, but there are many instances, where young men make what is to them a small fortune in Singapore, go back to China, return to Singapore a little older, re-commence their former work and drop dead between the shafts . . . I think it is the nature of the work, medical men have said so. Work of this nature should not be engaged in after forty years of age. No man above forty should run a race for instance.[20]

Older rickshaw coolies who did not slow down often did collapse and die, before the decision was made to kill themselves. See Koon Ang was standing in the door of her cubicle in Rochore Canal Road and her 45-year-old Hockchia husband, Ten Chow Ting, was sitting close by when he suddenly started breathing rapidly and expired from cardiac arrest. She informed the doctor that her husband was a rickshaw coolie and 'at times [he] complained the work was too severe'. Seah Ah Kau, a 55-year-old Hengwah, was found dying and unable to speak or walk on the five-footway in Joo Chiat Road in August 1933; he had been ill for weeks and had fallen over while walking along; similarly, Ang Kee, a 58-year-old rickshawman and 'lately a vagrant', was found dead on a verandah in Church Street covered in ulcerated sores.[21]

Some dropped out of rickshaw pulling before it was too late. They became coal coolies, labourers, or pig rearers and vegetable gardeners if they smoked opium.[22] Some switched to hawking to deal with the issues of ageing, economic hardship and loneliness, but could not get right off the streets:

Chiang was past forty and figured he could not pull a rickshaw any more. So he bought a basket rig to work as a street vendor selling a complete line of goods such as fruits, melons, peanuts, and cigarettes. But after doing this for two months he made a rough accounting and found he had not only come out short but was losing a great deal! He was accustomed to pulling a rickshaw and couldn't cope with the technique of selling things. Rickshaw pulling was a matter of picking up business when you met it. It's done once you get the job and if you don't get, never mind. It takes a great skill in bargaining to be a street vendor and he didn't know how to do it. . . .[23]

Chew Ah Kow was at first a rickshaw puller, then a hawker in old age. He stopped pulling at 53 years of age and opened a small fruit stall. He gave up due to pains in his legs which were sometimes swollen from syphilis and his associated difficulty in breathing.[24] For several years Lui Ah Lak's existence appeared as precarious as Chew Ah Kow's, but in 1925 his future was never more uncertain when he was forced to stop pulling his rickshaw. He was weak, and to make a living he played a flute and sold olives along Rochore Road, until he accidentally fell or deliberately leaped to his death from the upper storey of an eating-house.[25]

Rickshawmen over 40 were no longer young and brave as a group. For the most part they were a dogged, downtrodden bunch who, despite their age and ebbing strength, still had to eke out a meagre living day by day—rain or shine. In their twenties, pullers were robust, strong. In their thirties, they were still in their prime. But by about forty rickshaw coolies were old, clinging to their rickshaws with little or no future in front of them: 'Some of those over forty have been pulling rickshaws for only eight or ten years. They begin to slow down as their muscles deteriorate. Eventually they realize that they'll take a tumble and die in the street sooner or later.'[26] Their earnings decreased with time and they became impoverished both in material and social terms. Unhappy and lonely, many an aged puller became convinced that there was nothing for an old man to look forward to in Singapore, even the thought of China was depressing, and they had hardly any social relationships with younger men. The camaraderie formerly associated with visiting brothels no longer held the same attraction it once did, not even a pipe of opium could ease the bad dreams of an ageing man. Tang Koh Chi understood why the younger men neglected him. They had come to expect, as he once did when he was young and strong, that in the rush, stress, competition and aggression of Singapore street life, few among them gave a damn about coolies who were old. He was not as physically strong as he used to be and often experienced paralysis of the legs. Gone were the inner reserves of strength he used to be able to call upon in his youth. Gone too was his ability to summon up the split-second reflex action and explosive power that the average puller never possessed in the first place. Young rickshaw pullers he used to beat running on the streets just a few years ago left him behind:

> His running ... was still more skilled than most but he no longer ran as if his life were at stake. He was particularly cautious, almost excessively cautious, when turning corners and going up and down slopes. No matter how much he was teased and provoked by someone who wanted to race with him, he would hold his head down and silently keep on running at a steady pace. He seemed to have seen through the business of rickshaw pulling. He knew it for what it was and never thought about gaining glory from it again.[27]

Tang Koh Chi feared senility, losing the last ounce of his strength and mind, and being put away in an institution like the lunatic asylum, more than he feared pulmonary tuberculosis and syphilis. He was becoming a husk of a man. He kept on hiring rickshaws because it brought him more money than hawking or pig-rearing, but inside he knew the dream of his youth was dying, as so would he shortly.

Ling Ah Thui, a 41-year-old Hockchia, also expected his final years to be dismal, not worth living. He had been extremely ill for some time with a heart disease and was unable to pull his rickshaw except every now and then.[28] He survived on the earnings from the rickshaw pulling of his two brothers, but all three were barely living above the poverty line in 1925. The pain in his heart made him shudder and weep at times. He had consulted numerous *sinseh* but could find no cure. Ling Ah Thui was becoming old, and he resented it. He had lost most of his physical strength due to illness, and once he was strong and enjoyed doing the hard work of pulling a rickshaw. He was not used to the loss of strength and objected when the task of pulling a rickshaw showed that it was now beyond him. Ling Ah Thui could not quite believe that he could no longer carry a passenger a few blocks, accelerate and turn quickly at a broad junction, or even hold the rickshaw steady on a slow uphill climb. He was physically unfit and had psychological problems. There was no young part of him left, and he allowed himself to be depressed in the absence of his brothers pulling rickshaws on 29 December 1924. He remembered one of his brothers once reciting a Taoist saying, and it had stuck in the back of his mind: 'Life is a sea of suffering; turn but your head and you see the shore.' Ling Ah Thui got up from his bunk and slowly walked towards the latrine at the rear of the tenement. He stood on a stool and tied a stout rope to an old rickshaw wheel, the symbol of motion in his life and work, that had been stored above a beam across the top of the latrine. He then hanged himself in the lodging-house at No. 2 Angullia Road in colonial Singapore where the poor coolie could get rich, the rich *towkay* got richer, and the dream of Ling Ah Thui and his band of brothers comes true—not any more.

1. On the study of suicide see Emile Durkheim, *Suicide: A Study in Sociology* (Glencoe: Illinois Free Press, 1951); Maurice Halbwacks, *Les Causes du Suicide* (Paris: Alcan, 1930); Jack D. Douglas, *The Social Meanings of Suicide* (Princeton: Princeton University Press, 1967); Paul Bohannan (ed.), *African Homicide and Suicide* (Princeton: Princeton University Press, 1960); Richard Cobb, *Death in Paris 1795–1801* (London: Oxford University Press, 1978).

2. Low Ngiong Ing, *Chinese Jetsam on a Tropical Shore* (Singapore: Eastern Universities Press, 1974), p. 46.

3. Norman L. Farberow, 'Suicide: Psychological Aspects (2)', *International Encyclopedia of Social Science* (New York: Macmillan and Free Press, 1968), p. 393.

4. There is a large gap between 1908 and 1917 in the inquests. Some of the suicide cases of rickshawmen in that period show up in the views and dispositions but no inquest seems to have been held as the coroners felt they were clear cases of suicide.

5. SCII of Lui Ah Lak, No. 56, 29/1/25.

6. Farberow, 'Suicide: Psychological Aspects (1)', *International Encyclopedia of Social Science* (New York: Macmillan and Free Press, 1968), p. 386.

7. Plotting suicide rates accurately for Singapore's working class is especially difficult because in the early returns of disease and deaths in the government annual reports the figures were often calculated for all the Straits Settlements. However, the annual Police Reports do give a breakdown of the total number of recorded suicides accomplished and attempted by the 1920s, which, for example, rose from 91 accomplished in 1925 to 150 in the Depression-ridden Singapore of 1932. Under causes of death in the Straits Settlements Municipal Reports, a breakdown of statistics is also provided on the means of suicide from the turn of the century onwards. Macro-statistical information is also given on an annual basis for the number of deaths by suicide in the Criminal Prison and the Lunatic Asylum. However, vital micro-statistical data on age, sex, ethnicity, occupation, residential patterns, and identity is not available on a continual serial basis in these colonial records. On the historiographical significance of the statements of the next of kin and others called to an inquest see Cobb, op. cit., p. 102.

8. Lao She, *Rickshaw* (the novel *Lo-T'o Hsiang Tzu*), translated by Jean M. James (Honolulu: The University Press of Hawaii, 1979), p. 186.

9. *Singapore Free Press*, 11 January 1897.

10. Ibid.
11. SCII of Koh Kim Chwee, No. 677, 23/11/32.
12. SCII of Leong Ah Keng, No. 459, 1/11/21.
13. SSAR, Annual Medical Report on the Civil Hospitals, 1896, p. 552.
14. For details of cases of suicide by hanging due to illness see CCVS of Choo Tang Giok, No. 67, 31/10/08; and SCII of Wee Cheng, No. 231, 3/10/17; of Goh Ah Toh, No. 223, 7/6/22; and of Geok Lan, No. 328, 3/17/29.
15. CCVS of Hong Cha Bah, No. 7, 4/9/14; of an unknown Chinese, 2/2/14; of Hoh Monh, No. 133, 23/5/08; of Ling Kee Kee, No. 45, 25/5/07; and of Tan Ah Moh, No. 22, 12/12/13.
16. Memorandum of Dr R. M. Connolly, BMOC, Appendix LXXIII, p. 8116.
17. For details of cases of suicide by opium swallowing or the use of caustic soda due to venereal disease and opium addiction see SCII of Tan Chwee Chwee, No. 318, 10/7/25; of Ching Ah Hoot, No. 703, 23/12/35; of Koh Kim Chwee, No. 677, 23/11/32.
18. See SCII of Lui Ah Pek, No. 165, 18/9/08; of Lim Choon Huat, No. 664, 15/11/32; of Yau Chin Swee, No. 236, 26/6/24.
19. SCII of Tan Say Tee, No. 115, 23/9/03.
20. Evidence of Alex Gentle, SSOC, p. 325.
21. CCVS of Ten Chow Ting, No. 36, 25/9/18; of Seah Ah Kau, 10/8/33.
22. Evidence of Mr Goodlands, SSOC, p. 31.
23. Lao She, op. cit., p. 165.
24. SCII of Chew Ah Kow, No. 86, 14/2/38.
25. SCII of Lui Ah Lak, No. 56, 29/1/25.
26. Lao She, op. cit., p. 2.
27. Ibid., p. 201.
28. SCII of Ling Ah Thui, No. 516, 30/12/24.

Conclusion: Towards a People's History

THIS book has attempted to integrate the history of experience of rickshaw coolies into the larger history of Singapore in the period 1880–1940. These were decisive years. They witnessed the extraordinary economic development of vast potential for tin, rubber, oil palm and tobacco in the Malay peninsula and on the east coast of Sumatra under colonial rule, and the evolution of Singapore as a 'coolie town', with a colonial administrative heart and an entrepôt port, with the birth of the rickshaw and a stream of emigrants from China who poured in faster and faster to pull it. This floodtide of *singkeh* came to Singapore with the hope of forming a foundation for a new and prosperous life. Expanding Singapore, especially at this stage of its growth toward the end of the nineteenth century, was often considered by the migrants as a place of hope and betterment. There were in Singapore, tens of thousands of Cantonese, Hengwah, Hockchia and Foochow sojourners who hoped to find a pipeline to prosperity since the 1880s, when dire poverty and overpopulation plagued South-east China.

When *singkeh* decided to migrate to Singapore they were organized locally in terms of native-place ties which ranged from sub-county townships to groupings of provinces and/or speech groups in China. The kinship-centric nature of rickshaw pulling—how coolies closed the kin/non-kin gap by expanding fictive kinship roles outward to include friends, neighbours, and employers—shows up plainly in the use of the Coroner's evidence. This quantitative exposition is crucial too in identifying demographically and by occupation the immigrants and their place of origin.

On occasion they suffered considerable hardship on board sailing junks and tramp steamers in passage to the *Nanyang*. Upon arrival in Singapore, the newcomers joined forces within regionally-based ethnic and sub-ethnic groups to carve out an economic niche for themselves. Initially secret societies and later on speech groups sought to protect the monopolies of particular sub-communal groups in various trades and occupations, such as the Hengwah, Hockchia and Foochow in rickshaw pulling. The role that the societies and voluntary associations played in economic and social relations among rickshaw coolies was crucial. Their primary function was to provide financial assistance, social welfare and security for their members. In Singapore solidarity among rickshaw pullers was forged on the anvil of the society they knew in China. Native-place particularism and a network of voluntary associations helped to attract sojourners into Singapore, where through these associations they maintained special ties with the homeland as kinsmen and clansmen, and pursued special occupational interests like rickshaw pulling. The life of Singapore's rickshaw coolies as migrant labourers grew out of the expanding relationship between kinship or affinity and rent capital and labour.[1]

The Hengwah and Hockchia rickshaw coolies knew what they wanted. To begin with, facing poverty and deprivation in their own country, these *singkeh* had left their families behind in villages, counties, and prefectures in Fukien and Kwangtung provinces. Significantly, they had their own 'ambition', and some were given the strength of a bull and possibly a long life to use it. Their sole goal in migrating to all corners of the earth, especially to the promised city of Singapore, was to make money, and then return home to buy land and build a house. A beautiful dream, but one with a difference—Singapore offered the same hardships as rural China but with the promise of a future. The sojourners knew without such hope their life was not worth living at all. They seized the opportunity, and did the hard work of rickshaw pulling as the contraptions proved instantly popular, becoming an integral part of Singapore's history and of its society, economy, and life. The sojourning dream gave them physical strength and a sense of purpose, it encouraged them, they felt pulling rickshaws was a quick way of realizing their ambition. But in reality it was not as simple as that, their expectations were rarely if ever realized. On the contrary, rickshaw coolies often were proven to be wrong, very wrong. Rickshaw pulling was a menial, hazardous occupation, and a coolie's personal and economic well-being inevitably rested on a combination of factors including the attitude of the rickshaw owner, the state of a puller's health and standard of living, interference of relevant authorities, for example, a Malay peon's extortion of a rickshawman, and administrative and transport policy for the city.

The city was changing in the 1880s. Chinatown was fast on its way to having a population of several hundred thousand bachelor workers and destined to be called 'bullock cart water' in dialect—a filthy booming coolie town. The character of its transport and pattern of traffic also began to change. Motor cars and buses did not exist yet, and carriages drawn by high-stepping Java ponies and horses filled the streets. Most people walked. In 1880, a large consignment of Japanese manufactured rickshaws—'man-powered carriages'—made an impact on the then dominant mode of transport, horse carriage, and quickly became the popular means of transportation. Within the short space of five years, thousands of rickshaws were engaged day and night, negotiating the narrow backlanes of Chinatown or carrying goods short distances around the wholesale markets.

Ownership of rickshaws was normally separate from their operation. Most rickshaw coolies did not own their own vehicles. There were several types of rickshaw businesses. They usually operated in restricted areas of the city with a particularistically defined rental policy towards various sub-communal groups. Owners were sometimes *towkay*, small-time rent capitalists, such as shopkeepers and lodging-house proprietors, who kept and maintained several rickshaws as a side investment. *Singkeh* often just off the boat from China, who relied on their own strength, rented them on day and night shifts; each shift was 10 cents, which later increased to 30 cents by 1916. Another category of rickshaw business was half ownership–half operator, in other words, the puller owned the rickshaw and rented it out, usually to kin, when he was not using it. These rickshawmen were rarely encountered on the streets, though, as they were the exception, the cost of ownership ($160 for a new one in 1917) was prohibitive and most could not hope to save the sum necessary to become an owner. Frequently after a lifetime of trying to save to buy their own vehicle, coolies still had insufficient capital to settle their daily expenses and debts, let alone purchase a second-hand one. By far the most important category was the rickshaw entrepreneurs. They accounted for the vast majority of rickshaws that thronged the streets of Singapore. These individuals, who frequently owned between 30 and 50 rickshaws, derived their income from a monopoly of ownership and rentals. All their rickshaws were rented out to pullers. In some instances they did not restrict renting only to coolies of the same ethnic group; as long as members of other communities who wanted to ply for hire were considered trustworthy, the rickshaws were hired out.

Rickshaw fares were cheap. For a journey up to one mile the charge was 6 cents in 1897. The set fares were gazetted by the Rickshaw Department, but in fact, any distance was negotiable; bargaining went on between passenger and puller, and fares ranged from a few cents up according to distance, time of day, and weather. However, it was not unusual at the end of a journey for inexperienced pullers or those lacking in cunning to be either caught in a wrangle over the fare or be bilked.

A rickshaw coolie's daily earnings, after paying for the rental, netted 30–40 cents at the turn of the century. At that time basic commodities were cheap and with few wants, a rickshawman still had money left over to remit to kin in China. But among opium addicts, one could not find one in ten who still had cash left. Wee Choon Beok earned a daily income of $1, and tried to feed a family of three. After rent and food bills there was little left to take care of the family's needs. By the 1920s, government legislation freezing the wage of rickshaw pullers and soaring inflation, taken together, had affected the rickshaw coolies, particularly those with families, to an appreciable extent. Accommodation, rice, and staples such as salted vegetables and cooking oil were almost beyond their means.

In order not to mortgage their dreams and land in debt bachelors accepted a low standard of living and depended upon kin and clansmen. They shared rented rooms in filthy overcrowded tenements from landlords who, in many instances, were primarily rickshaw owners besides being proprietors of coolie lodges. In this cramped housing lived many pullers. Each had only a wooden bunk, or a bit of space on the floor; the rooms were extremely stark—dark, poorly ventilated, and unhygienic. The pattern of earnings and poverty was complex because it rested not only on what rickshaw coolies were paid, but also on personal circumstances. Whether they were married, the amount of rent, the number of children, the extent of opium addiction were all factors that determined if a man could manage on his income. By the late 1920s the hard facts on wages and living conditions were grim—food and rent for the rickshaw accounted for almost three-quarters of all that the poorest pullers spent daily, and food meant mostly rice and vegetables. As income continued to decline during the 1930s, so pullers ate less, and they ate worse, living on credit. Health worsened and debts mounted.

The men returned to China on an average of once every six to ten years with savings, to visit families, be reunited for a short period, perhaps take a bride, and then return to the *Nanyang* empty-handed to start again from scratch, pulling rickshaws in Singapore. Of course there were rickshawmen who worked extremely hard to make a living, whose wants were few and tastes inexpensive. They slowly accumulated the capital to become rickshaw owners or opened shops in the rickshaw trade. Today, some Hengwah descendants of this group, after several generations, are quite wealthy.

Rickshaws were the pride of the road at the turn of the century. By 1924 the actual number of rickshaws active was estimated at 28,800. An inexpensive and convenient mode of transport around town, it was patronized by people from all walks of life including schoolchildren, shoppers, hawkers, prostitutes, colonial officials and the indigent. Tourists relished the thrill of riding in such an exotic contraption, and the opportunity to see some interesting parts of town, with a better view than from the back seat of a carriage or taxi. A hard and garrulous lot, rickshaw pullers were adept at moving through heavy traffic. They also knew almost every alley and side-lane in their territory like the backs of their hands. Rickshaws were the principal public conveyance Singaporeans resorted to in moving themselves and their goods from place to place. Old photographs show that one could always expect to find scores of rickshaws around luxury hotels, major market-places, and the business district, catering to tourists, would-be shoppers, and *towkay*. They all turned to the rickshaw coolies, who sat idly by dressed in their bleached blue cottons and coarse straw hats—chatting, smoking, dozing—whenever they wanted a ride somewhere or to dispatch goods. During the monsoon rickshawmen endured driving downpours to provide trusted passage to and from schools, markets and hospitals; pullers had little protection against torrential rain. Their conical-shaped hats, so ideal for shielding their heads against the sun, were woefully inadequate against tropical wind and rain. Business was always brisk at this time of the year and in the commuter's mind the importance of rickshaws rose during floods. In such foul weather a rickshawman putting his back to the wheel was apt to charge more and get it too, as he sloshed his way right across Chinatown and back again in ankle-deep water.

The rapid increase in the number of motor vehicles after 1918 saw the puller gradually lose his traditional patronage. Fleets of buses running on regular schedules became a cheap dependable mode of transport, and an implacable competitor and foe. Motor vehicles became the bane of coolies as they padded along in the 'slow' lane on the left side of the road. Fast-moving motorists tended to drive where they pleased, dominating the centre, swerving to the sides, honking their horns quite oblivious of the presence of rickshaws. The traffic accident situation was perhaps most dangerous at night when a driver was apt to be drunk, the puller tired and lacking his usual traffic sense, and the lights of his rickshaw almost out. It was the coolies' responsibility to carry oil to power the lamps; few did this. The lucky ones who survived cursed their misfortune as a motor car surged out of the pitch dark to accidentally smash into the back or side of their rickshaw. The tragic condition of rickshaw pullers on the streets of Singapore can be seen from the number of fatal and near-fatal traffic accidents registered in the statistics of the Coroner's Court. The record of accidents amply affirms that rickshaw pulling was no simple matter by the 1920s; it was constantly open to risk of life and limb, especially if the bridge was narrow, the slope steep, or the traffic congested.

The rickshaw business that spread out over Singapore in the 1880s was unregulated. The government logic of 1892 in blaming rickshaws for traffic congestion was essentially correct. No matter how great the social need for rickshaws, the burgeoning industry had to be cleaned up, and the future of the trade as a whole reviewed. Obviously, higher numbers of rickshaws were justified in view of the city's unprecedented growth, but they could not be permitted to operate in an unregulated manner. This concern led to the formation of the Rickshaw Department under Mr Hooper in 1892. Legislation was enacted requiring the owners to renew licences every four months and produce their rickshaws in a good state of repair. Further the law directed that for certain street offences the owners were liable to have their licences suspended. The pullers were unlicensed and were not susceptible to punishment by the Registrar; the owners, much to their chagrin, being responsible for their conduct. The strike of 1897 occurred because of incessant pressure being exerted on vested interests of the Hockchew and Hengwah owners, who resided on the north side of the river in the neighbourhood of Victoria Street, Queen Street, and Rochore Road, to comply with the new regulations. The conspicuously bad quality and condition of the vehicles and their obstinate refusals to abide by the new laws led them to pull their rickshaws off the streets. The strike or 'lock out' was carefully planned and well orchestrated. The coolies, who were under strict orders from their *towkay*, refused to go out and ply for hire. The police prevented any serious damage being done by the more than 15,000 pullers out of employment, some of whom attempted to riot. The principal organizers were promptly deported. At the same time the rickshaw owners were invited to explain their grievances to a Committee of Commissioners. The report of the Committee contained much useful information on the subject of the rickshaw trade and rickshaw traffic and the working of the Ordinance of 1892, under which it was regulated and controlled.

The law did not put a ceiling on the number of rickshaws that could be licensed. In 1902 the number of licensed vehicles had risen to 22,629. Rickshaw pullers who crawled about and were ignorant of the rules of the road were dangerous, the government argued, and thus had to be removed from the streets which were jammed. On short notice, and at the personal behest of the Governor, the police started a drive against rickshaw pullers and owners. The movement of careless pullers in the main streets like North Bridge Road and South Bridge Road was banned to avoid traffic snarl-ups and accidents. This heavy handed action on behalf of traffic reform led to another strike by the owners. It was destined to fail. To demonstrate against the Government at the time was like 'throwing an egg against a rock'.[2] In the end, the major Hengwah instigator was deported for three years. During the first ten years of the working of the Ordinance the need for amendments became ever more apparent. The existing laws and regulations were ill-designed to cover offences of the puller. It seemed extraordinary to them that the strike led to the establishment of a Special Magistrate's Court under the Registrar's jurisdiction to deal specifically with offences of pullers. The amended Ordinance permitted the Registrar to levy fines ranging from 20 cents to several dollars on rickshaw coolies for interfering with traffic or loitering and causing obstruction; a law which also provided regulations against pullers covering physical condition, manner of dress, carriage of goods, right to step outside the shafts, and 'sundry offences'. Now it was left to the Registrar's discretion whether to increase the suspension time of rickshawmen who broke the rules. The Department's stipulation that rickshaws should be repaired every four months and new parts installed, otherwise they would be impounded or even destroyed, led to bankruptcy for some owners–operators as they were dispossessed of the means of their livelihood.

Worse than the threat of confiscation and destruction was the formation of a Malay traffic squad to implement the amended Act. It was this force added to the Registrar's well-stocked arsenal provided by the 'law' that made pullers feel isolated and powerless on the street. The Malay peons acted vigorously against men unfamiliar with the traffic rules. Limitations on the movement of rickshaw coolies in certain parts of the city was enforced. The advent of the Rickshaw Court saw peon exploitation and brutality. Shocking conduct of peons towards pullers, who were considered to be at the bottom of the heap, included graft and personal assault. They not only harassed ignorant and frightened coolies but also those familiar with the regulations and aware of their duties and rights. From a fiscal standpoint it was calculating to single out rickshaws as the sole target of the nit-picking traffic reforms of Mr Hooper's Court.

The tens of thousands of annual offenders, some of whom did not always get off with a light fine, made a major contribution to the Rickshaw Department's coffers every year.

By 1920 inflation, the unequal distribution of wealth and power, and the advent of a large-scale motorized transport system combined against the pullers' livelihood with a vengeance. The experience of the rickshaw pullers was in the inter-war years one of confrontation with the government and rickshaw owners, then 'temporary peace' through mediation and settlement, then resistance and strikes. The cycle repeated itself several times before culminating in the coolies' display of solidarity in the strike of 1938 when the authorities and owners sought to end their way of life. By the mid-1920s officials believed that rickshaws were an uneconomical, slow and hazardous mode of conveyance, and that they would ultimately have to go to improve the flow of public transport. From this time on the city's roads were restricted to motorized transport. The official argument was that rickshaws were slow-moving and snarled the flow of other vehicles. Thus, to free Singapore's public transport from traffic congestion restrictions on rickshaws had to be introduced. The rationale was all wrong. The plain fact was that the rickshaws were far more manoeuvrable in congested traffic than any other motor vehicle, rarely broke down like trams and buses, and handled most of the short-distance trips on small streets and alley-ways off the main roads where motorized public transport could not penetrate. There were no similar restrictions in these years on private cars and taxis despite an appalling increase in motor vehicle traffic accidents. The planners were not to be deterred. The systematic removal of rickshaws as 'slow-moving vehicles' began in 1928, but it did not improve the traffic situation on the main roads. From this time onward the future of the rickshaw coolie was bleak. The Rickshaw Department began to withdraw licences while at the same time neither issuing new ones nor renewing expired ones. This sudden removal of thousands of rickshaws and the services they provided caused disruption among those living at the lowest income levels, who had to count every cent, for there was no alternative system of transport except to walk.

For the rickshaw pullers the cuts over the next five years meant unemployment, reduced incomes, or being forced to return to the rural poverty and unrest of South-east China. On several occasions government officials had publicly stated that they would prefer to remove rickshaws from Singapore streets completely. Singapore's urban expansion continued in face of the world Depression. Urban planners believed that the march of progress was inexorable, that the antiquated rickshaw had to make way for modern motorized transport. The Government restricted their numbers to a licence quota of 4,000 and banned their movements in certain parts of the city. Social reformers joined in urging a ban on rickshaws for humanitarian reasons, but this would remove 90 per cent of the transport used by poorer Singaporeans. The rickshaw pullers and the users—schoolchildren, invalids, the elderly and commuters for whom rickshaws were an essential service—were hurt badly.

The rickshaw puller's future had been threatened before by owners, government officials, and planners, but now they were fighting for survival. As more rickshaws were pulled off the streets in an effort to restrict their numbers, the owners raised the rental fee. In 1938 a life and death struggle with the owners erupted over the rental fee and manipulation of the puller's contribution to the China Relief Fund to assist their countrymen who were in 'deep water and scorching fire'.[3] When the wage demands of the pullers were not met they closed ranks, demonstrating against owners, smashing their rickshaws. Their demand was simple: the right to continue doing what had become a way of life for them. The Government had not made a proper assessment of the social and economic impact of the plan to ban rickshaws. Their show of strength against the owners forced the Government to intervene. Thousands of rickshaws were impounded to prevent their wanton destruction as officials attempted to mediate the dispute. The results were a failure. The pullers refused to be silenced, but were made destitute and hungry as the strike dragged on for weeks on end. The Government and owners hoped to starve the pullers into submission by buying time. Hundreds of men, sensing the Government's total lack of sympathy, and hungry with families to feed, disappeared back to their villages in China with assisted passage. Rickshawmen who stayed behind were unable to enlist the support of other hard labourers with similar trade union demands and after six weeks the strike collapsed. The abolition of the rickshaw did inconvenience Singaporeans at the bottom end of the social scale, but the Government felt its departure would not greatly affect the majority. On the eve of the fall of Singapore the pragmatic interests of the owners and city planners had triumphed; the era of the rickshaw was at an end.

Rickshaw Coolie is a work that forces us to visit Singapore when life was hard for the sojourner at both ends of the migration process. The book moves to the rhythm of what was normal, describing the patterns and social networks of day-to-day life among the rickshaw coolies of Singapore. As a history of overseas Chinese work and industry it examines relations of the quality of life and quantity of work upon which the rickshaw puller was so dependent. From a unity of collective experience of individual rickshaw coolies flesh-and-bone characters emerge, events take shape over time paralleling their lives, and in doing so the narrative crosses the boundaries between life and work, kinship and culture, and politics and place in a Chinese city outside China. To move into this world meant discovering the humble facts and trivia of material life in the history of a Singapore which has largely disappeared. Such evidence was absolutely crucial for reconstructing the meaning of what it meant to be an impoverished teenager when a *singkeh* came to Singapore without skills or education, and to have no choice but to use one's strength to follow in the footsteps of thousands of others. The microsociological approach which hinges on building up layer upon layer of fully reliable detail has allowed this writer to provide an account of the process of learning to pull a rickshaw on the pavements of Singapore, and an ethnographic image of what actually happened to an overseas Chinese people in a particular time and place; we learn about what pullers routinely ate, how they dressed, the range of experience of their women and families, and of that flicker of a dream of owning a rickshaw, and letting days work into weeks and weeks into years with loneliness, hunger, sickness, old age and death following them—the evidence of one's eyes and heart that cannot be disregarded.

Terms such as 'History from below' and 'History of the inarticulate' have been used by historians to describe this approach to history writing. The structure of experience is discernible, but the historian must search for it in Singapore's past through the lens of a microscope. Historiographically, the danger lurks in relying solely on the telescope, the traditional method of historical inquiry, to discover, record and analyse the history of the underside of this cosmos. To be traditionally minded means that important elements in the cosmos of culture of rickshaw coolies, that have remained distantly remote or hidden from history, will be passed over or missed completely. To write about an occupation, workplace and life as lived, the social historian must devote attention to the concrete and specific, using the techniques of micro-sociology to see the past before him with new eyes. Scanning the puller's universe at point blank range allows the historian to explore a whole variety of contexts and key turning points in their lives. This technique provides a microscopic view, a window onto the world of the pullers' history and society in Singapore, and a rich source of detailed material to map out intensively the economic setting, urban terrain, specific character of rickshaw pulling, and acute sense of the complexity and variety of the rickshawmen's experiences.

It is this direct experience from the evidence of the Coroner's Records, oral testimony, photographs and social description of literature which enables us to learn about attitudes, the emotional reach and intensity of single events, and what was done as a rickshaw coolie's whole life, themes and incidents become interwoven with other aspects of the recent history of Singapore. We can, for instance, evoke an atmosphere of a city that was quietly devastating—the pullers' fear of being assaulted or hit and run over by a motor car in the pitch dark, of an elderly man's craving and not having money to purchase *chandu*, of dying in an empty cubicle or back lane as a 'vagrant' or 'unknown Chinese'; the chilling incongruities of wealthy tourists dancing in the Raffles at the height of the Depression while the pullers hovered about outside in the grip of misfortune, the rotten stench of sewage, the horrors of tenements, and the mortuaries piled with bodies of cholera victims. By portraying with great thoroughness, the changing character of the pullers' livelihood, the causes and impact of poverty in their economy and lives, and the nature of their interaction with the growth and change of the city, this approach and evidence provides the framework for a new kind of history of Singapore. A people's history focuses on the relationship between the rickshaw coolies and their patterns of individual behaviour and decisions, and on the macro-social, which examines the relationship between rickshaw pulling as an occupation, and certain urban characteristics of an all-encompassing city experiencing a whirlwind of change. This study of the rickshawmen shows at first hand what was happening in the structure of Singapore society as a whole. A powerful sense of the character of Singapore is conveyed. The economic growth of Singapore under colonial rule did not exist for them. For the rickshawmen in the 1920s especially, the setting was a city in decay. Singapore had one of the highest growth rates, but also one of the highest death rates and some of the worst health conditions and housing of any city of comparable size in Asia. Rickshawmen and their families suffered accidents and the violence of congested areas or sudden attacks of illness while living in the slums of a Coolie town. Most of them experienced loss of human dignity because of this social and physical environment and the reluctance of the authorities to change all this. Examination of the major sequential decisions made by the Colonial Government of Singapore in regard to housing, water supply, waste disposal and sewerage from the 1880s to the 1930s, shows that the city's rulers consistently chose alternatives that minimized costs at the expense of the coolie population. The tragedy was that these policies made the rickshawmen and their families vulnerable to disease, and left the pullers with very ill kin with the only option of standing helplessly and hopelessly by. They were aware that their medical problems were not just disease, but due to the social and physical environment of the city and the government policies that undermined their well-being. They felt the need to change things, but their failure to do so led some of them to lives which gave their kinsmen and clansmen anxiety. They quarrelled over rent, contracted tuberculosis or syphilis, or gambled away their savings. They cried out in anger and shame as the vision that was planted in China swept them up and spat them out, as circumstances drove them to the point of suicide.

Generalizations can be made about the nature of wider Singapore urban history and society. It is this methodological approach of linking detailed research of a local situation to wider issues of social history and theory in South-East Asia, with particular reference to 'experience', which underpins this work. Thus, an examination of the structure of life of rickshaw coolies at the micro-social level challenges certain generalizations which have been made about the nature of the urban evolution and history of Singapore. In addition, the long historical period of sixty years, from 1880 to 1940, reveals ways in which migration, economic transformation, population growth, colonial administration and influence, and labour were all reflected in the 'microcosm' of the experience of the rickshawmen.

History is a society's memory of its past. Therefore the historical concerns of *Rickshaw Coolie* are the concerns of Singapore society in the present. Lee Kwan Yew has said, 'To understand the present and anticipate the future, one must know enough of the past, enough to have a sense of a history of a people.'[4] This isn't nostalgia for the past. Today, the reclamation of heritage in Singapore has an urgency that is narcotic. Oral recollections and memories of rural forebears from southern Fukien and Kwangtung who were neither famous nor influential, and lived through the hardest times for Chinese in Singapore, are fast disappearing. In order to preserve and foster a sense of Singapore's past the Government has established an Oral History Department. Over the past several years this department has also organized a series of photographic exhibitions for Singaporeans to glimpse the past of Chinatown in its heyday. Pictorial books and albums about Singapore's history have become suddenly popular as the built-up history of the landscape sinks without a trace in the face of modern business and real estate demands.

The current of history has been remorseless, unswervingly deaf to persuasion when it has come to finding a place for rickshaw coolies and other hard labourers in Singapore's past. Their predominant presence in this past is all the more ironic as the rickshaw coolies appeared in the background of nearly every photograph or pictorial postcard in their time, yet in a very real sense remained 'hidden', invisible to the naked eye but not the camera. Except in old photographs and pictures of Singapore there are no further traces of rickshaws on the streets. Nor is there a rickshaw to be found in the possession of the National Museum. Now all that remains are the memories of what a few elderly rickshaw pullers have been through since coming from China and what they have endured in Singapore. In Westminster Abbey and in front of Victoria Memorial Hall in Singapore there are statues of Sir Stamford Raffles, and memorials have been built in the city to celebrate the memories and careers of successful Chinese *towkay*. But there is no monument, day of remembrance, commemorative stamp, or biography for such old men to reveal what they had done, and where they had worked. A surreal irony of Singapore history and history writing is that, the *singkeh* coolies are national—although still anonymous—heroes.

Today Singapore has another culture. It is far more cosmopolitan with consumer tastes and an educational system influenced by what is current in the West. The descendants of the rickshaw coolies belong to a radically different world from the Singapore of their grandfather's life and experience—a modern city-state, with an economy predicted on transnational capital, regional service, and trade. *Rickshaw Coolie* cannot give Singapore back what has been. But the book does describe the role that rickshaws and rickshaw coolies played in Singapore's history and the marginalized lives the pullers led. They can no longer be relegated to the back and side of the stage of Singapore history. Nor can they be seen as only the foundation of the stage. Now the experience, words and their voices come back to us—eighty or more years later—as their descendants in our time write a different epitaph on their past and life. *Rickshaw Coolie* is a means of looking at the future by reappraising the whole idea of Singapore history and its purpose. This book has tried to bring back to Singapore's own Chinese people and society, a *singkeh* coolie culture and history, which is, finally, their own—a People's History.

1. Maurice Freedman, *The Study of Chinese Society. Essays by Maurice Freedman* (Stanford: Stanford University Press, 1979), p. 243.

2. *The Heng Wah People and Their Development in Various Transport Trades* (Team project, History Department, Nanyang University, 1970–1), p. 38.

3. Ibid., p. 39.

4. *Singapore Retrospect through Postcards: 1900–1930* (Singapore: Sin Chew Jit Poh: Archives and Oral History Department, 1982), p. 7.

Appendices

APPENDIX 1

Rickshaw Owners

Name	*Sub-ethnic Group*	*No. and Street of Residence*	*No. of Rickshaws*	*Rate of Rickshaw Rental*	*Residence – Rickshaw Lodging*	*Inquest No.*	*Year*
Goh Chwee Kaye		86 Bencoolen Street	28 registered	10 cents	Yes	95	1902
Tay Choon	Hockchia	380 Victoria Street	14 registered	11 cents	Yes	116	1902
Quan Lock		248 Victoria Street				144	1902
Ling Hee Lye		19 Johore Road	1 registered		Yes	53	1907
Tan Ah Keong		43 Bain Street			Yes	241	1909
Leow Choon Seng		15 Angullia Road				170	1910
Chai Kit Leng	Hokkien	40 Park Road			Yes	233	1911
Koh Teng Hai	Hokkien	148 Queen Street	1 registered			170	1912
Lim Chong Chong	Foochow	102 Queen Street			Yes	56	1913
Tang Neo Kong	Teochiu	21 Omar Road				59	1913
Chee Kee Teng	Hockchew	51 Johore Road	7 registered		Yes	343	1918
Ho Seong		79 Duxton Road				137	1919
Tay Lian	Hengwah	56 Rochore Canal Road				46	1920
Ong Ee		85 Bencoolen Street			Yes	281	1920
Tee Tye	Hengwah	113 Middle Road			Yes	18	1921
Cheah Pin Soo (F)	Hokkien	Park Road			Yes	297	1923
Teng Ah Poon		72 Rochore Canal Road				397	1923
Tan Kin		14 Angullia Road				233	1924
Ho Ah Tak	Cantonese	14 Erskine Road			Yes	53	1925
Toy Kin Lian	Hengwah	56 Rochore Canal Road				183	1925
Ng Chi	Hengwah	111 Arab Street	1 registered			400	1926

Seah Ang Chang	Hokkien	5 Chetty Road		Yes	174	1927
Wong Song Song	Hockchia	147 New Market Road	14 registered	Yes	263	1929
Yeo Chong	Hokkien	249 Victoria Street		Yes	328	1929
Lim Swee Hin	Hokkien	14 Angullia Road		Yes	38	1930
Ling Kee Tou	Hockchia	151 New Market Road			309	1930
Poey Hiong Tey	Hockchia	158 New Market Road	12 registered		309	1930
Kuah Swee Kim	Hokkien	55 Sago Lane			385A	1930
Ho Kee Leong	Hokkien	22 Choon Guan Street	41 registered		231	1931
Ng Chong	Hokkien	22 Choon Guan Street			231	1931
Ling King Chew	Hockchia	13 Pitt Street		Yes	606	1931
Lim Ah Phong	Hockcha	2 Angullia Road	11 registered		220	1934
Seak Gin Gin	Hockchew	133 New Market Road	Many rickshaws		505	1934
Ng Ah Chan	Hengwah	6 Weld Road	2 registered		551	1934
Tan Pui Tin	Hockchia	23 Holloway Road			205	1936
Ch'ng Tian	Hokkien	35 Duxton Road			530	1937
Yeong Song Huay	Hockchia	54 Maude Road		Yes	88	1938
Tin Ah Soi	Hockchia	157 New Market Road			210	1938
Chor Kow Ern	Hengwah	1 Chitty Road			135	1939
Lim Nee Thong	Teochiu	23 Fisher Street	10 registered	Yes	491	1924

APPENDIX 2

Rickshaw Coolies: Kinship And Occupation

Name of Deceased Rickshaw Puller	*Age*	*Sub-ethnic Group*	*No. and Street of Residence*	*Name of Person who Identified the Deceased*	*Relation to Deceased*	*Occupation*	*Place of Residence*	*Inquest No.*	*Year*
Tan Sam Ong	20/25	Chawan	Mackenzie Road	Goh Chwee Kaye	None	Rickshaw owner	86 Bencoolen Street	95	1902
Ong Oh Kaw	About 28	Hockchia	380 Victoria Street	Ong Ah Chew	Elder brother	Rickshaw puller	380 Victoria Street	116	1902
Ng Yeak				Ng Gee	Younger brother	Rickshaw puller		144	1902
Tan Say Tee	32	Hockchew	126 Victoria Street	Tan Toh Kang	Younger brother	Rickshaw puller	126 Victoria Street	115	1903
Tan Ah Tong	About 33	Hokkien	72 Rochore Road	Tan Tock Hoh	Brother	Rickshaw puller	72 Rochore Road	54	1905
Tan Yeng Eng	About 24		22 Johore Road	Tan Ah Chay	Elder brother	Rickshaw puller	19-1 Johore Road	53	1907
Lim Tiew	About 50	Hokkien	109 Albert Street	Lim Yam	None			180	1907
Ting Lam Pee	45		261 Victoria Street	Teo Mak	Relative	Rickshaw puller	121 Victoria Street	164	1908
Lui Ah Pek	30	Hokkien	9 Spottiswoode Park Road	Hwe Ah Tat	None	Rickshaw puller/ proprietor of rickshaw lodging-house	9 Spottiswoode Park Road	165	1908

Tay Ah Sui	25/30		42 Bain Street	Tan Ah Keong	None	Rickshaw owner/ proprietor of rickshaw lodging-house	43 Bain Street	241	1909
Ling Poo Kiang	55		132 Queen Street	Ling Toh Kia	None/ Clansman	Rickshaw puller	132 Queen Street	58	1910
Teng Poh	About 30			Leow Choon Seng	None	Rickshaw owner	15 Angullia Road	170	1910
Keh Hoh Choon	49	Hokkien	12 Park Road	Hoon Ah Mui	Wife		12 Park Road	45	1912
Chew Ah Tong	30	Hokkien	Victoria Street	Koh Teng Hai	None	Rickshaw owner	148 Queen Street	170	1912
Chan Kay Swee	27	Hokkien	51 Duxton Road	Chan Whatt Seng	Older brother	Rickshaw puller	51 Duxton Road	206	1912
Koh Leh	30	Hokkien	21 Omar Road	Tang Neo Kong	None	Rickshaw owner	21 Omar Road	59	1913
Lim Tiang Soo	34	Teochiu	New Market Road	Lim Sing Soo	Younger brother	Ice-water hawker	New Market Road	179	1913
Teng Ah Poh	46	Hockchia	27 Angullia Road	Teng Ah Nge	Cousin	Keeper of an eating-shop	Holloway Lane	15	1914
Moh Ah Hee	About 25	Hockchia	27 Park Road	Ben Wan Poh	None/ Clansman	Rickshaw puller	27 Park Road	180	1914
Seah Wan Tan	About 29	Hokkien	45 Amoy Street	Seah Chui Seang	None/ Clansman	Rickshaw puller	45 Amoy Street	214	1914

(continued)

APPENDIX 2 (*continued*)

Name of Deceased Rickshaw Puller	*Age*	*Sub-ethnic Group*	*No. and Street of Residence*	*Name of Person who Identified the Deceased*	*Relation to Deceased*	*Occupation*	*Place of Residence*	*Inquest No.*	*Year*
Wong Cray Tee	37	Hockchia	27 Park Road	Lee Yong Moi	None	Rickshaw puller	12 Cheang Hong Lim Lane	36	1915
Koh Tee	36	Hengwah	12 Ban San Street	Koh Ah Pek	Relative	Rickshaw puller	12 Ban San Street	73	1916
Teng Ung	23	Hengwah	97 Weld Road	Ling Kim Piew	None	Rickshaw puller	97 Weld Road	95	1916
Tan Eu Moy	About 40	Hockchew	115 Queen Street	Teng Ong Ock	None	Rickshaw puller	115 Queen Street	130	1916
Ling Ah Teng	32	Hockchia	130-6 Victoria Street	Ling Ah Quee	Elder brother	Rickshaw puller	130-6 Victoria Street	69	1917
Yap Ma Yam	24	Hokkien	13 Duxton Road	Yap Hoa Tow	Cousin	Job Coolie	82 Duxton Road	202	1917
Wee Cheng	45	Hokkien	49-2 Rochore Road	Oo Sie	None	Rickshaw puller	48-2 Rochore Road	231	1917
Chee Moh Moh	40	Hockchew	51 Johore Road	Chee Kee Teng	None/ Clansman	Rickshaw owner	51 Johore Road	343	1918
Ng Kai	36	Hokkien	Craig Road	Ho Seong	None	Rickshaw owner	79 Duxton Road	137	1919
Teng Ah Tee	28	Hengwah	228 Victoria Street	Tan Hun Bow	None	Rickshaw puller	228 Victoria Street	11	1920

Ong Ah Choon	56	Hengwah	99 Weld Road	Kong Ah Fo	Cousin	Rickshaw puller	99 Weld Road	46	1920
Puah Ah Low	28	Hengwah	113 Middle Road	Puah Ah Pan	None/ Clansman	Rickshaw puller	113 Middle Road	18	1921
Ong Chew Kay	24	Hockcha	64 Telok Ayer Street	Ng Ah Kow	Uncle	Rickshaw puller	64 Telok Ayer Street	55	1921
Tan Chew Moi	35	Hockcha	22 Tras Street	Ting Cheng Soon	Brother	Rickshaw puller	22 Tras Street	78	1921
Ch'ng Chuan	42	Teochiu	Rochore Canal Road	Swee Kim Kam	None	Licensee of an opium smoking shop	8 Rochore Canal Road	395	1921
Leong Ah Keng	45	Cantonese	8 Erskine Road	Ng Ah Ng	None	Rickshaw puller	8 Erskine Road	459	1921
Tiew Tam	55	Hokkien	25 Duxton Road	Teow Choon Swee	Son	Rickshaw puller	25 Duxton Road	213	1922
Goh Ah Toh	27	Hokkien	38 People's Park	Goh Kang Soo	Elder brother	Rickshaw puller	38 People's Park	223	1922
Ng Pin	60	Hokkien	25 Banda Street	Ng Lam Seng	Nephew	Tea seller at a stall	25 Banda Street	393	1922
Lim Kee Lee	32	Hockchia	249 Victoria Street	Lim Ah Tee	Younger brother	Rickshaw puller	249 Victoria Street	59	1923
Low Nee	55	Hokkien	104 Queen Street	Low Ah Moey	Nephew	Rickshaw puller	96 Rochore Canal Road	266	1923
Kim Moh	35	Hockcha	Park Road	Cheah Pin Soo	None	Widow, Rickshaw owner	Park Road	297	1923

(continued)

APPENDIX 2 (*continued*)

Name of Deceased Rickshaw Puller	*Age*	*Sub-ethnic Group*	*No. and Street of Residence*	*Name of Person who Identified the Deceased*	*Relation to Deceased*	*Occupation*	*Place of Residence*	*Inquest No.*	*Year*
Ong Cha Bah	45	Hokkien	13 Park Road	Ong Yeok	Cousin	Hawker selling porridge	900-3 Tiong Bahru	303	1923
Lau Ah Chiew	20	Hengwah	89 Bencoolen Street	Lau See Lee	Older brother	Rickshaw puller	89 Bencoolen Street	370	1923
Chin Ah Ching	39	Hengwah	96 Sungei Road	Tong Ah Poon	None	Rickshaw owner	72 Rochore Canal Road	397	1923
Yau Chin Swee	34	Hokkien	96 Sungei Road	Tan Boon Tay	None	Rickshaw puller	96 Sungei Road	236	1924
Tang Ah Huat	20	Teochiu	23 Fisher Street	Lim Nee Thong	None	Rickshaw owner	23 Fisher Street	491	1924
Ling Ah Thui	41	Hockchia	2 Angullia Road	Lim Poh Kee	Younger brother	Rickshaw puller	2 Angullia Road	516	1924
Leung Chiu	28	Cantonese	14 Erskine Road	Hoh Ah Tak	None	Rickshaw owner	14 Erskine Road	33	1925
Teng Ah Yeok	39	Hengwah	22 Angullia Road	Teng Leng	None/ Clansman	Conduc-tor of bus	22 Angullia Road	99	1925
Hoh Oon	53	Hokkien	79 Duxton Road	Moh Choon Bok	Relative	Rickshaw puller	72 Duxton Road	162	1925
Toh Ah Soh	24	Hengwah	1 Ophir Road	Tay Ah Choo	Cousin	Rickshaw puller	1 Ophir Road	183	1925
Tan Chwee Chwee	42	Hockchew	33 Muar Road	Tang Kow Lee	None/ Clansman	Rickshaw puller	33 Muar Road	318	1925

Low Yah Cheong	39	Hengwah	Katong, East Coast Road	Low Aik	None	Rickshaw puller/ owner	Katong, East Coast Road	329	1925
Ling Ah Ngong	51	Hengwah	Rochore Canal Road	Yap Seah Hing	Wife		Rochore Canal Road	1	1926
Koh Lai Tee	49	Hockchia	377-1 Victoria Street	Koh Lai Moy	Younger brother	Rickshaw puller	Waterloo or Bencoolen Street	503	1926
Ee Ang Ang	46	Hockchia	Ophir Road	Ho Tai Cheang	Nephew	Rickshaw puller	106 Bencoolen Street	82	1927
Yu No Po	20	Hokkien	52 Victoria Street	Eu Tin See	Cousin	Rickshaw puller	52 Victoria Street	364	1927
Low Leong	48	Hengwah	209 Payah Road	Lee Leng	None	Keeper of a rickshaw pullers' house	209 Payah Road	399	1927
See Ah Heng	23	Hockchia	21 Lim Eng Bee Lane	See Mee Tee	Relative	Rickshaw puller	21 Lim Eng Bee Lane	414	1927
Siah Goh Seng	47	Hengwah	Joo Chiat Road	Ho Lee Ah	Wife		Joo Chiat Road	702	1928
Ong Teck Cheng	19	Hengwah	227 Jalan Sultan	Ong Teo Chong	Uncle	Rickshaw puller	227 Jalan Sultan	174	1929
Geok Lan	40	Hengwah	249 Victoria Street	Yeo Chong	None	Rickshaw owner	249 Victoria Street	328	1929
Teo Kow Seng	48	Hengwah	228 Victoria Street	Teo Kut Seng	Younger brother	Rickshaw puller	228 Victoria Street	436	1929
Ling Kong King	29	Hockchia	2 Ban San Street	Ling Nong Noey	None/ Clansman	Hawker	2 Ban San Street	380	1930

(continued)

APPENDIX 2 (*continued*)

Name of Deceased Rickshaw Puller	*Age*	*Sub-ethnic Group*	*No. and Street of Residence*	*Name of Person who Identified the Deceased*	*Relation to Deceased*	*Occupation*	*Place of Residence*	*Inquest No.*	*Year*
Leong Lam	38	Cantonese	Hokkien Street	Lee Hoong	None	Rickshaw puller	Hokkien Street	385A	1930
Ling Ah Liew	45	Hockchia	93 Chin Swee Road	Hong Ik Siew	None	Rickshaw owner	122 Chin Swee Road	360	1931
Ong Ah Siew	39	Hengwah	12 Angullia Road	Ong Ah Chan	Son	Rickshaw puller	12 Angullia Road	664	1931
Chung Ah Hoot	43	Hokkien	21 Duxton Road	Chung Ah Goon	Nephew	Rickshaw puller	21 Duxton Road	703	1931
Tang Koh Chi	45	Hockchia	161 New Market Road	Ling Ah Teh	None	Rickshaw puller	161 New Market Road	272	1932
Koh Kim Chwee	38	Hockchia	29 Angullia Road	Chong Swee Lin	Wife		29 Angullia Road	677	1932
Ong Seng Hong	32	Hengwah	34 Muar Road	Chua Kiong	None/ Fellow lodger	Rickshaw puller	34 Muar Road	410	1933
Lim Phua Sim	61	Hengwah	107 Prinsep Street	Lim Ang Ngong	Brother	Rickshaw puller	107 Prinsep Street	597	1933
Yat Ah Huat	41	Hengwah	532 Victoria Street	Low Ah Luang	None/Friend	Rickshaw puller	Victoria Street	199	1936
Koh Kong Cheng	42	Hengwah	17 Larut Road	Koh Keng Cheng	None/Friend	Rickshaw puller	17 Larut Road	99	1937
Lim Kim Cheok	50	Hokkien	Perak Road	Lim Sai Yoke	Daughter		117 Joo Chiat Road	506	1937

Chung Han Koh	30	Hokkien	69 Duxton Road	Ching Tian	Clansman	Rickshaw owner	35 Duxton Road	530	1937
Tee Yeok Choon	41	Hokkien	8 Craig Road	Tee Chew Kim	Brother	Rickshaw puller	8 Craig Road	568	1937
Ong Kwee Tiam	35	Hockchia	Victoria Street	Ong Ah Puan	Elder brother	Rickshaw puller	133 Victoria Street	584	1937
Ling Soh Kai	49	Hengwah	27 Dixon Road	Ling Choh Yew	Cousin	Rickshaw puller	44 Dixon Road	595	1937
Tan Nah Nai	51	Hockchew	99 Havelock Road	Tan Uh Kit	Younger brother	Rickshaw puller	99 Havelock Road	210	1938
Low Nong Nong	40	Hockchew	18-3 Johore Road	Yu Nan Nan	None	Principal tenant of lodging-house	18-3 Johore Road	597	1938
Ng Choon Quee	37	Hokkien	309 New Bridge Road	Quck Kee Moon	None	Principal tenant of lodging-house	309 New Bridge Road	692	1938

APPENDIX 3

Rickshaw Coolies: Residential Patterns

Name	*Age*	*Sub-ethnic Group*	*No. and Street of Residence*	*Private Residence*	*Rickshaw Coolie Lodging-house*	*Length of Time in Residence*	*Rent*	*Inquest No.*	*Year*
Tan Sam Ong	20/25	Chawan	Mackenzie Road	Coolie Lodging-house				95	1902
Ong Oh Kaw	About 28	Hockchia	380 Victoria Street		x	4 months		116	1902
Lim Ah Lock			No. unknown, Victoria Street		x			30	1903
Tan Say Tee	32	Hockchew	126 Victoria Street		x			115	1903
Tiang Seang	25		123 Bencoolen Street					30	1904
Teo Ah Say	35/40	Hokkien	219 Rochore Road					79	1904
Tan Ah Tong	About 33	Hokkien	72 Rochore Road		x			54	1905
Tan Yeng Eng	About 24		22 Johore Road					53	1907
Lim Tiew	About 50	Hokkien	109 Albert Street	Opium shop		1½ months	With board and *chandu* $8 per month	180	1907
Ting Lam Pee	45		261 Victoria Street		x			164	1908
Lui Ah Pek	30	Hokkien	9 Spottiswoode Park Road	x		Year		165	1908
Tay Ah Sui	25/30		42 Bain Street			About 3 months		241	1909

Ling Poo Kiang	55		132 Queen Street			58	1910
Keh Hoh Choon	49	Hokkien	12 Park Road		x	45	1912
Chew Ah Tong	30	Hokkien	Victoria Street			170	1912
Lee Low Chee		Hengwah	129-4 Victoria Street		x	170	1912
Koh Leh	30	Hokkien	21 Omar Road		x	59	1913
Lim Tiang Soo	34	Teochiu	New Market Road	x		179	1913
Teng Ah Poh	46	Hockchia	27 Angullia Road			15	1914
Moh Ah Hee	About 25	Hockchia	27 Park Road		x	180	1914
Seah Wah Tan	29	Hokkien	45 Amoy Street		x	214	1914
Wong Cray Tee	37	Hockchia	27 Park Road		x	36	1915
Lye Pho Ye	49	Cantonese	Hokkien Street	x		70	1916
Koh Tee	36	Hengwah	12 Ban San Street			73	1916
Teng Ung	23	Hengwah	97 Weld Road		x	95	1916
Tan Eu Moy	About 40	Hockchew	115 Queen Street			130	1916
Goh Wing Wah	49	Hockchia	10 Lim Eng Bee Lane			14	1917
Ling Ah Teng	32	Hockchia	130-6 Victoria Street			69	1917
Lee Ah Loi	25	Hengwah	94 Queen Street			183	1917
Yap Ma Yam	24	Hokkien	13 Duxton Road			202	1917
Wee Cheng	45	Hokkien	49-2 Rochore Road			231	1917
Chee Moh Moh	40	Hockchew	51 Johore Road		x	343	1918
Ng Kai	36	Hokkien	Craig Road			137	1919

(continued)

APPENDIX 3 (*continued*)

Name	*Age*	*Sub-ethnic Group*	*No. and Street of Residence*	*Private Residence*	*Rickshaw Coolie Lodging-house*	*Length of Time in Residence*	*Rent*	*Inquest No.*	*Year*
Teng Ah Tee	28	Hengwah	228 Victoria Street					11	1920
Ong Ah Choon	56	Hengwah	99 Weld Road	x				46	1920
Puah Ah Low	28	Hengwah	113 Middle Road		x			18	1921
Ong Chew Kay	24	Hockcha	64 Telok Ayer Street					55	1921
Tan Chew Moi	35	Hockcha	22 Tras Street		x			78	1921
Leong Ah Keng	45	Cantonese	8 Erskine Road					459	1921
Chen Loh Er	30		102 Arab Street	x				82	1922
Tiew Tam	55	Hokkien	25 Duxton Road					213	1922
Goh Kang Soo	27	Hokkien	People's Park No. 38	x				223	1922
Ng Pin	60	Hokkien	25 Banda Street					393	1922
Teo What Swee	26	Hokkien	49 Duxton Road					428	1922
Low Siang Quay	40	Hengwah	531-9 Queen Street					459	1922
Lim Kee Lee	32	Hockchia	249 Victoria Street		x			59	1923
Low Nee	55	Hokkien	104 Queen Street					266	1923
Kim Moh	35	Hockcha	Park Road		x			297	1923
Ong Cha Bah	45	Hokkien	13 Park Road		x	2 months		303	1923
Chin Ah Ching	39	Hengwah	96 Sungei Road					397	1923
Teng Tong	46	Hengwah	Lorong 20, Geylang Road					484	1923

Yau Chin Swee	34	Hokkien	96 Sungei Road		x	At least 6 months	$1.60 per month	236	1924
Gian Ah Kin	21	Hockcha	Waterloo Street					282	1924
Ng Liew	31	Hokkien	8 Pitt Street			6 months		386	1924
Ling Ah Thui	41	Hockchia	2 Angullia Road		x			516	1924
Liew Ah Cheong	28	Cantonese	14 Erskine Road		x			53	1925
Lui Ah Lak	40	Hengwah	136 Rochore Road	x		1 year		56	1925
Teng Ah Yeok	39	Hengwah	22 Angullia Road	x				99	1925
Hoh Oon	53	Hokkien	79 Duxton Road		x		$1.00 per month	162	1925
Toh Ah Soh	24	Hengwah	1 Ophir Road	x				183	1925
Tan Chwee Chwee	42	Hockchew	33 Muar Road		x			318	1925
Low Yah Cheong	39	Hengwah	Katong, East Coast Road					329	1925
Ling Ah Ngong	51	Hengwah	Rochore Canal Road	x				1	1926
Khoon Cheang	30	Hengwah	110-1 Queen Street	x				400	1926
Koh Lai Tee	49	Hockchia	377-1 Victoria Street		x			503	1926
Ee Ang Ang	46	Hockchia	Ophir Road					82	1927
Yu No Po	20	Hokkien	52 Victoria Street					364	1927
Low Leong	48	Hengwah	209 Payah Road		x			399	1927
See Ah Heng	23	Hockchia	21 Lim Eng Bee Lane					414	1927
Teng Ah Chin	45	Hengwah	12 Ban San Street					495	1927
Lee Ah Liang	40	Hengwah	95 Queen Street					59	1928

(*continued*)

APPENDIX 3 (*continued*)

Name	*Age*	*Sub-ethnic Group*	*No. and Street of Residence*	*Private Residence*	*Rickshaw Coolie Lodging-house*	*Length of Time in Residence*	*Rent*	*Inquest No.*	*Year*
Siah Hong Mee	30	Hockchia	Jalan Besar					588	1928
Siah Goh Seng	47	Hengwah	Joo Chiat Road	x				702	1928
Ching Chye Leng	41	Hokkien	82-1 Duxton Road		x			67	1929
Ong Teck Cheng	19	Hengwah	227 Jalan Sultan		x	Few months		174	1929
Geok Lan	40	Hengwah	249 Victoria Street		x			328	1929
Teo Kow Seng	48	Hengwah	228 Victoria Street		x			436	1929
Ling Kong King	29	Hockchia	2 Ban San Street	x				380	1930
Leong Lam	38	Cantonese	Hokkien Street		x			385A	1930
Kwok Nyong Pian	25	Hockchia	4 Johore Road					121	1931
Ling Ee Teng	22	Hockchia	1 Narcis Street					344	1931
Ling Ah Liew	45	Hockchia	93 Chin Swee Road	x				360	1931
Ong Ang Siew	39	Hengwah	12 Angullia Road	x				664	1931
Chung Ah Hoot	43	Hokkien	21 Duxton Road	x				703	1931
Tang Koh Chi	45	Hockchia	161 New Market Road		x			272	1932
Koh Kim Chwee	38	Hockchia	29 Angullia Road					677	1932
Ong Seng Hong	32	Hengwah	34 Muar Road	x				410	1933

Lim Phua Sim	61	Hengwah	107 Prinsep Street		x		597	1933
Yat Ah Huat	41	Hengwah	532 Victoria Street				199	1936
Teng Lau Ting	45	Hengwah	108 Albert Street	x			247	1936
Kwang Ah Lee	39	Hengwah	94 Sungei Road		x		392	1936
Koh Kong Cheng	42	Hengwah	17 Larut Road				99	1937
Lim Kim Cheok	50	Hokkien	Perak Road		x		506	1937
Chung Han Koh	30	Hokkien	69 Duxton Road				530	1937
Tee Yeok Choon	41	Hokkien	8 Craig Road		x		568	1937
Ong Kwee Tiam	35	Hockchia	Victoria Street				584	1937
Ling Soh Kai	49	Hengwah	27 Dixon Road				595	1937
Chew Ah Kow	54	Hokkien	24 Tiwari Street	x			86	1938
Tan Nah Nai	51	Hockchew	99 Havelock Road				210	1938
Low Nong Nong	40	Hockchew	18-3 Johore Road			1 month	597	1938
Ng Choon Quee	37	Hokkien	309 New Bridge Road				692	1938
Lim Boey Chong	29	Hockchia	12 Narcis Street				82	1939
Chee Hang Kee	37	Hockchia	8 Bolo Street	x			354	1939
Chong Guan	50	Hokkien	36 Muar Road				494	1939

APPENDIX 4

Rickshaw Coolies: Culpable Homicide And Assault

Name	*Age*	*Sub-ethnic Group*	*No. and Street of Residence*	*Identity of Assailant(s)*	*Ethnic/ Sub-ethnic Group*	*Date of Homicide*	*Time of Homicide*
Tan Sam Ong	20/25	Chawan	Mackenzie Road	Joseph Goin	French	6/7/02	3 a.m.
Ong Oh Kaw	About 28	Hockchia	380 Victoria Street	Some person or persons unknown	Hokkien	15/8/02	8 p.m.
Lim Ah Lock			Victoria Street	Some person or persons unknown	Hokkien	24/2/03	
Tan Yeng Eng	About 24		22 Johore Road	Teng Liong Hoh		31/3/07	8 p.m.
Teng Ho Hoo	About 28		Victoria Street	Teng Mah Koh and another unknown man, a Chinese coolie		18/8/08	
Tay Ah Sui	25/30		42 Bain Street	Abdullah Adam	Malay	27/12/09	7.40 p.m.
Teng Poh	30			Abu Osman	Malay	1/8/10	8 a.m.

APPENDIX 4 (*continued*)

Place of Homicide	*Whether Homicide Occurred while Pulling Rickshaw*	*Cause of Homicide*		*Death due to*		*Inquest No.*	*Year*
Keppel Road	Yes	Money (?)/ Fare	Accused had been drinking; possible altercation over fare	Stabbing	Haemorrhage from the jugular vein following stab wounds with razor	95	1902
Havelock Road	Yes	Unknown		Stabbing	Haemorrhage from the jugular vein following stab wound	116	1902
Thompson Road	Yes	Money/ Fare	Altercation over agreed price of fare with two Hokkien Chinese	Assault	General blood poisoning accelerated by the fracture of a rib – caused by the assault	30	1903
Johore Road	No	Money/Indebtedness	Deceased wanted to leave Liong Hoh's lodging-house, owed accused 3 or 4 dollars	Stabbing	Haemorrhage following stab wounds in the chest	53	1907
Rickshaw coolie lodging-house, Victoria Street	No	Money/Indebtedness	Altercation over money owed to Teng Mah Koh, rickshaw owner of Victoria Street	Assault	Cerebral abscess following injury to skull caused by blows from a hammer and plank	214	1908
Verandah of Boustead & Co. Godown	Yes	Money/ Fare	Accused ordered deceased to go faster/deceased stopped and demanded his fare	Stabbing	Haemorrhage from perforation of the aorta following stab wounds	241	1909
Coffee-shop in Orchard Road	Yes	Money/ Fare	Deceased asked money of the accused as he left shop in payment of rickshaw hire	Assault	Rupture of spleen and liver following an assault causing deceased to fall into a street drain	170	1910

(*continued*)

APPENDIX 4 (*continued*)

Name	*Age*	*Sub-ethnic Group*	*No. and Street of Residence*	*Identity of Assailant(s)*	*Ethnic/ Sub-ethnic Group*	*Date of Homicide*	*Time of Homicide*
Keh Hoh Choon	49	Hokkien	12 Park Road	Liew Kay	Hokkien	24/3/12	7.30 p.m.
Chew Ah Tong	30	Hokkien	Victoria Street	Lee Low Chee and another unknown man, a Chinese	Hengwah	31/10/12	Between 1 p.m. and 6 a.m. next morning
Wong Cray Tee	37	Hockchia	27 Park Road	Ho Lak Lee, Lo Hong Sai, Loh Tek Boo, Wee Ghee Hoo, Tan Yap Chin, Wee See Hye	Hylams	6/3/15	12.30 p.m.
Koh Tee	36	Hengwah	12 Ban San Street	Some person or persons unknown		24/4/16	8.30 p.m.
Ling Ah Teng	32	Hockchia	130-6 Victoria Street	Some person or persons unknown		11,12/ 4/17	Night of 11 or 12 April
Yap Ma Yam	24	Hokkien	13 Duxton Road	Lee Kwong	Cantonese	13/9/17	9 a.m.
Chee Moh Moh	40	Hockchew	51 Johore Road	Wan Pat	Cantonese	26/12/18	About midnight

APPENDIX 4 (*continued*)

Place of Homicide	*Whether Homicide Occurred while Pulling Rickshaw*	*Cause of Homicide*		*Death due to*		*Inquest No.*	*Year*
Cubicle in 9 Park Road	No	Money/Indebtedness	Deceased went out to collect some debts from Liew Kay. Deceased was assaulted	Assault	Peritonitis due to duodenal ulcer following blows inflicted by Liew Kay	45	1912
Payah Lebar Road	Yes	Personal	Accused, friend of deceased; possible personal involvement with wife of deceased	Stabbing	Haemorrhage from multiple injuries following stab wounds	170	1912
River Valley Road	Yes	Accidental, unknown	Hylams had a quarrel with the puller of another rickshaw. They struck the deceased when chasing this rickshaw coolie.	Assault	Rupture of small intestine following a severe blow on the abdominal wall from having been punched and kicked	36	1915
At or near bridge over Rochore Canal near Ban San Street	Yes	Unknown		Stabbing	Haemorrhage from brachial and axillary arteries following a stab wound	73	1916
At the side of Kim Keat Road	Yes	Theft(?)	The deceased took about 1 dollar a day; the lamps and cover were missing from the rickshaw.	Stabbing	Haemorrhage from stab wound	69	1917
Corner of Temple and Trengganu Streets	Yes	Accidental	Two rickshaws collided. The pullers fell down. The accused and deceased began to fight.	Assault	Haemorrhage from ruptured spleen following blows inflicted by Lee Kwong	202	1917
Tanjong Pagar	Yes	Money/Fare	Wan Pat refused to pay the puller so the two fought	Stabbing	Haemorrhage from stab wound of internal jugular vein	343	1918

(*continued*)

APPENDIX 4 (*continued*)

Name	*Age*	*Sub-ethnic Group*	*No. and Street of Residence*	*Identity of Assailant(s)*	*Ethnic/ Sub-ethnic Group*	*Date of Homicide*	*Time of Homicide*
Teng Ah Tee	28	Hengwah	228 Victoria Street	Tang Kang Sui	Hokkien	7/1/20	About midnight
Ong Chew Kay	24	Hockcha	64 Telok Ayer Street	Some unknown person, a Chinese	Baba	9/2/21	11.45 a.m.
Tan Chew Moi	35	Hockcha	22 Tras Street	Woon Mok Kay	Hockchia	26/2/21	8 a.m.
Chen Loh Er	30		102 Arab Street	Leng See Kwee		2/3/22	11 p.m.
Teo What Swee	26	Hokkien	49 Duxton Road	Lai Bee and six other unknown Chinese	Hockchew	27/8/22	7.30 a.m.
Ong Cha Bah	45	Hokkien	13 Park Road	Some person or persons unknown, Chinese		4/8/23	8 p.m.

APPENDIX 4 (*continued*)

Place of Homicide	*Whether Homicide Occurred while Pulling Rickshaw*	*Cause of Homicide*		*Death due to*		*Inquest No.*	*Year*
Near the junction of Victoria Street and Jalan Sultan	No	Accidental	Accidental quarrel at a food hawker's stall with a 'samseng'	Stabbing	Haemorrhage from brachial artery and vein following a stab wound	11	1920
Telok Ayer Street	Yes	Dispute	Deceased refused to take accused as a passenger as he was too ill to pull.	Assault	Haemorrhage from ruptured malarial spleen from having been kicked in abdomen	55	1921
22 Tras Street	No	Money/Indebtedness	Accused claimed some members of the house owed him about $60 and deceased and other members wanted him turned out.	Stabbing	Haemorrhage from stab wound of the abdomen	78	1921
102 Arab Street	No	Money/Loan	Deceased and accused had a quarrel over money. Deceased wanted to borrow money but accused refused to loan any	Accidental cut	Deceased cut his right foot on a piece of broken teapot, severing the right posterior fibial artery	82	1922
Everton Road	Yes	Dispute/Territorial	Deceased took a regular customer in a district usually served by pullers of another sub-communal group	Stabbing	Haemorrhage from stab wound of heart and kidney	428	1922
Park Road	No	Dispute/Secret society	Death of deceased suspected to be connected with secret society of Park Road or of the Sin Ghee Hin Society	Assault	Haemorrhage from ruptured spleen	303	1923

(*continued*)

APPENDIX 4 (*continued*)

Name	*Age*	*Sub-ethnic Group*	*No. and Street of Residence*	*Identity of Assailant(s)*	*Ethnic/ Sub-ethnic Group*	*Date of Homicide*	*Time of Homicide*
Lau Ah Chiew	20	Hengwah	89 Bencoolen Street	Some person or persons unknown, Rickshaw pullers	Hockcha	16/9/23	6.30 p.m.
Ng Liew	31	Hokkien	8 Pitt Street	Some unknown male person	Malay	1/10/24	8 a.m.
Teng Ah Yeok	39	Hengwah	22 Angullia Road	Some person or persons unknown		22/2/25	10.15 p.m.
Hoh Oon	53	Hokkien	79 Duxton Road	Hoh Giong Toh	Hokkien	3/4/25	8.30 p.m.
Khoon Cheang	30	Hengwah	110-1 Queen Street	Some person or persons unknown		22/8/26	
See Ah Heng	23	Hockchia	21 Lim Eng Bee Lane	Seak Ti Teng and others unknown	Hockchia	13/8/27	Midnight
Kow Wuh	27	Hockchia		Alib bin Undong	Malay	6/5/30	12.30 p.m.
Tan Chin Tee	30	Hockchia		Rik bin Awang	Malay	6/5/30	12.30 p.m.

APPENDIX 4 (*continued*)

Place of Homicide	*Whether Homicide Occurred while Pulling Rickshaw*	*Cause of Homicide*		*Death due to*		*Inquest No.*	*Year*
Waterloo Street	No	Dispute/ Clan society	Clan fight between Hengwah and Hockcha Rickshaw pullers	Stabbing	Haemorrhage from stab wounds	370	1923
Jalan Besar	Yes	Money/ Fare	Altercation over price of the fare, passenger kicked deceased in crotch	Assault	Shock from contusion of the perineum and testes and ruptured urethra from having been kicked	386	1924
Arab Street	Yes	Unknown		Assault	Haemorrhage from ruptured spleen	99	1925
79 Duxton Road	No	Money/ Rent	Deceased and accused quarrelled over payment of rent	Stabbing	Haemorrhage from stab wound of heart	162	1925
Crawfurd Street	Yes	Unknown		Assault	Acute cardiac dilation following fractured ribs and other injuries	400	1926
Eu Tong Seng Street, in front of the Southern Hotel	Yes	Dispute/ Territorial	Quarrel to prevent deceased from taking a passenger; assaulted by four other pullers	Assault	Septic meningitis following a penetrating wound of the skull	414	1927
Cornwall Street	Yes	Money/ Compensation	Payment for damage done to rickshaw in minor accident with automobile	Stabbing	Haemorrhage from stab wound of the abdomen	220	1930
Cornwall Street	Yes	Accidental	Deceased tried to aid fellow puller Kow Wuh who had been assaulted	Stabbing	Haemorrhage from stab wound of the abdomen	221	1930

(*continued*)

APPENDIX 4 (*continued*)

Name	*Age*	*Sub-ethnic Group*	*No. and Street of Residence*	*Identity of Assailant(s)*	*Ethnic/ Sub-ethnic Group*	*Date of Homicide*	*Time of Homicide*
Ch'ng Hay Koo	30	Hokkien	60 Duxton Road	Low Nian Mee, Low Sui Hoon and three other unknown Chinese	Hokkien	6/9/37	5.30 p.m.
Sia Sen Hert	37	Hockchia	8 Bolo Street	Some unknown person		15/6/39	6.00 a.m.

APPENDIX 4 (*continued*)

Place of Homicide	*Whether Homicide Occurred while Pulling Rickshaw*	*Cause of Homicide*		*Death due to*		*Inquest No.*	*Year*
Telok Ayer Basin	Yes	Accidental	Low Nian Mee had an altercation with another puller on previous day; deceased was mistaken for other rickshaw puller	Assault	Haemorrhage from fracture of skull following assault with pieces of wood	530	1937
Near Keng Cheow Street	No	Personal	Quarrel over relationship with a woman	Stabbing	Haemorrhage from stab wound of chest and abdomen	354	1939

APPENDIX 5

Wives Of Rickshaw Coolies: Suicide

Name	*Age*	*Sub-ethnic Group*	*No. and Street of Residence*	*Nature of Residence*	*State of Health*	*Husband's Name*	*Age*
Ngoh Ah Mui	39	Hockchia	99 Amoy Street	Cubicle – ground floor	Ill for some time (depressed)	Ling Ee Ngoh	
Sim Kwee Geok	35	Chawan	6 Kerbau Lane	Cubicle – upstairs	6 months pregnant (boy)	Lim Jin San	
Wee Choon Beoh	32	Hokkien	231 Waterloo Street	Small cubicle	Depressed over mother's death in China	Lim Ong	
Ler Cho Wing	28	Hengwah	129-6 Tiwary Street	Small cubicle – first floor/ rear	Poor health for 5 years	Tah Moon Heng	30
Gian Yeow Sun	19	Hockchia	32 Park Road	Small cubicle – first floor/ front	Good health	Ting Oh Tee	30
Teng Ah Poh	29	Hengwah	94 Sungei Road	Cubicle/ ground floor	Left hand, right leg deformed	Kwang Ah Lee	39

APPENDIX 5 (*continued*)

Sub-ethnic Group	*Length of Marriage*	*Number of Children*	*Date of Suicide*	*Cause of Suicide*	*Place of Suicide*	*Suicide due to*	*Inquest No.*	*Year*
Hockchew	22 yrs.	1 (died)	18/9/29	Illness	Cubicle	Asphyxia by hanging to the bedpost of the mosquito net frame	460	1929
Hokkien	2 yrs.	1 (died)	11/12/29	Quarrel–domestic/ financial	Cubicle	Drinking a quantity of liquid caustic soda	619	1929
Hokkien		2 small children		Death in family/no money for kin	Cubicle	Asphyxia by hanging from beam in cubicle	612	1930
Hengwah	11 yrs.	1 (M)–11 years old	10/7/35	Domestic/ financial	Cubicle	Asphyxia by hanging from an iron bar of the window	303	1935
Hockchia	1 yr.	None	17/7/35	Domestic/ financial	Cubicle	Asphyxia by hanging from the top of a partition at the side of the bed	319	1935
Hengwah	8/9 yrs.	None	10/7/36	Leprosy	Cubicle	Asphyxia by hanging from piece of wood attached to the partition	392	1936

APPENDIX 6

Rickshaw Coolies: Confirmed Cases of Death from Cholera among Cases Dumped, 1910/1911 and 1914

Name	*Speech/Dialect Group*	*Age*	*Description*	*Marks of Violence if any*
Unknown	Chinese	About 30		None, signs of cholera
Unknown	Chinese	About 30/35	Looks like a rickshaw puller	No external marks
Unknown	Hokkien	40		None
Unknown	Hokkien	40		None
Unknown	Hockchia	30		None
Unknown	Hokkien	45	Blue coat and pants	None
Unknown	Hockchia	40		None
Unknown	Hockchia	35	Blue clothes, red blanket	None
Unknown	Hockchia	34		None
Unknown	Hokkien	50		None
Unknown	Hockchia	37	Blue clothes, blanket, mat, water vessel	None
Unknown	Hockchia	30	Mat, blue clothes	None
Unknown	Hockchia	20	Red blanket	None
Unknown	Hockchia	40	Blue clothes, reddish mat	None
Unknown	Chinese	About 40		None
Unknown	Hockchew	About 25		None
Unknown	Hokkien	About 30		None
Unknown	Chinese	About 40		None
Unknown	Hokkien	About 35		None
Unknown	Hokkien	About 30		None

APPENDIX 6 (*continued*)

Where Found	*Cause of Death*	*Time of Death*	*Date of Death*
Dumped in verandah of lane off Queen Street	Cholera	Unknown	Around 12/8/10
Rochore Canal Road	Cholera	Unknown	Around 1/9/10
Muar Road	Cholera–dumped	Unknown	Around 4/10/11
Kubor Road	Cholera–dumped	Unknown	Around 7/10/11
Jalan Besar near Lavender Street	Cholera–dumped	Unknown	Around 7/10/11
Rochore Canal Road	Cholera–dumped	Unknown	Around 7/10/11
Johore Road	Cholera–dumped	Unknown	Around 7/10/11
133 Victoria Street	Cholera–dumped	Unknown	Around 8/10/11
Kubor Road	Cholera–dumped	Unknown	Around 9/10/11
3½ milestone Rallary Road	Cholera–dumped	Unknown	Around 14/10/11
Lane off Johore Road behind Victoria Street	Cholera–dumped	Unknown	Around 15/10/11
Verandah of Chinese temple, Victoria Street	Cholera–dumped	Unknown	Around 23/10/11
Johore Road	Cholera–dumped	Unknown	Around 24/10/11
Verandah 30 Johore Road	Cholera–dumped	Unknown	Around 29/10/11
Verandah of 27-2 Johore Road	Cholera	Unknown	Around 19/4/14
Side of Muar Road	Cholera–dumped	Unknown	27/4/14
On Johore Road	Cholera	Unknown	28/4/14
On Johore Road	Cholera–dumped	Unknown	2/5/14
Lane off Albert Street	Cholera	Unknown	Around 3/5/14
In lane off Johore Road	Cholera–dumped	Unknown	Around 3/5/14

(*continued*)

APPENDIX 6 (*continued*)

Name	*Speech/Dialect Group*	*Age*	*Description*	*Marks of Violence if any*
Unknown	Hockchia	About 30		None
Unknown	Hokkien	About 35		None
Sim Aye Koo	Teochiu	About 32		None
Unknown	Hokkien	About 30		None
Unknown	Hokkien	About 40		None
Unknown	Hokkien	About 40		None
Unknown	Hokkien	40		None
Unknown	Hokkien	About 41		None
Unknown	Chinese	About 40		None
Unknown	Hockchia	About 40		None
Unknown	Chinese	About 40		None
Unknown	Hokkien	About 35		None
Unknown	Hokkien	About 35		None

APPENDIX 6 (*continued*)

Where Found	*Cause of Death*	*Time of Death*	*Date of Death*
On Johore Road	Cholera	Unknown	Around 7/5/14
Lane off Johore Road	Cholera	Unknown	Around 14/5/14
7th mile Bukit Timah Road	Cholera	Unknown	Around 14/5/14
Verandah of 7 Victoria Street	Cholera	Unknown	Around 8/6/14
On Angullia Road	Cholera–dumped	Unknown	Around 8/6/14
Rochore Canal Road	Cholera–dumped	Unknown	Around 8/6/14
In a lane off Johore Road	Cholera–dumped	Unknown	Around 11/6/14
In the Rochore Canal at Arab Street Bridge	Cholera–dumped	Unknown	Around 13/6/14
Side of Rochore Canal Road	Cholera	Unknown	Around 27/6/14
Side of Rochore Canal Road	Cholera–dumped	Unknown	Around 28/6/14
Stamford Street and Waterloo Street	Cholera–stuffed in a box	Unknown	Around 9/7/14
Angullia Road	Cholera	Unknown	Around 12/7/14
Side of Rochore Canal Road	Cholera	Unknown	Around 22/7/14

APPENDIX 7

Rickshaw Coolies: Death Caused By Cardiac Arrest, 1906-1940

Name	*Speech/ Dialect Group*	*Age*	*Description*	*Marks of Violence if any*	*Where Found*	*Cause of Death*	*Time of Death*	*Date of Death*
Choi Ah Wong	Cantonese	35	Infirm	None	Banda Street where fell dead	Aortic disease	11.30 a.m.	13/3/08
Unknown	Hokkien	25 to 30	Normal	None	Avenue of Plantation home – fell dead	Aortic Valvular disease	11.30 a.m.	26/3/08
Chan Tee	Chinese	30	Normal	Abrasions on nose and forehead	Corner of Beach Road – fell dead	Acute dilation of heart	12.20 p.m.	30/6/08
Keng Ann	Hokkien	40	Opium smoker	None	Kou Non Road – fell dead	Acute dilation of heart	Unknown	Unknown
Unknown	Chinese	28 to 30	Normal	None	Waste ground – Havelock Road	Morbus cordismitral	Unknown	Assumed 2/4/09
Unknown	Chinese	28 to 30	Normal	None	Entrance to home, Kassip Road – fell dead	Dilation of heart	Midnight to early morning	22/5/09
Ong Lee Kaw	Chinese	48	Normal – healthy	A wound on the head from fall	New Bridge Road – fell dead	Dilation of heart	3.30 p.m.	22/5/09
See Li Mui	Chinese	35		None	Dr. Brooke's office – fell dead	Aneurism of the heart	10.30 a.m.	6/9/10
Chew Ging Chuan	Teochiu	35		None	Orchard Road – fell dead	Acute dilation of the heart	6.00 p.m.	8/2/14
Unknown	Hockchia	50		None	Rochore Road – fell dead	Morbus cordis (aortic)	10.05 a.m.	12/2/14
See Ah Chong	Hokkien	30		None	Temple Street – fell dead	Morbus cordis	Unknown	Around 30/8/14

Quong Ho Moi	Hokkien	About 30	None	In his rickshaw, Bencoolen Street	Rupture of aorta aneurism	Unknown	3/9/14
Ah Mua	Hokkien	About 30	None	Orchard Road – fell dead	Morbus cordis	2.00 p.m.	22/5/16
Hong Ho	Hokkien	39	None	In his rickshaw, New Bridge Road	Heart failure – arterial sclerosis	Unknown	About 21/10/16
Chan Au Nee	Hokkien	About 32	None	North Bridge Road – fell dead	Morbus cordis	1.30 p.m.	12/1/17
Loh Chye Lee	Teochiu	36	None	New Bridge Road – fell dead	Morbus cordis	Unknown	27/3/17
Cheang Chin Hoe	Cantonese	50	None	Hill Street – fell dead	Morbus cordis	2.30 p.m.	27/6/17
Sim Kay Say	Hockchia	40	None	Verandah Hill Street – fell dead	Cardiac Syncope/ syphelitic aortic	4.30 a.m.	22/9/17
Chong Ee Chong	Hockchia	24	None	New Bridge Road – fell dead	Morbus cordis	11.00 a.m. -2.00 p.m.	13/2/18
Unknown	Chinese	About 40	None	New Bridge Road – fell dead	Syphilitic Myocarditis	3.35 p.m.	4/5/18
Ten Chow Ting	Hockchia	45	None	72 Rochore Canal Road	Morbus cordis	4.30 p.m.	24/9/18
Unknown, possibly Pok Pua	Chinese	About 45	None	At Tan Tock Seng Hospital	Heart failure	Unknown	10/1/19
Unknown	Hockchia	About 70	None	Dunstan Street – fell dead	Morbus cordis	Unknown	8/3/19
Ho Ah Kee	Hockchia	21	None	Victoria Street – fell dead	Morbus cordis	Unknown	Around 8/6/19
Boh Ah Gee	Hengwah	35	None	Fell dead	Syncope-valvular disease	4.00 p.m.	7/2/20
Teo Hay Lan	Hockchia	47	None	Neil Road – fell dead	Cardiac failure	11.00 a.m.	15/4/26
Ah Choe	Hengwah	45	Abrasions right side of forehead	Jalan Sultan – fell dead	Syphilitic Aortitis	Unknown	Around 13/9/23

(*continued*)

APPENDIX 7 *(continued)*

Name	*Speech/ Dialect Group*	*Age*	*Description*	*Marks of Violence if any*	*Where Found*	*Cause of Death*	*Time of Death*	*Date of Death*
Koh Leong	Hokkien	55		None	Robinson Road – fell dead	Acute cardiac dilatation	9.00 p.m.	20/2/24
Leng Liah Kiah	Hockchia	43		None	New Market Road – fell dead	Heart failure	Unknown	12/10/28
Teo Ghee Sung	Hockchia	About 35		None	Waterloo Street	Syphilitic aortis	Unknown	7/11/24
Tan Chua	Hengwah	About 40		None	Ballister Road	Syphilitic aortis	Unknown	Around 25/2/24
Oh Chew	Hockchia	About 45		None	Victoria Street	Syphilitic aortis	Unknown	Around 29/5/25
Kho Hee Teh	Hockchia	26		None	Jalan Baar	Probably heart failure – from Syphilis	Unknown	21/8/25
Chou Keang	Hockchia	40		None	Serangoon Road – fell dead	Aortitis	Unknown	21/1/27
Foh Beng Lye	Chinese	About 27		Abrasions on forehead	Outram Road – fell dead	Cardiac failure	Unknown	21/11/29
Unknown	Chinese	About 35		None	Tanjong Pagar Road	Rupture of aortic aneurysm	Unknown	15/5/33
Seah Ah Kau	Chinese	55		Abrasions on forehead	Tan Tock Seng Hospital	Heart failure – arterial sclerosis	Unknown	10/8/33
Ah Hoo	Hengwah	About 30		None	Rochore Road – died in his rickshaw	Syphilitic aortis/ coronary obstruction	8.15 p.m.	3/9/33
Sim Chwee Kiat	Hokkien	65		None	Serangoon Road – fell dead	Aortic endocarditis	8.00 a.m.	29/3/34

Ch'ng Soi Bak Chew	Hokkien	About 45	None	Coleman Street – fell dead	Syphilitic aortitis	Unknown	Around 29/11/34
Goh Ah Chiang	Teochiu	48	None	Fisher Street – fell dead	Heart failure – Myocardial degeneration	Unknown	24/5/36
Thing Koe Lye	Chinese	About 45	None	In his rickshaw in Jalan Besar	Cardiac failure and Syphilis	Unknown	2/1/37
Teng Ah Peng	Hockcha	About 37	None	Rochore Road, dead in his rickshaw	Ruptured aortic aneurysm	Unknown	14/5/37
Tang Song Hye	Chinese	45	Star-shaped scar – left calf	Orchard Road – fell dead	Dilations of heart, natural causes	Unknown	12/11/38
Seng Ah Beo	Hokkien	36	Tattoo mark of Chinese lady on a horse	General Hospital–collapsed	Ruptured aortic aneurysm	3.30 p.m.	16/1/38
Tien Sang Kwai	Hengwah	57	None	Berman Street – dead in his rickshaw	Chronic aortitis with heart failure	Unknown	28/8/38
Unknown	Chinese	About 50	None	Fell Dead	Coronary Thrombosis	9.00 a.m.	19/2/39
Chew Jim	Teochiu	48	None	Tan Tock Seng Hospital	Endocarditition of aortic and mitric valves	2.20 a.m.	8/11/39
Chan Lui	Hengwah	38	None	Kallang Road	Ruptured aorta	Unknown	14/8/40

APPENDIX 8

Rickshaw Coolies: Traffic Accidents, 1898-1939

Name	*Age*	*Sub-ethnic Group*	*No. and Street of Residence*	*No. of Passengers in Rickshaw*	*Date of Accident*	*Place of Accident*	*Time of Accident and Weather Condition*
Ho Hee	45	Hokkien	4 Sungei Road	Empty	17/9/98	North Bridge Road/ Arab Street	8.00 a.m.
Tan Twah Sah	About 35	Hokkien		Empty	3/11/13	Havelock Road	2.30 p.m.
Teng Ah Poh	46	Hockchia	27 Angullia Road	One	14/1/14	Junction of Niven & Wilkie Roads	11 a.m.
Moh Ah Hee	About 25	Hockchia	27 Park Road	Two	2/8/14	Serangoon Road	7.30 p.m. clear evening
Lee Ah Loi	25	Hengwah	94 Queen Street	One	17/8/17	Orchard Road	9.00 a.m.
Ng Kai	36	Hokkien	Craig Road	Empty	3/6/19	Keppel Road	7.35 p.m.
Lim Hoon Keng	25	Hockcha		One	12/7/19	The Esplanade	1.35 a.m. clear evening/ moonlight
Ong Ah Choon	56	Hengwah	99 Weld Road	Empty	23/2/20	Private road close to Keppel Road	6.00 a.m.
Goh Chye Keh	30	Chawan	Middle Road	Empty	29/10/20	Junction of Hill & High Streets	12 p.m.
See Piong	26	Hokkien	37 Tanjong Pagar Road	Two	2/6/21	Junction of Cross Street & South Bridge Road	3.20 p.m.

APPENDIX 8 (*continued*)

Type of Vehicle Involved in Accident	*Name of Driver/ Puller*	*Cause of Accident*	*Death due to*	*Inquest No.*	*Year*
Bullock-cart loaded with planks	Sediah	Puller standing between shafts sideways/The cart coming from behind ran over his foot	Tetanus	128	1898
Bullock-cart	Choa Choa Bok	Rickshaw cut across the road, wheel of the bullock-cart collided with the shafts of rickshaw	Fractured skull. Right wheel of bullock-cart passing over the head of the deceased	175	1913
Car	Mrs Jane Downe	Deceased running downhill/due to impetus already acquired collided with Mrs Downe's car	Shock and haemorrhage	15	1914
Car/ Humber	Ong Boon Tat	Rickshaw puller crossed over Serangoon Road and was run into by the car. Motor car travelling at a fair speed from behind	Left leg injured. Right foot crushed. Shock from multiple injuries	180	1914
Car	Mohammed Noor bin Bedin	Deceased pulling rickshaw towards Tanglin, collided with car going towards town	Fractured skull. Shock from multiple injuries	183	1917
Car	Unknown	Deceased while proceeding towards town was knocked over from behind by a motor car, number and driver unknown	Fractured skull. Cerebral laceration	137	1919
Car	Samsul bin Mustapha	Motor car coming from opposite direction at a fast speed on the wrong side of the road ran into the rickshaw	Fractured skull. Cerebral haemorrhage	164	1919
Motor lorry	Omar bin Haji Salis	Motor lorry collided with the deceased causing death by a rash or negligent act	Shock and haemorrhage from multiple injuries	46	1920
Car/Buick	Lim Heng Wea	Car ran into the rickshaw, cut straight across in front of the car	Fractured skull	281	1920
Car	Chee bin Nordin	Deceased seems to have cut across the road and was hit by the car from behind.	Shock & haemorrhage from rupture of liver	209	1921

(*continued*)

APPENDIX 8 (*continued*)

Name	*Age*	*Sub-ethnic Group*	*No. and Street of Residence*	*No. of Passengers in Rickshaw*	*Date of Accident*	*Place of Accident*	*Time of Accident and Weather Condition*
Ch'ng Chuan	42	Teochiu	Rochore Canal Road	Empty	8/9/21	Stamford Road	4.25 a.m., just starting to rain
Eng Peng	60	Hokkien	25 Banda Street	One	26/9/22	Junction of Circular Road and New Bridge Road	9.30 a.m.
Low Siang Quay	40	Hengwah	531-9 Queen Street	One	4/11/22	Junction of Stamford Road and Beach Road	9.20 a.m.
Chin Ah Ching	39	Hengwah	96 Sungei Road	Two	7/10/23	Tanglin Road sloping towards Tanglin Junction	11.15 p.m.
Teng Tong	46	Hengwah	Lorong 20, Geylang Road	One	15/12/23	Entrance No. 3 Empire Dock, Tanjong Pagar	8 a.m.
Tang Ah Huat	20	Teochiu	23 Fisher Street	One	16/12/24	Patterson Road	9.45 a.m.
Toh Ah Soh	24	Hengwah	1 Ophir Road	One	18/4/25	Near junction of North Bridge Road and High Street	12.30 p.m.
Choi Bok Lee	52	Hockchia		Empty	26/4/25	Junction of Selegie Road, Prinsep Street and Dhoby Ghaut	5.45 p.m.
Low Yah Cheong	39	Hengwah	Katong, East Coast Road	Empty	15/7/25	Meyer Road	12.30 a.m.
Ling Ah Ngong	51	Hengwah	Rochore Canal Road	Two	2/1/26	New Bridge Road	6.00 p.m.

APPENDIX 8 (*continued*)

Type of Vehicle Involved in Accident	*Name of Driver/ Puller*	*Cause of Accident*	*Death due to*	*Inquest No.*	*Year*
Rickshaw	Unknown	Deceased's rickshaw and another collided; metal point of rickshaw shaft had gone into his stomach	Septicaemia from multiple abscesses	395	1921
Nightsoil motor lorry	Haji Densuri bin Patalah	Deceased came out of Circular Road, and cut across in front of the lorry and was on the wrong side of the road	Fractured pelvis and cystitis	393	1922
Rickshaw	Yew Teng	Other rickshaw tried to cut in front of deceased and collided with him–shaft of rickshaw injured left thigh	Tetanus–following a wound in the thigh	459	1922
Car	Khoo Boo Keng	Rickshaw came down incline and swerved into front of the car. Rickshaw shafts went through windscreen	Fractured skull	397	1923
Motor lorry	Koh Chow	Motor lorry came from behind collided with deceased's rickshaw; the lorry ran over him	Shock from fractured pelvis	484	1923
Unknown motor vehicle	Unknown	Deceased had been run into by a motor vehicle of some sort and then left on the road to die	Fractured skull	491	1924
Unknown motor bus and tram No. 3	Unknown	Unknown motor bus collided with deceased rickshaw puller, throwing him under Tram No. 3 which was in motion	Rupture of lungs, liver and stomach	183	1925
Car/Chevrolet	Mr Gaggino	Deceased darted out in front of car and was run over while returning from public latrine	Subdural haemorrhage	192	1925
Car	Mr Leuthold	Deceased was knocked down from behind by Mr Leuthold's car in a dark part of the road	Fractured skull	329	1925
Car	Chow Seh Woo	Accused turned his car to avoid hitting rickshaw coming towards the car	Shock from compound fracture of legs and injuries to head	1	1926

(*continued*)

APPENDIX 8 (*continued*)

Name	*Age*	*Sub-ethnic Group*	*No. and Street of Residence*	*No. of Passengers in Rickshaw*	*Date of Accident*	*Place of Accident*	*Time of Accident and Weather Condition*
Ee Ang Ang	46	Hockchia	Ophir Road	One	8/2/27	Junction of Queen Street and Ophir Road	12.00 a.m.
Ling Kow Kay	40	Hokkien			1/4/27	Balestier Road	6.00 a.m.
Ling Kheng Teh	40	Hengwah		One	18/1/28	New Bridge Road	4.40 p.m. Surface of road wet and extremely slippery
Lee Ah Liang	40	Hengwah	95 Queen Street	Five	21/1/28	Bukit Timah Road	2.30 p.m. Surface of road wet and muddy
Ong Teck Cheng	19	Hengwah	227 Jalan Sultan	One	4/4/29	Junction of Prinsep Street and Rochore Canal Road	4.35 p.m.
Teo Kow Seng	48	Hengwah	228 Victoria Street	Empty	3/9/29	Victoria Street	4.30 a.m.
Lim Kian Lye	40	Chawan		Empty	19/1/30	Serangoon Road	7 p.m. Rain had stopped but the road was wet
Leong Lam	38	Cantonese	Hokkien Street	Empty	19/10/30	Grove Road	2.45 a.m.
Ling Ah Liew	45	Hockchia	93 Chin Swee Road	One	28/6/31	Junction of Havelock Road and Kim Seng Road	3-4 p.m.
Yip Ah Kim	42	Hokkien		Two	12/4/33	Junction of Rochore Canal Road and Ophir Road	10.00 a.m.

APPENDIX 8 (*continued*)

Type of Vehicle Involved in Accident	*Name of Driver/ Puller*	*Cause of Accident*	*Death due to*	*Inquest No.*	*Year*
Motor bus	Kway Say Sung	Rickshaw going straight across Queen Street, the bus went straight into the rickshaw	Fractured skull	82	1927
Unknown motor car or lorry	Unknown	Rickshaw and puller had been struck by an oncoming vehicle	Fractured skull	174	1927
Trolley bus No. 28	Demin	Trolley bus skidded owing to slippery surface of road and collided with rickshaw of the deceased	Shock and haemorrhage from fractured ribs, rupture of liver and spleen	52	1928
Motor bus	Kang Ah Sek	Motor bus attempted to pass rickshaw and collided with it from behind	Shock and haemorrhage from fractured ribs and ruptured liver	59	1928
Motor bus	Chan Boon Seng	The puller was turning into Prinsep Street but the bus came on and hit the end of the rickshaw shafts	Shock following compound fracture of lower end of left femur	174	1929
Motor lorry	Osman bin Sulong	Lorry suddenly went across the road to its right, crashed into the rickshaw	Shock and haemorrhage from multiple injuries	436	1929
Motor car (taxi)	Ramasamy	Rickshaw cut across the road suddenly and taxi struck left side of rickshaw	Fractured skull	38	1930
Motor car	Mr Vaughan Jones	Car collided with rickshaw from behind; the rickshaw was too far out into the centre of the road	Fractured skull	385A	1930
Motor lorry	Tan Chwee	Lorry turned into Havelock Road and crashed into deceased & rickshaw	Fractured skull	360	1931
Motor lorry	Liew Guan Chua	The deceased started to cross the road and went in front of motor lorry and was knocked down	Fractured skull	177	1933

(*continued*)

APPENDIX 8 (*continued*)

Name	*Age*	*Sub-ethnic Group*	*No. and Street of Residence*	*No. of Passengers in Rickshaw*	*Date of Accident*	*Place of Accident*	*Time of Accident and Weather Condition*
Ah Kai	48	Cantonese			11/5/34	Jalan Besar	12.30 a.m.
Yat Ah Huat	41	Hengwah	532 Victoria Street		4/1/36	Junction of Lavender Street and Bendemeir Road	
Koh Kong Cheng	42	Hengwah	17 Larut Road	Three	10/2/37	Geylang Road	
Tan Moi Kah	45	Hengwah			23/4/37		8.00 p.m.
Lim Kim Cheok	50	Hokkien	Perak Road	Empty	25/8/37	Victoria Street	8–9 a.m. Raining, road was wet and slippery
Tee Yeok Choon	41	Hokkien	8 Craig Road	Two	27/9/37	Keppel Road	Evening
Ong Kwee Tiam	35	Hockchia	Victoria Street	Empty	4/10/37	Kallang Road	
Ling Soh Kai	49	Hengwah	27 Dixon Road			Junction of Serangoon, Selegie, Bukit Timah and Rochore Roads	9 p.m. Had been raining, road surface was wet
Tan Nah Nai	51	Hockchew	99 Havelock Road	Empty	14/4/38	New Bridge Road	6.00 a.m.
Teo Ah Lak	55	Hengwah		One	4/3/39	Serangoon Road	4.30 a.m. Little moonlight

APPENDIX 8 (*continued*)

Type of Vehicle Involved in Accident	*Name of Driver/ Puller*	*Cause of Accident*	*Death due to*	*Inquest No.*	*Year*
Car	Lieut. M. C. Munro	Deceased was run into by a car driven by Lieut. Munro	Fractured skull	220	1934
Car	Madin bin Latiff	Deceased was cutting the corner of Bendemier Road turning into Lavender Street and a car collided with his rickshaw	Fractured skull	199	1936
Unknown motor car or lorry	Unknown	Deceased was suddenly knocked by a vehicle into the drain by side of the road from behind	Fractured skull	99	1937
Motor lorry		Knocked down by lorry while pulling rickshaw	Shock and haemorrhage from multiple injuries	260	1937
Motor car	Unknown	Car knocked against the rickshaw in passing, throwing rickshaw puller on to five-footway	Fractured skull	506	1937
Motor car	Walter Lambert	Rickshaw struck by car while crossing road to railway station	Fractured skull	568	1937
Motor car	Ahmat bin Mohamed	Deceased ran in front of motor car; the vehicles collided	Fractured skull	584	1937
Motor car	Yeo Eng Song	Deceased when crossing junction collided with motor car	Sustained injuries which enhanced his death from TB	595	1937
Motor lorry	G. Somoo	Motor lorry collided with rickshaw, knocked deceased into a drain at the side of the road	Fractured skull	210	1938
Unknown motor car or lorry	Unknown	Motor vehicle struck rickshaw from behind	Fractured skull	135	1939

APPENDIX 9

Rickshaw Coolies: Suicide

Name	*Age*	*Sub-ethnic Group*	*No. and Street of Residence*	*Nature of Residence*	*State of Health*	*Opium Smoker*
Tan Say Tee	32	Hockchew	126 Victoria Street	Rickshaw coolie lodging-house/ cubicle	Suffering from V.D.	
Teo Ah Say	35/40	Hokkien	219 Rochore Road		Much debilitated, suffering from TB & diarrhoea	
Lim Tiew	About 50	Hokkien	109 Albert Street	Opium shop/ cubicle	Suffering from V.D./swollen legs	25¢ worth of *chandu*
Lui Ah Pek	30	Hokkien	9 Spottiswoode Park Road	Lodging-house/ upstairs cubicle	Poor health	30–40¢ worth of *chandu* per day
Wee Cheng	45	Hokkien	49-2 Rochore Road	Lodging-house/ cubicle	Poor health	
Leong Ah Keng	45	Cantonese	8 Erskine Road	Rickshaw coolie lodging-house/ cubicle downstairs	Ill for some time suffering severely with V.D.	
Tiew Tam	55	Hokkien	25 Duxton Road	Lodging-house		Did not smoke *chandu*
Goh Ah Toh	27	Hokkien	38 People's Park	Lodging-house	Suffering severely from Beri beri	Smoked *chandu*
Lim Kee Lee	32	Hockchia	249 Victoria Street	Rickshaw coolie lodging-house	Good	

APPENDIX 9 (*continued*)

Single/ Married	*Length of Marriage*	*No. of Children, Ages/Sex*	*Date of Suicide*	*Cause of Suicide*	*Place of Suicide*	*Suicide due to*	*Inquest No.*	*Year*
Single/ in Singapore over 8 years			23/9/03	Ill/unfit to work	The sea near the Esplanade, and the mouth of the Stamford Canal	Asphyxia by drowning	115	1903
Single			25/5/04	Illness	Native ward of the General Hospital	Strangulation	79	1904
Single			8/11/07	Ill over 1 month/ unable to work/in debt	Latrine in opium shop	Asphyxia by hanging from the roof of the latrine	180	1907
Single			18/9/08	Ill with fever, no money for *chandu*	Cubicle in lodging-house	Cut throat with small clasp knife	165	1908
Single			2/3/17	Ill/unfit to follow his occupation	Kitchen in lodging-house	Asphyxia by hanging by a rope from a rafter in the kitchen	231	1917
Single			1/11/21	Ill/unfit to follow his occupation	Cubicle in lodging-house	Cut throat with a razor	459	1921
Married		At least one son – a rickshaw puller	31/5/22			Opium poisoning	213	1922
Single			7/6/22	Ill/unfit to work	Outside the lodging-house	Asphyxia by hanging outside the house to the lattice-work	223	1922
Married			10/2/23	Domestic/ financial		Opium poisoning	59	1923

(*continued*)

APPENDIX 9 (*continued*)

Name	*Age*	*Sub-ethnic Group*	*No. and Street of Residence*	*Nature of Residence*	*State of Health*	*Opium Smoker*
Ling Ah Thui	41	Hockchia	2 Angullia Road	Rickshaw coolie lodging-house	Poor health for some time. Heart disease	
Tan Chwee Chwee	42	Hockchew	33 Muar Road	Rickshaw coolie lodging-house	Suffering severely from V.D.	Smoked *chandu*
Geok Lan	40	Hengwah	249 Victoria Street	Rickshaw coolie lodging-house	Very emaciated and filthy	Smoked *chandu*
Chung Ah Hoot	43	Hokkien	21 Duxton Road	Lodging-house		Smoked *chandu*
Tang Koh Chi	45	Hockchia	161 New Market Road	Rickshaw coolie lodging-house		
Lim Choon Huat	35	Teochiu	New Bridge Road	Lodging-house	Depressed/felt swindled out of money for kin	
Koh Kim Chwee	38	Hockchia	29 Angullia Road	Lodging-house	Good	
Teng Lau Ting	45	Hengwah	108 Albert Street	Barber shop/ lodging	Complained of not being well	Smoked *chandu*
Ng Choon Quee	37	Hokkien	309 New Bridge Road	Lodging-house		
Lim Boey Chong	29	Hockchia	12 Narcis Street	Lodging-house		

APPENDIX 9 (*continued*)

Single/ Married	*Length of Marriage*	*No. of Children, Ages/Sex*	*Date of Suicide*	*Cause of Suicide*	*Place of Suicide*	*Suicide due to*	*Inquest No.*	*Year*
Single			30/12/24	Ill/unfit to work	Latrine in lodging-house	Asphyxia by hanging by a rope tied to an old rick-shaw wheel stored across the top of the latrine	516	1924
Single			10/7/25	Ill/unfit to work for 9 days		Opium poison-ing	318	1925
Single			3/7/29	Ill/unfit to work for 2 weeks	Back lane of 249 Vic-toria Street	Asphyxia by hanging by a rope to a piece of wood used for drying clothes in back yard	328	1929
Married			23/12/31	Domestic/ financial no money for *chandu*	Kitchen in lodging-house	Asphyxia by hanging by a rope from a beam in the kitchen	703	1931
Single			3/5/32		Rickshaw coolie lodging-house	Asphyxia by hanging	272	1932
Single			15/11/32	Financial worries/ felt he was swindled	33 New Bridge Road, wine and spirits shop	Multiple stab wounds with a knife	664	1932
Married	3 years	1	23/11/32	Perhaps domestic/ financial	Took the opium just before he arrived home	Opium poison-ing	677	1932
Single			24/4/36	Gambling informer (?)	Sleeping platform at the back of the shop	Stab wounds of abdomen and neck with a knife	247	1936
Single			5/12/38		309 New Bridge Road	Asphyxia by hanging	692	1938
Single			5/2/39		12 Narcis Street	Asphyxia by hanging	82	1939

Bibliography

Unpublished Official Records

I. *England*

A. Public Records Office, Kew

CO 273 Straits Settlements, original correspondence, 1867–1941
CO 882 Confidential Print

B. Rhodes House Library, Oxford

Frederick George Bourne—Miscellaneous papers as Coroner of Singapore (Mss. Ind. Ocn. S. 203)

W. L. Blythe—Papers as Colonial Secretary, Singapore (Mss. Ind. Ocn. S. 116)

Sir William Peel—Notes covering his colonial service in Malaya, Singapore, and Hong Kong from 1897 to 1935 (typescript). (Mss. Brit. Emp. S. 208)

II. *Singapore*

A. National Archives and Records Centre

Straits Settlements Annual Reports, 1861–1941
Straits Settlements Legislative Council Proceedings, 1867–1941
Singapore Municipal Administration Reports, 1888–1939

B. Subordinate Court

Singapore Coroners Inquests and Inquiries, 1882–1939
Certificate of Coroners Views Singapore, 1906–1940

C. Archives and Oral History Department

Selected list of persons interviewed:

Mr Ho Bee Swee, February 1982, Duxton Road Community Leader
Mr Ng Kar Eng, November 1981, Rickshaw puller/trishaw rider
Mr Tan Ai Mai, November 1981, Rickshaw puller/trishaw rider
Mr Koh Teong Koo, November 1981, Rickshaw puller/trishaw rider

Published Official Records

Report of the Commissioners Appointed to Enquire into the State of Labour in the Straits Settlements and Protected Native States with Appendices and Papers in Continuation (Singapore: Government Printing Office, 1891).

W. J. Simpson, *Report on the Sanitary Condition of Singapore* (London: Waterloo and Sons Ltd., 1907).

Straits Settlements and Federated Malay States Opium Commission, 1908.

Proceedings and Report of the Commission Appointed to Inquire into the Cause of the Present Housing Difficulties in Singapore, and the Steps Which Should be Taken to Remedy Such Difficulties (Singapore: Government Printing Office, 1918).

Proceedings of the Committee Appointed by His Excellency the Governor and High Commissioner to Inquire into Matters Relating to the Use of Opium in British Malaya (Singapore: Government Printing Office, 1924).

Committee Appointed to Investigate the Hawker Question in Singapore (Singapore: Government Printing Office, 1932).

Newspapers and Periodicals

Malay Mail, 1965
Malaya Tribune, 1938
Singapore Free Press, 1897–1938
Straits Chinese Magazine, 1897–1907
Straits Echo, 1905

Books

Baker, Hugh D. R., *Chinese Family and Kinship* (London: The Macmillan Press, 1979).

Bilainkin, George, *Hail, Penang! Being the Narrative of Comedies and Tragedies in a Tropical Outpost, among Europeans, Chinese, Malays, and Indians* (London: Sampson Low, Marston and Company Ltd., 1932).

Blythe, W. L., *The Impact of the Chinese Secret Societies in Malaya: A Historical Study* (London: Oxford University Press, 1969).

Bohannen, Paul (ed.), *African Homicide and Suicide* (Princeton: Princeton University Press, 1960).

Braddell, Sir Roland St. J., *Chinese Marriages* (Singapore, 1921).

—— *The Laws of the Straits Settlements, A Commentary*, 2nd ed. (Singapore, 1931; reprinted Kuala Lumpur: Oxford University Press, 1982).

—— *The Lights of Singapore* (London: Methuen, 1934; reprinted Kuala Lumpur: Oxford University Press, 1982).

Britton, Nancy Pence, *East of the Sun* (Blackwood, 1956).

Brown, Edwin A., *Indiscreet Memories* (London: Kelly and Walsh, 1936).

Campbell, Psia C., *Chinese Coolie Emigration to Countries Within the British Empire* (London, 1923).

Castells, Manuel, *The Urban Question. A Marxist Approach* (London: Edward Arnold, 1979).

The Century Dictionary (London: The Times, 1899).

Chen Mong Hock, *The Early Chinese Newspapers of Singapore, 1881–1902* (Singapore: University of Malaya Press, 1967).

Chevalier, Louis, *Labouring Classes and Dangerous Classes in Paris during the First Half of the Nineteenth Century* (London: Routledge and Kegan Paul, 1973).

Chia, Felix, *The Babas* (Singapore: Times Books International, 1980).

Cobb, Richard, *Death in Paris 1795–1801* (London: Oxford University Press, 1978).

Condaminas, George, *L'Space Social a' propos de l'Asie de Sud-Est* (Paris: Flamarion, 1980).

Cook, Reverend J. A. Bethune, *Sunny Singapore. An Account of the Place and Its People, with a Sketch of the Results of Missionary Work* (London: Elliot Hock, 1907).

Cuylenburg, John, *Singapore through Sunshine and Shadow* (Singapore: Heinemann, 1982).

Davis, Fei-Ling, *Primitive Revolutionaries of China. A Study of Secret Societies in the late Nineteenth Century* (Hong Kong: Heinemann Books, 1977).

Dixon, A., *Singapore Patrol* (London, 1935).

Doeppers, Daniel F., *Manila 1900–1941 Social Change in a Late Colonial Metropolis* (Quezon City: Ateneo de Manila University Press, 1984).

Dogget, Marjorie, *Characters of Light. A Guide to the Buildings of Singapore* (Singapore: Donald Moore, 1957).

Douglas, Jack D., *The Social Meanings of Suicide* (Princeton: Princeton University Press, 1967).

Durkheim, Emile, *Suicide: A Study in Sociology* (Glencoe: Illinois Free Press, 1951).

Emerson, Rupert, *Malaysia* (Kuala Lumpur: University of Malaya Press, 1966).

Fairbank, John K., Reischauer, Edwin O. and Craig, Albert M., *East Asia. Tradition and Transformation* (London: George Allen and Unwin, 1973).

Foran, Robert W., *Malayan Symphony* (London: Hutchinson, 1935).

Fraser, J. M., *The Work of the Singapore Improvement Trust, 1927–1947* (Singapore, 1948).

Freedman, Maurice, *Chinese Family and Marriage in Singapore* (London: HMSO, 1957).

—— *Lineage Organisation in Southeastern China* (London, 1958).

—— *Chinese Lineage and Society; Fukien and Kwangtung* (London, 1966).

—— *The Study of Chinese Society. Essays by Maurice Freedman* (Stanford: Stanford University Press, 1979).

Gamble, Sydney, *Peking: A Social Survey Conducted under the Auspices of the Princeton University Center in China and the Peking Young Men's Christian Association* (New York: Doran, 1921).

—— *How Chinese Families Live in Peking* (New York: Funk and Wagnalls, 1933).

Garrad, Charles Goodricke, *The Acts and Ordinances of the Legislative Council of the Straits Settlements from the 1st April 1867 to 7th March 1898*, 2 vols. (London: Eyre and Spottiswoode, 1898).

Godley, Michael, *The Mandarin-Capitalists from Nanyang: Overseas Chinese Enterprise in the Modernization of China 1893–1911* (Cambridge: Cambridge University Press, 1981).

Halbwacks, Maurice, *Les causes du Suicide* (Paris: Alcan, 1930).

Jackson, R. N., *Immigrant Labour and the Development of Malaya, 1786–1920* (Kuala Lumpur: Government Press, 1961).

Kaye, Barrington, *Upper Nankin Street, Singapore. A Sociological Study of Chinese Households Living in a Densely Populated Area* (Singapore: University of Malaya Press, 1960).

Kiernan, V. G., *The Lords of Human Kind. European Attitudes to the Outside World in the Imperial Age* (London, 1972).

Lao She, *Rickshaw* (the novel *Lo-T'o Hsiang Tzu*), translated by Jean M. James (Honolulu: The University Press of Hawaii, 1979).

Le Roy Ladurie, Emmanuel, *Montaillou Cathars and Catholics in a French Village 1294–1324* (London: Penguin Books, 1980).

Lee Poh Ping, *Chinese Society in Nineteenth Century Singapore* (Kuala Lumpur: Oxford University Press, 1978).

Llewellyn-Jones, Derek, *Sex and V.D.* (London: Faber and Faber, 1974).

Lockhart, Bruce, *Return to Malaya* (New York: G. P. Putnam and Son, 1936).

Low Ngiong Ing, *Chinese Jetsam on a Tropical Shore* (Singapore: Eastern Universities Press, 1974).

Luscombe, F. M., *Singapore 1819–1930* (Singapore, 1930).

Macauley, Dr T. S., *Common Diseases of Coolies* (Singapore: Fraser and Neave, 1923).

Makepeace, W. E., Braddell, R. St. J., and Brooke, G. C. (eds.), *One Hundred Years of Singapore* (London, 1921).

Mak Lau Fong, *The Sociology of Secret Societies. A Study of Chinese Secret Societies in Singapore and Peninsular Malaysia* (Kuala Lumpur: Oxford University Press, 1981).

McGee, T. G. and Yeung, Y. M., *Hawkers in Southeast Asian Cities: Planning for the Bazaar Economy* (Ottawa: International Development Research Centre, 1977).

McKie, R. C. H., *This Was Singapore* (London, 1950).

McNeill, William H., *Plagues and Peoples* (London: Penguin Books, 1976).

Moore, Donald (ed.), *Where Monsoons Meet* (London: Harrap, 1956).

Onreat, Rene Henry de Solminihac, *Singapore, A Police Background* (London: Dorothy Crisp and Company, 1947).

Platt, Ambrose, *Magical Malaya* (Melbourne: Robertson and Mullen Ltd., 1931).

Pruitt, Ida, *Old Madam Yin. A Memoir of Peking Life 1926–1938* (Stanford: Stanford University Press, 1979).

Reith, George, *Handbook to Singapore* (Singapore, 1907; reprinted Singapore: Oxford University Press, 1985).

Rickshaws in Calcutta, UNNAYAN in association with T. H. Thomas (Calcutta: UNNAYAN, 1981).

Robertson, E. J., *Straits Memories—Incidents, People and Life in Singapore and the Straits a Generation Ago* (Singapore, 1910).

Robson, J. R., *Records and Recollections 1899–1934* (Kuala Lumpur: Kyle, Palmer, 1934).

Samuel, Raphael (ed.), *People's History and Socialist Theory* (London: Routledge and Kegan Paul, 1981).

Singapore Retrospect through Postcards: 1900–1930 (Singapore: Sin Chew Jit Poh: Archives and Oral History Department, 1982).

Skinner, G. William, *Chinese Society in Thailand: An Analytical History* (Ithaca: Cornell University Press, 1957).

Song Ong Siang, *One Hundred Years' History of the Chinese in Singapore* (London: Methuen, 1923; reprinted Kuala Lumpur: University of Malaya Press, 1967, and Singapore: Oxford University Press, 1984).

Spence, Jonathan D., *The Gate of Heavenly Peace* (N.Y.: The Viking Press, 1981).

Stenson, Michael R., *Industrial Conflict in Malaya: Prelude to the Communist Revolt of 1948* (London: Oxford University Press, 1970).

Stone, Lawrence, *The Past and the Present* (London: Routledge and Kegan Paul, 1981).

Sydney, R. H. J., *Malay Land* (London: Cecil Palmer, 1926).

Székely, Ladislao, *Tropic Fever. The Adventures of a Planter in Sumatra* (Kuala Lumpur: Oxford University Press, 1979).

Ta Chen, *Emigrant Communities in South China. A Study of Overseas Migration and its Influence on Standards of Living and Social Change* (New York: Secretariat, Institute of Pacific Relations, 1940).

Thompson, Paul, *The Voice of the Past. Oral History* (London: Oxford University Press, 1978).

Trocki, Carl, *Prince of Pirates: The Temenggongs and the Development of Johore and Singapore 1784–1885* (Singapore: Singapore University Press, 1979).

Turnbull, C. M., *The Straits Settlements 1826–67 Indian Presidency to Crown Colony* (Singapore: Oxford University Press, 1972).

—— *A History of Singapore 1819–1975* (Kuala Lumpur: Oxford University Press, 1977).

Vaughan, J. D., *The Manners and Customs of the Chinese of the Straits Settlements* (Kuala Lumpur: Oxford University Press, 1974).

Wickberg, Edgar, *The Chinese in Philippine Life 1850–1898* (New Haven: Yale University Press, 1965).

Wong Choon San, *A Gallery of Chinese Kapitans* (Singapore, 1964).

Wright, A., and Cartwright, H. (eds.), *Twentieth Century Impressions of British Malaya: Its History, People, Commerce, Industries and Resources* (London: Lloyds Greater Publishing Co. Ltd., 1908).

Wynne, M. L., *Triad and Tabut* (Singapore: Government Printing Office, 1941).

Yap Pheng Geck, *Scholar, Banker, Gentleman Soldier. The Reminiscences of Dr Yap Pheng Geck* (Singapore: Times Books International, 1982).

Articles

Becker, Howard, 'Photography and Sociology', *Studies in the Anthropology of Visual Communication*, VI (1974), pp. 3–26.

Blythe, W. L., 'Historical Sketch of Chinese Labour in Malaya', *Journal of the Malayan Branch of the Royal Asiatic Society*, XX, 1 (1947), pp. 64–114.

Butcher, John, 'The Demise of the Revenue Farm System in the Federated Malay States', *Modern Asian Studies*, Vol. 17, Part 3 (July 1983), pp. 387–412.

Caminada, Jerome, 'Topee and Rickshaw—Both were Doomed', *Straits Times Annual* (1975), pp. 124–8.

Crissman, Lawrence, 'The Segmentary Structure of Urban Overseas Chinese Communities', *Man*, 2 (1967), pp. 185–204.

'Economic Study of the Peking Ricsha Puller', *China Economic Monthly*, 3, 6 (June 1926), pp. 253–65.

Ee, Joyce, 'Chinese Migration to Singapore, 1896–1941', *Journal of Southeast Asian History*, 2 (1961), pp. 33–51.

Emmerson, Donald K., 'Issues in Southeast Asian History: Room for Introspection—A Review Article', *Journal of Asian Studies*, Vol. XL, No. 1 (November 1980), pp. 43–68.

Farberow, Norman L., 'Suicide: Psychological Aspects (1) and (2)', *International Encyclopedia of Social Science* (New York: Macmillan and Free Press, 1968), pp. 385–96.

Freedman, Maurice, 'Colonial Law and Chinese Society', *Journal of the Royal Anthropological Institute*, Vol. 80 (1950), pp. 97–126.

—— 'Immigrants and Associations: Chinese in 19th Century Singapore', *Comparative Studies in Society and History*, Vol. 3, No. 1 (1960), pp. 25–48.

—— 'Chinese Kinship and Marriage in Singapore', *The Journal of Southeast Asian History*, Vol. 3 (1962), pp. 65–73.

Freedman, Maurice and Topley, Marjorie, 'Religion and Social Realignments among the Chinese in Singapore', *Journal of Asian Studies*, 21, 1 (1961), pp. 3–23.

Gould, Harry A., 'Lucknow Rickawallas: The Social Organisation of an Occupational Category', *International Journal of Comparative Sociology*, VI, No. 1 (March 1965), pp. 24–47.

Khoo Kay Kim, 'The Great Depression: The Malaysian Context' in Khoo Kay Kim (ed.), *The History of South-East, South and East Asia. Essays and Documents* (Kuala Lumpur: Oxford University Press, 1977), pp. 78–94.

Kratoska, Paul H., 'Rice Cultivation and the Ethnic Division of Labour in British Malaya', *Comparative Studies in Society and History*, Vol. 24, No. 2 (1982), pp. 280–314.

Le Goff, J., 'Au Moyen Age, temps de l'Eglise et temps due marchand', *Annales: Economies Societies Civilisations*, 15 (1960), pp. 417–33.

O'Farrell, Patrick, 'Oral History: Facts and Fiction', *Quadrant* (November 1979), pp. 7–8.

Samuel, Raphael, 'Local History and Oral History', *History Workshop*, I (Spring 1976), pp. 192–208.

Saw Swee Hock, 'Population Trends in Singapore, 1819–1967', *Journal of Southeast Asian History*, Vol. 10, No. 1 (1969), pp. 36–49.

—— 'The Changing Population Structure in Singapore during 1824–1962', *Malayan Economic Review*, Vol. 9, No. 1 (1964), pp. 99–101.

Sidney, Richard, 'From a Singapore Verandah', *British Malaya* (November 1935), p. 170.

Strand, David, and Richard R. Weiner, 'Social Movements and Political Discourse in 1920's Peking: An Analysis of the Tramway Riot of October 22, 1929', in *Select Papers from the Center for Far Eastern Studies*, No. 3, edited by Susan Mann Jones (Chicago, 1978–9).

Strauch, Judith, 'Multiple Ethnicities in Malaysia: The Shifting Relevance of Alternative Chinese Categories', *Modern Asian Studies* (1981), pp. 235–60.

Thompson, E. P., 'Time, Work-Discipline and Industrial Capitalism', in M. W. Flinn and T. C. Smout (eds.), *Essays in Social History* (Oxford: Clarendon Press, 1974), pp. 39–77.

Wang Gungwu, 'Southeast Asian hua-ch'iao in Chinese History Writing', *Journal of Southeast Asian Studies*, Vol. XII, No. 1 (1981), pp. 1–14.

Warren, J., 'Rickshaw Coolie: An Exploration of the Underside of a Chinese City Outside China, Singapore, 1880–1940', *Itinerario Bulletin for the Leiden Center for the History of European Expansion*, Vol. 8, No. 2 (1984), pp. 80–91.

—— 'Living on The Razor's Edge: The Rickshawmen of Singapore between Two Wars, 1919–1939', *The Bulletin of Concerned Asian Scholars*, Vol. 16, No. 4 (October–December 1984), pp. 38–51.

—— 'The Singapore Rickshaw Pullers: The Social Organization of a Coolie Occupation', *Journal of Southeast Asian Studies*, Vol. 15, No. 1 (1985), pp. 1–15.

—— 'Social History and the Photograph: Glimpses of the Singapore Rickshaw Coolie in the Early 20th Century', *Journal of the Malaysian Branch of the Royal Asiatic Society*, Vol. 58, No. 1 (1985), pp. 29–43.

—— 'The Spiral of Failure: Suicide among the Singapore Rickshaw Coolies', *Southeast Asian Journal of Social Science*, Vol. 13, No. 2 (1985), pp. 47–66.

Wertheim, W. F., 'The Coolie Budget Report', *Pacific Affairs*, XXVI (1955), pp. 158–64.

Williams, Lea E., 'Chinese Leadership in Early British Singapore', *Asian Studies*, 2, 2 (1964), pp. 170–9.

Yen Ching-Hwang, 'Ching's Sale of Honours and the Chinese Leadership in Singapore and Malaya (1877–1912)', *Journal of Southeast Asian Studies* (September 1970), pp. 20–32.

—— 'Early Chinese Clan Organizations in Singapore and Malaya, 1819–1911', *Journal of Southeast Asian Studies*, 12, No. 1 (1981), pp. 62–92.

—— 'Ching Changing Images of the Overseas Chinese (1644–1912)', *Modern Asian Studies*, 15, 2 (1981), pp. 261–85.

Yong Ching Fatt, 'Chinese Leadership in Nineteenth Century Singapore', *Journal of the Island Society* (Hsin-she Hsiieh-pao), I (1967), pp. 1–18.

—— 'A Preliminary Study of Chinese Leadership in Singapore 1900–41', *Journal of Southeast Asian History* (September 1968), pp. 258–85.

—— 'Pang, Pang Organisations and Leadership in the Chinese Community of Singapore during the 1930s', *Journal of the South Seas Society*, Vol. 32, I and II (1977), pp. 31–50.

Zeng Shanti, 'Life and Crime', in *Reunion and Other Stories*, translated by Ly Singko (Singapore: Heinemann Asia, 1982), pp. 40–7.

Index

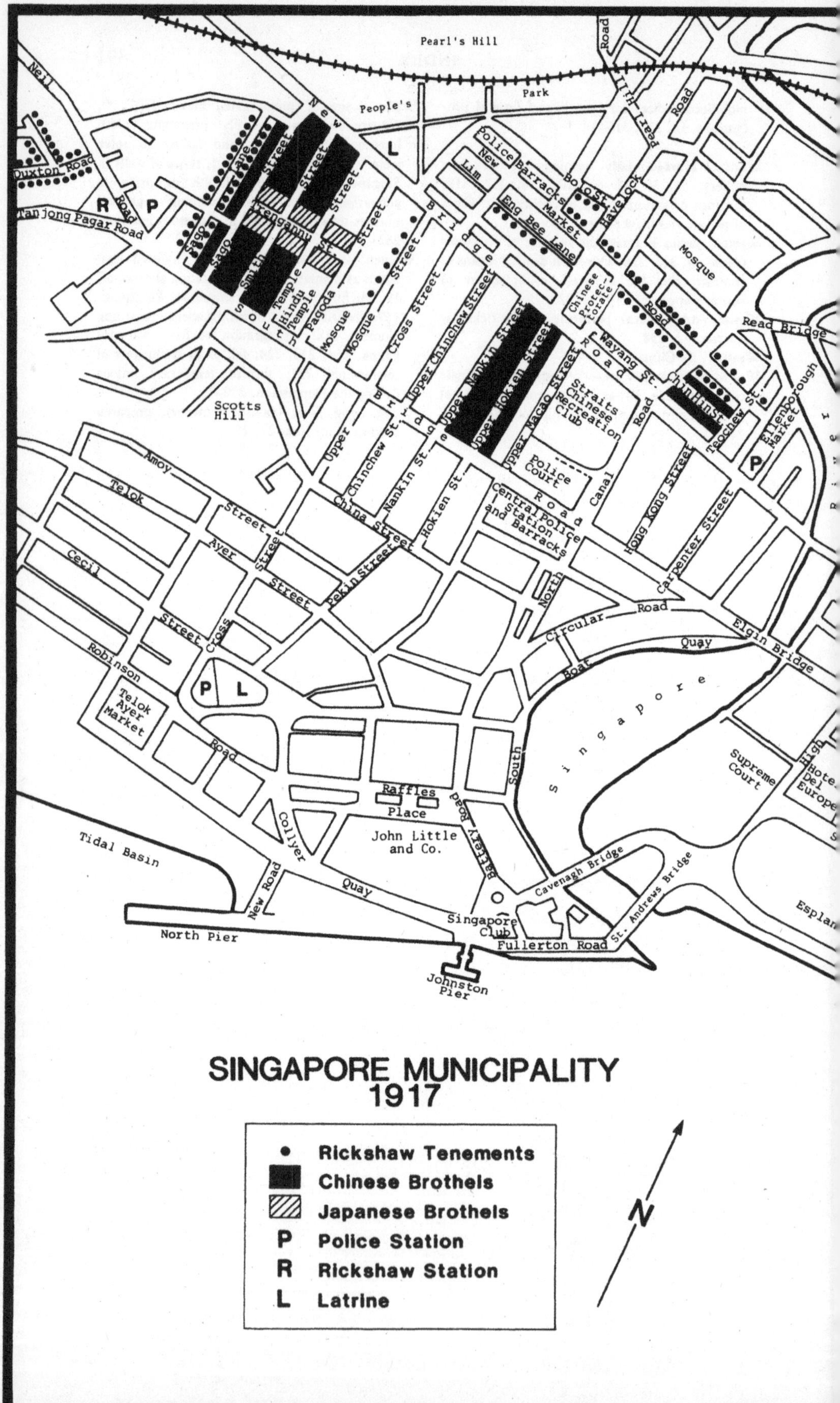

SINGAPORE MUNICIPALITY 1917

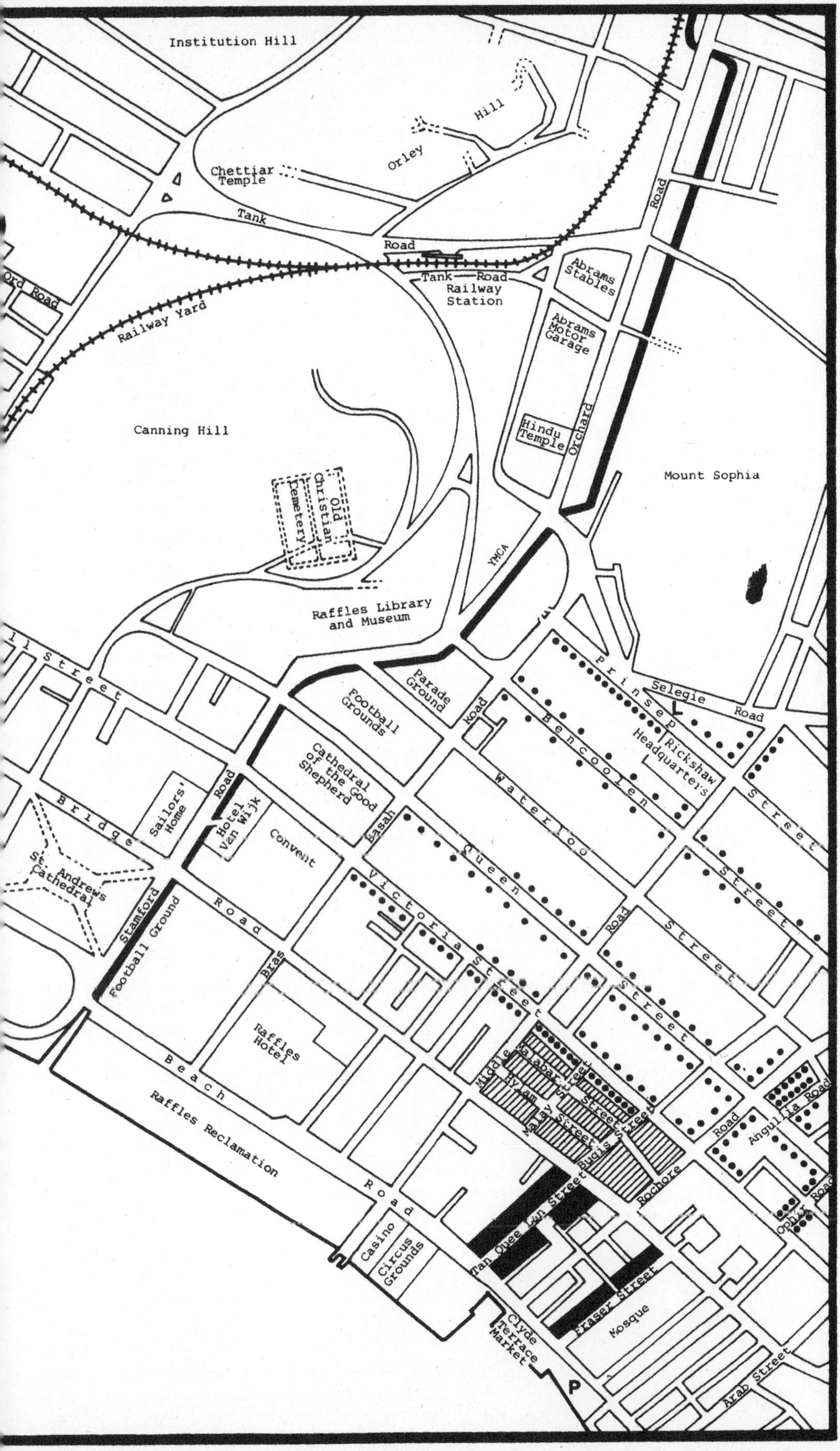
Institution Hill
Orley Hill
Chettiar Temple
Tank Road
Tank Road Railway Station
Abrams Stables
Abrams Motor Garage
Orchard Road
Hindu Temple
Railway Yard
Canning Hill
Old Christian Cemetery
Mount Sophia
YMCA
Raffles Library and Museum
Prinsep Street
Selegie Road
Parade Ground
Football Grounds
Rickshaw Headquarters
Bencoolen Street
Cathedral of the Good Shepherd
Waterloo Street
Sailors' Home
Hotel Van Wijk
Convent
Bridge Road
Basah Road
Queen Street
St. Andrews Cathedral
Stamford Road
Football Ground
Victoria Street
Bras Basah Road
Raffles Hotel
Middle Road
Malabar Street
Hylam Street
Malay Street
Bugis Street
Rochore Road
Angullia Road
Ophir Road
Beach Road
Raffles Reclamation
Casino
Circus Grounds
Tan Quee Lan Street
Fraser Street
Mosque
Clyde Terrace Market
Arab Street